Fodor's

SOUTHERN CALIFORNIA

T0049262

Welcome to Southern California

Balmy weather, blissful beaches, chic desert resorts, Hollywood glamour—Southern California delivers fun and relaxation year-round. Outdoor enthusiasts revel in the drama of the Mojave Desert and the Big Sur coast. Beach-goers appreciate the state's seemingly endless stretches of sand. In trendy Los Angeles and sunny San Diego, culture vultures enjoy superb restaurants, movie studio tours, and America's preeminent zoo. As you plan your trip, confirm that places are still open and let us know when we need to make updates by emailing editors@fodors.com.

TOP REASONS TO GO

★ **Cool Cities:** San Diego's bay, Los Angeles's movie lore, Palm Springs' spa resorts.

★ **Beaches:** For swimming, surfing, or tanning, the beaches can't be beat.

★ **Feasts:** Cutting-edge cuisine, food trucks, fusion flavors, farmers' markets.

★ **Theme Parks:** From Disneyland to Knott's Berry Farm, SoCal has some of the best.

★ **Outdoor Adventures:** Hiking, golfing, and national park excursions are all excellent.

★ **Road Trips:** The Pacific Coast Highway offers spectacular views and thrills aplenty.

Contents

Fodor's Features

Lions and Tigers and Bears:
The World-Famous San Diego Zoo.... 69

MAPS

Chapter 1

EXPERIENCE SOUTHERN CALIFORNIA

20 ULTIMATE EXPERIENCES

Southern California offers terrific experiences that should be on every traveler's list. Here are Fodor's top picks for a memorable trip.

1 Hike to the Hollywood Sign

The iconic Hollywood sign was originally erected in 1923 and read "Hollywoodland." The easiest path starts from the Griffith Park Observatory. *(Ch. 6)*

2 Find the weird at Venice Beach

California's counterculture—bodybuilders at Muscle Beach, head shops on the boardwalk—contrasts with multimillion-dollar homes along the Venice Canals. *(Ch. 6)*

3 Catch waves in Malibu

Surfrider Beach, a stretch of Malibu that includes the Malibu Pier, is popular with surfers and beach bums. On Zuma Beach, surfers share the water with sea lions. *(Ch. 6)*

4 Suspend disbelief at Universal Studios

Tour sets like *Jaws* and *Back to the Future*, or visit The Wizarding World of Harry Potter and Jurassic World. *(Ch. 6)*

5 Take the Ferry to Coronado

The 15-minute ferry ride between Downtown San Diego and Coronado provides great views of Downtown and Naval Air Station North Island. *(Ch. 4)*

6 Shop and Dine in Seaport Village

Situated along the water, the recently revitalized Seaport Village is a 14-acre, open-air shopping and dining complex that's home to shops and eateries, special events, and winding walking paths. *(Ch. 4)*

7 Book a Kayak Tour or Surf Lesson in La Jolla

One of the best local beaches for water sports, La Jolla Shores has rental and tour companies located just steps from the sand. There's surf or SUP lessons, as well as snorkel and kayak tours. *(Ch. 4)*

8 Explore Old Town San Diego

The city's oldest and most storied neighborhood is home to Mexican restaurants, souvenir shops, and cultural and historical attractions and celebrations. *(Ch. 4)*

9 Explore the Gaslamp Quarter

Covering more than 16 city blocks, this bustling neighborhood is great for shopping, dining, and nightlife. Guided walking tours of the historic district are available. *(Ch. 4)*

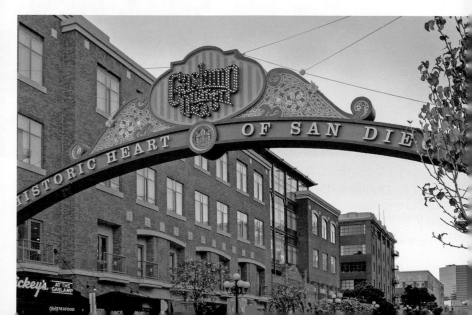

10 See Wildlife in San Diego

The San Diego Zoo and the San Diego Safari Park showcase wildlife without the claustrophobic animal cages. *(Ch. 4)*

11 Camp in Joshua Tree

Just east of Palm Springs is this national park, named for the yucca trees that Mormons named after the biblical Joshua, who raised his hands into the sky. *(Ch. 8)*

12 Traverse Death Valley

One of the hottest places on Earth, Death Valley sits on the eastern edge of California along the border with Nevada. *(Ch. 10)*

13 Tour Old Mission Santa Barbara

The "Queen of Missions"—one of the Central Coast's most photographed structures—also contains superb colonial Spanish/Mexican art. *(Ch. 11)*

14 Relive youth at Disneyland
This truly is the happiest place on Earth. *(Ch. 5)*

15 Tour Paramount Pictures
The only surviving major studio from Hollywood's golden age offers probably the most authentic tour, giving you a real sense of the film industry's history. *(Ch. 6)*

16 Go to a Show Taping in L.A.

Dozens of sitcoms, talk shows, and game shows film every day in Los Angeles, and you can get tickets to be an audience member. *(Ch. 6)*

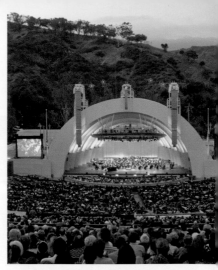

17 Enjoy a concert at the Hollywood Bowl

A live music amphitheater built into the side of the Hollywood Hills, the venue is known for its incredible acoustics. *(Ch. 6)*

18 See Stars on the Walk of Fame

The first stars were revealed in the early 1960s; today, more than 2,600 dot the Hollywood pavement. *(Ch. 6)*

19 Experience Opulence at the Hearst Castle

Once a celebrity hot spot hosting roaring '20s parties, you can tour the palace's zoo, gold-leaf Roman pool, and priceless art collection. *(Ch. 11)*

20 Get a bird's-eye view of Palm Springs

Ride the Palm Springs Aerial Tramway—the world's largest rotating tramway. At the top (8,516 feet) are restaurants and hiking trails. *(Ch. 7)*

California Today

"Has the Golden State Lost Its Luster?" "Is the California Dream Dead?" So read the inevitable rueful headlines in stories detailing the supposedly insurmountable obstacles—most notably a declining population, the high cost of living (especially housing), wildfires, drought, crime, traffic congestion, homelessness, and high taxes. So dire are some of the assessments that one might assume there's no reason to stay here, let alone come for a visit. This despite the fact that everything that has lured settlers and tourists from the get-go—breathtaking scenery, scintillating sightseeing, abundant natural resources, agricultural bounty, and a mostly hospitable climate—remains well in evidence.

Although California, like the rest of the nation and world, faces daunting challenges, the same gloomy predictions (often bearing precisely the same "lost its luster" and "dream dead" headlines) have appeared before: in the middle of the Great Recession (2009), after the first dot-com implosion (2000), all the way back to the gold and silver busts of the 19th century. And guess what? In every instance, the state bounced back, sometimes brilliantly.

Each allegedly ruinous calamity required reinvention, and each time residents rose to the occasion. Based on the past, there's no reason to think that the Golden State won't regain its luster—if it's even been lost.

POPULATION, POTENTIAL

California's birth rate and the pace of migration may have slowed, but they're hardly stagnant. For perspective, consider that the current population of about 39 million (about an eighth of the U.S. total) represents a net increase of nearly 2 million since 2010, albeit a pace behind Texas and Florida. While many residents departing California cite the high cost of living, recent transplants tend to perceive the same potential here as previous settlers.

HISTORICAL CONTEXT

By most accounts, the ancestors of California's indigenous peoples migrated from Asia, traversing a land bridge across the Bering Strait that formerly joined what's now Russia and Alaska. Some of these trailblazers continued south to California, flourishing off the fertile land for centuries. Many famous place names—Malibu, Napa, Ojai, Shasta, Sonoma—reflect this heritage.

Millennia later, Spanish explorers ventured north from Mexico searching for gold, with converts to Christianity the quest of 18th-century missionaries. Nineteenth-century miners rushed here from the world over also seeking gold—the state achieved statehood two years after the precious metal's 1848 discovery.

During the 20th century, successive, sometimes overlapping, waves of newcomers followed in their footsteps: real-estate speculators, would-be motion-picture actors and producers, Dust Bowl farmers and migrant workers, Asians fleeing poverty or chasing opportunity, sexual and gender pioneers, artists, dot-commers, venture capitalists, and these days AI practitioners.

POLITICS

The result is a population that leans toward idealism (some say utopianism)—without necessarily being as liberal as voter-registration statistics might lead one to think. California is Ronald Reagan's old stomping ground, after all. Herbert Hoover also thrived here, and Richard Nixon was a native son. Democrats hold a 2–1 registration advantage over Republicans, the latter essentially tied with "no party preference," but wander into some inland counties, and you may see signs proposing a breakaway, more conservative 51st State of Jefferson. Many residents in these areas supported a 2021 effort to recall Governor Gavin Newsom, a liberal Democrat. Early polls indicated the special-election race might be tight, but the governor prevailed by a substantial margin and was reelected to a second term in 2022.

DEMOGRAPHICS
As with politics, despite the stereotype of the blue-eyed, blond surfer, California's population isn't homogeneous either. Latino residents outnumber whites 40%–35%, with Asians (16%) and African Americans (6.5%) the next-largest groups. Residents here speak more than 220 languages, making California by far the nation's most linguistically diverse state.

ECONOMICS
Back to California's supposedly desperate situation: keep in mind that, in 2022, the Golden State reported a $98 billion budget *surplus,* hardly numbers to prompt despair and proving the Great Recession doomsayers predicting economic catastrophe way off the mark. (For the record, 2023 saw the state in the red to the tune of $30-plus billion.) California, responsible for 15% of the gross domestic product, leads all other states in income generated by agriculture, tourism, entertainment, and industrial activity. With a gross state product of approximately $3.6 trillion (median household income of about $79,000), by many estimates, California would have the world's fifth-largest economy—some say the fourth—were it an independent nation.

STILL DREAMIN'
A few years ago, dueling state-of-the-state analyses appeared within days of each other. A historian's *New York Times* opinion piece described California's declining population and loss of a congressional seat as among negative "firsts" for the state that had "sapped the collective sense of zealous optimism." The historian also predicted "decades of pain" if politicians didn't quickly produce solutions to California's pressing problems.

Two days before the *Times* piece ran, the University of California published a study suggesting pretty much the opposite: that the rate of residents moving out of state is neither unusual nor something to fret over; that residents by a 2–1 majority still believe in the California Dream; and that the state attracts more than half the nation's venture-capital investments, a sign that favorable economic conditions persist.

The naysayers may well be right about California's demise, but if history is any indication, the populace will likely shift gears as necessary. And again the next time it's required. In the meantime, the state's brigade of bucket-list attractions continues to supply the essentials for a dream vacation.

WHAT'S WHERE

1 San Diego. San Diego's Gaslamp Quarter and early California–theme Old Town have a human scale—but big-ticket animal attractions like the San Diego Zoo pull in visitors.

2 Disneyland and Orange County. A diverse destination with premium resorts and restaurants, strollable waterfront communities, and kid-friendly attractions.

3 Los Angeles. Go for the glitz of the entertainment industry, but stay for the rich cultural attributes and communities.

4 Palm Springs and the Desert Resorts. Golf on some of the West's most challenging courses, lounge at fabulous resorts, check out mid-century-modern architectural gems, and trek through primitive desert parks.

5 Joshua Tree National Park. Proximity to major urban areas—as well as world-class rock climbing and nighttime celestial displays—help make this one of the most visited national parks.

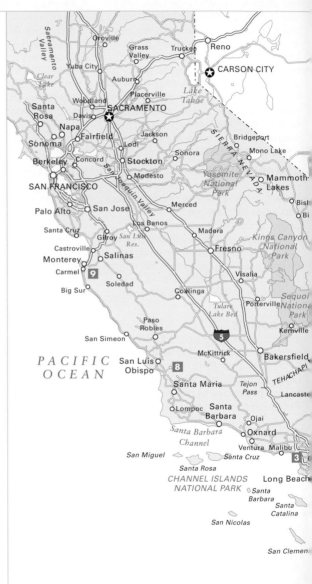

6 Mojave Desert.
Material pleasures are in
short supply here, but
Mother Nature's stark
beauty more than
compensates.

**7 Death Valley National
Park.** This vast, beautiful
national park is often the
hottest place in the
country.

8 The Central Coast.
Three of the state's top
stops—swanky Santa
Barbara, Hearst Castle,
and Big Sur—sit along the
scenic 200-mile route. A
quick boat trip away lies
scenic Channel Islands
National Park.

9 Monterey Bay Area.
Postcard-perfect
Monterey, Victorian-
flavored Pacific Grove,
and exclusive Carmel all
share this stretch of
California coast. To the
north, Santa Cruz boasts
a boardwalk, a UC
campus, ethnic clothing
shops, and plenty of
surfers.

What to Eat and Drink in Southern California

Avocado toast

CRAFT BEER
Dubbed the "Capital of Craft," San Diego has more than 150 craft breweries, a movement that began with Karl Strauss Brewing Company in 1989. Since then, the San Diego Brewers Guild established the San Diego Beer Week held every November, and a few neighborhoods have become craft brewery destinations in their own right.

L.A. HOT DOGS
While every major city in the country has their own take on street hot dogs, L.A.'s Mexican-inspired version is arguably the best. Wrapped in bacon and topped with grilled onions, bell peppers, ketchup, mustard, mayo, and jalapenos, it's practically a ritual for anyone stumbling home drunk to grab one. Look for street carts in areas with a lot of bars.

KOREAN BBQ TACOS
If you like Korean BBQ and you enjoy street tacos, then you might be ready for Korean BBQ tacos, one of the few culinary creations that originated in La La Land. They're exactly what they sound like—tacos but with Korean BBQ meats— and the best place to get them is from one of Roy Choi's legendary Kogi food trucks. To find a location, go to *kogibbq.com*.

FISH TACOS

There's a great debate about who makes the best fish tacos in San Diego. Rubio's Coastal Grill is credited with popularizing fish tacos in the U.S.; the original location is still in Pacific Beach. The original tacos have fried pollock, white sauce, salsa, cabbage, and a corn tortilla.

MEZCAL

Mezcal is made from the agave plant, typically in Oaxaca, Mexico, so naturally the best Oaxacan restaurant in L.A. (Guelaguetza) would have a top-shelf selection. Hollywood's Sassafrass Saloon has exquisite craft mezcals.

IN-N-OUT

No California food list is complete without the legendary In-N-Out. "Where's the closest In-N-Out?" is asked by just about every tourist the moment they arrive. In-N-Out burgers and fries are made fresh and made to order, which is why they're so good in the first place.

FRENCH DIP

Not only was the French Dip invented in Los Angeles, two different restaurants claim its origin. Philippe the Original in Downtown opened in 1908 and is a counter-style diner; Cole's, also opened in 1908, is (slightly) more upscale and features a hidden speakeasy in the back of the restaurant.

SEAFOOD FRESH FROM THE OCEAN

You don't have to go far to find a bounty of fresh seafood, most likely sourced from the waters off Southern California. Always check out the day's catch—served shucked and placed on ice or in a sandwich, salad, or other dish.

VEGETARIAN FOOD

Californians are generally known to be health conscious, eating lots of fresh local produce (including adding avocado to everything). There are abundant vegetarian and vegan options throughout most of Southern California.

TIKI COCKTAILS

Tiki culture has obvious parallels to San Diego's tropical, laid-back vacation vibe, so it's no surprise that the concept took root here with rum as the star spirit. Sure bets include The Grass Skirt and False Idol. If you're heading to Palm Springs, check out Bootlegger Tiki, Tonga Hut, or Toucans Tiki Lounge.

10 Best Beaches in San Diego

CORONADO

Often praised for its sparkling sand, the island is home to the Hotel del Coronado, a 135-year-old luxury hotel perfect for postbeach snacks; Del Beach, which is open to the public; and Dog Beach where pooches can run free sans leash.

MISSION BEACH

Located near SeaWorld San Diego, Mission Beach is home to a bustling boardwalk that's frequented by walkers, cyclists, and people-watchers. The bay is popular for water sports such as stand-up paddleboarding and Jet Skiing, but the beach is best known for Belmont Park, its oceanfront amusement park.

WINDANSEA BEACH

Seasoned surfers should head to La Jolla's Windansea Beach for powerful waves. Tucked away in a residential area, Windansea's entrance is marked by large rocks that make for a great place to watch or dry out, but recreational swimming is not advised here due to the strong surf.

TORREY PINES STATE BEACH

Situated at the base of a 1,500-acre natural reserve, La Jolla's Torrey Pines State Beach offers a long, narrow stretch of pristine beach framed by picturesque sea cliffs. Beachgoers can add a hike to their itinerary that starts or finishes on the sand, with plenty of lookout areas for great photo ops. Beyond the bluffs, a salt marsh provides seclusion from businesses and their associated street noise.

LA JOLLA SHORES

Pack up the whole family for a beach day in La Jolla Shores, which is known for its calm waves, two parks, and playground. Sea caves and underwater canyons that are part of La Jolla Underwater Park and Ecological Reserve—a marine protected area—attract kayakers and scuba divers.

DEL MAR CITY BEACH

In the upscale coastal neighborhood of Del Mar lie two beach parks that are popular for special events because of their stunning views of the Pacific. Seagrove Park is perched on the hill at the end of 15th Street, with benches for ocean gazing and winding paths along the bluffs. Farther north across the railroad tracks, Powerhouse Park offers easy beach access, a playground area, and a volleyball court.

SWAMI'S STATE BEACH

West of the magnificent Self-Realization Fellowship Temple and Meditation Gardens in Encinitas, this beach draws surfers and yogis in with its Zen vibes, while others treat the steep staircase leading down to the beach as a workout, with a rewarding view of sea cliffs waiting at the bottom. At low tide, shells and other sea creatures are left behind for beachcombers to easily discover.

FLETCHER COVE BEACH PARK

Nestled in the heart of Solana Beach, Fletcher Cove Beach Park doubles as a recreational park and beach access area. Here you'll find a basketball court, playground, lawn area, and picnic tables. A paved ramp leads down to the crescent-shape beach that's flanked by cliffs on both sides. For sweeping views of the ocean, position yourself at one of the lookouts outfitted with seating and/or binoculars—yup, binoculars are waiting for you.

BEACON'S BEACH

Follow the windy dirt path laden with switchbacks down to find Beacon's Beach in Encinitas, a well-known beach spot and favorite locals' hangout; on maps it may be labeled Leucadia State Beach. Since its entrance is hidden below sea cliffs on a one-way residential street, Beacon's Beach has an air of exclusivity. With plenty of space to spread out here, you won't have to infringe on sun-worshipping neighbors.

MOONLIGHT STATE BEACH

Fans of active beach days should head to this Encinitas beach. Volleyball courts, picnic tables, and playgrounds line the beach, with a concession stand, equipment rentals, and free Sunday concerts in high season.

10 Best Celebrity Hangouts in Los Angeles

CAFÉ GRATITUDE LARCHMONT
Round out your L.A. vacation with a plant-based meal at local chain Café Gratitude. For a celeb sighting, head to their Larchmont Boulevard location where Jake Gyllenhaal and Beyoncé obligingly declare what they're grateful for before digging in.

THE HOLLYWOOD ROOSEVELT
The Hollywood Roosevelt is one of L.A.'s oldest hotels, and has hosted numerous celebrities and dignitaries in its Spanish Colonial Revival rooms. Set in the heart of Hollywood, it offers a convenient location as well as a number of watering holes, including Tropicana Bar next to the pool.

PINZ BOWLING CENTER
For a bit of family-friendly fun, head to Pinz in Studio City, where bowling is more than just a game, it's also a neon- and black-light party. Celebrities often pop in here for bowling night, from A-listers like Vin Diesel and Jessica Alba to performers like Bruno Mars and Missy Elliott.

THE GROVE
L.A. may be strewn with outdoor malls, but it's The Grove that gets the highest billing, not just for its collection of mid- to high-end shops and restaurants, but also for its next-door neighbor, the Farmers Market. It's also one of the best places to see stars like Lena Headey, Zendaya, and Mario Lopez.

NOBU MALIBU
Nobu is a known A-list hot spot that's hosted everyone from Keanu Reeves to Kaia Gerber. Even if you don't spot a star, it's still worth the trip for its impeccable sushi and sashimi. Be warned, though: mingling with A-listers doesn't come cheap.

CATCH
Secure a table at the flora-cluttered Catch in West Hollywood and rub elbows with the likes of David Beckham and the Jenner-Kardashian clan. This eatery is as L.A. as you can get, with its alfresco setting, vegan and gluten-free offerings, and locally and sustainably grown ingredients.

CRAIG'S
A West Hollywood dining staple, Craig's plain facade provides a safe haven for the movie industry's most important names and well-known faces like John Legend and Chrissy Teigen. Just keep in mind this joint is always busy, so you might not even get a table. It's a good thing the food is worth the effort.

TOSCANA
Upscale Brentwood is home to many celebrities, and rustic trattoria Toscana is one of their neighborhood haunts. It may not be L.A.'s best Italian restaurant—for that, check out Osteria Mozza—but for star sightings, it's your best bet.

RUNYON CANYON
Of L.A.'s many beautiful hikes, Runyon Canyon gets the biggest share of celebrity regulars, probably because it's tucked between the Hollywood Hills, where many stars live, and the Sunset Strip. It's also a great place to get some fresh air and take panoramic sunset photos.

CHATEAU MARMONT
The Chateau Marmont is possibly L.A.'s best-known celebrity haunt. Come for brunch in the garden terrace or drop in at night for the Hollywood-inspired cocktails. Photos are not allowed.

What to Read and Watch

CHINATOWN

In this 1974 film noir, a young private eye (Jack Nicholson) in Depression-era Los Angeles gets in over his head with a client's case involving her husband's death. It's a tale of corruption and intrigue that incorporates fictionalized details of L.A.'s historic water wars.

FAST TIMES AT RIDGEMONT HIGH

Many don't know that this humorous, coming-of-age, cult classic was based on the journalistic efforts of *Rolling Stone* prodigy Cameron Crowe. He spent a year undercover at San Diego's Clairemont High School, and the resulting book (1981) and movie (1982) are accounts of this wild, adolescent period and its characters.

MULHOLLAND DRIVE

Surreal, psychotic, and artsy, David Lynch's 2001 film paints L.A. as a city of creepy fun house turns and blurs the lines between reality and cuts from a movie. Such dichotomies also exist in the two main characters: Betty, the blond Midwesterner fresh to L.A., and Rita, an amnesiac shrouded in darkness and mystery.

SUNSET BOULEVARD

This classic, 1950s, Billy Wilder movie offers a wild, entertaining glimpse at the film business and its eccentric characters. A has-been star and a young screenwriter hope to use each other in some way. But things get complicated, demonstrating that what happens behind the scenes in Hollywood isn't the same as what appears on the big screen.

ASK THE DUST BY JOHN FANTE

During the Great Depression, an Italian American writer lives in a seedy Los Angeles hotel and struggles with poverty, love, and creativity. Downtown is rendered well, and the character's relationship with Los Angeles is nuanced.

THE GANGSTER WE ARE ALL LOOKING FOR BY LE THI DIEM THUY

The characters of this novel, based on the author's own childhood, are Vietnamese refugees in the late '70s, adjusting to life in crowded bungalows and apartments of Normal Heights, Linda Vista, and east San Diego.

HAM ON RYE BY CHARLES BUKOWSKI

America's favorite degenerate poet writes an off-the-cuff novel about growing up in L.A. during the mid-20th century as the child of German immigrants. Told through Henry Chinaski, the author's alter ego and antihero, the book offers gritty takes on everything from family violence, alcoholism, and school-yard bullying to Model Ts and orange trees.

THE HOUSE OF BROKEN ANGELS BY LUIS ALBERTO AURREA

Focusing on three generations of a Mexican-American family, with a history in the California Territories since World War I, this robust, happy novel teems with big personalities and vivid characters.

THE REVOLT OF THE COCKROACH PEOPLE BY OSCAR ZETA ACOSTA

Grounded in real events, this story outlines aspects of east Los Angeles's Chicano movement through protests, marches, and court cases. The main protagonist is based on the fascinating author, an activist, lawyer/politician, and key player in the movement.

Chapter 2

TRAVEL SMART

Updated by
Daniel Mangin

★ **CAPITAL:**
Sacramento

👥 **POPULATION:**
39 million

💬 **LANGUAGE:**
English

$ **CURRENCY:**
U.S. dollar

☎ **COUNTRY CODE:**
1

⚠ **EMERGENCIES:**
911

🚗 **DRIVING:**
On the right

⚡ **ELECTRICITY:**
120–240 v/60 cycles;
plugs have two or three
rectangular prongs

🕐 **TIME:**
Three hours behind New
York

🌐 **WEB RESOURCES:**
www.visitcalifornia.com,
www.parks.ca.gov, dot.
ca.gov/travel,
travel.state.gov

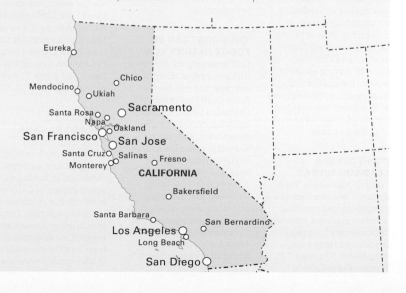

Know Before You Go

To help you prepare for a visit to the vast, diverse, unique state of California, below are tips about driving, destinations, the weather, saving money at restaurants and hotels, wildlife, cannabis tourism, and things to see and do that might save you time or money or increase peace of mind.

ROAD TRIPS TAKE TIME

California has some of the most scenic drives in the world. It's also the third-largest state behind Alaska and Texas and, in square miles, is similar in size to Sweden, Japan, or Paraguay. So, if you want to see all its beaches, deserts, mountains, and forests, you'll need a car—and, perhaps, a bit of patience.

A road trip through even half of the state takes several hours in the best of traffic (frequently not the case), and this doesn't count contending with winding, mountainous terrain, or coastal fog. Rule of thumb: factoring in an extra 20% or 25% more time than the GPS driving estimate lessens the chance you'll miss events or connections. Who knows? You might be surprised and arrive early—or at least on time.

DON'T LET GPS LEAD YOU ASTRAY

"Your GPS is Wrong: Turn Around," warns a sign on a steep dead-end road that some smartphone mapping apps mistake for a small mountain town's main drag below. Although GPS is generally reliable in cities and suburbs, it's less so in coastal, mountain, and desert areas, including some national and state parks. In addition to referencing the maps in this book, back yourself up with old-school atlases or fold-out paper maps.

If you plot out a trip and begin navigation while reception is good, you should still receive turning directions even if you move out of range. If you're already out of range when initiating a search, you won't be able to access route information.

THE COAST CAN BE FOGGY IN SUNNY CA

California rightfully earns its sunny reputation: on average, the sun shines more than two-thirds of the year in most regions, but with deserts, beaches, mountains, and forests, you should prepare for wide variations in temperature and conditions. This is especially true along the coast and at higher altitudes, where it's best to dress in layers year-round. On a day when it's 85° or 95° inland, the temperature along the coast can be 55° and windy.

In July and August, hot inland temperatures often cause cooler Pacific Ocean air—in the form of fog—to blanket areas nearest the shore. As a rule along the coast: the farther south you go, the drier and hotter the weather tends to be. The farther north you go, the cooler and wetter you'll likely find it.

"WINE COUNTRY" IS MORE THAN NAPA AND SONOMA

Modern California wine making got its start in Sonoma County, and Napa Valley wines raised the state's profile worldwide, but with about 4,800 bonded wineries from the Oregon border to San Diego County—the world's fourth-largest producer, making 80-plus percent of U.S. wines—the whole state's pretty much "Wine Country." Tasting rooms abound, even in unlikely places.

The state's most-planted red-wine grapes, in order, are Cabernet Sauvignon, Pinot Noir, Zinfandel, and Merlot. Among the whites, Chardonnay is by far the most grown, with French Colombard, Sauvignon Blanc, and Pinot Gris the runners-up.

NO NEED TO BREAK THE BANK

Away from coastal California or the eastern mountains on summer weekends or during ski season, much of California is affordable. In some cases, it's even a bargain. Tasting fees in lesser-known wine regions, for example, are at least half the price of those in high-profile ones, and some wineries even provide sips for free. In many inland areas, except for the fanciest bed-and-breakfasts, room rates trend lower than by the shore.

AVOIDING STICKER SHOCK AT RESTAURANTS

Even if you're not dining at temples of haute cuisine, eating out in California can induce sticker shock. There are several ways to avoid this. Have the day's fancy meal at brunch or lunch, when prices tend to be lower. Happy hour, when a restaurant might serve a signature appetizer or smaller version of a famous plate at a lower price, is another option. Even small towns in the interior are likely to have a purveyor or two of gourmet food to go, making picnicking in a park or eating back at your lodging a viable strategy.

AVOIDING STICKER SHOCK AT HOTELS

California's hotels, inns, and resorts are the most expensive from late spring to early fall. The easiest way to avoid sticker shock is to come during winter when prices are the least expensive except at ski resorts and a few desert hot spots. Year-round, you can save money by traveling midweek, when rates tend to drop. Visiting during the shoulder seasons of mid-to-late spring and mid-to-late fall, when the weather can be nice and the crowds less formidable, can also save you money.

Many travelers cut costs by booking a big-city business hotel on the weekend, when rates trend lower (with Sunday often the cheapest night of the week at such places). Conversely, weekend prices at beach or countryside resorts are generally high but sometimes drop midweek.

MAKERS AND MUSEUMS

The state's early-21st-century DIY types birthed what's come to be known as the maker movement, and throughout California you'll see evidence of this artisanal activity. Blue jeans, lasers, Apple computers, sourdough bread, Popsicles, McDonald's, Barbie Dolls, Hollywood movie glamour, and television all emerged from California. Nearly 3,000 museums (more than any other state) honor such accomplishments and more—if you can think of it, a museum here probably celebrates it.

PLAY BALL

Because the weather is basically great year-round, there's a dynamic sports culture in the Golden State. Spectacular (and often free) recreation areas and parks offer opportunities for surfing, skiing, hiking, and biking, among other activities.

If you're more into spectating, California supports more professional sports teams than any other state, including five MLB, four NBA (plus one WNBA), three NFL and NHL franchises, and several (men's and women's) soccer squads. You can witness athletic greatness at the highest levels any day of the week.

CALL OF THE WILDLIFE

Off the coast, creatures from gray and humpback whales to blue whales and orcas might come into view, along with sea lions, elephant seals, dolphins, and the occasional shark. Inland forests contain black bears, mountain lions, bobcats, beavers, and foxes. The desert supplies no end of reptiles, and the entire state is a birder's paradise.

Wild animals generally avoid interacting with humans, but contact is not unheard of. Most state and national parks post advice about steering clear of potentially dangerous encounters and what to do if you find yourself in one.

POT IS LEGAL, BUT…

Marijuana is legal in California for medical and recreational purposes. If you're 21 (or 18 with a doctor's order) and have proof of age or medical status, you can acquire and use marijuana, albeit not always in public. The California Cannabis Portal website maintains a searchable database (⊕ search. cannabis.ca.gov/retailers) of licensed dispensaries, where cannabis might come as flowers, edibles, and concentrates, among other things. The Cannabis Travel Association (⊕ cannabistravelasso-ciation.org) promotes "safe and responsible cannabis tourism" and provides general information.

Getting Here and Around

Air

Most national and many international airlines fly to California. Flying time to the state is about 6½ hours from New York and 4¾ hours from Chicago. Travel from London to either Los Angeles or San Francisco is 11½ hours and from Sydney approximately 14 hours. Flying between San Francisco and Los Angeles takes about 90 minutes.

Bus

Greyhound is the primary bus carrier in California. Regional bus service is available in metropolitan areas.

Car

A car is essential in most of California, the exceptions being parts of its largest cities, where it can be more convenient to use public transportation, taxis, or ride-sharing services. Two main north–south routes run through California: I–5 through the middle of the state, and U.S. 101, a parallel route closer to the coast. Slower but more scenic is Highway 1, which winds along much of the coast.

The state's main east–west routes are I–8, I–10, and I–15 (in the south) and I–80 (in the north). Much of California is mountainous, and you may encounter winding roads and steep mountain grades.

From Los Angeles To:	By Air	By Car
San Diego	55 mins	I–5 or I–405; 127 miles; 2 hrs
Las Vegas	70 mins	I–10 to I–15; 275 miles; 4 hrs
Death Valley	No flights	I–5 to Hwy. 14 to U.S. 395 to Hwy. 178 to Hwy. 190; 260 miles; 5 hrs
San Francisco	90 mins	I–5 to I–580 to I–80; 382 miles; 6 hrs
Monterey	70 mins	U.S. 101 to Hwy. 68 to Hwy. 1; 330 miles; 5 hrs
Santa Barbara	50 mins	U.S. 101; 95 miles; 1 hr 40 mins
Big Sur	No flights	U.S. 101 to Hwy. 1; 349 miles; 5 hrs 40 mins
Sacramento	90 mins	1–5; 385 miles; 6 hrs

Train

Amtrak provides rail service within California. On some trips, passengers board motor coaches part of the way.

Essentials

⚡ Activities

Athletic Californians often boast that it's possible to surf in the morning and ski in the afternoon (or vice versa) in the Golden State. With thousands of hiking, biking, and horse-riding trails and hundreds of lakes, rivers, and streams for fishing, swimming, and boating—not to mention sandy coastal strands for sunning and surfing and other beaches with dunes or rocks to explore—there's no shortage of outdoor fun to be had. One challenge on many a hiker's bucket list is the Pacific Crest Trail, which travels the length of the state. The National Park Service operates numerous parks and sites in California, and the state park system is robust. If you're interested in Native American heritage, Visit California's website (⊕ *visitcalifornia.com/native*) has a section devoted to indigenous cultural travel.

🍴 Dining

California has led the pack in bringing natural and organic foods to the forefront of American dining. Though rooted in European cuisine, California cooking sometimes has strong Asian and Latin influences. Wherever you go, you're likely to find that dishes are made with fresh produce and other local ingredients.

The restaurants we list are the cream of the crop in each price category. ⇨ *Restaurant reviews have been shortened. For full information, visit Fodors.com. For price information, see the Planning sections in each chapter.*

DISCOUNTS AND DEALS

The better grocery and specialty-food stores have grab-and-go sections, with prepared foods on par with restaurant cooking, perfect for picnicking.

MEALS AND MEALTIMES

Lunch is typically served from 11 or 11:30 to 2:30 or 3, with dinner service starting at 5 or 5:30 and lasting until 9 or later. Restaurants that serve breakfast usually open by 7, sometimes earlier, with some serving breakfast through the lunch hour. Most weekend brunches start at 10 or 11 and go at least until 2.

PAYING

Most restaurants take credit cards. Some accept cash, but others operate cashless. In most establishments tipping is the norm, but some include the service in the menu price or add it to the bill. ⇨ *For guidelines on tipping see Money, below.*

RESERVATIONS AND DRESS

It's a good idea to make a reservation when possible. Where reservations are indicated as essential, book a week or more ahead in summer and early fall. Large parties should always call ahead to check the reservations policy. Except as noted in individual listings, dress is informal.

➕ Health/Safety

If you have a medical condition that may require emergency treatment, be aware that many rural and mountain communities have only daytime clinics, not hospitals with 24-hour emergency rooms. Take the usual precautions to protect your person and belongings. In large cities, ask at your lodging about areas to avoid, and lock valuables in a hotel safe when not using them. Car break-ins are common in some larger cities, but it's always a good idea to remove valuables from your car or at least keep them out of sight.

Essentials

COVID-19

Most travel restrictions, including vaccination and masking requirements, have been lifted across the United States except in health-care facilities and nursing homes. Some travelers may still wish to wear a mask in confined spaces, including on airplanes, on public transportation, and at large indoor gatherings, but that is increasingly a personal choice. Be aware that some local mandates still exist and should be followed.

THE OUTDOORS

At beaches, heed warnings about high surf and deadly rogue waves, and don't fly within 24 hours of scuba diving. When hiking, stay on trails, and heed all warning signs about loose cliffs, predatory animals, and poison ivy or oak.

Before heading into remote areas, let someone know your trip route, destination, and estimated time and date of return. Make sure your vehicle is in good condition and equipped with a first-aid kit, snacks, extra water, jack, spare tire, tools, and a towrope or chain. Mind your gas gauge, keeping the needle above half if possible and stopping to top off the tank whenever you can.

In arid regions, stay on main roads, and watch out for wildlife, horses, and cattle. Don't enter mine tunnels or shafts. Not only can such structures be unstable, but they might also have hidden dangers such as pockets of bad air. Be mindful of sudden rainstorms, when floodwaters can cover or wash away roads and quickly fill up dry riverbeds and canyons. Never place your hands or feet where you can't see them: rattlesnakes, scorpions, and black widow spiders may be hiding there.

Sunscreen and hats are musts, and layered clothing is best as desert temperatures can fluctuate greatly between dawn and dusk. Drink at least a gallon of water a day (three gallons if you're hiking or otherwise exerting yourself). If you have a headache or feel dizzy or nauseous, you could be suffering from dehydration. Get out of the sun immediately, dampen your clothing to lower your body temperature, and drink plenty of water.

Although you might not feel thirsty in cooler, mountain climes, it's important to stay hydrated (drinking at least a quart of water during activities) at high altitudes, where the air is thinner, causing you to breathe more heavily. Always bring a fold-up rain poncho to keep you dry and prevent hypothermia. Wear long pants, a hat, and sturdy, closed-toe hiking boots with soles that grip rock. If you're going into the backcountry, bring a signaling device (such as a mirror), emergency whistle, compass, map, energy bars, and water purifier.

🛏 Lodging

California has inns, motels, hotels, and specialty accommodations to suit every traveler's fancy and finances. Retro motels recalling 1950s roadside culture but with 21st-century amenities are a popular trend, but you'll also see traditional motels and hotels, along with luxury resorts and boutique properties.

The state's more than 1,000 bed-and-breakfasts offer everything from simple home-stay options to lavish lodgings in historic hotels or homes. The California Association of Boutique and Breakfast Inns represents more than 200 member properties that you can locate and book through its website. In addition, you'll find listings for Airbnb and similar rentals throughout California.

The lodgings we review are the top choices in each price category. We don't specify whether the facilities cost extra; when pricing accommodations, ask what's included and what costs extra. ⇨ *For price information, see the Planning sections in each chapter. Hotels reviews have been shortened. For full information, visit Fodors.com.*

CHILDREN
Most hotels allow children under a certain age to stay in their parents' room at no extra charge, but others charge for them as additional adults; find out the cutoff age for discounts. Conversely, some accommodations aren't suitable for children, so check before you book.

RESERVATIONS AND CANCELLATIONS
Reservations are a good idea throughout the year, especially in summer. On weekends at smaller lodgings, minimum-stay requirements of two or three nights are common, though some places are flexible about this in winter.

Some properties allow you to cancel without a penalty—even if you prepaid to secure a discounted rate—if you cancel at least 24 hours in advance. Others require you to cancel a week in advance or penalize you the cost of one night. Small inns and B&Bs are most likely to require you to cancel far in advance.

💲 Money
On the coast, you'll pay top dollar for everything from gas and food to lodging and attractions. Aside from desert and ski resorts, inland prices tend to be lower.

Tipping Guidelines for California

Bartender	$1–$3 per drink, or 15%–20% per round
Bellhop	$2–$5 per bag, depending on the level of the hotel
Hotel Concierge	$5–$10 for advice and reservations, more for difficult tasks
Hotel Doorman	$3–$5 for hailing a cab
Valet Parking Attendant	$3–$5 when you get your car
Hotel Maid	$4–$6 per day (either daily or at the end of your stay, in cash)
Waiter	18%–22% (20%–25% is standard in upscale restaurants); nothing additional if a service charge is added to the bill
Skycap at Airport	$2 per bag
Hotel Room-Service Waiter	15%–20% per delivery, even if a service charge was added since that fee goes to the hotel, not the waiter
Tasting-room server	$5–$10 per couple basic tasting, $5–$10 per person hosted seated tasting
Taxi Driver	15%–20%, but round up the fare to the next dollar amount
Tour Guide	15% of the cost of the tour, more depending on quality

Essentials

In terms of gratuities, obviously the amount you tip (or if you tip at all) is a matter of personal preference. Remember, though, that in California, as in the rest of the United States, many people who work in the service industry rely on tips to earn a living wage. The degree and quality of service also come into play when considering what to tip.

TAXES

Depending on the city or county, you'll pay from 7.25% to 10.75% in sales tax, with larger urban areas toward the higher end. Exceptions include grocery-store food items and some takeout. Hotel taxes vary from 4% to 15%.

🧳 Packing

The California lifestyle emphasizes casual wear, and with the generally mild climate you needn't worry about packing cold-weather clothing unless you're going into mountainous areas. Jeans, walking shorts, and T-shirts are acceptable in most situations. Few restaurants require men to wear a jacket or tie, though a collared shirt is the norm at upscale establishments.

Summer evenings can be cool, especially near the coast, where fog often rolls in. Always pack a sweater or light jacket. If you're headed to state or national parks, packing binoculars, clothes that layer, long pants and long-sleeve shirts, sunglasses, and a wide-brimmed hat is wise. Pick up insect repellent, sunscreen, and a first-aid kit once in-state.

📅 When to Go

Expect high summer heat in the desert areas and low winter temperatures in the Sierra Nevada and other inland mountain ranges.

HIGH SEASON $$$–$$$$

High season lasts from late May through early September (a little later in wine regions and well into winter in desert resorts and ski areas). Expect higher hotel occupancy rates and prices.

LOW SEASON $$

From December to March, tourist activity slows. Except in the mountainous areas, which may see snowfall and an influx of skiers, winters here are mild, and hotels are cheaper.

VALUE SEASON $$–$$$

From April to late May and from late September to mid-November the weather is pleasant and hotel prices are reasonable.

Contacts

✈ Air

AIRLINES
CONTACTS Air Canada.
☎ 888/247–2262 ⊕ www.
aircanada.com. **Alaska Airlines/Horizon Air.**
☎ 800/252–7522 ⊕ www.
alaskaair.com. **American Airlines.** ☎ 800/433–7300
⊕ www.aa.com. **Delta Airlines.** ☎ 800/221–1212
for U.S. reservations,
800/241–4141 for international reservations
⊕ www.delta.com. **Frontier Airlines.** ☎ 801/401–9000
⊕ www.flyfrontier.com.
JetBlue. ☎ 800/538–2583
⊕ www.jetblue.com.
Southwest Airlines.
☎ 800/435–9792 ⊕ www.
southwest.com. **United Airlines.** ☎ 800/864–8331
⊕ www.united.com.

AIRLINE SECURITY ISSUES
CONTACTS Transportation Security Administration.
(TSA). ☎ 866/289–9673
⊕ www.tsa.gov.

AIRPORTS
Hollywood Burbank Airport.
☎ 818/840–8840 ⊕ www.
hollywoodburbankairport.
com. **John Wayne Airport,
Orange County.** ☎ 949/252–
5200 ⊕ www.ocair.
com. **Long Beach Airport.**
☎ 562/570–2600 ⊕ www.
lgb.org.

Los Angeles International Airport. ☎ 855/463–5252
⊕ www.flylax.com.
Ontario International Airport.
☎ 909/544–5300 ⊕ www.
flyontario.com. **San Diego International Airport.**
☎ 619/400–2400 ⊕ www.
san.org.

🚌 Bus
CONTACTS Greyhound.
☎ 800/231–2222 ⊕ www.
greyhound.com.

🚗 Car
ASSISTANCE American Automobile Association.
(AAA). ☎ 800/222–4357
⊕ www.aaa.com.

INFORMATION Caltrans Current Highway Conditions. ☎ 800/427–7623
⊕ quickmap.dot.ca.gov.
511 Traffic/Transit Alerts.
☎ 511.

MAJOR RENTAL AGENCIES Alamo.
☎ 800/462–5266
⊕ www.alamo.com.
Avis. ☎ 800/633–3469
⊕ www.avis.com. **Budget.**
☎ 800/218–7992 ⊕ www.
budget.com. **Hertz.**
☎ 800/654–3131 ⊕ www.
hertz.com.

National Car Rental.
☎ 844/382–6875 ⊕ www.
nationalcar.com.

SPECIALTY CAR AGENCIES Enterprise Exotic Car Rentals.
☎ 866/458–9227 ⊕ www.
enterprise.com.

🛏 Lodging
CONTACTS California Association of Boutique and Breakfast Inns. (CABBI).
☎ 800/373–9251 ⊕ www.
cabbi.com.

🚆 Train
CONTACTS Amtrak.
☎ 800/872–7245 ⊕ www.
amtrak.com.

Chapter 3

SOUTHERN CALIFORNIA'S BEST ROAD TRIPS

Updated by
Daniel Mangin

3

A California visit wouldn't be complete without taking a spin through the state's spectacular scenery. However, adding a road trip to your itinerary is not just a romantic idea: it's often a practical one, too—perhaps linking one urban area with another, say, or sampling some of this massive state's remote areas. Whether you have just a few days or longer to spare, these itineraries will help you hit the road.

SoCal for Kids and the Young at Heart, 7 Days

Southern California offers many opportunities to entertain the kids and the young at heart beyond the Magic Kingdom, this trip's last stop. San Diego's LEGOLAND is a blast for kids 12 and under, and the city's diverse attractions include a water park, the zoo, and several historic districts. Oh yes, and well-groomed La Jolla and other beach towns, too. If you can, fly into San Diego and out of Los Angeles to save time and maybe money.

DAYS 1–2: LEGOLAND
LEGOLAND's hotels are a 35-min drive from the airport.

Arrive at **San Diego** International Airport, pick up your rental car, and settle in at the **LEGOLAND Hotel** or the **Sheraton Carlsbad Resort & Spa,** perhaps taking a dip in the pool. In the late afternoon, drive south along the Pacific Coast Highway (PCH) past popular San Diego County surfing beaches. Stop in Solana Beach or Del Mar for a sunset cocktail, perhaps staying for dinner.

Getting an early start for an action-packed day at **LEGOLAND** is a breeze because both hotels offer direct access to the park. LEGOLAND has a water park, an aquarium, and LEGO-based rides, shows, and roller coasters. Little ones can live out their fairy-tale fantasies, and bigger ones can spend all day on waterslides, shooting water pistols, driving boats, or water fighting with pirates.

DAY 3: DOWNTOWN SAN DIEGO
Downtown is 35 mins from Carlsbad.

Check out of your LEGOLAND hotel in the late morning, taking the freeway south 35 minutes to **Downtown San Diego.** It'll probably be too early to check in (do it when convenient later in the afternoon), but park your car at your hotel and drop off your bags. Then proceed straight to the city's nautical heart, exploring the restored ships of the **Maritime Museum** and walking south along the waterfront. Victorian buildings—and plenty of other tourists—surround you on a stroll inland a few blocks to **Gaslamp Quarter,** where you can grab a happy-hour cocktail or mocktail before dining close to your hotel.

DAY 4: SEA WORLD, OLD TOWN, AND LA JOLLA

SeaWorld is 15 mins from Downtown; Old Town is 10 mins from SeaWorld; La Jolla is 20 mins from Old Town.

Two commercial and touristy sights are on the agenda, with a sunset cocktail the day's-end reward. With its walk-through shark tanks, **SeaWorld** delivers a ton of fun if you surrender to the experience. Also touristy, but with genuine historical significance, **Old Town** drips with Mexican and early Californian heritage. Soak it up in the plaza at **Old Town San Diego State Historic Park,** then browse the stalls and shops at **Fiesta de Reyes** and along San Diego Avenue. As the day winds down, make your way to **La Jolla Cove.** At the **Children's Pool,** look at, but don't go in the water, which is likely to be filled with barking seals. Have a sunset cocktail in La Jolla and dine there or Downtown.

DAY 5: SAN DIEGO ZOO

10 mins by car from Downtown San Diego.

Malayan tapirs in a faux-Asian rain forest, polar bears in an imitation Arctic, and orangutans and siamangs swinging through the trees—the **San Diego Zoo** maintains a vast and varied collection of creatures in a world-renowned facility comprised of meticulously designed habitats. Come early, and wear comfy shoes. If you have time, explore a little of **Balboa Park,** which contains the zoo. Have dinner in the Hillcrest neighborhood near the park, or dine Downtown.

DAYS 6–7: DISNEYLAND

90 mins by car from San Diego to Disneyland.

As early as you can get moving, hop onto I-5 and drive north. By the time you reach San Clemente, you'll be in **Orange County** (aka the O.C.). In less than an hour from there, you'll be in **Disneyland!** Skirt the lines at the box office with advance-purchased tickets in hand, and storm the gates of the Magic Kingdom. You can cram the highlights into a single day, but if you get a two-day ticket and stay the night, you can see the end-of-day parade and visit **Downtown Disney** before heading south. The **Grand Californian Hotel & Spa** is a top choice for lodging within the Disney Resort.

Hooray for Hollywood, 3 Days

If you are a movie fan, there's no better place to see it all than L.A. Keep your eyes peeled: you never know when you might spot a celebrity.

DAY 1: LOS ANGELES

Because of the time change, East Coast visitors flying into LAX often arrive well before noon. As soon as you land, make like a local, and hit the freeway to your hotel, dropping off your luggage even if your room isn't ready (it's safer). Even if L.A.'s top-notch art, history, and science museums don't tempt you, the mélange of art deco, Beaux Arts, and futuristic architecture begs at least a drive-by.

Wilshire Boulevard heading east from Santa Monica cuts through a historical and cultural cross section of the city. Two stellar sights on Wilshire's **Miracle Mile** are the encyclopedic **Los Angeles County Museum of Art** and the fossil-filled **La Brea Tar Pits.** Come evening, the open-air **Original Farmers Market** and its many eateries hum.

DAY 2: HOLLYWOOD AND THE MOVIE STUDIOS

Avoid driving to the studios during rush hr. Studio tours vary in length—plan at least a half day for the excursion.

Every L.A. tourist should experience at least one San Fernando Valley studio tour. For fun, choose the special-effects theme park at **Universal Studios Hollywood**; for the nitty-gritty, choose **Warner Bros. Studios.** Nostalgic musts in Hollywood itself include the **Hollywood Walk of Fame** along **Hollywood Boulevard** and the celebrity footprints cast in concrete outside **Grauman's Chinese Theatre** (now known as the TCL Chinese Theater). When evening arrives, the Hollywood scene includes a bevy of trendy restaurants and nightclubs.

DAY 3: THE GETTY, SANTA MONICA, VENICE, BEVERLY HILLS

15–20 mins by car between destinations, but considerably longer in traffic.

The **Getty Center**'s pavilion architecture, hilltop gardens, and frame-worthy L.A. views make it a dazzling destination—and that's before you experience the Brentwood museum's extensive art collection. From here, descend to the sea via Santa Monica Boulevard for a late lunch along the **Third Street Promenade,** followed by a ride on the historic **Santa Monica Pier Carousel.**

The buff and the bizarre meet at **Venice Beach's** Ocean Front Walk, an extension of Santa Monica's same-named boardwalk—strap on some back-in-vogue in-line skates if you want to join them.

Over in Beverly Hills, the **Rodeo Drive** shopping district specializes in exhibitionism with a hefty price tag, but voyeurs are still welcome. Have dinner in Beverly Hills or West Hollywood.

Palm Springs and the Desert, 5 Days

Many visitors consider the Palm Springs area pure paradise, and not just for the opportunity to get a good tan or play golf on championship courses. Expect fabulous and funky spas, a dog-friendly atmosphere, and sparkling stars at night.

DAY 1: ARRIVE AT PALM SPRINGS

Just over 2 hrs by car from LAX, without traffic.

Somehow in harmony with the harsh environment, mid-century-modern homes and businesses define the **Palm Springs** style. Although the desert cities—Rancho Mirage, Palm Desert, Indian Wells, Indio, and La Quinta—comprise a trendy destination with sumptuous hotels, multicultural cuisine, abundant nightlife,

and plenty of culture, a quiet atmosphere prevails. Fans of Palm Springs' legendary architecture won't want to miss the home tours, lectures, and other events at the annual Modernism Week held each February or the smaller fall preview event in October. If your visit doesn't coincide with these happenings, swing by the Palm Springs Visitor's Center for information on self-guided architecture tours.

The city seems far away when you hike in hushed **Tahquitz** or **Indian Canyon**; cliffs and palm trees shelter rock art, irrigation works, and other remnants of Agua Caliente culture. If your boots aren't made for walking, you can always practice your golf game or indulge in spa treatments at an area resort instead. Embrace the Palm Springs vibe, and park yourself at the modern-chic **Kimpton The Rowan Palm Springs Hotel** or the legendary **Parker Palm Springs.** Alternatively, base yourself at the desert oasis, **La Quinta Resort & Club,** about 40 minutes from downtown Palm Springs.

DAY 2: EXPLORE PALM SPRINGS

The Aerial Tram is 15 mins by car from central Palm Springs. Plan at least a half day for the excursion.

If riding a tram up an 8,516-foot mountain for a stroll or even a snowball fight above the desert sounds like fun, then show up at the **Palm Springs Aerial Tramway** before the first morning tram leaves (later, the line can get discouragingly long). Dress in layers, and wear decent footwear as it can be significantly colder at the top. Afterward, stroll through the **Palm Springs Art Museum,** with its shimmering display of contemporary studio glass, array of Native American baskets, and significant 20th-century sculptures by Henry Moore and others. After all that walking you may be ready for an early dinner. Nearly every restaurant in Palm Springs offers a happy hour, during which you can sip a cocktail and nosh on a light entrée, usually for half price.

DAY 3: JOSHUA TREE NATIONAL PARK

1 hr by car from Palm Springs.

Joshua Tree is among the most accessible of the national parks. You can see most of it in a day, entering the park at the town of Joshua Tree, exploring sites along **Park Boulevard,** and exiting at **Twentynine Palms.** With the signature trees, piles of rocks, glorious spring wildflowers, starlit skies, and colorful pioneer history, the experience is more like the Wild West than Sahara dunes. Whether planning to take a day hike or a scenic drive, load up on drinking water before entering the park.

DAY 4: INDIO AND THE SALTON SEA

Indio is about 30 mins by car from Palm Springs; the Salton Sea is 40 mins from Indio.

Head southeast from Palm Springs via I-10 to **Indio,** the state's date-growing capital and home to the famous Coachella music festival every April. En route, stop in the **Coachella Valley Preserve** for a glimpse of the desert before development. The **Shield's Date Garden & Café,** just 4 miles west of Indio on Highway 111, is a great place to grab a bite and sample dates, perhaps in the form of shakes, pancakes—even burgers.

The **Salton Sea,** about 40 miles southeast of Indio via Highway 86S, is one of the largest inland seas on Earth. Formed by the flooding of the Colorado River in 1905, it attracts thousands of migrating birds and bird-watchers every fall.

DAY 5: RETURN TO L.A.

LAX is just over 2 hrs by car from Palm Springs without traffic, but the drive often takes significantly more time.

If you intend to depart from LAX, plan for a full day of driving from the desert to the airport. Be prepared for heavy traffic at any time of day or night. If possible, fly out of Palm Springs International Airport or Ontario International Airport instead.

Southern PCH: Sand, Surf, and Sun, 4 Days

This tour along the southern section of the Pacific Coast Highway (PCH) is a beach vacation on wheels, taking in the highlights of the Southern California coast and its surfer-chic vibe. If the drive feels like something out of a movie, that's because it likely is—this is the California of Hollywood legend. And this segment is only the warm-up: after you get to Santa Barbara, you can keep heading north as far up the coast as time permits. Roll the top down on the convertible and let the adventure begin.

DAY 1: LAGUNA BEACH TO NEWPORT BEACH

1 hr by car.

Easily accessed off I–5, the PCH begins near Dana Point, a town famous for its harbor and whale-watching excursions, but you can just as easily start 10 miles north in **Laguna Beach.** Browse the art galleries, and enjoy lunch in the charming downtown before or after walking along the Pacific. Then head north a few miles to **Crystal Cove State Park.** When the tide's low, this is a wonderful spot for tide pooling. Don't miss the historic beach cottages dating as far back as 1935.

From the park, continue north a few more miles to **Newport Beach.** The affluent coastal cities of Orange County (aka the O.C.) are familiar to many thanks to *Arrested Development, The Real Wives of Orange County,* and other TV shows, though the yachts and multimillion-dollar mansions of Newport Beach may still take you by surprise. **Balboa Island,** a quaint, if expensive, getaway, sits in the middle of Newport Harbor. Browse the boutiques along Marine Avenue before hopping in a Duffy (electric boat) for a

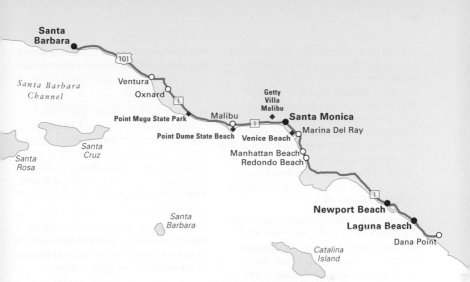

harbor tour. Back on land, enjoy a Balboa Bar—the ice-cream treat is virtually mandatory for all Balboa Island visitors. Spend the night on Balboa Island or elsewhere in Newport Beach.

DAY 2: NEWPORT BEACH TO SANTA MONICA

About 2 hrs by car without traffic, but plan on it.

From Newport Beach, eschew Highway 1, driving north on Highway 55 to the 405 freeway, also north. Exit at West 190th Street, following the signs to Redondo Beach, which—along with Hermosa and Manhattan beaches to the north—is popular with beach-volleyball enthusiasts. If time permits, follow Highway 1 through Marina del Ray; otherwise, skip this section of the PCH in favor of the 405 freeway. (As is always advisable near L.A., check current traffic reports before choosing your route.)

Get settled into a hotel near the **Santa Monica Pier,** then catch some of the action there before grabbing dinner along the **Third Street Promenade** or at Santa Monica Place.

DAY 3: SANTA MONICA TO SANTA BARBARA

About 2 hrs by car via Hwy. 1 and U.S. 101. Allow more time for beach stops when the weather's good.

Begin with a morning walk along **Santa Monica State Beach.** Check out of your hotel, but leave your bags to pick up later. Rent beach cruiser bikes and pedal south about 3 miles along the bike path to **Venice Beach.** When you've had your fill of skateboarders, bodybuilders, and street performers, head inland a few blocks to Abbott Kinney Boulevard for lunch at **Gjelina** and browsing in the local boutiques. Back in Santa Monica, drop off your bikes and begin the drive north to Santa Barbara. If you plan to visit the **Getty Villa Malibu** and its impressive antiquities collection and jaw-dropping setting overlooking the Pacific, spend less time on the bike ride. And be sure to obtain free timed-entry tickets—the last Getty Villa admission is at 3 pm—online before your arrival.

As you drive from Santa Monica through **Malibu** and beyond, chances are you'll experience déjà vu: mountains on one side, ocean on the other, opulent homes perched on hillsides. You've seen this piece of coast countless times on TV and film. In Malibu proper, affectionately christened "the 'bu," walk out on the **Malibu Pier** for a great photo op, then check out **Surfrider Beach,** with three famous points where perfect waves ignited a worldwide surfing rage in the 1960s. Continuing past Malibu, you'll experience miles of protected, largely unpopulated coastline. Scout for offshore whales at **Point Dume State Beach** during winter or early spring, or hike the trails at **Point Mugu State Park.**

On the north side of Oxnard, you'll trade Highway 1 for U.S. 101 (aka "the 101" and the Ventura Freeway) into **Ventura.** Approaching Ventura on a clear day, the Channel Islands are visible in the distance. If traffic hasn't held you up too much, stretch your legs on the **Ventura Oceanfront,** walking on San Buenaventura State Beach or around Ventura Harbor. Otherwise, continue to **Santa Barbara** and check into your hotel. Splurge on an overnight stay at the posh **Rosewood Miramar Beach** resort, or book a room at the **Santa Barbara Inn,** whose restaurant, **Convivo,** is a smart spot for dinner.

DAY 4: SANTA BARBARA
45 mins–1 hr by car.

Santa Barbara is a gem. Combining elegance with a laid-back coastal vibe, the city provides a tranquil escape from the congestion of Los Angeles and a dose of sophistication to the largely rural Central Coast.

Start your day at **Old Mission Santa Barbara,** known as the "Queen" of the 21 missions that comprise the California Mission Trail. Plan to spend some time here; if your visit doesn't coincide with one of the 60-minute docent-led tours, self-guided tours are also available. From here, head to the architecturally significant **Santa Barbara County Courthouse.** Don't miss the murals in the ceremonial

chambers or, from the tower, the incredible views of downtown's distinctive red-tile-roofed buildings and beyond them the Pacific Ocean.

Next up: the waterfront. Spend some time enjoying vast, sandy **East Beach,** and walk a little of **Stearns Wharf** before having lunch two blocks from the wharf at State Street's **Santo Mezcal** (upscale Mexican) or across the harbor at **Brophy Bros** (fresh, straightforward seafood with a view).

After lunch, peek into the nearby **Funk Zone**'s art galleries, and indulge in a wine tasting or two. Dine in this area, or head to **Montecito** for an elegant meal.

Santa Barbara Wine Country, 2 Days

It's been two decades since the movie *Sideways* brought the Santa Barbara Wine Country to the world's attention, and interest in this area continues to grow. This itinerary, best done from Thursday through Monday when most of the wineries and restaurants are open, makes a perfect add-on to a trip to Los Angeles and for those touring farther north along the coast.

DAY 1: BUELLTON, SOLVANG, AND LOS OLIVOS
Without stops, this route takes about 2 hrs by car. Plan to linger at—and detour down side roads to—the wineries.

Take the scenic drive along the coast on U.S. 101 toward **Buellton,** exiting west onto Santa Rosa Road and following it south less than ½ mile to the delightful **Vega Vineyard & Farm.** Before or after weekday lunch or weekend brunch, taste wine and commune with the cute farm animals.

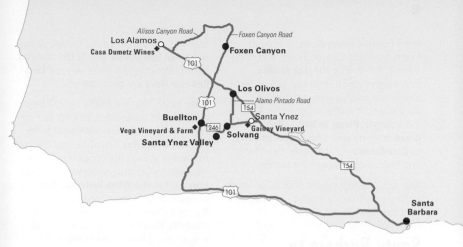

Santa Barbara Channel

From Vega, head north on U.S. 101 and east on Highway 246, signed as Mission Drive as it reaches central **Solvang.** Under its founder, **Alma Rosa Winery** pioneered cool-climate Chardonnays and Pinot Noirs from the Sta. Rita Hills AVA (west of U.S. 101 at Buellton), still a specialty, along with heftier reds from the Santa Ynez Valley AVA.

After tasting at Alma Rosa, head east on Mission Drive and north on Alamo Pintado Road to **Los Olivos,** where you can park the car and spend the rest of the day exploring on foot. Tasting rooms, galleries, boutiques, and restaurants have made this former stagecoach town wine-country chic. **Blair Fox Cellars** and **Coquelicot Estate Vineyard** are among the wineries with tasting rooms in town.

If you're staying at **Fess Parker's Wine Country Inn** or **The Inn at Mattei's Tavern,** eat at their restaurants—**Nella** and **Mattei's,** respectively—or nearby **Bar Le Côte.** Alternatively, check into **ForFriends Inn,** about 5 miles south in **Santa Ynez,** walking a few blocks to dinner at **Ellie's Tap & Vine.**

DAY 2: FOXEN CANYON AND THE SANTA YNEZ VALLEY
About 1 hr of driving to wineries and 45 mins to return to Santa Barbara via Highway 154.

Start the day with pastries in the Danish town of Solvang, whose windmills and distinct half-timber architecture are charming, if touristy. Walk a little of Solvang before hitting the road.

Los Olivos, Santa Ynez, and Solvang are located just a few minutes apart, with Santa Ynez Valley AVA wineries spread between them. A mile east of tiny Santa Ynez's commercial drag (4¼ miles east of Solvang) lies **Gainey Vineyard,** whose wines impress major critics.

From Gainey, head east on Highway 246 and northwest on Highway 154 (aka San Marcos Pass Road) a little past Los Olivos to Foxen Canyon Road, where the **Foxen Canyon Wine Trail** (⊕ *www.foxen-canyonwinetrail.net* for info and a map) extends to Santa Maria and has more than a dozen wineries.

From Foxen Canyon Road, turn south (right) on Alisos Canyon Road, and north on U.S. 101 to Exit 154, **Los Alamos,** following signs on Highway 135, called Bell Street once you're in the small downtown. If you're hungry, check out the vittles at **Plenty on Bell** or **Bob's Well Bread,** both on Bell. Otherwise, proceed to **Casa Dumetz** (Chardonnay, Pinot Noir, and Rhône-style reds) for a tasting.

Stay another night in the region, or return to Santa Barbara via scenic Highway 154 over the San Marcos Pass.

Santa Barbara to Big Sur, 3 Days

This drive is all about the Pacific Coast's jaw-dropping scenery. The human-made treasures include Hearst Castle, newspaper magnate William Randolph Hearst's opulent monument to his fabulousness. Book Big Sur lodgings weeks ahead, the castle at least several days ahead in summer.

DAY 1: SANTA BARBARA TO CAMBRIA
About 3 hrs by car, not counting stops.

Drive north from Santa Barbara on the combined Highway 1 and U.S. 101, exiting the latter when the former forks west (watch for signs to Lompoc and Vandenberg Air Force Base). For this stretch, Highway 1 is also signed as Cabrillo Highway. Stop for a spell at **Oceano Dunes State Vehicular Recreation Area,** where the enormous namesake dunes make for a fantastic sunny-day photo op. Highway 1 rejoins U.S. 101 at **Pismo Beach.** If you're

starving, detour for lunch, though downtown **San Luis Obispo** (aka SLO), 13 miles farther along, offers more variety. **Luna Red** and **Novo** are good choices.

After lunch, explore a little of SLO before, just north of downtown, picking up Highway 1 as it again separates west from the 101. **Morro Bay,** Cayucos, and tiny Harmony are among the fun potential stops en route to Cambria, where you'll spend the night at the **White Water Cambria** inn or elsewhere in town (nearby Morro Bay and Cayucos also have affordable options). End the day in Cambria with a walk along **Moonstone Beach** and a French-fusion dinner at **Madeline's.**

DAY 2: HEARST CASTLE TO BIG SUR
About 2 hrs by car, plus at least 2 hrs to tour Hearst Castle and additional time for hiking and vista stops.

At least a few days ahead (more in summer), make a reservation for one of the midmorning tours (the Grand Rooms Tour is good for first-timers) of **Hearst Castle,** 9 miles north of Cambria in **San Simeon.** Having traveled the surrounding coastline, you'll appreciate the bird's-eye perspective the castle provides. After the tour, have lunch down the hill at Hearst Ranch Winery, co-owned by one of William Randolph Hearst's great-grandsons. On your way north out of San Simeon, don't miss the **Piedras Blancas Elephant Seal Rookery.**

The drive through coastal **Big Sur** is justifiably one of the world's most famous stretches of road. The curves, endless views, and scenic waypoints are the stuff of road-trip legend. Keep your camera handy, fill the tank, and prepare to be wowed. Traffic can easily back up along the route, and you should be cautious while navigating the road's twists and turns. To fully experience the area, spend at least a night here. If room rates at the legendary **Post Ranch Inn** or **Alila Ventana Big Sur** exceed your budget, seek out one of the more rustic options. If not dining at your lodging, do so at **Nepenthe,** which offers decent food and gorgeous views. Time your reservation (again, made well ahead) to witness the sunset.

DAY 3: BIG SUR

About 1 hr by car, not counting stops for hikes, beach exploration, and photo ops.

Start the morning with a hike in southern Big Sur at **Julia Pfeiffer Burns State Park,** a draw for its dramatic waterfalls, which tumble 80 feet into the sea. There's no beach access due to trail erosion, but you can walk ½ mile to an overlook from a lot near the park's entrance. A pullout just to the north, near mile marker 36.2, also affords a view. Check the park's website for other trails open when you visit.

About 7½ miles north of the state park, watch for the odd-angled turnout for (the unmarked) Sycamore Canyon Road, which leads to **Pfeiffer Beach.** Following the road 2¼ miles toward the sea, you may question whether you are lost, but your perseverance will be rewarded when you reach the secluded beach and its signature rocky arch just offshore. Don't miss it!

If you're game for another hike, head into **Pfeiffer Big Sur State Park.** Near the Big Sur Lodge's restaurant are trailheads for a ¼-mile-loop, wheelchair-accessible self-guided nature walk and the Valley View Trail, a 2-mile moderate-to-strenuous loop past redwoods.

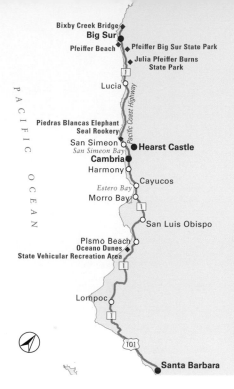

End your day 13 miles north of **Big Sur Lodge** (10 miles past the cluster of services known as Big Sur Village) at the extremely photogenic **Bixby Creek Bridge.** Pull over on the bridge's north side to get that perfect shot.

Most travelers continue north from here to Carmel-by-the-Sea or Monterey, either stopping there or returning to U.S. 101 via Highway 68 east from Monterey.

Chapter 4

SAN DIEGO

Updated by
Claire Deeks van der Lee,
Marlise Kast-Myers, and Jeff Terich

⊙ Sights	🍴 Restaurants	🛏 Hotels	🛍 Shopping	🍸 Nightlife
★★★★★	★★★★★	★★★★★	★★★★☆	★★★☆☆

WELCOME TO SAN DIEGO

TOP REASONS TO GO

★ **Sun and surf:** Legendary beaches and surfing in La Jolla, Coronado, and Point Loma.

★ **Good eats:** Brewpubs, a wide mix of ethnic cuisines, fresh seafood and produce, and modern cafés delight diners.

★ **Maritime history:** Climb aboard and explore a wide array of vessels from sailing ships to submarines.

★ **Family time:** Fun for all ages at LEGOLAND, Balboa Park, the San Diego Zoo, and more.

★ **Outdoor sports:** A perfect climate for golf, biking, hiking, sailing—anything—outdoors.

1 Downtown. This walkable area is home to the glam Gaslamp Quarter and the edgier East Village. Seaport Village, the Embarcadero, and Little Italy are nearby.

2 Balboa Park. The city's cultural heart has museums, stunning Spanish revival architecture, and the world-famous zoo. West of the park, Bankers Hill is a small neighborhood with gorgeous views.

3 Old Town and Uptown. California's first permanent European settlement is now a state historic park in Old Town. Uptown blends historical charm with modern urbanity.

4 Mission Bay and the Beaches. Home to SeaWorld and a 4,600-acre aquatic park perfect for water activities. Mission Beach and Pacific Beach—full of surf shops and beach bars—are nearby.

5 Point Loma Peninsula. Visit the site of the first European landfall on Point Loma.

6 Coronado. Home to the Hotel Del, Coronado's island-like isthmus is a favorite celebrity haunt.

7 La Jolla. The name of this luxe, bluff-top enclave fittingly means "the jewel."

PACIFIC OCEAN

```
0          2 mi
0     2 km
```

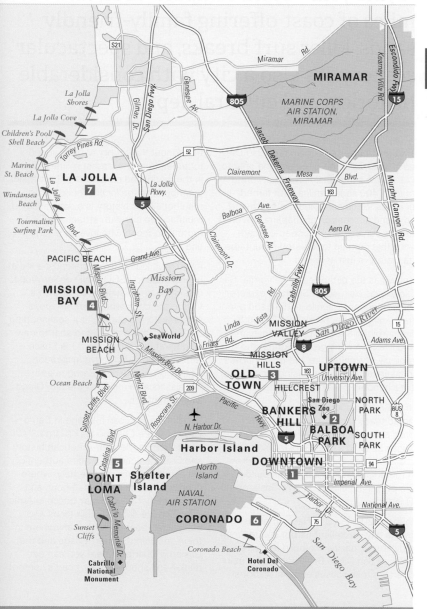

Miramar Rd.

MIRAMAR

MARINE CORPS
AIR STATION,
MIRAMAR

La Jolla
Shores

La Jolla Cove

Children's Pool/
Shell Beach

Marine
St. Beach

LA JOLLA 7

Windansea
Beach

Tourmaline
Surfing Park

Torrey Pines Rd.

La Jolla Pkwy.

Clairemont   Mesa   Blvd.

Balboa   Ave.

Aero Dr.

PACIFIC BEACH

Grand Ave.

Mission
Bay

MISSION
BAY 4

Clairemont Dr.

Linda   Vista   Rd.

MISSION
VALLEY 8

San Diego River

Adams Ave.

SeaWorld

MISSION
BEACH

Friars   Rd.

MISSION
HILLS

OLD
TOWN 3

UPTOWN
University Ave.

HILLCREST

Ocean Beach

Pacific   Hwy.

N. Harbor Dr.

San Diego
Zoo

BANKERS
HILL 2

NORTH
PARK

BALBOA
PARK

SOUTH
PARK

Harbor Island

DOWNTOWN 1

POINT
LOMA 5

Shelter
Island

North
Island

NAVAL
AIR STATION

CORONADO 6

Sunset
Cliffs

Cabrillo
National
Monument

Coronado Beach

Hotel Del
Coronado

San Diego Bay

Imperial Ave.

National Ave.

San Diego is a beach vacationer's paradise thanks to a laid-back vibe; idyllic year-round temperatures; and 70 miles of coast offering family-friendly sands, killer surf breaks, and spectacular scenery. It's also a city with considerable historical and cultural depth.

Though it has a small-town feel, San Diego is a big California city—second only to Los Angeles in population and covering roughly 400 square miles with famed beaches to the north and the south and an inland succession of chaparral-covered mesas punctuated with deep-cut canyons that step up to forested mountains. Its history is just as varied.

Known as the birthplace of California, San Diego was claimed for Spain by explorer Juan Rodríguez Cabrillo in 1542 and eventually came under Mexican rule. You'll find reminders of San Diego's Spanish and Mexican heritage throughout the region—in architecture and place-names, in distinctive Mexican cuisine, and in the time-honored buildings of Old Town.

In 1867 developer Alonzo Horton, who noted that town's bay front was "the prettiest place for a city I ever saw," began building a hotel, a plaza, and prefab homes on 960 Downtown acres. A remarkable number of these buildings are preserved in San Diego's Gaslamp Quarter.

In the 1920s, the U.S. Navy, impressed by the city's excellent harbor and temperate climate, decided to build a destroyer base on San Diego Bay. The military still operates many bases and installations throughout the county (which, added together, form the largest military base in the world) and continues to be a major contributor to the local economy. The result of all this history is a sophisticated, multifaceted city with attractions for more than those who love sun, sand, and surf.

If you have kids in tow (or are just a kid at heart), head to LEGOLAND or SeaWorld. Get in touch with your wild side on a visit to the city's world-famous zoo, a whale-watching outing, or a seal-spotting excursion. Take a simulated soar to new heights at the San Diego Air & Space Museum, or find creative inspiration while viewing Spanish-Baroque and Renaissance paintings at the San Diego Museum of Art.

Experience Mexican heritage in Barrio Logan, where Chicano Park's large murals depict Mexican-American history and Chicano activism, or find authentic old-country charm in Little Italy, where church bells ring on the half-hour, and people gather daily to play bocce in Amici Park. Sample delicious fish tacos and stellar craft beer just about anywhere in town, including Seaport Village and the Gaslamp Quarter, where you can eat, drink—and shop—to your heart's content.

Planning

Getting Here and Around

AIR

At San Diego International Airport (SAN), most airlines use Terminal 2. Terminal 1 is reserved for Southwest, Frontier, JetBlue, and a handful of smaller carriers. Free, color-coded shuttles loop the airport and match the parking lot they serve.

AIRPORT San Diego International Airport.
⊠ 3225 N. Harbor Dr., off I–5, San Diego ☎ 619/400–2400 ⊕ www.san.org.

AIRPORT TRANSFERS SuperShuttle.
⊠ San Diego ☎ 800/258–3826 ⊕ www. supershuttle.com.

CAR

You need a car to fully explore sprawling San Diego. Interstate 5, which stretches north–south from Oregon to the Mexican border, bisects San Diego. Interstate 8 provides access from Yuma, Arizona, and points east. Access from Los Angeles, Nevada, and mountain regions beyond is on I–15. During rush hours there are jams on I–5 and on I–15 between I–805 and Escondido.

Major highways in San Diego County have border-inspection stations, the largest of which is just north of Oceanside on I–5 near San Clemente. Travel with your driver's license, and, if you're an international traveler, your passport.

City parking is typically metered ($1.25 to $2.50 an hour) Monday through Saturday 10 to 8. Beach parking is generally free, though spots are hard to come by on sunny days.

PUBLIC TRANSPORTATION

To get route and timetable information for Metropolitan Transit System (MTS) buses—which connect with the iconic red San Diego trolleys—and North County Transit District (NCTD) buses, visit ⊕ www.511sd.com. One-way MTS bus

and trolley fares range from $2.50 to $5; NCTD bus fare is $2.50. Transfers aren't included. You can also buy single- or multi-day passes (starting at $6), which allow unlimited rides on non-premium regional buses and the trolley. The $12 Regional Plus Day Pass adds Coaster light-rail and premium bus-route service.

You can pay in cash when you board (exact change only) or purchase tickets at vending machines, which accept credit cards and cash and which generally return up to $5 in change. The easiest way to pay, however, is via the PRONTO phone app or PRONTO card ($2 initial-purchase charge) available from most vending machines and at the Downtown Transit Store and Albertsons markets.

NCTD buses connect with Coaster commuter trains between Oceanside and the Santa Fe Depot in San Diego. They serve points from Del Mar north to San Clemente, inland to Fallbrook, Pauma Valley, Valley Center, Ramona, and Escondido, with transfer points within the city of San Diego. The Sprinter light rail provides service between Oceanside and Escondido, with buses connecting to popular North County attractions.

FRED (FREE RIDE EVERYWHERE DOWNTOWN)

These open-air electric vehicles offer free rides throughout the Downtown area. Riders can make a pickup request through the FRED app, or simply flag one down. ⊕ www.thefreeride.com

CONTACTS North County Transit District.
☎ 760/966–6500 ⊕ www.gonctd.com. **San Diego 511.** ⊠ San Diego ☎ 855/467–3511 ⊕ www.511sd.com. **San Diego Metropolitan Transit System.** (MTS) ⊠ 102 Broadway, San Diego ☎ 619/234–1060 ⊕ www.sdmts.com.

TAXI AND RIDE SHARING

Cabs (about $2.80 for the first 1/10 mile, $3 each additional mile) are fine for short in-town jaunts. You can flag them Downtown; elsewhere, call for one or hire one at the taxi stands near hotels, major attractions, and shopping centers. ■**TIP➜ If you're heading to the airport from a hotel, ask about the flat rate; these vary by location but might be cheaper than the metered rate.**

App-driven ride-sharing services such as Uber and Lyft are popular in San Diego. Drivers are readily available from most in-town destinations and also service the airport.

TRAIN

Amtrak serves Downtown San Diego's Santa Fe Depot with daily trains to and from Los Angeles, Santa Barbara, and San Luis Obispo. The scenic *Pacific Surfliner* route delights with coastal views for much of the journey. Connecting service to Oakland, Seattle, Chicago, Texas, Florida, and points beyond is available in Los Angeles. In San Diego North County, Amtrak trains stop at Solana Beach and Oceanside. Recent track stabilization work has resulted in service modifications, so be sure to check the website for the most current schedules.

Hotels

In San Diego, you can plan a luxurious vacation at the beach, staying at a resort with ocean panoramas, private balconies, and a full-service spa. Or you can stay in action-packed Downtown, steps from the bustling Gaslamp Quarter, in a modern hotel featuring a lively rooftop pool, trendy restaurants, complimentary wine receptions, and high-tech entertainment systems.

Budget-friendly options can be found in smaller neighborhoods just outside the Gaslamp Quarter such as Little Italy. For families, Uptown and Old Town are both close to SeaWorld and the San Diego Zoo and offer good-value accommodations with extras like sleeper sofas and video games.

Though you'll need a car for stays in the beach communities, they are rich with lodging options. Coronado's hotels and resorts offer access to a stretch of glistening white sand that's one of the country's best beaches. La Jolla has many romantic, upscale, ocean-view hotels, as well as some of the area's best restaurants and shops. Surfers make themselves at home at casual inns and other budget properties in Pacific Beach and Mission Bay. If you're planning to fish, check out hotels near the marinas in Shelter Island, Point Loma, or Coronado.

Note that, if you're flexible, it's possible to get good deals at even pricey places. Consider, for instance, opting for a partial-view room, booking a hotel that's a quick drive from the action, or visiting in the fall when rates are at their lowest.

Restaurants

San Diego was on the cutting edge of the farm-to-table, Slow Food movement, and everything from fresh seafood to just-picked produce continues to be emphasized in dishes on local menus. The city's ethnically diverse neighborhoods, with their modest eateries offering affordable authentic international cuisines, have also traditionally added spice to the dining mix. This already well-regarded culinary scene got yet another boost when San Diego emerged as one of the world's top craft beer destinations. Artisan breweries and gastropubs have since opened almost everywhere.

In addition, each of the city's neighborhoods has its own distinct dining personality. The trendy Gaslamp Quarter delights with its broad range of innovative and international restaurants and nightspots, bustling Little Italy offers both affordable Italian eateries and posh new establishments, and modern restaurants and cafés thrive in East Village.

The Uptown neighborhoods centered on Hillcrest—an urbane district with San Francisco flavor—offer a mix of bars and independent restaurants, many specializing in ethnic cuisine. North Park, in particular, has a happening restaurant and craft beer scene, with laid-back prices to boot. And then there's La Jolla, where some of the city's best fine dining options often have dramatic water views.

⇨ *Restaurant and reviews have been shortened. For full information, visit Fodors.com. Restaurant prices are the average cost of a main course at dinner, or if dinner isn't served, at lunch. Hotel prices are the lowest cost of a standard double room in high season.*

What It Costs

	$	$$	$$$	$$$$
RESTAURANTS				
	under $20	$20–$30	$31–$40	over $40
HOTELS				
	under $200	$200–$350	$351–$500	over $500

Tours

You can get a great overview of the city from the water, and several companies offer a range of harbor cruises. Options for landlubbers include narrated trolley tours or guided walks of districts like the Gaslamp Quarter or Balboa Park.

Balboa Park Walking Tours

GUIDED TOURS | On Tuesday and select Fridays at 11 am, free, hour-long walks start from the Balboa Park Visitor Center. Tours explore the history of Balboa Park, its gardens and architecture. Reservations are not required, but no tours are scheduled between Thanksgiving and the New Year. Private, custom tours are also available for a fee, with proceeds going to the Balboa Park Conservancy. Contact the visitor center for details and to schedule. ⊠ *Balboa Park Visitor Center, 1549 El Prado, Balboa Park* ☎ *619/239–0512* ⊕ *www.balboapark.org* ✉ *Free; custom private tours from $60.*

Flagship Cruises and Events

BOAT TOURS | One- and two-hour tours of the San Diego Harbor loop north or south from the Broadway Pier throughout the day. Other offerings include dinner and dance cruises, brunch cruises, and winter whale-watching tours December–mid-April. ⊠ *990 N. Harbor Dr., Embarcadero* ☎ *619/234–4111* ⊕ *www.flagshipsd.com* ✉ *From $32.*

Gaslamp Quarter Historical Foundation

WALKING TOURS | Ninety-minute walking tours of the Downtown historic district depart from the William Heath Davis House at 1 pm on Thursday and 11 am on Saturday. ⊠ *410 Island Ave., San Diego* ☎ *619/233–4692* ⊕ *gaslampfoundation. org* ✉ *$25.*

Old Town Trolley Tours

GUIDED TOURS | **FAMILY** | Combining points of interest with local history, trivia, and fun anecdotes, this hop-on, hop-off trolley tour provides an entertaining overview of the city and offers easy access to all the highlights. The tour is narrated, and you can get on and off as you please. Stops include Old Town, Seaport Village, the Gaslamp Quarter, Coronado, Little Italy, and Balboa Park. The trolley leaves every 30 minutes, operates daily, and takes two hours to make a full loop. ⊠ *San Diego* ☎ *866/754–0966* ⊕ *www. trolleytours.com/san-diego* ✉ *From $49.*

Visitor Information

San Diego Tourism Authority. ✉ *750 B St., Suite 1500, San Diego* ☎ *619/232–3101* ⊕ *www.sandiego.org.*

When to Go

San Diego's weather is so ideal that most locals shrug off the high cost of living and relatively lower wages as a "sunshine tax." Along the coast, average temperatures range from the mid-60s to the high 70s, with clear skies and low humidity. Annual rainfall is minimal, less than 10 inches per year.

The peak season for sun seekers is July through October. In July and August, the mercury spikes and everyone spills outside. From mid-December to mid-March, whale-watchers can glimpse migrating gray whales frolicking in the Pacific. In spring and early summer, a marine layer hugs the coastline for much or all of the day (locals call it "June Gloom"), which can be dreary and disappointing for those who were expecting to bask in Southern California sunshine.

Downtown

Nearly written off in the 1970s, today Downtown San Diego is a testament to conservation and urban renewal. Once-derelict Victorian storefronts now house the hottest restaurants, and the *Star of India,* the world's oldest active sailing ship, almost lost to scrap, floats regally along the Embarcadero. Although many consider Downtown to be the 16½-block Gaslamp Quarter, it actually comprises eight neighborhoods, including East Village, Little Italy, and Embarcadero.

Gaslamp Quarter

The Gaslamp Quarter has the country's largest collection of commercial Victorian-style buildings. Despite this, when the move for Downtown redevelopment gained momentum in the 1970s, there was talk of bulldozing them and starting from scratch. In response, concerned history buffs, developers, architects, and artists formed the Gaslamp Quarter Council to clean up and preserve the quarter. Most of the landmark buildings are between Island Avenue and Broadway on 4th and 5th avenues, which are also peppered with the trendy nightclubs, swanky lounges, chic restaurants, and boisterous sports bars that make the district the liveliest in Downtown.

◉ Sights

Gaslamp Museum at the Davis-Horton House

HISTORIC HOME | The oldest wooden house in San Diego houses the Gaslamp Quarter Historical Foundation, the district's curator. Before developer Alonzo Horton came to town, Davis, a prominent San Franciscan, had made an unsuccessful attempt to develop the waterfront area. In 1850 he had this prefab saltbox-style house, built in Maine, shipped around Cape Horn and assembled in San Diego (it originally stood at State and Market Streets). Ninety-minute walking tours ($25) of the historic district leave from the house on Thursday at 1 pm (summer only) and Saturday at 11 am (year-round). If you can't time your visit with the tour, a self-guided tour map ($2) is available. ✉ *410 Island Ave., at 4th Ave., Gaslamp Quarter* ☎ *619/233–4692* ⊕ *www. gaslampfoundation.org* 🎬 *$5 self-guided, $10 with audio tour* ⊙ *Closed Mon.*

🍴 Restaurants

Breakfast Republic
$ | **AMERICAN** | Just because it's the most important meal of the day doesn't mean it can't also be flashy or innovative. Breakfast Republic adds some hipster flair to typical brunch fare with a menu that combines hearty Southern staples (grits, jambalaya), Mexican food (chilaquiles, breakfast burritos), and over-the-top treats such as Oreo pancakes and s'mores French toast. **Known for:** rich, gooey pancakes and French toast; kombucha flights; kitschy decor. [$] *Average main: $12* ✉ *707 G St., Gaslamp Quarter* ☎ *619/501–8280* 🌐 *www.breakfastrepublic.com* 🕒 *No dinner.*

Taka
$$ | **JAPANESE** | Pristine fish imported from around the world and presented creatively attracts crowds nightly to this intimate Gaslamp restaurant. Table service is available inside and outside where an *omakase* (tasting menu) or eight-piece rolls can be shared and savored; take a seat at the bar to watch one of the sushi chefs preparing appetizers. **Known for:** uni sushi topped with wasabi; omakase tasting menu; upscale sake offerings. [$] *Average main: $21* ✉ *555 5th Ave., Gaslamp Quarter* ☎ *619/338–0555* 🌐 *www.takasushi.com* 🕒 *No lunch.*

🛏 Hotels

★ Hard Rock Hotel San Diego
$$ | **HOTEL** | Self-billed as a hip playground for rock stars and people who want to party like them, the Hard Rock near Petco Park overlooks glimmering San Diego Bay with an interior that oozes laid-back sophistication and guest rooms that include branded Sleep Like a Rock beds and the option of renting a guitar. **Pros:** central location; energetic scene; luxurious rooms. **Cons:** pricey drinks; some attitude; party scene tends to be loud. [$] *Rooms from: $249* ✉ *207 5th Ave., Gaslamp Quarter* ☎ *619/702–3000, 866/751–7625* 🌐 *www.hardrockhotelsd.com* 🔑 *420 rooms* 🍽 *No Meals.*

★ Pendry San Diego
$$$$ | **HOTEL** | Opened in early 2017, the Pendry San Diego is the Gaslamp's newest stunner. **Pros:** well situated in Gaslamp Quarter; excellent dining options; complimentary coffee in the mornings. **Cons:** pricey room rates; meals are expensive; not very family-friendly. [$] *Rooms from: $510* ✉ *550 J St., Gaslamp Quarter* ☎ *619/738–7000* 🌐 *www.pendry.com* 🔑 *317 rooms* 🍽 *No Meals.*

★ The Sofia Hotel
$$ | **HOTEL** | This stylish and centrally located boutique hotel may have small rooms, but it more than compensates with pampering extras like motion-sensor temperature controls, a Zen-like 24-hour yoga studio, an updated lobby, and a brand-new spa suite. **Pros:** upscale amenities; historic building; near shops and restaurants. **Cons:** busy area; small rooms; spotty Wi-Fi. [$] *Rooms from: $257* ✉ *150 W. Broadway, Gaslamp Quarter* ☎ *619/234–9200, 800/826–0009* 🌐 *www.thesofiahotel.com* 🔑 *211 rooms* 🍽 *No Meals.*

★ The U.S. Grant, a Luxury Collection Hotel
$$ | **HOTEL** | The U.S. Grant may be more than 100 years old (it first opened in 1910) but thanks to a top-to-bottom renovation in 2017, this grand old dame is now one of the most glamorous hotels in Southern California. **Pros:** sophisticated rooms; great location; near shopping and restaurants. **Cons:** street noise can be heard from the guest rooms; no in-room minibars or coffeemakers; surrounded by many major construction projects Downtown. [$] *Rooms from: $334* ✉ *326 Broadway, Gaslamp Quarter* ☎ *619/232–3121, 800/325–3589* 🌐 *www.marriott.com* 🔑 *270 rooms* 🍽 *No Meals.*

▼ Nightlife

★ The Grant Grill

COCKTAIL LOUNGES | Though the Grant Grill—located on the ground floor of the historic U.S. Grant Hotel—is a full-service restaurant, it's built up a reputation in recent years for stepping up San Diego's craft cocktail game. The cocktail menu is updated seasonally with fresh ingredients and themes (one recently featured a mini "Voodoo" doll frozen inside of a large ice cube), all of which are both innovative and palate pleasant. The atmosphere is comfortable and elegant, even on its busiest nights. ⊠ *U.S. Grant Hotel, 326 Broadway, Gaslamp Quarter* ☎ *619/744–2077* ⊕ *www.grantgrill.com* ⊘ *No dinner on Sun. and Mon.*

★ Vin de Syrah

WINE BARS | This "spirit and wine cellar" sends you down a rabbit hole (or at least down some stairs) to a whimsical spot straight out of Alice in Wonderland. Behind a hidden door (look for a handle in the grass wall), you'll find visual delights (grapevines suspended from the ceiling, vintage jars with flittering "fireflies," cozy chairs nestled around a faux fireplace and pastoral vista) that rival the culinary ones—the wine list is approachable and the charcuterie boards are exquisitely curated. ■TIP➔ **This is more than just a wine bar: the cocktails are also worth a try.** ⊠ *901 5th Ave., Gaslamp Quarter* ☎ *619/234–4166* ⊕ *www.syrahwineparlor.com* ⊘ *Closed Mon.*

★ Westgate Hotel Plaza Bar

PIANO BARS | The old-money surroundings, including leather-upholstered seats, marble tabletops, and a grand piano, supply one of the most elegant and romantic settings for a drink in San Diego. ⊠ *1055 2nd Ave., Gaslamp Quarter* ☎ *619/238–1818* ⊕ *www.westgatehotel.com.*

Embarcadero

The bustle of Embarcadero comes less these days from the activities of fishing folk than from the throngs of tourists, but this waterfront walkway, stretching from the Convention Center to the Maritime Museum, remains the nautical soul of the city. There are several seafood restaurants here, as well as seafaring vessels of every variety—cruise ships, ferries, tour boats, and Navy destroyers.

A recent revitalization project transformed the northern Embarcadero area, adding parks, walkways, and art installations. The redevelopment plan is now focused south along the waterfront, and a major overhaul of Central Embarcadero and Seaport Village is slated for completion in 2028.

◉ Sights

★ Museum of Contemporary Art San Diego (MCASD)

ART MUSEUM | At the Downtown branch of the city's contemporary art museum (the space is under renovation so best to call ahead for hours), explore the works of international and regional artists in a modern, urban space. The Jacobs Building—formerly the baggage building at the historic Santa Fe Depot—features large gallery spaces, high ceilings, and natural lighting, giving artists the flexibility to create large-scale installations. MCASD's collection includes many pop art, minimalist, and conceptual works from the 1950s to the present. The museum showcases both established and emerging artists in temporary exhibitions, and has permanent, site-specific commissions by Jenny Holzer and Richard Serra. ⊠ *1100 and 1001 Kettner Blvd., Embarcadero* ☎ *858/454–3541* ⊕ *www.mcasd.org* ⧉ *$10; free 3rd Thurs. of month 5–7* ⊘ *Closed Wed.*

★ The New Children's Museum (NCM)

CHILDREN'S MUSEUM | FAMILY | The NCM blends contemporary art with unstructured play to create an environment that appeals to children as well as adults. The 50,000-square-foot structure was constructed from recycled building materials, operates on solar energy, and is convection-cooled by an elevator shaft. It also features a nutritious and eco-conscious café. Interactive exhibits include designated areas for toddlers and teens, as well as plenty of activities for the entire family. Several art workshops are offered each day, as well as hands-on studios where visitors are encouraged to create their own art. The studio projects change frequently and the entire museum changes exhibits every 18 to 24 months, so there is always something new to explore. The adjoining 1-acre park and playground is across from the convention center trolley stop. ✉ *200 W. Island Ave., Embarcadero* ☎ *619/233–8792* ⊕ *www.thinkplaycreate.org* 🍴 *$20* 🕑 *Closed Tues.*

Seaport Village

PEDESTRIAN MALL | FAMILY | You'll find some of the best views of the harbor at Seaport Village, three bustling shopping plazas designed to reflect the New England clapboard and Spanish Mission architectural styles of early California. On a prime stretch of waterfront the dining, shopping, and entertainment complex connects the harbor with hotel towers and the convention center. Specialty shops offer everything from a kite store and swing emporium to a shop devoted to hot sauces. You can dine at snack bars and restaurants, many with harbor views.

Live music can be heard daily from noon to 4 at the main food court. Additional free concerts take place every Sunday from 1 to 4 at the East Plaza Gazebo. The Seaport Village Carousel (🍴 *Rides $3*) has 54 animals, hand-carved and hand-painted by Charles Looff in 1895. Across the street, the Headquarters at Seaport Village converted the historic police headquarters into several trend-setting shops and restaurants. ✉ *849 W. Harbor Dr., Embarcadero* ☎ *619/530–0704 office and events hotline* ⊕ *www.seaportvillage.com.*

★ USS *Midway* Museum

MILITARY SIGHT | FAMILY | After 47 years of worldwide service, the retired USS *Midway* began a new tour of duty on the south side of the Navy pier in 2004. Launched in 1945, the 1,001-foot-long ship was the largest in the world for the first 10 years of its existence. The most visible landmark on the north Embarcadero, it now serves as a floating interactive museum—an appropriate addition to the town that is home to one-third of the Pacific fleet and the birthplace of naval aviation. A free audio tour guides you through the massive ship while offering insight from former sailors. As you clamber through passageways and up and down ladder wells, you'll get a feel for how the *Midway*'s 4,500 crew members lived and worked on this "city at sea."

Though the entire tour is impressive, you'll really be wowed when you step out onto the 4-acre flight deck—not only the best place to get an idea of the ship's scale, but also one of the most interesting vantage points for bay and city skyline views. An F-14 Tomcat jet fighter is just one of many vintage aircraft on display. Free guided tours of the bridge and primary flight control, known as "the Island," depart every 10 minutes from the flight deck. Many of the docents stationed throughout the ship served in the Navy, some even on the *Midway*, and they are eager to answer questions or share stories. The museum also offers multiple flight simulators for an additional fee, climb-aboard cockpits, and interactive exhibits focusing on naval aviation. There is a gift shop and a café with pleasant outdoor seating. This is a wildly popular stop, with most visits lasting several hours.

⚠ **Despite efforts to provide accessibility throughout the ship, some areas can only be reached via fairly steep steps; a video tour of these areas is available on the hangar deck.** ✉ *910 N. Harbor Dr., Embarcadero* ☎ *619/544–9600* 🌐 *www.midway.org* 🎟 *$31.*

🍴 Restaurants

★ Eddie V's Prime Seafood

$$$ | **SEAFOOD** | Don't be put off by the name, or that it is part of a small chain. This fine-dining restaurant at the Headquarters at Seaport in Downtown has won a devoted following for classic seafood, casual but sophisticated settings, and nightly live jazz. **Known for:** wallet-friendly happy hour deals; the shellfish tower, featuring oysters, crab, shrimp and Maine lobster; indulgent truffled mac and cheese. [$] *Average main: $40* ✉ *789 W. Harbor Dr., Embarcadero* ☎ *619/615–0281* 🌐 *www.eddiev.com* 🕒 *No lunch.*

★ Puesto

$ | **MEXICAN** | Bold graffiti graphics, chandeliers with tangled telephone wires, and beat-heavy music energize this Downtown eatery that celebrates Mexican street food with a modern twist. Settle into one of the interior rooms or the sunny patio under orange umbrellas to sip margaritas and other specialty cocktails, Baja wines, or fruity aguas frescas made daily. **Known for:** taco trio plates; unique Parmesan guacamole; fruit-infused margaritas made in-house. [$] *Average main: $16* ✉ *789 W. Harbor Dr., Embarcadero* ☎ *619/233–8880* 🌐 *www.eatpuesto.com.*

🛏 Hotels

★ InterContinental San Diego

$$ | **HOTEL** | A new addition to the waterfront skyline, InterContinental San Diego provides a more luxurious and stylish option for travelers in what's generally an area populated by more family-friendly lodging. **Pros:** stunning waterfront views; excellent dining options at Vistal and Garibaldi; close to both airport and attractions. **Cons:** a bit on the pricier side; pedestrian traffic can be hectic because of nearby shopping/boating areas; entrances and elevators are a bit confusing. [$] *Rooms from: $278* ✉ *901 Bayfront Ct., Embarcadero* ☎ *619/501–9400* 🌐 *www.intercontinentalsandiego.com/* 🛏 *400 rooms* 🍽 *No Meals.*

🛍 Shopping

★ The Headquarters at Seaport

MARKET | This new upscale shopping and dining center is in the city's former police headquarters, a beautiful and historic Mission-style building featuring an open courtyard with fountains. Restaurants and shops, many locally owned, occupy former jail facilities and offices. Pop into **Urban Beach House** for coastal-inspired fashion from popular surf brands for men and women, including accessories and home decor. **Perfume Gallery** offers more than 1,000 different scents in its extensive collection. **Madison San Diego** offers a great selection of leather goods and accessories, from apparel and handbags to belts and travel accessories. ✉ *789 W. Harbor Dr., Embarcadero* ☎ *619/235–4013* 🌐 *theheadquarters.com.*

East Village

The most ambitious of the Downtown projects is East Village, not far from the Gaslamp Quarter and encompassing 130 blocks between the railroad tracks up to J Street, and from 6th Avenue east to around 10th Street. Sparking the rebirth of this former warehouse district was the 2004 construction of the San Diego Padres' stunning 42,000-seat baseball stadium, Petco Park, where games are rarely rained out.

The Urban Art Trail has added pizzazz by transforming such things as trash cans and traffic controller boxes into works of art. As the city's largest Downtown neighborhood, East Village is continually broadening its boundaries with its urban design of redbrick cafés, spacious galleries, rooftop bars, sleek hotels, and warehouse restaurants.

Sights

Petco Park

SPORTS VENUE | FAMILY | Petco Park is home to the city's major league baseball team, the San Diego Padres. The ballpark is strategically designed to give fans a view of San Diego Bay, the skyline, and Balboa Park. Reflecting San Diego's beauty, the stadium is clad in sandstone from India to evoke the area's cliffs and beaches; the 42,000 seats are dark blue, reminiscent of the ocean, and the exposed steel is painted white to reflect the sails of harbor boats on the bay. The family-friendly lawnlike berm, "Park at the Park," is a popular and affordable place for fans to view the game. The ballpark underwent a huge effort to improve dining in the park, and local food vendors and craft breweries now dominate the dining options. Behind-the-scenes guided tours of Petco, including the press box and the dugout, are offered throughout the year. ✉ *100 Park Blvd., East Village* ☎ *619/795–5011 tour hotline* 🌐 *sandiego.padres.mlb.com* 🎟 *$30 tour.*

Restaurants

The Blind Burro

$$ | MODERN MEXICAN | FAMILY | East Village families, baseball fans heading to or from Petco Park, and happy-hour-bound singles flock to this airy restaurant with Baja-inspired food and drink. Traditional margaritas get a fresh kick from fruit juices or jalapeño peppers; other libations include sangria and Mexican beers, all perfect pairings for house-made guacamole, ceviche, or salsas with chips. **Known for:** house margarita with fruit infusions; surf-and-turf Baja-style tacos; gluten-free menu. [$] *Average main: $21* ✉ *639 J St., East Village* ☎ *619/795–7880* 🌐 *www.theblindburro.com.*

Nightlife

★ Noble Experiment

PIANO BARS | There are a handful of speakeasy-style bars in San Diego, though none deliver so far above and beyond the novelty quite like this cozy-yet-swank cocktail lounge hidden in the back of a burger restaurant. Seek out the hidden door (hint: look for the stack of kegs), tuck into a plush leather booth next to the wall of golden skulls, and sip on the best craft cocktails in the city. For even more exclusivity, check out the speakeasy-within-a-speakeasy Young Blood, which is an all-inclusive cocktail experience in an adjacent space for the up-front fee of $67. **■ TIP→ Reservations are almost always a must, so be sure to call ahead.** ✉ *777 G St., East Village* ☎ *619/888–4713* 🌐 *nobleexperimentsd.com.*

Little Italy

Home to many in San Diego's design community, Little Italy exudes a sense of urban cool and is a great place to wander. The main thoroughfare, India Street, is filled with lively cafés, gallery showrooms, chic shops, and trendy restaurants. The Saturday Mercato farmers' market is wildly popular, as are seasonal special events such as Artwalk in spring and FESTA! each fall.

The neighborhood is also marked by old-country charms: church bells ring on the half-hour, and Italians gather daily to play bocce in Amici Park. After an afternoon of gelati and espresso, you might just forget that you're in Southern California.

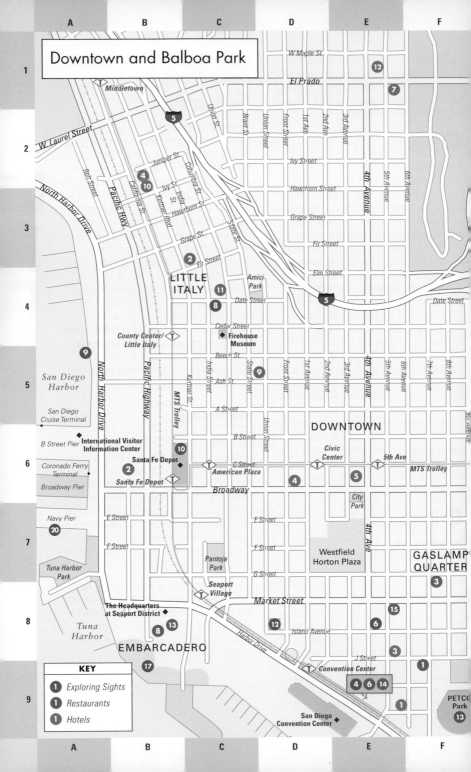

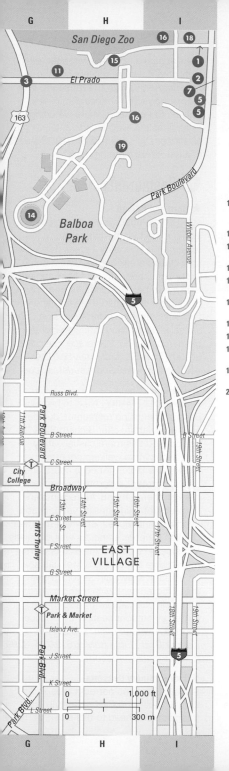

San Diego Zoo

El Prado

163

Park Boulevard

Wieber Avenue

Balboa
Park

5

Russ Blvd.

11th Avenue

Park Boulevard

B Street

B Street

19th Street

City
College

C Street

C Street

MTS Trolley

Broadway

13th St.

14th Street

15th Street

16th Street

17th Street

E Street

E Street

F Street

G Street

EAST
VILLAGE

Market Street

Park & Market

Island Ave.

18th Street

19th Street

Park Blvd.

J Street

5

K Street

Park Blvd.

L Street

0   1,000 ft

0   300 m

Sights ▼

1 Balboa Park Carousel....**I1**
2 Bea Evenson Fountain ...**I1**
3 Cabrillo Bridge **G1**
4 Chicano Park............. **E9**
5 Fleet Science Center.....**I2**
6 Gaslamp Museum at the
  Davis-Horton House..... **E8**
7 Inez Grant Parker
  Memorial Rose Garden
  and Desert Garden **I1**
8 Little Italy Mercato **C4**
9 Maritime Museum...... **A5**
10 Museum of
  Contemporary Art
  San Diego (MCASD).... **B6**
11 Museum of Us.......... **G1**
12 The New Children's
  Museum (NCM)......... **D8**
13 Petco Park............... **F9**
14 San Diego Air & Space
  Museum **G3**
15 San Diego
  Museum of Art.......... **H1**
16 San Diego Zoo **I1**
17 Seaport Village.......... **B9**
18 Spanish Village Art
  Center.....................**I1**
19 Spreckels Organ
  Pavilion **H2**
20 USS Midway
  Museum **A7**

Restaurants ▼

1 The Blind Burro **F9**
2 Born and Raised **C3**
3 Breakfast Republic **F8**
4 The Crack Shack........ **B2**
5 Craveology **I1**
6 Las Cuatros Milpas...... **E9**
7 Cucina Urbana **E1**
8 Eddie V's Prime
  Seafood.................. **B8**
9 Extraordinary
  Desserts **D5**
10 Herb & Wood............ **B2**
11 Little Italy Food Hall......**C4**
12 Mister A's **E1**
13 Puesto.................... **B8**
14 ¡Salud! **E9**
15 Taka **E8**
16 Tea Pavilion.............. **H2**

Hotels ▼

1 Hard Rock Hotel
  San Diego................. **E9**
2 InterContinental
  San Diego................. **B6**
3 Pendry San Diego **E8**
4 The Sofia Hotel.......... **D6**
5 The U.S. Grant, a
  Luxury Collection
  Hotel...................... **E6**

👁 Sights

Little Italy Mercato

MARKET | Each Saturday tourists and residents alike flock to the Little Italy Mercato, one of the most popular farmers' markets in San Diego. More than 150 vendors line Date Street selling everything from paintings and pottery to flowers and farm-fresh eggs. Come hungry, as several booths and food trucks serve prepared foods. Alternatively, the neighborhood's many cafés and restaurants are just steps away. The Mercato is a great opportunity to experience one of San Diego's most exciting urban neighborhoods. ⊠ *Date and India Sts., Little Italy* ⊕ *www.littleitalysd.com/events/mercato.*

★ Maritime Museum

MARINA/PIER | **FAMILY** | From sailing ships to submarines, the Maritime Museum is a must for anyone with an interest in nautical history. This collection of restored and replica ships affords a fascinating glimpse of San Diego during its heyday as a commercial seaport. The jewel of the collection, the *Star of India,* was built in 1863 and made 21 trips around the world in the late 1800s. Saved from the scrapyard and painstakingly restored, the windjammer is the oldest active iron sailing ship in the world. The newly constructed *San Salvador* is a detailed historic replica of the original ship first sailed into San Diego Bay by explorer Juan Rodriguez Cabrillo back in 1542, and the popular HMS *Surprise* is a replica of an 18th-century British Royal Navy frigate. The museum's headquarters are on the *Berkeley,* an 1898 steam-driven ferryboat, which served the Southern Pacific Railroad in San Francisco until 1958.

Numerous cruises of San Diego Bay are offered, including a daily 45-minute narrated tour aboard a 1914 pilot boat and three-hour weekend sails aboard the topsail schooner the *Californian,* the state's official tall ship, and 75-minute tours aboard a historic swift boat, which highlights the city's military connection. Partnering with the museum, the renowned yacht *America* also offers sails on the bay, and whale-watching excursions are available in winter. ⊠ *1492 N. Harbor Dr., Little Italy* ☎ *619/234–9153* ⊕ *www.sdmaritime.org* 🎫 *$20.*

🍴 Restaurants

★ Born and Raised

$$$$ | **STEAKHOUSE** | The name is cheeky if a little morbid; the title refers to the restaurant's speciality—steak. It's a twist on a classic steak house, with a menu full of aged, prime cuts of beef served with a number of sauces, or perhaps try the table-side-prepared steak Diane with flambéed jus. **Known for:** table-side Caesar salad; aged New York steak; cheeky, glamorous decor. 💲 *Average main: $45* ⊠ *1909 India St., Little Italy* ☎ *619/202–4577* ⊕ *www.bornandraisedsteak.com.*

★ The Crack Shack

$ | **AMERICAN** | **FAMILY** | Next to his successful fine-dining restaurant, Juniper and Ivy, celebrity chef Richard Blais has opened this more casual eatery complete with a walk-up counter, picnic-style tables, a bocce court, and a giant rooster—a nod to the egg- and chicken-theme menu. Ingredients are sourced from high-quality vendors and used for sandwiches, of which the fried chicken varieties shine, as well as salads and sides like fluffy minibiscuits with a miso-maple butter and a Mexican spin on poutine. **Known for:** Señor Croque fried chicken sandwich with smoked pork belly; biscuits with miso-maple butter; all-outdoor seating with bocce court. 💲 *Average main: $13* ⊠ *2266 Kettner Blvd., Little Italy* ☎ *619/795–3299* ⊕ *www.crackshack.com.*

★ Extraordinary Desserts

$ | **CAFÉ** | For Paris-perfect cakes and tarts embellished California-style with fresh flowers, head to this sleek, serene branch of Karen Krasne's pastry shop and café. The space with soaring ceilings hosts breakfasts, lunches, and light dinners, accompanied by a wide selection of teas, coffee, organic wines, and craft beers. **Known for:** blueberry coffee cake for breakfast; chocolate dulce de leche cake; house-made dips including onion dip and Parmesan pesto. $ *Average main: $17* ⊠ *1430 Union St., Little Italy* ☎ *619/294–7001* ⊕ *www.extraordinarydesserts.com.*

★ Herb & Wood

$$ | **AMERICAN** | Design lovers will fall for celebrity chef Brian Malarkey's sprawling restaurant, a former art store that has been refashioned into four luxe spaces in one—an entryway lounge, outdoor lounge, fireplace-dotted patio, and the main dining room, which is flanked by beaded chandeliers, lush banquettes, and paintings in rich jewel tones. The menu is heavy on wood-roasted dishes, many of which are apt for sharing, like the roasted baby carrots or hiramasa with crispy quinoa. **Known for:** roasted baby carrots with cashew sesame dukkah; pillow-soft oxtail gnocchi; the secret menu Parker House rolls topped with Maldon sea salt. $ *Average main: $22* ⊠ *2210 Kettner Blvd., Little Italy* ☎ *619/955–8495* ⊕ *www.herbandwood.com* ⊘ *No lunch Mon.–Sat.*

Little Italy Food Hall

$ | **FUSION** | **FAMILY** | A recently opened, chic update on the food court, Food Hall brings together a half dozen different innovative food counters to offer quick bites vastly more interesting than mall fare. Among its offerings are the fried chicken sandwiches at Coo-Coos Nest and pizza at Ambrogio15, and an update on a local delicacy, Not Not Tacos. **Known for:** fusion tacos; bustling crowds of Mercato shoppers; beer/wine cart dispensing refreshments in the outdoor seating area. $ *Average main: $10* ⊠ *550 W. Date St., Suite B, Little Italy* ☎ *619/269–7187* ⊕ *www.littleitalyfoodhall.com.*

ⓨ Nightlife

Ballast Point Brewing Co.

$ | **AMERICAN** | **FAMILY** | Until recently, you had to head to the Miramar/Scripps Ranch area for a tasting at Ballast Point, but now there's a spacious (and popular) local taproom in Little Italy. The Sculpin IPA is outstanding, as are the blue cheese duck nachos. **Known for:** duck nachos; truffalo wings; more than three-dozen beers on tap. $ *Average main: $18* ⊠ *2215 India St., Little Italy* ☎ *619/255–7213* ⊕ *www.ballastpoint.com.*

★ False Idol

COCKTAIL LOUNGES | A walk-in refrigerator harbors the secret entrance to this tiki-theme speakeasy, which is attached to the full-service restaurant Craft & Commerce. Beneath fishing nets full of puffer-fish lights and elaborate tiki-head wall carvings, the knowledgeable staff serves up creative takes on tropical classics with the best selection of rums in town. ■TIP→ **The bar fills up quickly, especially on weekends. Make a reservation online a week or more in advance.** ⊠ *675 W. Beech St., Little Italy* ⊕ *falseidoltiki.com.*

Karl Strauss' Brewing Company

$ | **AMERICAN** | **FAMILY** | San Diego's first microbrewery now has multiple locations, but the original one remains a staple. This locale draws an after-work crowd for German-inspired pub food and pints of Red Trolley Ale and later fills with beer connoisseurs from all walks of life to try Karl's latest concoctions. **Known for:** beer pretzels with ale cheese dip; beeramisu dessert, made with Imperial Stout; more than a dozen rotating and seasonal beers on tap. $ *Average main: $17* ⊠ *1157 Columbia St., Little Italy* ☎ *619/234–2739* ⊕ *www.karlstrauss.com.*

Barrio Logan

San Diego's Mexican-American community is centered on Barrio Logan, under the San Diego–Coronado Bay Bridge on the Downtown side. Chicano Park, spread along National Avenue from Dewey to Crosby streets, is the barrio's recreational hub. It's worth taking a short detour to see the huge murals of Mexican history painted on the bridge supports at National Avenue and Dewey Street; they're among the best examples of folk art in the city. The district is also becoming a hub for artists and has Art enthusiasts a burgeoning gallery scene.

◉ Sights

★ Chicano Park
PUBLIC ART | FAMILY | The cultural center of the Barrio Logan neighborhood, Chicano Park—designated a National Historic Landmark in 2017—was born in 1970 from the activism of local residents who occupied the space after the state rescinded its promise to designate the land a park. Signed into law a year later, the park is now a protected area that brings together families and locals for both public and private events, a welcoming gathering space as well as an outdoor gallery featuring large murals documenting Mexican-American history and Chicano activism. Every year Chicano Park Day is held on April 21, filling the park with the sights and sounds of music, dancers, vintage cars, and food and clothing vendors. ⊠ *Logan Ave. and Cesar Chavez Pkwy., Barrio Logan* ⊕ *chicano-park.com; www.chicanoparksandiego.com.*

🍴 Restaurants

Las Cuatros Milpas
$ | MEXICAN | One of the oldest restaurants in San Diego, having opened in 1933, Las Cuatros Milpas feels like a closely held secret in Barrio Logan. Open daily until 3 pm, it almost inevitably attracts a big lunchtime rush, though the wait is worth it for the homemade tortillas, beans with chorizo, and rolled tacos. **Known for:** homemade tortillas; checkered picnic tables; chorizo con huevos. $ *Average main: $5* ⊠ *1857 Logan Ave., Barrio Logan* ☎ *619/234–4460* ⊕ *www. las-cuatro-milpas.com* ▬ *No credit cards* ⊘ *Closed Sun.*

★ ¡Salud!
$ | MEXICAN | The line that inevitably wraps around the building is indicative of the quality of the tacos and the large selection of local craft beers on tap. Indeed, these are some of the best tacos in all of San Diego, ranging from the classic carne asada and Baja fish tacos to fried-shell beef tacos and Califas, which features French fries inside the tortilla. **Known for:** Baja-style street tacos; Pruno de Piña (beer and fermented pineapple); churros and ice cream. $ *Average main: $4* ⊠ *2196 Logan Ave., Barrio Logan* ☎ *619/255–3856* ⊕ *saludtacos.com* ⊘ *Closed Mon.*

Balboa Park

Overlooking Downtown and the Pacific Ocean, 1,200-acre Balboa Park is the cultural heart of San Diego, home to most of the city's museums and art galleries in addition to the Globe Theatres. The park is also where you'll find the world-famous San Diego Zoo, as well as enchanting gardens and captivating architecture.

Buildings dating from San Diego's 1915 Panama–California International Exposition line the park's main east–west thoroughfare, El Prado, which leads from 6th Avenue eastward over the Cabrillo Bridge, the park's official gateway. If you're a cinema fan, many of the buildings may be familiar—Orson Welles used exteriors of several to represent the

Xanadu estate of Charles Foster Kane in his 1941 classic, *Citizen Kane*. Prominent among them was the California Building, whose 200-foot tower, housing a 100-bell carillon that tolls the hour, is El Prado's tallest structure. Missing from the black-and-white film, however, was the magnificent blue of its tiled dome shining in the sun.

West of Balboa Park, Bankers Hill is a small neighborhood with gorgeous views that stretch from the park's greenery in the east to the San Diego Bay in the west. It's become one of San Diego's hottest restaurant destinations.

◉ Sights

★ Balboa Park Carousel

AMUSEMENT RIDE | FAMILY | Suspended an arm's length away on this antique merry-go-round is the brass ring that could earn you an extra free ride (it's one of the few carousels in the world that continue this bonus tradition). Hand-carved in 1910, the carousel features colorful murals, big-band music, and bobbing animals including zebras, giraffes, and dragons; real horsehair was used for the tails. ⊠ *1889 Zoo Pl., behind zoo parking lot, Balboa Park* ☎ *619/239–0512* ⊕ *www. balboapark.org* ⊡ *$3* ⊙ *Closed weekdays Labor Day–mid-June.*

Bea Evenson Fountain

FOUNTAIN | A favorite of barefoot children, this fountain shoots cool jets of water upward of 50 feet. Built in 1972 between the Fleet Center and Natural History Museum, the fountain offers plenty of room to sit and watch the crowds go by. ⊠ *Balboa Park* ⊹ *East end of El Prado* ⊕ *www.balboapark.org.*

Cabrillo Bridge

BRIDGE | The official gateway into Balboa Park soars 120 feet above a canyon floor. Pedestrian-friendly, the 1,500-foot bridge provides inspiring views of the California Tower and El Prado beyond.

■ **TIP→ This is a great spot for photo-capturing a classic image of the park.** ⊠ *Balboa Park* ⊹ *On El Prado, at 6th Ave. park entrance* ⊕ *www.balboapark.org.*

Fleet Science Center

SCIENCE MUSEUM | FAMILY | Interactive exhibits here are artfully educational and for all ages: older kids can get hands-on with inventive projects in Studio X, while the five-and-under set can be easily entertained with interactive play stations like the Ball Wall and Fire Truck in the center's Kid City. The IMAX Dome Theater, which screens exhilarating nature and science films, was the world's first, as was the Fleet's "NanoSeam" (seamless) dome ceiling that doubles as a planetarium. ⊠ *1875 El Prado, Balboa Park* ☎ *619/238–1233* ⊕ *www.fleetscience.org* ⊡ *The Fleet experience includes gallery exhibits and 1 IMAX film $25; additional cost for special exhibits or add-on 2nd IMAX film or planetarium show; virtual reality simulation rides $10 add-on.*

★ Inez Grant Parker Memorial Rose Garden and Desert Garden

GARDEN | These neighboring gardens sit just across the Park Boulevard pedestrian bridge and offer gorgeous views over Florida Canyon. The award-winning formal rose garden contains 1,600 roses representing nearly 130 varieties; peak bloom is usually in April and May but the garden remains beautiful and worthy of a visit year-round. The adjacent Desert Garden provides a striking contrast, with 2½ acres of succulents and desert plants seeming to blend into the landscape of the canyon below. ⊠ *2525 Park Blvd., Balboa Park* ⊕ *www.balboapark.org.*

★ Museum of Us

VIEWPOINT | FAMILY | Originally known as San Diego Museum of Man, the name was changed in efforts to reflect values of equity, inclusion, and decolonization. If the facade of this building—the landmark California Building—looks familiar, it's because filmmaker Orson Welles used it and its dramatic tower as the principal features of the Xanadu estate in his 1941 classic, *Citizen Kane*. Closed for 80 years, the tower was recently reopened for public tours. An additional timed ticket and a climb up 125 steps is required, but the effort will be rewarded with spectacular 360-degree views of the coast, Downtown, and the inland mountains. Back inside, exhibits at this highly respected anthropological museum focus on Southwestern, Mexican, and South American cultures. Carved monuments from the Mayan city of Quirigua in Guatemala, cast from the originals in 1914, are particularly impressive. Exhibits might include examples of intricate beadwork from across the Americas, the history of Egyptian mummies, or the lifestyles of the Kumeyaay, indigenous peoples of the present-day San Diego area. ⊠ *California Bldg., 1350 El Prado, Balboa Park* ☎ *619/239–2001* ⊕ *www.museumofus. org* ⊠ *$20; tower tour $10 extra plus admission* ⊘ *Closed Mon. and Tues.* ☞ *Tower tours are timed-entry and can be booked in advance through website or on arrival at museum.*

★ San Diego Air & Space Museum

SCIENCE MUSEUM | FAMILY | By day, the streamlined edifice looks like any other structure in the park; at night, outlined in blue neon, the round building appears—appropriately enough—to be a landed UFO. Every available inch of space in the rotunda is filled with exhibits about aviation and aerospace pioneers, including examples of enemy planes from the World Wars. In all, there are more than 60 full-size aircraft on the floor and hanging in the rafters. In addition to exhibits from the dawn of flight to the jet age, the museum displays a growing number of space-age exhibits, including the actual *Apollo 9* command module. To test your own skills, you can ride in a two-seat Max Flight simulator or try out the Talon Racing simulator. Movies in the 3D/4D theater are included with admission. ⊠ *2001 Pan American Plaza, Balboa Park* ☎ *619/234–8291* ⊕ *www. sandiegoairandspace.org* ⊠ *$25; flight simulators $8–$10.*

★ San Diego Museum of Art

ART MUSEUM | Known for its Spanish baroque and Renaissance paintings, including works by El Greco, Goya, Rubens, and van Ruisdael, San Diego's most comprehensive art museum also has strong holdings of South Asian art, Indian miniatures, and contemporary California paintings. The museum's exhibits tend to have broad appeal, and if traveling shows from other cities come to town, you can expect to see them here. Free docent tours are offered throughout the day. An outdoor Sculpture Court and Garden exhibits both traditional and modern pieces. Enjoy the view over a craft beer and some locally sourced food in the adjacent Panama 66 courtyard restaurant. ⊠ *1450 El Prado, Balboa Park* ☎ *619/232–7931* ⊕ *www.sdmart.org* ⊠ *$20; sculpture garden is free* ⊘ *Closed Wed.*

★ San Diego Zoo

ZOO | FAMILY | Balboa Park's—and perhaps the city's—most famous attraction is its 100-acre zoo. Nearly 12,000 animals of some 650 diverse species roam in hospitable, expertly crafted habitats that replicate natural environments as closely as possible. The flora in the zoo, including many rare species, is even more dear than the fauna. Walkways wind over bridges and past waterfalls ringed with tropical ferns; elephants in a sandy plateau roam so close you're tempted to pet them.

Exploring the zoo fully requires the stamina of a healthy hiker, but open-air double-decker buses that run throughout the day let you zip through three-quarters of the exhibits on a guided 35- to

Continued on page 74

Polar bear, San Diego Zoo

LIONS AND TIGERS AND BEARS:
The World-Famous San Diego Zoo

From diving polar bears and 6-ton elephants to swinging great apes, San Diego's most famous attraction has it all. Nearly 12,000 animals representing 650 species roam the 100-acre zoo in expertly crafted habitats that replicate the animals' natural environments. Once world-famous for its Giant Panda program (they have since returned home to China), the zoo has many other celebrity residents to see, from beloved baby hippos and giraffes to its very own axolotl. But it's not all just fun and games. Known for its exemplary conservation programs, the zoo educates visitors on how to go green and explains its efforts to protect endangered species.

SAN DIEGO ZOO TOP ATTRACTIONS

❶ Wildlife Explorers Basecamp. The newest section of the zoo delights visitors of all ages with its rope bridges and exciting play spaces set alongside its 4 distinct habitat zones: desert, marsh, woods and rainforest. Here you can observe a colony of leaf cutter ants, meet a sloth, or spot the rare resident axoltl.

❷ Komodo Kingdom and Hummingbird Habitat. Get an up-close look at a pair of modern day dragons in the dry, rocky landscape of Komodo Island. Next door, observe several species of hummingbirds as you wind your way through the orchids, palms and water features of this lush habitat.

❸ Monkey Trails and Forest Tales (Lost Forest). Follow anelevated trail at treetop leveland trek through the forestfloor observing African mandrill monkeys, Asia's cloudedleopard, the rare pygmy hippopotamus, and Visayan warty pigs.

❹ Orangutan and Siamang Exhibit (Lost Forest). Orangutans and siamangs climb and swing in this lush, tropical environment lined with 110-foot-long and 12-foot-high viewing windows.

❺ Scripps, Parker, and Owens Aviaries (Lost Forest). Wandering paths climb through the enclosed aviaries where brightly colored tropical birds swoop between branches inches from your face.

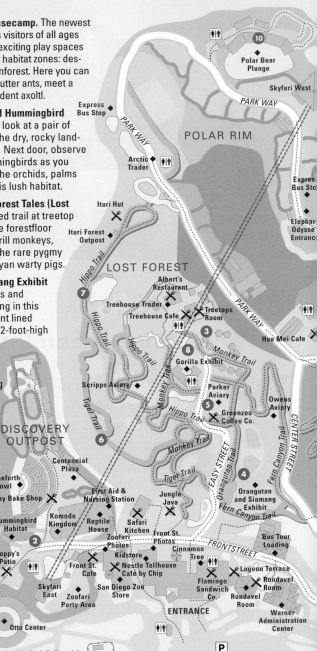

6 Tiger Trail (Lost Forest). The mist-shrouded trails of this simulated rainforest wind down a canyon. Tigers, Malayan tapirs, and Argus pheasants wander among the exotic trees and plants.

7 Hippo Trail (Lost Forest). Glimpse huge but surprisingly graceful hippos frolicking in the water through an underwater viewing window and buffalo cavorting with monkeys on dry land.

8 Gorilla Exhibit (Lost Forest). The gorillas live in one of the zoo's bio-climatic zone exhibits modeled on their native habitat with waterfalls, climbing areas, and an open meadow. The sounds of the tropical rain forest emerge from a 144-speaker sound system that plays CDs recorded in Africa.

9 Africa Rocks. This massive exhibit consists of six different rocky habitats designed to showcase the diversity of topography and species on the African continent. Penguins, meerkats, and a band of baboons are just a few of the animals that call this ambitious exhibit home.

Lories at Owen's Aviary

10 Polar Bear Plunge (Polar Rim). Watch polar bears take a chilly dive from the underwater viewing room. There are also Siberian reindeer, white foxes, and other Arctic creatures here. Kids can learn about the Arctic and climate change through interactive exhibits.

11 Elephant Odyssey. Get a glimpse of the animals that roamed Southern California 12,000 years ago and meet their living counterparts. The 7.5-acre, multispecies habitat features elephants, California condors, jaguars, and more.

12 Koala Exhibit (Outback). The San Diego Zoo houses the largest number of koalas outside Australia. Walk through the exhibit for photo ops of these marsupials from Down-Under curled up on their perches or dining on eucalyptus branches.

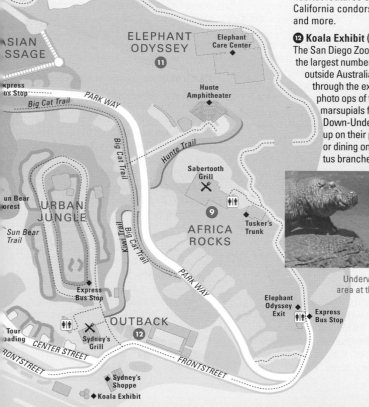

ASIAN
SSAGE

ELEPHANT
ODYSSEY
11

Elephant
Care Center

xpress
us Stop

Big Cat Trail

PARK WAY

Big Cat Trail

Hunte Trail

Hunte
Amphitheater

un Bear
orest

URBAN
JUNGLE

*Sun Bear
Trail*

Sabertooth
Grill

Big Cat Trail

9

AFRICA
ROCKS

Tusker's
Trunk

Express
Bus Stop

Tour
oading

CENTER STREET

OUTBACK
12

Sydney's
Grill

PARK WAY

Elephant
Odyssey
Exit

Express
Bus Stop

RONT STREET

FRONT STREET

Sydney's
Shoppe

Koala Exhibit

Underwater viewing area at the Hippo Trail

MUST-SEE ANIMALS

❶ GORILLA

This troop of primates engages visitors with their human-like expressions and behavior. The youngsters are sure to delight, especially when hitching a ride on mom's back. Up-close encounters might involve the gorillas using the glass partition as a backrest while peeling cabbage. By dusk the gorillas head inside to their sleeping quarters, so don't save this for your last stop.

❷ ELEPHANT

Asian and African elephants coexist at the San Diego Zoo. The larger African elephant is distinguished by its big flapping ears—shaped like the continent of Africa—which it uses to keep cool. An elephant's trunk has over 40,000 muscles in it—that's more than humans have in their whole body.

❸ ORANGUTAN

Bornean and Sumatran orangutans have been entertaining San Diego visitors since 1928. The exhibit has rope climbing structures, a man-made "termite mound" that's often filled with treats, rocky caves, and tall "sway poles" that allow the orangutans to swing like they would in trees. Don't be surprised if the orangutans come right up to the glass to observe the humans observing them!

❹ KOALA

While this collection of critters is one of the cutest in the zoo, don't expect a lot of activity from the koala habitat. These guys spend most of their day curled up asleep in the branches of the eucalyptus tree—they can sleep up to 20 hours a day. Although eucalyptus leaves are poisonous to most animals, bacteria in koalas' stomachs allow them to break down the toxins.

❺ POLAR BEAR

The trio of polar bears is one of the San Diego Zoo's star attractions, and their brand-new exhibit gets you up close and personal. Visitors sometimes worry about polar bears living in the warm San Diego climate, but there is no cause for concern. The San Diego-based bears eat a lean diet, thus reducing their layer of blubber and helping them keep cool.

Did You Know?

Red pandas aren't actually pandas, but more like skunks or raccoons in your backyard. With the giant pandas gone from the San Diego Zoo though, the red pandas are an adorable alternative.

40-minute, 3-mile tour. There are also express buses, used for quick transportation, that make five stops around the grounds and include some narration. The Skyfari Aerial Tram, which soars 170 feet above the ground, gives a good overview of the zoo's layout and, on clear days, a panorama of the park, Downtown San Diego, the bay, and the ocean, far beyond the San Diego–Coronado Bridge.

■ TIP→ **Unless you come early, expect to wait for the regular bus, and especially for the top tier—the line can take more than 45 minutes; if you come at midday on a weekend or school holiday, you'll be doing the in-line shuffle for a while. Don't forget the San Diego Safari Park, the zoo's 1,800-acre extension to the north at Escondido.**

✉ *2920 Zoo Dr., Balboa Park* ☎ *619/234–3153* ⊕ *www.sandiegozoowildlifealliance.org* 💲 *$71* ☞ *Multiday and combination tickets available.*

★ Spanish Village Art Center

ART GALLERY | More than 200 local artists, including glassblowers, enamel workers, wood-carvers, sculptors, painters, jewelers, and photographers work and give demonstrations of their craft on a rotating basis within and outside of these red tile–roof studio-galleries that were set up for the 1935–36 exposition in the style of an old Spanish village. The center is a great source for memorable gifts. ✉ *1770 Village Pl., Balboa Park* ☎ *619/233–9050* ⊕ *spanishvillageartcenter.com* 💲 *Free.*

★ Spreckels Organ Pavilion

PLAZA/SQUARE | The 2,400-bench-seat pavilion, dedicated in 1915 by sugar magnates John D. and Adolph B. Spreckels, holds the 4,518-pipe Spreckels Organ, the largest outdoor pipe organ in the world. You can hear this impressive instrument at one of the year-round, free, 2 pm Sunday concerts, regularly performed by the city's civic organist Raúl Prieto Ramírez and guest artists—a highlight of a visit to Balboa Park. On Monday evening from late June to mid-August,

internationally renowned organists play evening concerts. At Christmastime the park's Christmas tree and life-size Nativity display turn the pavilion into a seasonal wonderland. ✉ *2211 Pan American Rd., Balboa Park* ☎ *619/702–8138* ⊕ *spreckelsorgan.org.*

🍴 Restaurants

Craveology

$ | **AMERICAN** | **FAMILY** | Enjoy views of the Bea Evenson Fountain from the patio of this quick lunch option outside the Fleet Science Center. The menu offers everything from flatbreads, sandwiches, and soups to smoothies, specialty coffees, and soft-serve ice cream. **Known for:** fountain views; smoothies and specialty coffees; color-changing ice-cream spoons. 💲 *Average main: $9* ✉ *1875 El Prado, Balboa Park* ✛ *Outside Fleet Science Center* ☎ *619/238–1233* ⊕ *www.fleetscience.org.*

★ Cucina Urbana

$$ | **ITALIAN** | Twentysomethings mingle with boomers in this convivial Bankers Hill dining room and bar, one of the most popular restaurants in town. The open kitchen turns out innovative Italian food with a California sensibility including a selection of small plates and family-style pasta dishes alongside traditional entrées. **Known for:** in-house wine shop with reasonably priced bottles and $9 corkage fee; seasonal polenta with ragu; ricotta-stuffed zucchini blossoms. 💲 *Average main: $27* ✉ *505 Laurel St., Bankers Hill* ☎ *619/239–2222* ⊕ *www.cucinaurbana.com* 🕙 *Closed Mon. No lunch.*

★ Mister A's

$$$$ | **CONTEMPORARY** | For decades, this venerable 12th-floor dining room with panoramic views and polished service has reigned as a celebratory fine-dining destination. A recent renovation following the passing of the torch from former owner Betrand Hug to his longtime employee Ryan Thorsen has resulted in an exciting refresh of this enduring landmark. **Known for:** iconic "special occasion" destination; popular bar and lounge space; stunning panoramic bay and city views. $ *Average main: $45* ✉ *2550 5th Ave., 12th fl., Bankers Hill* 🕾 *619/239–1377* ⊕ *www.asrestaurant.com* ⊗ *No lunch Mon. and Tues.* ⏶ *Business casual dress code strictly enforced.*

Tea Pavilion
$ | **JAPANESE** | Grab some noodles, sushi, or Japanese tea and treats at this pavilion located in the center of the park. The large outdoor patio is a great place to rest and recharge before seeking tranquility in the adjacent Japanese Friendship Garden. **Known for:** spacious patio; extensive tea selection; Japanese snacks and sweets. $ *Average main: $9* ✉ *2215 Pan American Way, Balboa Park* 🕾 *619/231–0048* ⊕ *www.cohnrestaurants.com* ⊗ *Closed Mon. and Tues. No dinner.*

🎭 Performing Arts

★ Globe Theatres
THEATER | This complex, comprised of the Sheryl and Harvey White Theatre, the Lowell Davies Festival Theatre, and the Old Globe Theatre, offers some of the finest theatrical productions in Southern California. Theater classics such as *Into the Woods* and *Dirty Rotten Scoundrels,* and more recent hits like *Bright Star* and *Meteor Shower,* premiered on these famed stages and went on to perform on Broadway. The Old Globe presents a renowned summer Shakespeare Festival with three to four plays in repertory. The theaters, done in a California version of Tudor style, sit between the sculpture garden of the San Diego Museum of Art and the California Tower. If you can't catch a show, daytime one-hour behind-the-scenes tours offer a close-up look at the theaters as well as the intricacies of set and costume design. ✉ *1363 Old Globe Way, Balboa Park* 🕾 *619/234–5623* ⊕ *www.theoldglobe.org* 🎟 *Tours $7* ⊗ *Box office closed Mon.*

Old Town and Uptown

The city's Spanish and Mexican roots are most evident in Old Town and the surrounding hillside of Presidio Park. Old Town San Diego State Historic Park re-creates life during the early settlement, while San Diego Avenue buzzes with galleries, gift shops, festive restaurants, as well as open-air stands selling inexpensive Mexican handicrafts.

Nearby Uptown is composed of several smaller neighborhoods near Downtown and around Balboa Park. Vibrant Hillcrest, Mission Hills, North Park, and South Park showcase their unique blend of historical charm and modern urban community.

👁 Sights

★ Fiesta de Reyes
PLAZA/SQUARE | FAMILY | North of San Diego's Old Town Plaza lies the area's unofficial center, built to represent a colonial Mexican plaza. The collection of more than a dozen shops and restaurants around a central courtyard in blossom with magenta bougainvillea, scarlet hibiscus, and other flowers in season reflects what early California might have looked like from 1821 to 1872. Mariachi bands and folklorico dance groups frequently perform on the plaza stage—check the website for times and upcoming special events.

■**TIP**→ **Casa de Reyes is a great stop for a margarita and some chips and guacamole.** ✉ *4016 Wallace St., Old Town* 🕾 *619/297–3100* ⊕ *www.fiestadereyes.com.*

★ Old Town San Diego State Historic Park
MUSEUM VILLAGE | FAMILY | The six square blocks on the site of San Diego's original pueblo are the heart of Old Town. Most of the 20 historic buildings preserved or re-created by the park cluster are around

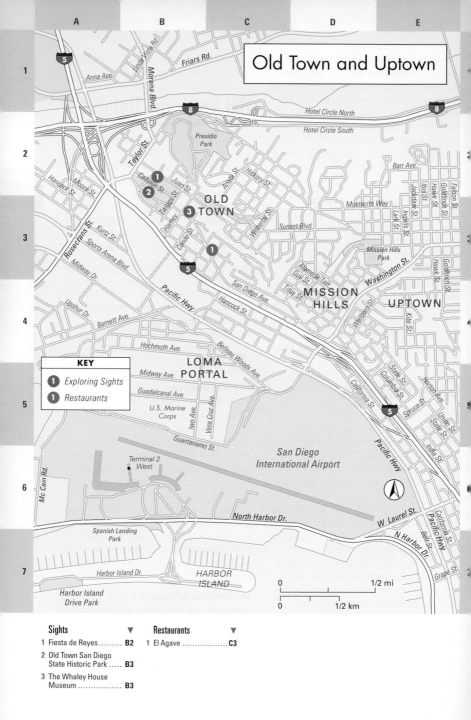

Old Town and Uptown

Old Town Plaza, bounded by Wallace Street on the west, Calhoun Street on the north, Mason Street on the east, and San Diego Avenue on the south. The plaza is a pleasant place to rest, plan your tour of the park, and watch passersby. San Diego Avenue is closed to vehicle traffic here.

Some of Old Town's buildings were destroyed in a fire in 1872, but after the site became a state historic park in 1968, reconstruction and restoration of the remaining structures began. Five of the original adobes are still intact. La Casa de Estudillo, La Casa de Machado y Stewart, La Casa de Machado y Silvas, the Pedrorena-Altamirano House, and La Casa de Bandini (now the Cosmopolitan Hotel).

Facing Old Town Plaza, the **Robinson-Rose House** was the original commercial center of Old San Diego, housing railroad offices, law offices, and the first newspaper press. The largest and most elaborate of the original adobe homes, the **Casa de Estudillo** was occupied by members of the Estudillo family until 1887 and later gained popularity for its billing as "Ramona's Marriage Place" based on a popular novel of the time. Albert Seeley, a stagecoach entrepreneur, opened the Cosmopolitan Hotel in 1869 as a way station for travelers on the daylong trip south from Los Angeles. Next door to the Cosmopolitan Hotel, the **Seeley Stable** served as San Diego's stagecoach stop in 1867 and was the transportation hub of Old Town until 1887, when trains became the favored mode of travel.

Several reconstructed buildings serve as restaurants or as shops purveying wares reminiscent of those that might have been available in the original Old Town. Racine & Laramie, a painstakingly reproduced version of San Diego's first cigar store in 1868, is especially interesting.

Pamphlets available at the Robinson-Rose House give details about all the historic houses on the plaza and in its vicinity. Free tours of the historic park are offered daily at 11:30 and 2; they depart from the Robinson-Rose House.

■ **TIP**➜ **The covered wagon located near the intersection of Mason and Calhoun Streets provides a great photo op.** ⊠ *Visitor center (Robinson-Rose House), 4002 Wallace St., Old Town* ☎ *619/220–5422* ⊕ *www.parks.ca.gov* ⊠ *Free.*

★ The Whaley House Museum
HISTORIC HOME | A New York entrepreneur, Thomas Whaley came to California during the gold rush. He wanted to provide his East Coast wife with all the comforts of home, so in 1857 he had Southern California's first two-story brick structure built, making it the oldest double-story brick building on the West Coast. The house, which served as the county courthouse and government seat during the 1870s, stands in strong contrast to the Spanish-style adobe residences that surround the nearby historic plaza and marks an early stage of San Diego's "Americanization." A garden out back includes many varieties of prehybrid roses from before 1867. The place is perhaps most famed, however, for the ghosts that are said to inhabit it. You can tour on your own during the day, but must visit by guided tour after 4:30 pm. The evening tours are geared toward the supernatural aspects of the house. Tours start at 5 pm and are offered every half hour, with the last tour departing at 9:30 pm. ⊠ *2476 San Diego Ave., Old Town* ☎ *619/273–5824* ⊕ *www.whaleyhousesandiego.com* ⊠ *From $13.*

🍴 Restaurants

El Agave
$$$ | MEXICAN | Not a typical San Diego taco shop, this Mexican eatery is upstairs in a shopping complex in the middle of a tequila museum with some 2,000 bottles dating from the 1930s. The owners are equally serious about food, calling their cuisine Hispanic-Mexican Gastronomy,

which means meat and fish dishes with lots of unusual spicy chilies, herbs, spices, and moles. **Known for:** impressive tequila selection and tequila flights; variety of mole dishes; upscale option in generally casual Old Town. $ *Average main: $32* ✉ *2304 San Diego Ave., Old Town* ☎ *619/220–0692* ⊕ *www.elagave. com.*

Shopping

Bazaar del Mundo Shops

SHOPPING CENTER | With a Mexican villa theme, the Bazaar hosts riotously colorful gift shops such as Ariana, for ethnic and artsy women's fashions; Artes de Mexico, which sells handmade Latin American crafts and Guatemalan weavings; and The Gallery, which carries handmade jewelry, Native American crafts, collectible glass, and original silk-screen prints. The Laurel Burch Gallerita carries the complete collection of its namesake artist's signature jewelry, accessories, and totes. ✉ *4133 Taylor St., at Juan St., Old Town* ☎ *619/296–3161* ⊕ *www.bazaardelmundo.com.*

Mission Bay and the Beaches

This area serves as San Diego's aquatic playground. Mission Bay is home to both SeaWorld and a 4,600-acre park with grassy areas, protected waters, and 19 miles of beaches, making it the perfect place for water sports and picnics. Mission Beach is a famous and lively fun zone, where, if it isn't party time at the moment, it will be five minutes from now. Pathways here are lined with vacation homes, many for rent by the week or month.

North of Mission Beach is Pacific Beach—fondly referred to as "PB"—a laid-back surfing mecca that also attracts skateboarders, beach cruisers, and other free-spirited locals. The energy level rises considerably during happy hour, when PB's cluster of nightclubs, bars, and restaurants welcome those who are ready to party.

Sights

★ Belmont Park

AMUSEMENT PARK/CARNIVAL | FAMILY | The once-abandoned amusement park between the bay and Mission Beach boardwalk is now a shopping, dining, and recreation complex. Twinkling lights outline the Giant Dipper, an antique wooden roller coaster on which screaming thrill seekers ride more than 2,600 feet of track and 13 hills (riders must be at least 4 feet, 2 inches tall). Created in 1925 and listed on the National Register of Historic Places, this is one of the few old-time roller coasters left in the United States.

Other Belmont Park attractions include miniature golf, a laser maze, video arcade, bumper cars, a tilt-a-whirl, and an antique carousel. The zipline thrills as it soars over the crowds below, while the rock wall challenges both junior climbers and their elders.

The **Plunge** indoor swimming pool was the largest—60 feet by 125 feet—saltwater pool in the world when it opened in 1925; it's had freshwater since 1951. Johnny Weismuller and Esther Williams are among the stars who were captured on celluloid swimming here. After an extensive renovation, the pool now features expansive windows and a retractable glass ceiling, and is once again a San Diego landmark. Open to the public, its many lap lanes and a large inflatable obstacle course make the Plunge a popular choice for athletes and recreational swimmers alike. ✉ *3146 Mission Blvd., Mission Bay* ☎ *858/488–1549 for rides* ⊕ *www.belmontpark.com* 🎟 *Unlimited ride day package from $60, individual ride tickets available from $10; Plunge pass from $15.*

★ Crystal Pier

MARINA/PIER | Stretching out into the ocean from the end of Garnet Avenue, Crystal Pier is Pacific Beach's landmark. In the 1920s, it was a classic amusement park complete with ballroom. Today, it's mainly comprised of a series of quaint cottages that are all a part of the Crystal Pier Hotel. Guests have access to fishing, as well as the intersecting Mission Beach boardwalk. For those that aren't hotel guests, you may access the pier through a side gate from 8 am to sunset. ⊠ *Pacific Beach* ⊹ *At end of Garnet Ave.*

★ Mission Bay Park

CITY PARK | San Diego's monument to sports and fitness, this 4,600-acre aquatic park has 27 miles of shoreline including 19 miles of sandy beaches. Playgrounds and picnic areas abound on the beaches and low, grassy hills. On weekday evenings, joggers, bikers, and skaters take over. In the daytime, swimmers, water-skiers, paddleboarders, anglers, and boaters—some in single-person kayaks, others in crowded powerboats—vie for space in the water. ⊠ *2688 E. Mission Bay Dr., Mission Bay* ⊹ *Off I–5 at Exit 22, E. Mission Bay Dr.* ☏ *858/581–7602 park ranger's office* ⊕ *www.sandiego.gov/park-and-recreation* ⊠ *Free.*

★ Mission Beach Boardwalk

PROMENADE | The cement pathway lining the sand from the southern end of Mission Beach north to Pacific Beach is always bustling with activity. Cyclists ping the bells on their beach cruisers to pass walkers out for a stroll alongside the oceanfront homes. Vacationers kick back on their patios while friends play volleyball in the sand. The activity picks up alongside Belmont Park, where people stop to check out the action at the amusement park and beach bars. ⊠ *Mission Beach* ⊹ *Alongside sand from Mission Beach Park to Pacific Beach.*

SeaWorld San Diego

THEME PARK | **FAMILY** | Spread over 189 tropically landscaped bay-front acres, SeaWorld is one of the world's largest marine-life amusement parks. The majority of its exhibits are walk-through marine environments like Shark Encounter, where guests walk through a 57-foot acrylic tube and come face-to-face with a variety of sharks that call the 280,000-gallon habitat home. Turtle Reef offers an incredible up-close encounter with the green sea turtle, while the moving sidewalk at Penguin Encounter whisks you through a colony of nearly 300 penguins.

The park also wows with its recent heavy investment in adventure rides like the Electric Eel, a shocking multi-launch coaster that sends riders twisting forward and backward 150 feet in the air at speeds reaching 60 mph, and the Emperor, a floorless dive coaster with a 14-story face-down vertical drop. The newest addition is Arctic Rescue, a straddle coaster simulating a perilous animal rescue mission aboard a snowmobile at speeds of 40 mph. For a comparatively milder thrill, Journey to Atlantis water coaster splashes down a 60-foot plunge. Younger children will enjoy the rides, climbing structures, and splash pads at the Sesame Street Bay of Play.

SeaWorld is most famous for its large-arena entertainments, but this is an area in transition. The park's latest orca experience features a nature-inspired backdrop and demonstrates orca behaviors in the wild, part of SeaWorld's efforts to refocus its orca program toward education and conservation. Other live-entertainment shows feature dolphins, sea lions and otters. Several upgraded animal encounters are available including the Dolphin Interaction Program, which gives guests the chance to interact with SeaWorld's bottlenose dolphins in the water. The hour-long program (20 minutes in the water), during which visitors can feed,

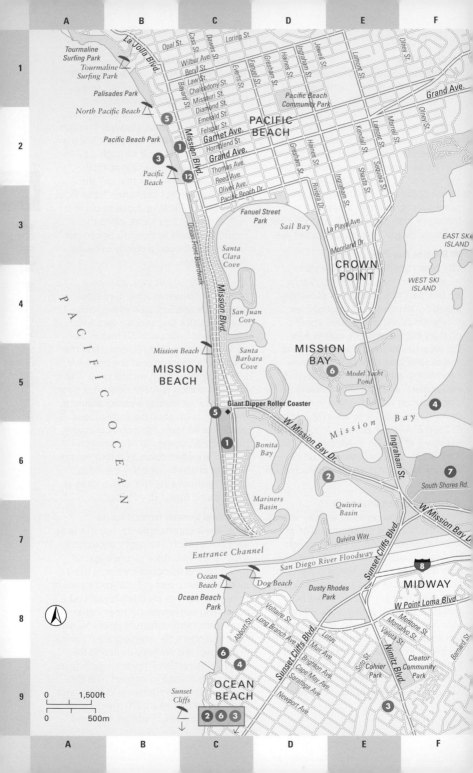

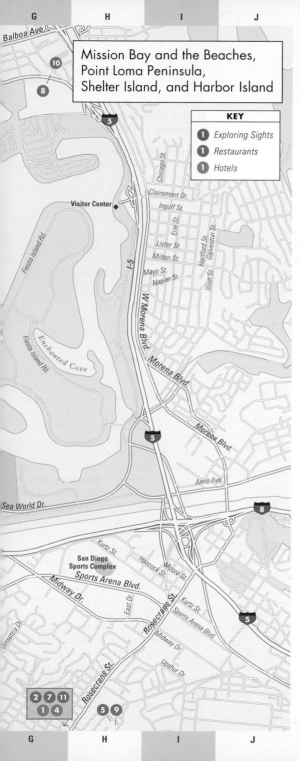

Mission Bay and the Beaches, Point Loma Peninsula, Shelter Island, and Harbor Island

KEY

1 Exploring Sights
1 Restaurants
1 Hotels

4

San Diego MISSION BAY AND THE BEACHES

touch, and give behavior signals, costs $215. ✉ *500 SeaWorld Dr., near west end of I–8, Mission Bay* ☎ *619/222–4732* ⊕ *www.seaworld.com* ✉ *$110; advanced purchase discounts available online; parking $30.*

 Beaches

Mission Beach

BEACH | FAMILY | With an amusement park and rows of eclectic local shops, this 2-mile-long beach has a carnival vibe and is the closest thing you'll find to Coney Island on the West Coast. It's lively year-round but draws a huge crowd on hot summer days. A wide boardwalk paralleling the beach is popular with walkers, joggers, skateboarders, and bicyclists. To escape the crowds, head to South Mission Beach. It attracts surfers, swimmers, and volleyball players, who often play competitive pickup games on the courts near the north jetty. The water near the Belmont Park roller coaster can be a bit rough but makes for good body-boarding and bodysurfing. For free parking, you can try for a spot on the street, but your best bets are the two big lots at Belmont Park. **Amenities:** lifeguards; parking (no fee); showers; toilets. **Best for:** surfing; swimming; walking. ✉ *3000 Mission Blvd., Mission Bay* ✛ *Parking near roller coaster at West Mission Bay Dr.* ⊕ *www.sandiego.gov/lifeguards/ beaches/mb.*

Pacific Beach/North Pacific Beach

BEACH | This beach, known for attracting a young college-age crowd and surfers, runs from the northern end of Mission Beach to Crystal Pier. The scene here is lively on weekends, with nearby restaurants, beach bars, and nightclubs providing a party atmosphere. In PB (as the locals call it) Sundays are known as "Sunday Funday," and pub crawls can last all day, although drinking is no longer allowed on the beach. The mood changes just north of the pier at North Pacific Beach, which attracts families and surfers. Although not quite pillowy, the sand at both beaches is nice and soft, which makes for great sunbathing and sandcastle building.

■ **TIP** → **Kelp and flies can be a problem on this stretch, so choose your spot wisely.**

Parking at Pacific Beach can also be a challenge. A few coveted free angle parking spaces are available along the boardwalk, but you'll most likely have to look for spots in the surrounding neighborhood. **Amenities:** food and drink; lifeguards; parking (no fee); showers, toilets. **Best for:** partiers; surfing; swimming. ✉ *4500 Ocean Blvd., Pacific Beach* ⊕ *www.sandiego.gov/lifeguards/beaches/ pb.*

Tourmaline Surfing Park

BEACH | Offering slow waves and frequent winds, this is one of the most popular beaches for surfers. For windsurfing and kiteboarding, it's only sailable with northwest winds. The 175-space parking lot at the foot of Tourmaline Street normally fills to capacity by midday. Just like Pacific Beach, Tourmaline has soft, tawny-color sand, but when the tide is in the beach becomes quite narrow, making finding a good sunbathing spot a bit of a challenge. Parking will be difficult on evenings and weekends. **Amenities:** seasonal lifeguards; parking (no fee); showers; toilets. **Best for:** surfing; windsurfing. ✉ *600 Tourmaline St., Pacific Beach.*

🍴 Restaurants

The Baked Bear

$ | BAKERY | FAMILY | This build-your-own ice-cream-sandwich shop a block from Pacific Beach is a local favorite thanks to its homemade cookies and diverse array of ice-cream flavors, from birthday cake to peanut butter fudge. Don't miss out on their hot pressed ice-cream sandwiches! **Known for:** Bear Bowls made of cookies; doughnut ice-cream sandwiches; long lines on summer evenings. Ⓢ *Average main: $7* ✉ *4516 Mission Blvd., Suite C,*

Pacific Beach ☎ *858/886–7433* 🌐 *www.thebakedbear.com.*

Rubio's Coastal Grill

$ | **SEAFOOD** | Credited with popularizing fish tacos in the United States, Ralph Rubio brought the Mexican staple to San Diego, opening his first restaurant in Pacific Beach where it still stands today. The original beer-battered fish tacos have fried pollock topped with white sauce, salsa, and cabbage atop a corn tortilla. **Known for:** the original fish taco; Taco Tuesday deals—$1.99 fish taco; $8 lunch specials. [$] *Average main: $10* ✉ *4504 E. Mission Bay Dr., Pacific Beach* ☎ *858/272–2801* 🌐 *www.rubios.com.*

★ Sushi Ota

$$ | **SUSHI** | One fan called it "a notch above amazing"—an accolade not expected for a Japanese eatery wedged in a strip mall in Pacific Beach. But it's a destination for lovers of high-quality, superfresh raw fish from around San Diego and abroad; reservations strongly encouraged. **Known for:** velvety hamachi belly; sea urchin specials; chef's omakase tasting menu. [$] *Average main: $25* ✉ *4529 Mission Bay Dr., Pacific Beach* ☎ *858/880–8778* 🌐 *www.sushi-ota.com* 🕒 *Closed Mon. No lunch weekends.*

★ Waterbar

$$ | **SEAFOOD** | Occupying a prime oceanfront lot just south of Crystal Pier, the views from the raised dining room are impressive. Throw in an excellent raw bar, a wide selection of shared plates, and a buzzy bar scene and you get Waterbar's "social seafood" concept. **Known for:** "Boardwalk hour" oyster specials; boozy weekend brunch; ocean views. [$] *Average main: $29* ✉ *4325 Ocean Blvd., Pacific Beach* ☎ *858/888–4343* 🌐 *www.waterbarsd.com.*

Hotels

Hyatt Regency Mission Bay Spa and Marina

$$$ | **RESORT** | **FAMILY** | This bayside property has many desirable amenities, including balconies with excellent views of the garden, bay, ocean, or swimming pool courtyard. **Pros:** proximity to water sports; 120-foot waterslides in pools, plus kiddie slide; several suite configurations good for families. **Cons:** daily resort fee; not centrally located; some common areas and bay building rooms are in need of updates. [$] *Rooms from: $409* ✉ *1441 Quivira Rd., Mission Bay* ☎ *619/224–1234, 800/233–1234* 🌐 *www.hyatt.com* 🛏 *429 rooms* 🍴 *No Meals* ☞ *$35 resort fee.*

Pacific Terrace Hotel

$$$$ | **HOTEL** | Travelers love this terrific beachfront hotel and the ocean views from most rooms as well as the pool; it's a perfect place for watching sunsets over the Pacific. **Pros:** beach views; large rooms; friendly service. **Cons:** busy and sometimes noisy area; expensive in peak season; resort fee. [$] *Rooms from: $699* ✉ *610 Diamond St., Pacific Beach* ☎ *858/581–3500, 800/344–3370* 🌐 *www.pacificterrace.com* 🛏 *73 rooms* 🍴 *No Meals* ☞ *$18 Resort Fee.*

Paradise Point Resort & Spa

$$$ | **RESORT** | **FAMILY** | Minutes from SeaWorld but hidden in a quiet part of Mission Bay, the beautiful landscape of this 44-acre resort offers plenty of space for families to play and relax. **Pros:** water views; five pools; sprawling grounds. **Cons:** not centrally located; motel-thin walls; parking and resort fees. [$] *Rooms from: $474* ✉ *1404 Vacation Rd., Mission Bay* ☎ *858/240–4913* 🌐 *www.paradisepoint.com* 🛏 *462 rooms* 🍴 *No Meals* ☞ *$39 Resort Fee.*

🍸 Nightlife

Amplified Ale Works

BREWPUBS | Pacific Beach often veers between the trendy and the tawdry, so this genuine craft brewhouse offers a more casual middle ground. Amplified serves more than a dozen in-house-brewed beers and healthy, vegan-friendly Mediterranean/Californian food at its scenic outdoor beer garden with breathtaking ocean views. ✉ *4150 Mission Blvd., No. 208, Pacific Beach* ☎ *858/270–5222* ⊕ *www.amplifiedales.com.*

★ The Grass Skirt and Captain's Quarters

COCKTAIL LOUNGES | This pair of speakeasies delights guests with high-theme decor and engaging menus. Entering the nondescript storefront, a sign above the desk in the seemingly cluttered travel agency reads "Other World Travel," but the working kitchen behind offers a hint that all is not as it seems. Accessed through a false freezer door on the left, the Grass Skirt tiki bar serves a wide selection of rum-based tropical cocktails and a menu of shareable pupus in delightfully kitsch surroundings. Venturing through the hidden door to the right transports travelers to the refined Captain's Quarters of a 17th-century sailing vessel where small bites are served alongside a gin-centric cocktail menu. Be sure to reserve a table through the website—these hidden gems are no secret! ✉ *910 Grand Ave., Pacific Beach* ☎ *858/412–5237* ⊕ *www.thegrassskirt. com.*

JRDN

BARS | This contemporary lounge (pronounced "Jordan") occupies the ground floor of Pacific Beach's chicest boutique hotel, TOWER23, and offers a more sophisticated vibe in what is a very party-happy neighborhood. Sleek walls of windows and an expansive patio overlook the boardwalk. ✉ *723 Felspar St., Pacific Beach* ☎ *858/270–2323* ⊕ *www.t23hotel. com.*

🏃 Activities

If you're a novice surfer, consider paddling in the waves off Mission Beach, Pacific Beach, and Tourmaline Surfing Park. Several outfitters offer year-round lessons as well as surf camps in the summer months and during spring break.

Easily accessible kelp forests and protected marine areas off the coast offer divers ample opportunities to explore. Classes are available for beginners, while experienced divers will appreciate the challenges of local wreck and canyon dives. Water temperatures can be chilly, so check with a local outfitter for the appropriate gear before setting out.

A bike ride along the Mission Beach boardwalk is a great way to take in a classic California scene. Keep in mind that this often-crowded route is more for cruising than hard-core cycling. Mission Bay has a 10-mile loop of cement paths that are good for leisurely bike rides or walks beside big green lawns, playgrounds, and picnic spots.

Cheap Rentals

SURFING | One block from the boardwalk, this place has good daily and weekly prices for surfboards, paddleboards, kayaks, snorkel gear, skateboards, coolers, umbrellas, chairs, and bike rentals, including beach cruisers, tandems, hybrids, and two-wheeled baby carriers. Kids' bikes are also available. Demand is high during the busy season (May through September) so call to reserve equipment ahead of time. ✉ *3689 Mission Blvd., Mission Beach* ☎ *858/488–9070* ⊕ *www.cheap-rentals. com* 🎟 *Season passes $350, unlimited daytime pass $40, unlimited weekend pass $60.*

Mission Bay Aquatic Center

BOATING | FAMILY | One of the world's largest instructional waterfront facilities offers lessons in wakeboarding, sailing, surfing, waterskiing, rowing, kayaking, and windsurfing. Equipment rental is also available, but the emphasis is on instruction, and most rentals require a minimum two-hour orientation lesson before you can set out on your own. Reservations are recommended, particularly during the summer. Skippered keelboats and boats for waterskiing or wakeboarding can be hired with reservations. Free parking is available but keep an eye out for signage—not all the parking spots are free or overnight. ✉ *1001 Santa Clara Pl., Mission Beach* ☎ *858/488–1000* ⊕ *www.mbaquaticcenter.com.*

★ Seaforth Boat Rentals

BOATING | The Mission Bay outpost of this popular rental company offers a wide variety of motorized and nonmotorized craft. Jet Skis, SUPs, kayaks, and fishing skiffs are available alongside sailboats and powerboats of all sizes. For added relaxation, charter a skippered pontoon party boat, some with waterslides for added fun. ✉ *1641 Quivira Rd., Mission Bay* ☎ *888/834–2628* ⊕ *www.seaforthboatrental.com.*

Point Loma Peninsula

The hilly Point Loma peninsula protects the San Diego Bay from the Pacific's tides and waves. Here you'll find sandy beaches, private marinas, and prominent military installations. Nestled between Coronado and Point Loma, Harbor and Shelter islands have bars and restaurants that are great places to take in views of Downtown San Diego across the bay.

Point Loma

The high elevations and sandy cliffs of Point Loma, which curves west and south into the Pacific, provide incredible views. Early San Diego history is marked here at the Cabrillo National Monument, the site where Spanish explorer Juan Rodríguez Cabrillo landed in 1542. The peninsula's maritime roots—from its ties to the U.S. Navy to its bustling sportfishing and sailing marinas—are also evident. The funky community of Ocean Beach coexists alongside the stately homes of Sunset Cliffs.

⊙ Sights

★ Cabrillo National Monument

VIEWPOINT | FAMILY | This 166-acre preserve marks the site of the first European visit to San Diego, made by 16th-century Spanish explorer Juan Rodríguez Cabrillo when he landed at this spot on September 15, 1542. Today the site, with its rugged cliffs and shores and outstanding overlooks, is one of the most frequently visited of all the national monuments. There's a good visitor center and useful interpretive stations along the cliff-side walkways. Highlights include the moderately difficult Bayside Trail, the Old Point Loma Lighthouse, and the tide pools (at low tide only). There's also a sheltered viewing station where you can watch the gray whales' yearly migration (December–February) from Baja California to Alaska (including high-powered telescopes). ✉ *1800 Cabrillo Memorial Dr., Point Loma* ☎ *619/523–4285* ⊕ *www.nps.gov/cabr* 🎫 *$20 per car, $10 per person on foot/bicycle, entry good for 7 days.*

Ocean Beach Pier

MARINA/PIER | Constructed in 1966, this T-shape pier is the West Coast's longest concrete pier. It's the perfect place to take in views of the harbor, the surfers, the ocean, and Point Loma Peninsula. It's also a popular fishing spot and home to the Walking On Water Cafe and a small tackle shop; however, a winter storm in 2023 caused severe damage to the pier, resulting in its closure (as well as that of the café and shop) until at least 2026 when construction is expected to start. Surfers flock to the waves that break just below. ✉ *1950 Abbott St., Ocean Beach.*

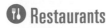

Beaches

Sunset Cliffs

BEACH | As the name would suggest, this natural park near Point Loma Nazerene University is one of the best places in San Diego to watch the sunset thanks to its cliff-top location and expansive ocean views. Some limited beach access is accessible via an extremely steep stairway at the foot of Ladera Street. Beware of the treacherous cliff trails and pay attention to warning signs since the cliffs are very unstable. If you're going to make your way to the narrow beach below, it's best to go at low tide when the southern end, near Cabrillo Point, reveals tide pools teeming with small sea creatures. Farther north the waves lure surfers, and Osprey Point offers good fishing off the rocks. Keep your eyes peeled for migrating California gray whales during the winter months. Check WaveCast (🌐 *www.wavecast.com/socal*) for tide schedules. **Amenities:** parking (no fee). **Best for:** solitude; sunset; surfing. ✉ *Sunset Cliffs Blvd., between Ladera St. and Adair St., Point Loma* 🌐 *www.sunsetcliffs.info.*

Restaurants

★ Cesarina

$$ | **ITALIAN** | A wall of mason jars with pickled vegetables and brined olives transports you to an Italian market in Rome where the owner's mother perfected generations of recipes that have made their way into this Point Loma eatery. Since its 2019 opening, customers have lined up for generous portions of homemade Italian staples including pasta, gnocchi, meatballs, sausage, bread, and decadent desserts. **Known for:** nearly everything made from scratch; authentic Italian cuisine; excellent vegan options. [$] *Average main: $25* ✉ *4161 Voltaire St., Point Loma* ☎ *619/226–6222* 🌐 *www.cesarinarestaurant.com.*

★ Hodad's

$ | **BURGER** | **FAMILY** | Surfers with big appetites, and fans of Food Network's *Diners, Drive-ins and Dives,* chow down on huge, messy burgers, fries, onion rings, and shakes at this funky, hippie beach joint adorned with beat-up surfboards, stickers, and license plates from almost every state. Don't be put off by lines out the door—they move quickly and the wait is worth it, especially for the Guido Burger; inspired by Guy Fieri, it's topped with pastrami, onions, pickles, and Swiss cheese. **Known for:** legendary bacon cheeseburgers and thick-cut onion rings; surf-shack vibe; a little sass with your burger. [$] *Average main: $12* ✉ *5010 Newport Ave., Ocean Beach* ☎ *619/224–4623* 🌐 *www.hodadies.com.*

★ Liberty Public Market

$ | **INTERNATIONAL** | **FAMILY** | The city's former Naval Training Center is home to more than 30 vendors so even the pickiest of diners will be pleased. Options include tacos and quesadillas at Cecilia's Taqueria; fried rice, pad Thai, and curries at Mama Made Thai; lavender lattes from Westbean Coffee Roasters; fried chicken and fries from Fluster Cluck; sweet and savory crepes from Olala; more than a dozen Argentinean empanadas at Paraná; and croissants, éclairs, and macarons at Le Parfait Paris. **Known for:** cuisines from around the world; lively kid- and dog-friendly patio; the best regional foods under one roof. [$] *Average main: $10* ✉ *2820 Historic Decatur Rd., Liberty Station* ☎ *619/487–9346* 🌐 *www.libertypublicmarket.com.*

★ Little Lion Cafe

$$ | **MODERN AMERICAN** | Amid surf shacks and hippie beach bars, this restaurant perched on stunning Sunset Cliffs feels like a hidden European bistro. The sisters who run the show come from a long line of successful local restaurateurs and have brought their passed-down expertise to the thoughtful service and simple, healthy menu that features entrées like plant-based tacos, quinoa bowls, and the Bistro Burger with Hatch Chile cheddar on a brioche bun. **Known for:** eggs Benedict; cozy bistro setting; chocolate hazelnut scone. $ *Average main: $20* ✉ *1424 Sunset Cliffs Blvd., Ocean Beach* ☎ *619/756–6921* ⊕ *www.thelittlelioncafe. com* ⊗ *Closed Tues. No dinner.*

Point Loma Seafoods

$$ | **SEAFOOD** | **FAMILY** | When fishing boats unload their catch on-site, a seafood restaurant and market earns the right to boast that they offer "the freshest thing in town." In the late 1950s, mostly sportfishermen came here, but word got out about the just-caught fried fish on San Francisco–style sourdough bread, and now locals and visitors come to enjoy bay views, sunshine, and a greatly expanded menu of seafood dishes. A friendly, efficient crew takes orders for food and drinks at the counter, keeping the wait down even on the busiest days. **Known for:** San Francisco–style seafood on sourdough; dockside bay views; hickory-wood smoked fish. $ *Average main: $20* ✉ *2805 Emerson St., Point Loma* ☎ *619/223–1109* ⊕ *www.pointlomaseafoods.com.*

Stone Brewing World Bistro & Gardens—Liberty Station

$$ | **ECLECTIC** | **FAMILY** | This 50,000-square-foot monument to beer and good food is a crowd-pleaser, especially for fans of San Diego's nationally known craft beer scene. The global menu features dishes like the Bavarian pretzel and Brewmaster's Beef Dip that pair perfectly with on-tap and bottled beers from around the world and Stone's famous IPAs. **Known for:** massive outdoor patio; brew-friendly eats; artisanal burgers. $ *Average main: $22* ✉ *2816 Historic Decatur Rd., Liberty Station* ☎ *619/269–2100* ⊕ *www.stone-libertystation.com.*

🛏 Hotels

★ Homewood Suites San Diego Airport Liberty Station

$$ | **HOTEL** | **FAMILY** | With amenities like kitchens and a business center, most guests stay at least four nights, turning this all-suites hotel into a home. **Pros:** outstanding central location near attractions; close to paths for joggers and bikers; complimentary airport shuttle. **Cons:** breakfast area can get crowded; $19 parking fee and $75 pet fee; far from nightlife. $ *Rooms from: $249* ✉ *2576 Laning Rd., Liberty Station* ☎ *619/222–0500* ⊕ *www.homewoodsuites.com* ⇥ *150 suites* ⦿ *Free Breakfast.*

Inn at Sunset Cliffs

$$ | **HOTEL** | At this 1950s former apartment complex, every room at the U-shape hotel gets a glimpse of the ocean, meaning you can fall asleep to the sound of the crashing waves and wake up to the sight of surfers paddling just in front of the hotel. **Pros:** midweek rates from $175; rooms remodeled in 2022; Rooms 114, 201, and 214 have full ocean views. **Cons:** rooms are tiny; no elevator; thin walls. $ *Rooms from: $315* ✉ *1370 Sunset Cliffs Blvd., Ocean Beach* ☎ *619/222–7901, 866/786–2543* ⊕ *www.innatsunsetcliffs.com* ⇥ *24 rooms* ⦿ *No Meals.*

🏃 Activities

★ Bayside Trail at Cabrillo National Monument

HIKING & WALKING | Driving here is a treat in itself, as a vast view of the Pacific unfolds before you. The view is equally enjoyable on Bayside Trail (2½ miles round-trip), which is home to the same coastal sagebrush that Juan Rodriguez Cabrillo saw when he first discovered the California coast in the 16th century. After the hike, you can explore nearby tide pools, the monument statue, and the Old Point Loma Lighthouse. Don't worry if you don't see everything on your first visit; your entrance receipt ($20 per car) is good for seven days. ✉ *1800 Cabrillo Memorial Dr., Point Loma* ✣ *From I–5, take Rosecrans exit and turn right on Canon St. then left on Catalina Blvd. (also known as Cabrillo Memorial Dr.); follow until end* ☎ *619/523–4285* 🌐 *www.nps.gov/cabr* 🅿 *Parking $20* ☞ *No restrooms or water along the trail; pets and bikes are not allowed.*

Shelter Island

In 1950, San Diego's port director decided to raise the shoal that lay off the eastern shore of Point Loma above sea level with the sand and mud dredged up during the course of deepening a ship channel in the 1930s and '40s. The resulting peninsula is Shelter Island. Today, it's a yacht-building hub, and vessels in every stage of construction are visible in its boat yards.

A long sidewalk runs past the marinas and resorts—some with retro, 1950s, Polynesian details—that line the inner shore, facing Point Loma. On the bay side, fishermen launch their boats and families relax at picnic tables along the grass, where there are fire rings and permanent barbecue grills.

🍴 Restaurants

Bali Hai

$$ | **HAWAIIAN** | For more than 50 years, generations of San Diegans and visitors have enjoyed this Polynesian-theme icon with its stunning bay and city skyline views. The menu is a fusion of Hawaiian and Asian cuisines with standouts like the crispy ahi tuna, wok-fried bass, and pan-seared scallops with macadamia nut butter. **Known for:** potent Bali Hai mai tais; Sunday brunch buffet with a DIY sundae bar; Happy hours Monday–Thursday 3–5. [$] *Average main: $25* ✉ *2230 Shelter Island Dr., Shelter Island* ☎ *619/222–1181* 🌐 *www.balihairestaurant.com* 🕓 *No lunch Sun.*

🛏 Hotels

★ Kona Kai Resort & Spa

$$ | **RESORT** | A $30 million renovation took this Shelter Island resort up a notch, with remodeled rooms, a new pool, spa, gym, and lobby—making the marina view an added bonus rather than the main focus. **Pros:** private beach with firepits; near marina with water view; on-site sports rental equipment. **Cons:** not centrally located; resort fees; popular for business meetings and weddings. [$] *Rooms from: $269* ✉ *1551 Shelter Island Dr., Shelter Island* ☎ *619/221–8000, 800/566–2524* 🌐 *www.resortkonakai.com* 🔑 *170 rooms* 🍽 *No Meals.*

🍸 Nightlife

Humphrey's Concerts by the Bay

LIVE MUSIC | From June through September, this dining and drinking oasis surrounded by water hosts the city's best outdoor jazz, folk, and light-rock concert series and is the stomping ground of such musicians as the Cowboy Junkies, Kenny G, Dolly Parton, and Chris Isaak. The rest of the year the music moves indoors for first-rate jazz (on Sunday), blues, classic rock, and more. ✉ *2241 Shelter Island Dr., Shelter Island* ☎ *619/224–3577* 🌐 *www.humphreysconcerts.com* ☞ *Cover charge from $5.*

Harbor Island

Following the successful creation of Shelter Island, in 1961 the U.S. Navy used the residue from digging berths deep enough to accommodate aircraft carriers to build Harbor Island, a 1½-mile-long peninsula adjacent to the airport. Restaurants and high-rise hotels dot the inner shore while the bay shore is lined with pathways, gardens, and scenic picnic spots. On the west point, the restaurant Tom Ham's Lighthouse has a U.S. Coast Guard–approved beacon shining

Sights

1 Coronado Ferry Landing **C2**

2 Orange Avenue...... **B3**

Restaurants

1 Clayton's Coffee Shop......... **B4**

2 Coronado Brewing Company.... **B2**

3 Mootime Creamery ... **B4**

Hotels

1 Coronado Island Marriott Resort & Spa **C3**

2 Hotel del Coronado ... **B4**

3 1906 Lodge at Coronado Beach....... **B4**

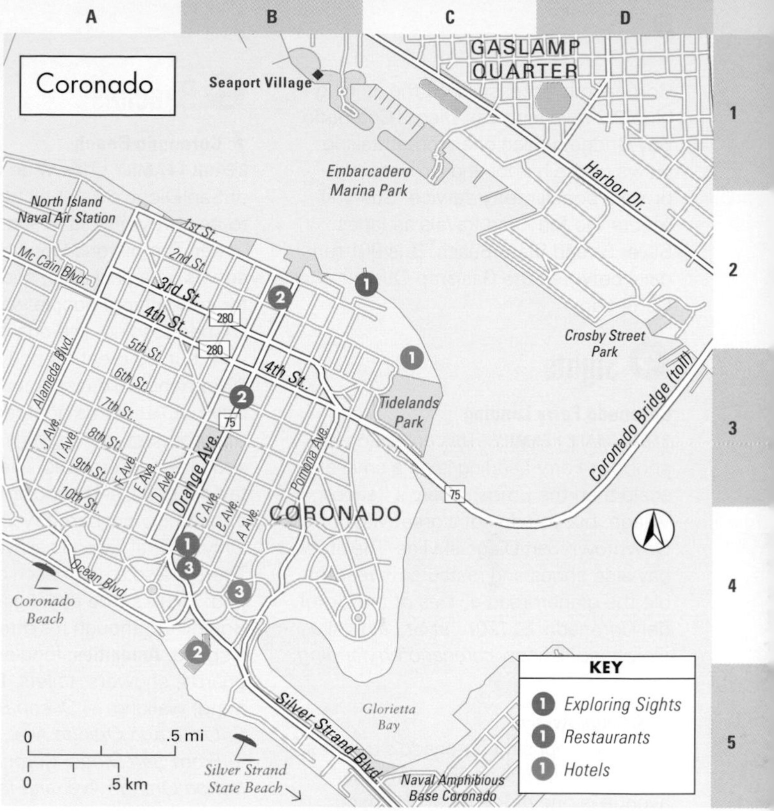

from its tower and a sweeping view of San Diego's bay front.

🍴 Restaurants

Tom Ham's Lighthouse

$$ | **SEAFOOD** | It's hard to top this longtime Harbor Island restaurant's incredible views across San Diego Bay to the Downtown skyline and Coronado Bridge. An alfresco dining deck and a contemporary seafood-focused menu ensure the dining experience at this working lighthouse doesn't take a back seat to the scenery. **Known for:** Sunday brunch; alfresco dining deck with skyline and Coronado bridge views; fresh seafood and beer-battered cod. [$] *Average main: $30* ✉ *2150 Harbor Island Dr., Harbor Island* ☎ *619/291–9110* 🌐 *www.tomhamslighthouse.com.*

Coronado

Coronado's quaint appeal is captured in its old-fashioned storefronts, well-manicured gardens, and charming Ferry Landing Marketplace. Its streets are wide, quiet, and friendly, and many of today's residents live in grand Victorian homes handed down for generations. Naval Air Station North Island, established in 1911 across from Point Loma, was the site of Charles Lindbergh's departure on the transcontinental flight that preceded his famous solo flight across the Atlantic. Coronado's long relationship with the U.S. Navy has made it an enclave for military personnel; it's said to have more retired admirals per capita than anywhere else in the United States.

Coronado is accessible via the arching blue 2.2-mile-long San Diego–Coronado Bay Bridge, which offers breathtaking views of the harbor and Downtown, or via a popular ferry service. Bus 904 meets the ferry and travels as far as Silver Strand State Beach. Bus 901 runs daily between the Gaslamp Quarter and Coronado.

Sights

Coronado Ferry Landing

STORE/MALL | FAMILY | This collection of shops at Ferry Landing is on a smaller scale than the Embarcadero's Seaport Village, but you do get a great view of the Downtown San Diego skyline. The little bay-side shops and restaurants resemble the gingerbread domes of the Hotel del Coronado. ⊠ *1201 1st St., at B Ave., Coronado* ⊕ *www.coronadoferrylanding. com.*

★ Orange Avenue

TOWN | Comprising Coronado's business district and its village-like heart, this avenue is one of the most charming spots in Southern California. Slow-paced and very "local" (the city fights against chain stores), it's a blast from the past, although entirely up-to-date in other respects. The military presence—Coronado is home to the U.S. Navy Sea, Air, and Land (SEAL) forces—is reflected in shops selling military gear and places like McP's Irish Pub, at No. 1107. A family-friendly stop for a good, all-American meal, it's the unofficial SEALs headquarters. Many clothing boutiques, home-furnishings stores, and upscale restaurants cater to visitors with deep pockets, but you can buy plumbing supplies, too, or get a genuine military haircut at Crown Barber Shop, at No. 947. If you need a break, stop for a latte at the sidewalk café of Bay Books, San Diego's largest independent bookstore, at No. 1007. ⊠ *Orange Ave., near 9th St., Coronado.*

⛱ Beaches

★ Coronado Beach

BEACH | FAMILY | This wide beach is one of San Diego's most picturesque thanks to its soft white sand and sparkly blue water. The historic Hotel del Coronado serves as a backdrop, and it's perfect for sunbathing, people-watching, and Frisbee tossing. The beach has limited surf, but it's great for bodyboarding and swimming. Exercisers might include Navy SEAL teams or other military units that conduct training runs on beaches in and around Coronado. There are picnic tables, grills, and popular fire rings, but don't bring lacquered wood or pallets. Only natural wood is allowed for burning. There's also a dog beach on the north end. There's free parking along Ocean Boulevard, though it's often hard to snag a space. **Amenities:** food and drink; lifeguards; showers; toilets. **Best for:** swimming; walking. ⊠ *Ocean Blvd., between S. O St. and Orange Ave., Coronado* ⛳ *From San Diego–Coronado bridge, turn left on Orange Ave. and follow signs.*

Silver Strand State Beach

BEACH | FAMILY | This quiet beach on a narrow sand spit allows visitors a unique opportunity to experience both the Pacific Ocean and San Diego Bay. The 2½ miles of the ocean side is great for surfing and other water sports while the bay side, accessible via foot tunnel under Highway 75, has calmer, warmer water and great views of the San Diego skyline. Lifeguards and rangers are on duty year-round, and there are places for biking, volleyball, and fishing. Picnic tables, grills, and firepits are available in summer, and the Silver Strand Beach Cafe is open Memorial Day through Labor Day. The beach is close to Loews Coronado Bay Resort and the Coronado Cays, an exclusive community popular with yacht owners. You can reserve RV sites ($65 beach; $50 inland) online. Three day-use parking lots provide room for 800 cars. **Amenities:** food and drink; lifeguards; parking (fee);

showers; toilets. **Best for:** surfing; swimming; walking. ✉ *5000 Hwy. 75, Coronado* ✣ *4½ miles south of city of Coronado* ☎ *619/435–5184* 🌐 *www.parks.ca.gov/silverstrand* 🎫 *Parking from $10.*

🍴 Restaurants

Clayton's Coffee Shop
$ | **AMERICAN** | **FAMILY** | A classic diner with bar seating in a circle, Clayton's is a great lunch or breakfast spot with a menu that ranges from classic American fare to Mexican-inspired dishes like the popular breakfast burrito. Just don't forget dessert! **Known for:** bottomless coffee; breakfast burrito; gooey cinnamon roll sundae. [$] *Average main: $10* ✉ *979 Orange Ave., Coronado* ☎ *619/435–5425* 🌐 *www.claytonscoffeeshop.com.*

Coronado Brewing Company
$ | **AMERICAN** | **FAMILY** | Perfect for beer lovers with kids, this popular, laid-back Coronado brewpub offers a menu that features large portions of basic bar food like burgers, sandwiches, pizza, and salads. Enjoy a brew at a pair of sidewalk terraces or belly up to the bar and a new batch being made such as the Islander Pale Ale (IPA) or Mermaid's Red Ale. **Known for:** a good selection of house-crafted beers; kids' menu; more strollers than bar stools. [$] *Average main: $12* ✉ *170 Orange Ave., Coronado* ☎ *619/437–4452* 🌐 *www.coronadobrewing.com.*

Mootime Creamery
$ | **CAFÉ** | **FAMILY** | For a deliciously sweet pick-me-up, check out the rich ice cream, frozen yogurt, and sorbet made fresh daily on the premises. Dessert nachos made from waffle-cone chips are an unusual addition to an extensive sundae menu. Just look for the statue of Elvis on the sidewalk in front. **Known for:** daily house-made ice cream, yogurt, and sorbet; dessert nachos; "moopies" sandwiches, with ice cream between two cereal bars. [$] *Average main: $5* ✉ *1025 Orange Ave., Coronado* ☎ *619/435–2422* 🌐 *www.mootimecreamerysd.com* 💳 *No credit cards.*

🛏 Hotels

★ Coronado Island Marriott Resort & Spa
$$ | **RESORT** | **FAMILY** | Near San Diego Bay, this snazzy hotel has rooms with great Downtown skyline views. **Pros:** spectacular views; on-site spa; close to water taxis. **Cons:** not in downtown Coronado; resort fee; expensive self-parking. [$] *Rooms from: $329* ✉ *2000 2nd St., Coronado* ☎ *619/435–3000* 🌐 *www.marriott.com/hotels/travel/sanci-coronado-island-marriott-resort-and-spa* 🔑 *300 rooms* 🍴 *No Meals.*

★ Hotel del Coronado
$$$ | **RESORT** | **FAMILY** | As much of a draw today as it was when it opened in 1888, the Victorian-style "Hotel Del" is always alive with activity, as guests—including U.S. presidents and celebrities—and tourists marvel at the fanciful architecture and ocean views. **Pros:** 17 on-site shops; on the beach; well-rounded spa. **Cons:** some rooms are small; expensive dining; hectic public areas. [$] *Rooms from: $500* ✉ *1500 Orange Ave., Coronado* ☎ *800/468–3533, 619/435–6611* 🌐 *www.hoteldel.com* 🔑 *757 rooms* 🍴 *No Meals.*

★ 1906 Lodge at Coronado Beach
$$ | **B&B/INN** | Smaller but no less luxurious than the sprawling beach resorts of Coronado, this lodge—whose name alludes to the main building's former life as a boardinghouse built in 1906—welcomes couples for romantic retreats two blocks from the ocean. **Pros:** most suites feature Jacuzzi tubs, fireplaces, and porches; historic property; free underground parking. **Cons:** too quiet for families; no pool; limited on-site dining options. [$] *Rooms from: $329* ✉ *1060 Adella Ave., Coronado* ☎ *619/437–1900, 866/435–1906* 🌐 *www.1906lodge.com* 🔑 *17 rooms* 🍴 *Free Breakfast.*

A surfer prepares to head out before sunset at La Jolla's Torrey Pines State Beach and Reserve.

Activities

The Gondola Company

BOATING | You don't have to travel to Venice to be serenaded by a gondolier. This company features authentic Venetian gondola rides that depart daily from the picturesque Coronado Cays. ⊠ *503 Grand Caribe Causeway, Suite C, Coronado* ☎ *619/429–6317* ⊕ *www.gondolacompany.com* ⌦ *From $129 for 2 people.*

Holland's Bicycles

BIKING | This is a great bike rental source on Coronado Island, so you can ride the Silver Strand Bike Path on an electric bike, beach cruiser, road bike, or tandem. ⊠ *977 Orange Ave., Coronado* ☎ *619/435–3153* ⊕ *www.hollandsbicycles.com* ⌦ *From $10.*

SUP & Saddle

KAYAKING | While La Jolla's Bike & Kayak Tours, under the same ownership, offers a Leopard Shark Encounter snorkeling tour ($59 per person), where adventuresome travelers can see the shy spotted creatures up close, the Coronado location has you embarking on a kayak tour ($40 per person) underneath the Coronado Bridge at dusk to enjoy incredible views of Downtown San Diego. The Coronado branch also offers stand-up paddleboards for as little as $39 per person. ⊠ *1201 1st St., Suite 215, Coronado* ☎ *619/880–6236* ⊕ *www.supandsaddle.com* ⌦ *From $39.*

La Jolla

La Jolla (pronounced la *hoy*-a) means "the jewel" in Spanish and appropriately describes this small, affluent village and its beaches. Downtown La Jolla is more commercialized, with high-end stores great for browsing. La Jolla Shores, a mile-long beach, lies in the more residential area to the north. The beach and cove are La Jolla's prime charms—the cove's seals and underwater kelp beds are big draws for kayakers and nature lovers.

◉ Sights

Birch Aquarium at Scripps

AQUARIUM | FAMILY | Affiliated with the world-renowned Scripps Institution of Oceanography, this excellent aquarium sits at the end of a signposted drive leading off North Torrey Pines Road and has sweeping views of La Jolla coast below. More than 60 tanks are filled with colorful saltwater fish, and a 70,000-gallon tank simulates a La Jolla kelp forest. A special exhibit on seahorses features several examples of the species, plus mesmerizing sea dragons and a seahorse nursery. Besides the fish themselves, attractions include interactive educational exhibits based on the institution's ocean-related research and a variety of environmental issues. ⊠ *2300 Expedition Way, La Jolla* ☎ *858/534–3474* ⊕ *www. aquarium.ucsd.edu* ⛦ *$25* ⛬ *Reservations required.*

★ Museum of Contemporary Art San Diego

ART MUSEUM | Driving along Coast Boulevard, it is hard to miss the mass of watercraft jutting out from the rear of the Museum of Contemporary Art San Diego (MCASD) La Jolla location. *Pleasure Point* by Nancy Rubins is just one example of the mingling of art and locale at this spectacular oceanfront setting.

The oldest section of La Jolla's branch of San Diego's contemporary art museum was originally a residence, designed by Irving Gill for philanthropist Ellen Browning Scripps in 1916. In the mid-1990s the compound was updated and expanded by architect Robert Venturi, who respected Gill's original geometric structure and clean Mission-style lines while adding his own distinctive touches. An expansion in 2020 quadrupled existing gallery space. The result is a striking contemporary building that looks as though it's always been here.

The light-filled Axline Court serves as the museum's entrance and does triple duty as reception area, exhibition hall, and forum for special events, including The Gala each September, attended by the town's most fashionable folk. Inside, the museum's artwork gets major competition from the setting: you can look out from the top of a grand stairway onto a landscaped garden that contains permanent and temporary sculpture exhibits as well as rare 100-year-old California plant specimens and, beyond that, to the Pacific Ocean.

Artists from San Diego and Tijuana figure prominently in the museum's permanent collection of post-1950s art, but the museum also includes examples of every major art movement through the present—works by Andy Warhol, Robert Rauschenberg, Frank Stella, Joseph Cornell, and Jenny Holzer, to name a few. The museum also gets major visiting shows. Head to the museum's shop for unique cards and gifts. The street-facing plaza at the museum café is a great spot to relax and recharge.

■**TIP→** Free tours are offered at 2 on Sunday. ⊠ *700 Prospect St., La Jolla* ☎ *858/454–3541* ⊕ *www.mcasd.org* ⛦ *$25; MCASD is free on 2nd Sun. and 3rd Thurs. of every month* ☉ *Closed Mon.–Wed.*

San Diego-La Jolla Underwater Park Ecological Reserve

REEF | Four habitats across 6,000 acres make up this underwater park and ecological reserve. When the water is clear, this is a diver's paradise with reefs, kelp beds, sand flats, and a submarine canyon reaching depths up to 600 feet. Plunge to see guitarfish rays, perch, sea bass, anchovies, squid, and hammerhead sharks. Snorkelers, kayakers, and stand-up paddleboarders are likely to spot sea lions, seals, and leopard sharks. The Seven La Jolla Sea Caves, 75-million-year-old sandstone caves, are at the park's edge.

■**TIP→** While the park can be explored on your own, the best way to view it is with a professional guide. ⊠ *La Jolla* ⚓ *La Jolla Cove.*

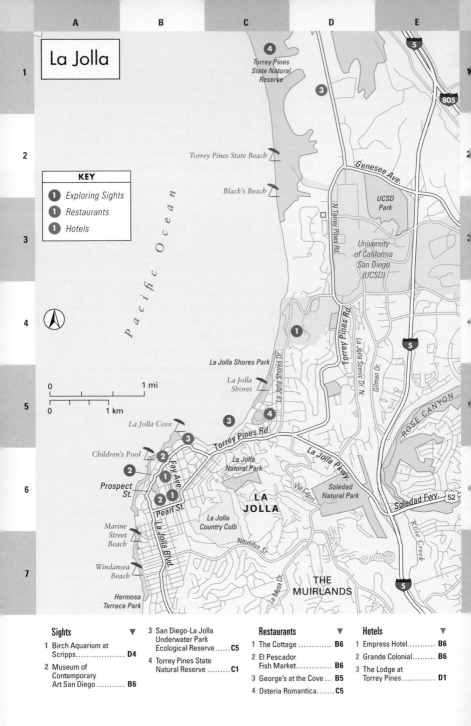

La Jolla

KEY

1 *Exploring Sights*

1 *Restaurants*

1 *Hotels*

Pacific Ocean

Torrey Pines State Natural Reserve

Torrey Pines State Beach

Black's Beach

Genesee Ave.

UCSD Park

University of California San Diego (UCSD)

N Torrey Pines Rd.

Torrey Pines Rd.

La Jolla Scenic Dr. N.

Gilman Dr.

ROSE CANYON

0 ——— 1 mi

0 ——— 1 km

La Jolla Shores Park

La Jolla Shores

La Jolla Shores Dr.

La Jolla Cove

Children's Pool

Prospect St.

Fay Ave.

Pearl St.

La Jolla Natural Park

La Jolla Pkwy.

Soledad Natural Park

Via Capri

Soledad Fwy. 52

Rose Creek

Marine Street Beach

La Jolla Blvd.

LA JOLLA

La Jolla Country Culb

Nautilus St.

Windansea Beach

Hermosa Terrace Park

La Mesa Dr.

THE MUIRLANDS

★ Torrey Pines State Natural Reserve

NATURE PRESERVE | *Pinus torreyana,* the rarest native pine tree in the United States, enjoys a 1,500-acre sanctuary at the northern edge of La Jolla. About 6,000 of these unusual trees, some as tall as 60 feet, grow on the cliffs here. The park is one of only two places in the world (the other is Santa Rosa Island, off Santa Barbara) where the Torrey pine grows naturally. The reserve has several hiking trails leading to the cliffs, 300 feet above the ocean; trail maps are available at the park station. Wildflowers grow profusely in spring, and the ocean panoramas are always spectacular. From December to March, whales can be spotted from the bluffs. When in this upper part of the park, respect the restrictions. Not permitted: picnicking, camping, drones, smoking, leaving the trails, dogs, alcohol, or collecting plant specimens.

You can unwrap your sandwiches, however, at Torrey Pines State Beach, just below the reserve. When the tide is out, it's possible to walk south all the way past the lifeguard towers to Black's Beach over rocky promontories carved by the waves (avoid the bluffs, however; they're unstable). **Los Peñasquitos Lagoon** at the north end of the reserve is one of the many natural estuaries that flow inland between Del Mar and Oceanside. It's a good place to watch shorebirds. Volunteers lead guided nature walks at 10 on most weekends and holidays. ⊠ *12600 N. Torrey Pines Rd., La Jolla* ⊹ *N. Torrey Pines Rd. exit off I–5 onto Carmel Valley Rd. going west, then turn left (south) on Coast Hwy. 101* ☎ *858/755–2063* ⊕ *www.torreypine.org* 🖼 *Parking from $20.*

Beaches

Black's Beach

BEACH | The powerful waves at this beach attract world-class surfers, and the strand's relative isolation appeals to nudist nature lovers (although by law nudity is prohibited). Backed by 300-foot-tall cliffs whose colors change with the sun's angle, Black's can be accessed from Torrey Pines State Beach to the north, or by a narrow path descending the cliffs from Torrey Pines Glider Port. Be aware that the city has posted a "do not use" sign there because the cliff trails are unmaintained and highly dangerous, so use at your own risk. If you plan to access Black's from the beaches to the north or south, do so at low tide. High tide and waves can restrict access. Strong rip currents are common—only experienced swimmers should take the plunge. Lifeguards patrol the area only between spring break and mid-October. Also keep your eyes peeled for the hang gliders and paragliders who ascend from atop the cliffs. Parking is available at the Glider Port and Torrey Pines State Beach. **Amenities:** none. **Best for:** nudists; solitude; surfing. ⊠ *Between Torrey Pines State Beach and La Jolla Shores, La Jolla* ⊹ *2 miles south of Torrey Pines State Beach parking lot* ⊕ *www.sandiego.gov/ lifeguards/beaches/blacks.*

★ La Jolla Cove

BEACH | **FAMILY** | This shimmering blue-green inlet surrounded by cliffs is what first attracted everyone to La Jolla, from Native Americans to the glitterati. "The Cove," as locals refer to it, beyond where Girard Avenue dead-ends into Coast Boulevard, is marked by towering palms that line a promenade where people strolling in designer clothes are as common as Frisbee throwers. Ellen Browning Scripps Park sits atop cliffs formed by the incessant pounding of the waves and offers a great spot for picnics with a view. The Cove has beautiful white sand that is a bit coarse near the water's edge, but the beach is still a great place for sunbathing and lounging. At low tide, the pools and cliff caves are a destination for explorers. With visibility at 30-plus feet, this is the best place in San Diego for snorkeling, where bright-orange garibaldi fish and other marine life populate the waters of the San Diego–La Jolla Underwater Park Ecological Reserve. From above water, it's not uncommon to spot sea lions and birds basking on the rocks, or dolphin fins just offshore. The cove is also a favorite of rough-water swimmers, while the area just north is best for kayakers wanting to explore the Seven La Jolla Sea Caves. **Amenities:** lifeguards; showers; toilets. **Best for:** snorkeling; swimming; walking. ✉ *1100 Coast Blvd., east of Ellen Browning Scripps Park, La Jolla* 🌐 *www.sandiego.gov/lifeguards/beaches/cove.*

La Jolla Shores

BEACH | FAMILY | This is one of San Diego's most popular beaches due to its wide sandy shore, gentle waves, and incredible views of La Jolla Peninsula. There's also a large grassy park, and adjacent to La Jolla Shores lies the San Diego–La Jolla Underwater Park Ecological Reserve, 6,000 acres of protected ocean bottom and tidelands, bordered by the Seven La Jolla Sea Caves. The white powdery sand at La Jolla Sands is some of San Diego's best, and several surf and scuba schools teach here. Kayaks can also be rented nearby. A concrete boardwalk parallels the beach, and a boat launch for small vessels lies 300 yards south of the lifeguard station at Avenida de Playa. Arrive early to get a parking spot in the lot near Kellogg Park at the foot of Calle Frescota. Street parking is limited to one or two hours. **Amenities:** lifeguards; parking (no fee); showers; toilets. **Best for:** surfing; swimming; walking. ✉ *8200 Camino del Oro, in front of Kellogg Park, La Jolla* ✣ *2 miles north of downtown La Jolla* 🌐 *www.sandiego.gov/lifeguards/beaches/shores.shtml.*

★ Windansea Beach

BEACH | With its rocky shoreline and strong shore break, Windansea stands out among San Diego beaches for its dramatic natural beauty. It's one of the best surf spots in San Diego County. Professional surfers love the unusual A-frame waves the reef break here creates. Although the large sandstone rocks that dot the beach might sound like a hindrance, they actually serve as protective barriers from the wind, making this one of the best beaches in San Diego for sunbathing. The beach's palm-covered surf shack built in 1946 is a protected historical landmark, and a seat here at sunset may just be one of the most romantic spots on the West Coast. The name Windansea comes from a hotel that burned down in the late 1940s. You can usually find nearby street parking. **Amenities:** lifeguards (seasonal); toilets. **Best for:** solitude; sunset; surfing. ✉ *Neptune Pl. at Nautilus St., La Jolla* 🌐 *www.sandiego.gov/lifeguards/beaches/windan.shtml.*

🍴 Restaurants

The Cottage

$ | AMERICAN | FAMILY | A cozy beach cottage sets the stage for American comfort food with a California twist at this La Jolla staple. The restaurant serves lunch, but it's the well-loved daily breakfast that has locals and visitors happily queuing—sometimes up to two hours on weekends. **Known for:** daily breakfast that people line up for; substantial portions to keep you satisfied; great patio seating. [$] *Average main: $17* ✉ *7702 Fay Ave., La Jolla* ☎ *858/454–8409* 🌐 *www.cottagelajolla.com* ⏲ *No dinner.*

El Pescador Fish Market

$ | SEAFOOD | This bustling café first opened as a full-service fish market in 1974, and has been popular with locals ever since. Order the char-grilled, locally caught halibut, swordfish, or yellowtail on a toasted torta roll to enjoy in-house or to go for an oceanfront picnic at nearby La Jolla Cove. **Known for:** clam chowder; bustling on-site fish market; daily-caught cuts to go. [$] *Average main: $17* ✉ *634 Pearl St., La Jolla* ☎ *858/456–2526* 🌐 *www.elpescadorfishmarket.com.*

George's at the Cove

$$$ | **AMERICAN** | La Jolla's ocean-view destination restaurant is like two dining experiences in one with Level2 bar and the rooftop Ocean Terrace. Prepare for spectacular views and an innovative menu featuring maple leaf duck with tangerine marmalade and salmon with braised lentils at the outdoor-only Ocean Terrace, while the Level2 lounge has unique craft cocktails like "Spa Day" with cucumber-mint infused vodka and elderflower. **Known for:** outstanding California coastal cuisine; excellent ocean views; attention to detail for special-occasion dinners. [$] *Average main: $37* ✉ *1250 Prospect St., La Jolla* ☎ *858/454–4244* 🌐 *www.georgesatthecove.com.*

Osteria Romantica

$$ | **ITALIAN** | Between music by Pavarotti, the checkered tablecloths, and the sight of homemade pasta and free-flowing vino, you'll swear you've died and gone to Italy. At this cozy La Jolla Shores eatery, northern and southwestern Italian flavors have fused into culinary magic—housemade breads, sauces, gnocchi, and pastas like pappardelle with braised lamb, and linguine with mussels—since 2004. **Known for:** tender lamb pappardelle; cozy Italian vibe; homemade pasta, breads, and sauces. [$] *Average main: $20* ✉ *2151 Av. de la Playa, La Jolla* ☎ *858/551–1221* 🌐 *www.osteriaromantica.com* 🕒 *No lunch Mon.*

Hotels

Empress Hotel

$ | **HOTEL** | A few blocks from the ocean and Girard Avenue's upscale shops, this five-story hotel blends Southern California beach style with a touch of European flair, making it one of the more affordable and convenient options in La Jolla. **Pros:** near shops, restaurants, and beach; free coffee and muffins in the lobby; friendly staff. **Cons:** not exciting for kids; $35 pet fee; small bathrooms. [$] *Rooms from: $149* ✉ *7766 Fay Ave., La Jolla* ☎ *858/454–3001* 🌐 *www.empress-hotel.com* 🛏 *73 rooms* 🍴 *No Meals.*

★ Grande Colonial

$$$ | **HOTEL** | This white-wedding-cake-style hotel in the heart of La Jolla Village has ocean views and charming European details that include chandeliers, mahogany railings, a wooden elevator, crystal doorknobs, and French doors. **Pros:** the Village's only four-diamond hotel; superb restaurant; hospitality extras included in rate. **Cons:** small pool; no fitness center; valet parking only. [$] *Rooms from: $369* ✉ *910 Prospect St., La Jolla* ☎ *888/828–5498* 🌐 *www.thegrandecolonial.com* 🛏 *97 rooms* 🍴 *No Meals.*

The Lodge at Torrey Pines

$$$ | **RESORT** | Best known for its location adjacent to two 18-hole championship golf courses, this beautiful Craftsman-style lodge sits on a bluff between La Jolla and Del Mar with commanding coastal views, excellent service, a blissful spa, and the upscale A. R. Valentien restaurant (named after a San Diego artist of the early 1900s), which serves farm-to-table California cuisine. **Pros:** spacious upscale rooms; remarkable service; adjacent to the famed Torrey Pines Golf Course; warm decor with Craftsman accents and hardwoods. **Cons:** not centrally located; expensive; $40 daily parking fee. [$] *Rooms from: $452* ✉ *11480 N. Torrey Pines Rd., La Jolla* ☎ *858/529–5641* 🌐 *www.lodgetorreypines.com* 🛏 *170 rooms* 🍴 *No Meals.*

Nightlife

Manhattan of La Jolla

PIANO BARS | Lovingly referred to as the "Manhattan Lounge" by locals, this underrated and largely undiscovered bar neighbors the Italian steak house inside the Empress Hotel. The dark, old-school interior is perfect for sipping martinis and listening to live music Wednesday through Sunday. ✉ *7766 Fay Ave., La Jolla* ☎ *858/459–0700* 🌐 *www.*

manhattanoflajolla.com ☞ *Jazz Wed., Thurs.–Sun. piano or guest musicians.*

The Spot

BARS | Nightlife can be kind of sleepy in affluent La Jolla, but in-the-know locals keep this sports bar buzzing on any given night thanks to powerful cocktails like the Killer Old Fashioned and the bar grub that's served late into the evening—one of the few spots that's open in La Jolla in the wee hours. ⊠ *1005 Prospect St., La Jolla* ☎ *858/459–0800* ⊕ *www.thespotonline.com.*

Activities

Hike Bike Kayak Adventures

KAYAKING | This shop offers several kayak tours, from easy excursions in La Jolla Cove that are well suited to families and beginners to more advanced jaunts. Tours include kayaking the caves off La Jolla coast, and whale-watching (from a safe distance) December through February. Tours last 90 minutes to two hours and require a minimum of four people. ⊠ *2222 Av. de la Playa, La Jolla* ☎ *858/551–9510* ⊕ *www.hikebikekayak.com* ⊠ *From $50.*

Scuba San Diego

SCUBA DIVING | This center is well regarded for its top-notch instruction and certification programs, as well as for guided dive tours. Scuba Adventure classes for noncertified divers are held daily in Mission Bay, meeting near Mission Point. Trips for certified divers depart from La Jolla and include dives to kelp reefs in La Jolla Cove, shipwrecks, and night diving at La Jolla Canyon. They also have snorkeling tours to La Jolla's Sea Caves. ⊠ *8008 Girard St., La Jolla* ☎ *619/260–1880* ⊕ *www.scubasandiego.com* ⊠ *From $80* ☞ *Scuba Adventure*

meeting point is 2615 Bayside La. in South Mission Bay, near Mission Point.

★ Surf Diva Surf School

SURFING | Check out clinics, surf camps, and private lessons especially formulated for girls and women. Most clinics and trips are for women only, but there are some coed options. Guys can also book group or private lessons from the nationally recognized staff. Surf Diva is also home to a boutique that sells surf and stand-up paddleboard equipment. They also offer surf retreats in Costa Rica. ⊠ *2160 Av. de la Playa, La Jolla* ☎ *858/454–8273* ⊕ *www.surfdiva.com* ⊠ *Group lessons $105 per person; private lessons $150.*

★ Torrey Pines Golf Course

GOLF | Due to its cliff-top location overlooking the Pacific and its classic championship holes, Torrey Pines is one of the best public golf courses in the United States. The course was the site of the 2008 and 2021 U.S. Open and has been the home of the Farmers Insurance Open since 1968. The par-72 South Course, redesigned by Rees Jones in 2001, receives rave reviews from touring pros; it is longer, more challenging, and more expensive than the North Course. Tee times may be booked up to 90 days in advance and are subject to an advance booking fee ($47). ⊠ *11480 N. Torrey Pines Rd., La Jolla* ☎ *858/452–3226, 800/985–4653* ⊕ *www.torreypinesgolfcourse.com* ⊠ *South: from $278. North: from $176; $45 for golf cart* ⚲ *South: 18 holes, 7707 yards, par 72. North: 18 holes, 7258 yards, par 72.*

Chapter 5

DISNEYLAND AND ORANGE COUNTY

Updated by
Jill Weinlein

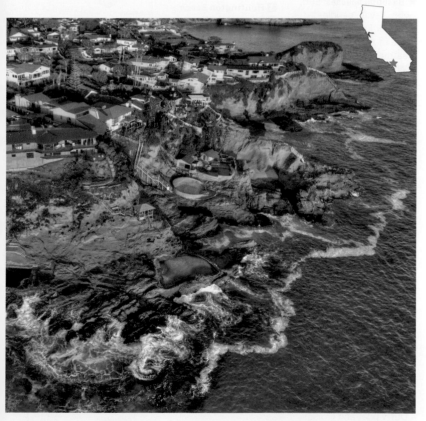

👁 Sights	🍴 Restaurants	🛏 Hotels	💼 Shopping	🍸 Nightlife
★★★★★	★★★★☆	★★★★★	★☆☆☆☆	★☆☆☆☆

WELCOME TO DISNEYLAND AND ORANGE COUNTY

TOP REASONS TO GO

★ **Disneyland:** Walking down Main Street, U.S.A., with Sleeping Beauty Castle straight ahead, you really will feel like you're in one of the happiest places on Earth.

★ **Beautiful beaches:** Surf, swim, kayak, paddleboard, or just relax on some of the state's most breathtaking stretches of coastline. Calm coves offer clear water for snorkeling and scuba diving.

★ **Santa Catalina Island:** Just 22 miles from the mainland, Santa Catalina Island is the only inhabited island of the Channel Islands chain. A fast and easy cruise away on a high-speed catamaran, once there you can explore the Mediterranean-inspired small town of Avalon, dive or snorkel through the state's first underwater park, or explore the unspoiled beauty of the island's wild interior.

★ **Family fun:** Ride roller coasters, eat ice cream and frozen chocolate-dipped bananas, bike on oceanfront paths, fish off ocean piers, or rent a Duffy boat and cruise around the calm harbors.

1 Disneyland Resort. Southern California's top draw is now a megaresort, with more attractions spilling over into Disney's California Adventure.

2 Knott's Berry Farm. Think thrill rides, the *Peanuts* gang, and lots of fried chicken and boysenberry pie.

3 Huntington Beach. This resort destination is known as Surf City U.S.A.

4 Newport Beach. There's something for every taste here, from glamorous boutiques to simple snack huts.

5 Corona del Mar. No matter your preferred outdoor activity, you'll find it on one of the beaches here.

6 Laguna Beach. With 30 beaches and coves to explore, there's plenty to keep visitors busy.

7 San Juan Capistrano. Take a trip back in time exploring a historic Spanish mission.

8 Catalina Island. Just off the Orange County coast is an island paradise with walkable streets filled with shops and restaurants in the charming town of Avalon. Beyond is a large land and underwater nature preserve to explore.

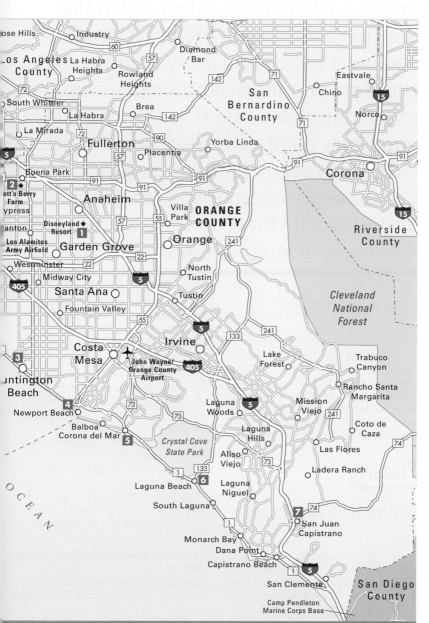

With its tropical flowers and palm trees, the stretch of coast between Seal Beach and San Clemente is often called the Southern California Riviera. Upscale Newport Beach and artsy Laguna are the stars, but lesser-known gems on the glistening coast—such as Corona del Mar and Dana Point—are also worth visiting. Offshore, meanwhile, lies picturesque Catalina Island, an unspoiled paradise and a favorite for tourists, boaters, divers, and backpacking campers alike.

Few of the citrus groves that gave Orange County its name remain. This region south and east of Los Angeles is now ruled by tourism and high-tech business rather than agriculture. Despite a building boom that began in the 1990s, the area is still a place to find wilderness trails, canyons, greenbelts, and natural environs. Just offshore is a deep-water wilderness that's possible to explore via daily whale-watching excursions.

Planning

Getting Here and Around

AIR
Orange County's main facility is John Wayne Airport Orange County (SNA), which is served by 12 airlines. Long Beach Airport (LGB) is served by four airlines and is 30 minutes by car to Anaheim.

The best way to get to your destination from one of the airports is logging into Lyft or Uber for door-to-door service.

BUS
The Orange County Transportation Authority will take you virtually anywhere in the county, but it will take time; download the OC Bus app to purchase a one-day (or more) bus pass and find bus times and bus stop locations. OC buses go from Knott's Berry Farm and Disneyland to Newport Beach. Anaheim offers Anaheim Resort Transportation (ART) service that connects hotels to Disneyland Resort, downtown Anaheim, Buena Park, and the Metrolink train center. Download the A-Way WeGo app. One-way rides are $4 or $6 for a full-day pass.

CONTACTS Anaheim Resort Transportation (ART). ⊠ *2099 S. State College Blvd., Suite 600, Anaheim* ☎ *714/563–5287* ⊕ *rideart.org.* **Orange County Transportation**

Authority. ⊠ *550 S. Main St., Anaheim* ☎ *714/636–7433* ⊕ *www.octa.net.*

CAR

Driving is the most convenient option to explore Orange County. Download the Waze app to get the best directions to your destination. The San Diego Freeway (I–405) is the coastal route, and the Santa Ana Freeway (I–5) is more inland running north–south through Orange County. South of Laguna, I–405 merges into I–5 (called the San Diego Freeway south from this point). A toll road, Highway 73, runs 15 miles from Newport Beach to San Juan Capistrano; prices fluctuate on weekdays, weekends, and off-peak hours, and this option is usually less jammed than the regular freeways. Do your best to avoid all Orange County freeways during rush hours (6:30 am–9 am and 3:30 pm–6:30 pm). Highway 55 leads to Newport Beach. The Pacific Coast Highway (Highway 1) allows easy access to beach communities and is the most scenic route, but expect it to be crowded, especially on summer weekends and holidays.

FERRY

There are two ferries that service Catalina Island: Catalina Express runs multiple departures daily from San Pedro, Long Beach, and Dana Point; from each port, it takes about 70 minutes to reach the island. The Catalina Flyer runs from Newport Beach to Avalon in about 75 minutes. Reservations are strongly advised for summer months and weekends. During the winter months, ferry crossings are not as frequent.

TRAIN

Amtrak Pacific Surfliner makes five Orange County stops. The easiest stop without a car is the San Juan Capistrano station, which puts you within easy walking distance of lodging, restaurants, shopping, and the California Mission. Metrolink is a weekday commuter train that runs to and from Los Angeles and Orange County. On weekends the train offers a $10 Weekend Day Pass. Download the Metrolink app.

CONTACTS Amtrak. ⊠ *2626 E. Katella Ave., Anaheim* ☎ *800/872–7245* ⊕ *www.amtrak.com.* **Metrolink.** ⊠ *800 N. Alameda St., Los Angeles* ☎ *800/371–5465* ⊕ *www.metrolinktrains.com.*

Hotels

Lodging prices tend to be high along the coast, and there are some remarkable luxury resorts and smaller boutique hotels. Splurge and stay at Laguna Beach's Montage resort to swim in the mosaic tile pool. For an exclusive California beach club experience, an overnight at the Waldorf Astoria Monarch Beach will give you a taste of the O.C. glam life. The Resort at Pelican Hill is an idyllic place to stay and enjoy lunch, brunch, or dinner at its Coliseum Grill overlooking the world's largest circular pool and the ocean beyond. For nautical scenery, stay overnight overlooking multimillion-dollar yachts in Newport harbor at the Balboa Bay Resort. If you're looking for value, consider a hotel that's inland along the I–405 freeway corridor. In most cases, you can take advantage of some of the facilities of the high-end resorts, such as restaurants and spas, even if you aren't an overnight guest.

Restaurants

Guests dining at restaurants in Orange County generally wear beach-casual or resort wear, although at top resorts and fine-dining venues, guests usually choose to dress up. Of course, there's also a swath of casual places along the beachfronts—seafood takeout, taquerias, burger joints—that won't mind if you wear shorts and flip-flops. Reservations are recommended for the nicest restaurants.

⇨ *Restaurant and hotel reviews have been shortened. For full information, visit Fodors.com. Restaurant prices are the average cost of a main course at dinner or, if dinner is not served, at lunch. Hotel prices are the lowest cost of a standard double room in high season.*

What It Costs			
$	$$	$$$	$$$$
RESTAURANTS			
under $20	$20–$30	$31–$40	over $40
HOTELS			
under $200	$200–$350	$351–$500	over $500

Visitor Information

Visit Anaheim is an excellent resource for both leisure and business travelers and can provide materials on transportation and special offers on many area attractions. Visit California has an Orange County section on their site that is helpful and informative.

CONTACTS Orange County Visitors Association. ⊕ *www.travelcostamesa. com/visittheoc.* **Visit Anaheim.** ✉ *2099 S. State College Blvd., Suite 600, Anaheim* 🕿 *714/765–2800* ⊕ *www.visitanaheim. org.*

Disneyland Resort

26 miles southeast of Los Angeles, via I–5.

The snowcapped Matterhorn, the centerpiece of Disneyland, punctuates the skyline of Anaheim. Since 1955, when Walt Disney chose this once-quiet farming community for the site of his first amusement park, Disneyland has attracted more than 650 million visitors and tens of thousands of workers, and Anaheim has been their host.

Today, there are more than 60 attractions and adventures in the park's nine themed lands: Fantasyland; Adventureland; Tomorrowland; Frontierland; Main Street, U.S.A.; New Orleans Square; Critter Country; Mickey's Toontown; and Star Wars: Galaxy's Edge. The sprawling resort complex not only includes Disney's two amusement parks (Disneyland and Disney's California Adventure) but also three hotels and Downtown Disney, a shopping, dining, and entertainment promenade.

GETTING HERE

Disney is about a 30-mile drive from either LAX or Downtown. From LAX, follow Sepulveda Boulevard south to the I–105 freeway and drive east 16 miles to the I–605 north exit. Exit at the Santa Ana Freeway (I–5) and continue south for 12 miles to the Disneyland Drive exit. Follow signs to the resort. From Downtown, follow I–5 south 28 miles and exit at Disneyland Drive.

SAVING TIME AND MONEY

If you plan to visit one of the parks, each guest is required to have a theme park reservation and ticket (as of January 2024, date-based tickets will not require reservations). For more than a day, you can save money by buying multiday Park Hopper tickets that grant same-day "hopping" privileges between Disneyland and Disney's California Adventure. Start at one park, and then enter the other park at a certain time and go between parks (based on availability).

Single-day and Park Hopper admission prices vary by date. A one-day Park Hopper pass usually costs approximately $154–$214 for anyone 10 or older, $149–$209 for kids ages three to nine. Admission to either park (but not both) is approximately $104–$179 for adults or $98–$169 for kids three to nine; kids two and under are free.

In addition to tickets, parking is $30 (unless your hotel has a shuttle or is within walking distance), and meals in the parks and at Downtown Disney range from $15 to $75 per person.

Disneyland

★ Disneyland

AMUSEMENT RIDE | FAMILY | Disneyland is the only place where guests visit nine imaginative lands, from a galaxy far, far away in the *Star Wars* land; to a world of pirates in search of Jack Sparrow from the *Pirates of the Caribbean* series; and ride the Storybook Land Canal Boats, passing miniature replicas of animated Disney scenes from classics such as *Frozen* and *Alice in Wonderland*. Beloved Disney characters appear for autographs and photos throughout the day; times and places are posted at the entrances and on the Disneyland mobile app. Live shows, parades, strolling musicians, fireworks (on weekends and during the summer and holidays), and endless creative snack choices add to the carnival atmosphere. You can also meet some of the animated icons at one of the character meals served at the three Disney hotels (open to the public, but reservations are needed). Belongings can be stored in lockers just off Main Street while stroller rentals, wheelchairs, and Electric Conveyance Vehicles (ECV) are at the entrance gate as convenient options for families with mobility challenges. The park's popularity means there are always crowds, especially during the holidays and summer months, so take advantage of the Disney Genie+ and Lightning Lane to spend less time waiting in lines. Some rides offer Single Rider Lanes which are also much shorter. Also be sure to make dining reservations at least three weeks before your visit to guarantee a table without a wait. The park is expertly run, with perfectly maintained grounds and a helpful staff ("cast members" in the Disney lexicon). ⊠ *Disneyland Park, 1313 S. Disneyland Dr., between Ball Rd. and Katella Ave., Anaheim* ☎ *714/781–4636*

guest information ⊕ *disneyland.disney. go.com* ✉ *From $97; parking $20.*

PARK NEIGHBORHOODS
MAIN STREET, U.S.A.

Walt's hometown of Marceline, Missouri, was the creative inspiration behind this romanticized small-town America, circa 1900. The sidewalks are lined with a penny arcade, magic shop, and an endless supply of colorful confections in the candy store. Disney-themed clothing and a photo shop that offers souvenirs created via Disney's PhotoPass (on-site photographers capture memorable moments digitally—you can access them in person or online via the Disneyland app). Main Street opens half an hour before the rest of the park, so it's a good place to explore if you're getting an early start to beat the crowds (it's also open an hour after the other attractions close, so you may want to save your shopping for the end of the day).

Step into City Hall to receive a complimentary button showcasing whatever you're celebrating (your first visit, a birthday, a marriage, or just Disney in general); throughout the day, Disney cast members will congratulate you with friendly smiles and well wishes. Main Street Cinema offers a cool respite from the crowds and six classic Disney animated shorts, including *Steamboat Willie*. There's rarely a wait to enter. Grab a cappuccino and fresh-made pastry at the Jolly Holiday bakery to jump-start your visit. Board the Disneyland Railroad, an authentic steam-powered train located at the entrance that makes stops in the park's different lands. The 20-minute scenic round-trip gives you unique behind-the-scenes views of Star Wars: Galaxy's Edge, Autopia, the Grand Canyon, and Rivers of America.

Beyond Main Street, U.S.A., is Sleeping Beauty's Castle sparkling in platinum, gold, pink, and blue colors. Two new majestic water fountains create excitement in the moat.

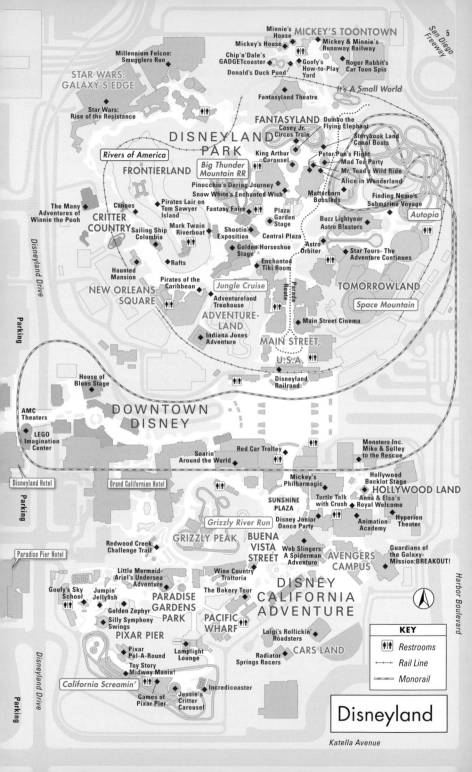

Disneyland

NEW ORLEANS SQUARE

It's Mardi Gras every day at New Orleans Square French Quarter with larger-than-life masks and decorations providing a festive atmosphere. Stroll through the narrow streets and hidden courtyards to Tiana's Place. Walk into "Eudora's Chic Boutique" featuring Tiana's Gourmet Secrets. Inspired by the movie *The Princess and the Frog* is a new retail store that Tiana opened with her mother, Eudora. Opening in 2024, Tiana's Bayou Adventure is a new theme attraction. Listen to live street performances near the Cajun-inspired Blue Bayou Restaurant set inside the Pirates of the Caribbean ride. While dining, watch visitors float on a weathered barge ride to discover Jack Sparrow and his band of pirates among enhanced special effects and battle scenes (complete with cannonball explosions). Be sure to stop for a pillowy Mickey beignet and refreshing nonalcoholic mint julep drink at the Mint Julep Bar. It's located next to Tiana's Place and the Disneyland Railroad Depot, and the nearby Haunted Mansion. This popular attraction continues to spook guests with its stretching walls and "doombuggy" ride through a house of happy ghosts. Tim Burton's *Nightmare Before Christmas* holiday overlay is an annual tradition that starts in the fall and extends throughout the holidays to the end of January. Enjoy a Monte Cristo sandwich at Cafe Orleans. Food carts offer everything from just-popped popcorn to churros, fresh fruit, beverages, and Mickey Mouse–shaped ice cream chocolate bars.

FRONTIERLAND

Between Adventureland and next to New Orleans Square, Frontierland transports you to the wild, wild West with wood sidewalks and swinging door buildings, a shooting gallery, foot-stompin' The Golden Horseshoe dance hall, and a pretty Spanish-tile courtyard with a fountain. The marquee attraction, Big Thunder Mountain Railroad, is a relatively tame roller coaster ride (no steep descents) that takes the form of a runaway mine car as it rumbles and turns through desert canyons and an old mining town. Be sure to take a ride on the beautifully restored 19th-century Mark Twain Riverboat. The 14-minute paddleboat cruises around Pirate's Lair and Tom Sawyer Island. Another boat ride is the Sailing Ship Columbia, a full-scale replica of a merchant ship that once sailed the globe (usually limited to weekends and select seasons only). Families enjoy taking a motorized raft over to Pirate's Lair on Tom Sawyer Island, where you can explore pirate-themed caves, go on a treasure hunt, and climb a fort. Dine outside at the River Belle Terrace for a variety of shrimp and catfish Cobb salad, fried chicken sandwich, or sweet and sticky pulled pork. This restaurant also offers three plant-based options that include BBQ tofu and meatballs with grits for lunch and dinner. Or take a seat on the festive Mexican terrace at the quick-service Rancho del Zocalo for a trio of street tacos, fire-grilled citrus-marinated chicken, plant-based cauliflower tacos, and cinnamon crisps for dessert. There is a Disney Kids menu.

CRITTER COUNTRY

Iconic Splash Mountain was the biggest draw to this down-home country-themed area, but the ride closed in 2023 to make way for Tiana's Bayou Adventure, scheduled to open in 2024. In the meantime, little ones love to take a peek through Winnie the Pooh's Hundred-Acre Wood, and families paddling along the Rivers of America on Davy Crockett's Explorer Canoes stop at Tom Sawyer Island to explore the interactive Pirate's Lair.

GALAXY'S EDGE

This 14-acre expansive land has guests step into the planet Batuu, designed from architectural locations in Morocco, Turkey, and Israel. Star Wars storytelling has expanded to include new tales and characters, including the legendary bounty hunter Boba Fett and mercenary

Best Tips for Disneyland

Download the Disneyland mobile app on your smartphone. Buy entry tickets here in advance or at nearby Disney Good Neighbor hotels or through Disney's website. Get the complimentary Disney Genie service loaded with features to enhance your visit. This stores your tickets, and informs you about attraction wait times, character visits, and parade times. You can view restaurant menus and make dining reservations; preorder and pay for contactless pickup at both parks; and download and share Disney PhotoPass photos.

Best Days to Visit: Midweek. Weekends (especially during the summer, Halloween, and winter holidays) are often the busiest times to visit. A rainy winter weekday is often the least crowded time to check out the parks.

Plan your times to hit the most popular rides. Get to the park as early as possible, even before the gates open, and make a beeline for the top rides before the crowds reach a critical mass. Staying at one of the three Disneyland hotels qualifies you for early admission. Later in the evening the parks thin out and you can catch a special show or parade. Save the quieter attractions for midafternoon.

Purchase Disney Genie+ starting at $25 to move forward on your favorite rides and save time in line. Another purchase is the new Discover Magic Band+. Pair it to your smartphone and Disneyland app for additional enhancement experiences.

Avoid peak mealtime crowds. Outside food and beverages in nonglass containers are allowed inside the parks, but dining at one of the park's many theme restaurants can be an experience to remember. For any sit-down establishment, be sure to make dining reservations months in advance, especially for the Blue Bayou Restaurant in Disneyland's New Orleans Square or Carthay Circle at Disney California Adventure. You can make a reservation up to 60 days in advance online or via the Disneyland app. If you just need a quick recharge, Disney carts offer creative snacks including popcorn in souvenir buckets, Mickey Mouse–shaped pretzels, cute cake pops, and a variety of ice cream. It's always a good idea to bring water, juice boxes, and snacks for little ones.

Check the daily events schedule online, on the Disneyland app, or at the park entrance. During parades, fireworks, and other special events, sections of the parks are filled with crowds. This distraction can work in your favor to take advantage of shorter lines at dining venues and rides. It also can work against you in maneuvering around a section of the park, so plan ahead.

Fennec Shand, as well as late-2023 additions, The Mandalorian and Grogu.

Ride **Star Wars: Rise of the Resistance** to accept a mission from the Resistance to fight against the First Order. You can also take a thrilling interactive ride in a six-person cockpit on **Millennium Falcon:** **Smugglers Run,** where you will be given the task of a pilot, gunner, or engineer, as you soar into hyperspace on a smuggling mission. Purchase a MagicPlus+ band to follow the lights and vibration down the right path to your bounty. The Droid Depot offers a build-your-own-droid workshop stocked with colorful parts, chips, and tech items. Starting at $119.99, you will receive a basket and blueprint to build your droid. Another treasure to purchase and take home is a hand-built lightsaber at Savi's Workshop.

For dining, popular Oga's Cantina is good for coffee, all-day light snacks, and unique cocktails for grown-ups. Galactic food and drink options can be found at the Milk Stand, where guests can sample blue and green beverages similar to what Luke Skywalker drank in the movies. Docking Bay 7 Food and Cargo offers lunch and dinner fare starting at $14.99. Ronto Roasters has roasted meats and savory grilled sausages.

ADVENTURELAND

Modeled after the lands of Africa, Polynesia, and Arabia, this tiny tropical paradise is worth braving the crowds that flock here for the ambience and better-than-average food. Sing along with the animatronic birds and tiki gods in the Enchanted Tiki Room, sail the rivers of the world with joke-cracking skippers on Jungle Cruise, and climb the new Adventureland Treehouse that Walt Disney and his Imagineers built in the early 1960s as a tribute to the Disney movie Swiss Family Robinson. Follow the wood rope stairway up to the boughs of the tree to explore various rooms.

Cap off the visit with a wild jeep ride at the recently refurbished Indiana Jones Adventure. Some of the best fast-casual dining options include The Tropical Hideaway along the open-air dock overlooking the Jungle Cruise ride. Snacks include pineapple, mango, or strawberry Dole Whip, plus Dole Whip floats and Asian-style *bao* buns. Skewers and rice plates, plus a vegetarian hummus trio, are available at Bengal Barbecue. The Tiki Juice Bar has pineapple juice and pineapple Dole Whip.

FANTASYLAND

Sleeping Beauty Castle marks the entrance to Fantasyland where guests can climb steps and walk inside to explore the epic tale of Princess Aurora. There are sounds, 3D displays, and exciting special effects. Beyond the castle is a visual wonderland of princesses, spinning teacups, flying elephants, and other classic storybook characters. Bibbidi Bobbidi Boutique offers princess makeovers for ages 3–12, with hair, makeup, nails, and even a princess dress for purchase. Fantasy Faire is a fairy-tale-style village where Disney princesses gather together for photos and autographs. Each has her own reception nook in the Royal Hall.

Restaurants in this area of the park include the fairy-tale Red Rose Taverne, inspired by Belle's provincial town in Beauty and the Beast. Families with tots love It's a Small World on the east end of Fantasyland with its dancing animatronic dolls from every country, cuckoo clock–covered walls, and variations of the song everyone knows in different languages. Other memorable rides include the King Arthur Carrousel with 68 hand-painted horses and fancy chariot. Look up to see to see nine hand-painted vignettes of Disney's animated Sleeping Beauty fairy tale. Ride Casey Jr. Circus Train to tour miniature-scale sites from some of Disney's most popular movies from a higher vantage than on Storybook Land Canal Boats. This is also home to some of the first rides at Disneyland, including Mr. Toad's Wild Ride, Peter Pan's Flight, Snow White's Enchanted Wish, and Pinocchio's Daring Journey. They are all classic movie-theater-dark rides that immerse riders in Disney fairy tales. Keep an eye out for the Abominable Snowman when he pops up on the Matterhorn Bobsleds, a fun roller coaster that twists and turns up and around on a made-to-scale model of the real Swiss mountain.

Did You Know?

The plain purple teacup in Disneyland's Mad Tea Party ride spins the fastest—though no one knows why.

MICKEY'S TOONTOWN

Mickey's Toontown is reimagined with new experiences for families with small kids. CenTOONial Park is ideal for little ones to run around the grassy lawn. There is a pretty fountain featuring water tables for guests to have a sensory experience and a dreaming tree for children to crawl and explore the sculpted tree roots. Inside the El CapiTOON Theater, is the new Mickey & Minnie's Runaway Railway. Engineer Goofy takes guests on a wacky ride filled with twists and turns through a fun adventure. The cartoonlike downtown is where Mickey, Donald, Goofy, and other classic Disney characters hang their hats. Over near Goofy's house, watch honey drip from a beehive into a chute that travels into his home. Step inside to help Goofy make treats with his new candy-making interactive contraption with silly appliance sounds. Outside is the new Goofy How-To-Play-Yard where kids can explore an elevated off-the-ground clubhouse. There is a whimsical sound garden to hear some funny noises. Over at Donald's Duck Pond little ones can get wet near the spinning water lilies, balance on beams and rocking toys, and see bubbles in the porthole windows on Donald's Boat. One of the most popular attractions is Roger Rabbit's Car Toon Spin—board Lenny the Cab for a twisting, turning cab ride through the Toontown of *Who Framed Roger Rabbit?* Head over to Chip 'n' Dale's GADGETcoaster for a low-key thrill ride. Little ones love to walk inside Mickey's and Minnie's homes to meet and be photographed with these famous mice.

For food, the new Cafe Daisy has Daisy Duck serve kid classic fare at her new sidewalk table eatery. Toontown offers fresh Farmers Market items at Good Boy! Grocers, a grab-and-go roadside stand offering treats and drinks.

TOMORROWLAND

This popular section of the park continues to tinker with its future, adding and enhancing rides regularly. Nemo's Submarine Voyage allows guests to search for the beloved clown fish Nemo, and friends Dory, Marlin, and other characters from the Disney-Pixar film. Star Wars–themed attractions can't be missed, like the immersive, 3D Star Tours – The Adventures Continue, where you can join the Rebellion in a galaxy far, far away. The interactive Buzz Lightyear Astro Blasters lets you zap laser beams and compete with others for the highest score. Hurtle through the cosmos at fast speeds in the dark on Space Mountain or check out mainstays like driving along a miniature motorway road trip on Autopia powered by Honda, with a working gas pedal and steering wheel to maneuver curves and inclines. Soar on futuristic Astro Orbiter rockets. Disneyland Monorail and Disneyland Railroad both have stations here.

Go to the Disneyland app to discover daily live-action shows; parades are always crowd-pleasers.

■TIP➔ **Arrive early to secure a good view; if there are two shows scheduled for the day, the second one tends to be less crowded. A fireworks display lights up weekends and most summer evenings.**

Disney California Adventure

★ **Disney California Adventure**
AMUSEMENT PARK/CARNIVAL | FAMILY | The sprawling Disney California Adventure, adjacent to Disneyland (their entrances face each other), pays tribute to the Golden State with multiple theme areas. Take your park experience to the next level of fun with Play Disney Parks, a mobile app with entertaining games, activities, and trivia. Admire the vintage art-deco architectural shops and dining venues along Buena Vista Street and learn about movie magic at Hollywood Land.

Avengers Campus is home for a new generation of superheroes, focusing on the characters of the Marvel Cinematic Universe. Ride on Web-Slingers: A Spider-Man Adventure, where guests of all ages can help wrangle Spider-Bots while wearing 3D glasses and accumulate points. Screams can be heard around the park from the free-falling Guardians of the Galaxy–Mission: BREAKOUT! See your favorite characters from several hit Pixar films when crossing over Pixar Pier. Ride the superfast Incredicoaster, and collect points playing along the interactive Toy Story Midway Mania ride. Stop to win a prize playing games at the carnival area in Pixar Pier. The 12-acre Cars Land features Radiator Springs Racers, a speedy trip in six-passenger speedsters through scenes featured in the blockbuster hit. The Single Rider Lane saves time to experience the thrills quicker. At night the park takes on neon hues as glowing signs light up Route 66 in Cars Land and Pixar Pal-A-Round, a giant Ferris wheel.

Cocktails, craft beers, and premium wines from California are available in the Pacific Wharf dining area. This area in the park is being reimagined into San Fransokyo from the movie *Big Hero 6,* where East meet West. There is a place to meet Baymax, plus new dining and shopping venues. Live nightly entertainment features a 1930s jazz troupe and seasonal entertainers throughout the year. The MagicBand+ is a new way to unlock Disney storytelling. This hands-free wearable on your wrist enhances your park experience in exciting new ways with color-changing and gesture-recognition features. Certain rides have Lightning Lanes with Disney's Genie+ to save time in line. Be sure to stay for the World of Color-One, a light-and-sound show celebrating Walt Disney's 100 Years of Wonder storytelling. ✉ *1313 S. Disneyland Dr., between Ball Rd. and Katella Ave., Anaheim* ☎ *714/781–4636* ⊕ *disneyland.disney.go.com* 🚊 *From $114 during the week and $150 on weekends; parking $30.*

PARK NEIGHBORHOODS
BUENA VISTA STREET
California Adventure's grand entryway re-creates the 1920s Los Angeles that Walt Disney encountered when he moved to the Golden State. There's a Red Car trolley (modeled after Los Angeles's bygone streetcar line); hop on for the brief ride to Hollywood Land. Buena Vista Street is also home to a Starbucks outlet—within the Fiddler, Fifer and Practical Café—and the upscale Carthay Circle Restaurant and Lounge, which serves modern craft food, cocktails, and beer. The comfy booths of the Carthay Circle restaurant on the second floor feel like a relaxing world away from the theme park outside. Keep an eye out for Officer Blue; he is known to give guests a citation to take home as a unique souvenir. The circle with a fountain in the middle has live entertainment throughout the day, ride times, and park information.

GRIZZLY PEAK
This woodsy land celebrates California's national parks and the great outdoors. Test your skills on the Redwood Creek Challenge Trail, a challenging trek across net ladders and suspension bridges. Grizzly River Run mimics the river rapids of the Sierra Nevada; be prepared to get soaked.

Soarin' Around the World is a spectacular simulated hang-gliding ride over internationally known landmarks like Switzerland's Matterhorn and India's Taj Mahal.

There is an entrance into Disney's Grand Californian Hotel & Spa from this area in Disney's California Adventure Park.

HOLLYWOOD LAND
Movie moments take place along a main street modeled after Hollywood Boulevard, with a fake sky backdrop, and real sound stages guests can step into. Monsteropolis offers an exciting Monsters, Inc. Mike & Sulley To The Rescue ride to return Boo home. Sorcerer's Workshop is where Disney Animation gives you an

insider's look at how animators create characters and what character is most like you. Turtle Talk with Crush lets kids have an unscripted chat with a computer-animated Crush, the sea turtle from *Finding Nemo*. Grab a bite at Award Weiners for gourmet hot dogs and fries. Delicious fruit smoothies are blended at Schmoozies! Grab-and-go snacks and drinks are available at Studio Catering Co.

CARS LAND

Amble down Route 66, the main thoroughfare of Cars Land, and discover a pitch-perfect re-creation of the vintage highway. Hop onto Mater's Junkyard Jamboree spinning ride and the Italian-theme Luigi's Rollickin' Roadsters. One of the most popular rides in Cars Land is Radiator Springs Racers. Strap into a nifty sports car and meet the characters of Pixar's *Cars* before a speedy auto race through a red rock canyon featuring a waterfall and desert in Radiator Springs. There is a Single Rider Lane and Lightning Lane for quicker wait times. Quick, creative eats are found at the Cozy Cone Motel (in an orange, tepee-shaped motor court) while Flo's V8 café serves hearty comfort food. Fresh fruit, vegetables, and drinks are available in the psychedelic Fillmore's Taste-In service station.

■ TIP→ **To bypass the line, there's a single-rider option for Radiator Springs Racers.**

PACIFIC WHARF

In the midst of the California Adventure you'll find multiple dining options, from light snacks to full-service restaurants at the new San Fransokyo. The San Francisco Bay theme and Tokyo Bay–inspired design is from Disney's *Big Hero 6* animated film. They kept many of guests' favorite food court options such as Lucky Fortune Cafe, Ghirardelli Soda Fountain and Chocolate Shop, and Pacific Wharf Cafe, with breads by Boudin, San Francisco's world-famous artisanal bakery. They sell loaves of Mickey Mouse–shaped sourdough bread.

PARADISE GARDENS PARK

The far corner of California Adventure is a mix of floating and flying rides. Soar via the Silly Symphony Swings; Goofy's Sky School rollicks and rolls through a cartoon-inspired landscape; and the sleek retro-style gondolas of the Golden Zephyr mimic 1920s movies and their sci-fi adventures. Journey through Ariel's colorful world on The Little Mermaid—Ariel's Undersea Adventure. The best views of the nighttime music, water, and light show, World of Color, are from the paths along Paradise Bay. FastPass tickets are available. Or for a guaranteed spot, book dinner at the Wine Country Trattoria that includes a ticket to a viewing area to catch all the show's stunning visuals.

PIXAR PIER

The most popular ride in this area is Toy Story Midway Mania! This fun 4D shooting game usually has a wait. This is a re-creation of California's famous seaside piers, featuring Pixar films' beloved characters. Join the Incredibles family on the Incredicoaster, a fast-moving roller coaster that zooms from zero to 55 mph in about four seconds. Riders scream through tunnels, steeply angled drops, and a 360-degree loop. Pixar Pal-A-Round is a giant Ferris wheel with gondolas named after Disney and Pixar characters. Hop in one and soar 150 feet in the air. Some of the gondolas spin and sway for an extra thrill while overlooking the park. There are also carnival games to win prizes, an aquatic-themed carousel, and Inside Out Emotional Whirlwind ride. Dining options include soft-serve ice cream, turkey legs, popcorn, and churros for quick snacking. At the Lamplight Lounge adults can chill out and overlook the action while sipping on craft cocktails.

AVENGERS CAMPUS

Assemble with fellow superfans and prepare to spring into action at this training ground for superheroes of the Marvel Cinematic universe. Team up with your favorite Avenger while exploring the mysterious ancient sanctum to learn the secrets of Doctor Strange. Help Spider-Man wrangle rogue Spider-Bots while on the Web-Slinger ride and join Rocket to rescue the Guardians of the Galaxy in an accelerated drop tower dark ride. Watch the mightiest heroes spring into action throughout the day at Avengers Headquarters and train with Black Panther's loyal bodyguards in Wakanda.

OTHER ATTRACTIONS
★ **Downtown Disney District**
PEDESTRIAN MALL | **FAMILY** | The exciting Downtown Disney District is a walking promenade filled with international dining, shopping, and lively entertainment that connects the resort's hotels and theme parks. More than a dozen new and reimagined establishments include the popular Asian restaurant Din Tai Fung, specializing in Taiwanese soup dumplings, and grab-and-go Earl of Sandwich along with the sit-down Earl of Sandwich Tavern. Jazz Kitchen Coastal Grill & Patio offers Southern-inspired food and live music on welcoming patios, verandas, and dining rooms. Be sure to try their signature seasonal flavor beignets that can be dipped, drizzled, and sprinkled. Southern California's iconic Porto's Bakery and Cafe offering Cuban-California–inspired pastries, desserts, and specialty items is set to open later in 2023. Enjoy a cold beer at Ballast Point Brewery and gourmet burger at Black Tap Craft Burgers. Save room for sweet treats at Salt and Straw for gourmet ice cream flavors such as honey lavender and oat milk and cookies, and Sprinkles for decadent frosted cupcakes.

Disney merchandise, souvenirs, and artwork are showcased at the brightly lit World of Disney store. At the megasize LEGO Store there are bigger-than-life LEGO creations, hands-on demonstrations, and space to play with the latest LEGO creations.

All visitors must pass through a security checkpoint and metal detectors before entering. ⊠ *1580 Disneyland Dr.,*

Anaheim ☎ *714/781–4565* ⊕ *disneyland. disney.go.com/downtown-disney* ⊠ *Free.*

🍴 Restaurants

Anaheim White House
$$$ | **ITALIAN** | **FAMILY** | The owner and executive chef Bruno Serato is one of the most beloved and famous philanthropists in Anaheim, known as much for his mission to feed America's hungry children as for his fine-dining Italian restaurant where standout dishes include lobster ravioli, Italian gourmet pizza, and his signature steamed salmon "chocolat" served with Belgium white-chocolate mashed potatoes. Grilled hanger steak dazzles with a green chimichurri sauce, and the Angus beef filet mignon is served with a savory Italian porcini sauce. **Known for:** classic Mediterranean cuisine; celebratory fine-dining venue; celeb chef. Ⓢ *Average main: $40* ⊠ *887 S. Anaheim Blvd., Anaheim* ☎ *714/772–1381* ⊕ *www.anaheimwhitehouse.com* ⊙ *Closed Mon. and Tues.*

★ Napa Rose
$$$$ | **AMERICAN** | Done up in a handsome Craftsman style, the upscale dinner venue Napa Rose prepares rich seasonal cuisine paired with an extensive wine list. For a look into the open kitchen, sit at the counter and watch the chefs as they whip up signature dishes such as warm duck confit salad, sautéed diver scallops, and beef filet mignon. **Known for:** upscale food and wine; kid-friendly options; gorgeous dining room and lounge. Ⓢ *Average main: $60* ⊠ *Disney's Grand Californian Hotel, 1600 Disneyland Dr., Anaheim* ☎ *714/781-4636* ⊕ *disneyland.disney.go.com/ grand-californian-hotel/napa-rose.*

🛏 Hotels

Anaheim Majestic Garden Hotel
$ | **HOTEL** | **FAMILY** | This sprawling replica of an English Tudor estate is a little prince or princess's dream hotel. **Pros:** large, attractive lobby; spacious rooms with comfortable beds; shuttle to the theme

parks. **Cons:** confusing layout; hotel sits close to a busy freeway; decor is dated. [$] *Rooms from: $150* ✉ *900 S. Disneyland Dr., Anaheim* ☎ *714/778–1700, 844/227–8535* 🌐 *www.majesticgarden-hotel.com* 🛏 *489 rooms* 🍴 *No Meals.*

★ Courtyard by Marriott Anaheim Theme Park Entrance

$$$ | RESORT | FAMILY | Near the entrance to both Disney parks, and featuring a Surfside Waterpark with a fun splash zone, waterslides, and a heated swimming pool, this is not your typical Courtyard by Marriott. **Pros:** fun waterpark; family-friendly rooms; prime location by Disney parks. **Cons:** valet parking only; no sit-down restaurant; water park requires reservations. [$] *Rooms from: $329* ✉ *1420 S. Harbor Blvd., Anaheim* ☎ *714/254–1442* 🌐 *www.marriott.com/en-us/hotels/snadt-courtyard-anaheim-theme-park-entrance* 🛏 *200 rooms* 🍴 *No Meals* ☞ *Valet parking only $35 per day.*

★ Disneyland Hotel

$$$$ | HOTEL | FAMILY | Staying at one of the happiest places on Earth is almost as fun as visiting Disney's two parks. **Pros:** early entrance into parks; pools, slides, and Disney characters; great location. **Cons:** this magic does not come cheap; pool's crowded in the summer; restaurants require reservations. [$] *Rooms from: $650* ✉ *1150 Magic Way, Anaheim* ☎ *714/778–6600* 🌐 *disneyland.disney.go.com* 🛏 *970 rooms including 71 suites* 🍴 *No Meals.*

★ Disney's Grand Californian Hotel and Spa

$$$$ | RESORT | FAMILY | The most opulent of Disneyland's three hotels, the Craftsman-style Grand Californian offers views of Disney California Adventure and Downtown Disney. **Pros:** early entrance into parks; family-friendly with three beautiful pools; direct access to California Adventure. **Cons:** expensive; valet parking is $65 a day; reserve dining in advance. [$] *Rooms from: $850* ✉ *1600 S. Disneyland Dr., Anaheim* ☎ *714/635–2300* 🌐 *disneyland.disney.go.com/grand-californian-hotel* 🛏 *1,019 rooms* 🍴 *No Meals.*

Hilton Anaheim

$ | HOTEL | FAMILY | Attached to the Anaheim Convention Center, this busy Hilton is the largest hotel in Orange County. **Pros:** good location; special hotel packages; large resort with amenities. **Cons:** dated decor; not a lot of green space; megasize parking lot maze. [$] *Rooms from: $175* ✉ *777 Convention Way, Anaheim* ☎ *714/750–4321* 🌐 *www.hiltonanaheimhotel.com* 🛏 *1,572 rooms* 🍴 *No Meals.*

★ JW Marriott, Anaheim Resort

$$ | RESORT | FAMILY | This luxury four-diamond hotel is just blocks from Disneyland and the Anaheim Convention Center. **Pros:** Tocca Ferro Italian Chophouse; great fireworks views; luxury amenities. **Cons:** rooftop views from lower-level rooms; no Disneyland-themed rooms; pricey valet parking and added daily fees. [$] *Rooms from: $350* ✉ *1775 S. Clementine St., Anaheim* ☎ *714/294–7800* 🌐 *www.marriott.com* 🛏 *468 rooms* 🍴 *No Meals.*

Park Vue Inn

$$ | HOTEL | FAMILY | Watch the frequent fireworks from the rooftop sundeck at this bougainvillea-covered Spanish-style inn, one of the closest lodgings to the Disneyland Resort main gate. **Pros:** easy walk to Disneyland, Downtown Disney, and Disney California Adventure; free parking until midnight on checkout day; some rooms have bunk beds. **Cons:** all rooms face the parking lot; no breakfast on-site; inefficient room air conditioners. [$] *Rooms from: $250* ✉ *1570 S. Harbor Blvd., Anaheim* ☎ *714/772–3691, 800/334–7021* 🌐 *www.parkvueinn.com* 🛏 *86 rooms* 🍴 *No Meals.*

★ The Viv Hotel

$$ | HOTEL | FAMILY | This family-friendly hotel offers spacious guest rooms and Disney magic throughout, from the blue fiberglass-and-resin life-size Star Wars Stormtroopers who greet guests arriving from the parking garage to the Fantasia-style hallway carpet and the views of Disneyland and Disney California Adventure Park from some rooms. **Pros:** heated family pool with fun water features; rooftop restaurant, bar, and outdoor lounge; family-friendly, spacious rooms. **Cons:** not a prime location; some freeway noise in rooms facing Disneyland; hard to enter driveway by car. [$] *Rooms from: $250* ✉ *1601 S. Anaheim Blvd., Anaheim* ☎ *714/408–2787* 🌐 *www.thevivhotelanaheim.com* 🛏 *326 rooms* 🍴 *No Meals.*

★ Westin Anaheim
$$$ | **RESORT** | Opened in 2021, and within walking distance of the parks, this convention-friendly hotel was designed by the same architect who designed the Mirage and Wynn hotels in Las Vegas, and the ground-level heated swimming pool and hot whirlpool with fountain feature and cabanas definitely bring Las Vegas vibes. **Pros:** ideal location for Disney parks and Convention Center; lots of dining options; rooftop bar with views. **Cons:** valet parking is $45; lacks Disney vibes; pool can get crowded in prime season. [$] *Rooms from: $425* ✉ *1030 W. Katella Ave., Anaheim* ☎ *657/279–9786* 🌐 *www.westinanaheim.com* 🛏 *618 rooms* 🍴 *No Meals.*

Activities

Los Angeles Angels of Anaheim
BASEBALL & SOFTBALL | **FAMILY** | Professional baseball's Los Angeles Angels of Anaheim have called Anaheim and Angel Stadium home since 1966. An "Outfield Extravaganza" celebrates great plays on the field, with fireworks and a geyser exploding over a model evoking the California coast. ✉ *Angel Stadium, 2000 E. Gene Autry Way, Anaheim* ☎ *714/940–2000* 🌐 *www.mlb.com/angels/ballpark* [M] *Metrolink Angels Express.*

Anaheim Ducks
HOCKEY | **FAMILY** | The National Hockey League's Anaheim Ducks, winners of the 2007 Stanley Cup, play at Honda Center. Concerts are also hosted here. ✉ *Honda Center, 2695 E. Katella Ave., Anaheim* ☎ *877/945–3946* 🌐 *nhl.com/ducks.*

Knott's Berry Farm

25 miles south of Los Angeles, via I–5, in Buena Park.

The iconic Knott's Berry Farm theme park appeals to all ages. Explore the Ghost Town, ride some thrilling roller coasters, and save room for fried chicken and boysenberry treats.

Sights

Knott's Berry Farm
AMUSEMENT PARK/CARNIVAL | **FAMILY** | This lively amusement park is fun for all ages. Once a 160-acre boysenberry farm, it's now an entertainment complex with close to 40 rides, dozens of restaurants and shops, arcade games, live shows, and a brick-by-brick replica of Philadelphia's Independence Hall. Take a step back into the 1880s while walking through Knott's Old West Ghost Town. Ride on a horse-drawn stagecoach or board a steam engine to start your journey into the park; just keep your valuables close to you, as bandits might enter your train car and put on quite a show. Camp Snoopy has plenty of rides to keep small children occupied as they explore 15 kid-friendly attractions. There are awesome thrill rides in the Boardwalk area, including the zooming HangTime that pauses dramatically then drops nearly 15 stories, and the exhilarating steel moto-coaster Pony Express that goes from zero to 35 mph in less than three seconds.

Be sure to get a slice of boysenberry pie, as well as boysenberry soft-serve ice cream, jam, juice, you name it. There's even a Boysenberry Food Festival once a year. In the fall, part of the park is turned into Knott's Scary Farm, a popular activity for teens and adults. Buy adult tickets online for a discount. Buy a bundle for parking and food included with your ticket. FastLane wristbands give you quicker access to the most popular rides. Nearby Knott's Soak City is open during the summer for guests who want to float on the lazy river, go down waterslides, and swim in the wave pool.

Fun fact: In 1934, Cordelia Knott began serving chicken dinners on her wedding china to supplement her family's income. The dinners and her boysenberry pies proved more profitable than her husband Walter's berry farm, so the two moved first into the restaurant business and then into the entertainment business. ⊠ *8039 Beach Blvd., Buena Park* ✛ *Between La Palma Ave. and Crescent St., 2 blocks south of Hwy. 91* ☏ *714/220–5200* ⊕ *www.knotts.com* ⊠ *$80* ⚲ *Purchase online* ☞ *Parking is $25.*

Knott's Soak City

WATER SPORTS | FAMILY | Knott's Soak City Waterpark is directly across from Knott's Berry Farm on 15 acres offering speed tubes, family rafting, a lazy river, and body slides. Pacific Spin is an oversize waterslide that drops riders 75 feet into a catch pool. There's also a children's pool, a 750,000-gallon wave pool, and a fun house. Soak City's season runs mid-May through September and is a separate admission ticket. ⊠ *8200 Beach Blvd., Buena Park* ☏ *714/220–5200* ⊕ *www. knotts.com/soak-city* ⊠ *$49.99* ⊙ *Open mid-May through Sept.*

PARK NEIGHBORHOODS
THE BOARDWALK

Thrill rides and skill-based games dominate the scene at the Boardwalk. Roller coasters including Coast Rider, Surfside Glider, and Pacific Scrambler surround a pond that keeps things cooler on hot days. HangTime towers 150 feet above the Boardwalk as coaster cars hang, invert, and drop the equivalent of 15 stories. The Boardwalk is also home to a string of test-your-skill games that are fun to watch whether you're playing or not. Dining options include the all-American diner Johnny Rockets.

CAMP SNOOPY

Kids love this miniature High Sierra wonderland where the *Peanuts* gang hangs out. Tykes can push and pump their own mini-mining cars on Huff and Puff, soar around on Charlie Brown's Kite Flyer, and hop aboard Woodstock's Airmail, a kids' version of the park's Supreme Scream ride. Most of the rides here are geared toward kids only, leaving parents to cheer them on and take photos from the sidelines. Sierra Sidewinder, a roller coaster near the entrance of Camp Snoopy, is aimed at older children, with spinning saucer-type vehicles that go a maximum speed of 37 mph.

FIESTA VILLAGE

The renovated Fiesta Village has brand-new experiences, entertainment, shopping, dining, and thrills. Along vibrant Fiesta Mercado, inspired by Olvera Street in Downtown Los Angeles, shop for authentic and unique souvenirs, and wander among pretty fountains and magenta bougainvillea flowers. Order fresh Mexican fare with a *cerveza* or margarita at the full-service Casa California restaurant and Cantina Del Sur. The Fiesta Stage has been transformed, offering live-entertainment shows. Thrill seekers will want to ride the next chapter in Montezooma's Revenge—MonteZOOMa: The Forbidden Fortress.

GHOST TOWN

Stop and chat with a blacksmith, crack open a geode, and visit Sad-Eye Joe sitting in the town jail while you walk among authentic old buildings relocated from their original mining-town sites in this town. Step inside a circa-1879 one-room schoolhouse for another step-back-in-time experience, as well as riding on an original horse-pulled Butterfield stagecoach. Looming over the area is GhostRider, Orange County's first wooden roller coaster. Traveling up to 56 mph and reaching 118 feet at its highest point, it's one of the park's biggest attractions. On the Western-themed Silver Bullet, riders are sent to a height of 146 feet and then back down 109 feet. Riders spiral, corkscrew, fly into a cobra roll, and experience overbanked curves. The Calico Mine ride descends into a replica of a re-created working gold mine complete with 50 animatronic figures. The Timber Mountain Log Ride is a visitor favorite: the flume ride tours through pioneer scenes before splashing down. Also found here is the Pony Express, a roller coaster that lets riders saddle up on packs of "horses" tethered to a steel platform before taking off on a series of hairpin turns at speeds of 38 mph. Take a step inside the Western Trails Museum, a dusty old gem full of Old West memorabilia and rural Americana, plus menus from the original chicken restaurant and an impressive antique button collection. Calico Railroad departs regularly from Ghost Town station for a round-trip tour of the park (bandit holdups notwithstanding). You can order a boysenberry soft-serve ice-cream cone nearby afterward. This section is also home to Big Foot Rapids, a splash-fest of white-water river rafting over towering cliffs, cascading waterfalls, and wild rapids.

INDIAN TRAILS

Celebrate Native American traditions through interactive exhibits like tepees and daily dance and storytelling performances.

🍴 Restaurants

★ Mrs. Knott's Chicken Dinner Restaurant

$$ | AMERICAN | FAMILY | Cordelia Knott's fried chicken and boysenberry pies drew crowds so big in the 1930s, that Knott's Berry Farm built a park to keep the hungry customers occupied while they waited. The Western-theme restaurant serves crispy home-style fried chicken, along with handmade biscuits, mashed potatoes, gravy, and Mrs. Knott's signature chilled cherry-rhubarb compote. **Known for:** famous fried chicken; long waits especially on weekends; pies and desserts. [$] *Average main: $22* ✉ *Knott's Berry Farm Marketplace, 8039 Beach Blvd., Buena Park* ☎ *714/220–5200* 🌐 *www.knotts.com/california-marketplace/mrs-knott-s-chicken-dinner-restaurant.*

🛏 Hotels

Knott's Berry Farm Hotel

$$ | HOTEL | FAMILY | This newly renovated hotel next to Knott's Berry Farm offers farm-theme-designed guest rooms with mini-refrigerators, two tennis courts, a basketball court, and swimming pool. **Pros:** easy access to Knott's Berry Farm; swimming pool; on-site dining. **Cons:** can be noisy; parking $15 a day; lower level has no view of park. [$] *Rooms from: $230* ✉ *7675 Crescent Ave., Buena Park* ☎ *714/995–1111, 866/752–2444* 🌐 *www.knotts.com/knotts-berry-farm-hotel* 🛏 *249 rooms* 🍴 *No Meals* ☞ *Bed and Breakfast package and Room and Knott's Berry Farm ticket packages are available.*

Huntington Beach

40 miles southeast of Los Angeles.

Huntington Beach is commonly referred to as Surf City U.S.A. This town offers a range of luxury and boutique hotels overlooking or just a block away from its broad white-sand beaches. Take a walk along the long wood pier to watch surfers glide across the surface on sometimes-towering waves. At the beginning and end of the lively pier are a few restaurants. Other shops and restaurants can be discovered on Main Street. A

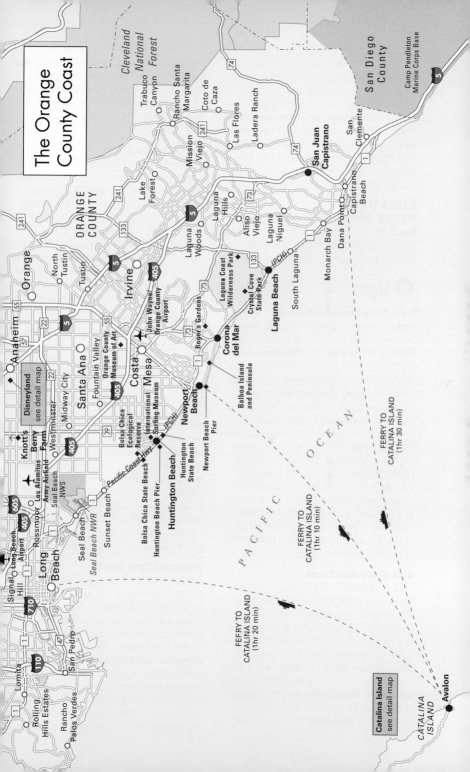

The Orange County Coast

Cleveland National Forest

San Diego County

Camp Pendleton Marine Corps Base

ORANGE COUNTY

Anaheim

Orange

Santa Ana

Disneyland
see detail map

Knott's
Berry
Farm

North Tustin

Tustin

Irvine

Lake Forest

Laguna Woods

Laguna Hills

Mission Viejo

Rancho Santa Margarita

Trabuco Canyon

Coto de Caza

Ladera Ranch

Las Flores

San Juan Capistrano

San Clemente

San Capistrano Beach

Dana Point

Monarch Bay

Laguna Niguel

Aliso Viejo

South Laguna

Laguna Beach

Crystal Cove State Park

Laguna Coast Wilderness Park

Corona del Mar

Roger's Gardens

Balboa Island and Peninsula

Newport Beach

Newport Beach Pier

Costa Mesa

John Wayne Orange County Airport

Orange County Museum of Art

Fountain Valley

Midway City

Westminster

Rossmoor

Los Alamitos Army Airfield

Seal Beach NWS

Seal Beach

Sunset Beach

Bolsa Chica Ecological Reserve

Bolsa Chica State Beach

Huntington Beach Pier

Huntington Beach

Huntington State Beach

Pacific Coast Hwy.

(PCH)

Long Beach

Long Beach Airport

Signal Hill

San Pedro

Lomita

Rolling Hills Estates

Rancho Palos Verdes

PACIFIC OCEAN

FERRY TO CATALINA ISLAND
(1hr 20 min)

FERRY TO CATALINA ISLAND
(1hr 10 min)

FERRY TO CATALINA ISLAND
(1hr 30 min)

Catalina Island
see detail map

CATALINA ISLAND

Avalon

draw for surf fans is the U.S. Open professional surf competition, which brings a festive atmosphere to town annually in late July. There's even a Surfing Walk of Fame, with plaques set in the sidewalk around the intersection of PCH and Main Street. Surf City Nights are every Tuesday with the first three blocks of Main Street closed to cars for a weekly farmers' market, street fair, and kids activities.

ESSENTIALS

VISITOR INFORMATION Visit Huntington Beach. ⊠ *155 Fifth St., Suite 111, Huntington Beach* ☎ *714/969–3492, 800/729–6232* ⊕ *www.surfcityusa.com.*

⊙ Sights

Bolsa Chica Ecological Reserve

WILDLIFE REFUGE | FAMILY | Wildlife lovers and bird-watchers flock to Bolsa Chica Ecological Reserve, which has more than 1,300 acres of salty marshland home to 200 different bird species—including great blue herons, snowy and great egrets, and brown pelicans. Throughout the reserve are easy-to-walk trails for bird-watching along a 1½-mile loop. There are two entrances off the Pacific Coast Highway: one close to the Interpretive Center and a second 1 mile south on Warner Avenue, opposite Bolsa Chica State Beach. Each parking lot connects to 4 miles of walking and hiking trails with scenic overlooks. ⊠ *3842 Warner Ave., Huntington Beach* ☎ *714/846–1114* ⊕ *www.bolsachica.org* ⊠ *Free.*

Bolsa Chica State Beach

BEACH | FAMILY | In the northern section of the city, Bolsa Chica State Beach is usually less crowded than its southern neighbors. The sand is somewhat gritty and not the cleanest, but swells make it a hot surfing spot. The Huntington Beach bike trail runs along the edge of the sand for 7 miles north to the south of Huntington Beach. Picnic sites can be reserved in advance. Firepits attract beachgoers most nights. **Amenities:** food and drink;

lifeguards; parking; showers; toilets. **Best for:** sunset; surfing; swimming; walking. ⊠ *Pacific Coast Hwy., between Seapoint St. and Warner Ave., Huntington Beach* ☎ *714/377-5691* ⊕ *www.parks.ca.gov* ⊠ *$15 parking.*

Huntington Beach Pier

MARINA/PIER | FAMILY | This municipal pier stretches 1,856 feet out to sea, past the powerful waves that gave Huntington Beach the title of "Surf City U.S.A." Well above the waves, it's a prime vantage point to watch the dozens of surfers in the water below. On the pier you'll find a snack shop and a shop where you can buy fishing rod rentals, tackle, and bait to fish off the pier. ⊠ *Pacific Coast Hwy., Huntington Beach* ⊕ *www.surfcityusa.com.*

Huntington City Beach

BEACH | FAMILY | Stretching for 3½ miles from Bolsa Chica State Beach to Huntington State Beach, Huntington City Beach is most crowded around the pier where amateur and professional surfers brave the waves daily. There are 100 fire rings, numerous concession stands, bike paths, and well-raked white sand. Surfboard rental shops make this a popular beach year-round. **Amenities:** food and drink; lifeguards; parking; showers; toilets. **Best for:** sunset; surfing; swimming; walking. ⊠ *Pacific Coast Hwy., from Beach Blvd. to Seapoint St., Huntington Beach* ☎ *714/536–5281, 714/536–9303 surf report* ⊕ *www.huntingtonbeachca.gov/ residents/beach_info* ⊠ *Parking from $15.*

Huntington State Beach

BEACH | FAMILY | This peaceful state beach offers 121 sandy acres and 200 firepits, so it's popular during the day and evening. There are changing rooms, and two new concession stands—the Huntington Beach House and Sahara Sandbar. There are year-round surf lessons, lifeguards, Wi-Fi access, and ample parking. An 8½-mile bike path connects Huntington to Bolsa Chica State Beach. Picnic areas can be reserved in advance for a fee depending on location; otherwise it's first come,

Lively Huntington Beach is a center for surfing on the coast.

first served. On hot days, expect crowds at this broad, soft-sand beach. **Amenities:** food and drink; lifeguards; parking; showers; toilets. **Best for:** sunset; surfing; swimming; walking. ✉ *21601 E. Pacific Coast Hwy., from Beach Blvd. south to Santa Ana River, Huntington Beach* ☎ *714/536–1454* 🌐 *www.parks.ca.gov/?page_id=643* 🎟 *$15 parking.*

International Surfing Museum
HISTORY MUSEUM | **FAMILY** | Just up Main Street from Huntington Pier, in an iconic art-deco building, the International Surfing Museum pays tribute to the sport's greats with an impressive collection of surfboards and related memorabilia. Exhibits are designed to encourage families to learn about the history of surfing. Highlights include Duke Kahanamoku's surfboard and the "World's Largest Surfboard" measuring 42 feet long, 11 feet wide, 16 inches thick, and weighing 1,300 pounds. ✉ *411 Olive Ave., Huntington Beach* ☎ *714/960–3483* 🌐 *www.huntingtonbeachsurfingmuseum.org* 🎟 *$3* 🕒 *Closed Mon.*

🍴 Restaurants

Duke's
$$$$ | **SEAFOOD** | **FAMILY** | Freshly caught seafood reigns supreme at this homage to surfing legend Duke Kahanamoku; it's also a prime people-watching spot right at the beginning of Huntington Beach Pier. Choose from several fish-of-the-day selections—many topped with Hawaiian ingredients—and shellfish like lobster, king crab, and shrimp. **Known for:** Hawaiian-style decor; gorgeous sunset views; mai tai cocktails. [$] *Average main: $45* ✉ *317 Pacific Coast Hwy., Huntington Beach* ☎ *714/374–6446* 🌐 *www.dukeshuntington.com.*

Wahoo's Fish Taco
$ | **MEXICAN FUSION** | **FAMILY** | Proximity to the ocean makes this eatery's seafood-filled tacos and burritos taste even better. The healthy fast-food chain—tagged with dozens of surf stickers—brought Baja's fish tacos north of the border to quick success. **Known for:** organic ingredients; Hawaiian onion ring burrito;

casual beachy ambience. [$] *Average main: $13* ✉ *120 Main St., Huntington Beach* ☎ *714/536–2050* 🌐 *www.wahoos.com.*

Hotels

Hyatt Regency Huntington Beach Resort and Spa

$$$ | RESORT | FAMILY | The Mediterranean design of this sprawling resort incorporates arched courtyards, beautiful tiled fountains, and firepits, all a nod to California's Mission period. **Pros:** close to beach with exclusive access; variety of pool areas; some rooms have private firepits. **Cons:** some partial ocean-view rooms; resort and daily valet fees; some rooms can hear the traffic on PCH. [$] *Rooms from: $400* ✉ *21500 Pacific Coast Hwy., Huntington Beach* ☎ *714/698–1234* 🌐 *www.hyatt.com* 🛏 *517 rooms* 🍴 *No Meals.*

★ Kimpton Shorebreak Resort

$$$ | HOTEL | FAMILY | This surfer-style Kimpton hotel is not only across the street from the beach, but it's the closest hotel to the Huntington Beach Pier and Main Street. **Pros:** proximity to beach and shops; free surfboard storage; quiet rooms despite central location. **Cons:** $35 valet parking fee; courtyard rooms have uninspiring alley views; additional resort fee to receive best perks. [$] *Rooms from: $450* ✉ *500 Pacific Coast Hwy., Huntington Beach* ☎ *714/861–4470, 877/212–8597* 🌐 *www.shorebreakhotel.com* 🛏 *157 rooms* 🍴 *No Meals.*

Pasea Hotel & Spa

$$$ | RESORT | FAMILY | Painted in shades of coastal blue, the contemporary-style Pasea is eight stories offering ocean views from almost every guest room, with balconies to take in the fresh breezes. **Pros:** excellent ocean views; pet friendly; supercomfortable beds. **Cons:** pool can get crowded; $40 valet parking fee; noise issues from nearby bars at Pacific City. [$] *Rooms from: $500* ✉ *21080 Pacific Coast Hwy., Huntington Beach* ☎ *866/478–9702* 🌐 *www.meritagecollection.com/pasea-hotel* 🛏 *250 rooms* 🍴 *No Meals.*

The Waterfront Beach Resort, a Hilton Hotel

$$$ | RESORT | FAMILY | This two-tower resort offers a variety of amenities for families, couples, and business travelers alike. **Pros:** quick walk to beach and pier; fun surf decor; oceanfront views from rooms. **Cons:** different towers have different vibes; overnight valet parking $48; crowded pool and deck during summer. [$] *Rooms from: $475* ✉ *21100 Pacific Coast Hwy., Huntington Beach* ☎ *714/845–8000,* 🌐 *www.waterfrontresort.com* 🛏 *290 rooms* 🍴 *No Meals.*

Shopping

Huntington Surf and Sport

SPORTING GOODS | FAMILY | The largest surf-gear source in town is Huntington Surf and Sport, right across from Huntington Pier. Staffed by true surf enthusiasts, it's also one of the only surf shops with a Java Point coffee counter inside. Surfboard rentals are $15 an hour or $50 all day, while soft-top boards are $10 per hour or $30 a day. They also rent wet suits for $15 a day. ✉ *300 Pacific Coast Hwy., Huntington Beach* ☎ *714/841–4000* 🌐 *www.hsssurf.com.*

Activities

SURFING

Corky Carroll's Surf School

SURFING | FAMILY | Learn the fundamentals of both longboard and shortboard surfing at Bolsa Chica State Beach. Run by the 1960s first professional surfer Corky Carroll, the surf school organizes beginning and more experienced surfing lessons, and provides hard- and soft-top boards and wet suits to rent during your lesson. ✉ *18581 E. Pacific Coast Hwy., Huntington Beach* ☎ *714/969–3959* 🌐 *www.surfschool.net.*

Dwight's Beach Concession

BIKING | **FAMILY** | You can rent surrey or cruiser bikes, wet suits, surfboards, bodyboards, umbrellas, and beach chairs at Dwight's, one block south of Huntington Pier. They also serve casual beach food, including their world-famous cheese strips. ⊠ *201 Pacific Coast Hwy., Huntington Beach* ☎ *714/536–8083* ⊕ *www.dwightsbeachconcession.com.*

Zack's HB

LOCAL SPORTS | **FAMILY** | This go-to sport rental and quick food spot is steps from the pier and Main Street. Zack's rents beach equipment, surfboards, wet suits, and bicycles. There is a walk-up window to purchase a quick hamburger, corn dog, grilled fish sandwich, fries, slush puppy, and ice cream. Zack's also has a gift shop with sunglasses, hats, and shirts. ⊠ *405 Pacific Coast Hwy., at Main St., Huntington Beach* ☎ *714/536–0215* ⊕ *www. zackssurfcity.com.*

Newport Beach

Just south of Huntington Beach, Newport Beach has evolved from a simple seaside village to a sophisticated coastal playground, featuring 10 distinctive neighborhoods. Newport Harbor is home to million-dollar yachts, adorable Duffy boats, kayaks, and stand-up paddleboarders enjoying the largest recreational harbor on the West Coast. Biking and walking are popular along the serene coastal wetlands in the Back Bay, while Fashion Island is a premier shopping and dining destination. Some of the most luxurious and unique boutique hotels are located in each neighborhood, except the residential Balboa Island, a short car ferry ride from the historic Balboa Peninsula. The Balboa Island loop is just over a 2½-mile walk around two connected islands in the middle of Newport Harbor. Stroll the public sidewalk along the waterfront and visit some of the unique shops and restaurants while admiring the million-dollar homes and boats docked in their backyards. Maybe you can't live here but you can enjoy Balboa Island's frozen treats—a Balboa Bar (vanilla or chocolate ice cream on a stick rolled in sprinkles, nuts, or other toppings) and frozen bananas dipped in chocolate.

ESSENTIALS

VISITOR INFORMATION Visit Newport Beach Concierge. ⊠ *Atrium Ct. at Fashion Island, 1600 Newport Center Dr., Newport Beach* ☎ *949/719–6100* ⊕ *www. newportbeachandco.com.*

◉ Sights

★ Balboa Island

ISLAND | **FAMILY** | This sliver of terra firma in Newport Harbor boasts quaint streets tightly packed with impossibly charming multimillion-dollar cottages. The island's main drag, Marine Avenue, is lined with picturesque cafés, frozen chocolate banana shops, and apparel, decor, and souvenir stores. There are bicycle and walking paths encircling much of the island for an easy and scenic visit. Rent a bike or walk the 2½-mile bike path and boardwalk that encircles much of the island for an easy and scenic visit.

To get here, you can either park your car on the mainland side of the PCH in Newport Beach and walk or bike over the bridge onto Marine Avenue, or take the Balboa Island Ferry, the country's longest-running auto ferry. The one-way fare is $1.50 for an adult pedestrian; $1.75 for an adult with a bike; and $2.50 to take your car on board. ⊠ *Marine Ave., Newport Beach* ☎ *949/719–6100* ⊕ *www. visitnewportbeach.com.*

Balboa Peninsula

BEACH | **FAMILY** | Newport's best beaches are on a 3-mile stretch called Balboa Peninsula. The picturesque Newport Harbor is on one side, and sandy, broad beaches on the other. The most intense spot for bodysurfing in Orange County, and arguably on the West Coast, known

Newport Beach is another popular place in the O.C. to catch waves.

as the Wedge, is at the south end of the peninsula. It was created by accident in the 1930s when the Federal Works Progress Administration built a jetty to protect Newport Harbor. ⚠ **Rip currents and punishing waves mean it's strictly for the pros—but it sure is fun to watch an experienced local ride it.** ✉ *Newport Beach* ⊕ *www.visitnewportbeach.com/ beaches-and-parks/the-wedge.*

Newport Beach Pier

BEACH | FAMILY | Jutting out into the ocean near 21st Street, Newport Pier is a popular fishing spot. Below is 5 miles of sandy beach for sunbathing, surfing, and walking along the beach. Street parking is difficult, so grab the first space you find and be prepared to walk. Early on Wednesday–Sunday morning you're likely to encounter dory fishermen hawking their predawn catches, as they've done for generations. On weekends the area is alive with kids of all ages on in-line skates, skateboards, and bikes dodging pedestrians and whizzing past fast-food joints and classic dive bars. Skate, bike,

and surfboard rental shops are nearby. ✉ *70 Newport Pier, Newport Beach* ☎ *949/644–3309* ⊕ *www.visitnewport-beach.com.*

★ Newport Harbor

BODY OF WATER | FAMILY | Sheltering nearly 9,000 small boats, Newport Harbor may seduce even those who don't own a yacht. Spend an afternoon exploring the charming shops and restaurants along the boat slips. California's shortest auto ferry takes visitors across to Balboa Island, which is popular with pedestrians, joggers, and bicyclists. Several grassy areas on the primarily residential Lido Isle have views of the water. To truly experience the harbor, rent a kayak or an electric Duffy boat for a pleasant picnic cruise or try stand-up paddleboarding to explore the sheltered waters. ✉ *Pacific Coast Hwy., Newport Beach* ⊕ *www. balboaislandferry.com.*

Orange County Museum of Art

ART MUSEUM | FAMILY | Founded by 13 visionary women in 1962 and one of the earliest contemporary art museums in California, the OCMA opened in late 2022 in its new $94 million home at the Segerstrom Center for the Arts in Costa Mesa. Designed by Pritzker Prize–winning architect Thom Mayne, OCMA's striking 53,000-square-foot building has 25,000 square feet of free-flowing gallery space to house its extensive collection of more than 4,500 works produced in the 20th and 21st centuries by artists with ties to California. Outside, a grand staircase provides amphitheater seating and serves as a community gathering point, inspired by the steps at the Metropolitan Museum of Art in New York. There is a bar, café, and sculpture terrace on Level 2. Programs include Art + Play for little ones and Art Happy Hour & Pop-Up Talks for adults. ✉ *3333 Ave. of the Arts, Costa Mesa* ☎ *71471/714/780–2130* 🌐 *www.ocma.art* 🎫 *Free* 🕒 *Closed Mon.*

Sculpture Exhibition in Civic Center Park
PUBLIC ART | **FAMILY** | This outdoor "museum without walls" is a favorite walking spot for locals and visitors. Located in the Newport Beach Civic Center, there is a car-free walking path displaying meaningful and whimsical public art sculptures. Take a self-guided walking tour by downloading the MyNB app in advance of your visit. ✉ *1000 Avocado Ave., Newport Beach* ☎ *949/717–3802* 🌐 *www.newportbeachca.gov.*

🍴 Restaurants

Basilic Restaurant
$$$$ | **BRASSERIE** | This intimate French–Swiss bistro adds a touch of old-world elegance to Balboa Island with its white linen and flower-topped tables. Chef Bernard Althaus grows the herbs used in his classic French dishes. **Known for:** French classics; fine wine; old-school ambience. [$] *Average main: $50* ✉ *217 Marine Ave., Balboa Island* ☎ *949/673–0570* 🌐 *www.basilicrestaurant.com* 🕒 *Closed Sun. and Mon.*

★ **Bear Flag Fish Co.**
$ | **SEAFOOD** | **FAMILY** | Expect long lines in summer at this indoor–outdoor dining spot serving up the freshest local fish (swordfish, sea bass, halibut, and tuna) and a wide range of creative seafood dishes (the Hawaiian-style poke salad with ahi tuna is a local favorite). Order at the counter, which doubles as a seafood market, and sit inside or outside on a grand patio. **Known for:** fresh catches thanks to restaurant fishing boat; fish tacos with homemade hot sauce; craft beers. [$] *Average main: $15* ✉ *Newport Peninsula, 3421 Via Lido, Newport Beach* ☎ *949/673–3474* 🌐 *www.bearflagfishco.com.*

Bluewater Grill
$$$ | **SEAFOOD** | **FAMILY** | On the site of an old sportfishing dock, this popular spot offers a variety of seasonal seafood, shellfish, meat, and poultry. There's a tranquil bay view from either the dining room, which is adorned with early-1900s fishing photos, or the waterfront patio. **Known for:** boat and harbor views; happy hour specials; daily-changing menu of fresh fish. [$] *Average main: $35* ✉ *Lido Peninsula, 630 Lido Park Dr., Newport Beach* ☎ *949/675–3474* 🌐 *www.bluewatergrill.com.*

The Cannery
$$$ | **SEAFOOD** | This 1920s cannery building still teems with fish, but now they go into dishes on the eclectic seafood menu rather than being packed into crates. Many diners arrive by boat, as there's a convenient dock at the front entrance. **Known for:** waterfront views; seafood specialties; craft cocktails. [$] *Average main: $40* ✉ *3010 Lafayette Rd., Newport Beach* ☎ *949/566–0060* 🌐 *www.cannerynewport.com.*

Gulfstream
$$$ | **SEAFOOD** | **FAMILY** | Established in 1999, this trendy restaurant has an open kitchen, comfortable booths, and outdoor seating. The patio is a fantastic place to hang out to enjoy a shrimp cocktail and

glass of wine. **Known for:** oysters on the half shell; local hangout; outdoor patio. [$] *Average main: $40* ✉ *850 Avocado Ave., Newport Beach* ☎ *949/718–0188* 🌐 *www.gulfstreamrestaurant.com.*

Sugar 'N Spice

$ | ICE CREAM | FAMILY | Stop by ice cream parlor Sugar 'N Spice for a Balboa Bar—a slab of vanilla ice cream dipped first in chocolate and then in a topping of your choice such as hard candy, chopped nuts, or Oreo crumbs. Other parlors serve the concoction, but Sugar 'N Spice claims to have invented it back in 1945. **Known for:** inventor of the Balboa Bar; frozen banana; local institution. [$] *Average main: $6* ✉ *310 Marine Ave., Balboa Island* ☎ *949/673–8907.*

Hotels

Balboa Bay Resort

$$$$ | RESORT | FAMILY | Once a private club that was a luxury hangout for Humphrey Bogart, Lauren Bacall, and Ronald Reagan, this esteemed waterfront resort now offers contemporary coastal elegance and one of the best harbor bay views, especially from the spacious bayview guest rooms. **Pros:** exquisite bayfront views; comfortable beds; local-favorite restaurant. **Cons:** swimming pool in the middle of the resort has no views; $35 nightly hospitality fee; some rooms don't face the bay. [$] *Rooms from: $550* ✉ *1221 W. Coast Hwy., Newport Beach* ☎ *949/645–5000* 🌐 *www.balboabayresort.com* 🛏 *160 rooms* 🍴 *No Meals.*

Hyatt Regency Newport Beach

$$$ | RESORT | FAMILY | The best aspect of this beloved resort-style Newport hotel is its lushly landscaped acres: 26 of them, all overlooking the Back Bay. The casually elegant architecture, spread over the generous grounds, will appeal to travelers weary of high-rise hotels. **Pros:** good amenities and activities; centrally located for shopping; pet-friendly hotel. **Cons:** $36 self-parking is far from main property; 10-minute drive to beach; $40 daily resort fee. [$] *Rooms from: $379* ✉ *1107 Jamboree Rd., Newport Beach* ☎ *949/729–1234* 🌐 *www.hyatt.com* 🛏 *410 rooms* 🍴 *No Meals.*

★ Lido House, Autograph Collection

$$$$ | RESORT | FAMILY | This Marriott Autograph Collection resort is located at the gateway of the exclusive Lido Island and three blocks from the beach. **Pros:** large hot tub and pool deck; lively hotel pub-style bar; free bikes to cruise the nearby boardwalk. **Cons:** no beach or water view; $35 resort fee; $49 valet parking. [$] *Rooms from: $500* ✉ *3300 Newport Blvd., Balboa Island* ☎ *949/524–8500* 🌐 *www.lidohousehotel.com* 🛏 *130 rooms, 5 cottages* 🍴 *No Meals.*

Newport Beach Hotel

$$$ | B&B/INN | FAMILY | This charming historic home turned into a boutique hotel offers direct views of the Pacific Ocean and Catalina Island and is the closest lodging to the beach and Newport Beach pier. **Pros:** beach- and ocean-view guest rooms; in a lively area near restaurants; steps to the pier and beach. **Cons:** some rooms are small; not all rooms have views; parking is $30 a day. [$] *Rooms from: $450* ✉ *2306 W. Oceanfront, Newport Beach* ☎ *949/673–7030* 🌐 *www.thenewportbeachhotel.com* 🛏 *20 rooms* 🍴 *Free Breakfast.*

★ VEA Newport Beach Marriott Hotel and Spa

$$$$ | RESORT | FAMILY | This centrally located, newly renovated property is across the street from the popular Fashion Island shopping-and-dining complex. **Pros:** spectacular views; gorgeous swimming pool, deck, and lounge; central location across from Fashion Island. **Cons:** sprawling floor plan; walk by conference rooms to get to Sky Suites; valet parking $55 a day. [$] *Rooms from: $500* ✉ *900 Newport Center Dr., Newport Beach* ☎ *949/640–4000* 🌐 *www.marriott.com* 🛏 *400 rooms* 🍴 *No Meals.*

A whimbrel hunts for mussels at Crystal Cove State Park.

Shopping

★ Fashion Island

STORE/MALL | The ritzy Fashion Island outdoor mall is designed with a cluster of archways and courtyards complete with koi pond, fountains, and a mix of high-end shopping and chain stores. Multiple dining venues include Fleming's Steak House, True Food Kitchen, and Sushi Roku. Well-known department store anchors include Macy's, Neiman Marcus, Nordstrom, and Bloomingdale's, plus boutiques like St. John, Brandy Melville, and See's Candies. ✉ 401 Newport Center Dr., between Jamboree and MacArthur Blvds., off PCH, Newport Beach ☎ 949/721–2000 ⊕ www.fashion-island.com 🎫 free.

Activities

BOAT RENTALS

★ Boat Rentals of America

BOATING | **FAMILY** | Pack a picnic with food and drinks to enjoy while touring the waterways surrounding Lido and Balboa Islands on either a power motorboat ($175 for two hours for up to six people), or an electric Duffy boat ($220 for two hours for up to eight people). ✉ 510 E. Edgewater Ave., Balboa Island ☎ 949/673–7200 ⊕ www.boats4rent.com.

BOAT TOURS

Catalina Flyer

BOATING | **FAMILY** | The Catalina Flyer, the largest passenger-carrying catamaran on the West Coast, operates a 75-minute round-trip catamaran ferry passage daily to Catalina Island for $78. Reservations are required; check the schedule for times, as crossings may be rescheduled due to weather or annual maintenance.

All-day parking is up to $30 a day in a nearby Newport Beach lot. Payment is made at self-serve pay stations. ✉ *400 Main St., Balboa Island* ☎ *949/673–5245* ⊕ *www.catalinainfo.com.*

★ **City Experiences Cruises and Events**
ENTERTAINMENT CRUISE | **FAMILY** | This operator books two-hour harbor cruises, Sunday brunch cruises, and weekend dinner cruises with dancing. The trips traverse the scenic waters of Newport Harbor with barking seals, million-dollar yachts, and water-view homes and restaurants. ✉ *2431 W. Coast Hwy., Newport Beach* ☎ *949/650–2412* ⊕ *www.cityexperiences.com.*

FISHING
Davey's Locker
FISHING | **FAMILY** | In addition to a complete tackle shop, Davey's Locker offers two-hour whale-watching cruises starting at $34, and half-day deep-sea fishing trips starting at $65. They also offer Duffy electric boats and skiff rentals. ✉ *Balboa Pavilion, 400 Main St., Balboa Island* ☎ *949/673–1434* ⊕ *www.daveyslocker.com.*

GOLF
Newport Beach Golf Course
GOLF | **FAMILY** | This 18-hole executive Newport Beach Golf Course is a walking course starting at $26 on Monday–Thursday, and $29 on Friday–Sunday and holidays. A pull cart is $5, and an electric cart is $24. They do offer a discount to junior and senior golfers. Reservations are accepted up to one week in advance, but walk-ins are accommodated when possible. Note: The front 9 holes are shorter and the back 9 holes are more challenging. ✉ *3100 Irvine Ave., Newport Beach* ☎ *949/474–4424* ⊕ *www.newportbeachgolfcoursellc.com* ⛳ From $18 🏌 *18 holes, 3180 yards, par 59.*

Corona del Mar

Coronal del Mar is often referred to as a small jewel on the Pacific Coast, but its name translated from Spanish is actually "The Crown of the Sea," which is fitting considering the area includes some of Orange County's most expensive residential areas surrounding a trendy seaside village. Corona del Mar is 2 miles south of Newport Beach and known for its exceptional beaches. One of the best sunset view spots is Little Corona Beach with its rocky cliffs and coastal vegetation.

⊙ Sights

★ **Corona del Mar State Beach**
BEACH | **FAMILY** | This half-mile beach is actually made up of two beaches, Little Corona and Big Corona, separated by a cliff and rocky jetty. Both have soft, golden-hue sand to set up chairs and towels for the day. You can find a parking spot on the street on weekdays. **Amenities:** lifeguards; parking; showers; toilets. **Best for:** snorkeling; sunset; swimming. ✉ *3100 Ocean Blvd., Corona del Mar* ☎ *949/718–1859* ⊕ *www.parks.ca.gov* ⛳ *Free.*

★ **Crystal Cove State Park**
STATE/PROVINCIAL PARK | **FAMILY** | Midway between Corona del Mar and Laguna Beach is Crystal Cove State Park, a favorite of local beachgoers and wilderness trekkers. It encompasses a 3.2-mile stretch of unspoiled beach and has some of the best tide-pooling in Southern California. Here you can see starfish, crabs, and sea anemones near the rocks. The park's 2,400 acres of backcountry are ideal for hiking and mountain biking, but stay on the trails to preserve the beauty. The Moro Campground offers campsites with picnic tables, including spots designated for RVs and trailers. ✉ *8471 N. Coast Hwy., Laguna Beach* ☎ *949/494–3539* ⊕ *www.parks.ca.gov/crystalcove* ⛳ *$15 parking.*

The Park Store at Crystal Cove Cottages
STORE/MALL | Located in Crystal Cove's Historic District, The Park Store carries fine art works by local plein air artists, as well as sea glass and ocean-themed jewelry, children's toys, snacks, and beach toys and apparel. ✉ *State Park Historic District, Newport Coast* ☎ *949/376–6200* 🌐 *www.crystalcove.org/visit/things-to-do/store-gallery.*

Roger's Gardens
GARDEN | **FAMILY** | One of the largest retail gardens in Southern California, Roger's showcases some of the best garden ideas and holiday decorations during Easter, Halloween, and Christmas. The on-site Farmhouse at Roger's Gardens restaurant is popular with visitors and locals during lunchtime and dinner. The chefs prepare locally sourced menu items to enjoy while overlooking the bucolic gardens. ✉ *2301 San Joaquin Hills Rd., Corona del Mar* ☎ *949/640–5800* 🌐 *www.rogersgardens.com* 🎟 *Free.*

Sherman Library and Gardens
GARDEN | **FAMILY** | This 2½-acre botanical garden and library specializes in the history of the Pacific Southwest. You can wander among cactus gardens, rose gardens, a cool fern garden, and a tropical conservatory. There's a good garden gift shop, and a restaurant named 698 Dahlia that serves lunch on Wednesday through Sunday from 11 am to 2 pm. ✉ *2647 E. Pacific Coast Hwy., Corona del Mar* ☎ *949/673–2261* 🌐 *www.thesherman.org* 🎟 *$5.*

🍴 Restaurants

The Beachcomber Cafe at Crystal Cove
$$ | **SEAFOOD** | Beach culture flourishes in this Crystal Cove Historic District restaurant, thanks to its umbrella-laden deck just a few steps above the white sand. This is where you can sip a really good mai tai at the Bootlegger Bar, while waiting for your chance to sample ahi tacos, Maine lobster pasta, or blue crab–stuffed salmon. **Known for:** beachside cocktails; fresh seafood; big crowds and long waits. [$] *Average main: $30* ✉ *15 Crystal Cove, Corona del Mar* ☎ *949/376-6900* 🌐 *www.thebeachcombercafe.com.*

Shake Shack at Crystal Cove
$ | **DINER** | **FAMILY** | This Southern California landmark sitting on a bluff off the PCH is the perfect spot to get a quick breakfast burrito or pancake combo. During lunch and dinner they make tasty Cove burgers served with a side of French fries or coleslaw, fish-and-chips, and a seared ahi sandwich. **Known for:** more than 30 different shake flavors; incredible ocean views; small parking lot with 30-minute limit. [$] *Average main: $15* ✉ *7703 E. Coast Hwy., Newport Coast* ☎ *949/464–0100* 🌐 *www.crystalcoveshakeshack.com.*

🛏 Hotels

Crystal Cove Historic District Cottages
$ | **HOUSE** | The Crystal Cove Historic District is home to a collection of unique and historic cottages decorated and furnished to reflect the 1935 to 1955 beach culture that flourished here. **Pros:** beachfront; great views and location; affordable for this location. **Cons:** in demand so reservations require advance planning; some cottages are dorm-style; not all cottages offer the same decor and outdoor space. [$] *Rooms from: $94* ✉ *35 Crystal Cove, Corona del Mar* ☎ *800/444–7275 reservations* 🌐 *www.reservecalifornia.com* 🛏 *24 cottages* 🍽 *No Meals.*

★ The Resort at Pelican Hill
$$$$ | **RESORT** | **FAMILY** | Built on a protected coastal enclave across the PCH from Crystal Cove State Park, this upscale Italian Renaissance–style resort is one of the most spectacular resorts in Orange County and features a dramatic domed rotunda and Tuscan columns and pilasters in the lobby. **Pros:** ocean-view paradise for golfers; spectacular swimming pool (the largest of its kind in the world); great spa and dining options. **Cons:** one of the

most expensive resorts in Orange County; swimming pool can get very crowded during the holidays; pricey resort fee. $ *Rooms from: $1,000* ⊠ *22701 S. Pelican Hill Rd., Newport Coast* ☎ *833/260–8926* ⊕ *www.pelicanhill.com* ⤴ *204 rooms, 128 villas* ⭗ *No Meals.*

🛍 Shopping

Crystal Cove Promenade
STORE/MALL | FAMILY | This Mediterranean-inspired upscale strip mall is across the street from Crystal Cove State Park, with the shimmering Pacific Ocean in plain view. Crystal Cove Promenade offers a mix of well-known storefronts such as Williams Sonoma and Trader Joe's, plus unique boutiques, and popular restaurants that include Javier's, Mastro's Ocean Club, and Bear Flag Fish Co. ⊠ *7845–8085 E. Coast Hwy., Newport Beach* ⊕ *www.shopirvinecompany.com.*

Laguna Beach

10 miles south of Newport Beach on PCH, 60 miles south of Los Angeles, I–5 south to Hwy. 133, which turns into Laguna Canyon Rd.

Driving in along Laguna Canyon Road from the I–405 freeway gives you the chance to cruise through one of the most gorgeous coastal communities with 30 unique coves and beaches to explore and some of the clearest water in Southern California. During the summer, there's a convenient and free trolley service that cruises from North Laguna to Main Beach and all the way to the picturesque Ritz Carlton Laguna Niguel.

Laguna's welcome mat is legendary. On the corner of Forest and Park Avenues is a gate proclaiming, "This gate hangs well and hinders none, refresh and rest, then travel on." Art galleries dot the village streets, and there's usually someone daubing en plein air on the bluff in Heisler

Park. Along the Pacific Coast Highway you'll find dozens of clothing boutiques, jewelry stores, cafés, and seafood restaurants.

ESSENTIALS
VISITOR INFORMATION Visit Laguna Beach Visitors Center. ⊠ *381 Forest Ave., Laguna Beach* ☎ *949/497–9229, 800/877–1115* ⊕ *www.visitlagunabeach.com.*

👁 Sights

Festival of Arts and Pageant of the Masters
ARTS CENTER | An outdoor amphitheater near the mouth of the canyon hosts the annual Pageant of the Masters, Laguna's signature art event. Local participants arrange tableaux vivants, in which live models and carefully orchestrated backgrounds merge in striking mimicry of classical and contemporary paintings. The pageant is part of the Festival of Arts, held in July and August; tickets are in high demand, so plan ahead. ⊠ *650 Laguna Canyon Rd., Laguna Beach* ☎ *800/489–3378* ⊕ *www.foapom.com* 💲 *Tickets: $40–$110.*

Heisler Park
CITY PARK | FAMILY | One of the most picturesque parks in Laguna Beach, Heisler Park offers plenty of fun and relaxation. There is a picnic beach with tables overlooking palm trees and panoramic ocean views. Take the stairs down to Diver's Cove for snorkeling, scuba diving, and tide-pool exploring. Take the paved walking path along the cliff all the way to Laguna's Main Beach. There are public restrooms and outdoor showers. This is also a popular area for plein air artists to set up an easel and chair and paint for hours. ⊠ *400 Cliff Dr., Laguna Beach* ⊕ *www.visitlagunabeach.com* 💲 *Free.*

Laguna Art Museum
ART MUSEUM | This museum displays work by California artists from all time periods, representing scenery in Laguna, and life and history of the Golden State

Looking for shells on Laguna Beach, one of the nicest stretches of sand in Southern California.

in general. Special exhibits change quarterly. ✉ *307 Cliff Dr., Laguna Beach* 🖷 *949/494–8971* ⊕ *www.lagunaartmuseum.org* 🖾 *$12* ⊗ *Closed Mon.*

Laguna Coast Wilderness Park

HIKING & WALKING | FAMILY | With easy, moderate, and difficult trails spread over 7,000 acres of canyon to coastal territory, Laguna Coast Wilderness Park is a hiker's paradise. The 40 miles of trails offer expansive views and are also popular with mountain bikers. Trails open daily at 7 am and stay open until sunset, weather permitting. No dogs are allowed in the park. ✉ *18751 Laguna Canyon Rd., Laguna Beach* 🖷 *949/923–2235* ⊕ *www.ocparks.com/parks/lagunac* 🖾 *$3 parking.*

Beaches

★ Main Beach Park

BEACH | FAMILY | Centrally located in the main town of Laguna Beach near multiple dining venues, art galleries, and shops, Main Beach Park has a fitting name. Walk along this soft-sand beach to Bird Rock and explore nearby tide pools or just sit on one of the benches and watch people bodysurfing, play beach volleyball, or scramble around two half-basketball courts. The beach also has a children's play area with climbing equipment. Most of Laguna's hotels are within a short (but hilly) walk. **Amenities:** lifeguards; showers; toilets. **Best for:** sunrise, sunset; swimming. ✉ *Broadway at S. Coast Hwy., Laguna Beach* ⊕ *www.visitlagunabeach.com.*

1,000 Steps Beach

BEACH | FAMILY | Off South Coast Highway at 9th Street, 1,000 Steps Beach isn't too hard to find and actually only has 217 steps. It's one of the many coves in Laguna Beach offering a long stretch of soft sand, waves, and dramatic rock formations. Sea caves and tide pools enhance the already beautiful natural spot. Walking back up to your car, you will feel like you got a good workout. **Amenities:** showers. **Best for:** snorkeling; surfing; swimming. ✉ *S. Coast Hwy., at 9th St., Laguna Beach* ⊕ *www.visitlagunabeach.com.*

Wood's Cove

BEACH | **FAMILY** | Off South Coast Highway, Wood's Cove is especially quiet during the week. Big rock formations hide lurking crabs. This is a prime scuba-diving spot, and at high tide much of the beach is underwater. Climbing the steps to leave, you can see a Tudor-style mansion that was once home to Bette Davis. Street parking is free yet limited. **Amenities:** none. **Best for:** snorkeling; scuba diving; sunset. ✉ *Diamond St. and Ocean Way, Laguna Beach* 🌐 *www.visitlagunabeach.com.*

🍴 Restaurants

The Cliff

$$$ | **SEAFOOD** | **FAMILY** | Walk through the quaint Laguna Beach artist village to get to the Cliff and its 180-degree views of Main Beach and the Pacific coastline. The multilevel dining patios serve hearty breakfasts and coastal seafood favorites for lunch and dinner. **Known for:** some of Laguna Beach's best ocean-view dining; reservations necessary; splurge-worthy seafood towers. [$] *Average main: $40* ✉ *577 S. Coast Hwy., Laguna Beach* ☎ *949/494–1956* 🌐 *www.thecliffrestaurant.com.*

Gelato Paradiso

$ | **EUROPEAN** | **FAMILY** | Each morning this gelato shop makes fresh small batches of artisanal gelatos and dairy-free sorbettos in a variety of appealing flavors. Located in back of the charming Peppertree Lane shopping center, there is a small outdoor patio where people gather to enjoy the authentic Italian gelato after a day at the beach or to cap off an evening. **Known for:** authentic Italian gelato; fruit flavors; patio gathering spot. [$] *Average main: $6* ✉ *Peppertree La., 448 S. Coast Hwy., Laguna Beach* ☎ *949/464–9255* 🌐 *www.gelatoparadiso.com.*

★ Las Brisas

$$$$ | **MEXICAN FUSION** | **FAMILY** | Located in what used to be the Victor Hugo Inn, Las Brisas is now a Laguna Beach landmark restaurant. Sit on the expansive patio to take in the spectacular coastline views while enjoying signature margaritas and coastal Mexican cuisine with a California twist. **Known for:** fresh seafood; panoramic coastal views; reservations a must. [$] *Average main: $45* ✉ *361 Cliff Dr., Laguna Beach* ☎ *949/497–5434* 🌐 *www.lasbrisaslagunabeach.com.*

The Rooftop Lounge

$$$ | **INTERNATIONAL** | Another popular sunset view venue in South Laguna, The Rooftop Lounge at the top of Casa del Camino top floor is a hot seat for sunset cocktails, so plan ahead. Snag a table to enjoy a variety of different flavor mojitos or a pomegranate martini along with a cheese board, spicy fish-and-chips, or a veggie sandwich. **Known for:** spectacular sunset views; craft cocktails; burgers, pasta, salads, and sandwiches. [$] *Average main: $40* ✉ *1289 S. Coast Hwy., Laguna Beach* ☎ *949/497–2446* 🌐 *www.rooftoplagunabeach.com.*

Sapphire and The Pantry

$$ | **INTERNATIONAL** | **FAMILY** | This Laguna Beach establishment set in a historic Craftsman-style building is part gourmet pantry (a must-stop for your every picnic need) and part global dining adventure. Enjoy comfort cuisine from around the world paired with an eclectic wine and beer list. **Known for:** sapphire salad; weekend brunch; pet-friendly patio. [$] *Average main: $30* ✉ *The Old Pottery Place, 1200 S. Coast Hwy., Laguna Beach* ☎ *949/715–9888* 🌐 *www.sapphirelagunabeach.com.*

★ Selanne Steak Tavern

$$$$ | **STEAKHOUSE** | Located inside a historic 1934 home along Pacific Coast Highway, and named after one of the owners—Hockey Hall of Famer and six-time Olympian Teemu Selanne—Selanne Steak Tavern serves modern steak-house fare paired with stellar Napa Valley wines. There is a cozy Carrara-topped tavern-style bar where bartenders make artisanal cocktails and martinis, and a formal fine-dining experience upstairs.

Known for: variety of dining settings; prime cuts of meat; Monkey Bread dessert. [$] *Average main: $70* ✉ *1464 S. Coast Hwy, Laguna Beach* 🌐 *www.selannesteaktavern.com.*

The Stand Natural Foods

$ | **VEGETARIAN** | **FAMILY** | Since 1975, this old-school, artsy eatery in Laguna provides healthy, organic vegan salads, bowls, burritos, tamales, veggie burgers, pita pocket sandwiches, fresh fruit soft serve, and smoothies. **Known for:** 100% plant-based vegan food; brown rice burritos; nut-milk shakes. [$] *Average main: $15* ✉ *238 Thalia St., Laguna Beach* ☎ *949/494–8101* 🌐 *www.thestandnaturalfoods.com.*

Taco Loco

$ | **MEXICAN** | **FAMILY** | This may look like a fast-food taco stand with salads, quesadillas, and nachos on the menu, but the quality of the food here equals that in many higher-price restaurants. Some Mexican standards get a seafood twist, like swordfish, calamari, and shrimp tacos. **Known for:** vegetarian and vegan tacos; sidewalk seating; surfer clientele. [$] *Average main: $16* ✉ *640 S. Coast Hwy., Laguna Beach* ☎ *949/497–1635* 🌐 *www.lagunabeachmexicanfood.com.*

Urth Caffe

$$ | **BAKERY** | **FAMILY** | A local favorite in the morning and throughout the day for organic heirloom coffee and hand-blended fine organic teas, Urth also serves health-conscious food as well as pastries outside on the charming garden patio looking out at the Laguna Art Museum across the street. For lunch and dinner, they offer a variety of salads, soups, bowls, pizzas, and signature sandwiches. **Known for:** health-conscious cuisine; organic coffee and tea; long lines on the patio during peak hours and weekends. [$] *Average main: $20* ✉ *308 N. Pacific Coast Hwy., Laguna Beach* ☎ *949/376–8888* 🌐 *www.urthcaffe.com.*

Zinc Café and Market

$$ | **AMERICAN** | **FAMILY** | It's always brunch time at his small Laguna Beach institution where—from 7 am to 4 pm—you will find reasonably priced breakfast-to-lunch (okay, brunch) items that include everything from signature quiches, poached eggs, and homemade granolas, to healthy salads, homemade soups, quesadillas, and pizza. All the sweets are homemade, including the megasize brownies. **Known for:** gourmet pastries, some gluten-free; coffee bar; busy outdoor patio. [$] *Average main: $20* ✉ *350 Ocean Ave., Laguna Beach* ☎ *949/494–6302* 🌐 *www.zinccafe.com.*

🛏 Hotels

★ Inn at Laguna Beach

$$$$ | **HOTEL** | **FAMILY** | This golden local landmark is stacked neatly on the hillside at the north end of Laguna's Main Beach and it's one of the few hotels in the area set almost on the sand. **Pros:** rooftop with fabulous ocean views; beach essentials provided; beachfront location. **Cons:** ocean-view rooms are pricey; tiny hot tub; nonrefundable $100 pet fee and daily amenity fee. [$] *Rooms from: $650* ✉ *211 N. Coast Hwy., Laguna Beach* ☎ *949/497–9722, 800/544–4479* 🌐 *www.innatlagunabeach.com* 🛏 *70 rooms* 🍴 *No Meals.*

La Casa del Camino

$$$ | **HOTEL** | The look is Old California at the 1929-built La Casa del Camino, with dark woods, arched doors, wrought iron, and a beautiful tiled fireplace in the recently refreshed lobby. **Pros:** breathtaking views from rooftop lounge; beach lovers will appreciate surf-theme rooms; steps to the beach. **Cons:** some rooms face the highway; no pool; $25 resort fee but it includes parking. [$] *Rooms from: $400* ✉ *1289 S. Coast Hwy., Laguna Beach* ☎ *949/497–2446* 🌐 *www.lacasadelcamino.com* 🛏 *36 rooms* 🍴 *Free Breakfast.*

★ Montage Laguna Beach

$$$$ | RESORT | FAMILY | Built on a picturesque coastal bluff above the Pacific Ocean and Treasure Island Beach, this elegant Craftsmen-style resort features 30 acres of grassy lawns, soft sand beaches, and a stunning mosaic tile swimming pool. **Pros:** picturesque coastal location; stunning tiled mosaic swimming pool; residential style villas with sweeping ocean views. **Cons:** one of the area's priciest resorts, especially during holidays or summer weekends; $75 valet parking per night; $65 daily resort fee and $220 nonrefundable pet fee. $ *Rooms from: $1,100* ⊠ *30801 S. Coast Hwy., Laguna Beach* ☎ *949/715–6000, 866/271–6953* ⊕ *www.montagehotels.com/lagunabeach* ⤳ *258 rooms* ❚❂❚ *No Meals.*

★ The Ranch at Laguna Beach

$$$$ | RESORT | Set in an incredible lush canyon landscape, just a short walk from a stunning stretch of coastline, the Ranch at Laguna Beach offers morning yoga by the heated pool, 9 holes of golf on a verdant course nestled between two canyons, and two-story contemporary beach cottages. **Pros:** incredible setting; sustainable hotel; immersive activities. **Cons:** no ocean view; parking $25 a day; $46 daily resort fee. $ *Rooms from: $550* ⊠ *31106 S. Coast Hwy, Laguna Beach* ☎ *888/316–0959* ⊕ *www.theranchlb.com* ⤳ *97 rooms* ❚❂❚ *No Meals.*

★ Surf and Sand Resort

$$$$ | RESORT | FAMILY | One mile south of downtown, on an exquisite stretch of beach with sometimes thundering waves, this is a getaway for those who want a boutique hotel experience with surf and sand. **Pros:** easy sandy beach access; intimate boutique resort; good restaurant with wonderful views. **Cons:** pricey valet parking; surf can be loud; no air-conditioning (but overhead fans help). $ *Rooms from: $650* ⊠ *1555 S. Coast Hwy., Laguna Beach* ☎ *877/579–8554* ⊕ *www.surfandsandresort.com* ⤳ *167 rooms* ❚❂❚ *No Meals.*

🛍 Shopping

Candy Baron

CANDY | FAMILY | Get your sugar fix at the time-warped Candy Baron, filled with old-fashioned goodies like gumdrops, licorice, bull's-eyes, sugar-free candies, and more than 50 flavors of saltwater taffy. ⊠ *231 Forest Ave., Laguna Beach* ☎ *877/798–2339* ⊕ *www.thecandybaron.com.*

San Juan Capistrano

5 miles north of Dana Point, 60 miles north of San Diego.

San Juan Capistrano is best known for its historic mission, where the swallows traditionally return each year, migrating from their winter haven in Argentina. The town offers charming antiques stores, fun restaurants, boutique hotels, and lively night venues.

GETTING HERE AND AROUND

If you arrive by train, which is far more romantic and restful than battling freeway traffic, you'll be dropped off across from the mission at the San Juan Capistrano depot. With its appealing brick café and preserved Santa Fe cars, the depot retains much of the magic of early American railroads. If driving, park near Ortega and Camino Capistrano, the city's main streets.

◉ Sights

★ Los Rios Historic District

MUSEUM VILLAGE | FAMILY | Take a walk back in time on the oldest residential street in Southern California, where houses date to the 1790s. The Silvas Adobe is a typical example of the dozen or more one-room adobes in the area. It's located near Mission San Juan Capistrano, the first Californian mission to allow workers to live outside the mission grounds. On the street you'll also find the Historical Society Museum and the ZOOMARS

Mission San Juan Capistrano was founded in 1776.

petting zoo for families. Shopping and dining options line this lovely community on the National Register of Historic Places. ✉ *31831 Los Rios St., San Juan Capistrano* ☎ *949/493–8444* 🌐 *www.sanjuancapistrano.net* 🎫 *free.*

★ Mission San Juan Capistrano

HISTORIC SIGHT | FAMILY | Founded in 1776 by Father Junípero Serra (consecrated as St. Serra), Mission San Juan Capistrano was one of two Roman Catholic outposts between Los Angeles and San Diego. The Great Stone Church, begun in 1797, is the largest structure created by the Spanish in California. After extensive retrofitting, the golden-hued interiors are open to visitors who may feel they are touring among ruins in Italy rather than the O.C. Many of the mission's adobe buildings have been restored to illustrate mission life, with exhibits of an olive millstone, tallow ovens, tanning vats, metalworking furnaces, and the padres' living quarters. The beautiful gardens, with their fountains and koi pond, are a lovely spot in which to wander. The bougainvillea-covered Serra Chapel is believed to be the oldest church still standing in California and is the only building remaining in which St. Serra actually led Mass. Enter via a small gift shop in the gatehouse. ✉ *26801 Ortega Hwy., San Juan Capistrano* ☎ *949/234–1300* 🌐 *www.missionsjc.com* 🎫 *$18* 🕑 *Closed Mon.* ✍ *Advance online tickets are encouraged.*

🍴 Restaurants

Cedar Creek Inn

$$$ | AMERICAN | FAMILY | Just across the street from Mission San Juan Capistrano, this restaurant has a patio that's perfect for a late lunch or a romantic dinner. The menu is fairly straightforward, with dishes that are tasty and portions that are substantial—try the "Brown Derby" Cobb salad or Cedar Creek burger at lunch, or the prime rib for dinner. **Known for:** view of the historic mission; coconut cake; comfortable seating and patio. [$] *Average main: $40* ✉ *26860 Ortega Hwy., San Juan Capistrano*

☎ *949/240–2229* 🌐 *www.cedarcreekinn.com.*

L'Hirondelle

$$$ | **FRENCH** | Locals have romanced at cozy tables for decades at this delightful restaurant directly across from the San Juan Capistrano Mission. Such classic dishes as beef bourguignon and a New York strip in a black-peppercorn-and-brandy sauce are the hallmarks of this French and Belgian restaurant, whose name means "the little swallow." The extensive wine list is matched by an impressive selection of Belgian beers. **Known for:** popular Sunday brunch; traditional French and Belgian cuisine; good Belgian beer selection. [$] *Average main: $39* ✉ *31631 Camino Capistrano, San Juan Capistrano* ☎ *949/661–0425* 🌐 *www.lhirondellesjc.com* 🕒 *Closed Mon.; brunch only on Sun.*

The Ramos House Cafe

$$$$ | **AMERICAN** | It may be worth hopping the Amtrak to San Juan Capistrano just for the chance to have breakfast or lunch at one of Orange County's most beloved restaurants, located in a historic board-and-batten home dating back to 1881. This café sits practically on the railroad tracks across from the depot—nab a table on the patio and dig into a hearty breakfast featuring seasonal items, such as the smoked bacon scramble with wilted rocket and apple fried potatoes. **Known for:** Southern specialties; weekend brunch; historic setting. [$] *Average main: $45* ✉ *31752 Los Rios St., San Juan Capistrano* ☎ *949/443–1342* 🌐 *www.ramoshouse.com* 🕒 *Closed Wed. No dinner.*

Hotels

★ Inn at the Mission San Juan Capistrano

$$$ | **HOTEL** | **FAMILY** | This family-friendly hacienda-style boutique hotel is located across the street from the famed San Juan Capistrano Mission. **Pros:** great location next to the mission; terrific culinary program; luxury rooms and suites. **Cons:** guests may hear freeway noise; beach is almost 3 miles away; daily amenity fee and expensive parking. [$] *Rooms from: $500* ✉ *26907 Old Mission Rd., San Juan Capistrano* ☎ *949/503–5700* 🌐 *www.marriott.com* 🛏 *135 rooms* 🍴 *No Meals.*

★ The Ritz-Carlton, Laguna Niguel

$$$$ | **RESORT** | **FAMILY** | Located on an oceanfront bluff with an unparalleled view of the Pacific Ocean, and offering the Ritz's signature top-tier service, you are in the lap of luxury at this resort. **Pros:** beautiful grounds and views; excellent dining options; sophisticated service. **Cons:** some rooms are small for the price; in-house dining prices are high; $60 daily resort fee. [$] *Rooms from: $1,000* ✉ *1 Ritz-Carlton Dr., Dana Point* ☎ *949/240–2000, 800/542–8680* 🌐 *www.ritzcarlton.com/en/hotels/california/laguna-niguel* 🛏 *396 rooms* 🍴 *No Meals.*

Nightlife

Coach House

LIVE MUSIC | A roomy, premier entertainment venue, Coach House draws music crowds of varying ages for dinner and entertainment. Make a dinner reservation and receive priority seating to listen to the next hip new band, popular cover bands, and legacy musicians. The calendar of shows is online. ✉ *33157 Camino Capistrano, San Juan Capistrano* ☎ *949/496–8930* 🌐 *www.thecoachhouse.com.*

Swallow's Inn

BARS | Across the way from Mission San Juan Capistrano you may spot a line of Harleys in front of the down-home and downright funky Swallow's Inn. Despite a somewhat tough look, it attracts all kinds—bikers, surfers, modern-day cowboys, and grandparents—for a drink, a casual bite, and live entertainment. Happy hour is all day on Monday, and the rest of the week from 4 to 7 pm. ✉ *31786 Camino Capistrano, San Juan Capistrano* ☎ *949/493–3188* 🌐 *www.swallowsinn.com.*

Catalina Island

Just 22 miles across from Orange County and Long Beach, Catalina is a Mediterranean-looking and-feeling island offering unspoiled mountains, canyons, coves, and beaches.

Water sports are a big draw, as divers and snorkelers come for the exceptionally clear water surrounding the island. Kayakers are attracted to the calm cove waters and thrill seekers book the eco-themed zipline that traverses a deep canyon. The beach community of the main town of Avalon is where yachts and pleasure boats bob in the crescent bay. Wander beyond the pedestrian waterfront and find brightly painted little bungalows and million-dollar homes up in the hills. Bicycles and golf carts are the preferred mode of transportation.

In 1919, William Wrigley Jr., the chewing-gum magnate, purchased a controlling interest in the company developing Catalina Island, whose most famous landmark, the Casino, was built in 1929 under his orders. Because he owned the Chicago Cubs baseball team, Wrigley made Catalina the team's spring training site, an arrangement that lasted until 1951.

In 1975, the Catalina Island Conservancy, a nonprofit foundation, acquired about 88% of the island to help preserve the area's natural flora and fauna, including the bald eagle and the Catalina Island fox. These days the conservancy is restoring the rugged interior country with plantings of native grasses and trees. The organization helps oversee the interior's 50 miles of bike trails and 165 miles of hiking trails and helps protect the island's 60 endemic species. Along the coast you might spot oddities like electric perch, saltwater goldfish, and flying fish.

GETTING HERE AND AROUND
FERRY BOAT TRAVEL

Set sail to Catalina Island with four convenient port locations. Two companies offer ferry service to Catalina Island—Catalina Express and Catalina Flyer. These boats have both indoor and outdoor seating and snack bars. There is an extra fee for bicycles and surfboards. The waters around Catalina can occasionally get a little rough, so if you're prone to seasickness, come prepared. During the summer there are more departures. Winter, holiday, and weekend schedules vary, so reservations are strongly recommended.

Catalina Express makes an hour-long run from Long Beach or San Pedro to Avalon and a 90-minute run to Two Harbors. It also has a boat that leaves from Dana Point to Avalon. Round-trip fares begin at $77, with discounts for seniors and kids. On busy days, a $40 upgrade to the Commodore Lounge, when available, is worth it. You also receive a complimentary snack and nonalcohol or alcoholic beverage. Service from Newport Beach to Avalon is available through the *Catalina Flyer*. The boat leaves from Balboa Pavilion at 9 am (in season), takes 75 minutes to reach the island, and costs $78 round-trip. Reservations are required for the *Catalina Flyer* and recommended for all weekend and summer trips.

■ TIP→ **Keep an eye out for dolphins, which sometimes swim alongside the ferries.**

FERRY CONTACTS Catalina Express. ⊠ *320 Golden Shore, Long Beach* ☎ *562/485–3200* ⊕ *www.catalinaexpress.com.* **Catalina Flyer.** ⊠ *Balboa Pier, 400 Main St., Newport Beach* ☎ *949/673–5245* ⊕ *www.catalinainfo.com.*

GOLF CARTS

Golf carts constitute the island's main form of transportation other than walking or biking to sightsee in the area. Some parts of town are off-limits, as is the island's interior. Drivers 25 and over with

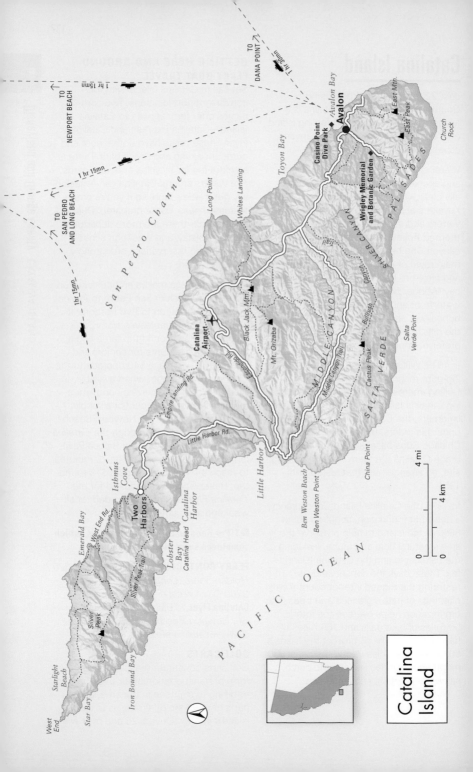

Catalina Island

valid driver's license can rent them along Avalon's Crescent Avenue and Pebbly Beach Road. Four passenger carts are $120 for two hours, with a $60 refundable deposit, payable via cash only. A few six-passenger carts are available on a first-come, first-served basis.

GOLF CART RENTALS Catalina Island Vacation Rentals. ⊠ *212 Catalina Ave., Avalon* ☎ *855/631–5280* ⊕ *www.catalinavacations.com.*

TOURS

Santa Catalina Island Company runs both land tours that include a Bison Expedition and Ridgetop Eco Adventure. Ocean tours include the *Flying Fish* boat trip (summer evenings only) and a glass-bottom boat. The eco-themed zipline tour traverses a scenic canyon; and a fast Cyclone boat tour takes you to the less populated center of the island, Two Harbors. Reservations are highly recommended for all tours. Tours range in cost $18 to $139.

CONTACTS Catalina Adventure Tours. ⊠ *302 Pebbly Beach Rd., Avalon* ☎ *562/432–8828* ⊕ *www.catalinaadventuretours.com.* **Catalina Island Conservancy.** ⊠ *708 Crescent Ave., Avalon* ☎ *310/510–2595* ⊕ *www.catalinaconservancy.org.* **Santa Catalina Island Company.** ⊠ *150 Metropole Ave., Avalon* ☎ *310/510–2000* ⊕ *www.visitcatalinaisland.com.*

Avalon

A ferry ride from Long Beach, San Pedro, Newport Beach, or Dana Point.

Avalon, Catalina's only real town, extends from the shore of its natural harbor to the surrounding hillsides. Its resident population is about 3,800, but it swells with tourists on weekends and during the summer months. Most of the city's activity, however, is centered on the pedestrian mall on Crescent Avenue, and most sights are easily reached on foot. Rental golf carts and bicycles and electric bikes can be rented from shops along Crescent Avenue.

⊙ Sights

★ Casino

NOTABLE BUILDING | Built in 1929, this iconic circular white structure is an architectural masterpiece. The entrance offers Spanish-inspired Catalina tile and painted murals in marine blue, sand, and sea foam green colors. This *casino* was named after the Italian word for "gathering place," not gambling. The circular ballroom with a soaring 50-foot dome ceiling once famously hosted 1940s big bands and is still used for jazz festivals and gala events. The Santa Catalina Island Company leads two different types of guided walking tours of the Casino. On the lower level is the historic Avalon Theatre with more than 1,000 seats; first-run movies show here on the weekend. Look up to see one of the most beautiful art deco murals by John Gabriel Beckman. ⊠ *1 Casino Way, Avalon* ☎ *310/510–0179* ⊕ *www.visitcatalinaisland.com.*

Casino Point Dive Park

WILDLIFE REFUGE | The crystal clear waters of the Casino Point Dive Park are home to protected marine life. This is where moray eels, bat rays, spiny lobsters, harbor seals, and brilliant orange garibaldi (California's state marine fish) cruise around kelp forests and along the sandy bottom. It's a terrific site for scuba diving, with some shallow areas suitable for snorkeling. Equipment can be rented on-site next to the world-famous Catalina Casino. Water temperature ranges in the low 70s during the summer, with September to mid-October being the warmest. Glass-bottom-boat tours and a submarine tour take guests to the shallow waters of Lover's Cove, across the harbor, another spot filled with marine life. ⊠ *1 Casino Way, Avalon* ⊕ *www.divingcatalina.com.*

Did You Know?

You can take a tour of Avalon's Scenic Drive for 7½ miles of panoramic views and a lesson in Catalina Island folklore.

Catalina Island Museum

PUBLIC ART | **FAMILY** | Inside this local art and history interactive museum, visitors can learn about the island's native Chumash people, Catalina Island's owner and creative developer William Wrigley Jr., his baseball team, his Hollywood celebrity friends and and love for big band music. The exterior of the Catalina Island Museum is a beautiful Spanish Mission style with art deco enhancements. Upstairs the rooftop and gardens are a pretty event space with native plants and colorful glass art. There is a gift shop worth exploring for Catalina-themed souvenirs and reproductions of the island's signature colorful Catalina pottery tiles. The first Friday of the month they sponsor a "Culture between Cocktails" event from 5 to 7 pm. ✉ *217 Metropole Ave., Avalon* ☎ *310/510–2414* 🌐 *www.catalinamuseum.org* 🎟 *$18* 🕒 *Closed Mon.*

Green Pleasure Pier

MARINA/PIER | Head to the Green Pleasure Pier for a good vantage point of Avalon Harbor. On the pier you can find a visitor information office, fish-and-chip snack stands, a bait shop, a tour boat ticket stand and gathering spot, plus rental boat and water sport rentals. ✉ *1 Green Pleasure Pier, Avalon* 🌐 *www.lovecatalina.com.*

Wrigley Memorial and Botanic Garden

GARDEN | **FAMILY** | Two miles south of the bay is Wrigley Memorial and Botanic Garden, home to many plants native only to Southern California and the Channel Islands. Today there are five different sections where you can see Catalina ironwood, wild tomato, and rare Catalina mahogany. The Wrigley family commissioned the garden as well as the monument, which has a grand staircase and a Spanish-style mausoleum inlaid with colorful Catalina tile. Wrigley Jr. was once buried here but his remains were moved to Glendale, California, during World War II. You'll find great views at the top. ✉ *Avalon Canyon Rd., Avalon* ☎ *310/510–2897* 🌐 *www.catalinaconservancy.org* 🎟 *$12.*

🍴 Restaurants

Bluewater Grill

$$$ | **SEAFOOD** | **FAMILY** | Overlooking the entire harbor, this open-to-the-sea-air patio is the preferred spot to dine on freshly caught fish, savory chowders, and all manner of shellfish. Order a swordfish steak, the lobster roll, or the sand dabs if they are on the menu. **Known for:** fresh local fish; handcrafted cocktails; overwater harbor views. [$] *Average main: $35* ✉ *306 Crescent Ave., Avalon* ☎ *310/510–3474* 🌐 *www.bluewatergrill.com.*

Catalina Coffee & Cookie Company

$ | **AMERICAN** | **FAMILY** | There is no Starbucks on the island, so the Catalina Coffee & Cookie Company is very popular in the morning. While you're grabbing your coffees, lattes, and mochas, you may want to kick-start the day with fresh-baked pastries, a hot breakfast burrito, or one of their custom made-to-order bagel sandwiches. **Known for:** popular breakfast spot; bagel sandwiches; dark chocolate pistachio bars. [$] *Average main: $10* ✉ *205 Crescent Ave., Avalon* ☎ *310/510–2447* 🌐 *www.catcookieco.com* ☞ *Open daily 6–4.*

★ Descanso Beach Club

$$ | **AMERICAN** | **FAMILY** | Set on an expansive deck overlooking the water and a few boats, Descanso Beach Club serves a wide range of favorites: grilled burgers, street tacos, clam chowder, salads, and layered nachos, along with the island's sweet signature cocktail, Buffalo Milk—a mix of fruit liqueurs, vodka, and whipped cream. Firepits and chic beach cabanas add to the scene, as does the sound of happy and terrified screams from the zipliners in the canyon above the beach. **Known for:** tropical beach vibe; scenic views; chic cabana rentals. [$] *Average main: $20* ✉ *Descanso Beach, 1 Descanso Ave., Avalon* ☎ *310/510–7410* 🌐 *www.visitcatalinaisland.com.*

★ Eric's on the Pier

$$ | **AMERICAN** | Grab a stool at this little snack bar on the Green Pleasure Pier for people-watching while drinking a draft beer and munching on a burrito, fish-and-chips, or signature buffalo burger. **Known for:** comfort foods; quick eats; beachside location. [$] *Average main: $20 ✉ 4 Green Pier, Avalon ☎ 310/510–2550 🌐 www.lovecatalina.com/listing/erics-on-the-pier/23 ⏱ No dinner.*

★ The Lobster Trap

$$$ | **SEAFOOD** | Seafood rules at the popular Lobster Trap, because the restaurant's owner has his own boat and fishes for the catch of the day and, in season, spiny lobster. Ceviche is a great starter, always fresh and brightly flavored. **Known for:** locally caught seafood; convivial atmosphere; local hangout. [$] *Average main: $35 ✉ 128 Catalina St., Avalon ☎ 310/510–8585 🌐 catalinalobstertrap.com.*

Steve's Steakhouse and Seafood

$$$ | **STEAKHOUSE** | **FAMILY** | A hop, skip, and a jump from the bay, this popular second-floor restaurant keeps regulars happy with sizzling steaks and locally caught swordfish and shrimp. The sultry black-and-blue decor and old-fashioned supper club feel creates a romantic atmosphere set off with stunning harbor views. **Known for:** friendly staff; water views; steak and seafood dinners. [$] *Average main: $40 ✉ 417 Crescent Ave., Avalon ☎ 310/510–0333 🌐 www.stevessteakhouse.com.*

Hotels

Aurora Hotel

$$$ | **HOTEL** | In a town dominated by historic properties, the Aurora is refreshingly contemporary, with a hip attitude and sleek furnishings. **Pros:** comfortable rooms; quiet location off main drag; close to restaurants. **Cons:** standard rooms are small; no elevator; two-night minimum stay required. [$] *Rooms from: $350 ✉ 137 Marilla Ave., Avalon ☎ 310/510–0454 🌐 www.auroracatalina.com 🛏 18 rooms 🍴 Free Breakfast.*

The Avalon Hotel

$$$$ | **B&B/INN** | This charming boutique hotel one block from the beach, decorated with photos and artifacts of Avalon, has clean and well-maintained rooms and a showstopper rooftop lounge area to luxuriate in Avalon Bay views and breezes. **Pros:** unique and quaint; good location; rooftop lounge overlooking Avalon Bay. **Cons:** some rooms are noisy; no elevator; rooms are small. [$] *Rooms from: $500 ✉ 124 Whittley Ave., Suite 706, Avalon ☎ 310/510–7070 🌐 www.theavalonhotel.com 🛏 15 rooms 🍴 Free Breakfast.*

Bellanca Hotel

$$ | **HOTEL** | One of the closest boutique hotels to the Catalina Casino and the beach, this sea theme hotel also offers a communal rooftop lounge area where guests can enjoy a cup of coffee and take in the 180-degree views of Avalon. **Pros:** romantic setting; close to beach; expansive sundeck with comfortable lounge furniture. **Cons:** ground-floor rooms can hear golf carts drive by; some rooms are on the small side; no elevator. [$] *Rooms from: $299 ✉ 111 Crescent Ave., Avalon ☎ 310/510–0555, 888/510–0555 🌐 www.bellancahotel.com 🛏 35 rooms 🍴 No Meals.*

★ Hotel Atwater

$$$ | **HOTEL** | **FAMILY** | Located one block from the beach in the heart of Avalon, Hotel Atwater originally opened in 1920 and was recently redesigned in 2019, to honor Helen Atwater Wrigley (daugher-in-law of famed local William Wrigley). **Pros:** elegant hotel featuring historical decor; central location; nice amenities. **Cons:** some rooms have street noise; $40 daily destination fee; not on the beach. [$] *Rooms from: $400 ✉ 125 Sumner Ave., Avalon ☎ 310/510–1673, 877/778–8322 🌐 www.visitcatalinaisland.com 🛏 95 rooms 🍴 No Meals.*

Hotel Vista del Mar

$$$ | **HOTEL** | **FAMILY** | On the bay-facing Crescent Avenue, this third-floor property is steps from the beach, so complimentary towels, chairs, and umbrellas await guests as do rooms with balconies, views, and fireplaces. **Pros:** comfortable and luxurious; central location; rooms have fireplaces. **Cons:** no restaurant or spa facilities; few rooms with ocean views; no elevator. $ *Rooms from: $450 ⊠ 417 Crescent Ave., Avalon ☎ 310/510–1452, 800/601–3836 ⊕ www.hotel-vistadelmar.com ⇨ 14 rooms* ⦿ *Free Breakfast.*

★ Mt. Ada

$$$$ | **B&B/INN** | A stay in the 1921 mansion that William Wrigley Jr. built includes breakfast, lunch, beverages, an evening wine and charcuterie plate, gelato, house-made cookies, and snacks—all the comforts of a millionaire's home. **Pros:** timeless charm; all-inclusive services, including complimentary shuttle from ferry dock; incredible canyon, bay, and ocean views. **Cons:** some rooms and bathrooms are small; a far walk into town; pricey for the amenities available. $ *Rooms from: $600 ⊠ 398 Wrigley Rd., Avalon ☎ 877/778–8322 ⊕ www. visitcatalinaisland.com ⇨ 6 rooms* ⦿ *All-Inclusive.*

★ Pavilion Hotel

$$$ | **HOTEL** | This mid-century modern hotel is steps from the sand and water. **Pros:** steps to the beach and harbor; lower level rooms have semiprivate patios; shabby-chic decor. **Cons:** no pool; $40 daily destination fee; no elevator. $ *Rooms from: $450 ⊠ 513 Crescent Ave., Avalon ☎ 310/510–1788, 877/778–8322 ⊕ www. visitcatalinaisland.com ⇨ 71 rooms* ⦿ *No Meals.*

Snug Harbor Inn

$$$ | **B&B/INN** | Calm, comfort, and charm await at this adults-only escape where you will find picturesque mountain, harbor, or ocean views from Cape Cod–chic rooms. **Pros:** great location; wine and hors d'oeuvres each evening; breakfast brought to your room. **Cons:** small and reserves quickly; some rooms showing wear; some rooms are quite snug. $ *Rooms from: $495 ⊠ 108 Sumner Ave., Avalon ☎ 310/510–8400 ⊕ snugharbor-inn.com ⇨ 6 rooms* ⦿ *Free Breakfast.*

★ Zane Grey Pueblo Hotel

$$$ | **HOTEL** | Best-selling Western novelist Zane Grey built his home as a retreat to take in the views of Avalon while writing more than 100 books; his home was turned into this quaint boutique hotel with suites named after Zane Grey book titles. **Pros:** breathtaking views; complimentary continental breakfast; the only ocean-view hotel with a swimming pool. **Cons:** older rooms are dark; a hike up a hill from town; bell tower chimes can be loud for some people. $ *Rooms from: $400 ⊠ 199 Chimes Tower Rd., Avalon ☎ 310/510–0966 ⊕ www.zanegreyhotel. com ⇨ 16 rooms* ⦿ *Free Breakfast.*

🏃 Activities

BICYCLING

Brown's Bikes

BIKING | **FAMILY** | Look for Brown's Bike rentals near the Catalina Express boat pier on Pebbly Beach Road. Beach cruisers start at $30 per day, mountain bikes are $40 per day, and electric bikes are $65 for a day rental, and a good choice to explore Catalina's steep hills. They also rent tandem bikes, strollers, and wheelchairs. ⊠ *107 Pebbly Beach Rd., Avalon ☎ 310/510–0986 ⊕ www.catalinabiking. com.*

DIVING AND SNORKELING

Catalina Divers Supply

SCUBA DIVING | Head to Catalina Divers Supply to rent equipment, sign up for guided scuba and snorkel tours, and attend certification classes. It also has an outpost at the Dive Park at Casino Point and one on the Green Pleasure Pier. Both offer gear rental and tank air fills. ⊠ *1 Casino Way, Avalon* ☎ *310/510–0330* ⊕ *www.catalinadiverssupply.com.*

HIKING
The Trailhead

HIKING & WALKING | FAMILY | Permits from the Catalina Island Conservancy are required for hiking into Santa Catalina Island's rugged interior, where there are more than 165 miles of trails of all levels to explore. If you plan to backpack overnight, you'll need a camping reservation. The interior is dry and desertlike; bring plenty of water, sunblock, a hat, and all necessary supplies. The permits are free or you can make a donation to the Conservancy. It's also possible to hike between Avalon and Two Harbors, starting at the Hogsback Gate, above Avalon, but the 28-mile journey has an elevation gain of 3,000 feet and is not for the weak. A popular hike is the three- to five-day, 38.5 mile Trans-Catalina Trail for which you will need a permit. You don't need a permit for shorter hikes, such as the 20-minute one from Avalon to the Wrigley Botanical Garden. There is a great restaurant, Toyon Grill, up on the second floor overlooking the Green Pleasure Pier, Harbor and Casino. Bluewater Avalon teamed up with the Catalina Island Conservancy to offer a casual, sit-down spot with a full bar. Try the Island's own Rusack Vineyard wines by Wrigley and Geoff Rusack. The vineyards are located at Middle Ranch (Wrigley's family horse ranch) in the island's interior. ■**TIP**➜ **For a pleasant 4-mile hike out of Avalon, take Avalon Canyon Road to the Wrigley Botanical Garden and follow the trail to Lone Pine. At the top there's an amazing view of the Palisades cliffs and, beyond them, the sea.** ⊠ *708 Crescent Ave., Avalon* ☎ *310/510–2595* ⊕ *www.catalinaconservancy.org.*

PARASAILING
Catalina Parasailing

PARASAILING | FAMILY | Sail up, up, and away in a brightly colored parasail from Catalina Tours, until you are suspended up to 800 feet above the clear blue Pacific Ocean taking in the dolphins and bobbing boats in the harbor blow. Get fitted in a harness and vest for a solo, tandem, or three-at-a-time ride. If floating is not your thing, you can also pay $25 to just ride in the boat and enjoy the view. Sails take about one hour 15 minutes and depart from Green Pleasure Pier. ⊠ *20 Pleasure Pier, Avalon* ☎ *310/510–9280* ⊕ *islandwatercharters.com* ⊠ *$69.*

Chapter 6

LOS ANGELES

Updated by
Paul Feinstein, Michelle Rae Uy,
and Candice Yacono

👁 Sights	🍴 Restaurants	🛏 Hotels	👜 Shopping	🍸 Nightlife
★★★★★	★★★★★	★★★★★	★★★★★	★★★★☆

WELCOME TO LOS ANGELES

TOP REASONS TO GO

★ **Seeing stars:** Both through the telescope atop Griffith Park and among the residents of Beverly Hills.

★ **Good eats:** From food trucks to fine dining, an unparalleled meal awaits your palate.

★ **Beaches and boardwalks:** The dream of '80s Venice is alive in California.

★ **Shopping:** Peruse eclectic boutiques or window-shop on Rodeo Drive.

★ **Architecture:** Art-deco wonders to Frank Gehry masterpieces abound.

★ **Scenic drives:** You haven't seen the sunset until you've seen it from a winding L.A. road.

1 Santa Monica, Venice, and Brentwood. Expect a beach scene with a raffish mix of artists, beach punks, and yuppies. Upscale Brentwood has the Getty museum complex.

2 Beverly Hills. The glamour here includes Rodeo Drive's excesses—both wretched and ravishing.

3 West Hollywood and Fairfax. Here you can shop, eat, and be merry.

4 Hollywood and the Studios. Glitzy and tarnished, good and bad—Hollywood mirrors the entertainment business.

5 Mid-Wilshire and Koreatown. Mid-Wilshire has Museum Row. Koreatown has great restaurants and bars.

6 Downtown Los Angeles. An older district with stunning modern architecture.

7 Los Feliz, Silver Lake, and the Eastside. Head east for everything young, cool, and hip.

8 Pasadena. Arts and Crafts homes and two stellar museums mark this genteel area.

9 Malibu and the Beaches. En route to chichi Malibu, spy on sea lions at a white-sand beach.

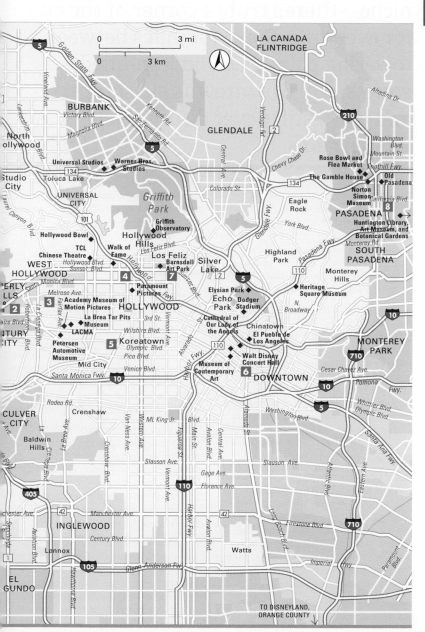

LA CANADA
FLINTRIDGE

BURBANK
Victory Blvd.

GLENDALE

Los Angeles is a polarizing place, but those who hate it just haven't found their niche—there's truly a corner of the city for everyone. Drive for miles between towering palm trees, bodega-lined streets, and Downtown's skyscrapers, and you'll still never discover all of L.A.'s hidden gems.

Of course, no trip to L.A. would be complete without spending time on a beach. Malibu is worth hitting if only for the drive along the Pacific Coast Highway. Santa Monica and Venice are closer, though less serene. Whether you're a surfer, skater, or volleyball player, however, there's a sandy stretch for you here.

It's impossible to deny that this is very much an "industry" town, even if the industry has more glam than grit. You'll see evidence of it while driving past hilltop mansions in Beverly Hills and while touring soundstages and sets at Warner Bros. or Universal Studios. You might even catch a glimpse of an A-lister eating lunch at the studio commissary. (Just remember to keep your cool with any celeb encounter—after all, this isn't a safari, and they're not animals.)

You might think that you'll have to spend most of your visit in a car along traffic-clogged freeways, but that shouldn't always be the case. There are plenty of walkable pockets like Venice's Abbot Kinney. In fact, exploring by foot is the only way to really get to know the various fringe neighborhoods and mini-cities that make up the vast L.A. area.

Regardless, no single locale—whether it's Malibu, Downtown, Beverly Hills, or Burbank—fully embodies Los Angeles. It really is in the mix that you can discover the city's character.

Planning

Getting Here and Around

AIR

Los Angeles International Airport (LAX) is served by more than 65 major airlines. All arrivals are from the lower level while departures are on the upper level. There's no Metro in or out of the airport, but it's coming in the not-too-distant-future.

Secondary airports include Hollywood Burbank Airport close to Downtown L.A. and the equally convenient Long Beach Airport. Flights to Orange County's John Wayne Airport are often more expensive than those to the other secondary airports. Also check out L.A./Ontario International Airport.

It will take you 20 minutes to get to Santa Monica, 30 minutes to Beverly Hills, and at least 45 minutes to Downtown L.A. In heavy traffic it can take much longer. From Burbank Airport, it's 30 minutes to Hollywood and Downtown. Plan on at least 45 minutes from Long Beach Airport and an hour from John Wayne Airport or L.A./Ontario International Airport.

If you're not renting a car, a taxi is the most convenient airport-transfer option. There's a flat rate of $50.50 between LAX and Downtown. Fares from LAX to other destinations (and from other airports) vary and may be metered. Alternatively, do what most Angelenos do: use Lyft or another ride-share service. The app estimates the cost (be mindful of surge pricing at busy times) before you accept the ride. Free LAX-it shuttles will take you from the airport to the nearby ride-share and taxi lots.

Shuttles are more cost-effective ($17 to $35) option, but you might need to book in advance. FlyAway buses, which travel between LAX and Van Nuys and Union Station in Downtown L.A., are the best deal at $9.75 (payable only by credit or debit card).

AIRPORTS Hollywood Burbank Airport. (*BUR*) ✉ *2627 N. Hollywood Way, near I–5 and U.S. 101, Burbank* ☎ *818/840– 8840* ⊕ *www.hollywoodburbankairport. com.* **John Wayne Airport.** (*SNA*) ✉ *18601 Airport Way, Santa Ana* ☎ *949/252–5200* ⊕ *www.ocair.com.* **L.A./Ontario International Airport.** (*ONT*) ✉ *2500 E. Airport Dr., off I–10, Ontario* ☎ *909/544–5300* ⊕ *www.flyontario.com.* **Long Beach Airport.** (*LGB*) ✉ *4100 Donald Douglas Dr., Long Beach* ☎ *562/570–2600* ⊕ *www. lgb.org.* **Los Angeles International Airport.** (*LAX*) ✉ *1 World Way, off Hwy. 1, Los Angeles* ☎ *855/463–5252* ⊕ *www.flylax. com.*

SHUTTLES FlyAway. ✉ *Los Angeles* ☎ *714/507–1170* ⊕ *www.flylax.com/en/ flyaway-bus.* **SuperShuttle.** ✉ *Los Angeles* ☎ *800/258–3826* ⊕ *www.supershuttle. com.*

BUS

Many local trips can, with time and patience, be made on Los Angeles County Metropolitan Transit Authority buses. In certain cases—visiting the Getty Center or Universal Studios—they might even be your best option. There's also a special Dodger Stadium Express that shuttles passengers between Union Station and the world-famous ballpark.

Metro Buses cost $1.75, which includes a two-hour window for a transfer to another bus or the subway. A one-day pass costs $3.50 and a weekly pass, valid from Sunday through Saturday, is $12.50 for unlimited travel on all buses and trains. For the fastest service, look for the red-and-white Metro Rapid buses, which stop less frequently and can extend green lights. There are 25 Bus Rapid Transit (BRT) routes, including along Wilshire and Vermont Boulevards.

DASH minibuses cover six circular routes in Hollywood, Mid-Wilshire, and Downtown. You pay 50¢ every time you get on. The Santa Monica Municipal Bus Line, also known as the Big Blue Bus, is a pleasant and inexpensive ($1.10) way to move around the Westside.

On MTA, Santa Monica, and Culver City buses you can pay fares with cash, but you must have exact change. You can also buy MTA TAP cards at Metro Rail stations, customer centers throughout the city, and some convenience and grocery stores.

CONTACTS Culver CityBus. ✉ *Los Angeles* ☎ *310/253–6510* ⊕ *www.culvercitybus. com.* **DASH.** ✉ *Los Angeles* ☎ *310/808– 2273* ⊕ *www.ladottransit.com.* **Los Angeles County Metropolitan Transit Authority.** ✉ *Los Angeles* ☎ *323/466–3876* ⊕ *www. metro.net.* **Santa Monica Big Blue Bus.** ✉ *Los Angeles* ☎ *310/451–5444* ⊕ *www. bigbluebus.com.*

CAR

Unless you're used to urban driving, navigating L.A. can be unnerving. That said, unlike many older big cities, L.A. has evolved with drivers in mind. Streets are wide, and parking garages abound.

Be very specific when inputting addresses into a GPS or asking for directions as L.A. has plenty of identically or similarly named streets (e.g., Beverly Boulevard and Beverly Drive). In addition, expect sudden changes in addresses as streets pass through neighborhoods, then incorporated cities, then back into neighborhoods. This can be most bewildering on Robertson Boulevard, a useful north–south artery that crosses through L.A., West Hollywood, and Beverly Hills.

■ TIP➜ If you get discombobulated while on the freeway, remember: even-numbered freeways run east and west, odd-numbered freeways run north and south.

Parking rules are strictly enforced, and illegally parked cars are ticketed or towed quickly, so read signs carefully. Parking rates vary from 25¢ (meters and public lots) to $2 per 15-minutes (private lots). Downtown and Century City rates may be as high as $25 an hour. At some shops, most restaurants, and hotels, valet parking is virtually assumed. The cost is $6 to $16 for restaurants, but can be as high as $70 for hotels. Keep small bills on hand to tip the valets.

METRO/PUBLIC TRANSPORT

Metro Rail covers only a small part of L.A., but it's convenient, frequent, and inexpensive. Most popular with visitors is the underground B Line, which runs from Downtown's Union Station through Mid-Wilshire, Hollywood, and Universal City en route to North Hollywood, stopping at popular tourist destinations along the way. Other key lines are the light-rail C Line (LAX and Redondo Beach–Norwalk), the partially underground A Line (Azusa–Long Beach), the D Line (Union Station–Wilshire/Western), and the E Line (East Los Angeles–Santa Monica).

Daily service is offered from about 4:30 am to 1:30 am, with departures every 5 to 15 minutes. On weekends trains run until 2 am. Buy tickets from station vending machines; fares are $1.75 or $3.50 for an all-day pass.

CONTACTS Los Angeles County Metropolitan Transit Authority. ✉ *Los Angeles* ☎ *323/466–3876* ⊕ *www.metro.net.*

TAXI /RIDE SHARING

Instead of trying to hail a taxi on the street, phone one of the many taxi companies. The Curb Taxi app allows for online hailing of L.A. taxis. The metered rate is $2.70 per mile, plus a $2.85 per-fare charge and an additional $2 curb fee. Taxi rides from LAX have an additional $4 surcharge. Be aware that distances are greater than they might appear on the map so fares add up quickly.

Request a ride using apps like Lyft or Uber, and a driver will usually arrive within minutes. Note, though, that fares increase during busy times.

CONTACTS Beverly Hills Cab Co. ✉ *Los Angeles* ☎ *800/273–6611* ⊕ *www.beverlyhillscabco.com.* **Independent Cab Co.** ✉ *Los Angeles* ☎ *800/521–8294* ⊕ *www.lataxi.com/new.* **United Checker Cab.** ✉ *Los Angeles* ☎ *877/201-8294* ⊕ *www.unitedcheckercab.com/taxi-los-angeles.html.* **Yellow Cab Los Angeles.** ✉ *Los Angeles* ☎ *424/222–2222* ⊕ *www.layellowcab.com.*

TRAIN

Downtown's Union Station is the place to catch an Amtrak, Metrolink commuter train, or Metro B and D lines. It's also one of the great American railroad terminals, with comfortable seating, restaurants, and bars.

Among Amtrak's Southern California routes are 13 daily trips to San Diego and 5 to Santa Barbara. The luxury *Coast Starlight* travels along the spectacular coastline from Seattle to Los Angeles in just a day and a half (though it's often a little late). The *Sunset Limited* arrives from New Orleans, and the *Southwest Chief* comes from Chicago.

CONTACTS Metrolink. ✉ *Los Angeles* ☎ *800/371–5465* ⊕ *www.metrolinktrains. com.* **Union Station.** ✉ *800 N. Alameda St., Downtown* ☎ *213/683–6979* ⊕ *www. unionstationla.com* Ⓜ *Union Station.*

Hotels

Hotels in Los Angeles today are more than just a place to rest your head; they're a key part of the experience. From luxurious digs in Beverly Hills and along the coast to budget boutiques in Hollywood, hotels are stepping up service, upgrading amenities, and trying all-new concepts, like upscale hostels and retro-chic motels.

Taxes will add 10%–14% to your bill depending on where in Los Angeles County you stay. Some hoteliers tack on energy, service, or occupancy surcharges—ask about customary charges when you book your room.

Don't write off the pricier establishments immediately. Specials abound, particularly in Downtown on the weekends. Many hotels have packages that include breakfast, theater tickets, spa services, or luxury rental cars. Pricing is competitive, so always check with the hotel for current special offers, including online exclusives.

Restaurants

Los Angeles may be known for its beach living and star-studded backdrop, but it was once a farm town. The hillsides were covered in citrus orchards and dairy farms, and agriculture was a major industry. Today, even as L.A. is urbanized, the city's culinary landscape has reembraced a local, sustainable, and seasonal philosophy at many levels—from fine dining to street snacks.

Although the status of the chef carries weight in this town (people follow the culinary zeitgeist with the same fervor

as celebrity gossip), international eats continue to be a backbone of the dining scene. People head to Koreatown for epic Korean cooking and late-night coffeehouses and to West L.A. for phenomenal sushi. Latin food is particularly well represented, with everything from Guatemalan eateries and Peruvian restaurants to nouveau Mexican bistros and Tijuana-style taco trucks.

⇨ *Restaurant and hotel reviews have been shortened. For full information, visit Fodors.com. Restaurant prices are the average cost of a main course at dinner, or if dinner isn't served, at lunch. Hotel prices are the lowest cost of a standard double room in high season.*

What It Costs			
$	$$	$$$	$$$$
RESTAURANTS			
under $20	$20–$30	$31–$40	over $40
HOTELS			
under $200	$200–$350	$351–$500	over $500

Tours

Tours are a great way to experience L.A.'s individual neighborhoods, allowing for greater insight on the city as a whole. Of course, you'll be spoiled for choice in terms of celebrity-themed offerings, including behind-the-scenes options at the movie studios.

Access Hollywood Celebrity Homes Tours
SPECIAL-INTEREST TOURS | FAMILY | This company takes groups in an open-air van through the glitzy streets of Beverly Hills where you can see homes belonging to the likes of A-listers like Mick Jagger, Tom Cruise, Katy Perry, and many more. ✉ *Los Angeles* ☎ *323/472–7938* ⊕ *www. accesshollywoodtours.com* 🎫 *From $39* ☞ *2-person minimum for tickets.*

Neon Cruise

DRIVING TOURS | Soak up the glow of classic neon signs around L.A. from an open double-decker bus on tours offered by the Museum of Neon Art. There are also walking tours through different neighborhoods like Chinatown, the Broadway Theatre District, Hollywood, and more. ⊠ *Los Angeles* ☎ *818/696–2149* ⊕ *www. neonmona.org/neon-cruise* ☞ *$65.*

Sidewalk Food Tours

SPECIAL-INTEREST TOURS | For food lovers, the Sidewalk Food Tours are unique walking tours around Los Angeles that let you explore this incredible city through its many cuisines. Tours are broken up between West Hollywood and Downtown L.A., run for 2½ hours, and hit five to seven different food outlets along the way. ⊠ *1933 Bronson Ave., Los Angeles* ☎ *877/568–6877* ⊕ *www.sidewalkfoodtours.com/los-angeles* ☞ *$75.*

Starline Tours

GUIDED TOURS | FAMILY | Operating double-decker and open-roof-van tours, Starline Tours offers hop-on/off tours around town. Passengers are picked up from the TCL Chinese Theatre and in Santa Monica. ⊠ *6801 Hollywood Blvd., Hollywood* ☎ *323/463–3333* ⊕ *www.starlinetours. com* ☞ *From $39* Ⓜ *Hollywood/Highland.*

Visitor Information

CONTACTS **Discover Los Angeles.** ⊠ *Los Angeles* ☎ *213/624–7300* ⊕ *www.discoverlosangeles.com.*

When to Go

Almost any time of the year is the right time to go to Los Angeles; the climate is mild and pleasant year-round. Winter brings crisp, sunny, unusually smogless days from about November to May (expect brief rains from December to April). Los Angeles summers, which are virtually rainless, can lead to air-quality alerts. Prices skyrocket and reservations are a must when tourism peaks from July through early October.

Santa Monica, Venice, and Brentwood

Pedestrian-friendly Santa Monica and Venice are two of the region's most iconic destinations, but while Santa Monica has its eyes firmly on the future thanks to Silicon Beach, California's tech hub, Venice enjoys indulging a bit in its past. To spend the day like an A-lister, head to nearby Brentwood, where you'll find high-end shopping, fine dining, and the Getty Center museum complex.

Santa Monica

◉ Sights

★ **Santa Monica Pier**

AMUSEMENT PARK/CARNIVAL | FAMILY | Souvenir shops, carnival games, arcades, eateries, an outdoor trapeze school, a small amusement park, and an aquarium all contribute to the festive atmosphere of this truncated pier at the foot of Colorado Boulevard below Palisades Park. The pier's trademark 46-horse Looff Carousel, built in 1922, has appeared in several films, including *The Sting.* The Soda Jerks ice-cream fountain (named for the motion the attendant makes when pulling the machine's arm) inside the carousel building is a pier staple, and the MariaSol restaurant at the end of the pier serves great fajitas. Free concerts are held on the pier in the summer. ⊠ *Colorado Ave., Santa Monica* ☎ *310/458–8901* ⊕ *www. santamonicapier.org.*

Third Street Promenade and Santa Monica Place

BUSINESS DISTRICT | Stretch your legs along this pedestrian-only, three-block stretch of 3rd Street, close to the Pacific,

Santa Monica Pier's West Coaster and Pacific Wheel provide incredible ocean views.

lined with jacaranda trees, ivy-topiary dinosaur fountains, strings of lights, and branches of many major U.S. retail chains; indeed, it always seems to house the most-coveted brands for each generation of teens. Outdoor cafés, street vendors, movie theaters, and a rich nightlife make this a main gathering spot for locals, visitors, street artists and musicians, and performance artists, though it has yet to return to its pre-2020 level of bustle. Plan a night just to take it all in or take an afternoon for a long people-watching stroll. There's plenty of parking in city structures on the streets flanking the promenade. Santa Monica Place, at the south end of the promenade, is a sleek outdoor mall and foodie haven. Its three stories are home to Nordstrom, Louis Vuitton, Coach, and other upscale retailers. Don't miss the ocean views from the rooftop food court. ⊠ *3rd St., between Colorado and Wilshire Blvds., Santa Monica* ⊕ *www. downtownsm.com.*

🜄 Beaches

Santa Monica State Beach

BEACH | FAMILY | The first beach you'll hit after the Santa Monica Freeway (Interstate 10) runs into the Pacific Coast Highway, wide and sandy Santa Monica is *the* place for sunning and socializing. The Strand, which runs across the beach and for 22 miles in total, is popular among walkers, joggers, and bicyclists. Be prepared for a mob scene on summer weekends, when parking becomes an expensive ordeal. Swimming is fine (with the usual poststorm-pollution caveat); for surfing, go elsewhere. For a memorable view, climb up the stairway over PCH to Palisades Park, at the top of the bluffs. Free summer concerts are held on the pier on Thursday evenings. **Amenities:** food and drink; lifeguards; parking; showers; toilets; water sports. **Best for:** partiers; sunset; surfing; swimming; walking. ⊠ *1642 Promenade, PCH at California Incline, Santa Monica* ☎ *310/458–8573* ⊕ *www.smgov.net/portals/beach* 🚗 *Parking from $7 winter/$15 summer.*

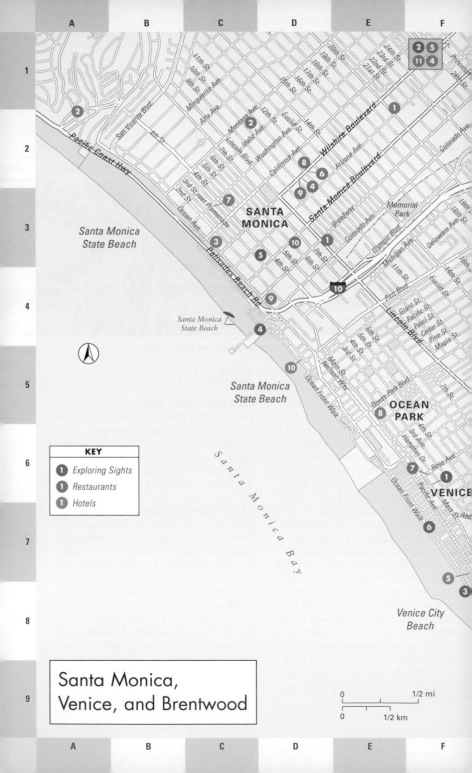

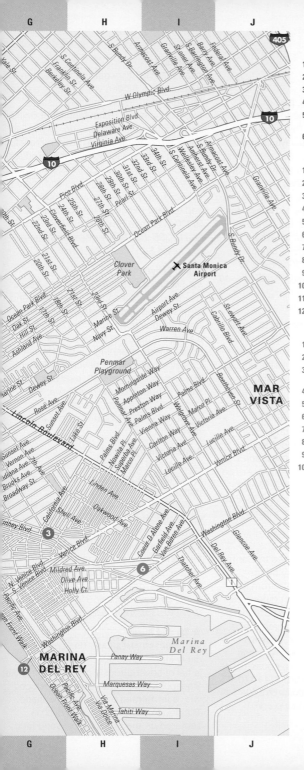

6

Los Angeles SANTA MONICA, VENICE, AND BRENTWOOD

Sights ▼

1 Binoculars Building **F6**
2 The Getty Center.................... **F1**
3 Muscle Beach **F8**
4 Santa Monica Pier................ **D4**
5 Third Street Promenade and
   Santa Monica Place.............. **D3**
6 Venice Beach Boardwalk **F7**

Restaurants ▼

1 Bay Cities Italian Deli **D3**
2 Father's Office **C2**
3 Gjelina........................... **G7**
4 Huckleberry Bakery and Cafe.... **D2**
5 Lady Chocolatt **F1**
6 Mélisse **D2**
7 Rose Cafe.......................... **F6**
8 Rustic Canyon..................... **D2**
9 Santa Monica Seafood **D2**
10 Tar and Roses **D3**
11 Toscana........................... **F1**
12 Venice Whaler **G8**

Hotels ▼

1 The Ambrose **E2**
2 Channel Road Inn.................. **A2**
3 Fairmont Miramar Hotel and
   Bungalows Santa Monica.........**C3**
4 Hotel Bel-Air **F1**
5 Hotel Erwin **F7**
6 The Kinney.......................... **I7**
7 Palihouse Santa Monica...........**C3**
8 Sea Shore Motel.................... **E5**
9 Shore Hotel........................ **D4**
10 Shutters on the Beach **D5**

🍴 Restaurants

★ Bay Cities Italian Deli

$ | **SANDWICHES** | Part deli, part market, Bay Cities has been home to incredible Italian subs since 1925. This renowned counter-service spot is always crowded (best to order ahead), but monster subs run the gamut from the mighty meatball to the signature Godmother, made with prosciutto, ham, capicola, mortadella, Genoa salami, and provolone. **Known for:** market with rare imports; old-school, deli-style service; huge sandwiches. [$] *Average main: $10* ✉ *1517 Lincoln Blvd., Santa Monica* ☎ *310/395–8279* 🌐 *www.baycitiesitaliandeli.com* 🕒 *Closed Mon. and Tues.*

Father's Office

$ | **AMERICAN** | Distinguished by its vintage neon sign, this gastropub is famous for handcrafted beers and a brilliant signature burger (along with a substantial and excellent menu). Topped with Gruyère and Maytag blue cheeses, arugula, caramelized onions, and applewood-smoked bacon compote, the Office Burger is a guilty pleasure worth waiting in line for, which is usually required. **Known for:** addictive sweet potato fries; strict no-substitutions policy; 36 craft beers on tap. [$] *Average main: $15* ✉ *1018 Montana Ave., Santa Monica* ☎ *310/736–2224* 🌐 *www.fathersoffice.com* 🕒 *Closed Mon. No lunch weekdays.*

Huckleberry Bakery and Cafe

$ | **AMERICAN** | **FAMILY** | Founded by Santa Monica natives, Huckleberry brings together the best ingredients from local farmers and growers to craft diner-style comfort food with a chic twist. Nearly everything is made on-site, even the hot sauce and almond milk. **Known for:** from-scratch diner-style breakfast options; delectable pastries; house-made cold brew. [$] *Average main: $14* ✉ *1014 Wilshire Blvd., Santa Monica* ☎ *310/451–2311* 🌐 *www.huckleberrycafe.com.*

★ Mélisse

$$$$ | **FRENCH** | It's a gem tucked within a treasure box: hidden within Citrin, a one-Michelin-star restaurant, is Mélisse, a two-Michelin-star restaurant. Chef-owner Josiah Citrin entrusts chef de cuisine Ian Scaramuzza to blend his modern French cooking with seasonal California produce at this Santa Monica institution. **Known for:** the epitome of freshness and inventiveness; only 14 seats; contemporary and elegant decor. [$] *Average main: $399* ✉ *1104 Wilshire Blvd., Santa Monica* ☎ *310/395–0881* 🌐 *www.melisse.com* 🕒 *Closed Sun.–Tues. No lunch.*

Rustic Canyon

$$$ | **MODERN AMERICAN** | A Santa Monica mainstay, the seasonally changing menu at this farm-to-table restaurant consistently upends norms and has even earned a Michelin nod. The homey, minimalist space offers sweeping views of Wilshire Boulevard. **Known for:** never-ending wine list; knowledgeable staff; everything is made in-house. [$] *Average main: $40* ✉ *1119 Wilshire Blvd., Santa Monica* ☎ *310/393–7050* 🌐 *www.rusticcanyonrestaurant.com.*

Santa Monica Seafood

$$ | **SEAFOOD** | **FAMILY** | A Southern California favorite that seems like a tourist trap at first blush but decidedly isn't, this Italian seafood haven has been serving up fresh fish since 1939. This freshness comes from its pedigree as the largest seafood distributor in the Southwest. **Known for:** deliciously seasoned fresh entrées; oyster bar; historic fish market. [$] *Average main: $20* ✉ *1000 Wilshire Blvd., Santa Monica* ☎ *310/393–5244* 🌐 *www.santamonicaseafood.com.*

★ Tar and Roses

$$$ | **MODERN AMERICAN** | This small and dimly lit, romantic spot in Santa Monica is full of adventurously global options, like Singaporean chili crab cake or black cod with a fermented black bean marinade. The new American cuisine, which is centered on the restaurant's wood-fired

oven, also features standouts like braised lamb shank with sweet potato, pomegranate, *labneh, zhough,* and flatbread. **Known for:** phenomenal oxtail dumplings; global inspirations; ever-changing menu. $ *Average main: $36 ⊠ 602 Santa Monica Blvd., Santa Monica* ☎ *310/587–0700* ⊕ *www.tarandroses.com.*

🛏 Hotels

The Ambrose

$$$ | HOTEL | Tranquility pervades the airy, California Craftsman–style, four-story Ambrose, which blends right into its mostly residential Santa Monica neighborhood. **Pros:** partial ocean views; "green" practices like nontoxic cleaners and recycling bins; nice amenities (like car service and wine reception) for a $25 extra fee. **Cons:** quiet, residential area of Santa Monica; parking fee ($39); not walking distance to beach. $ *Rooms from: $389 ⊠ 1255 20th St., Santa Monica* ☎ *310/315–1555, 877/262–7673* ⊕ *www.ambrosehotel.com* 🛏 *77 rooms* ❌ *No Meals.*

★ Channel Road Inn

$$$ | B&B/INN | A quaint surprise in Southern California, the Channel Road Inn is every bit the country retreat bed-and-breakfast lovers adore, with four-poster beds, fluffy duvets, and a cozy living room with a fireplace. **Pros:** free wine-and-cheese hour each afternoon; home-cooked breakfast included; meditative rose garden on-site. **Cons:** no pool; need a car (or Uber) to get around; decidedly non-L.A. decor is not for everyone. $ *Rooms from: $365 ⊠ 219 W. Channel Rd., Santa Monica* ☎ *310/459–1920* ⊕ *www.channelroadinn.com* 🛏 *15 rooms* ❌ *Free Breakfast.*

Fairmont Miramar Hotel and Bungalows Santa Monica

$$$$ | HOTEL | A mammoth Moreton Bay fig tree dwarfs the main entrance of the 5-acre, beach-adjacent Santa Monica wellness retreat and lends its name to the inviting on-site Mediterranean-inspired restaurant, FIG, which focuses on local ingredients and frequently refreshes its menu. **Pros:** coveted central location with a private club feel; swanky open-air cocktail spot, the Bungalow, on-site; retrofitted '20s and '40s bungalows. **Cons:** all this luxury comes at a big price; standard rooms are on the small side; breakfast not included. $ *Rooms from: $599 ⊠ 101 Wilshire Blvd., Santa Monica* ☎ *310/576–7777, 866/540–4470* ⊕ *www. fairmont.com/santamonica* 🛏 *297 rooms* ❌ *No Meals.*

Palihouse Santa Monica

$$$ | HOTEL | Tucked in a posh residential area three blocks from the sea and lively Third Street Promenade, Palihouse Santa Monica caters to design-minded world travelers, with spacious rooms and suites decked out in whimsical antiques. **Pros:** Apple TV in rooms; walking distance to Santa Monica attractions; fully equipped kitchens. **Cons:** no pool; decor might not appeal to more traditional travelers; parking fee ($45). $ *Rooms from: $450 ⊠ 1001 3rd St., Santa Monica* ☎ *310/394–1279* ⊕ *www.palihousesantamonica.com* 🛏 *38 rooms* ❌ *No Meals.*

Sea Shore Motel

$$ | HOTEL | On Santa Monica's busy Main Street, the Sea Shore (family-owned for five decades) is a charming throwback to Route 66 and to '60s-style roadside motels, nestled in an ultratrendy neighborhood. **Pros:** close to beach and restaurants; free Wi-Fi, parking, and use of beach equipment; popular rooftop deck. **Cons:** street noise; motel-style decor and beds; not the Santa Monica style a lot of people are looking for. $ *Rooms from: $200 ⊠ 2637 Main St., Santa Monica* ☎ *310/392–2787* ⊕ *www.seashoremotel. com* 🛏 *25 rooms* ❌ *No Meals.*

Shore Hotel

$$$ | HOTEL | With views of the Santa Monica Pier, this hotel with a friendly staff offers eco-minded travelers stylish rooms with a modern design, just steps from the sand and sea. **Pros:** near beach and Third Street Promenade; rainfall showerheads; solar-heated pool and hot tub. **Cons:** expensive rooms and parking fees; fronting busy Ocean Avenue; some sharing a room may be wary of the see-through shower. $ *Rooms from: $399* ✉ *1515 Ocean Ave., Santa Monica* ☎ *310/458–1515* ⊕ *shorehotel.com* ⇥ *164 rooms* ⦿ *No Meals.*

★ Shutters on the Beach

$$$$ | **HOTEL** | **FAMILY** | Set right on the sand, this Cape Cod–inspired inn has become synonymous with staycations, with the beachfront location and show-house decor making it one of SoCal's most popular luxury hotels. **Pros:** built-in cabinets filled with art books and curios; restaurants you'll never tire of dining in; bathrooms come with whirlpool tubs. **Cons:** have to pay for extras like beach chairs; very expensive; breakfast not included. $ *Rooms from: $675* ✉ *1 Pico Blvd., Santa Monica* ☎ *310/458–0030, 800/334–9000* ⊕ *www.shuttersonthebeach.com* ⇥ *198 rooms* ⦿ *No Meals.*

🍸 Nightlife

★ Chez Jay

BARS | Around since 1959, this dive bar and steak joint continues to be a well-loved place in Santa Monica. Everyone from the young to the old (including families) frequents this historical landmark, where Marilyn Monroe is said to have once canoodled with JFK. It's a charming place, from the well-worn booths with their red-checkered tablecloths to the ship's wheel near the door. Photographs are discouraged, but if you ask politely, you can learn how one of the restaurant's famous free peanuts ended up on a trip to the Moon. The backyard lounge is perfect for warm, low-key days; the grub's solid, with a more contemporary menu, and the happy hour is popular amongst locals and tourists alike. ✉ *1657 Ocean Ave., Santa Monica* ☎ *310/395–1741* ⊕ *www.chezjays.com.*

The Galley

BARS | Nostalgia reigns at this true neighborhood fixture, which opened in 1934 and has had the same owner for more than 30 years. As Santa Monica's oldest restaurant and bar, the Galley has a consistent nautical theme inside and out: the boatlike exterior features wavy blue neon lights and porthole windows. Inside, fishing nets and anchors adorn the walls, and the whole place is aglow with colorful string lights. Most patrons tend to crowd the center bar, with the more dinner-oriented folks frequenting the booths. The back patio is also a solid choice in good weather, especially for weekend brunch. And strangely enough, the secret-recipe salad dressing is justifiably famous. ✉ *2442 Main St., Santa Monica* ☎ *310/452–1934* ⊕ *www. thegalleyrestaurant.net.*

🛍 Shopping

Brat

MIXED CLOTHING | If your trip to La La Land has you itching to upgrade your wardrobe with a little attitude, look no further than Brat. No matter what your proclivity—be it rockabilly, Goth, punk, or cottagecore—Brat has that unique item you didn't even know you needed. It's also a perfect place to find something "L.A. cool" for folks back home. ✉ *1938 14th St., Santa Monica* ☎ *310/452–2480* ⊕ *www. bratstore.com.*

Venice

👁 Sights

Binoculars Building

NOTABLE BUILDING | Frank Gehry is known around the world for his architectural masterpieces. In L.A. alone he's responsible for multiple houses and buildings like the Gehry Residence, Loyola Law School, and Walt Disney Hall. But one of his most interesting creations, completed in 1991, is the Binoculars Building, a quirky Venice spot that is exactly as advertised: a giant set of binoculars standing on their end. The project was originally designed for the Chiat/Day advertising agency and today is home to one of Google's Silicon Beach offices. While you can't tour the building, you can take a clever Instagram shot out front. ✉ *340 Main St., Venice.*

Muscle Beach

OTHER ATTRACTION | Bronzed young men bench-pressing five girls at once, weightlifters doing tricks on the sand—the Muscle Beach facility fired up the country's imagination from the get-go. There are actually two spots known as Muscle Beach. The original Muscle Beach, just south of the Santa Monica Pier, is where bodybuilders Jack LaLanne and Vic and Armand Tanny used to work out in the 1950s. When it was closed in 1959, the bodybuilders moved south along the beach to Venice, to a city-run facility known as "the Pen," and the Venice Beach spot inherited the Muscle Beach moniker. The spot is probably best known now as a place where a young Arnold Schwarzenegger first came to flex his muscles in the late '60s and began his rise to fame. The area now hosts a variety of sports and gymnastics events, along with occasional "beach babe" beauty contests that always draw a crowd. But stop by any time during daylight for an eye-popping array of beefcakes (and would-be beefcakes). ✉ *1800 Ocean Front Walk, Venice* 🌐 *www.musclebeach.net.*

★ Venice Beach Boardwalk

PROMENADE | The surf and sand of Venice are fine, but the main attraction here is the boardwalk scene, which is a cosmos all its own. Go on weekend afternoons for the best people-watching experience; you'll see everything from Baywatch wannabes to break-dancers to TikTok influencers to would-be messiahs. You can also swim, fish, surf, and skateboard, or have a go at racquetball, handball, shuffleboard, and basketball (the boardwalk is the site of hotly contested pickup games). Or you can rent a bike or in-line skates and hit the Strand bike path, then poke around the gloriously tacky tourist and souvenir shops before pulling up a seat at a sidewalk café and watching the action unfold. ✉ *1800 Ocean Front Walk, west of Pacific Ave., Venice* ☎ *310/392–4687* 🌐 *www.venicebeach.com.*

🍴 Restaurants

★ Gjelina

$$ | **AMERICAN** | Walk through the rustic wooden door and into a softly lit dining room with long communal tables and a lively crowd; come later in the night and the place heats up with an enthusiastic post-pub crowd lured by the seasonal menu and outstanding small plates, charcuterie, pastas, and pizza. Begin with a pizza made with house-made chorizo, grilled pear with burrata and prosciutto, or Snow Island oysters. **Known for:** lively crowd on the patio; late-night menu; Michelin-recommended restaurant. [$] *Average main: $22* ✉ *1429 Abbot Kinney Blvd., Venice* ☎ *310/450–1429* 🌐 *www.gjelina.com.*

Rose Cafe

$$ | **MODERN AMERICAN** | **FAMILY** | This indoor–outdoor restaurant has served Venice for more than four decades but constantly reinvents itself, serving mouthwatering California cuisines and offering multiple patios, a full bar, and a bakery. Creative types sip espressos and tap on keyboards under the macramé chandeliers, while young families gather out back to snack on smoked radiatore carbonara and crispy brussels sprouts. **Known for:** sophisticated but unpretentious vibe; location in the heart of Venice; lively patio seating. [$] *Average main: $25* ✉ *220 Rose Ave., Venice* ☎ *310/399–0711* 🌐 *www.rosecafevenice.com.*

Venice Whaler

$ | AMERICAN | This beachfront bar has been the local watering hole for musicians like the Beatles, the Doors, and the Beach Boys since 1944. It boasts an amazing view and serves tasty California pub food like fish tacos, pulled-pork sliders, and avocado toast with a basic selection of beers. **Known for:** rock and roll history; great pub food; fun brunch. $ *Average main: $15* ⊠ *10 W. Washington Blvd., Venice* ☏ *310/821–8737* ⊕ *www.venicewhaler.com.*

Hotels

Hotel Erwin

$$$ | HOTEL | A boutique hotel a block off the Venice Beach Boardwalk, the Erwin will make you feel like a hipper version of yourself. **Pros:** dining emphasizing fresh ingredients; playful design in guest rooms; free Wi-Fi and use of hotel bikes and beach equipment. **Cons:** some rooms face a noisy alley; no pool; $49 valet parking. $ *Rooms from: $395* ⊠ *1697 Pacific Ave., Venice* ☏ *310/452–1111, 800/786–7789* ⊕ *www.hotelerwin.com* ⇘ *119 rooms* ⃝ *No Meals.*

★ The Kinney

$$ | HOTEL | Walking distance to Venice Beach and Abbot Kinney's artsy commercial strip, this playful hotel announces itself boldly with wall murals by Melissa Scrivner before you even enter the lobby. **Pros:** affordable, artistic rooms; Ping-Pong area; Jacuzzi bar. **Cons:** valet parking is a must ($15); hotel can get loud; some hipper-than-thou vibes. $ *Rooms from: $239* ⊠ *737 Washington Blvd., Venice* ☏ *310/821–4455* ⊕ *www.thekinneyvenicebeach.com* ⇘ *68 rooms* ⃝ *No Meals.*

🛍 Shopping

Coutula

WOMEN'S CLOTHING | Owner Carrie Hauman of Coutula (a portmanteau of "Couture L.A.") travels around the globe to hand-select the clothing, accessories, jewelry, and home furnishings sold in her light-filled, airy Abbot Kinney 1930s cottage. Nab anything from a $10 bracelet to a $6,000 necklace here, along with floaty sundresses that look much more expensive than they are, handmade Cut n Paste leather handbags, and bliss-inducing Tyler candles. ⊠ *1204 Abbot Kinney Blvd., Venice* ☏ *310/581–8010* ⊕ *www.coutula.com.*

General Store

GENERAL STORE | Right at home in the beachy, bohemian neighborhood, this well-curated shop is a decidedly contemporary take on the concept of general stores. The very definition of "California cool," General Store offers beauty and bath products loaded with organic natural ingredients, handmade ceramics, linen tea towels, and a spot-on selection of art books. Featuring an impressive number of local makers and designers, the boutique also sells modern, minimalist clothing and has a kids' section that will wow even the hippest moms and dads. ⊠ *1801 Lincoln Blvd., Venice* ☏ *310/751–6393* ⊕ *www.shop-generalstore.com.*

Brentwood

◉ Sights

★ The Getty Center

ART MUSEUM | FAMILY | Architect Richard Meier's Getty Center features stunning design, uncommon gardens, and fascinating art collections. The complex's rough-cut travertine marble skin seems to soak up the light on a sunny day. From the underground parking structure at the base of the hill, walk or take a smooth, computer-driven tram up the steep slope, checking out the Bel Air estates across the 405 freeway. From the courtyard, plazas, and walkways, you can survey the city from the San Gabriel Mountains to the ocean. In a ravine separating the museum and the Getty Research Institute, artist Robert Irwin created the

Central Garden in stark contrast to Meier's geometrical designs. Though the two sniped at each other during construction (Irwin stirred the pot with every loose twist his garden path took), the result is a refreshing garden walk whose focal point is an azalea maze—some insist the Mickey Mouse shape is on purpose—in a reflecting pool.

Inside the pavilions are permanent collections of European paintings, drawings, sculpture, illuminated manuscripts, and decorative arts, as well as world-class temporary exhibitions and photographs gathered internationally. The collection of French furniture and decorative arts, especially from the early years of Louis XIV to the end of the reign of Louis XVI, is renowned for its quality and condition. You'll also find works by Rembrandt, Van Gogh, Monet, and James Ensor. Dining options include the upscale restaurant and the cafeteria with panoramic window views, plus outdoor coffee carts. ■ **TIP→ On-site parking is subject to availability and can fill up by midday on holidays and in the summer, so try to come early in the day or after lunch.** ✉ *1200 Getty Center Dr., Brentwood* ☎ *310/440–7300* 🌐 *www.getty.edu* 🎟 *Free; parking $15* 🕒 *Closed Mon.*

🍴 Restaurants

Lady Chocolatt

$ | BELGIAN | The purveyor of the finest Belgian chocolate in all of Los Angeles, Lady Chocolatt is the perfect answer to the age-old question of what to gift on any special occasion. The ornate display case is filled with dark chocolate truffles, hazelnut pralines, Grand Marnier ganaches, and so much more, all handcrafted by a Master Chocolatier in Belgium. **Known for:** Belgian chocolate; Italian espresso; tasty sandwiches. [$] *Average main: $5* ✉ *12008 Wilshire Blvd., Brentwood* ☎ *310/442–2245* 🕒 *Closed Sun.*

Toscana

$$$ | ITALIAN | This rustic trattoria along San Vicente has been a favorite celebrity haunt for decades. Expect elevated sensory offerings, from its cozy atmosphere to its mouthwatering Tuscan and Italian fare (including carpaccio and gnocchi primavera) and excellent wine list. **Known for:** excellent wine list; seasonal menu; great celeb-spotting. [$] *Average main: $35* ✉ *11633 San Vicente Blvd., Brentwood* ☎ *310/820–2448* 🌐 *www.toscanabrentwood.com.*

🛏 Hotels

★ Hotel Bel-Air

$$$$ | HOTEL | This Spanish Mission–style icon has been a discreet hillside retreat for celebrities and society types since 1946 and was given a face-lift by star designers Alexandra Champalimaud and David Rockwell. **Pros:** shuttle available within 3-mile radius of hotel; perfect for the privacy-minded; alfresco dining at Wolfgang Puck restaurant. **Cons:** not walking distance to restaurants or shops; hefty price tag; controversial ownership by the Sultan of Brunei. [$] *Rooms from: $1,175* ✉ *701 Stone Canyon Rd., Bel Air* ☎ *310/472–1211* 🌐 *www.dorchestercollection.com/en/los-angeles/hotel-bel-air* 🔑 *103 rooms* 🍽 *No Meals.*

🛍 Shopping

Brentwood Country Mart

SHOPPING CENTER | This family-friendly faux country market was first built in the postwar boom of the 1940s and remains a staple of the community. Among the dozens of stores are Goop (Gwyneth Paltrow's lifestyle brand's gorgeous first brick-and-mortar store), Turpan (for luxury home goods), James Perse (for laid-back cotton knits), Jenni Kayne (for a curated mix of modern clothing, housewares, and gifts), and Malia Mills (for American-made swimwear separates). Grab a chicken basket at Reddi Chick and chow down on the open-air patio. ✉ *225 26th St., at San Vicente Blvd., Brentwood* ☎ *310/458–6682* ⊕ *www.brentwood-countrymart.com.*

Beverly Hills

The rumors are true: Beverly Hills delivers on a dramatic, cinematic scale of wealth and excess. A known celebrity haunt, come here to daydream or to live like the rich and famous for a day. Window-shop or splurge at tony stores, and keep an eye out for filming locales; just walking around here will make you feel like you're on a movie set.

👁 Sights

Museum of Tolerance
HISTORY MUSEUM | **FAMILY** | A museum that unflinchingly confronts bigotry and racism, one of its most affecting sections covers the Holocaust, with film footage of deportations and concentration camps. Upon entering, you are issued a "passport" bearing the name of a child whose life was dramatically changed by the Nazis; as you go through the exhibit, you learn the fate of that child. Another exhibit called *Anne: The Life and Legacy of Anne Frank* brings her story to life through immersive environments, multimedia presentations, and interesting artifacts, while Simon Wiesenthal's Vienna office is set exactly as the famous "Nazi hunter" had it while conducting his research that brought more than 1,000 war criminals to justice.

Interactive exhibits include The Forum where visitors can examine and debate solutions to controversial topics facing our nation today such as immigration, policing, homelessness, the pandemic, and bigotry; We the People, which looks at U.S. history from the 1600s up to the attack on the Capitol on January 6th, 2021, with an immense interactive wall; and the Point of View Experience,

a four-sided glass cube that presents a different individual's perspective on a particular situation facing society.

■ **TIP→ Plan to spend at least three hours touring the museum; making a reservation is especially recommended for Sunday and holiday visits.** ✉ *9786 W. Pico Blvd., south of Beverly Hills, Beverly Hills* ☎ *310/772-2505 for reservations* ⊕ *www.museumoftolerance.com* 🎟 *From $16* ⊙ *Closed Fri. and Sat.*

★ Rodeo Drive
STREET | The ultimate shopping indulgence, Rodeo Drive is one of L.A.'s bona fide tourist attractions. The art of window-shopping (and reenacting your *Pretty Woman* fantasies) is prime among the retail elite: Tiffany & Co., Gucci, Jimmy Choo, Valentino, Harry Winston, Prada—you get the picture. Near the southern end of Rodeo Drive is Via Rodeo, a curvy cobblestone street designed to resemble a European shopping area and the perfect backdrop to pose for your Instagram feed. To give your feet a rest, free trolley tours depart from the southeast corner of Rodeo Drive and Dayton Way from 11:30 to 4:30. They're a terrific way to get an overview of the neighborhood. ✉ *Rodeo Dr., Beverly Hills* ⊕ *www.rodeodrive-bh.com.*

Greystone Mansion
HISTORIC HOME | Built in 1928, this stunning mansion resides in a discreet residential part of Beverly Hills, surrounded by 18 acres of manicured grounds that are open to the public. The historic house was built by oil magnate Ned Doheny (inspiration for the Daniel Day-Lewis character in *There Will Be Blood*) and has been featured in a number of films like *The Big Lebowski*, *Spider-Man*, *The Social Network*, and *X-Men*. Park rangers offer tours for $20 where you can gawk at the 46,000-square-foot estate with a bowling alley, secret panels for liquor, and even a screening room. ✉ *905 Loma Vista Dr., Beverly Hills* ☎ *310/286–0119* ⊕ *www.greystonemansion.org.*

🍴 Restaurants

Crustacean

$$$ | **VIETNAMESE** | A Euro–Vietnamese fusion gem in the heart of Beverly Hills, Crustacean allows you to walk on water above exotic fish and see the kitchen preparing your perfect garlic noodles through a glass window. Standouts (besides the noodles) include Dungeness crab, A5 Wagyu beef, tuna cigars, and hearts-of-palm crab cakes. **Known for:** sake-simmered dishes; no-grease garlic noodles; unique cocktails like artichoke old-fashioneds. $ *Average main: $36* ✉ *468 N. Bedford Dr., Beverly Hills* ☎ *310/205–8990* ⊕ *crustaceanbh.com* ⊗ *Closed Mon.*

★ Gucci Osteria da Massimo Bottura

$$$$ | **ITALIAN** | Legendary Italian chef Massimo Bottura opened this spot, his first L.A. eatery, to loads of fanfare and celebrity sightings. The restaurant mirrors the Florence, Italy, location of the same name with a menu filled with favorites like a mouthwatering tortellini with Parmigiano Reggiano crema. **Known for:** excellent pastas; great people-watching; avant-garde design. $ *Average main: $80* ✉ *347 N. Rodeo Dr., Beverly Hills* ☎ *424/600–7490* ⊕ *www.gucci.com/us/en/st/capsule/gucci-osteria-beverly-hills.*

Nate 'n' Al's

$ | **SANDWICHES** | A longtime refuge from California's lean cuisine, Nate 'n' Al's serves up steaming pastrami, matzo ball soup, and potato latkes. Big-time media and entertainment insiders are often seen kibbitzing at this old-time East Coast–style establishment. **Known for:** matzo ball soup; killer pastrami; long waits. $ *Average main: $18* ✉ *414 N. Beverly Dr., Beverly Hills* ☎ *310/274–0101* ⊕ *www.natenals.com.*

Polo Lounge

$$$$ | **AMERICAN** | Nothing says Beverly Hills quite like the Polo Lounge inside the Beverly Hills Hotel. This classic, monied spot is home to Hollywood royalty and entertainment luminaries noshing on lobster Nicoise or the famed Wagyu burger during power lunches. **Known for:** celebrity sightings; mouthwatering Wagyu burgers; dress code of no ripped jeans or baseball caps. $ *Average main: $45* ✉ *The Beverly Hills Hotel, 9641 Sunset Blvd., Beverly Hills* ☎ *310/887–2777* ⊕ *www.dorchestercollection.com/en/los-angeles/the-beverly-hills-hotel/restaurants-bars/the-polo-lounge.*

★ Spago Beverly Hills

$$$ | **MODERN AMERICAN** | Wolfgang Puck's flagship restaurant is a modern L.A. classic. Spago centers on a buzzing red-brick outdoor courtyard (with retractable roof) shaded by 100-year-old olive trees, and a daily-changing menu that offers dishes like smoked salmon pizza or off-menu schnitzel. **Known for:** great people-watching; off-menu schnitzel; sizzling smoked salmon pizza. $ *Average main: $35* ✉ *176 N. Canon Dr., Beverly Hills* ☎ *310/385–0880* ⊕ *www.wolfgangpuck.com* ⊗ *Closed Mon.*

🛏 Hotels

Beverly Wilshire, a Four Seasons Hotel

$$$$ | **HOTEL** | Built in 1928, this Rodeo Drive–adjacent hotel is part Italian Renaissance (with elegant details like crystal chandeliers) and part contemporary. **Pros:** complimentary car service; Wolfgang Puck restaurant on-site; first-rate spa. **Cons:** small lobby; valet parking is $65/night; might be too sceney for some. $ *Rooms from: $735* ✉ *9500 Wilshire Blvd., Beverly Hills* ☎ *310/275–5200, 800/427–4354* ⊕ *www.fourseasons.com/beverlywilshire* ⇆ *395 rooms* ⦿ *No Meals.*

★ L'Ermitage Beverly Hills

$$$$ | **HOTEL** | This all-suites hotel is the picture of luxury: French doors open to a mini-balcony with views of the Hollywood sign; inside the very large rooms you'll find soaking tubs and oversize bath towels. **Pros:** stellar on-site restaurant;

free shuttle service within 2-mile radius; all rooms are large suites with balconies. **Cons:** small spa and pool; valet $60/night; a bit of a trek to Beverly Hills shopping. [$] *Rooms from: $595* ✉ *9291 Burton Way, Beverly Hills* ☎ *310/278–3344* 🌐 *www.lermitagebeverlyhills.com* 🛏 *116 rooms* 🍴 *No Meals.*

★ The Maybourne Beverly Hills

$$$$ | HOTEL | The nine-story, Mediterranean-style palazzo is dedicated to welcoming those who relish luxury, providing classic style and exemplary service. **Pros:** Italian cocktail bar on the roof; obliging, highly trained staff; one-of-a-kind spa. **Cons:** breakfast not included with standard rooms; not all rooms have balconies; valet parking $60/night. [$] *Rooms from: $995* ✉ *225 N. Canon Dr., Beverly Hills* ☎ *310/860–7800* 🌐 *www.maybournebeverlyhills.com* 🛏 *201 rooms* 🍴 *No Meals.*

★ Peninsula Beverly Hills

$$$$ | HOTEL | This French Riviera–style palace overflowing with antiques and art is a favorite of boldface names, and visitors consistently describe a stay here as near perfect. **Pros:** 24-hour check-in/check-out policy; sunny pool area with cabanas; complimentary Rolls-Royce takes you to nearby Beverly Hills. **Cons:** valet parking $65/night; room decor might feel too ornate for some; room views are limited to a private garden or city streets. [$] *Rooms from: $980* ✉ *9882 S. Santa Monica Blvd., Beverly Hills* ☎ *310/551–2888, 800/462–7899* 🌐 *www.peninsula.com/en/beverly-hills/5-star-luxury-hotel-beverly-hills* 🛏 *195 rooms* 🍴 *No Meals.*

SLS Hotel Beverly Hills

$$$ | HOTEL | From the sleek, Philippe Starck–designed lobby and lounge with fireplaces, hidden nooks, and a communal table to luxurious poolside cabanas, this hotel offers a cushy, dreamlike stay. **Pros:** outstanding rooftop views; complimentary house car for use within 3-mile radius; dreamy Ciel spa. **Cons:** standard rooms are compact; valet parking $70/night; on a busy intersection outside Beverly Hills. [$] *Rooms from: $440* ✉ *465 S. La Cienega Blvd., Beverly Hills* ☎ *310/247–0400* 🌐 *slshotels.com/beverlyhills* 🛏 *297 rooms* 🍴 *No Meals.*

Sonder The Crescent Beverly Hills

$ | HOTEL | Built in 1927 as a dorm for silent-film actors, the Crescent is now a fanciful boutique hotel with a great location—within the Beverly Hills shopping triangle—and with an even better price (for the area). **Pros:** incredible prints throughout hotel; lively on-site restaurant, Crescent Bar and Terrace; cheapest room rates in Beverly Hills. **Cons:** no direct phone to the hotel; no elevator; rooms on the small side. [$] *Rooms from: $175* ✉ *403 N. Crescent Dr., Beverly Hills* ☎ *310/247–0505* 🌐 *www.sonder.com/destinations/los_angeles* 🛏 *35 rooms.*

Shopping

Alo Yoga

SPORTING GOODS | In a city that takes its yoga seriously, it only makes sense that this locally designed activewear brand would take its very first Los Angeles storefront to the next level. For Alo Yoga's flagship, that means an 8,000-square-foot space complete with an organic coffee bar, kombucha on tap, and a rooftop deck that hosts daily sweat-and-stretch sessions. As for the clothing, the model-favorite line offers stylish leggings, sports bras, tanks, and more pieces that look as cool outside the fitness studio as they do during downward dog. ✉ *370 N. Canon Dr., Beverly Hills* ☎ *310/295–1860* 🌐 *www.aloyoga.com.*

Neiman Marcus

DEPARTMENT STORE | This couture salon frequently trots out designer trunk shows, and most locals go right to the shoe department, which features high-end footwear favorites like Giuseppe Zanotti and Christian Louboutin. A café on the third floor keeps your blood sugar high during multiple wardrobe changes, while a bar on the fourth is for celebrating those perfect finds with a glass of champagne. ⊠ *9700 Wilshire Blvd., Beverly Hills* ☎ *310/550–5900* ⊕ *www. neimanmarcus.com.*

Taschen

BOOKS | Philippe Starck designed the Taschen space to evoke a cool 1920s Parisian salon—a perfect showcase for the publisher's design-forward coffee-table books about architecture, travel, culture, and photography. A suspended glass cube gallery in back hosts art exhibits and features limited-edition books. ⊠ *354 N. Beverly Dr., Beverly Hills* ☎ *310/274–4300* ⊕ *www.taschen.com.*

West Hollywood and Fairfax

West Hollywood is less about sightseeing and more about doing—gallery hopping, dining, clubbing. Since the end of Prohibition, the Sunset Strip has been Hollywood's nighttime playground, where stars headed to such glamorous nightclubs as the Trocadero, the Mocambo, and Ciro's. Crowds still file into well-established spots like Whisky A Go Go, and paparazzi still stake out the members-only Soho House, but hedonism isn't all that drives West Hollywood.

Also thriving is an important interior design and art gallery trade exemplified by the Cesar Pelli–designed Pacific Design Center. Progressive West Hollywood is also one of the most gay-friendly cities anywhere, with a large LGBTQ+ community and one of the nation's largest Gay Pride parades each June.

Running from Sunset Strip all the way down to Wilshire (and beyond), the Fairfax District is where you'll find the historic Farmers Market and The Grove shopping mall—both great places to people-watch over breakfast or to shop for ethnic eats and designer wares.

◉ Sights

★ The Grove

STORE/MALL | **FAMILY** | Come to this popular outdoor mall for familiar names like Apple, Nike, and Nordstrom; stay for the central fountain with "dancing" water and light shows, people-watching from the trolley, and, during the holiday season, artificial snowfall and a winter wonderland. Feel-good pop blasting over the loudspeakers aims to boost your mood while you spend, and a giant cineplex gives shoppers a needed break with the latest box office blockbusters. ⊠ *189 The Grove Dr., Fairfax District* ☎ *323/900–8080* ⊕ *www.thegrovela.com.*

Holocaust Museum LA

HISTORY MUSEUM | A museum dedicated solely to the Holocaust, it uses its extensive collections of photos and artifacts as well as award-winning audio tours and interactive tools to evoke European Jewish life in the 20th century. The mission is to commemorate the lives of those who perished and those who survived the Holocaust. The building is itself a marvel, having won two awards from the American Institute of Architects. Throughout the week, the museum hosts talks given by Holocaust survivors, while other events include a lecture series, educational programs, and concerts. ⊠ *100 The Grove Dr., Los Angeles* ☎ *323/651–3704* ⊕ *www.holocaustmuseumla.org* 🎫 *Free.*

★ The Original Farmers Market

MARKET | **FAMILY** | Called the Original Farmers Market for a reason, this special piece of land brought out farmers to sell their wares starting in 1934. Today, the market has more permanent residences, but fresh produce still abounds among the dozens of vendors. Some purveyor standouts include gourmet market Monsieur Marcel, Bob's Coffee & Doughnuts, and Patsy D'Amore's Pizzeria, which has been serving slices since 1949. The market is adjacent to The Grove shopping center, and locals and tourists flock to

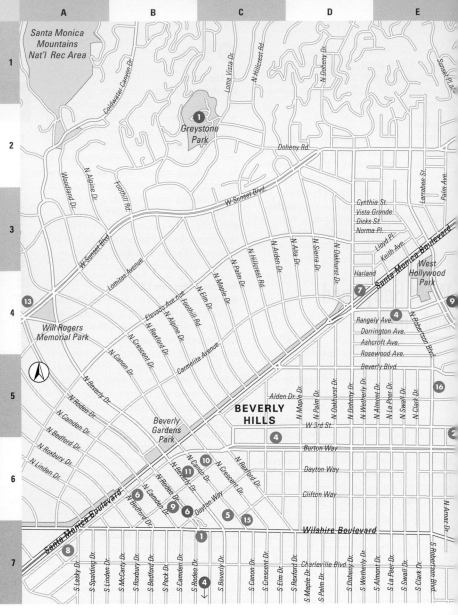

A   B   C   D   E

Santa Monica Mountains Nat'l Rec Area

Greystone Park

Will Rogers Memorial Park

Beverly Gardens Park

BEVERLY HILLS

West Hollywood Park

Beverly Hills, West Hollywood, and Fairfax

WEST HOLLYWOOD

PARK LA BREA

Pan Pacific Park

Hancock Park

2,000 ft

500 m

From celebrity mansions to rock-and-roll lore, Sunset Boulevard is a drive through Hollywood history.

both in droves. ✉ *6333 W. 3rd St., Fairfax District* ☎ *323/933–9211* ⊕ *www.farmers-marketla.com.*

Santa Monica Boulevard

STREET | From Fairfax Avenue in the east to Doheny Drive in the west, Santa Monica Boulevard is the commercial core of West Hollywood's gay community, with restaurants and cafés, bars and clubs, bookstores and galleries, and other establishments catering largely to the LGBTQ+ scene. Twice a year—during June's L.A. Pride and on Halloween—the boulevard becomes an open-air festival. ✉ *Santa Monica Blvd. between Fairfax Ave. and Doheny Dr., West Hollywood* ☎ *323/848–6400* ⊕ *weho.org.*

Sunset Boulevard

STREET | One of the most fabled avenues in the world, Sunset Boulevard began humbly enough in the 18th century as a route from El Pueblo de Los Angeles to the Pacific Ocean. Today, as it passes through West Hollywood, it becomes the sexy and seductive Sunset Strip, where rock and roll had its heyday and cocktail

bars charge a premium for the views. It slips quietly into the tony environs of Beverly Hills and Bel Air, twisting and winding past gated estates and undulating vistas. ✉ *Sunset Blvd., West Hollywood* ⊕ *www.weho.org.*

West Hollywood Design District

STORE/MALL | More than 200 businesses—art galleries, antiques shops, fashion outlets (including Rag & Bone and James Perse), and interior design stores—are found in the design district. There are also about 30 restaurants, including the famous paparazzi magnet, the Ivy. All are clustered within walking distance of each other—rare for L.A. ✉ *West Hollywood* ✛ *Melrose Ave. and Robertson and Beverly Blvds.* ☎ *310/289–2534* ⊕ *westhollywooddesigndistrict.com.*

🍽 Restaurants

★ Angelini Osteria

$$$ | **ITALIAN** | With a buzzy indoor dining room and ample outdoor seating, this is one of L.A.'s most celebrated Italian restaurants. The keys are chef-owner Gino Angelini's consistently impressive dishes, like whole branzino, *tagliolini al limone,* veal chop *alla* Milanese, as well as lasagna oozing with *besciamella* (Italian béchamel sauce). **Known for:** large Italian wine selection; bold flavors; savory pastas. $ *Average main: $40* ⊠ *7313 Beverly Blvd., Beverly–La Brea* ☎ *323/297–0070* ⊕ *www.angelinirestaurantgroup.com.*

A.O.C.

$$ | **MEDITERRANEAN** | Not to be confused with the congresswoman from New York, the acronym here stands for Appellation d'Origine Contrôlée, the regulatory system that ensures the quality of local wines and cheeses in France. Fittingly, A.O.C. upholds this standard of excellence in its shared plates and perfect wine pairings in the stunning exposed-brick and vine-laden courtyard. **Known for:** amazing cocktail hour; quaint outdoor courtyard; charming indoor fireplaces. $ *Average main: $30* ⊠ *8700 W. 3rd St., West Hollywood* ☎ *310/859–9859* ⊕ *www.aocwinebar.com.*

Canter's

$ | **SANDWICHES** | **FAMILY** | This granddaddy of L.A. delicatessens (it opened in 1931) cures its own corned beef and pastrami and features delectable desserts from the in-house bakery. It's not the best (or friendliest) deli in town, but it's a classic. **Known for:** location adjacent to Kibitz Room bar; plenty of seating and short wait times; open 24 hours. $ *Average main: $18* ⊠ *419 N. Fairfax Ave., Fairfax District* ☎ *323/651–2030* ⊕ *www.cantersdeli.com.*

Craig's

$$$ | **AMERICAN** | Behind the unremarkable facade is an übertrendy—yet decidedly old-school—den of American cuisine that doubles as a safe haven for the movie industry's most important names and well-known faces. Be aware that this joint is always busy so you might not even get a table and reservations are hard to come by. **Known for:** lots of celebrities; delicious chicken Parm; strong drinks. $ *Average main: $35* ⊠ *8826 Melrose Ave., West Hollywood* ☎ *310/276–1900* ⊕ *craigs.la* ☾ *No lunch Mon.–Sat. No dinner Sun.*

★ Crossroads

$$ | **VEGETARIAN** | From its famous Impossible Burger (you can't believe it's not meat) to its Sicilian pepperoni pizza (again, not meat), Crossroads's level of plant-based inventiveness knows no bounds. The space itself is dimly lit, with red-leather booths and a full bar illuminating its A-list clientele. **Known for:** high-end plant-based cuisine; great bar menu; popular celebrity hangout. $ *Average main: $24* ⊠ *8284 Melrose Ave., West Hollywood* ☎ *323/782–9245* ⊕ *www.crossroadskitchen.com.*

Dan Tana's

$$$ | **ITALIAN** | If you're looking for an Italian vibe straight out of *Goodfellas,* your search ends here. Checkered tablecloths cover the tightly packed tables as Hollywood players dine on the city's best chicken and veal Parm, and down Scotches by the finger. **Known for:** elbow-room-only bar; lively atmosphere; celeb spotting. $ *Average main: $35* ⊠ *9071 Santa Monica Blvd., West Hollywood* ☎ *310/275–9444* ⊕ *www.dantanasrestaurant.com* ☾ *No lunch.*

★ El Coyote Mexican Food

$ | **MEXICAN** | **FAMILY** | Open since 1931, this landmark spot is perfect for those on a budget or anyone after an authentic Mexican meal. The traditional fare is decadent and delicious while the margaritas are sweetened to perfection. **Known for:** affordable, quality cuisine; festive atmosphere; being an L.A. staple. $ *Average main: $18* ⊠ *7312 Beverly Blvd., Beverly–La Brea* ☎ *323/939–2255* ⊕ *www.elcoyotecafe.com* ☾ *Closed Mon. and Tues.*

★ MozzaPlex

$$$ | **ITALIAN** | A trio of restaurants by star chef Nancy Silverton, MozzaPlex

consists of Pizzeria Mozza, a casual pizza and wine spot; Osteria Mozza, an upscale Italian restaurant with incredible pastas; and chi SPACCA, an Italian steak house with succulent cuts of steak. The restaurant complex is one of the most beloved in the whole city and if you're craving any kind of Italian food, you'll want to get yourself inside. **Known for:** great pizzas; intimate atmosphere; the chi SPACCA burger. [$] *Average main: $31* ✉ *641 N. Highland Ave., Beverly–La Brea* ☎ *323/297–1130* 🌐 *www.mozzarestaurantgroup.com.*

★ Pink's Hot Dogs
$ | **HOT DOG** | **FAMILY** | Since 1939, Angelenos and tourists alike have been lining up at this roadside hot dog stand. But Pink's is more than just an institution, it's a beloved family-run joint that serves a damn good hot dog. **Known for:** the famous Brando Dog; late-night dining; chili fries. [$] *Average main: $7* ✉ *709 N. La Brea Ave., Hollywood* ☎ *323/931–4223* 🌐 *www.pinkshollywood.com.*

Pura Vita
$$ | **VEGETARIAN** | At the first 100% plant-based Italian restaurant and wine bar in the whole country, chef Tara Punzone makes you believe her caprese has real mozzarella, her meatballs come from cows, and her *cacio e pepe* is filled with dairy. The food is exceptional, the atmosphere screams New York, and the best part is that no animals were harmed for any of it. **Known for:** all-vegan cuisine; incredible pastas; stellar wine list. [$] *Average main: $20* ✉ *8247 Santa Monica Blvd., West Hollywood* ☎ *323/688–2303* 🌐 *www.puravitalosangeles.com* ⏲ *Closed Mon.*

Sushi Tama
$$ | **JAPANESE** | A calming effect comes over you as you enter this simple sushi bar on one of L.A.'s most fashionable streets. Chef Yoshimoto actually sharpened his skills inside Tokyo's Tsukiji Fish Market where he learned what the best quality fish really means, resulting in sushi that transports you to Japan. **Known for:** fresh fish; donburi bowls; traditional sushi. [$] *Average main: $25* ✉ *116 N. Robertson Blvd., West Hollywood* ☎ *424/249–3009* 🌐 *www.sushitama-la.com.*

🛏 Hotels

Chamberlain
$$ | **HOTEL** | On a leafy residential side street, the Chamberlain is steps from Santa Monica Boulevard and close to the Sunset Strip, bringing in fashionable young professionals and 24-hour party people looking to roam West Hollywood. **Pros:** excellent guests-only dining room and bar; suites come with fireplace and balcony; 24-hour fitness center. **Cons:** compact bathrooms; uphill climb to the Sunset Strip; party-friendly crowds might be too noisy for some. [$] *Rooms from: $249* ✉ *1000 Westmount Dr., West Hollywood* ☎ *310/657–7400, 888/377–7181* 🌐 *www.chamberlainwesthollywood.com* 🛏 *114 suites* 🍴 *Free Breakfast.*

Chateau Marmont
$$$$ | **HOTEL** | Built in 1929 as a luxury apartment complex, the Chateau is now one of the most unique see-and-be-seen hotel hot spots in all of the city. **Pros:** private and exclusive vibe; famous history; beautiful pool. **Cons:** some may find it pretentious; celeb guests will take priority over you; some of the rooms are underwhelming. [$] *Rooms from: $595* ✉ *8221 Sunset Blvd., West Hollywood* ☎ *323/656–1010* 🌐 *www.chateaumarmont.com* 🛏 *63 rooms* 🍴 *No Meals.*

Mondrian Los Angeles
$$$ | **HOTEL** | The Mondrian has a city club feel; socializing begins in the lobby bar and lounge and extends from the restaurant to the scenic patio and pool, where you can listen to music underwater, and the lively Skybar. **Pros:** acclaimed Skybar on property; flirty social scene; best views in the city. **Cons:** pricy valet parking; late-night party scene not for

everyone; Alice in Wonderland theme might be too much for some. $ *Rooms from: $352* ⊠ *8440 Sunset Blvd., West Hollywood* ☎ *323/650–8999, 800/606–6090* ⊕ *www.mondrianhotel.com* ⇆ *236 rooms* ⦿ *No Meals.*

Palihotel Melrose Avenue

$$ | HOTEL | A mostly young and creative clientele flocks here, to one of the only boutique hotels on Melrose Avenue. **Pros:** great decor; walking distance to Melrose shops and restaurants; good on-site dining. **Cons:** no gym, spa, or pool; the area can be unsafe after dark; need to request alarm clocks and phones from front desk. $ *Rooms from: $269* ⊠ *7950 Melrose Ave., West Hollywood* ☎ *323/272–4588* ⊕ *www.pali-hotel.com* ⇆ *33 rooms* ⦿ *No Meals.*

★ Sunset Marquis Hotel and Villas

$$$ | HOTEL | If you're in town to cut your new hit single, you'll appreciate this near-the-Strip hidden retreat in the heart of WeHo, with two on-site recording studios. **Pros:** favorite among rock stars; 53 villas with lavish extras; exclusive Bar 1200. **Cons:** rooms can feel dark; small balconies; no direct car access to the Sunset Strip. $ *Rooms from: $450* ⊠ *1200 N. Alta Loma Rd., West Hollywood* ☎ *310/657–1333, 800/858–9758* ⊕ *www.sunsetmarquis.com* ⇆ *152 rooms* ⦿ *No Meals.*

▼ Nightlife

★ The Abbey

DANCE CLUBS | The Abbey in West Hollywood is one of the most famous LGBTQ+ bars in the world. And rightfully so. Seven days a week, a mixed and very good-looking crowd comes to eat, drink, dance, and flirt. Creative cocktails are whipped up by buff bartenders with a bevy of theme nights and parties each day. ⊠ *692 N. Robertson Blvd., West Hollywood* ☎ *310/289–8410* ⊕ *www.theabbeyweho.com.*

Comedy Store

COMEDY CLUBS | Three stages give seasoned and unseasoned comedians a place to perform and try out new material, with big-name performers dropping by just for fun. The front bar along Sunset Boulevard is a popular hangout after or between shows, oftentimes with that night's comedians mingling with fans. ⊠ *8433 Sunset Blvd., West Hollywood* ☎ *323/650–6268* ⊕ *www.thecomedystore.com.*

Laugh Factory

COMEDY CLUBS | Top stand-up comics regularly appear at this Sunset Boulevard mainstay, often working out the kinks in new material in advance of national tours. Stars such as Tiffany Haddish and Dan Ahdoot sometimes drop by unannounced, and theme nights like Chocolate Sundaes and Tehran Thursdays are extremely popular, with comics performing more daring sets. ⊠ *8001 W. Sunset Blvd., West Hollywood* ☎ *323/656–1336* ⊕ *www.laughfactory.com.*

Rainbow Bar and Grill

BARS | Its location next door to a long-running music venue, the Roxy, helped cement this bar and restaurant's status as a legendary watering hole for musicians (as well as their entourages and groupies). The Who, Guns N' Roses, Poison, Kiss, and many others have all passed through the doors. ⊠ *9015 W. Sunset Blvd., West Hollywood* ☎ *310/278–4232* ⊕ *www. rainbowbarandgrill.com.*

★ The Troubadour

LIVE MUSIC | The intimate vibe of the Troubadour helps make this club a favorite with music fans. Around since 1957, this venue has a storied past where legends like Elton John and James Taylor have graced the stage. These days, the eclectic lineup is still attracting crowds, with the focus mostly on rock, indie, and folk music. Those looking for drinks can imbibe to their heart's content at the adjacent bar. ⊠ *9081 Santa Monica Blvd., West Hollywood* ⊕ *www.troubadour.com.*

The Viper Room

LIVE MUSIC | This 21-plus rock club on the edge of the Sunset Strip has been around for more than 30 years and is famously known as the site of much controversial Hollywood history—River Phoenix overdosed and died here, and Johnny Depp used to be a part owner. Today the venue books rising alt-rock acts, and covers typically range from $10 to $15, but its history has also seen legends like Tom Petty and Lenny Kravitz on the stage. ⊠ *8852 Sunset Blvd., West Hollywood* ☎ *310/358–1881* ⊕ *www.viperroom.com.*

Whisky A Go Go

LIVE MUSIC | The hard-core metal and rock scene is alive and well at the legendary Whisky A Go Go (the full name includes the prefix "World Famous"), where Janis Joplin, Led Zeppelin, Alice Cooper, Van Halen, the Doors (they were the house band for a short stint), and Frank Zappa have all played. On the Strip for more than five decades, the club books both underground acts and huge names in rock. ⊠ *8901 W. Sunset Blvd., West Hollywood* ☎ *310/652–4202* ⊕ *www.whiskyagogo.com.*

👜 Shopping

★ American Rag Cie

SECOND-HAND | Half the store features new clothing from established and emerging labels, while the other side is stocked with well-preserved vintage clothing organized by color and style. You'll also find plenty of shoes and accessories being picked over by the hippest of Angelenos. ⊠ *150 S. La Brea Ave., West Hollywood* ☎ *323/935–3154* ⊕ *americanrag.com.*

Beverly Center

MALL | This eight-level shopping center is home to luxury retailers like Gucci, Louis Vuitton, and Salvatore Ferragamo but also offers plenty of outposts for more affordable brands including Aldo, H&M, and Uniqlo. Don't miss the bevy of great dining options like Eggslut, an extraordinarily popular breakfast joint; Angler, an upscale and modern seafood haven; and Yardbird, a fried-chicken lovers' favorite, plus many, many more. ⊠ *8500 Beverly Blvd., West Hollywood* ☎ *310/854–0070* ⊕ *www.beverlycenter.com.*

Book Soup

BOOKS | One of the best independent bookstores in the country, Book Soup has been serving Angelenos since 1975. Given its Hollywood pedigree, it's especially deep in books about film, music, art, and photography. Fringe benefits include an international newsstand, a bargain-book section, and author readings several times a week. ⊠ *8818 Sunset Blvd., West Hollywood* ☎ *310/659–3110* ⊕ *www.booksoup.com.*

★ Fred Segal

MIXED CLOTHING | One of the most well-known boutiques in all of Los Angeles, Fred Segal is a fashion design mecca that has been clothing the rich, famous, and their acolytes since the 1960s. Since moving from its original location on Melrose, the flagship store sits atop Sunset Boulevard with more than 21,000 square feet of space that showcases innovative brands and high-end threads. ⊠ *8500 Sunset Blvd., West Hollywood* ☎ *310/432–0560* ⊕ *www.fredsegal.com.*

★ Maxfield

WOMEN'S CLOTHING | This modern concrete structure is one of L.A.'s most desirable destinations for ultimate high fashion. The space is stocked with sleek offerings from Givenchy, Saint Laurent, Valentino, and Rick Owens, plus occasional pop-ups by fashion's labels-of-the-moment. For serious shoppers (or gawkers) only. ⊠ *8825 Melrose Ave., West Hollywood* ☎ *310/274–8800* ⊕ *www.maxfieldla.com.*

★ Melrose Trading Post

MARKET | Hollywood denizens love this hip market, where you're likely to find recycled rock T-shirts or some vinyl to complete your collection in addition to antique furniture and quirky arts and crafts. Live music and fresh munchies entertain vintage hunters and collectors. The market is held 9 to 5 every Sunday—rain or shine—in Fairfax High School's parking lot and admission is $5. ⊠ *Fairfax Ave. and Melrose Ave., Fairfax District* ☎ *323/655–7679* ⊕ *www.melrosetradingpost.org.*

The Way We Wore

WOMEN'S CLOTHING | Beyond the over-the-top vintage store furnishings, you'll find one of the city's best selections of well-cared-for and one-of-a-kind items, with a focus on sequins and beads. Upstairs, couture from Halston, Dior, and Chanel can cost up to $20,000. ⊠ *334 S. La Brea Ave., Beverly–La Brea* ☎ *323/937–0878* ⊕ *www.thewaywewore.com.*

Hollywood and the Studios

The Tinseltown mythology was born in Hollywood, still one of L.A.'s largest and most vibrant neighborhoods. In the Hollywood Hills to the north of Franklin Avenue sit some of the most marvelous mansions the moguls ever built; in the flats below Sunset and Santa Monica boulevards are the classic bungalows where studio workers once resided. Reputation aside, though, Paramount is the only studio still located in what is now, essentially, a workaday district.

To find many of the places that have made L.A. so famous, you must head over the Hollywood Hills to San Fernando Valley (known locally as just "the Valley"). Here, Universal City—an unincorporated area of the city that nevertheless has its own zip code and subway station—is home to Universal Studios Hollywood and Hollywood CityWalk. Due west of it is Studio City, which has several smaller film and TV studios.

Northeast of Universal City is Burbank, which longtime host Johnny Carson used to ironically refer to as "beautiful downtown Burbank." Today, however, all joking is set aside: this is one of L.A.'s most desirable suburbs. It's also home to Warner Bros. Studios, Disney Studios, Burbank Studios (formerly NBC Studios), and the Bob Hope Airport.

Hollywood

⊙ Sights

Dolby Theatre

PERFORMANCE VENUE | More than just a prominent fixture on Hollywood Boulevard, the Dolby Theatre has a few accolades under its belt as well, most notably as home to the Academy Awards. The theater is a blend of the traditional and the modern, where an exquisite classical design inspired by the grand opera houses of Europe meets a state-of-the-art sound and technical system for an immersive, theatrical experience. Watch a concert or a show here to experience it fully, but before you do, take a tour for an informative, behind-the-scenes look and to step into the VIP lounge where celebrities rub elbows on the big night. ⊠ *6801 Hollywood Blvd., Hollywood* ☎ *323/308–6300* ⊕ *www.dolbytheatre. com* ⊠ *Tour $25.*

★ Hollywood Bowl

PERFORMANCE VENUE | For those seeking a quintessential Los Angeles experience, a concert on a summer night at the Bowl, the city's iconic outdoor venue, is unsurpassed. The Bowl has presented world-class performers since it opened in 1920. The L.A. Philharmonic plays here from June to September; its performances and other events draw large crowds. Parking is limited near the venue, but there are additional remote parking locations serviced by shuttles. You can bring food and drink to any event, which Angelenos often do, though you can only BYOB to L.A. Phil

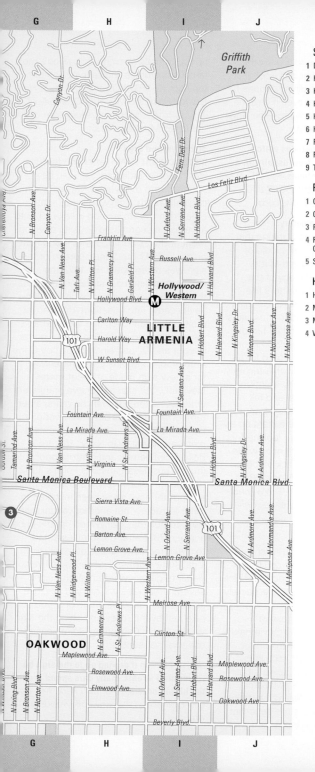

Sights ▼

1 Dolby Theatre **C4**
2 Hollywood Bowl **C2**
3 Hollywood Forever Cemetery **G7**
4 Hollywood Museum **C4**
5 Hollywood Sign **D1**
6 Hollywood Walk of Fame **E4**
7 Pantages Theatre.................. **F4**
8 Paramount Pictures **F8**
9 TCL Chinese Theatre **C4**

Restaurants ▼

1 Cactus Taquerias #1.............. **E7**
2 Gwen............................. **D5**
3 Providence **E8**
4 Roscoe's House of
Chicken and Waffles **F5**
5 Salt's Cure **C6**

Hotels ▼

1 Hollywood Roosevelt Hotel........ **C4**
2 Magic Castle Hotel **B3**
3 Mama Shelter Los Angeles........ **D4**
4 W Hollywood **E4**

performances and some rock and other shows. (Bars do, however, sell alcohol at all events, and there are dining options.) It's wise to bring a jacket even if daytime temperatures have been warm—the Bowl can get quite chilly at night.

■ TIP → **Visitors can sometimes watch the L.A. Phil practice for free, usually on a weekday; call ahead for times.** ✉ *2301 N. Highland Ave., Hollywood* ☎ *323/850–2000* ⊕ *www.hollywoodbowl.com.*

★ Hollywood Forever Cemetery

CEMETERY | One of the many things that makes this cemetery in the middle of Hollywood so fascinating is that it's the final resting place of many of the Hollywood greats, from directors like Cecil B. DeMille and actors like Douglas Fairbanks and Judy Garland to musicians like Johnny Ramone. Beyond its famous residents, however, the Hollywood Forever Cemetery is also frequented for its serene grounds peppered with intricately designed tombstones, not to mention by cinephiles in the summer and fall months for the outdoor movie screenings that take place under the stars on the Fairbanks Lawn. If you're looking for both tourist and local experiences while in town, this sight lets you tick off both in one visit. ✉ *6000 Santa Monica Blvd., Hollywood* ☎ *866/706–4826* ⊕ *www.hollywoodforever.com* ✉ *Free; check online for film screenings.*

★ Hollywood Museum

HISTORY MUSEUM | Don't let its kitschy facade turn you off: the Hollywood Museum, nestled at the busy intersection of Hollywood and Highland, is worth it, especially for film aficionados. A museum deserving of its name, it boasts an impressive collection of exhibits from the moviemaking world, spanning several film genres and eras. Start in its pink, art deco lobby where the Max Factor exhibit pays tribute to the cosmetics company's pivotal role in Hollywood, make your way to the dark basement, where the industry's penchant for the macabre is on full display, and wrap up your visit by admiring Hollywood's most famous costumes and set props on the top floor. ✉ *1660 N. Highland Ave., at Hollywood Blvd., Hollywood* ☎ *323/464–7776* ⊕ *www.thehollywoodmuseum.com* ✉ *$15* ⊗ *Closed Mon. and Tues.*

★ Hollywood Sign

HISTORIC SIGHT | With letters 50 feet tall, Hollywood's trademark sign can be spotted from miles away. The icon, which originally read "Hollywoodland," was erected in the Hollywood Hills in 1923 to advertise a segregated housing development and was outfitted with 4,000 light bulbs. In 1949 the "land" portion of the sign was taken down. By 1973 the sign had earned landmark status, but because the letters were made of wood, its longevity came into question. A makeover project was launched and the letters were auctioned off (rocker Alice Cooper bought an "O" and singing cowboy Gene Autry sponsored an "L") to make way for a new sign made of sheet metal. Inevitably, the sign has drawn pranksters who have altered it over the years, albeit temporarily, to spell out "Hollyweed" (in the 1970s, to push for more lenient marijuana laws), "Go Navy" (before a Rose Bowl game), and "Perotwood" (during businessman Ross Perot's 1992 presidential bid). A fence and surveillance equipment have since been installed to deter intruders, but another vandal managed to pull the "Hollyweed" prank once again in 2017 after Californians voted to make recreational use of marijuana legal statewide. And while it's still very illegal to get anywhere near the sign, several area hikes will get you as close as possible for some photo ops; you can hike just over 6 miles up behind the sign via the Brush Canyon trail for epic views, especially at sunset.

⚠ **Use caution if driving up to the sign on residential streets; many cars speed around the blind corners.** ✉ *Griffith Park, Mt. Lee Dr., Hollywood* ⊕ *www.hollywoodsign. org.*

Hollywood Walk of Fame

OTHER ATTRACTION | Along Hollywood Boulevard (and part of Vine Street) runs a trail of affirmations for entertainment-industry overachievers. On this mile-long stretch of sidewalk, inspired by the concrete handprints in front of TCL Chinese Theatre, names are embossed in brass, each at the center of a pink star embedded in dark gray terrazzo. They're not all screen deities; many stars commemorate people who worked in a technical field, such as sound or lighting. The first eight stars were unveiled in 1960 at the northwest corner of Highland Avenue and Hollywood Boulevard: Olive Borden, Ronald Colman, Louise Fazenda, Preston Foster, Burt Lancaster, Edward Sedgwick, Ernest Torrence, and Joanne Woodward (some of these names have stood the test of time better than others). Since then, more than 2,000 others have been immortalized, though that honor doesn't come cheap—upon selection by a special committee, the personality in question (or more likely his or her movie studio or record company) pays about $30,000 for the privilege. To aid you in spotting celebrities you're looking for, stars are identified by one of five icons: a motion-picture camera, a radio microphone, a television set, a record, or a theatrical mask. ⊠ *Hollywood Blvd. and Vine St., Hollywood* ⊕ *www.walkoffame. com.*

Pantages Theatre

PERFORMANCE VENUE | Besides being home to the Academy Awards for a decade in the '50s, this stunning art deco–style theater near Hollywood and Vine has been playing host to many of the musical theater world's biggest and greatest productions, from the classics like *Cats*, *West Side Story*, and *Phantom of the Opera* to modern hits like *Hamilton* and *Wicked*. During your Los Angeles jaunt, see a show or two in order to really experience its splendor. While guided tours are not being offered to the public, an annual open house is available to season pass holders for an exclusive and informative tour of the theater and its history. ⊠ *6233 Hollywood Blvd., Hollywood* ☎ *323/468–1770* ⊕ *www.broadwayinhollywood.com.*

★ Paramount Pictures

FILM/TV STUDIO | With a history dating to the early 1920s, the Paramount lot was home to some of Hollywood's most luminous stars, including Mary Pickford, Rudolph Valentino, Mae West, Marlene Dietrich, and Bing Crosby. Director Cecil B. DeMille's base of operations for decades, Paramount offers probably the most authentic studio tour, giving you a real sense of the film industry's history. This is the only major studio from film's golden age left in Hollywood—all the others are now in Burbank, Universal City, or Culver City.

Memorable movies and TV shows with scenes shot here include *Sunset Boulevard, Forrest Gump,* and *Titanic.* Many of the *Star Trek* movies and TV series were shot entirely or in part here, and several seasons of *I Love Lucy* were shot on the portion of the lot Paramount acquired in 1967 from Lucille Ball. You can take a two-hour studio tour or a 4½-hour VIP tour, led by guides who walk and trolley you around the backlots. As well as gleaning some gossipy history, you'll spot the sets of TV and film shoots in progress. Reserve ahead for tours, which are for those ages 10 and up.

■ **TIP→ You can be part of the audience for live TV tapings (tickets are free), but you must book ahead.** ⊠ *5515 Melrose Ave., Hollywood* ☎ *323/956–1777* ⊕ *www. paramountstudiotour.com* 🎟 *$63.*

TCL Chinese Theatre

HISTORIC HOME | The stylized Chinese pagodas and temples of the former Grauman's Chinese Theatre have become a shrine both to stardom and the combination of glamour and flamboyance that inspire the phrase "only in Hollywood." Although you have to buy a movie ticket

A concert at the Hollywood Bowl is a summertime tradition for Angelenos.

to appreciate the interior trappings, the courtyard is open to the public. The main theater itself is worth visiting, if only to see a film in the same setting as hundreds of celebrities who have attended big premieres here.

And then, of course, outside in front are the oh-so-famous cement hand- and footprints. This tradition is said to have begun at the theater's opening in 1927, with the premiere of Cecil B. DeMille's *King of Kings,* when actress Norma Talmadge just happened to step in wet cement. Now more than 160 celebrities have contributed imprints for posterity, including some oddball specimens, such as casts of Whoopi Goldberg's dreadlocks. ✉ *6925 Hollywood Blvd., Hollywood* ☎ *323/461–3331* 🌐 *www.tclchinesetheatres.com* 🎫 *Tour $16.*

🍴 Restaurants

Cactus Taqueria #1

$ | MEXICAN | FAMILY | A humble taco shack on the side of the road, Cactus offers up $4 tacos with all types of meat you could imagine, even beef tongue. They also have carne asada and chicken for the less adventurous. **Known for:** California burritos; delicious fries; excellent street-style tacos. [$] *Average main: $11* ✉ *950 Vine St., Hollywood* ☎ *323/464–5865* 🌐 *www.cactustaqueriainc.com.*

★ Gwen

$$$$ | STEAKHOUSE | Heaven for carnivores, this upscale European-style butcher shop and fine-dining restaurant serves wood-fire-cooked meats in a copper-and-marble art deco setting. From Australian celeb-chef Curtis Stone and his brother, Luke, and named for their grandmother, Gwen's butcher shop serves up quality cuts of humanely raised meats to locals during the day, while the elegant dining space within view of the glass-enclosed dry-age rooms, charcuterie curing, and roaring firepit elevates the smoking, searing, and roasting of those quality meats to an art form by night. **Known for:** house-made charcuterie; wood-fire grilled steaks; strong cocktails and good wine list. [$] *Average main: $50* ✉ *6600 Sunset Blvd., Hollywood* ☎ *323/946–7513* 🌐 *www.gwenla.com.*

★ Providence

$$$$ | **SEAFOOD** | This is widely considered one of the best seafood restaurants in the country, and chef-owner Michael Cimarusti elevates sustainably driven fine dining to an art form. The elegant space is the perfect spot to sample exquisite seafood with the chef's signature application of French technique, traditional American themes, and Asian accents. **Known for:** fresh seafood; honey and zero-waste chocolate programs; exquisite dessert options. [$] *Average main: $150* ✉ *5955 Melrose Ave., Hollywood* ☎ *323/460–4170* 🌐 *www.providencela.com* 🕒 *Closed Sun. and Mon.*

Roscoe's House of Chicken and Waffles

$ | **SOUTHERN** | **FAMILY** | Roscoe's is *the* place for down-home Southern cooking in Southern California. Just ask the patrons who drive from all over L.A. for bargain-priced fried chicken and waffles. The name of this casual eatery honors a late-night combo popularized in Harlem jazz clubs. **Known for:** simple yet famous chicken and waffles; classic soul food dishes; eggs with cheese and onions. [$] *Average main: $15* ✉ *1514 N. Gower St., Hollywood* ☎ *323/466–7453* 🌐 *www.roscoeschickenandwaffles.com.*

Salt's Cure

$$ | **AMERICAN** | **FAMILY** | Featuring all locally sourced meat, seafood, and produce, an all-day lunch menu, and a popular patio, this former West Hollywood spot proves that despite appearances, Californians love traditional meat-based staples and cocktails just as much as they love their kale salads and smoothies. If you're in doubt, just take a good look at this joint's hearty sandwiches. **Known for:** oatmeal griddle cakes; hearty sandwiches; all California-grown ingredients. [$] *Average main: $20* ✉ *1155 N. Highland Ave., Hollywood* ☎ *323/465–7258* 🌐 *www.saltscure.com* 🕒 *Closed Mon. and Tues.*

🛏 Hotels

★ Hollywood Roosevelt Hotel

$$$ | **HOTEL** | The historic, party-centric Hollywood Roosevelt Hotel, known for hosting the first Academy Awards ceremony, has played host and been home to some of the movie industry's most important people and events. **Pros:** refreshed rooms with great amenities; pool is a popular weekend hangout; great burgers at the on-site 25 Degrees restaurant. **Cons:** reports of noise and staff attitude; stiff parking fees ($45); busy location. [$] *Rooms from: $365* ✉ *7000 Hollywood Blvd., Hollywood* ☎ *323/856–1970* 🌐 *www.hollywoodroosevelt.com* 🛏 *300 rooms* 🍴 *No Meals.*

★ Magic Castle Hotel

$$ | **HOTEL** | **FAMILY** | Guests at the hotel can secure advance dinner reservations and attend magic shows at the Magic Castle, a private club in a 1908 mansion next door for magicians and their admirers. **Pros:** heated pool and lush patio; central location near Hollywood & Highland; access to fun Magic Castle shows. **Cons:** strict dress code; no elevator; highly trafficked street. [$] *Rooms from: $250* ✉ *7025 Franklin Ave., Hollywood* ☎ *323/851–0800, 800/741–4915* 🌐 *magiccastlehotel.com* 🛏 *43 rooms* 🍴 *Free Breakfast.*

★ Mama Shelter Los Angeles

$$ | **HOTEL** | Mama Shelter Los Angeles is not just a cool hotel, it's an attitude, with its tropical rooftop bar populated with beautiful people having fun, a lively lobby restaurant and café, and eclectic, playful design, throughout like masks in rooms and a foosball table in the lobby. **Pros:**

delicious food and cocktails on the property; affordable rooms that don't skimp on style; a block from Hollywood Boulevard. **Cons:** some rooms are noisy; creaky elevators; bar and restaurant often get crowded. $ *Rooms from: $265* ✉ *6500 Selma Ave., Hollywood* ☎ *323/785–6600* ⊕ *www.mamashelter.com/en/los-angeles* ⇥ *70 rooms* ⦿ *No Meals.*

W Hollywood
$$$ | **HOTEL** | This centrally located, ultra-modernly lit location is outfitted for the wired traveler and features a rooftop pool deck and popular on-site bars, like the Station Hollywood and the mod Living Room lobby bar. **Pros:** Metro stop outside the front door; comes with in-room party necessities, from ice to cocktail glasses; comfy beds with petal-soft duvets. **Cons:** small pool; pricey dining and valet parking; location in noisy part of Hollywood. $ *Rooms from: $479* ✉ *6250 Hollywood Blvd., Hollywood* ☎ *323/798–1300, 888/625–4988* ⊕ *www.marriott.com/en-us/hotels/laxwh-w-hollywood* ⇥ *305 rooms* ⦿ *No Meals.*

Nightlife

Burgundy Room
BARS | Around since 1919, Burgundy Room attracts a fiercely loyal crowd of locals, as well as the occasional wandering tourist. The bar is supposedly haunted (check out the Ouija boards toward the back), but that just adds to its charm. Its rock-and-roll vibe, strong drinks, and people-watching opportunities make this a worthy detour on any night out on the town. ✉ *1621½ N. Cahuenga Blvd., Hollywood* ☎ *323/465–7530.*

★ Good Times at Davey Wayne's
BARS | It's a fridge; it's a door; it's the entrance to Davey Wayne's, a bar and lounge that pulls out all the stops to transport you back in time to the '70s. The interior is your living room; the outside is an ongoing backyard barbecue with all your friends. Come early to beat the crowds or be prepared to get up close and personal with your neighbors. ✉ *1611 N. El Centro Ave., Hollywood* ☎ *323/498–0859* ⊕ *www.goodtimesat-daveywaynes.com.*

Hotel Cafe
LIVE MUSIC | This intimate venue caters to fans of folk, indie rock, and music on the softer side. With red velvet backdrops, hardwood furnishings, and the occasional celebrity surprise performance—notably John Mayer—music lovers will not only be very happy but will receive a respite from the ordinary Hollywood experience. ✉ *1623½ N. Cahuenga Blvd., Hollywood* ⊕ *www.hotelcafe.com.*

★ Musso and Frank Grill
GATHERING PLACES | **FAMILY** | The prim and proper vibe of this old-school steak house won't appeal to those looking for a raucous night out; instead, its appeal lies in its history and sturdy drinks. Established over a century ago, its dark wood decor, red tuxedo–clad waiters, and highly skilled bartenders can easily shuttle you back to its Hollywood heyday when Marilyn Monroe, F. Scott Fitzgerald, and Greta Garbo once hung around and sipped martinis. ✉ *6667 Hollywood Blvd., Hollywood* ☎ *323/467–7788* ⊕ *www.mussoandfrank.com.*

No Vacancy
BARS | At first glance, No Vacancy might convey an air of exclusivity and pretentiousness, but its relaxed interiors and welcoming staff will almost instantly make you feel like you're at a house party. You know, the kind with burlesque shows, tightrope performances, a speakeasy secret entrance, and mixologists who can pretty much whip up any drink your heart desires. ✉ *1727 N. Hudson Ave., Hollywood* ☎ *323/465–1902* ⊕ *www.novacancyla.com.*

Sassafras Saloon
DANCE CLUBS | Put on your dancing shoes (or your cowboy boots) and step back in time. The Sassafras boasts not only

an oddly cozy, Western atmosphere, but also plenty of opportunities to strut your moves on the dance floor. Indulge in exquisite craft mezcal, whiskey, and tequila cocktails for some liquid courage before you two-step the night away. ⊠ 1233 N. Vine St., Hollywood 🕿 323/467–2800 ⊕ www.sassafrassaloon.com.

🛍 Shopping

★ Amoeba Music

MUSIC | Touted as the "World's Largest Independent Record Store," Amoeba is a playground for music lovers, with a knowledgeable staff and a focus on local artists. Catch free in-store appearances and signings by artists and bands that play sold-out shows at venues down the road. There's a massive and eclectic collection of vinyl records, CDs, and cassette tapes, not to mention VHS tapes, DVDs, and Blu-Ray discs. It's a paradise for both music and movie lovers. ⊠ 6200 Hollywood Blvd., Hollywood 🕿 323/245–6400 ⊕ www.amoeba.com.

Ovation Hollywood

SHOPPING CENTER | If you're on the hunt for unique boutiques, look elsewhere. However, if you prefer the biggest retail chains America has to offer, Ovation Hollywood is a great spot for a shopping spree. Sadly, the original courtyard that pays tribute to the city's film legacy is no longer there, replaced by a more modern space, but if you head to the north-facing balconies, you will find a picture-perfect view of the Hollywood sign. Heads up that this place is a huge tourist magnet. ⊠ 6801 Hollywood Blvd., at Highland Ave., Hollywood ⊕ www.ovationhollywood.com.

Larry Edmunds Bookshop

BOOKS | Cinephiles have long descended upon this iconic 70-plus-year-old shop that in addition to stocking tons of texts about motion picture history offers film fans the opportunity to pick up scripts, posters, and photographs from Hollywood's golden era to the present. ⊠ 6644 Hollywood Blvd., Hollywood 🕿 323/463–3273 ⊕ www.larryedmunds.com.

The Record Parlour

MUSIC | Vinyl records and music memorabilia abound in this hip yet modest record store–slash–music lover magnet that also touts vintage audio gear and retro jukeboxes. A visit here is usually a multi-hour affair, one that involves more than just browsing through display cases, digging through wooden carts of used vinyls, and playing your picks at the listening station. ⊠ 6408 Selma Ave., Hollywood 🕿 323/464–7757 ⊕ www.facebook.com/therecordparlour.

🏃 Activities

★ Runyon Canyon Trail and Park

HIKING & WALKING | Is Runyon Canyon the city's most famous trail? To the world, it just might be, what with so many A-listers frequenting it. Many folks visiting L.A. take the trail specifically for celebrity spotting. But, if that's not something you're into, this accessible trail right in the middle of Hollywood is also a good place to hike, run, see the Hollywood sign, photograph the city skyline, or simply get a bit of fresh air. If you just happen to run into a famous face, well that's just the cherry on the cake. ⊠ 2000 N. Fuller Ave., Hollywood 🕿 323/644–6661 Park Ranger ⊕ www.laparks.org/runyon.

Universal City

👁 Sights

★ Universal Studios Hollywood

THEME PARK | **FAMILY** | A theme park with classic attractions like roller coasters and thrill rides, Universal Studios Hollywood also provides that unique brand of thrill you get from the magic of the movies, with tours of sets and movie-themed rides. Unlike other amusement parks, this one is centered around the biggest blockbusters, with rides like Jurassic World –The Ride and Harry Potter and the Forbidden Journey as well as worlds like the brand-new Super Nintendo World, which boasts the fun and highly interactive Mario Kart: Bowser's Challenge and is, in and of itself, a game—exactly the kind of experience that Super Mario fans truly enjoy. If you're in town in October, the park's Halloween Horror Nights is a must-visit, featuring mazes full of monsters, murderers, and jump scares.

The world-famous Studio Tour takes you around the Universal backlot, home to working soundstages and exterior sets where many popular movies and shows have been filmed. During the tram tour, you'll witness King Kong save you from massive predators, see the airplane wreckage from *War of the Worlds,* ride along with the cast of the *Fast and the Furious,* and have a close call with Norman Bates from *Psycho.*

■ TIP→ The tram ride is usually the best place to begin your visit, because the lines become longer as the day goes on.

Geared more toward adults, CityWalk is a separate venue run by Universal Studios, where you'll find shops, restaurants, nightclubs, and movie theaters. ✉ *100 Universal City Plaza, Universal City* ☎ *800/864–8377* 🌐 *www.universalstudioshollywood.com* 🎫 *$139.*

🛏 Hotels

Sheraton Universal

$$ | **HOTEL** | **FAMILY** | With large meeting spaces and a knowledgeable staff, this Sheraton buzzes year-round with business travelers and families, providing easy access to the free shuttle that takes guests to adjacent Universal Studios and CityWalk. **Pros:** pool area with cabanas and bar; convenient for visitors to Universal Studios; family friendly. **Cons:** parking is pricey; touristy crowd; chain hotel feel. [$] *Rooms from: $250* ✉ *333 Universal Hollywood Dr., Universal City* ☎ *818/980–1212, 888/627–7184* 🌐 *www.sheratonuniversal.com* 🛏 *461 rooms* 🍴 *No Meals.*

Studio City

🍴 Restaurants

Asanebo

$$ | **JAPANESE** | One of L.A.'s finest sushi restaurants, Asanebo is an inviting, no-frills establishment serving top-quality sushi and a wealth of innovative dishes to an A-list clientele. The affable chefs will regale you with memorable specialties such as succulent seared *toro* (tuna belly), halibut truffle sashimi, or just simple morsels of pristine fish dusted with sea salt. **Known for:** omakase (chef's choice) dinners; halibut truffle; excellent sushi. [$] *Average main: $30* ✉ *11941 Ventura Blvd., Studio City* ☎ *818/760–3348* 🌐 *www.asanebo-restaurant.com.*

Firefly

$$$ | **AMERICAN** | One minute you're in an old library quickly converted into a lounge, the next you're in the cabana of a modest country club. Yet Firefly's eclectic design is part of its appeal, and its excellent, if a bit pricey, French-American fare will make you forget all about it. **Known for:** prix-fixe and à la carte dining; reputation as a date spot; seasonal fare. [$] *Average main: $34* ✉ *11720 Ventura Blvd., Studio City* ☎ *818/762–1833* 🌐 *www.fireflystudiocity.com.*

Good Neighbor Restaurant

$ | **DINER** | Its walls may be heavy with framed photographs of film and TV stars, and folks from the biz might regularly grace its tables, but this Studio City diner is every bit as down-to-earth as your next-door neighbor, even after 40-some years. It gets pretty busy, but a plateful of that home cooking is worth the wait; or if you're in a mad dash, grab a caffeine or fruit smoothie fix from the Neighbarista. **Known for:** craft-your-own omelet; cottage fries; excellent breakfast food. $ *Average main: $15* ✉ *3701 Cahuenga Blvd. W, Studio City* ☎ *818/761–4627* ⊕ *good-neighborrestaurant.com* ⊘ *Closed Mon.*

▽ Nightlife

Baked Potato
LIVE MUSIC | Baked Potato might be a strange name to give a world-famous jazz club that's been holding performances of well-known acts (Allan Holdsworth and Michael Landau) under its roof since the '70s, but it only takes a quick peek at the menu to understand. Twenty four different types of baked potatoes dominate its otherwise short menu, each of which come with sour cream, butter, and salad to offset all that carb intake. ✉ *3787 Cahuenga Blvd., Studio City* ☎ *818/980–1615* ⊕ *www.thebakedpotato.com.*

Burbank

⊙ Sights

★ Warner Bros. Studios
FILM/TV STUDIO | **FAMILY** | Tour an actual working studio, visit hot sets, and marvel at the costumes and props from the biggest blockbusters at Warner Bros. Studios. The exterior sets and soundstages here have been used to film some of the most famous TV shows and films in Hollywood, making a visit here a vital part of the Los Angeles experience.

After a short film on the studio's movies and TV shows, hop aboard a tram for a ride through the sets and soundstages used for classics such as *Casablanca* and *Rebel Without a Cause.* You'll see the bungalows where Marlon Brando, Bette Davis, and other icons relaxed between takes, and the current production offices for famous directors. You might even spot a celeb or see a shoot in action— tours change from day to day depending

on the productions taking place on the lot. Finally, you can spend a couple of hours pretending like you're part of your favorite shows and movies, whether it's at a working replica of Central Perk from *Friends* or taking part in a Sorting Hat ceremony from the Harry Potter movies. ✉ *3400 W. Riverside Dr., Burbank* ☎ *818/977–8687* ⊕ *www.wbstudiotour. com* ⊠ *From $69.*

⊕ Restaurants

Bea Bea's
$ | **DINER** | **FAMILY** | Just because Bea Bea's is a no-nonsense kind of place, it doesn't mean the food isn't special. This diner serves breakfast food that is about as close to extraordinary as the most important meal of the day can be. **Known for:** pancakes and French toast; friendly staff; classic diner grub. $ *Average main: $15* ✉ *353 N. Pass Ave., Burbank* ☎ *818/846– 2327* ⊕ *www.beabeas.com.*

Centanni Trattoria
$$ | **ITALIAN** | In a city full of adventurous restaurants touting innovation and all things new and gimmicky, Centanni Trattoria focuses on executing traditional, comforting fare to perfection. From lasagna and ravioli to tiramisu, this authentic dinner spot offers reasonably priced, delicious food. **Known for:** pumpkin ravioli; risotto di funghi; great appetizers. $ *Average main: $23* ✉ *117 N. Victory Blvd., Burbank* ☎ *818/561–4643* ⊕ *www. centannila.com.*

Los Amigos
$ | **MEXICAN** | **FAMILY** | If you're in the mood for good old-fashioned fun coupled with hearty Mexican fare and delicious margaritas, then you'll want to consider Los Amigos, whose legendary fruity margaritas alone are worth the drive. Pair those with something from the Platillos Mexicanos menu on karaoke night, and you're guaranteed a good time until the wee hours of the night. **Known for:** classic Mexican food; massive portions; casual

dining. $ *Average main: $18* ✉ *2825 W. Olive Ave., Burbank* ☎ *818/842–3700* ⊕ *www.losamigosbarandgrill.com.*

Porto's Bakery
$ | **CUBAN** | **FAMILY** | Waiting in line at Porto's is as much a part of the experience as is indulging in one of its roasted pork sandwiches or chocolate-dipped croissants. This Cuban bakery and café has been an L.A. staple for more than 50 years, often drawing crowds during lunch. **Known for:** famous potato balls; must-try desserts; fast-moving counter service. $ *Average main: $8* ✉ *3614 W. Magnolia Blvd., Burbank* ☎ *818/846–9100* ⊕ *www.portosbakery.com.*

Hotels

Hotel Amarano Burbank
$$ | **HOTEL** | Close to Burbank's TV and movie studios, the smartly designed Amarano feels like a Beverly Hills boutique hotel, complete with 24-hour room service, a homey on-site restaurant and lounge, and lovely rooms. **Pros:** amenities include saltwater pool and complimentary bike rentals; convenient to studios and restaurants; lively bar. **Cons:** some street noise; away from most of the city's action; $25 amenity fee. $ *Rooms from: $280* ✉ *322 N. Pass Ave., Burbank* ☎ *818/842–8887* ⊕ *www.hotelamarano. com* ➵ *132 rooms* ⍩ *No Meals.*

Nightlife

Flappers Comedy Club
COMEDY CLUBS | Even though this live comedy club doesn't exactly have as long a history as others in town (it opened in 2010), it's attracted an impressive list of big names like Jerry Seinfeld, Maria Bamford, and Adam Sandler thanks to its Celebrity Drop-In Tuesdays. The food and drinks are good though not great, but you're here for the laughs not the grub. ✉ *102 E. Magnolia Blvd., Burbank* ☎ *818/845–9721* ⊕ *www.flapperscomedy.com.*

Shopping

It's a Wrap
OTHER SPECIALTY STORE | For nearly four decades, the wardrobe departments of movie and TV studios and production companies have been shipping clothes and props here daily. Besides scoring occasional gems from designers like Georgio Armani, Versace, Chanel, and more for between 35% and 95% off retail price, insiders flock here to get their hands on a piece of history. Good news for the serious collectors: your purchase includes the title and code from the production it was used on, so you can properly place each piece of memorabilia. ✉ *3315 W. Magnolia Blvd., Burbank* ☎ *818/567–7366* ⊕ *www.itsawraphollywood.com.*

Magnolia Park Vintage
NEIGHBORHOODS | Melrose Avenue might be Los Angeles's most well-known vintage shopping destination, but to many locals, especially those on the Eastside, Burbank's Magnolia Park is, in many ways, better. Spanning several blocks around Magnolia Avenue, this revitalized area blends vintage, thrift, and antiques shopping opportunities with the laid-back small-town vibe that Melrose lacks. Great dining spots and modern coffee shops abound, as well as foot and nail spas for a bit of pampering. ✉ *W. Magnolia Blvd., between N. Niagara and N. Avon St., Burbank* ⊕ *www.visitmagnoliapark.com.*

Playclothes Vintage Fashions
MIXED CLOTHING | Productions including *Mad Men, Austin Powers,* and *Catch Me If You Can* (among many, many others) have turned to this vintage shop for mint-condition pieces from the 1930s through the 1980s. Ladies who love the pinup look will adore the selection of curve-hugging pencil skirts, cardigans, and lingerie, while men will have their pick of Hawaiian shirts, suits, and skinny ties. The time-warped interior also features decorative home accents and

furniture from decades past. ⊠ *3100 W. Magnolia Blvd., Burbank* ☎ *818/557–8447* ⊕ *www.vintageplayclothes.com.*

Mid-Wilshire and Koreatown

While they're two distinctly different neighborhoods, Mid-Wilshire and Koreatown sit side by side and offer Angelenos some of the most interesting sights, sounds, and bites in the city.

Mid-Wilshire is broadly known for its wide variety of museums, but there's also a strip called Little Ethiopia, where you can find incredible cuisine. Koreatown, meanwhile, is not only a haven for Seoul food (pun intended) but also for multiethnic dining, with spots that are often at the top of many best-restaurant lists. Once your stomach is sated, check out a Korean spa, where scrubbing and pampering can close out a perfectly long day.

Mid-Wilshire

◉ Sights

★ Academy Museum of Motion Pictures
OTHER MUSEUM | FAMILY | The long-awaited Academy Museum of Motion Pictures sits on the corner of Wilshire and Fairfax, and is highlighted by a giant spherical dome that features a 1,000-seat theater and stunning terrace with views of the Hollywood Hills. Inside, the museum has seven floors of exhibition space that delves into the history of cinema with interactive exhibits, features on award-winning storytellers, multiple theaters, and immersive experiences. Dedicated to the art and science of movies, the Academy Museum is the premier center that is a must-stop for film buffs and casual moviegoers alike. ⊠ *6067 Wilshire Blvd., Mid-Wilshire* ☎ *323/930–3000* ⊕ *www.academymuseum.org* ⊡ *$25.*

La Brea Tar Pits Museum
NATURE SIGHT | FAMILY | Show your kids where Ice Age fossils come from by taking them to the stickiest park in town. The area formed when deposits of oil rose to the earth's surface, collected in shallow pools, and coagulated into asphalt. In the early 20th century, geologists discovered that all that goo contained the largest collection of Pleistocene (Ice Age) fossils ever found at one location: more than 600 species of birds, mammals, plants, reptiles, and insects. Roughly 100 tons of fossil bones have been removed in excavations during the last 100 years, making this one of the world's most famous fossil sites. You can see most of the pits through chain-link fences, and the Excavator Tour gets you as close as possible to the action.

Pit 91 and Project 23 are ongoing excavation projects; tours are offered, and you can volunteer to help with the excavations in the summer. Several pits are scattered around Hancock Park and the surrounding neighborhood; construction in the area has often had to accommodate them, and in nearby streets and along sidewalks, little bits of tar occasionally ooze up. The museum displays fossils from the tar pits and has a glass-walled laboratory that allows visitors to view paleontologists and volunteers as they work on specimens.

■ TIP→ **Museum admission is free for L.A. County residents weekdays 3–5 pm.** ⊠ *5801 Wilshire Blvd., Miracle Mile* ☎ *323/934–7243* ⊕ *www.tarpits.org* ⊡ *$15* ⊙ *Closed 1st Tues. of every month and every Tues. in Sept.* ☞ *Excavator Tour 1 pm weekdays and 10 am weekends.*

★ Los Angeles County Museum of Art (LACMA)
ART MUSEUM | Los Angeles has a truly fabulous museum culture and everything that it stands for can be epitomized by the massive, eclectic, and ever-changing Los Angeles County Museum of Art. Opened at its current location in 1965,

today the museum boasts the largest collection of art in the western United States with more than 135,000 pieces from 6,000 years of history across multiple buildings atop more than 20 acres. Highlights include the *Urban Light* sculpture by Chris Burden (an Instagram favorite), *Levitated Mass* by Michael Heizer, and prominent works by Frida Kahlo, Wassily Kandinsky, Henri Matisse, and Claude Monet. With an illustrative permanent collection to go along with an ever-rotating array of temporary exhibits, film screenings, educational programs, and more, the museum is a beacon of culture that stands alone in the middle of the city.

■ **TIP→ Temporary exhibitions sometimes require tickets purchased in advance.** ✉ *5905 Wilshire Blvd., Miracle Mile* ☎ *323/857–6000* 🌐 *www.lacma.org* 🎟 *$20* 🕒 *Closed Wed.*

Petersen Automotive Museum

OTHER MUSEUM | FAMILY | L.A. is a mecca for car lovers, which explains the popularity of this museum with a collection of more than 300 automobiles and other motorized vehicles. But you don't have to be a gearhead to appreciate the Petersen; there's plenty of fascinating history here for all to enjoy. Learn how Los Angeles grew up around its freeways, how cars evolve from the design phase to the production line, and how automobiles have influenced film and television. To see how the vehicles, many of them quite rare, are preserved and maintained, take the 90-minute self-guided tour of the basement-level Vault. ✉ *6060 Wilshire Blvd., Mid-Wilshire* ☎ *323/964–6331* 🌐 *www.petersen.org* 🎟 *From $25.*

🍴 Restaurants

★ Meals by Genet

$$ | ETHIOPIAN | In a tucked-away stretch along Fairfax Avenue is Little Ethiopia, where Angelenos of all stripes flock for the African country's signatures like *tibs*, *wat*, and *kitfo*. And while there is a plethora of Ethiopian options, no one does the cuisine justice quite like Meals by Genet. **Known for:** authentic Ethiopian cuisine; jovial atmosphere; unreal tibs. [$] *Average main: $20* ✉ *1053 S. Fairfax Ave., Mid-Wilshire* ☎ *323/938–9304* 🌐 *www.mealsbygenetla.com* 🕒 *Closed Mon.–Wed.*

★ République

$$$ | FRENCH | FAMILY | This stunning expansive space, originally built for Charlie Chaplin back in the 1920s, serves French delicacies for breakfast, lunch, and dinner every day of the week. The scent of homemade croissants wafts through the building in the morning; steak frites can be enjoyed at night. **Known for:** French classics; unbeatable pastries; nice bar menu. [$] *Average main: $35* ✉ *624 S. La Brea Ave., Beverly–La Brea* ☎ *310/362–6115* 🌐 *www.republiquela.com* 🕒 *No dinner Sun. or Mon.*

Sky's Gourmet Tacos

$ | MEXICAN | If you're searching for some of the spiciest and most succulent tacos in L.A., look no further than Sky's. This quaint taco joint offers up beef, chicken, turkey, seafood, and vegan options that will leave your mouth on fire and your belly full in all the best ways possible. **Known for:** amazing tacos with a variety of fillings (including breakfast tacos); lots of spices; jovial atmosphere. [$] *Average main: $10* ✉ *5303 W. Pico Blvd., Mid-Wilshire* ☎ *323/672–4062* 🌐 *www.skysgourmettacos.com.*

Koreatown

🍴 Restaurants

The Boiling Crab

$$ | SEAFOOD | FAMILY | Put on your bib and prepare to get messy, because this crab shack is not for stodgy eaters. Choices of blue, Dungeness, snow, and king are brought out in plastic bags where you can rip, tear, twist, and yank the meaty goodness out of their shells. **Known for:** giant crab legs; unfussy environment; long lines. $ *Average main: $21* ⊠ *3377 Wilshire Blvd., Suite 115, Koreatown* ☎ *213/389–2722* ⊕ *www.theboilingcrab. com* Ⓜ *Wilshire/Normandie Station.*

Guelaguetza

$$ | **MEXICAN** | **FAMILY** | A classic L.A. Mexican eatery, Guelaguetza serves the complex but not overpoweringly spicy cooking of Oaxaca, one of Mexico's most renowned culinary capitals. **Known for:** mole; chili-marinated pork; family-owned restaurant. $ *Average main: $21* ⊠ *3014 W. Olympic Blvd., Koreatown* ☎ *213/427–0608* ⊕ *www.ilovemole.com* ☾ *Closed Mon.*

★ Kobawoo House

$$$ | **KOREAN** | **FAMILY** | Nestled into a dingy strip mall, this Korean powerhouse is given away by the lines of locals waiting outside. Once inside, scents of grilled meats and kimchi immediately fill your nostrils, and soon enough, your table will be littered with sides, *kalbi* beef, *dolsot* bibimbap, *wang bosam* (cabbage wraps with boiled pork), and tall bottles of Hite beer. **Known for:** perfect kalbi beef; long lines; cheap eats. $ *Average main: $35* ⊠ *698 S. Vermont Ave., Suite 109, Koreatown* ☎ *213/389–7300* ⊕ *www.kobawoo-house.com* ☾ *Closed Mon.* Ⓜ *Wilshire/Vermont.*

🛏 Hotels

Hotel Normandie

$$ | **HOTEL** | Originally built in 1926, this Renaissance Revival gem has been renovated to today's standards and is now a hip and not-terribly-pricey spot to post up in the ever-booming center of Koreatown. **Pros:** Michelin-starred French restaurant; daily wine reception; historic burger joint. **Cons:** feels dated; tiny bathrooms; neighborhood can be dangerous at night. $ *Rooms from: $250* ⊠ *605 Normandie Ave., Koreatown* ☎ *213/388–8138* ⊕ *www.hotelnor-mandiela.com* ⇋ *92 rooms* ⦿⃝ *No Meals* Ⓜ *Wilshire/Normandie.*

The Line

$$ | **HOTEL** | This boutique hotel pays homage to its Koreatown address with dynamic dining concepts and a hidden karaoke speakeasy. **Pros:** Room service by Michelin chef Josiah Citrin; unique decor; fun bars on-site (ask about the speakeasy). **Cons:** valet parking $54/night; lobby bar crowds public spaces; hotel is a bit isolated from common tourist attractions. $ *Rooms from: $210* ⊠ *3515 Wilshire Blvd., Koreatown* ☎ *213/381–7411* ⊕ *www.thelinehotel.com* ⇋ *384 rooms* ⦿⃝ *No Meals* Ⓜ *Wilshire/Normandie Station.*

Nightlife

Dan Sung Sa

BARS | Step through the curtained entrance and back in time to 1970s Korea at Dan Sung Sa, which gained wider popularity after Anthony Bourdain paid a visit. At this quirky time-capsule bar, wood-block menus feature roughly 100 small eats. You'll see much that looks familiar, but fortune favors the bold. Take a chance on corn cheese, or try the *makgeolli*: a boozy Korean rice drink you sip from a bowl. It pairs perfectly with good conversation and snacking all night long. ⊠ *3317 W. 6th St., Koreatown* ☎ *213/487–9100* ⊕ *dansungsala.com* Ⓜ *Wilshire/Vermont.*

★ HMS Bounty

BARS | This super-kitschy nautical-theme bar in the heart of Koreatown offers drink specials and food at prices that will make you swoon. Come for the wings, all-day breakfast specials, cheap drinks, and very eclectic crowds. ⊠ *3357 Wilshire Blvd., Koreatown* ☎ *213/385–7275* ⊕ *www.the-hmsbounty.com* Ⓜ *Wilshire/Normandie.*

The Prince

BARS | *Mad Men* and *New Girl* both had multiple scenes filmed in this Old Hollywood relic, which dates back to the early

1900s. The Prince is trimmed with vintage fabric wallpaper and bedecked with a stately mahogany bar; the grand piano waits in the wings. Squire lamps punctuate red-leather booths where you can enjoy Korean fare and standard cocktails, wine, and beer. Whatever you do, get the deep-fried chicken. ⊠ *3198 W. 7th St., Koreatown* ☎ *213/389–1586* ⊘ *Closed Sun.* Ⓜ *Wilshire/Vermont Station.*

Activities

Aroma Spa & Sports

SPAS | It's not difficult to find amazing spa experiences throughout Koreatown. Most places will offer up standard scrubs, hot and cold baths, dry and wet saunas, and more. Aroma takes things to another level as the spa is just the centerpiece of an entire entertainment complex. Spa services include all the traditional treatments, but when you're done getting pampered, the rest of the facility includes a gym, a swimming pool, restaurants, and a state-of-the-art golf driving range. ⊠ *3680 Wilshire Blvd., Koreatown* ☎ *213/387–2111* ⊕ *www. aromaresort.com* Ⓜ *Wilshire/Western.*

★ Wi Spa

SPAS | Koreatown is filled with endless spa experiences, but there are a few that rise above the rest. Wi Spa is a 24/7 wonderland of treatments that includes hot and cold baths, unique sauna rooms, and floors for men, women, or co-ed family spa fun. Signature sauna rooms vary from intense 231-degree thermotherapy to salt-enriched stations and specialty clay imported from Korea. Just remember, Korean spas are not for the shy at heart—you will be nude, you will get scrubbed, and you will feel like a million bucks after. ⊠ *2700 Wilshire Blvd., Koreatown* ☎ *213/487–2700* ⊕ *www.wispausa. com* ▨ *For services under $150, there is an admission fee of $30* Ⓜ *Wilshire/Vermont.*

Downtown Los Angeles

If there's one thing Angelenos love, it's a makeover, and city planners have put the wheels in motion for a dramatic revitalization of this area in recent years. Downtown is both glamorous and gritty, epitomizing L.A.'s complexity as a whole.

On the glamorous side, this area offers a dizzying variety of experiences showcasing the artistic, historic, ethnic, and sports-loving aspects of the city. On the gritty side, nowhere is L.A.'s homelessness problem more prevalent than in Downtown. Tent encampments often flank sparkling new high-rises, highlighting the dichotomy of the city's rich and poor. Walking around this area at night can be dangerous; drugs and crime are an unfortunate byproduct of the overwhelming number of people on the streets.

⊙ Sights

★ Angels Flight Railway

HISTORIC SIGHT | The turn-of-the-20th-century funicular, dubbed "the shortest railway in the world," operated between 1901 and 1969, when it was dismantled to make room for an urban renewal project. Almost 30 years later, Angels Flight returned with its original orange-and-black wooden cable cars hauling travelers up a 298-foot incline from Hill Street to the fountain-filled Watercourt at California Plaza. Your reward is a stellar view of the neighborhood. Tickets are $1 each way, but you can buy a souvenir round-trip ticket for $2 if you want something to take home with you. ⊠ *351 S. Hill St., between 3rd and 4th Sts., Downtown* ☎ *213/626–1901* ⊕ *www.angelsflight.org.*

Bradbury Building

NOTABLE BUILDING | Stunning wrought-iron railings, ornate plaster moldings, pink marble staircases, a birdcage elevator, and a skylighted atrium that rises almost 50 feet—it's easy to see why the Bradbury Building leaves visitors awestruck. Designed in 1893 by a novice architect who drew his inspiration from a science-fiction story and a conversation with his dead brother via an Ouija board, the office building was originally the site of turn-of-the-20th-century sweatshops, but now it houses a variety of businesses. Scenes from *Blade Runner*, *Chinatown*, and *500 Days of Summer* were filmed here, which means there's often a barrage of tourists snapping photos. Visits are limited to the lobby and the first-floor landing.

■TIP→ **Historic Downtown walking tours hosted by the L.A. Conservancy cost $15 and include the Bradbury Building.** ⊠ *304 S. Broadway, Downtown* ☎ *213/626–1893* ⊕ *www.laconservancy.org/locations/bradbury-building* Ⓜ *Pershing Square Station.*

★ **The Broad Museum**

ART MUSEUM | The talk of Los Angeles's art world when it opened in 2015, this museum in an intriguing, honeycomb-looking building was created by philanthropists Eli and Edythe Broad (rhymes with "road") to showcase their stunning private collection of contemporary art, amassed over five decades and still growing. With upward of 2,000 pieces by more than 200 artists, the collection has in-depth representations of the work of such prominent names as Jean Michel Basquiat, Jeff Koons, Ed Ruscha, Cindy Sherman, Cy Twombly, Kara Walker, and Christopher Wool. The "veil and vault" design of the main building integrates gallery space and storage space (visitors can glimpse the latter through a window in the stairwell): the veil refers to the fiberglass, concrete, and steel exterior; the vault is the concrete base. Temporary exhibits and works from the permanent collection are arranged in the small first-floor rooms and in the more expansive third floor of the museum, so you can explore everything in a few hours. Next door to the Broad is a small plaza with olive trees and seating, as well as the

museum restaurant, Otium. Admission to the museum is free, but book timed tickets in advance to guarantee entry. ⊠ *221 S. Grand Ave., Downtown* ☎ *213/232–6200* ⊕ *www.thebroad. org* Free ⊗ *Closed Mon.* Tickets required in advance Ⓜ *Civic Center/Grand Park Station.*

California African American Museum

ART MUSEUM | With more than 4,500 historical artifacts, this museum showcases contemporary art of the African diaspora. Artists represented here include Betye Saar, Charles Haywood, and June Edmonds. The museum has a research library with more than 6,000 books available for public use.

■TIP→ **If possible, visit on a Sunday or Thursday, when there's almost always a diverse lineup of speakers and performances.** ⊠ *600 State Dr., Exposition Park* ☎ *213/744–7432* ⊕ *www.caamuseum.org* Free; parking $15 ⊗ *Closed Mon. and Tues.* Ⓜ *Expo/Vermont Station.*

California Science Center

SCIENCE MUSEUM | **FAMILY** | You're bound to see excited kids running up to the dozens of interactive exhibits here that illustrate the prevalence of science in everyday life. Clustered in different "worlds," the center keeps young guests busy for hours. They can design their own buildings and learn how to make them earthquake-proof; watch GLOBAL ZONE, where you can see Earth's global cycles of air, water, land, and life exhibited on a giant interactive globe. One of the exhibits in the Air and Space section shows how astronauts Pete Conrad and Dick Gordon made it to outer space in the Gemini 11 capsule in 1966. The IMAX theater screens science-related large-format films that change throughout the year. ⊠ *700 Exposition Park Dr., Exposition Park* ☎ *323/724–3623* ⊕ *www. californiasciencecenter.org* Permanent exhibits free; fees for some attractions, special exhibits, and IMAX screenings vary; parking $15 Ⓜ *Expo/Vermont.*

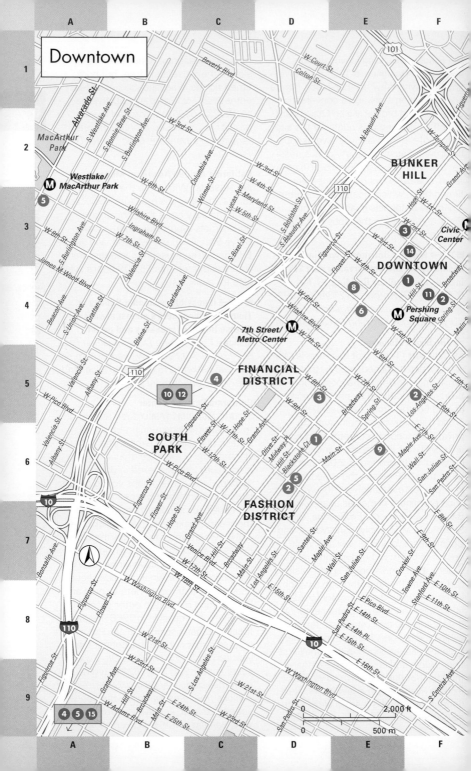

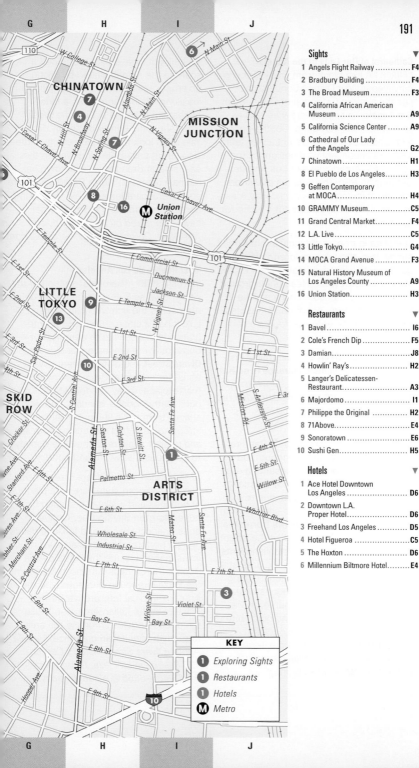

KEY

🔴 *Exploring Sights*

🔴 *Restaurants*

🔴 *Hotels*

Ⓜ *Metro*

Cathedral of Our Lady of the Angels

CHURCH | A half block from Frank Gehry's curvaceous Walt Disney Concert Hall sits the austere Cathedral of Our Lady of the Angels—a spiritual draw as well as an architectural attraction. Controversy surrounded Spanish architect José Rafael Moneo's unconventional design for the seat of the Archdiocese of Los Angeles. But judging from the swarms of visitors and the standing-room-only holiday masses, the church has carved out a niche for itself in Downtown L.A.

The plaza in front is glaringly bright on sunny days, though a children's play garden with bronze animals mitigates the starkness somewhat. Head underground to wander the mausoleum's mazelike white-marble corridors. Free self-guided tours start at the entrance fountain at 1 pm on weekdays.

■TIP→ **There's plenty of underground visitors' parking; the vehicle entrance is on Hill Street.** ⊠ *555 W. Temple St., Downtown* ☎ *213/680–5200* ⊕ *www.olacathedral.org* 🖾 *Free* Ⓜ *Civic Center/Grand Park.*

Chinatown

HISTORIC DISTRICT | Smaller than San Francisco's Chinatown, this neighborhood near Union Station still represents a slice of East Asian life. Sidewalks are usually jammed with tourists, locals, and residents hustling from shop to shop picking up goods, spices, and trinkets from small shops and mini-plazas that line the street. Although some longtime establishments have closed in recent years, the area still pulses with its founding culture. During Chinese New Year, giant dragons snake down the street. And, of course, there are the many restaurants and quick-bite cafés specializing in Chinese feasts. In recent years, a slew of hip eateries like Howlin' Ray's and Majordomo have injected the area with vibrancy.

An influx of local artists has added a spark to the neighborhood by taking up empty spaces and opening galleries along Chung King Road, a faded pedestrian passage behind the West Plaza shopping center between Hill and Yale. Also look for galleries along a little side street called Gin Ling Way on the east side of Broadway. Chinatown has its main action on North Broadway. There are several garages available for parking here that range from $15 to $25 per day. ⊠ *Bordered by the 110, 101, and 5 freeways, Downtown* ⊕ *chinatownla.com* Ⓜ *Union Station.*

★ El Pueblo de Los Angeles

HISTORIC SIGHT | The oldest section of the city, known as El Pueblo de Los Angeles, represents the rich Mexican heritage of L.A. It had a close shave with disintegration in the early 20th century, but key buildings were preserved, and eventually **Olvera Street,** the district's heart, was transformed into a Mexican American marketplace. Today vendors still sell puppets, leather goods, sandals, and woolen shawls from stalls lining the narrow street. You can find everything from salt and pepper shakers shaped like donkeys to gorgeous glassware and pottery.

At the beginning of Olvera Street is the Plaza, a Mexican-style park with plenty of benches and walkways shaded by a huge Moreton Bay fig tree. On weekends, mariachi bands and folkloric dance groups perform. Nearby places worth investigating include the historic Avila Adobe, the Chinese American Museum, the Plaza Firehouse Museum, and the America Tropical Interpretive Center. Exhibits at the Italian American Museum of Los Angeles chronicle the area's formerly heavy Italian presence. ⊠ *Avila Adobe/Olvera Street Visitors Center, 125 Paseo De La Plaza, Downtown* ☎ *213/485–6855* ⊕ *elpueblo.lacity.org*

Free for Olvera St. and self-guided tours; fees at some museums.

Geffen Contemporary at MOCA

ART MUSEUM | The Geffen Contemporary is one of architect Frank Gehry's boldest creations. One of three MOCA branches, the 40,000 square feet of exhibition space was once used as a police car warehouse. The museum's permanent collection includes works from artists like Willem de Kooning, Franz Kline, Jackson Pollock, Mark Rothko, and Cindy Sherman.

■TIP➔ **Present your TAP metro card to get two-for-one admission.** ⊠ *152 N. Central Ave., Downtown* ☎ *213/626–6222* ⊕ *www.moca.org/visit/geffen-contemporary* *Free; special exhibitions $18 or free every Thurs. 5–8; parking $9* ⊘ *Closed Mon.*

GRAMMY Museum

OTHER MUSEUM | The GRAMMY Museum brings the music industry to life. Throughout four floors and 30,000 square feet of space, the museum showcases rare footage of GRAMMY performances, plus rotating and interactive exhibits on award-winning musicians and the history of music. A 200-seat theater is great for live events that include screenings, lectures, interviews, and intimate music performances. ⊠ *800 W. Olympic Blvd., Downtown* ☎ *213/765–6800* ⊕ *www.grammymuseum.org* *$18* ⊘ *Closed Tues.* Ⓜ *Pico.*

★ Grand Central Market

MARKET | With options that include handmade white-corn tamales, warm olive bread, dried figs, Mexican fruit drinks, and much more, this mouthwatering gathering place is the city's largest and most active food market. The spot bustles nonstop with locals and visitors surveying the butcher shop's display of everything from lambs' heads to pigs' tails. Produce stalls are piled high with locally grown avocados and heirloom tomatoes. Stop by Chiles Secos at stall No. 30 for a remarkable selection of rare chilies and spices; Ramen Hood at No. 23, for sumptuous vegan noodles and broth; or Sticky Rice at stall No. 24, for fantastic Thai-style chicken. Even if you don't plan on buying anything, it's a great place to browse and people-watch. ⊠ *317 S. Broadway, Downtown* ☎ *213/624–2378* ⊕ *www.grandcentralmarket.com* *Free* Ⓜ *Pershing Square.*

L.A. Live

PLAZA/SQUARE | The mammoth L.A. Live entertainment complex was opened in 2007 when there was little to do or see in this section of Downtown. Since its inception, this once creepy ghost town has become a major hub for sports, concerts, award shows, and more. The first things you'll notice as you emerge from the parking lot are the giant LED screens and sparkling lights, and the buzz of crowds as they head out to dinner before or after a Lakers game, movie, or live show at the Microsoft Theater. There are dozens of restaurants and eateries here, including Los Angeles favorite Katsuya, the spot for sizzling Kobe beef platters and excellent sushi (the crab rolls are not to be missed).

■TIP➔ **Park for free on weekdays from 11 am to 2 pm if you eat at one of the dozen or so restaurants here.** ⊠ *800 W. Olympic Blvd., Downtown* ☎ *213/763–5483* ⊕ *www.lalive.com* Ⓜ *Pico.*

★ Little Tokyo

HISTORIC DISTRICT | One of three official Japantowns in the country—all of which are in California—Little Tokyo is blossoming again thanks to the next generation of Japanese Americans setting up small businesses. Besides dozens of sushi bars, tempura restaurants, and karaoke bars, there's a lovely garden at the Japanese American Cultural and Community Center and a renovated 1925 Buddhist temple with an ornate entrance at the Japanese American National Museum.

On 1st Street you'll find a strip of buildings from the early 1900s. Look down when you get near San Pedro Street to see the art installation called *Omoide no Shotokyo* ("Remembering Old Little Tokyo"). Embedded in the sidewalk are brass inscriptions naming the original businesses, quoted reminiscences from residents, and steel time lines of Japanese American history up to World War II. Nisei Week (a *nisei* is a second-generation Japanese American) is celebrated every August with traditional drums, dancing, a carnival, and a huge parade.

■TIP➔ **Docent-led walking tours are available by appointment on occasional Saturdays starting at 10:15 am. The cost is $15 and should be reserved in advance at** ⊕ *littletokyohs.org.* ⊠ *Bounded by 1st and 3rd Sts., the 101 and 110 freeways, and L.A. River, Downtown* ☎ *213/880–6875* ⊕ *www.visitlittletokyo.com* Ⓜ *Civic Center/Grand Park Station.*

MOCA Grand Avenue

ART MUSEUM | The main branch of the Museum of Contemporary Art, designed by Arata Isozaki, contains underground galleries and presents elegant exhibitions. A huge Nancy Rubins sculpture fashioned from used airplane parts graces the museum's front plaza. The museum gift shop offers apothecary items, modernist ceramics, and even toys and games for children to appease any art lover.

■TIP➔ **Take advantage of the free audio tour.** ⊠ *250 S. Grand Ave., Downtown* ☎ *213/626–6222* ⊕ *www.moca.org* 🎟 *General admission free; special exhibitions $18 or free Thurs. 5–8* ⊗ *Closed Mon.* Ⓜ *Civic Center/Grand Park.*

Natural History Museum of Los Angeles County

HISTORY MUSEUM | FAMILY | The hot ticket at this Beaux Arts–style museum completed in 1913 is the Dinosaur Hall, whose more than 300 fossils include adult, juvenile, and baby skeletons of the fearsome *Tyrannosaurus rex*. The Discovery Center lets kids and curious grown-ups touch real animal pelts, and the Insect Zoo gets everyone up close and personal with the white-eyed assassin bug and other creepy crawlers. A massive hall displays dioramas of animals in their natural habitats. Also look for pre-Columbian artifacts and crafts from the South Pacific, or priceless stones in the Gem and Mineral Hall. Outdoors, the 3½-acre Nature Gardens shelter native plant and insect species and contain an expansive edible garden.

■TIP➔ **Don't miss out on the Dino lab, where you can watch paleontologists unearth and clean real fossils.** ⊠ *900 W. Exposition Blvd., Exposition Park* ☎ *213/763–3466* ⊕ *www.nhm.org* 🎟 *$15* ⊗ *Closed 1st Tues. of the month* Ⓜ *Expo/Vermont.*

Union Station

TRAIN/TRAIN STATION | Even if you don't plan on traveling by train anywhere, head here to soak up the ambience of a great rail station. Envisioned by John and Donald Parkinson, the architects who also designed the grand City Hall, the 1939 masterpiece combines Spanish Colonial Revival and art deco elements that have retained their classic warmth and quality. The waiting hall's commanding scale and enormous chandeliers have provided the backdrop for countless scenes in films, TV shows, and music videos. Recently added to the majesty are the Homebound Brew Haus and the Traxx Bar, two bars that pay homage to the station's original architecture while serving homemade brews and inventive classic cocktails. ■TIP➔ **Walking tours of Union Station are on Saturday at 11 and cost $15.** ⊠ *800 N. Alameda St., Downtown* ⊕ *www.unionstationla.com* Ⓜ *Union Station.*

⊕ Restaurants

★ Bavel

$$$$ | **MIDDLE EASTERN** | Fans of Bestia have been lining up for stellar Mediterranean cuisine at this Arts District hot spot, which is owned by the same restaurateurs. Rose-gold stools give way to marble tabletops as the open kitchen bangs out hummus and baba ghanoush spreads, along with flatbreads and lamb-neck shawarma. **Known for:** delicious Mediterranean cuisine; reservations recommended; great vibes. $ Average main: $50 ⊠ 500 Mateo St., Downtown 🕾 213/232–4966 ⊕ baveldtla.com.

★ Cole's French Dip

$ | **AMERICAN** | There's a fight in Los Angeles over who created the French dip sandwich. The first contender is Cole's, whose sign on the door says it's the originator of the salty, juicy, melt-in-your-mouth meats. **Known for:** historic L.A. dining; one of the top contenders for best French dip sandwich in the country; secret speakeasy in back. $ Average main: $18 ⊠ 118 E. 6th St., Downtown 🕾 213/622–4090 ⊕ www.pouringwithheart.com/coles.

Damian

$$$ | **MODERN MEXICAN** | The Arts District in DTLA continues to trot out some of the most exciting restaurants in all of Los Angeles, and Damian is simply the latest and greatest example to enter the space. Across from Bestia, the Enrique Olvera–helmed joint serves contemporary Mexican fare combined with California's bounty of excellent produce. **Known for:** modern Mexican cuisine; great cocktails; buzzy spot. $ Average main: $40 ⊠ 2132 E. 7th Pl., Downtown 🕾 213/270–0178 ⊕ www.damiandtla.com ⊗ Closed Mon. and Tues. ☞ Open for brunch weekends.

★ Howlin' Ray's

$ | **SOUTHERN** | **FAMILY** | Don't let the hour-long waits deter you—if you want the best Nashville fried chicken in L.A., Howlin' Ray's is worth the effort. Right in the middle of Chinatown, this tiny chicken joint consists of a few bar seats, a few side tables, and a kitchen that sizzles as staff yell out "yes, chef" with each incoming order. **Known for:** spicy fried chicken; classic Southern sides; long waits. $ Average main: $15 ⊠ 727 N. Broadway, Suite 128, Downtown 🕾 213/935–8399 ⊕ www.howlinrays.com ⊗ Closed Mon. and Tues. Ⓜ Union Station.

★ Langer's Delicatessen-Restaurant

$$ | **SANDWICHES** | **FAMILY** | This James Beard Award winner not only has the look and feel of a no-frills Jewish deli from New York, it also has the food to match. The draw here is the hand-cut pastrami: lean, peppery, robust—and with a reputation for being the best in town. **Known for:** #19 sandwich; Jewish deli classics like matzo ball soup and rugelach; no-frills atmosphere. $ Average main: $23 ⊠ 704 S. Alvarado St., Downtown 🕾 213/483–8050 ⊕ www.langersdeli.com ⊗ Closed Sun. No dinner Ⓜ Westlake/MacArthur Park.

★ Majordomo

$$$$ | **ECLECTIC** | You would never just stumble upon this out-of-the-way spot in Chinatown, but world-famous celeb chef David Chang likes it that way. The beautifully designed minimal spot with spacious patio, an exposed-duct ceiling, and elongated wood bar has a cuisine style that defies any singular category. **Known for:** chuck short rib; rice-based drinks; hard-to-get reservations (try to eat at the bar). $ Average main: $55 ⊠ 1725 Naud St., Downtown 🕾 323/545–4880 ⊕ www.majordomo.la ⊗ Closed Mon. and Tues.

★ Philippe the Original
$ | AMERICAN | FAMILY | First opened in 1908, Philippe's is one of L.A.'s oldest restaurants and claims to be the originator of the French dip sandwich. While the debate continues around the city, one thing is certain: the dips made with beef, pork, ham, lamb, or turkey on a freshly baked roll stand the test of time. Join locals as they chow down at communal tables while debating Dodgers games and politics. **Known for:** 50¢ coffee; communal tables; post–Dodgers game eats. [$] *Average main: $11* ✉ *1001 N. Alameda St., Downtown* ☎ *213/628–3781* 🌐 *www.philippes.com* [M] *Union Station.*

71Above
$$$$ | ECLECTIC | As its name suggests, this sky-high dining den sits on the 71st floor, 950 feet above ground level. With that elevation comes the most stunning views of any restaurant in L.A., and the food is close to matching it. **Known for:** sky-high views; fine dining with a seafood focus; classy atmosphere and loosely enforced dress code (no shorts or flip-flops). [$] *Average main: $45* ✉ *633 W. 5th St., 71st fl., Downtown* ☎ *213/712–2683* 🌐 *www.71above.com* 🕒 *No lunch* [M] *Pershing Square Station.*

Sonoratown
$ | MEXICAN | Paying homage to the Mexican border town where owner Teo Diaz-Rodriguez Jr. grew up, Sonoratown is a Downtown L.A. joint that serves some of the best tacos in the entire city. Handmade tortillas, mesquite wood-fired carne asada, and supercheap prices have made this spot a neighborhood favorite and a must-have on any trip Downtown. **Known for:** excellent Sonoran-style tacos; great prices; friendly neighborhood spot. [$] *Average main: $8* ✉ *208 E. 8th St., Downtown* ☎ *213/628–3710* 🌐 *www.sonoratown.com.*

Sushi Gen
$$ | JAPANESE | Consistently rated one of the top sushi spots in L.A., Sushi Gen continues to dole out the freshest and tastiest fish in town. Sit at the elongated bar and get to know the sushi masters while they prepare your lunch. **Known for:** chef-recommended sushi selections; limited seating; great lunch specials. [$] *Average main: $25* ✉ *422 E. 2nd St., Downtown* ☎ *213/617–0552* 🌐 *www.sushigen-dtla.com* 🕒 *Closed Sun. and Mon. No lunch Sat.*

🛏 Hotels

★ Ace Hotel Downtown Los Angeles
$ | HOTEL | The L.A. edition of this bohemian-chic hipster haven is at once a hotel, theater, and poolside bar (called Upstairs), housed in the gorgeous Spanish Gothic–style United Artists building in the heart of Downtown. **Pros:** lively rooftop lounge/pool area; gorgeous building and views; location in the heart of Downtown. **Cons:** expensive parking rates compared to nightly rates ($55); some kinks in the service; compact rooms. [$] *Rooms from: $165* ✉ *929 S. Broadway, Downtown* ☎ *213/623–3233* 🌐 *www.acehotel.com/losangeles* 🛏 *183 rooms* 🍴 *No Meals.*

★ Downtown L.A. Proper Hotel
$$ | HOTEL | The new Downtown L.A. Proper Hotel is a design-lover's dream as renowned interior decorator Kelly Wearstler infuses the property with touches of Mexican modernism to Moroccan and Spanish flourishes. **Pros:** stunning interior design; restaurants and bars by renowned L.A. chefs; speakeasy off lobby. **Cons:** parking $55/night; smallish rooms; the area can be dangerous at night. [$] *Rooms from: $269* ✉ *1100 S. Broadway, Downtown* ☎ *213/806–1010* 🌐 *www.properhotel.com/downtown-la* 🛏 *147 rooms* 🍴 *No Meals.*

★ Freehand Los Angeles
$ | HOTEL | Part hotel, part shared accommodation space, the Freehand is one of the newer hotels in Downtown Los Angeles and also one of the coolest. **Pros:** range of affordable rooms from

lofts to bunk beds; active social scene; great rooftop pool and bar. **Cons:** area can be dangerous at night; free lobby Wi-Fi attracts nonhotel guests; most affordable rooms are shared accommodations. [$] *Rooms from: $77* ✉ *416 W. 8th St., Downtown* ☎ *213/612–0021* 🌐 *freehandhotels.com/los-angeles* 🛏 *59 shared rooms* 🍴 *No Meals* [M] *Pershing Square.*

Hotel Figueroa

$$ | **HOTEL** | The 12-story Hotel Figueroa was originally built in 1926, and touches of that originality are still seen throughout with original skylights, wood beams, and tiles. **Pros:** a short walk to L.A. Live and the convention center; great poolside bar; buzzy nightlife scene. **Cons:** the area can be dangerous at night; expensive parking ($52/night); smallish pool. [$] *Rooms from: $219* ✉ *939 S. Figueroa St., Downtown* ☎ *866/734–6018* 🌐 *www.hotelfigueroa.com* 🛏 *268 rooms* 🍴 *No Meals* [M] *Olympic/Figueroa.*

The Hoxton

$$ | **HOTEL** | One of the chicest Downtown hotels, the Hoxton is an open-house hotel where the lobby is the hub of activity and welcoming to all, and has thoughtful design touches that permeate throughout. **Pros:** stellar restaurant; welcoming lobby; great rooftop pool. **Cons:** area can be dangerous at night; no gym; some rooms on the small side. [$] *Rooms from: $249* ✉ *1060 S. Broadway, Downtown* ☎ *213/725–5900* 🌐 *www.thehoxton.com/downtown-la* 🛏 *174 rooms* 🍴 *No Meals.*

Millennium Biltmore Hotel

$ | **HOTEL** | As the local headquarters of John F. Kennedy's 1960 presidential campaign and the location of some of the earliest Academy Awards ceremonies, this Downtown treasure, with its gilded 1923 Beaux Arts design, exudes ambience and history. **Pros:** 24-hour fitness center; tiled indoor pool; impressive history. **Cons:** business groups can overwhelm common areas; standard rooms are compact; some decor feels outdated. [$] *Rooms from: $150* ✉ *506 S. Grand Ave., Downtown* ☎ *213/624–1011, 866/866–8086* 🌐 *www.millenniumhotels.com* 🛏 *683 rooms* 🍴 *No Meals* [M] *Pershing Square.*

Nightlife

Broadway Bar

BARS | This watering-hole-meets-dive sits in a flourishing section of Broadway (neighbors include the swank Ace Hotel). Bartenders mix creative cocktails while DJs spin tunes nightly. The two-story space includes a smoking balcony overlooking the street. The crowd is often dressed to impress. ✉ *830 S. Broadway, Downtown* ☎ *213/614–9909* 🌐 *www.broadwaybarla.com.*

★ Golden Gopher

BARS | Craft cocktails, beers on tap, an outdoor smoking patio, and retro video games—this bar in the heart of Downtown is not to be missed. With one of the oldest liquor licenses in Los Angeles (issued in 1905), the Golden Gopher is the only bar in Los Angeles with an on-site liquor store for to-go orders—just in case you want to buy another bottle before you head home. ✉ *417 W. 8th St., Downtown* ☎ *213/614–8001* 🌐 *www.pouringwithheart.com/golden-gopher* [M] *7th Street/Metro Center.*

Redwood Bar & Grill

LIVE MUSIC | If you're looking for a place with potent drinks and a good burger, this kitschy bar fits the bill perfectly. Known today as the "pirate bar" because of its nautical decor, the place dates back to the 1940s, when it was rumored to attract mobsters, politicians, and journalists due to its proximity to city hall, the Hall of Justice, and the original location of the *Los Angeles Times*. There's nightly live music, though it comes with a cover charge. ✉ *316 W. 2nd St., Downtown* ☎ *213/680–2600* 🌐 *www.theredwoodbar.com* [M] *Civic Center/Grand Park.*

★ Resident

LIVE MUSIC | Catch a lineup of indie taste-makers inside this converted industrial space, or hang outdoors in the beer garden while trying bites from on-site food truck KTCHN (on cooler evenings you can congregate around the firepits). A wide variety of draft beers and a specially curated cocktail program are available inside at the bar or at the trailer bar outside. ✉ *428 S. Hewitt St., Downtown* ☎ *213/628–7503* ⊕ *www.residentdtla. com.*

★ Seven Grand

BARS | The hunting lodge vibe makes you feel like you need a whiskey in hand—luckily, this Downtown establishment stocks more than 700 of them. Attracting whiskey novices and connoisseurs, the bartenders here are more than willing to help you make a selection. Live jazz, blues, folk, and other bands play almost every night, so even if you're not a big drinker, there's still some appeal (although you're definitely missing out). For a more intimate setting, try the on-site Bar Jackalope, a bar within a bar, which has a "whiskey tasting library" specializing in Japanese varieties and seats only 18. ✉ *515 W. 7th St., 2nd fl., Downtown* ☎ *213/614–0736* ⊕ *www. sevengrandbars.com* Ⓜ *7th Street/Metro Center.*

🆕 Performing Arts

Ahmanson Theatre

THEATER | The largest of L.A.'s Center Theatre Group's three theaters, the 2,100-seat Ahmanson Theatre presents larger-scale classic revivals, dramas, musicals, and comedies like *Into the Woods,* which are either going to or coming from Broadway and the West End. The ambience is a theater lover's delight. ✉ *135 N. Grand Ave., Downtown* ☎ *213/972–7211* ⊕ *www.musiccenter. org/visit/Our-Venues/ahmanson-theatre* Ⓜ *Civic Center/Grand Park Station.*

★ Dorothy Chandler Pavilion

CONCERTS | Though half a century old, this theater maintains the glamour of its early years, richly decorated with crystal chandeliers, classical theatrical drapes, and a 24-karat gold dome. Part of the Los Angeles Music Center, this pavilion is home to the L.A. Opera though a large portion of programming is made up of dance and ballet performances as well. Ticket holders can attend free talks that take place an hour before opera performances.

■ **TIP** ➜ **Reservations for the talks aren't required, but it's wise to arrive early, as space is limited.** ✉ *135 N. Grand Ave., Downtown* ☎ *213/972–0711* ⊕ *www. musiccenter.org/visit/Our-Venues/dorothy-chandler-pavilion* Ⓜ *Civic Center/ Grand Park.*

Microsoft Theater

CONCERTS | The Microsoft Theater is host to a variety of concerts and big-name awards shows—the Emmys, American Music Awards, BET Awards, and the ESPYs. This theater and the surrounding L.A. Live complex are a draw for those looking for a fun night out. The building's emphasis on acoustics and versatile seating arrangements means that all 7,100 seats are good, whether you're at an intimate acoustic concert or an awards show. Outside, the L.A. Live complex is home to restaurants and attractions, including the GRAMMY Museum, to keep patrons entertained before and after shows (though it's open whether or not there's a performance). ✉ *777 Chick Hearn Ct., Downtown* ☎ *213/763–6030* ⊕ *www.microsofttheater.com* Ⓜ *Pico.*

Orpheum Theatre

CONCERTS | Opened in 1926, the opulent Orpheum Theatre played host to live attractions including classic comedians, burlesque dancers, jazz greats like Lena Horne, Ella Fitzgerald, and Duke Ellington, and later on rock-and-roll performers such as Little Richard. After extensive restorations, the Orpheum once again revealed a stunning white-marble lobby, majestic auditorium with fleur-de-lis panels, and two dazzling chandeliers. A thick red velvet and gold-trimmed curtain opens at showtime, and a white Wurlitzer pipe organ (one of the last remaining organs of its kind from the silent movie era) is at the ready. The original 1926 rooftop neon sign again shines brightly, signaling a new era for this theater. Today the theater plays host to live concerts, comedy shows, and movie screenings. ⊠ *842 S. Broadway, Downtown* ☎ *877/677–1386* ⊕ *www.laorpheum. com/events.*

Shrine Auditorium

CONCERTS | Since opening in 1926, the auditorium has hosted nearly every major awards show at one point or another, including the Emmys and the GRAMMYs. Today, the venue and adjacent Expo Hall hosts concerts, film premieres, award shows, pageants, and special events. The Shrine's Moorish Revival–style architecture is a spectacle all its own. ⊠ *665 W. Jefferson Blvd., Downtown* ☎ *213/748–5116* ⊕ *www.shrineauditorium.com.*

★ Walt Disney Concert Hall

CONCERTS | One of the architectural wonders of Los Angeles, the 2,265-seat hall is a sculptural monument of gleaming, curved steel designed by Frank Gehry. It's part of a complex that includes a public park, gardens, shops, and two outdoor amphitheaters, one of them atop the concert hall. The acoustically superlative venue is the home of the city's premier orchestra, the Los Angeles Philharmonic, whose music director, Gustavo Dudamel, is an international celebrity in his own right. The orchestra's season runs from late September to early June, before it heads to the Hollywood Bowl for the summer. ⊠ *111 S. Grand Ave., Downtown* ☎ *323/850–2000* ⊕ *www.laphil.org* ⛟ *Free self-guided tours* Ⓜ *Civic Center/ Grand Park.*

🛍 Shopping

★ Olvera Street

MARKET | FAMILY | Known as the birthplace of Los Angeles, this redbrick walkway is lined with historic buildings and overhung with grapevines. At dozens of clapboard stalls you can browse south-of-the-border goods—leather sandals, woven blankets, and devotional candles, as well as cheap toys and souvenirs—and sample outstanding tacos. With the musicians and cafés providing the soundtrack, the area is constantly lively. Annual events include a tree-lighting ceremony and Día de los Muertos celebrations. ⊠ *Downtown* ✛ *Between Cesar Chavez Ave. and Arcadia St.* ⊕ *www.olvera-street.com* Ⓜ *Union Station.*

Row DTLA

SHOPPING CENTER | The city's newest shopping, food, and cultural destination in the venerable L.A. Arts District, Row DTLA is spread across an entire campus, with around 100 curated boutique stores like Poketo, Bodega, A+R, Flask & Field, and Tokyo Bike. Additionally, new restaurants like Rappahannock Oyster Bar and Michelin-starred Hayato seem to be popping up weekly. A weekend highlight is Smorgasburg, where every Sunday dozens of food stalls pop up in the next-door parking lot serving tasty favorites across every cuisine imaginable. ⊠ *777 Alameda St., Downtown* ☎ *213/988– 8890* ⊕ *rowdtla.com.*

The Santee Alley

NEIGHBORHOODS | Situated in the Fashion District, the Santee Alley is known for back-alley deals on knockoffs of designer sunglasses, jewelry, handbags, shoes, and clothing. Be prepared to haggle, and don't lose sight of your wallet. Weekend crowds can be overwhelming, but there's plenty of street food to keep your energy up. ⊠ *Santee St. and Maple Ave. from Olympic Blvd. to 12th St., Downtown* ☎ *213/488–1153* ⊕ *www.fashiondistrict. org/santee-alley.*

Los Feliz, Silver Lake, and the Eastside

The neighborhoods in L.A.'s Eastside are talked about with the same oh-my-god-it's-so-cool reverence by Angelenos as Brooklyn is by New Yorkers. These streets are dripping with trendiness—which will delight some and enrage others.

Almost 20 years ago, now-affluent Los Feliz, in the rolling hills below the Griffith Observatory, was the first of these rediscovered neighborhoods. Next came came Silver Lake, followed by Echo Park. As each became more expensive, the cool kids relocated, leaving behind their style and influence. Although the epicenter will no doubt shift yet again, Highland Park is currently the nexus of the oh-so-hip universe.

Los Feliz

◉ Sights

Barnsdall Art Park

CITY PARK | FAMILY | The panoramic view of Hollywood alone is worth a trip to this hilltop cultural center. On the grounds you'll find the 1921 **Hollyhock House,** a masterpiece of modern design by architect Frank Lloyd Wright. It was commissioned by philanthropist Aline Barnsdall to be the centerpiece of an arts community. While Barnsdall's project didn't turn out the way she planned, the park now hosts the L.A. Municipal Art Gallery and Theatre, which provides exhibition space for visual and performance artists.

Wright dubbed this style "California Romanza" (*romanza* is a musical term meaning "to make one's own form"). Stylized depictions of Barnsdall's favorite flower, the hollyhock, appear throughout the house in its cement columns, roof line, and furnishings. The leaded-glass windows are expertly placed to make the most of both the surrounding gardens and the city views. On summer weekends, there are wildly popular wine tastings and outdoor movie screenings. Self-guided tours are available Thursday through Sunday from 11 to 4. ✉ *4800 Hollywood Blvd., Los Feliz* ☎ *323/913–4030* ⊕ *www.barnsdall.org* 🎟 *Free; house tours $7* ⊗ *House closed Sun.–Wed.* ⚲ *Advance tickets required for house.*

★ Griffith Observatory

OBSERVATORY | Most visitors barely skim the surface of this gorgeous spot in the Santa Monica Mountains, but those in the know will tell you there's more to the Griffith Observatory than its sweeping views and stunning Greek Revival architecture. The magnificence of the cosmos and humankind's ingenuity to explore the deepest depths of the universe are in the spotlight here, with its space-focused exhibits, the free public telescopes, and shows at the Leonard Nimoy Event Horizon Theater and the Samuel Oschin Planetarium. For visitors who are looking to get up close and personal with the cosmos, monthly star-viewing parties with local amateur astronomers are also on hand. In the early mornings, the extensive trails of Griffith Park are the perfect venue to partake in L.A.'s favorite pastime: hiking.

■ TIP➔ **For a fantastic view, come at sunset to watch the sky turn fiery shades of red with the city's skyline silhouetted.** ✉ *2800 E. Observatory Ave., Los Feliz* ☎ *213/473–0800* ⊕ *www.griffithobservatory.org* ⊗ *Closed Mon.* ☞ *Observatory grounds and parking are open daily.*

★ Griffith Park

CITY PARK | FAMILY | One of the country's largest municipal parks, the 4,210-acre Griffith Park is a must for nature lovers, the perfect spot for respite from the hustle and bustle of the surrounding urban areas. Plants and animals native to Southern California can be found within the park's borders, including deer and coyotes. Bronson Canyon (where the Batcave from the 1960s *Batman* TV series is located) and Crystal Springs are favorite picnic spots.

The park is named after Colonel Griffith J. Griffith, a mining tycoon who donated 3,000 acres to the city in 1896. As you might expect, the park has been used as a film and television location for at least a century. Here you'll find the Griffith Observatory, the Los Angeles Zoo, the Greek Theater, two golf courses, hiking and bridle trails, a swimming pool, a merry-go-round, and an outdoor train museum. ✉ *4730 Crystal Springs Dr., Los Feliz* ☎ *323/644–2050* 🌐 *www.laparks.org/dos/parks/griffithpk* 🎟 *Free; attractions inside park have separate admission fees.*

🍴 Restaurants

Kismet
$$ | **MEDITERRANEAN** | You may feel like you're about to walk into a sauna rather than a restaurant because of its minimalist light-color wood on white-paint interior, but you'll find nothing but colorful, gorgeous, Middle Eastern dishes here at Kismet. This James Beard nominee perfectly blends comforting Middle Eastern and Israeli cuisine with California flavors and plant-based flair, all served in a modern space. **Known for:** Persian crispy rice; tasty lamb meatballs; Middle Eastern classics with a Cali twist. [$] *Average main: $20* ✉ *4648 Hollywood Blvd., Los Feliz* ☎ *323/409–0404* 🌐 *www.kismetla.com.*

Little Dom's
$$ | **ITALIAN** | With a vintage bar and dapper barkeep who mixes up seasonally inspired retro cocktails, an attached Italian deli where you can pick up a pizza kit to take back to your Airbnb or kitchenette, and a $25 Monday-night supper, it's not surprising that Little Dom's is a neighborhood gem. Cozy and inviting, with big leather booths you can sink into for the night, the restaurant puts a modern spin on classic Italian dishes such as rice balls, fish piccata, and spaghetti and meatballs. **Known for:** ricotta cheese and fresh blueberry pancakes; excellent pizza margherita; fun weekend brunch. [$] *Average main: $25* ✉ *2128 Hillhurst Ave., Los Feliz* ☎ *323/661–0055* 🌐 *www.littledoms.com.*

🍸 Nightlife

Dresden Room
PIANO BARS | This bar's 1940s lounge decor makes it a favorite with folks in Los Angeles. Another reason to wander in is the Blood and Sand cocktail, self-proclaimed to be "the world's most tantalizing drink." ✉ *1760 N. Vermont Ave., Los Feliz* ☎ *323/665–4294* 🌐 *www.thedresden.com.*

🛍 Shopping

Skylight Books
BOOKS | A neighborhood bookstore through and through, Skylight has excellent sections devoted to kids, fiction, travel, and food; it even has a live-in cat. The space also hosts book discussion groups, panels, and author readings with hip literati. Art lovers can peruse texts on design and photography, graphic novels, and indie magazines at Skylight's annex a few doors down. ✉ *1818 N. Vermont Ave., Los Feliz* ☎ *323/660–1175* 🌐 *www.skylightbooks.com.*

Soap Plant/Wacko
SOUVENIRS | This pop-culture supermarket offers a wide range of items, including rows of books on art and design. But it's the novelty stock that makes the biggest impression, with ant farms, X-ray specs, and anime figurines for sale. An adjacent gallery space, La Luz de Jesus, focuses on underground art. ✉ *4633 Hollywood Blvd., Los Feliz* ☎ *323/663–0122* 🌐 *www.soapplant.com.*

Spitfire Girl

SOUVENIRS | When the person you're shopping for is the nontraditional type, you can count on this quirky boutique to provide unique goods including taxidermy, printed wood flasks, white magic spell kits, and cheeky socks, much of which is created by Spitfire Girl's own house label. ✉ *1939½ Hillhurst Ave., Los Feliz* ☎ *323/912–1977* 🌐 *www.spitfiregirl.com.*

Activities

Bronson Canyon

HIKING & WALKING | Bronson Canyon—or more popularly, Bronson Caves—is one of L.A.'s most famous filming locations, especially for Western and sci-fi flicks. This section of Griffith Park, easily accessible through a trail that's less than half a mile, is a great place to visit whether you're a film buff or an exercise junkie. ✉ *3200 Canyon Dr., Hollywood.*

Silver Lake

Restaurants

Creamo by Donut Friend

$ | **ICE CREAM** | Started by former music producer and Donut Friend creator Mark Trombino, Creamo is to ice cream as Donut Friend is to doughnuts (and if you don't get those L.A. references, it's what In-N-Out is to burgers). Everything is vegan in the shop; nonetheless, non-vegans will love its 16 soy-based flavors, many of which are named after pop-punk and emo bands. **Known for:** Donut Friend doughnuts; vegan shakes and ice cream sandwiches; vegan ice cream. [$] *Average main: $5* ✉ *3534 Sunset Blvd., Silver Lake* ☎ *213/863–0979* 🌐 *creamoicecream.com* ⏲ *Closed Mon.*

Gingergrass

$ | **VIETNAMESE** | **FAMILY** | With minimalist decor marked by tropical wood banquettes, Silver Lake's bohemian past and ubertrendy present converge at Gingergrass. Traditional Vietnamese favorites emerge from the café's open kitchen, sometimes with a California twist. **Known for:** roasted pork chop with rice; bánh mì sandwiches; great desserts. [$] *Average main: $15* ✉ *2396 Glendale Blvd., Silver Lake* ☎ *323/644–1600* 🌐 *www.gingergrass.com.*

★ Night + Market Song

$ | **THAI** | There are a lot of Thai restaurants in Los Angeles, but none have quite reached the level of cult status of Night + Market Song. Tucked between a free clinic, a small clothing store, and a tax office, this second rendition of chef Kris Yenbamroong's popular WeHo restaurant might be easy to miss, but keep an eye out, as its authentic (and properly spicy) Thai dishes are practically mandatory when you're in the neighborhood. **Known for:** Moo Sadoong ("startled pig"); khao soi; long weekend lines. [$] *Average main: $17* ✉ *3322 W. Sunset Blvd., Silver Lake* ☎ *323/665–5899* 🌐 *www.nightmarketsong.com* ⏲ *Closed Wed.*

Pine and Crane

$ | **TAIWANESE** | **FAMILY** | This is not the typical Chinese restaurant you might expect; it's a fast-casual, often locally sourced Taiwanese restaurant housed in a modern setting. The menu changes based on season, the wine and beer list updates constantly, and the tea menu is carefully curated. **Known for:** dan dan noodles; traditional panfried omelet; friendly staff. [$] *Average main: $15* ✉ *1521 Griffith Park Blvd., Silver Lake* ☎ *323/668–1128* 🌐 *www.pineandcrane.com* ⏲ *Closed Tues.*

Silverlake Ramen

$ | **RAMEN** | Now a franchise with several locations around Los Angeles (and a random one in Concord, NC), this spot in the heart of the city's hipsterville is the original and the best. The go-to ramen joint for Silverlake and Echo Park denizens is just the ticket if you're in dire need of some comfort food while also partaking in L.A.'s multicultural food scene. **Known for:** The Blaze, a spicy Tonkotsu ramen; crispy rice with spicy tuna; hearty Japanese fare. $ *Average main: $16* ⊠ *2927 Sunset Blvd., Silver Lake* ☎ *323/660–8100* ⊕ *www.silverlakeramen.com.*

Playita Mariscos

$ | **MEXICAN** | Essentially just a concrete shack with a roofed outdoor dining space populated by picnic tables, no-frills Playita Mariscos is a beloved local joint lauded for its Baja-style tacos. You'll also find beer-battered fish and shrimp tacos that evoke feelings of the sun-dappled Baja Mexico coast. Be sure to add the *aguachile* and ceviche to your order. **Known for:** beer-battered fish and shrimp tacos; aguachile; local haunt. $ *Average main: $12* ⊠ *3143 Sunset Blvd., Silver Lake* ☎ *323/928–2028* ⊕ *www.playitamariscos.com.*

🍸 Nightlife

Akbar

BARS | Recently updated Akbar is not your fancy L.A. cocktail bar filled with sipping model types and beautiful celebrity-adjacent people. This local haunt is every inch a neighborhood bar, one that serves fast, cheap, and strong drinks; is inclusive of all people; and engages the local community through fun, unapologetically outrageous events like Craftaoke, Gaymer Night, and queer disco nights. ⊠ *4356 W. Sunset Blvd., Silver Lake* ☎ *323/665–6810* ⊕ *www.akbarsilverlake.com.*

★ 4100

BARS | With swaths of fabric draped from the ceiling, this low-lit bar with a bohemian vibe is the perfect backdrop (and mood) for a date. Groups of locals also come through for the night, making for a good mix of people and energy. The bartenders pour drinks that are both tasty and potent. There's plenty of seating at the tables and stools along the central bar, which gets crowded on the weekends. ⊠ *1087 Manzanita St., Silver Lake* ☎ *213/784–6595* ⊕ *www.4100bar.com.*

Silverlake Lounge

LIVE MUSIC | Rock bands, burlesque performances, comedy sets, and LTGBQ+ nights all have a home at the cross section of Sunset and Silver Lake at a little dive bar called the Silverlake Lounge. This small-yet-famous venue, which received a recent refresh, is a neighborhood spot in the best way possible, with cheap drinks and local talent deserving of their time in the limelight. There are 10 signature cocktails, many of which are riffs on classics, and quite a few tequilas and mezcals on offer. If you come hungry, you can bring food in from the pizza place across the street or look for a restaurant pop-up in the newly updated back patio. ⊠ *2906 W. Sunset Blvd., Silver Lake* ☎ *323/741–0032* ⊕ *www.thesilverlakelounge.com.*

🛍 Shopping

Mohawk General Store

MIXED CLOTHING | Filled with a brilliant combination of indie and established designers, this upscale boutique is a mainstay for the modern minimalist. Pick up the wares of local favorites as well as internationally loved labels like Acne Studios, Issey Miyake, and Levi's. The Sunset Boulevard store stocks goods for men and women as well as children, plus accessories and some home goods. ⊠ *4011 W. Sunset Blvd., Silver Lake* ☎ *323/669–1601* ⊕ *www.mohawkgeneralstore.com.*

★ Yolk

SOUVENIRS | Woman-owned Yolk is the perfect spot to shop for home and lifestyle goods that are trendy in Los Angeles, stocked with all the nice things that you will want to buy as gifts for others, but will struggle to give away. Most of the offerings here are locally made and, therefore, hard to find elsewhere, and there's also a carefully curated selection of lovely designer goods. Look for unique kids' toys and furnishings, exquisite home accessories, stationery, and handcrafted items from California artisans. ✉ *3910 W. Sunset Blvd., Silver Lake* ☎ *323/426–9391* 🌐 *www.shopyolk.com.*

Echo Park

👁 Sights

★ Dodger Stadium

SPORTS VENUE | FAMILY | Home of the Dodgers since 1962, Dodger Stadium is the third-oldest baseball stadium still in use and has had quite the history in baseball, including Sandy Koufax's perfect game in 1965 and Kirk Gibson's 1988 World Series home run. Not only has it played host to the Dodgers' ups and downs and World Series runs, it's also been the venue for some of the biggest performers in the world, including the Beatles, Madonna, and Beyoncé. The stadium can be tough to get into on game day, so consider getting dropped off in the park and walking up. Alternately, you can arrive early, as locals tend not to roll up until the third inning. If you have the opportunity to take in a Friday night game, make sure to stick around for the fireworks show that follows—if you're patient, you can even wait in line and watch it from the field. ✉ *1000 Vin Scully Ave., Echo Park* ☎ *866/363–4377* 🌐 *mlb.com/dodgers/ballpark.*

Elysian Park

HIKING & WALKING | FAMILY | Though not Los Angeles's biggest park—that honor belongs to Griffith Park—Elysian comes in second, and also has the honor of being the city's oldest. It's also home to one of L.A.'s busiest and most beloved attractions, Dodger Stadium, the home field to the Los Angeles Dodgers. For this reason, baseball fans flock to this 600-acre park for tailgate parties. The rest of the time, however, Elysian Park serves as the Echo Park residents' backyard, thanks to its network of hiking trails, picnic spaces, and public playgrounds. ✉ *929 Academy Rd., Echo Park* ☎ *213/485–5054* 🌐 *www.laparks.org/park/elysian.*

🍴 Restaurants

★ Guisados

$ | MEXICAN | Family-owned Guisados has achieved cult status in L.A. with locations throughout the city (DTLA, Boyle Heights, WeHo) to accommodate its popularity. This Echo Park spot is worshipped and well supported locally for Nana's slow-cooked stew recipes, cooked to perfection for five to six hours and slapped on house-grilled tortillas. **Known for:** tacos with slow-cooked meats; breakfast tacos; cult favorite. [$] *Average main: $12* ✉ *1261 W. Sunset Blvd., Echo Park* ☎ *213/250–7600* 🌐 *www.guisados.la.*

Lady Byrd Cafe

$ | AMERICAN | Walking into woman-owned Lady Byrd Cafe is like walking through a portal to a fairy-tale land filled with whimsical decor, inventive greenhouse-sheltered tables, and grandma tableware, which explains its Insta-famous status. But, it's much more than just a pretty place to eat; dishes are pretty delectable. **Known for:** lemon poppy seed pancakes; variety of eggs Benedicts; juices and smoothies. [$] *Average main: $18* ✉ *2100 Echo Park Ave., Echo Park* ☎ *323/922–1006* 🌐 *ladybyrdcafe.com.*

Masa of Echo Park

$$ | PIZZA | FAMILY | While Masa of Echo Park does do excellent "bistro pizzas," as the restaurant calls them, it's mostly known for the delectable deep-dish pies that may just be the best you'll find this side of Chicago. Be prepared, though—it can take a while to get seated and up to 45 minutes to get that deep dish you ordered, so it might be best to call ahead. **Known for:** vegan menu options; family-style dining; deep-dish pizza. $ *Average main: $24* ⊠ *1800 W. Sunset Blvd., Echo Park* ☎ *213/989–1558* ⊕ *www.masaofechopark.com* ⊗ *Closed Mon. and Tues.*

Spoon and Pork

$ | FILIPINO | In a city where food trucks can be successful enough to have their own brick-and-mortar spaces, and where Filipino food has quickly become a craze, it's no surprise that Spoon and Pork has found its rightful place in the neighborhood. With a name that cleverly plays on the traditional Filipino way of eating (using both spoon and fork), this modern Filipino food spot is the perfect introduction to the cuisine. **Known for:** adobo pork belly; lechon kawali; Filipino comfort food. $ *Average main: $16* ⊠ *3131 W. Sunset Blvd., Echo Park* ☎ *323/922–6061* ⊕ *www.spoonandpork.com* ⊗ *Closed Mon.*

ⓨ Nightlife

★ The Echo

LIVE MUSIC | Echo Park is peppered with music venues, but if you want to be in the heart of the neighborhood's live music scene, you should head to the Echo. With a full bar and recurring theme nights, the spot hosts cutting-edge music from both up-and-coming local and touring acts as well as well-known bands. ⊠ *1822 Sunset Blvd., Echoplex entrance at 1154 Glendale Blvd., Echo Park* ☎ *213/413–8200* ⊕ *theecho.com.*

★ Mohawk Bend

PUBS | There are plenty of reasons to stop by Mohawk Bend: 72 craft beers on tap, a wide range of California-only liquor, a vegetarian and vegan-friendly menu that includes tailored-to-your-wants pizza, and a buffalo cauliflower that—rumor has it—started the whole trend. There might be a long line to get into this 100-year-old former theater in the evenings, but it's worth it. ⊠ *2141 Sunset Blvd., Echo Park* ☎ *213/483–2337* ⊕ *mohawk.la.*

★ 1642

LIVE MUSIC | This romantically lit hole-in-the-wall is easy to miss, but you should aim to check it out if you're a discerning wine connoisseur or looking to experience the best of California's microbreweries. Perfect for first dates, come here to experiment with craft beers or to warm up with wine while listening to some live old-time fiddle tunes. ⊠ *1642 W. Temple St., Echo Park* ☎ *213/989–6836* ⊕ *www.1642bar.com.*

⬤ Shopping

Stories Books and Café

BOOKS | With an off-the-beaten-path collection of new and used literature, a café catering to freelancers and freethinkers, and a back patio that showcases singer-songwriters, Stories Books and Café is an authentic reflection of Echo Park. Readings, signings, and other events are a regular occurrence. ⊠ *1716 Sunset Blvd., Echo Park* ☎ *213/413–3733* ⊕ *www.storiesla.com.*

Time Travel Mart

OTHER SPECIALTY STORE | FAMILY | You probably won't find anything useful in the Time Travel Mart and that's exactly the point. From dinosaur eggs to robot milk, this is a store that touts the absurdly hilarious—all of which should bring back memories of your childhood and maybe a little bit of joy. That's because the store holds a secret: it's really a fundraiser for the nonprofit 826LA, which tutors neighborhood kids in the back section. So even when you're buying something unnecessary but absolutely wonderful, remember it's for a noble and worthy cause. ⊠ *1714 W. Sunset Blvd., Echo Park* ☎ *213/556–4861* ⊕ *timetravelmart.com.*

Highland Park

Sights

Heritage Square Museum

HISTORY MUSEUM | Looking like a prop street set up by a film studio, Heritage Square resembles a row of bright dollhouses in the modest Highland Park neighborhood. Five 19th-century residences, a train station, a church, a carriage barn, and a 1909 boxcar that was originally part of the Southern Pacific Railroad, all built between the Civil War and World War I, were moved to this small park from various locations in Southern California to save them from the wrecking ball. The latest addition, a re-creation of a World War I–era drugstore, has a vintage soda fountain and traditional products. Docents dressed in period costume lead visitors through the lavish homes, giving an informative picture of Los Angeles in the early 1900s. Don't miss the unique 1893 Octagon House, one of just a handful of its kind built in California. ✉ *3800 Homer St., Highland Park* ☎ *323/225–2700* 🌐 *www.heritagesquare.org* 🎟 *$10* 🕒 *Closed Tues.–Fri. and federal holiday Mon.*

Restaurants

Cafe Birdie

$$ | **MEDITERRANEAN** | This spacious 1920s-style spot along a quickly revitalizing stretch of Figueroa has established itself as a neighborhood bistro frequented by Highland Park residents, as well as folks from all over Los Angeles. The eclectic menu skillfully blends elements of European, North African, Southern, and Asian cuisines, tying them together with a fresh California flair and a gorgeously lush interior inspired by a fictional meeting-of-two-souls narrative. **Known for:** Moroccan-spiced fried chicken; seasonal cocktails; modern and luxurious yet lush and airy. [$] *Average main: $22* ✉ *5631 N. Figueroa St., Highland Park* ☎ *323/739–6928* 🌐 *www.cafebirdiela.com.*

★ Donut Friend

$ | **BAKERY** | When this music-influenced doughnut shop first opened on York Boulevard in the early days of Highland Park's renaissance, there wasn't much there, and its arrival helped shape the now-bustling strip and its vegan inclinations. Donut Friend has evolved into a destination in its own right, touting both a signature and limited menu of purely vegan doughnuts—which also happen to be inspired by the pop punk and emo music scene. **Known for:** fun flavors like Green Teagan and Sara (with matcha tea glaze); all-vegan ingredients; ice cream and shakes. [$] *Average main: $4* ✉ *5107 York Blvd., Highland Park* ☎ *213/908–2745* 🌐 *www.donutfriend.com.*

El Huarache Azteca

$ | **MEXICAN** | **FAMILY** | While you definitely should try the flat shoe-shaped dish El Huarache Azteca is named after—think somewhere between a flatbread and a tostada—you cannot go wrong with any of the other options at this family restaurant that's been a fixture in the area for the last couple of decades. Just be aware there's often a wait for the food to come out. **Known for:** no-frills Mexican dishes; agua fresca; super huarache. [$] *Average main: $15* ✉ *5225 York Blvd., Highland Park* ☎ *323/478–9572* 🌐 *orderelhuaracheazteca.com.*

★ Knowrealitypie

$ | **BAKERY** | The award-winning Knowrealitypie, hidden in a shop the size of a large walk-in closet, is truly a passion project, with co-owner Tracy Ann DeVore furiously paddling beneath the water's surface to make those homemade pies on her own. That's why it's only open from Thursday through Saturday until it sells out, which it often does. **Known for:** triple berry Cabernet pie; salted caramel mango rum pie; vegan and gluten-free options on request. [$] *Average main: $6* ✉ *5106 Townsend Ave., Highland Park*

☎ *916/799–5772* ⊕ *www.knowrealitypie. com* ⊘ *Closed Mon.–Thurs.*

Polka Polish Cuisine

$ | POLISH | Polka Polish Cuisine, like most restaurants in L.A., went through a makeover during the lockdown, and now boasts a more modern interior and an airy patio that offers outdoor seating. But the food here—traditional Polish fare like pierogi, schnitzel, and stuffed cabbage rolls—is just as delicious and comforting as ever. **Known for:** hearty Polish comfort food; traditional pierogi and kielbasa; mom-and-pop ambience. $ *Average main: $20* ⊠ *4112 Verdugo Rd., Highland Park* ☎ *323/255–7887* ⊕ *www.polkares-taurant.com* ⊘ *Closed Mon. and Tues.*

▶ Nightlife

★ Highland Park Bowl

THEMED ENTERTAINMENT | FAMILY | Once an ambitious restoration project, Highland Park Bowl now serves as a massive throwback to its Prohibition-era roots as an alcohol-prescribing doctor's office and drugstore with its own bowling alley. That bowling alley remains, complete with the original pin machine. The hooch-pushing doctor and druggist, however, are long gone. But now there's an Italian restaurant that serves excellent pizza made from scratch using a mother dough brought all the way from Italy. ⊠ *5621 N. Figueroa St., Highland Park* ☎ *323/257–2695* ⊕ *www.highlandparkbowl.com.*

The York

PUBS | Since 2007, before Highland Park became trendy, the York has been holding its own as the ultimate neighborhood bar. It's not just that the aesthetic gives off that neighborhood vibe (think exposed brick and chalkboard menus), but the craft beers on tap are great, and the pub food is delicious—the cheddar burger and the fish-and-chips are favorites. ⊠ *5018 York Blvd., Highland Park* ☎ *323/255–9675* ⊕ *www.they-orkonyork.com.*

🛍 Shopping

Galco's Soda Pop Stop

OTHER FOOD & DRINK | FAMILY | A local fixture in Highland Park for decades, Galco's is in some ways a trip down memory lane, carrying more than 600 sodas—most of which harken back to the days when soda was a regional affair—and options from all over the world. They also have a collection of retro candies, a soda creation station with more than 100 syrups to choose from, and a selection of alcohol that would put most liquor stores to shame. ⊠ *5702 York Blvd., Highland Park* ☎ *323/255–7115* ⊕ *sodapopstop. com.*

Permanent Records

MUSIC | Part of the vinyl resurgence since 2013, Permanent Records stocks new and used vinyl for every musical taste and does it without any snobbery. The record store, which often has in-store performances, also runs its own label that focuses on local bands, limited-edition runs, and reissues. ⊠ *1906 Cypress Ave., Highland Park* ☎ *323/332–2312* ⊕ *www.permanentrecordsla.com.*

Pasadena

Although seemingly absorbed into the general Los Angeles sprawl, Pasadena is a separate and distinct city. It's best known for the Tournament of Roses, or more commonly, the Rose Bowl, seen around the world every New Year's Day. But the city has sites worth seeing year-round—from gorgeous Craftsman homes to exceptional museums, particularly the Norton Simon and the Huntington Library, Art Museum, and Botanical Gardens. Note that the Huntington and the Old Mill reside in San Marino, a well-heeled, 4-square-mile residential area just over the Pasadena line.

👁 Sights

The Gamble House

HISTORIC HOME | Built by Charles and Henry Greene in 1908, this American Arts and Crafts bungalow illustrates the incredible craftsmanship that went into early L.A. architecture. The term "bungalow" can be misleading, since the Gamble House is a huge three-story home. To wealthy Easterners such as the Gambles (as in Procter & Gamble), this type of vacation home seemed informal compared with their mansions back home. Admirers swoon over the teak staircase and cabinetry, the Greene and Greene–designed furniture, and an Emil Lange glass door. The dark exterior has broad eaves, with sleeping porches on the second floor. An hour-long, docent-led tour of the Gamble's interior will draw your eye to the exquisite details. For those who want to see more of the Greene and Greene homes, there are guided walks around the historic Arroyo Terrace neighborhood. Advance tickets are highly recommended.

■ TIP➜ **Film buffs might recognize this as Doc Brown's house from** *Back to the Future.* ✉ *4 Westmoreland Pl., Pasadena* ☎ *626/793–3334* ⊕ *gamblehouse.org* 🎟 *$15* ◔ *Closed Mon. and Wed.*

★ Huntington Library, Art Museum, and Botanical Gardens

GARDEN | If you have time for just one stop in the Pasadena area, be sure to see this sprawling estate built for railroad tycoon Henry E. Huntington in the early 1900s. Henry and his wife, Arabella (who was also his aunt by marriage), voraciously collected rare books and manuscripts, botanical specimens, and 18th-century British art. The institution they established became one of the most extraordinary cultural complexes in the world.

The library contains more than 700,000 books and 4 million manuscripts, including one of the world's biggest history of science collections and a Gutenberg Bible.

Don't resist being lured outside into the 130-acre Botanical Gardens, which extend out from the main building. The 10-acre Desert Garden has one of the world's largest groups of mature cacti and other succulents (visit on a cool morning or late afternoon). The Shakespeare Garden, meanwhile, blooms with plants mentioned in Shakespeare's works. The Japanese Garden features an authentic ceremonial teahouse built in Kyoto in the 1960s, and will soon see the addition of another historic building. A waterfall flows from the teahouse to the ponds below. The Chinese Garden, which is among the largest outside China, sinews around waveless pools. The Bing Children's Garden lets tiny tots explore the ancient elements of water, fire, air, and earth. Several on-site dining options are available, including the Rose Garden Tea Room, where afternoon tea is served (reserve in advance).

A 1¼-hour guided tour of the Botanical Gardens is led by docents at posted times, and a free brochure with a map and property highlights is available in the entrance pavilion. Tickets for a monthly free-admission day are snapped up within minutes online, so plan carefully. ✉ *1151 Oxford Rd., San Marino* ☎ *626/405–2100* ⊕ *www.huntington.org* 🎟 *From $25; free admission 1st Thurs. of every month with advance ticket* ◔ *Closed Tues.*

★ Norton Simon Museum

ART MUSEUM | As seen in the New Year's Day Tournament of Roses Parade, this low-profile brown building is one of the finest midsize museums anywhere, with a collection that spans more than 2,000 years of Western and Asian art. It all began in the 1950s when Norton Simon (Hunt-Wesson Foods, McCalls Corporation, and Canada Dry) started collecting works by Degas, Renoir, Gauguin, and Cézanne. His collection grew to include works by old masters and impressionists, modern works from Europe, and Indian and Southeast Asian art. Today the museum is richest in works by Rembrandt, Picasso, and, most of all, Degas.

Head down to the bottom floor to see temporary exhibits and phenomenal Southeast Asian and Indian sculptures and artifacts, where pieces like a Ban Chiang blackware vessel date back to well before 1000 BC. Don't miss a living artwork outdoors: the garden, conceived by noted Southern California landscape designer Nancy Goslee Power. The tranquil pond was inspired by Monet's gardens at Giverny. ⊠ 411 W. Colorado Blvd., Pasadena ☎ 626/449–6840 ⊕ www. nortonsimon.org ⊠ $15 ⊙ Closed Tues. and Wed.

The Old Mill (El Molino Viejo)

NOTABLE BUILDING | Built in 1816 as a gristmill for the San Gabriel Mission, the mill is the state's oldest commercial building and one of the last remaining examples in Southern California of Spanish Mission architecture. The thick adobe walls and textured ceiling rafters give the interior a sense of quiet strength. Be sure to step into the back room, now a gallery with rotating quarterly exhibits. Outside, a chipped section of the mill's exterior reveals the layers of brick, ground seashell paste, and ox blood used to hold the structure together. The surrounding gardens are reason enough to visit, with a flower-decked arbor and old sycamores and oaks. In summer, the Capitol Ensemble performs in the garden. ⊠ 1120 Old Mill Rd., San Marino ☎ 626/449–5458 ⊕ www.old-mill.org ⊠ Free ⊙ Closed Mon.

Old Town Pasadena

NEIGHBORHOOD | This 22-block historic district contains a vibrant mix of restored 19th-century brick buildings interspersed with contemporary architecture. Chain stores have muscled in, but there are still some homegrown shops, plenty of tempting cafés and restaurants, and a bustling beer scene. In recent years, a vibrant Asian food scene has popped up in the vicinity as well. In the evening and on weekends, the streets are packed with people. Old Town's main action takes place on Colorado Boulevard between Pasadena Avenue and Arroyo Parkway. ⊠ Pasadena ☎ 626/356–9725 ⊕ www.oldpasadena.org.

★ Rose Bowl and Flea Market

MARKET | With an enormous rose on its exterior, this 90,000-plus-seat stadium is home to the UCLA Bruins and the annual Rose Bowl Game on New Year's Day, and also regularly sees performances from the biggest recording artists in the world. Set at the bottom of a wide arroyo in Brookside Park, the facility is closed except during games, concerts, and special events like its famed Flea Market, a Southern California institution. The massively popular and eclectic event, which happens the second Sunday of each month (rain or shine), deservedly draws crowds that come to find deals from more than 2,500 vendors on goods including mid-century and antique furniture, vintage clothing, pop culture collectibles, books, and music. Food and drink options are on hand to keep shoppers satiated, parking is free, and general admission is just $9, but VIP/early-bird options are available for a little extra. Crowds tend to peak midday. Bring cash to avoid an inevitable line at the ATM, and feel free to try your hand at haggling. ⊠ 1001 Rose Bowl Dr., Pasadena ☎ 626/577–3100 ⊕ www.rosebowlstadium.com.

🍴 Restaurants

Pie 'n Burger

$$ | **DINER** | Since 1963, this small and charming diner has done two things really well—pies and burgers. Most seats are counter-style, with a griddle searing up patties. **Known for:** simple burgers; enormous pie slices; retro-style decor. [$] *Average main: $14* ✉ *913 E. California Blvd., Pasadena* ☎ *626/795–1123* 🌐 *pien-burger.com.*

The Raymond 1886

$$$ | **MODERN AMERICAN** | The coolest kid on the Pasadena block, the Raymond 1886 is carved out of an old Craftsman cottage and has an expansive patio with long wooden tables and hanging lights. Chefs dish out everything from roasted acorn squash with "forbidden" rice to braised beef cheeks with mole sauce. **Known for:** solid happy hour; great bar food; expansive patio. [$] *Average main: $36* ✉ *1250 S. Fair Oaks Ave., Pasadena* ☎ *626/441–3136* 🌐 *theraymond.com* 🕒 *Closed Mon.*

🛍 Shopping

Vroman's Bookstore

BOOKS | Southern California's oldest and largest independent bookseller is justly famous for its great service. A newsstand, café, literary-themed wine bar, and stationery store add to the appeal, and it's a favorite with locals for its on-trend, eclectic gift selection. A regular rotation of events including trivia night, kids' story time, author meet and greets, crafting sessions, discussions, and more get the community actively involved. ✉ *695 E. Colorado Blvd., Pasadena* ☎ *626/449–5320* 🌐 *www.vromansbookstore.com.*

Malibu and the Beaches

The beaches and coastal areas of Los Angeles are an iconic symbol of the region's casual friendliness and endless optimism, and the local love for them is as much a trope as it is a reality. The coast is where Angelenos come to play, and getting some sand on the floor of your car is a rite of passage here.

Like some of its most ardent fans, this stretch of the Pacific is known for its beauty: cosmetically enhanced in some areas and ruggedly pristine in others. From the hillside mansions of Malibu, where even the air is rarified, to the cultural dynamism of Long Beach, the gently arching shore tells an L.A. story all its own as it transitions from ultrarich to bohemian to working class. Through it all, the sand remains the center of the action.

Malibu

👁 Sights

Malibu Pier

MARINA/PIER | **FAMILY** | This rustically chic, 780-foot fishing dock is a great place to drink in the sunset, take in some coastal views, or watch local fishermen reel up a catch. Some tours also leave from here. A pier has jutted out on this spot since the early 1900s; storms destroyed the last one in 1995, and it was rebuilt in 2001. Over the years, private developers have worked with the state to refurbish the pier, which now yields a gift shop, water-sport and beach rentals, a jeweler housed in a vintage Airstream trailer, and a wonderful farm-to-table restaurant with stunning views and locations at both ends of the pier. ✉ *Pacific Coast Hwy. at Cross Creek Rd., Malibu* 🌐 *www.malibupier.com.*

Beaches

Malibu Lagoon State Beach

BEACH | Bird-watchers, take note: in this 5-acre marshy area near Malibu Beach Inn you can spot egrets, blue herons, avocets, and gulls. (You need to stay on the boardwalks so as not to disturb their habitats.) The path leads out to a rocky stretch of Surfrider Beach and makes for a pleasant stroll. The sand is soft, clean, and white, and you're also likely to spot a variety of marine life. Look for the signs to help identify these sometimes exotic-looking creatures. The lagoon is particularly enjoyable in the early morning and at sunset—and even more so now, thanks to a restoration effort that improved the lagoon's scent. The parking lot has limited hours, but street-side parking is usually available at off-peak times. The on-site Malibu Lagoon Museum reveals local history, and close by are shops and a theater. **Amenities:** lifeguards; parking (fee); showers; toilets. **Best for:** sunset; walking. ⊠ *23200 Pacific Coast Hwy., Malibu* ☎ *310/457–8143* ⊕ *www.parks.ca.gov/?page_id=835* ⊠ *Parking $12.*

Westward Beach–Point Dume State Beach

BEACH | This famed promontory is a Malibu pilgrimage for any visitor to the area. Go tide-pooling, fishing, snorkeling, or bird-watching (prime time is late winter to early spring). Hike to the top of the sandstone cliffs at Point Dume to whale-watch—their migrations can be seen between December and April—and take in dramatic coastal views. Westward is a favorite surfing beach, but the steep surf isn't for novices. The Sunset restaurant is between Westward and Point Dume (at 6800 Westward Beach Road). Otherwise, bring your own food, since the nearest concession is a long hike away. **Amenities:** food and drink; lifeguards; parking (fee); showers; toilets. **Best for:** surfing; walking. ⊠ *71030 Westward Beach Rd., Malibu* ☎ *310/305–9503* ⊕ *www.parks.ca.gov/?page_id=623* ⊠ *Parking $15.*

Zuma Beach Park

BEACH | This 2-mile stretch of white sand, usually dotted with tanning teenagers, has it all, from fishing and kitesurfing to swings and volleyball courts. Beachgoers looking for quiet or privacy should head elsewhere. Stay alert in the water: the surf is rough and inconsistent, and riptides can surprise even experienced swimmers. A new metered parking program limits visits to 90 minutes at a time. **Amenities:** food and drink; lifeguards; parking; showers; toilets. **Best for:** partiers; sunset; swimming; walking. ⊠ *30000 Pacific Coast Hwy., Malibu* ☎ *310/305–9522* ⊕ *beaches.lacounty.gov/zuma-beach* ⊠ *Metered parking: $0.50 per 15 mins (90-min max).*

Restaurants

★ Nobu Malibu

$$$$ | **JAPANESE** | At famous chef-restaurateur Nobu Matsuhisa's coastal outpost, superchic clientele sails in for morsels of the world's finest fish. It's hard not to be seduced by the oceanfront property; stellar sushi and ingenious specialties match the upscale setting. **Known for:** exotic fish; A-list celebrity chef; exceptional views. Ⓢ *Average main: $46* ⊠ *22706 Pacific Coast Hwy., Malibu* ☎ *310/317–9140* ⊕ *www.noburestaurants.com.*

Reel Inn

$ | **SEAFOOD** | **FAMILY** | Escape the glitz and glamour at this decades-old, down-home Malibu institution. Long wooden tables and booths are often filled with fish-loving families chowing down on mahimahi sandwiches and freshly caught swordfish. **Known for:** easy-to-miss spot on PCH; fresh catches; dog-friendly patio. Ⓢ *Average main: $19* ⊠ *18661 Pacific Coast Hwy., Malibu* ☎ *310/456–8221* ⊕ *www.reelinnmalibu.com.*

🛏 Hotels

★ Malibu Beach Inn

$$$$ | **B&B/INN** | Set right on exclusive Carbon Beach in a stretch known as Billionaire's Beach, Malibu's hideaway for the superrich remains the room to nab along the coast, with an ultrachic look thanks to designer Waldo Fernandez and an upscale restaurant and wine bar perched over the Pacific. **Pros:** views of the ocean from your private balcony; walking distance to the pier; epitome of beachside luxury. **Cons:** added fee for the health club across the way; some in-room noise from PCH; no pool, gym, or hot tub. **$** *Rooms from: $749* ✉ *22878 Pacific Coast Hwy., Malibu* ☎ *310/456–6444* ⊕ *www.malibubeachinn.com* ⤳ *47 rooms* ❑ *No Meals.*

🍸 Nightlife

Duke's Barefoot Bar

BARS | With a clear view of the horizon from almost everywhere, a sunset drink at Duke's Barefoot Bar inside Duke's Restaurant is how many beachgoers like to end their day. The entertainment is in keeping with the bar's theme, with Hawaiian dancers as well as live music by Hawaiian artists on Aloha Friday nights. The menu features island favorites like poke tacos, macadamia-crusted fish, and kalua pork. Indulge in a Sunday brunch buffet from 10 to 2. Just don't expect beach-bum prices, unless you stop by the happy hour weekday events like Taco Tuesday (bargain-priced fish, kalua pork, or grilled chicken tacos and beers). ✉ *21150 Pacific Coast Hwy., Malibu* ☎ *310/317–0777* ⊕ *www.dukes-malibu.com.*

Moonshadows

COCKTAIL LOUNGES | This indoor-outdoor lounge attracts customers with its modern look and views of the ocean. Think dark woods, cabana-style draperies, and ambient lighting in the Blue Lounge, open late on weekends. DJs are constantly spinning in the background, and there's never a cover charge. Sunday afternoons perfectly blend the laid-back ambience with good vibes. There's also a full-service restaurant on-site; try a sunset dinner or the lobster roll and dessert lineup to go with your cocktails. ✉ *20356 Pacific Coast Hwy., Malibu* ☎ *310/456–3010* ⊕ *www.moonshadowsmalibu.com.*

🛍 Shopping

Malibu Country Mart

SHOPPING CENTER | Stop by this outdoor outpost for the ultimate Malibu lifestyle experience, complete with browsing on-trend clothing (Nati, Ron Herman, or Madison) and eclectic California housewares and gifts (Malibu Colony Co.), picking up body-boosting wellness goodies (SunLife Organics), and finishing the day off with dinner at long-standing eatery Tra di Noi, reputed to be a favorite of Barbra Streisand. If you can squeeze in a workout, there are multiple studios to choose from, plus tarot readings at metaphysical outpost Malibu Shaman. Then reward yourself for your good health habits by stopping at K Chocolatier by Diane Krön for some of her famed truffles, derived from a Hungarian family recipe. ✉ *3835 Cross Creek Rd., Malibu* ☎ *310/456–7300* ⊕ *www.malibucountrymart.com.*

Manhattan Beach, Redondo Beach, and Long Beach

⊙ Sights

★ Aquarium of the Pacific

AQUARIUM | FAMILY | Sea lions, zebra sharks, and penguins—oh my! This aquarium focuses on creatures of the Pacific Ocean and is home to more than 12,000 animals. The main exhibits include large tanks of sharks, stingrays, and ethereal sea dragons, which the aquarium has successfully bred in captivity. The museum's first major expansion in years, Pacific Visions, features a 29,000-square-foot multisensory experience in which attendees can immerse themselves in humankind's relationship with the natural world through video projections, sound-scapes, tactile exhibits, a touchscreen wall, interactive game tables, rumbling theater seats, and more. The aquarium focuses on its local environment in its refreshed Southern California Gallery, where you'll explore kelp forests, learn about local species, and learn about the aquarium's conservation efforts. Special events for kids, teens, and families abound; if you're interested in offsetting your travels with some local eco efforts, the whole family can join in local wetlands habitat restoration efforts held by the aquarium. Whale-watching trips on Harbor Breeze Cruises depart from the dock adjacent to the aquarium; summer sightings of blue whales are an unforgettable thrill. ⊠ *100 Aquarium Way, Long Beach* ☎ *562/590–3100* ⊕ *www. aquariumofpacific.org* ⊠ *$45.*

★ Queen Mary

NAUTICAL SIGHT | FAMILY | The beautifully preserved art deco–style ocean liner, the *Queen Mary,* was launched in 1936 and made 1,001 transatlantic crossings before finally berthing in Long Beach in 1967. Today, it is a unique and historic hotel, one of Long Beach's top tour attractions, and an impressive example of 20th-century cruise ship opulence.

Take one of several daily themed tours such as the informative Glory Days historical walk, a traipse into the boiler rooms on the Steam and Steel Tour, or the downright spooky Haunted Encounters tour. (Spirits have reportedly been spotted in the pool and engine room.) You can add on a Winston Churchill exhibit and other holiday and special events, from a haunted Halloween experience to an annual Scottish festival. Stay for dinner at one of the ship's restaurants (call ahead to reserve), then listen to live jazz or order a cocktail in the Observation Bar (the sumptuous original first-class lounge). Even better, plan to spend the night in one of the 347 wood-paneled cabins. The ship's neighbor, a geodesic dome originally built to house Howard Hughes's *Spruce Goose* aircraft, now serves as a terminal for Carnival Cruise Lines, making the *Queen Mary* the perfect pit stop before or after a cruise. ⊠ *1126 Queens Hwy., Long Beach* ☎ *877/342–0738* ⊕ *www.queenmary. com* ⊙ *Tours from $10.*

Beaches

Manhattan Beach

BEACH | A wide, sandy strip with good swimming and rows of volleyball courts, Manhattan Beach is the preferred destination of fit, tanned young professionals. There are also such amenities as a bike path, a playground, a bait shop, fishing equipment for rent, and a sizable fishing pier with a free aquarium at the end. It's the perfect place to unwind during a long layover at LAX. **Amenities:** food and drink; lifeguards; parking (fee); showers; toilets. **Best for:** swimming; walking. ⊠ *Manhattan Beach Blvd. at N. Ocean Dr., Manhattan Beach* ☎ *310/372–2166* ⊕ *beaches.lacounty.gov/manhattan-beach* 🅿 *Metered parking; long- and short-term lots.*

Redondo Beach

BEACH | The pier here marks the starting point of this wide, busy beach along a heavily developed shoreline community. Restaurants and shops flourish along the pier; excursion boats and privately owned crafts depart from launching ramps; and a reef formed by a sunken ship creates prime fishing and snorkeling conditions. If you're adventurous, you might try to kayak out to the buoys and hobnob with pelicans and sea lions. A series of free rock and jazz concerts takes place at the pier every summer. **Amenities:** food and drink; lifeguards; parking; showers; toilets; water sports. **Best for:** snorkeling; sunset; swimming; walking. ⊠ *Torrance Blvd. at Catalina Ave., Redondo Beach* ☎ *310/372–2166* ⊕ *www.redondopier.com.*

Chapter 7

PALM SPRINGS

Updated by
Carrie Bell

◉ Sights	🍴 Restaurants	🛏 Hotels	🛍 Shopping	🍸 Nightlife
★★★★★	★★★★☆	★★★★★	★★☆☆☆	★★☆☆☆

WELCOME TO PALM SPRINGS

TOP REASONS TO GO

★ **Year-round sunshine:** With more than 300 days of sun each year and mild winters, the weather is ideal for teeing off at one of the area's 120 golf courses or pedaling around neighborhoods full of mid-century modern marvels.

★ **Spa after dark:** In addition to all-day self-care menus, several spas offer nighttime services including outdoor soaks and treatments.

★ **Personal pampering:** The resorts here have it all—beautifully appointed rooms packed with amenities, professional staff, immaculate grounds, stiff drinks, sublime spas, and delicious dining options.

★ **Divine desert scenery:** The area is a feast for the eyes, with sometimes snowcapped 10,000-foot mountains that envelop the flat desert floor, towering palm trees, secluded canyons, and blue skies that turn violet at dusk.

★ **The Hollywood connection:** Palm Springs has more celebrity ties than any other resort community, so expect to spy stars.

1 Palm Springs. A mid-century modern vibe and many restaurants, bars, and galleries line the avenues of Palm Springs. Hiking trails and an aerial tramway lead from the desert floor up to the San Jacinto Mountain peaks.

2 Cathedral City. Slightly less swanky than most of its neighbors, Cat City, just south of Palm Springs, has a younger demographic, affordable lodging, a thriving public art initiative, and gorgeous canyon hikes.

3 Rancho Mirage. This upscale residential community has resorts, golf courses, and gated mansions, as well as Sunnylands Center & Gardens, a historical estate visited by numerous dignitaries and open for public tours.

4 Palm Desert. The mile-long El Paseo shopping, gallery, and restaurant district is the heart of this peaceful community also known for its challenging golf courses and the Living Desert Zoo and Gardens.

5 Indian Wells. Exclusive Indian Wells hosts national tennis and pickleball championships at posh resorts, where spas and restaurants pamper players and spectators alike.

6 La Quinta. When Coachella Valley's first golf course opened here in 1920, the area alongside the sprawling resort and club grew into a quaint town obsessed with the sport.

7 Indio. The nation's date capital lures visitors with tasty date shakes and thriving palm orchards.

8 Salton Sea. Positioned on the Pacific Flyway, bird-watchers flock to its shores and the nearby Sonny Bono National Wildlife Refuge hoping to spot more than 400 species.

9 Desert Hot Springs. At the base of the San Bernardino Mountains north of Palm Springs, the community nicknamed Spa City has numerous hotels that harness the therapeutic mineral waters from a network of hot springs. It's a great place to stop before, or even better, after a hike in Joshua Tree National Park.

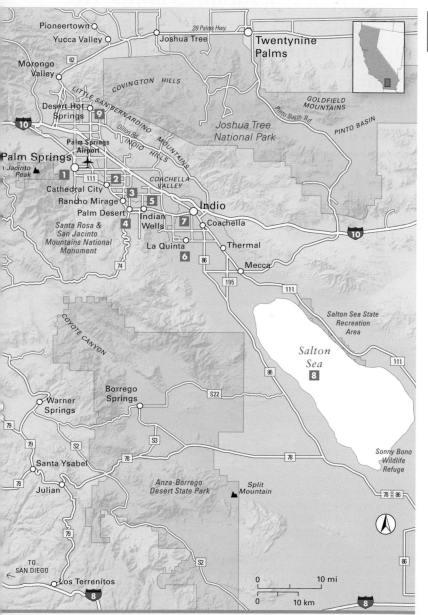

With year-round sunshine, breathtaking scenery, luxurious resorts and spas, chef-driven restaurants, Atomic Age aesthetics, and see-and-be-seen pool parties, it's no wonder that Hollywood A-listers, as well as weekend warriors, make the Palm Springs area a regular getaway.

Less than three hours from Los Angeles, the region has long been a playground for the rich and famous. In the 1920s, Al Capone opened the Two Bunch Palms Hotel in Desert Hot Springs; Marilyn Monroe was discovered poolside in the late 1940s at a downtown Palm Springs tennis club; the Rat Pack partied and performed here almost as often as they did in Las Vegas; Elvis and Priscilla Presley honeymooned here—the list goes on.

Today's stars are just as smitten. Many come for the annual film festival in January or April's mega music festivals Coachella and Stagecoach. Thankfully, the opportunities for pampering rest and relaxation or energizing swimsuit-clad recreation splendor aren't reserved just for marquee names.

Fill your days shopping for vintage caftans and crystal decanters, getting a massage with a poultice foraged in the desert scrub, or lounging in a poolside chaise while sipping frozen umbrella drinks. Alternatively, take an architecture tour or view works at museums, and art galleries. If you feel restless, practice your golf swing on a legendary course, hike to hot springs and palm-dotted oases, go bird-watching at the Salton

Sea, or bike from one brightly colored Insta-famous door to the next.

Nights are best spent at tiki bars, steak houses, drag shows, by your hotel's firepit with s'mores and a telescope (stargazing is primo here, especially in nearby Joshua Tree National Park), or on a dance floor or at a concert in Acrisure Arena. At some point, though, be sure to take everything in while riding the aerial tramway up to snowy San Jacinto peaks.

MAJOR REGIONS
Palm Springs and the Southern Desert Resorts. The city of Palm Springs is within the Colorado Desert, on the western edge of Coachella Valley and at the northwestern end of Highway 111. To the southeast are resort-filled desert communities like Cathedral City, Rancho Mirage, Palm Desert, Indian Wells, La Quinta, and Indio. Farther south is the Salton Sea.
Desert Hot Springs to Twentynine Palms Highway. Northwest of Palm Springs, off I–10 and Scenic California Highway 62, is the community of Desert Hot Springs, after which Highway 62 becomes Twentynine Palms Highway en route to Joshua Tree National Park.

Planning

Getting Here and Around

AIR

Palm Springs International Airport (PSP), roughly 3 miles from downtown, serves California's desert communities. Air Canada, Alaska, Allegiant, American, Delta, Flair, JetBlue, Southwest, Sun Country, United, and WestJet all fly to Palm Springs, some only seasonally. Cab and rideshare companies serve the airport. In addition, Sunline Transit Agency has two bus stops within three blocks of the airport. There's also a stop at the terminal's north end for Basin Transit buses.

AIRPORT INFORMATION Palm Springs International Airport. ⊠ *3400 E. Tahquitz Canyon Way, Palm Springs* ☎ *760/318–3800 general information* ⊕ *palmsprings-airport.com.*

BUS

Greyhound provides service to Palm Springs from many cities and also has stations in Desert Hot Springs and Indio. SunLine Transit Agency buses travel the entire Coachella Valley, from Desert Hot Springs to Mecca. Basin Transit buses serve the Morongo Basin, including Yucca Valley, Joshua Tree, and Twentynine Palms.

BUS CONTACTS Basin Transit. ☎ *760/366–2395* ⊕ *basin-transit.com.* **SunLine Transit Agency.** ☎ *760/343–3451* ⊕ *www.sunline. org.*

CAR

The desert resort communities occupy a 20-mile stretch between I–10 to the east and Palm Canyon Drive (Highway 111) to the west. The region is about a two-hour drive (up to a four-hour drive during rush hour and on weekends when traffic is heavy) east of Los Angeles and a three-hour drive northeast of San Diego. From Los Angeles, take the San Bernardino Freeway (I–10) east to Highway 111. From San Diego, I–15 north connects with the Pomona Freeway (Highway 60), leading to the San Bernardino Freeway east.

TAXI

City Cab, Coachella Valley Taxi, and Yellow Cab of the Desert serve the entire Coachella Valley. The fare is $4 to enter a cab and about $4 per mile. There is also an additional airport fee for all rides to or from PSP.

CONTACTS City Cab. ⊠ *19345 N. Indian Canyon Dr., Palm Springs* ☎ *760/328–3000* ⊕ *citycabride.com.* **Coachella Valley Taxi** ⊠ *Palm Springs* ☎ *760/992–5337* ⊕ *coachellavalleytaxi.com.*

TRAIN

The Amtrak *Sunset Limited*, which runs between Florida and Los Angeles, and *Texas Eagle* (Chicago to Los Angeles) stop in Palm Springs. Amtrak buses also meet *Pacific Surfliner* trains in Fullerton to ferry passengers to the Palm Springs region.

Hotels

In general, Palm Springs has the widest variety of lodgings, from tiny bed-and-breakfasts and historic inns to brand-name business hotels, sprawling resorts, and hiply updated roadside motels. Massive resort properties dominate in down-valley communities, such as Palm Desert and Rancho Mirage. You can stay in the desert for as little as $100 or splurge on luxury digs for more than $1,000 a night. ■TIP➜ **Take care when considering budget lodgings; other than reliable chains, they may not be up to par.**

Rates vary widely by season, day of the week, and expected occupancy. For example, a $200 room midweek can jump to $500 on Saturday, and rates can drop by up to 50% in summer and early fall. Expect to a pay a premium and book well ahead for stays during popular events such as Modernism Week or

Coachella, when, despite higher prices, coveted lodgings fill up far in advance.

Most hotels charge a daily resort fee of up to $60; this and, possibly, other fees aren't necessarily included in the room rate, so ask about them when booking. Many hotels are pet-friendly and offer special services, though these also typically cost extra. Discounts are sometimes given for extended stays, and casino hotels often offer promotional deals.

■TIP→ Ask your accommodation of choice if it sells day passes for its pool(s) or spa; if so, it will be harder to find peace—not to mention a chaise by the pool—or to get spa appointments.

Restaurants

The meat-and-potatoes crowd still has plenty of options, but an influx of talented chefs gives new meaning to the term "food desert" by making it possible to find fresh, superbly prepared seafood, contemporary Californian, French, Asian, Indian, and vegetarian cuisine. As with the rest of the state, Mexican food is plentiful.

Many restaurants host early-bird happy hours with discounted drinks and special menus. More savings can be had during the annual Restaurant Week in June in which participating restaurants offer prix-fixe coursed meals, special offers, and wine pairings. Some restaurants close or offer limited service in July and August.

⇨ Restaurant and hotel reviews have been shortened. For full information, visit Fodors.com. Restaurant prices are the average cost of a main course at dinner, or if dinner isn't served, at lunch. Hotel prices are the lowest cost of a standard double room in high season.

What It Costs

	$	$$	$$$	$$$$
RESTAURANTS				
	under $20	$20–$30	$31–$40	over $40
HOTELS				
	under $200	$200–$350	$351–$500	over $500

Tours

Big Wheel Bike Tours

BICYCLE TOURS | FAMILY | This company rents all manner of bicycles—from cruisers to mountain and e-bikes—at hotels and other locations in Palm Springs and Palm Desert. If you want something more structured, join escorted full- or half-day biking, hiking, or combo tours, all of which can be customized to your interests and skill levels. Those who prefer not to pedal can go off-roading in a Jeep instead. ⌧ *Palm Springs* ☎ *760/779–1837 Palm Desert, 760/548–0500 Palm Springs* ⊕ *bwbtours.com* ⌧ *From $119.*

Palm Springs Mod Squad

SPECIAL-INTEREST TOURS | Get immersed in the wonderful world of brise-soleil, cantilevered roofs, Sputnik chandeliers, and Plexiglass furniture with designer/reporter/bon vivant Kurt Cyr as your expert escort around what is generally considered the mecca of the mid-century modern movement. The Rat Pack–theme excursion ends, appropriately, with mid-day martinis, the era's cocktail of choice. ⌧ *Palm Springs* ☎ *760/469–9265* ⊕ *www. psmodsquad.com* ⌧ *From $75.*

Red Jeep Tours

ADVENTURE TOURS | FAMILY | This outfit's two- to six-hour Jeep, SUV, or van tours, some of which include hiking, explore Joshua Tree National Park, Indian Canyons and their indigenous history, Mecca Hills Wilderness Area, or the San Andreas Fault. The groups are small and the guides are knowledgeable.

Departures are from Indio Hills, Palm Springs, and Coachella depending on which tour you've booked. ⊠ *Palm Desert* ☎ *760/324–5337* ⊕ *www.red-jeep.com* ✆ *From $135.*

When to Go

Late November through April is the height of the visitor season. The desert weather is best during this time, and it's when many of the area's numerous big-deal festivals and special events take place. Early fall is nearly as lovely but things are generally less crowded and less expensive. Summer, a popular time with European visitors, offers the best deals because daytime temperatures regularly rise above 110°F. (Evenings often cool to the mid-70s.) Keep in mind that some attractions and restaurants close or reduce their hours during summer.

FESTIVALS AND EVENTS

Coachella Valley Music and Arts Festival. One of Southern California's biggest parties draws hundreds of thousands of music fans to Indio each April for two weekends of live (and generally sold-out) concerts, art installations, and DJ sets. ⊕ *www.coachella.com*

Greater Palm Springs Pride Festival. Events at this three-day November festival in downtown Palm Springs include street fairs, concerts, and dance parties. ⊕ *www.pspride.org*

La Quinta Art Celebration. Hundreds of jury-selected painters, sculptors, ceramicists, and other artists participate each March in a four-day show that's considered one of the best in the West. ⊕ *www.laquintaartcelebration.org*

Modernism Week. This 11-day mid-February program highlights the area's mid-century architecture with lectures, cocktail parties, films, and home and garden tours. A four-day mini-Mod happens in October. ⊕ *modernismweek.com*

Palm Springs International Film Festival. In mid-January, this 12-day festival brings stars, feature films, and panel discussions to various venues around town. The weeklong ShortFest, North America's largest short film festival and market, takes place in June. ⊕ *www.psfilmfest.org*

Riverside County Fair & National Date Festival. Indio celebrates its raison d'être in February at the fairgrounds with 10 days of exhibits on local dates, cooking demos, amusement rides, live music, a rodeo, and monster truck shows. ⊕ *www.datefest.org*

Stagecoach Festival. Country music's answer to Coachella is held at Indio's Empire Polo Field over three days in April. ⊕ *www.stagecoachfestival.com*

Palm Springs

A tourist destination since the late 19th century, Palm Springs evolved into an ideal hideaway for early Hollywood celebrities who slipped into town to play tennis, lounge poolside, attend a party or two, and, unless things got out of hand, steer clear of gossip columnists. But the area really blossomed in the 1930s, after actors Charlie Farrell and Ralph Bellamy bought 200 acres of land for $30 an acre and opened the Palm Springs Racquet Club, which soon listed Ginger Rogers, Humphrey Bogart, and Clark Gable among its members.

Today, Palm Springs embraces its glory days. Owners of resorts, bed-and-breakfasts, and galleries have renovated mid-century modern buildings, luring a new crop of celebs and high-powered executives. LGBTQ+ travelers, twentysomethings, and families also sojourn here.

Pleasantly touristy Palm Canyon Drive is packed with alfresco restaurants, along with indoor cafés, vintage boutiques, and souvenir shops. Farther west is the

Uptown Design District, which offers even chicer and more retro shopping options—many specializing in furniture and home goods—as well as art galleries and lively eateries. Within blocks of the safe and walkable downtown lie resorts and boutique hotels complete with energetic pool scenes, decadent spas, exclusive dining establishments, and trendy bars.

GETTING HERE AND AROUND

Palm Springs is 90 miles southeast of Los Angeles on I–10. Most visitors arrive in the area by car from Los Angeles or San Diego area via this freeway, which intersects with Highway 111 north of Palm Springs. Tahquitz Canyon Way marks the division between north and south on major streets (e.g., North and South Palm Canyon Drive).

VISITOR INFORMATION

CONTACTS Greater Palm Springs Conven-tion & Visitors Bureau. ⊠ *Visitor center, 70–100 Hwy. 111, at Via Florencia, Ran-cho Mirage* ☎ *760/770–9000, 800/967–3767* ⊕ *www.visitgreaterpalmsprings. com.* **Palm Springs Bureau of Tourism.** ⊠ *277 N. Av. Cabelleros, Palm Springs* ☎ *760/325–6611* ⊕ *www.visitpalm-springs.com.*

◉ Sights

Agua Caliente Casino Palm Springs

CASINO | This 24-hour downtown casino has 1,000 slot machines, as well as table games, a high-limit room, a coffeehouse, a steak house, and two bars—including a sports-theme one with mammoth screens displaying live games and matches. For dancing and live enter-tainment, head to the casino's Cascade Lounge. ⊠ *401 E. Amado Rd., at N. Calle Encilia, Palm Springs* ☎ *888/999–1995* ⊕ *aguacalientecasinos.com/properties/palm-springs.*

★ Indian Canyons

INDIGENOUS SIGHT | FAMILY | The Indian Canyons are the ancestral home of the Agua Caliente Band of Cahuilla Indians. While hiking three canyons open to the public, you can see remnants of their ancient life, including rock art, house pits and foundations, irrigation ditches, dams, and food-preparation areas. Trails vary in length from 1.2 to 4.7 miles long, are classified as easy or moderate, and are lined with palm oases, waterfalls, rock formations, and, in spring, wildflowers. Tree-shaded picnic areas are abundant.

The Trading Post at the entrance to Palm Canyon, noted for its stand of Washing-tonia palms, has trail maps and refresh-ments as well as Native American crafts. Endangered Peninsular Bighorn Sheep call Murray Canyon home. Fan palms and tall willows contrast with strange rock formations in Andreas Canyon. Rang-er-led hikes and talks are included with paid admission, but only they occur from October through June. Note that no ani-mals are allowed. ■TIP➜ **While exploring the canyons, remember you are a guest amid the still-sacred tribal lands.** ⊠ *38520 S. Palm Canyon Dr., south of Acanto Dr., Palm Springs* ☎ *760/323–6018* ⊕ *www. indian-canyons.com* ☎ *$12* ⊗ *Closed Mon.–Thurs. from July 5–Sept. 30.*

Moorten Botanical Garden

GARDEN | FAMILY | In 1938, Chester "Cac-tus Slim" Moorten, an original Keystone Cop, and his wife, Patricia, opened this showplace for desert plants—now numbering in the thousands—that include an ocotillo, a massive elephant tree, and a boojum tree. Be sure to stroll through the Cactarium, the world's first as the Moortens coined the term, to spot rare finds such as the welwitschia, which originated in southwestern Africa's Namib Desert. ⊠ *1701 S. Palm Canyon Dr., Palm Springs* ☎ *760/327–6555* ⊕ *www.moortengarden.com* ☎ *$5* ⊗ *Closed Wed.*

Morongo Casino

CASINO | A 20-minute drive west of Palm Springs, this casino has nearly 4,000 slot machines, high-limit gaming, big-money tournaments, table games, a poker room, and some fast-casual dining options. It sits on 44 acres alongside a 308-room luxury resort, a pool with sandy beach and lazy river, a full-service spa and salon, a coffee shop, Cielo restaurant, 12,000 square feet of meeting space, and a state-of-the-art venue that draw big names in music and comedy. ⊠ *49500 Seminole Dr., off I–10, Cabazon* ☎ *800/252–4499* ⊕ *www.morongocasinoresort.com.*

★ Palm Springs Aerial Tramway

VIEWPOINT | **FAMILY** | A trip on the world's largest rotating tram car provides a 360-degree view of the desert as it makes the 2½-mile ascent through Chino Canyon and up to an elevation of 8,516 feet in 10 minutes. On clear days, which are common, the view stretches 75 miles from Mt. San Gorgonio in the north to the Salton Sea in the south. In winter, stepping out into the snow at the top, a bit below Mt. San Jacinto's peak, is a treat. In summer, the summit's much cooler temperature is a welcome respite from punishing lower-elevation heat.

Year-round attractions at Mountain Station include observation decks, two restaurants, a cocktail lounge, a gift shop, picnic facilities, a small natural history museum, and two theaters that screen movies on the attraction's construction and on Mount San Jacinto State Park, which is also on the mountain and has 50 miles of hiking trails. In addition, you can take advantage of free guided weekend nature walks, or rent skis and snowshoes at the Adventure Center.

■**TIP→** Ride-and-dine packages are available after 4 pm. To avoid long waits, buy tickets online in advance or arrive 30 minutes before the first car leaves in the morning. ⊠ *1 Tram Way, off N. Palm Canyon Dr. (Hwy. 111), Palm Springs* ☎ *888/515–8726* ⊕ *pstramway.com* ⊠ *From $30* ⊘ *Closed 2 wks in Sept. for maintenance.*

★ Palm Springs Air Museum

HISTORY MUSEUM | **FAMILY** | This impressive collection of aircraft spans from World War II and Vietnam through the War on Terror and includes showpieces like a B-17 Flying Fortress bomber, a King Cobra, F-117A Nighthawk, and Grumman cats. In addition to planes, there are cool murals and exhibits on women in aviation, the Tuskegee Airman, and important battles and military operations of the last 100 years including a Tom Brokaw–narrated Pearl Harbor diorama.

There are no ropes, so you can crawl into or walk under aircraft and feel the metal. You can also watch mechanics rehab flying machines and see a flight demonstration. If you dare and can afford the splurge, take advantage of the museum's coolest offering: a flight in a vintage warbird like the T-28 Trojan, T-33 Thunderbird, and P-51 Mustang. ⊠ *745 N. Gene Autry Trail, Palm Springs* ☎ *760/778–6262* ⊕ *palmspringsairmuseum.org* ⊠ *$22; free for active-duty military and their immediate family.*

Palm Springs Art Museum

ART MUSEUM | **FAMILY** | This world-class art museum, housed in a building by famed architect E. Stewart Williams, focuses on photography, modern architecture, contemporary glass, and fine art. Outside, you're greeted by several large-scale works, including Seward Johnson's 26-foot, 34,000-pound *Forever Marilyn* statue, which depicts the actress in the iconic, billowing-dress *Seven Year Itch* pose. Inside, 28 bright, open galleries contain permanent-collection works and photos by such artists as Dale Chihuly, Allen Houser, Deborah Butterfield, Ginny Ruffner, Mark Di Suvero, Julius Shulman, and William Morris. Other highlights include enormous Native American baskets, as well as furniture handcrafted by the late actor George Montgomery.

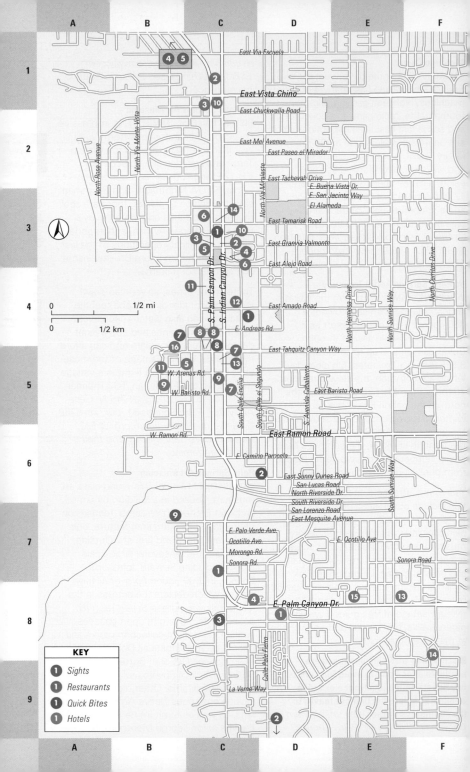

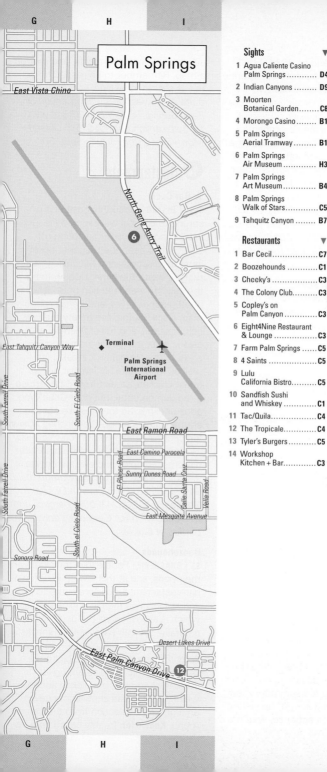

Palm Springs

Sights ▼

1 Agua Caliente Casino Palm Springs **D4**
2 Indian Canyons **D9**
3 Moorten Botanical Garden **C8**
4 Morongo Casino **B1**
5 Palm Springs Aerial Tramway **B1**
6 Palm Springs Air Museum **H3**
7 Palm Springs Art Museum **B4**
8 Palm Springs Walk of Stars **C5**
9 Tahquitz Canyon **B7**

Restaurants ▼

1 Bar Cecil **C7**
2 Boozehounds **C1**
3 Cheeky's **C3**
4 The Colony Club **C3**
5 Copley's on Palm Canyon **C3**
6 Eight4Nine Restaurant & Lounge **C3**
7 Farm Palm Springs **C5**
8 4 Saints **C5**
9 Lulu California Bistro **C5**
10 Sandfish Sushi and Whiskey **C1**
11 Tac/Quila **C4**
12 The Tropicale **C4**
13 Tyler's Burgers **C5**
14 Workshop Kitchen + Bar **C3**

Quick Bites ▼

1 Café La Jefa **C3**
2 Townie Bagels **D6**

Hotels ▼

1 Ace Hotel & Swim Club **D8**
2 Alcazar Palm Springs ... **C3**
3 ARRIVE Palm Springs ... **C1**
4 Azure Sky **C8**
5 Casa Cody **C5**
6 The Colony Palms Hotel **C3**
7 Drift Palm Springs **C5**
8 Kimpton The Rowan Palm Springs **C5**
9 Korakia Pensione **B5**
10 Movie Colony Hotel **C3**
11 Orbit In Hotel **B5**
12 Parker Palm Springs **I9**
13 The Saguaro **E8**
14 Smoke Tree Ranch **F8**
15 Sparrows Lodge **E8**
16 Willows Historic Palm Springs Inn **B5**

A 433-seat theater and an 85-seat hall present plays, concerts, lectures, operas, and other cultural events while two gardens are filled with sculptures. There's a great gift shop for classier souvenirs. Free Thursday nights are accompanied by DJ performances. Note, too, that the museum operates a separate Architecture and Design Center (✉ *300 S. Palm Canyon Dr.*), which, coincidentally, is housed within a former savings-and-loan office also built by Williams. ✉ *101 Museum Dr., off W. Tahquitz Canyon Dr., Palm Springs* ☎ *760/322–4800* 🌐 *www.psmuseum.org* 🎟 *$16, free Thurs. 5–8* 🕒 *Closed Mon.–Wed.*

Palm Springs Walk of Stars

OTHER ATTRACTION | FAMILY | More than 400 bronze stars are embedded in the sidewalks (à la Hollywood Walk of Fame) around downtown to honor celebrities with a Palm Springs connection. The Chairman of the Board, Elvis, Bob Hope, Marilyn Monroe, Dinah Shore, Ginger Rogers, Liz Taylor, and Liberace are among those who have received their due. Started on Palm Canyon Drive in 1992, stars have spread to Museum Way and Tahquitz Canyon Way. ✉ *Palm Canyon Dr., around Tahquitz Canyon Way, and Tahquitz Canyon Way, between Palm Canyon and Indian Canyon Drs., Palm Springs* ☎ *760/325–1577* 🌐 *www.palmsprings.com/walk-of-stars.*

Tahquitz Canyon

CANYON | FAMILY | Hikers who power through the strenuous 1.8-mile trail, 350 feet of elevation gain, and approximately 100 steep rock steps in this secluded restroom-less canyon on the Agua Caliente Reservation will be rewarded with a spectacular 60-foot waterfall, rock art, ancient irrigation systems, and native flora and fauna. Venture out on your own or join ranger-led walks (free with admission), which are conducted four times a day except during the summer when there is only one at 8 am. At the visitor center at the canyon entrance, watch a short video, look at artifacts, and pick up a map. Remember to be respectful as this is sacred tribal land. ✉ *500 W. Mesquite Ave., west of S. Palm Canyon Dr., Palm Springs* ☎ *760/323–6018* 🌐 *www.tahquitzcanyon.com* 🎟 *$15* 🕒 *Closed Mon.–Thurs. from July 5–Sept. 30.*

🍴 Restaurants

★ Bar Cecil

$$$$ | BISTRO | Since this posh bistro sprung to colorful wallpapered life just beyond downtown in the spring of 2021, it has been the toughest ticket in town to score—and Michelin agrees that it's worth the hype. Hoping to be the culinary manifestation of British photographer, artist, and Renaissance man, Cecil Beaton, the meaty menu is rich, flavorful, and full of financial and caloric splurges (caviar-topped deviled eggs, Wagyu tomahawk steaks), as well as fundamentally familiar dishes (roast chicken, steak frites, Bibb-lettuce salad, lemon tarts), but chef Gabe Woo adds unexpected touches like seasonal chutney atop a smoked pork chop. **Known for:** charming patio where you might spy celebrities; perfect vegetable accompaniments; complex and elegant cocktails, including a $50 martini. [$] *Average main: $45* ✉ *1555 S. Palm Canyon Dr., Palm Springs* ☎ *442/332–3800* 🌐 *barcecil.com* 🕒 *Closed Mon.* ☞ *Cash only; only serves parties of 6 or less.*

Boozehounds

$$ | BRASSERIE | People love traveling with their pups, and at this inventive uptown bar–restaurant, Fido is welcome to join you at tables on the big enclosed patio, which is accessed via the doggy door, naturally! You can savor spirits, snacks, and more substantial plates—many with Asian/Filipino leanings, like blistered shishitos, garlic noodles with *galbi* (Korean short ribs), or chicken adobo—while your dog can chow-chow down on a gourmet selection from the canine menu. **Known for:** freshly baked cookies

and milk (or milk punch); happy hour daily in high season and Friday–Sunday in summer; Instagram-worthy design. $ *Average main: $27* ✉ *2080 N. Palm Canyon Dr., Palm Springs* ☎ *760/656–0067* ⊕ *boozehoundsps.com* ☽ *Closed Tues. and Wed. in summer.*

★ Cheeky's

$ | **AMERICAN** | **FAMILY** | The flavored bacon flight, hangover-halting Bloody Marys, and the rest of the self-described "quirky comfort cuisine" have attracted legions to this casual breakfast and lunch joint for more than a decade, which results in epic waits on weekends (no reservations accepted for groups smaller than 10). Once seated, the well-oiled service machine is fast and furious—just pray the homemade cinnamon roll-croissant hybrids haven't sold out yet. **Known for:** pastries baked daily; juices pressed in-house; eggs collected from Cheeky's own chickens which eat a special diet; spacious outdoor patio. $ *Average main: $14* ✉ *622 N. Palm Canyon Dr., at E. Granvia Valmonte, Palm Springs* ☎ *760/327–7595* ⊕ *www.cheekysps.com* ☽ *No dinner.*

The Colony Club

$$$$ | **MODERN AMERICAN** | Discerning diners, even those whose names don't appear on the registry of The Colony Palms Hotel, know to book a table here for contemporary takes on white tablecloth staples like beef Stroganoff (here, made with short ribs and fresh pappardelle), green beans almondine (jazzed up with a brown-butter-and-cider glaze), or shrimp "cocktail" (barely recognizable but lip-lickin' good). Now overseen by chef Michael Hung—who cut his teeth at Daniel, Aquavit, Jardiniere, and La Folie— the restaurant emphasizes California seasonality and sourcing from farms and aquaculture operations to pack punch into everything from the small—say, preserved lemon compote and ginger scallion relish—to the large, like chicken schnitzel or vegan meatloaf. **Known for:**

Wine Wednesdays with discounted bottles; attentive, knowledgeable service; chic dining room dinners, sunny poolside brunches. $ *Average main: $50* ✉ *The Colony Palms Hotel, 572 N. Indian Canyon Dr., Palm Springs* ☎ *760/969–1818* ⊕ *colonypalmshotel.com.*

Copley's on Palm Canyon

$$$ | **AMERICAN** | Chef Andrew Manion Copley prepares decadent dishes with flavors and techniques he picked up at past posts in Europe, Australia, and Hawaii in a setting that's straight out of Hollywood—a hacienda once owned by Cary Grant. Dine in the clubby house or in the garden under the stars and with mountain views. **Known for:** romantic patio dining; fresh seafood and meats bathed in rich sauces; sweet and savory herb ice creams. $ *Average main: $37* ✉ *621 N. Palm Canyon Dr., at E. Granvia Valmonte, Palm Springs* ☎ *760/327–9555* ⊕ *www.copleyspalmsprings.com* ☽ *Closed July and Aug. No lunch.*

Eight4Nine Restaurant & Lounge

$$$ | **AMERICAN** | No matter what time or day it is, this swanky restaurant in the Uptown Design District buzzes with pals toasting promotions and celebrating birthdays, couples on dates sharing beet carpaccio and oysters, singles mingling in the lounge, and tourists who were lured from the street by the jovial sounds and tantalizing smells wafting out of the polished white (with pops of Barbie pink) rooms and expansive patio. The look may be a little late-'90s, early-aughts Miami, but the menu is pure Pacific Coast with favorites like ahi tuna poke with house-made kimchi, steelhead niçoise salad, mesquite-smoked carne asada, and curried-cauliflower steak. **Known for:** colorful plates made from scratch; energetic scene; Brandini toffee s'mores fondue will knock your socks off. $ *Average main: $33* ✉ *849 N. Palm Canyon Dr., Palm Springs* ☎ *760/325–8490* ⊕ *eight-4nine.com.*

★ Farm Palm Springs

$$$$ | FRENCH | At this charmer of a bistro in downtown's historic La Plaza, you can cross the pond without a passport by tucking into Provençal-style staples like sweet or savory crepes, bouillabaisse, croque-monsieur sandwiches, and omelets—all made from scratch using true-to-the-name ingredients, plenty of dairy products, and *amour*. Savor breakfast and lunch daily as the sun warms your skin; the setting becomes even more magical after dark thanks to string lights, clinking wine glasses, a gurgling fountain, and a five-course prix-fixe dinner offering. **Known for:** seating in a fragrant, flower-filled courtyard; house-made jams, French press coffee, baked-Brie board; boozy brunch. $ *Average main: $67* ⊠ *6 La Plaza, Palm Springs* ☎ *760/322–2724* ⊕ *farmpalmsprings.com* ☽ *No dinner Wed. and Thurs.*

4 Saints

$$$$ | AMERICAN | Perched on the seventh-floor rooftop of The Rowan hotel, where stunning mountain and city views unfold from nearly every table, 4 Saints serves modern American farm-to-table dishes in a distinguished dining room crafted from leather, wood, and metal and on the outdoor patio. The menu features hearty, sophisticated steak, seafood, and pasta dishes made with global flair and fresh-daily produce. **Known for:** creative and classic cocktails; see-and-be-seen scene; attentive service. $ *Average main: $43* ⊠ *100 W. Tahquitz Cyn. Way, Palm Springs* ☎ *760/392–2020* ⊕ *www. 4saintspalmsprings.com* ☽ *Closed Mon. and Tues. No lunch.*

Lulu California Bistro

$$ | MODERN AMERICAN | For more than a decade, Lulu has been feeding desert denizens and vacationers a little bit of everything—seriously, if you can't find something on the lengthy menu of soups, salads, pasta dishes, burgers, sandwiches, pizzas, seafood, other star proteins like pork ribs and filet mignon, and desserts (cotton candy!), you likely don't eat human food. Dine in the spacious, quirky multilevel dining room or outside on the terrace with prime Palm Canyon people-watching. **Known for:** separate vegetarian/vegan and gluten-free menus; three-course, prix-fixe weekend brunch ($28); local art collection. $ *Average main: $23* ⊠ *200 S. Palm Canyon Dr., Palm Springs* ☎ *760/327–5858* ⊕ *lulupalmsprings.com* ☽ *No breakfast weekdays.*

Sandfish Sushi and Whiskey

$$$ | SUSHI | The idea of eating raw fish in a landlocked desert might give some people pause, but be assured that a meal at Sandfish—an uptown sushiya melding Japanese techniques, Scandinavian plating, and a sexy minimalist earth-tone aesthetic—is a gastronomical leap of faith worth taking. Chef Engin Onural studied at the reputable Sushi Chef Institute, so he obviously has classic rolls, nigiri, maki, and sashimi on lock, but not trying his original creations that incorporate unusual ingredients like black-truffle zest, coconut flakes, or fried-potato threads would be a rookie mistake, as would skipping the cocktails made with desert botanicals and titular whiskey. **Known for:** decadent omakase chef's tasting menu; largest Japanese whiskey collection in the valley; the best-selling Venue Roll. $ *Average main: $34* ⊠ *1556 N. Palm Canyon, Palm Springs* ☎ *760/537–1022* ⊕ *www.sandfishsushiwhiskey.com* ☽ *No lunch.*

★ Tac/Quila

$$ | MODERN MEXICAN | FAMILY | Tac/Quila is what happens when two lawyers dare to dream out loud and switch gears mid-career—judging from the crowds at this always humming joint, they made the right decision. The setting features flower-laden "living" walls and a blend of mid-century modern and classic-Mexican design elements, but the menu is all Mexican, with Jalisco-style appetizers, tacos, ceviches, and meat dishes, as

well as a surprising number vegetarian and vegan copycats. **Known for:** flavored margarita and craft-beer flights; fun, sharable appetizers like aqua chile oysters and tempura avocado nuggets; convenient location. $ *Average main: $21* ✉ *415 N. Palm Canyon Dr., Palm Springs* ☎ *760/417–4471* ⊕ *tacquila.com.*

The Tropicale

$$$ | **ECLECTIC** | This popular watering hole and fine-dining eatery is part mid-century supper club (some nights feature live jazz), part Miami kitsch (pops of pink neon, marlin wall art, and apps served in glass seashells), and all good time. Sip from the extensive martini and mojito list; bask in the gorgeous glow of a flambéed baked Alaska from one of the main dining room's tall leather booths; or nosh on protein-packed salads, pork chops, pizzas, or Sunday sushi amid tropical plants and water features in the outdoor area. **Known for:** globe-trotting menu; happy hour (all night on Wednesday); celebrating special occasions. $ *Average main: $36* ✉ *330 E. Amado Rd., at N. Calle Encilia, Palm Springs* ☎ *760/866–1952* ⊕ *www.thetropicale.com.*

★ **Tyler's Burgers**

$ | **AMERICAN** | **FAMILY** | Since 1996, families, working stiffs, and couples have trusted Tyler's to supply simple lunch fare in a convenient downtown location, one that happens to be housed in a converted 1936 gas station. Expect mid-20th-century America's greatest hits: heaping burgers, hot dogs, tuna melts, stacks of fries, grilled cheeses, floats, and milk shakes. **Known for:** house-made cole slaw and potato salad; feeding carnivores and vegetarians alike; long weekend waits. $ *Average main: $12* ✉ *149 S. Indian Canyon Dr., at La Plaza, Palm Springs* ☎ *760/325–2990* ⊕ *www.tylersburgers. com* ⊙ *Closed Sun. and July and Aug.*

★ **Workshop Kitchen + Bar**

$$$$ | **AMERICAN** | Chef Michael Beckman's Uptown Design District hot spot pairs high-quality California cuisine and classic and creative cocktails with sleek, utilitarian, concrete-and-leather design inside a repurposed historical theater and outside on a lively patio. Everything is delicious, but this team particularly excels at anything involving duck, from duck fried rice to duck breast with beet and blood orange jus. **Known for:** most ingredients sourced from within a 100-mile radius; house-made ice cream and sorbet; communal seating options. $ *Average main: $43* ✉ *800 N. Palm Canyon Dr., at E. Tamarisk Rd., Palm Springs* ☎ *760/459–3451* ⊕ *www.workshopkitch- enbar.com* ⊙ *No lunch.*

☕ Coffee and Quick Bites

★ **Café La Jefa**

$ | **CAFÉ** | **FAMILY** | Thanks to its misted patio, fast Internet connection, plethora of seating, and, most importantly, fine selection of caffeinated hot and cold drinks, this is a great work-from-café option on the main drag in uptown. The colorful, independently owned, Latina-influenced coffeehouse serves Sisters Coffee out of Oregon, local Townie bagels, Lotus Energy elixirs, fresh-daily pastries, and filling breakfast plates, including smoked salmon toast and chorizo *con papas*. **Known for:** chai chatas and chagaccinos; wraparound patio with shaded section; healthy grab-and-go nibbles and locally made snacks. $ *Average main: $14* ✉ *750 N. Palm Canyon Dr., Palm Springs* ✛ *Inside Flannery Exchange* ☎ *760/673–7456* ⊕ *cafelajefa.com* ⊙ *No dinner.*

Townie Bagels

$ | **BAKERY** | **FAMILY** | Tucked into the Warm Sands neighborhood is the brick-and-mortar realization of a bagel dream for two dudes who started selling baked goods out of their home and at the weekend farmers' market. Using non-additive flours and old-school methods like boiling in malted water, they create their round mounds of goodness daily in 22 rotating flavors, from the expected poppy and cinnamon raisin to the less common like the black Russian. **Known for:** basic but comfortable location; take-away fresh bread and crackers; special weekend-only bagel flavors (like olive fennel or pretzel). [$] *Average main: $7* ✉ *650 E. Sunny Dunes Rd., Palm Springs* ☎ *760/459–4555* 🌐 *www.towniebagels.com* 🕒 *Closed Tues.*

Hotels

Ace Hotel & Swim Club
$$ | **RESORT** | The good times always seem to be rolling at this former Howard Johnson's that was brilliantly transformed into a buzzy boho boutique hotel by the hipster, Seattle-based Ace brand. **Pros:** King's Highway restaurant serves elevated diner food; stargazing deck above the clubhouse; roster of cultural and musical events. **Cons:** party atmosphere not for everyone; limited amenities; casual staff and service. [$] *Rooms from: $299* ✉ *701 E. Palm Canyon Dr., Palm Springs* ☎ *760/325–9900* 🌐 *acehotel.com/palm-springs* 🛏 *173 rooms* 🍴 *No Meals.*

Alcazar Palm Springs
$$ | **HOTEL** | At the crossroads of the Uptown Design District and the Movie Colony neighborhood, Alcazar, with its ample, modern, blazing-white guest rooms that wrap around a sparkling pool, does hip, simple, and comfortable well—and at a more affordable price point than most of its competitors. **Pros:** walking distance of downtown; on-site parking included with low resort fee; Townie bikes available. **Cons:** set between two very busy streets; wall a/c units; sleek room decor could feel sterile to some. [$] *Rooms from: $209* ✉ *622 N. Palm Canyon Dr., Palm Springs* ☎ *760/318–9850* 🌐 *alcazarpalmsprings.com* 🛏 *34 rooms* 🍴 *Free Breakfast.*

★ ARRIVE Palm Springs
$$ | **HOTEL** | By day, sip cocktails at the indoor–outdoor bar (which doubles as the reception desk), lounge in the pool while a live DJ spins nearby, or browse the trendy gift shop while slurping scoops of Coachella Valley Date from the in-store ice cream counter; at night, relax in the pool-sized hot tub, socialize around communal firepits (half of the rooms also have private patios and fireplaces), play drag-queen bingo (every other Thursday), or cozy up in your king-size bed amid tasteful urbane furnishings and boldly patterned wallpaper. **Pros:** private cabanas with misting systems; great on-site restaurant and local coffee shop; easy access to Uptown Design District shops, restaurants, galleries. **Cons:** only king rooms available; shower offers little privacy; adults-only party scene may not suit everyone. [$] *Rooms from: $325* ✉ *1551 N. Palm Canyon Dr., Palm Springs* ☎ *760/507–1650* 🌐 *www.arrivehotels.com* 🛏 *32 rooms* 🍴 *No Meals.*

★ Azure Sky
$$$ | **HOTEL** | It's easy to fall in love with this new-in-2022, adults-only Acme Hospitality property in a restored mid-century jewel of an apartment complex—we're talking sun-dappled breezeways, clerestory windows, carved doors, a low-slung roof, and a full-wall white-brick fireplace fronted by a shag rug in the lobby living room. **Pros:** quiet residential neighborhood close enough to bike to downtown; rooms stocked with artisan snacks, booze, tea, and coffee; has both pool and lawn courtyards. **Cons:** no TVs or telephones in room; limited designated parking; platform bed corners are pretty but painful to run into. [$] *Rooms from: $399* ✉ *1661 S. Calle Palo Fierro, Palm Springs* ☎ *760/469-4498* 🌐 *azureskyhotel.com* 🛏 *14 rooms* 🍴 *Free Breakfast.*

★ Casa Cody
$$$ | **B&B/INN** | Boutique hospitality firm Casetta dusted off a hodgepodge of buildings—including an early-1900s adobe, a rare 1932 Olympic cottage, and a hacienda hotel once run by Buffalo Bill Cody's cousin, Harriet—to create the kind of exceptional lodging where you

can easily lose track of time floating in one of two pools, eating fruit plucked off a property tree and sipping tea or coffee (available all day) in the bougainvillea-covered arcade, or watching sunlight and shadows crawl across the walls from your snuggly, never-want-to-leave bed. **Pros:** easy walk to restaurants, hikes, museums; some rooms have kitchenettes, private patios, and fireplaces; fancy Parachute linens. **Cons:** very few parking stalls; limited on-site amenities; noise carries through old windows and walls. [$] *Rooms from: $489* ✉ *175 S. Cahuilla Rd., Palm Springs* ☎ *760/320–9346* 🌐 *www.casacody.com* 🛏 *30 rooms* 🍴 *Free Breakfast.*

The Colony Palms Hotel

$$$$ | **HOTEL** | A hip place to stay since the 1930s, when gangster Al Wertheimer built it to front his casino, bar, and brothel, this Spanish colonial–style property later became the Howard Hotel (hosting a young Frank Sinatra, Elizabeth Taylor, and Liberace) and has now been been returned it to its art deco roots and further gussied up for the social-media age to once again attract tastemakers, pretty young things, and other adults with the desire (and budget) to live the good life. **Pros:** etched personalized nameplates on doorways is a nice touch; attentive, affable staff; rooms with outdoor tubs, fireplaces, and private patios. **Cons:** can get noisy especially near the pool; valet parking only; uneven sidewalks hard to navigate with luggage. [$] *Rooms from: $760* ✉ *572 N. Indian Canyon Dr., Palm Springs* ☎ *760/969–1800* 🌐 *colonypalmshotel.com* 🛏 *57 rooms* 🍴 *No Meals.*

★ Drift Palm Springs

$$ | **HOTEL** | **FAMILY** | Opened in 2023, the third hotel from a thriving new name in West Coast hospitality is a neutral-toned nirvana that combines a touch of Tulum with mid-century nods and offers a desirable, convenient location; suites and studios that can accommodate individuals and couples or families and other groups of varying sizes; desert-sojourn musts like a refreshing pool, yoga, lawn games, firepits, and photogenic cacti; and such mod cons as digital check-in, coded room entry, pour-over coffee equipment, and steamers that actually work. **Pros:** large pool deck with lots of chaises and daybeds; breakfast chilaquiles and churros; quiet spaces with fountains or lending libraries to escape pool crowds. **Cons:** minimal hangers, hooks, or storage; high resort fee ($60); only valet parking. [$] *Rooms from: $275* ✉ *284 S. Indian Canyon Dr., Palm Springs* ☎ *888/976–4487* 🌐 *www.drifthotels.co* 🛏 *39 units* 🍴 *No Meals.*

★ Kimpton The Rowan Palm Springs

$$$ | **HOTEL** | **FAMILY** | As the tallest building in town, this upscale boutique dazzles locals and guests (especially the under-45 set) with stunning mountain, museum-installation, and twinkling, after-dark, urban views from guest rooms and suites, the bar, the seventh-story restaurant, and the deck that surrounds the city's lone rooftop pool. **Pros:** PUBLIC bikes to ride around town; no extra fees for pets; both self and valet parking. **Cons:** no spa, though in-room services can be arranged; allow nonguests to rent cabanas; Juniper Table breakfast option is overpriced. [$] *Rooms from: $389* ✉ *100 W. Tahquitz Canyon Way, Palm Springs* ☎ *760/904–5015* 🌐 *www.rowanpalmsprings.com* 🛏 *153 rooms* 🍴 *No Meals.*

★ Korakia Pensione

$$$ | **B&B/INN** | This incredibly unique, Moroccan–Mediterranean mashup comprises Scottish painter Gordon Coutts' 1924 Tangier-inspired villa, a southern Europe–styled 1930s home once owned by silent film star J. Carol Naish, and a 1918 California adobe spread across 1½ acres on both sides of a quiet street a couple of blocks from downtown's main drag. **Pros:** two pools that never close; outdoor movie nights with popcorn; sound baths and yoga on weekends. **Cons:** woo-woo vibe won't appeal to business hotel loyalists; no TVs or phones in rooms; limited parking. $ *Rooms from: $379* ✉ *257 S. Patencio Rd., Palm Springs* ☎ *760/864–6411* ⊕ *www.korakia.com* ⬩ *28 rooms* ¶◎¶ *Free Breakfast.*

Movie Colony Hotel

$$ | **HOTEL** | Designed in 1935 by Albert Frey, this intimate, adults-only hotel leans hard into the mid-century minimalist aesthetic throughout its gleaming-white, balcony-studded, two-story buildings and its residential-style rooms, where the accents and bright colors are era-accurate. **Pros:** architectural icon; cool vibe; property-wide remodel in 2019. **Cons:** close quarters, small pool area; basic breakfast; staff not available 24/7. $ *Rooms from: $280* ✉ *726 N. Indian Canyon Dr., Palm Springs* ☎ *760/284–1600* ⊕ *www.moviecolonyhotel.com* ⬩ *17 rooms* ¶◎¶ *Free Breakfast.*

Orbit In Hotel

$$ | **B&B/INN** | The exterior architecture—nearly flat roofs, wide overhangs, glass everywhere—of this hip, adults-only, Herbert Burns–designed inn on a quiet street dates from its 1955 opening, and the period feel continues inside, where rooms, some with kitchenettes, all have patios and are appointed with mid-mod furnishings by Charles and Ray Eames, Marcel Breuer, and other contemporaries. **Pros:** saltwater pool; nightly cocktail hour with signature Orbitinis; free breakfast and snacks served poolside. **Cons:** no on-site restaurant (though area eateries are just a stroll away); no prepared hot items like eggs at breakfast; staff not available 24 hours. $ *Rooms from: $249* ✉ *562 W. Arenas Rd., Palm Springs* ☎ *760/323–3585* ⊕ *www.orbitin.com* ⬩ *9 rooms* ¶◎¶ *Free Breakfast.*

★ Parker Palm Springs

$$$$ | **RESORT** | At what is definitely not your grandad's luxury hotel, a cacophony of color, retro accessories, Moroccan textiles, and flamboyant art masterfully assembled by designer Jonathan Adler is paired with lush, mazelike grounds; attentive service; and amenities that include three saltwater pools, cozy firepits, free EV charging, clay tennis courts, pétanque, morning barista services, and a huge spa that looks like a Wes Anderson film set. **Pros:** celebrity sightings happen regularly; on-site restaurants, bars, and spa; guests can use the spa facilities without booking a treatment. **Cons:** pricey drinks and food; have to drive to downtown; resort fee ($45). $ *Rooms from: $1,049* ✉ *4200 E. Palm Canyon Dr., Palm Springs* ☎ *760/770–5000* ⊕ *www.parkerpalmsprings.com* ⬩ *144 rooms* ¶◎¶ *No Meals.*

The Saguaro

$ | **HOTEL** | Manhattan-based architects Peter Stamberg and Paul Aferiat took a ho-hum Holiday Inn of yore and turned it into a rainbow-bright stay for sunseekers, where the proudly loud palette—said to be inspired by the surrounding desert's wildflowers—is carried through the grounds, the pool area (which always seems to be mid-party), and the rooms. **Pros:** weekend yoga; Taco Tuesday and Thursday at on-site cantina; cool artist collaborations for decor, uniforms, and a merch line. **Cons:** a few miles from downtown; pool area can be noisy and crowded; $42 resort fee. $ *Rooms from: $139* ✉ *1800 E. Palm Canyon Dr., Palm Springs* ☎ *760/323–1711* ⊕ *thesaguaro.com* ⬩ *244 rooms* ¶◎¶ *No Meals.*

Smoke Tree Ranch

$$$ | **RESORT** | **FAMILY** | A laid-back retreat since the mid-1930s for some of the world's foremost families, including Walt Disney's, the area's most under-the-radar resort occupies 385 pristine desert acres, is surrounded by mountains and unspoiled vistas, and provides a wholesome, family-friendly experience with a touch of the Old West. **Pros:** priceless privacy; wood-burning fireplaces for cold desert nights; rustic yet refined. **Cons:** no glitz; limited entertainment options; family atmosphere not for everyone. $ *Rooms from: $490* ✉ *1850 Smoke*

Tree La., Palm Springs ☎ *800/787–3922* 🌐 *www.smoketreeranch.com* 🕑 *Closed May–Oct.* 🛏 *49 cottages* 🍴 *All-Inclusive.*

Sparrows Lodge
$$$ | B&B/INN | Rustic earthiness meets haute design (rusted rolled-steel roof, open shelving, concrete-pebble floors, gallery walls, and so many accent pillows) at the adults-only Sparrows, a restored 1950s retreat originally built by actor Don Castle just off the main drag. **Pros:** interiors overhauled in 2022; intimate property; some rooms have private patios. **Cons:** not family-oriented; a little too far to walk to downtown shopping and dining; no TVs in rooms. [$] *Rooms from: $399* ✉ *1330 E. Palm Canyon Dr., Palm Springs* ☎ *760/327–2300* 🌐 *www.sparrowslodge.com* 🛏 *20 rooms* 🍴 *Free Breakfast.*

★ Willows Historic Palm Springs Inn
$$$$ | B&B/INN | Set in two adjacent, opulent, Mediterranean-style mansions built in the 1920s to host the rich and famous friends (Clark Gable, Shirley Temple, Albert Einstein) of millionaire William Mead, this sumptuous hillside B&B has gleaming hardwood floors, stone fireplaces, frescoed ceilings, hand-painted tiles, iron balconies, and a 50-foot waterfall that splashes down outside the dining room window providing breakfast entertainment. **Pros:** short walk to art museum, restaurants, shops; interesting architecture and fabulous Hollywood history; expansive breakfast and afternoon wine hour. **Cons:** closed from June to September; pricey (but no daily resort fee); some rooms on the small side. [$] *Rooms from: $545* ✉ *412 W. Tahquitz Canyon Way, Palm Springs* ☎ *760/320–0771* 🌐 *thewillowspalmsprings.com* 🕑 *Closed June–Sept.* 🛏 *17 rooms* 🍴 *Free Breakfast.*

🍸 Nightlife

BARS AND DANCE CLUBS

★ Bootlegger Tiki
BARS | This uptown drinking den picks up where tiki bar founding father Don the Beachcomber left off—first, by occupying its former space where Frank Sinatra guzzled navy grog by the quart and second, by delivering both classic cocktails like zombies and mai tais and fruit-forward, rum-heavy originals decorated with umbrellas, chunks of honeycomb, and flamingos. It's dark, full of kitsch (it's hard not to love the pufferfish lights), and has both late-afternoon and last-call happy hours daily. ✉ *1101 N. Palm Canyon Dr., Palm Springs* ☎ *760/318–4154* 🌐 *www.bootleggertiki.com.*

Tailor Shop
BARS | Uptown and next door to Bootleggers, this moody, sophisticated establishment was opened in late 2021 by the folks behind Sandfish—which accounts for the extensive collection of high-end whiskies and the Japanese-leaning snacks and sushi menu—to service serious cocktail connoisseurs. It has a New York air, with tufted banquettes, dim lights, leather-covered menus, a wraparound marble bar, and waxed-canvas-apron-clad bartenders who sometimes roll over the bar cart to muddle and shake in your personal space. ✉ *140 W. Via Lola, Suite A, Palm Springs* 🌐 *www.tailorshopps.com.*

Tonga Hut
BARS | The younger sibling of L.A.'s oldest still-operating tiki bar (opened in 1958 in North Hollywood) transports guests from Palm Springs to Polynesia with groovy tunes, pupu platters, and umbrella drinks. Most of drinks, both classic and original, are powered by rum, but gin hounds, rye or dies, and vodka lovers have a few options, too. The bar is on the second floor of a building in the thick of

Palm Springs Modernism

Some of the world's most forward-looking architects designed and constructed buildings around Palm Springs between 1940 and 1970. Described these days as mid-century modern—you'll also see the term "desert modernism" used—these structures, which were popular elsewhere in California, too, in the years after World War II, are ideal for desert living because they minimize the separation between indoors and outdoors. Houses with glass exterior walls are common, as are oversize flat roofs that provide shade from the sun. The style is also notable for elegant informality, simple landscaping, and clean lines that often mirror the shapes of surrounding topography.

Noteworthy examples include three 1960s buildings that are part of the Palm Springs Aerial Tramway complex. Albert Frey, a Swiss-born architect, designed the soaring A-frame Tramway Gas Station, visually echoing the pointed peaks behind it. Frey also created the glass-walled Valley Station, from which you get your initial view of the Coachella Valley before you board the tram to the Mountain Station, designed by E. Stewart Williams.

Frey, a Palm Springs resident for more than 60 years, also designed the indoor-outdoor City Hall, Fire Station No. 1, and numerous houses.

His second home, atop stilts on a hill above the Palm Springs Art Museum, affords a sweeping Coachella Valley view through glass walls. The classy Movie Colony Hotel, one of Frey's first desert designs, might seem like a typical 1950s motel, with rooms surrounding a swimming pool, but when it was built in 1935, it was years ahead of its time.

Donald Wexler, who honed his vision with Los Angeles architect Richard Neutra, brought new ideas about the use of materials to the desert, where he teamed up with William Cody on projects such as the terminal at the Palm Springs Airport. Wexler also experimented with steel framing back in 1961, but the metal proved too expensive. Seven of his steel-frame houses can be seen in a neighborhood off Indian Canyon and Frances drives.

The Palm Springs Modern Committee website has lots of information and resources, including a downloadable app (⊕ *psmodcom.org/mid-century-modern-tour-app*) that guides you to the most interesting buildings. Note, too, that the desert communities celebrate the Palm Springs "look" during mid-February's Modernism Week (⊕ *modernismweek.com*), an 11-day event featuring lectures, films, and home and garden tours. A shorter preview week happens in October.

downtown, so try to nab a table on the lanai to watch the action from above. Private parties can reserve a shagadelic room hidden behind a phone booth. ✉ *254 N. Palm Canyon Dr., Palm Springs* ☎ *760/322–4449* ⊕ *www.tongahut.com* ⊗ *Closed Mon.*

★ The Village

DANCE CLUBS | Going strong since 1995, with themed happenings and live entertainment or DJs most nights, this popular sports bar/nightclub/restaurant caters to a young crowd and visiting bachelor/bachelorette posses who want to dress sexy, drink seriously (and cheaply during happy hour), and play hard. ⊠ *266 S. Palm Canyon Dr., at Baristo Rd., Palm Springs* ☎ *760/323–3265* ⊕ *thevillagepalmsprings.com.*

GAY AND LESBIAN CLUBS
Chill Bar Palm Springs
DANCE CLUBS | Dance, drink, drag, and dine at this nightclub in a strip mall in the heart of the gay-centric Arenas Road district. By day, it's quite civilized. Socialize on the patio, share a watermelon feta salad, and play games. When the sun goes down, it's time to get down on the large dance floor to the hypnotic electronic beats of live spinners, enjoy drag performers, or marvel at the go-go dancers. Alcohol flows all day, every day no matter the theme. ⊠ *217 E. Arenas Rd., Palm Springs* ☎ *760/676–9493* ⊕ *www. chillbarpalmsprings.com.*

Hunters
DANCE CLUBS | A young energetic gay and straight crowd comes to this club-scene mainstay for bar grub, drag bingo, bottle service, and Speedo-sporting studs. ⊠ *302 E. Arenas Rd., at Calle Encilia, Palm Springs* ☎ *760/323–0700* ⊕ *hunterspalmsprings.com.*

★ Toucans Tiki Lounge
CABARET | A welcoming place with botanical prints, vibrant colors, carved totems, and globe pendants, Toucans is the longtime go-to for those who love drag queens, cabaret, and festive drinks. ⊠ *2100 N. Palm Canyon Dr., at W. Via Escuela, Palm Springs* ☎ *760/416–7584* ⊕ *toucanstikilounge.com* ⊘ *Closed Tues. and Wed.*

THEMED ENTERTAINMENT
Ace Hotel and Swim Club
THEMED ENTERTAINMENT | Events are held at the hotel's bar, pool, or restaurant nearly every night, including film screenings, full moon parties, concerts, DJ sets, and trivia/bingo nights. Many are free, most are casual, and some are even family-friendly. ⊠ *701 E. Palm Canyon Dr., at Calle Palo Fierro, Palm Springs* ☎ *767600/325–9900* ⊕ *acehotel.com.*

🛍 Shopping

DISTRICTS
Backstreet Art District
ART GALLERIES | A collective of galleries such as Galleria Marconi and Artize Gallery, working studios, and art-adjacent businesses like framers showcase works across multiple disciplines by a number of highly acclaimed artists. Support local artists new to the biz at the Stephen Baumbach Gallery. ■**TIP**➔ **On the first Wednesday of the month, the galleries stay open from 5 to 7 for Artwalk.** ⊠ *2600 S. Cherokee Way, Palm Springs* ⊕ *www. backstreetartdistrict.com* ⊘ *Several galleries are closed Mon. and Tues.*

★ Uptown Design District
NEIGHBORHOODS | Like-minded boutiques, secondhand shops, furniture stores, galleries, and lively restaurants line this stretch of street north of downtown. The theme here is decidedly retro. Some places sell mid-century modern furniture and decor and photos of neon signs and stylish soirees while others carry vintage (or vintage-knockoff) designer clothing, pool party gear, and estate jewelry. One spot definitely worth a peek is The Shag Store, the gallery of fine art painter Josh Agle. If you dig the mid-mod aesthetic, breeze through the furnishings at Towne Palm Springs or a La MOD INC. Find several independent sellers under one E. Stewart Williams–designed roof at The Shops At Thirteen Forty Five. ⊠ *N. Palm Canyon Dr., between Alejo and Vista Chino, Palm Springs.*

MALLS
★ Desert Hills Premium Outlets
OUTLET | **FAMILY** | About 20 miles west of Palm Springs lies one of California's largest outlet malls, which hawks everything from bikinis and bags to sunglasses and stilettos. The complex's 180 stores include Jimmy Choo, Samsonite, Levi's,

Saint Laurent, J. Crew, Armani, Gucci, lululemon, and Prada. ⊠ *48400 Seminole Dr., off I–10, Cabazon* ☏ *951/849–6641* ⊕ *www.premiumoutlets.com.*

Flannery Exchange

SHOPPING CENTER | In the Uptown Design District, Flannery Exchange is a photogenic mixed-use minimall with on-trend boutiques, an art gallery, the Café La Jefa coffeehouse, and Bar Chingona (which serves modern Latin food and sassy cocktails from an Airstream trailer). Grab a chaga-charged latte to sip and stroll through the shelves of stationery (Bobo Palm Springs), zero-waste goods (it refills), vintage threads (Joyful Living), and jewelry and gifts (Covet). Or pop open a canned kombucha to enjoy in a swinging chair on the sunny patio. Each vendor has different hours so check before you go. ⊠ *750 N. Palm Canyon Dr., Palm Springs* ☏ *760/364–9611* ⊕ *flanneryexchange.com.*

The Shops At Thirteen Forty Five

SHOPPING CENTER | Several independently owned, high-end, and Goop-approved boutiques coexist in an iconic E. Stewart Williams building to supply those with good taste in need of ceramics, abstract art, statement swimwear and sunglasses, planters, linens, throw pillows, jewelry, and so much more. ⊠ *1345 N. Palm Canyon Dr., Palm Springs* ☏ *760/464–0480* ⊕ *www.theshopsat1345.com* ⊗ *Closed Tues. and Wed.*

SPECIALTY STORES
Hadley Fruit Orchards

FOOD | **FAMILY** | Just off I–10 near the Desert Hills outlet mall, stock up on dried fruit, nuts, candy, and other road-trip treats at what was once a roadside stand owned by the folks who invented trail mix. Although the café serves sandwiches and other quick bites, a must-order is the date shake made with caramel-tasting, California-grown, Deglet Noor dates. (A vegan version is available, too.) ⊠ *47993 Morongo Trail, Cabazon* ☏ *951/849–5255* ⊕ *hadleyfruitorchards.com.*

★ Just Fabulous

SOUVENIRS | **FAMILY** | Find coffee-table books, greeting cards, home decor with cheeky and naughty sayings, candles, wearable souvenirs, and other eclectic items at this fun gift shop that celebrates the area's retro-modern lifestyle and desert dolce vita. ⊠ *515 N. Palm Canyon Dr., Palm Springs* ☏ *760/864–1300* ⊕ *bjustfabulous.com.*

★ Mojave Flea Trading Post

SOUVENIRS | **FAMILY** | This 10,000-square-foot marketplace filled with boho bits and baubles, prints and other art, clothing, foodstuffs, dried bouquets, candles, and toiletries—created mostly by artisans and makers from Joshua Tree, the Coachella Valley, and elsewhere in California—feels like a brick-and-mortar Etsy. ⊠ *383 N. Indian Canyon Dr., Palm Springs* ☏ *760/232–6132* ⊕ *shoptradingpost.com.*

On The Mark

FOOD | **FAMILY** | At this downtown fine-foods market, shelves and displays are filled with small-batch snacks, sauces, and sweets that make great edible souvenirs. There's also a selection of wine and beer, and the deli case—well-stocked with nitrate-free cold cuts, cheeses from boutique creameries around the world, pickled veggies, and fancy condiments—provides the starting point for yummy sandwiches and trendy charcuterie boards that would be perfect for a picnic or a pool party. ⊠ *111 N. Palm Canyon Dr., Suite 155, Palm Springs* ☏ *760/832–8892* ⊕ *www.onthemark-palmsprings.com.*

★ Trina Turk | Mr Turk

MIXED CLOTHING | Celebrity designer Trina Turk's candy-color empire takes up a city block in the Uptown Design District. Designed by Kelly Wearstler, the light and bright adjoining showrooms create the perfect platform to display the splashy patterns, vibrant colors, and sophisticated poolside cocktail party aesthetic Trina Turk is famous for—in her resortwear as well as her accessories, pets, and home

Home to more than 100 courses, the Palm Springs area is a golfer's paradise.

lines. It's the place to go if you forgot to pack a floppy hat, caftan, or a two-piece floral cabana set. ⊠ *891 N. Palm Canyon Dr., Palm Springs* ☎ *760/416–2856* ⊕ *www.trinaturk.com.*

 Activities

GOLF

Indian Canyons Golf Resort

GOLF | Operated by the Aqua Caliente Band of Cahuilla Indians, this spot at the base of the mountains includes two 18-hole courses open to the public. In the 1960s, this was *the* place to play when visiting the desert. The North Course, designed by William F. Bell, is adjacent to homes once owned by Walt Disney and has six water hazards. The South Course, redesigned in 2004 by Casey O'Callaghan with input from the LPGA player Amy Alcott, has four ponds, 850 palm trees, and five par-5 holes. Discounted twilight rates are available on both after 1 pm. ⊠ *1097 E. Murray Canyon Dr., at Kings*

Rd. E, Palm Springs ☎ *760/833–8724* ⊕ *www.indiancanyonsgolf.com* ⊠ *North Course, $65; South Course, $190* ⚐ *North Course: 18 holes, 6943 yards, par 72; South Course: 18 holes, 6582 yards, par 72.*

Tahquitz Creek Golf Resort

GOLF | Conveniently located within minutes of the airport, this resort has two popular courses, a 50-stall driving range, a chipping green, and two putting greens. Golfers have been walking the Legend course with its challenging back nine for more than 60 years. The newer Resort course, designed by Ted Robinson, offers sweeping mountain views, undulating fairways, and cheeky hole names like Wet Banana and Terminator. ⊠ *1885 Golf Club Dr., at 34th Ave., Palm Springs* ☎ *760/328–1005* ⊕ *tahquitzgolfresort.com* ⊠ *Legend Course, $71; Resort Course, $111* ⚐ *Legend Course: 18 holes, 6815 yards, par 71; Resort Course: 18 holes, 6705 yards, par 72.*

HORSEBACK RIDING
Smoke Tree Stables
HORSEBACK RIDING | FAMILY | Explore desert canyons, stream beds, and palm groves on horseback like the earliest pioneers. Two-hour tours depart three times a day, and private outings can be booked for riders age seven and older. ⊠ *2500 S. Toledo Ave., Palm Springs* ☎ *760/327–1372* ⊕ *www.smoketreestables.com* ⊠ *From $160* ⊘ *Closed Wed. and Thurs.*

SPAS
Estrella Spa
SPAS | The Avalon Hotel's spa earns top honors each year for the indoor–outdoor experience it offers. Housed in the garden bungalow at the back of the property, check-in is handled in the divine-smelling living room with bubbles, services are performed in six regal rooms where crown molding and navy duvets add a touch of Old Hollywood glamour, and pre- and post-hanging can be spent in the private courtyard with a whirlpool tub and shaded daybeds. Compared to other area spas, the treatment list is a wee bit skimpy, but a CBD massage or a hydrating scalp treatment are well worth a visit. ⊠ *Avalon Hotel, 415 S. Belardo Rd., Palm Springs* ☎ *760/318–3000* ⊕ *www.avalon-hotel.com/palm-springs/estrella-spa* ⊠ *Massages and facials from $195, body treatments from $175* ⊘ *Closed Wed., by appointment only Mon. and Tues.*

Palm Springs Yacht Club
SPAS | It's only fitting that a hotel as quirky and hip as the Parker has a spa that feels like the set of a Wes Anderson movie thanks to its all-encompassing whimsical nautical theme brought to life with stripes, sailing flags, life-preserver art, front-desk "quartermasters" who refer to guests as captain, locker room portholes, rope-print carpet, and a relaxation area that looks like the lido deck of a vintage steamer. The style is backed up with self-care substance. After a cucumber-infused vodka shot, head to one of the 15 treatment rooms (named after America's Cup winners!) for massages, facials, scrubs, or wraps. (Some of these, like the salty sea buffing, are also themed.) PSYC also offers nail care, a gym, a pool, sauna and steam facilities, a boutique, and hot tubs. ⊠ *4200 E. Palm Canyon Dr., Palm Springs* ☎ *760/321–4606* ⊕ *www.parkerpalmsprings.com/palm-springs-yacht-club* ⊠ *Massages from $175, facials from $225, body treatments from $225, packages from $500.*

★ The Spa at Séc-he
SPAS | Palm Springs has long been a popular wellness destination, and it has *Séc-he,* an ancient geothermal spring that sits 8,000 feet below the city, and the Agua Caliente Band of Cahuilla Indians, who shared the mineral-laden waters with the area's first settlers and vacationers, to thank for it. This exquisite, completely renovated, 73,000-square-foot pamper palace offers state-of-the-art serenity. As in the old days, you can "take the waters," but you now have a variety of ways to do so: 22 private bubbling baths, larger shared mineral hot tubs in the men's and women's locker areas, and an even bigger zero-edge mineral pool outside near the bar–café. In addition to standard services and amenities (massages, facials, scrubs, wraps, saunas, steam rooms), the spa also offers halotherapy salt caves, float tanks, a cryotherapy chamber, relaxation areas with vibrational loungers, grounded tranquility rooms with zero-gravity conductive chairs, a cupping treatment, a quartz bed, a full-service hair and nail salon with scalp-treatment beds, and a fitness center. There's also a resort-style pool deck with a waterfall pool, whirlpools, cabanas, and daybeds. ⊠ *200 E. Tahquitz Canyon Way, Palm Springs* ☎ *866/777–3243* ⊕ *thespaatseche.com* ⊠ *Massages from $230, facials from $235, body treatments from $225, packages from $320.*

St. Somewhere Spa

SPAS | Whether you're a devoted Parrothead or someone who'd like to throw that last shaker of salt at the radio whenever Jimmy Buffet comes on, the spa at the Margaritaville Resort—the largest hotel spa within city limits with 18 treatment rooms—is a worthy place to be wasting away an afternoon getting a massage, an Intraceuticals vitamin C facial, a milk bath, or a body treatment. And it's an egalitarian place at that with its validated valet parking, theme monthly specials, weekday happy-hour pricing, and date-night rates on Thursday when the spa stays open late for couples. You can even bring your dog along as there's a separate menu of treatments for Fido. Before or after the service, relax in the dimly lit sanctuary, the Blue Haven Lounge, where a waterfall's steady cascade lulls you into an even more languorous tempo while you float in the Watsu pool or spa. Fun fact: the Margaritaville was the Riviera in a past life, and the old nightclub was where the Rat Pack and Elvis held court in the 1960s. ✉ *1600 N. Indian Canyon Dr., Palm Springs* ☎ *760/778–6690* 🌐 *www.margaritavilleresorts.com/margaritaville-resort-palm-springs* 🎫 *Massages from $100, facials from $155, body treatments from $150.*

Cathedral City

5½ miles southeast of Palm Springs.

While surveying a Colorado Desert canyon in 1855, Colonel Henry Washington remarked that the rock formations reminded him of European cathedrals. The name stuck, and today those same natural wonders are still wowing hikers on trails in Cat City, as it is colloquially known. The town itself began as an artists' colony, and a public arts initiative has placed works around the city, which is also home to the Perez Road Art & Design District, a great place to shop for decorative items.

GETTING HERE AND AROUND

Cathedral City lies due east of the Palm Springs International Airport. It's main streets running north and south are Landau and Date Palm; those running west to east are Ramon Road, Dinah Shore, and Highway 111.

🍴 Restaurants

Luchador Brewing Company

$ | **MEXICAN** | **FAMILY** | In addition to strong cervezas, which are brewed on-site (or at the larger, Chino Hills flagship) in four 10-barrel tanks, this taproom serves up Tijuana-style street food (tacos, tortas, churros, esquites) from a built-in, vintage food truck. **Known for:** beer cocktails and adult slushies; crowlers to go; Mexican brunch on weekends. [$] *Average main: $9* ✉ *68510 E. Palm Canyon Dr., Suite 140, Cathedral City* ☎ *760/797–2337* 🌐 *www.luchadorbrew.com.*

Sol y Sombra

$$ | **SPANISH** | Head to a poolside, historical adobe building in the center of The Paloma Resort for Spanish tapas incorporating local delicacies like dates, chiles, and citrus and big plates designed to feed two, as well as tequila and mezcal cocktails. Breakfasts have a foreign flair with wine-soaked French toast and Iberico ham Benedicts, lunches feature options like Manchego-cheese beef sliders and blue-cheese Serrano fries, and dinners focus on protein-heavy dishes. **Known for:** three kinds of paella nightly; date nights and after-work drinks; Instagram-worthy decor and design. [$] *Average main: $25* ✉ *The Paloma Resort, 67670 Carey Rd., Cathedral City* ☎ *760/864–1177* 🌐 *thepalomaresort.com/dining* 🕒 *No dinner Mon. Closed Sun. and Tues. in summer.*

🛏 Hotels

The Paloma Resort

$$ | RESORT | Tucked into a quiet neighborhood just off Highway 111, what was once a date farm and then a 1950s-era Elizabeth Arden spa is now a small but colorful palm-dotted resort with sizeable, comfortable, and fun suites and stand-alone bungalows. **Pros:** poolside day suite perfect for group hangs; well-curated in-room snacks and spirits; fantastic Spanish restaurant from successful local chef. **Cons:** not within comfortable walking distance to restaurants or shopping; motel-style buildings lack privacy; design might be too loud for some. $ *Rooms from: $295* ✉ *67670 Carey Rd., Cathedral City* ☎ *760/864–1177* ⊕ *thepalomaresort. com* ⇆ *66 units* ⊚ *No Meals.*

🛍 Shopping

Perez Road Art & Design District

NEIGHBORHOODS | In-the-know interior designers, incognito celebrities, and other fashionable folk who are in the market for orange rotary phones, Italian ceramics, new rugs, peacock chairs, or a piece of statement art, head to this 30,000-square-foot treasure trove tucked behind the Agua Caliente Casino. Here, expertly sourced vintage and contemporary art, decor, and furniture are sold in a handful of stores including Hedge, Object Culture, Spaces, and JC Studio. ✉ *68929 Perez Rd., Cathedral City* ⊕ *perezartdistrict.com* ⇆ *Hrs vary by shop/gallery; some are open on weekends only.*

Rancho Mirage

4½ miles southeast of Cathedral City.

Rancho Mirage's rich and famous live in beautiful estates, drive fancy cars, and patronize fancy local amenities. Here, visitors can dabble in champagne wishes and caviar dreams by sleeping in high-thread count sheets at an elegant resort, indulging in an anti-aging scrub at a restorative spa, and enjoying a meal at a fine-dining restaurant.

Although many mansions here are concealed behind gated community walls and country club hedges, the grandest of them all, Sunnylands, is open to the public. The city's golf courses host high-profile tournaments and hobbyists alike.

GETTING HERE AND AROUND

Rancho Mirage stretches from Ramon Road in the north to the hills south of Highway 111. The western border is Da Vall Drive; the eastern one is Monterey Avenue. Major east–west cross streets are Frank Sinatra Drive and Country Club Drive. Most shopping and dining spots are on Highway 111.

👁 Sights

Rancho Mirage Library and Observatory

OBSERVATORY | FAMILY | Get a good look the night sky at this city-owned observatory next to the public library. The complex includes five high-powered telescopes—four on the deck and a main telescope in the 360-degree observatory dome that's designed to look like a comet. There is a 3 pm tour on weekdays, and stargazing parties are usually scheduled two times a week. Astronomy lectures are also held regularly. ✉ *71–100 Hwy. 111, Rancho Mirage* ☎ *760/341–7323* ⊕ *www.ranchomiragelibrary.org* ⇆ *Free* ⊘ *Closed Sun.*

★ Sunnylands Estate, Center & Gardens

HISTORIC HOME | Despite being an active retreat venue, the stunning 200-acre winter home of the late Ambassadors Walter and Leonore Annenberg, which has welcomed eight presidents and first ladies, royalty, numerous world leaders, and countless celebrities, is open to the public for free. You could easily spend a day taking a self-guided audio tour of 9 acres of art-filled grounds; viewing art exhibits; watching a film about the estate and the desert diplomacy that has happened here; grabbing a bite in the café; and participating in wellness activities, classes, or other programs. For an insightful peek inside the 25,000-square-foot mid-century marvel, book a 90-minute Historic House Tour. Guided estate (shuttle and walking options) and birding tours are also available. ✉ *37977 Bob Hope Dr., south of Gerald Ford Dr., Rancho Mirage* ☎ *760/202–2222* 🌐 *www.sunnylands.org* 🎫 *House tour $55; historic walking tour $26; guided birding tour $39; open-air shuttle tour of grounds $28; visitor center, gardens, and parking are free* 🕑 *Closed Mon. and Tues. Closed early June–mid-Sept. and during retreats.*

🍴 Restaurants

Babe's Bar-B-Que and Brewery

$$$ | BARBECUE | FAMILY | Though the late founder Donald Callender made his name as a purveyor of pie with the Marie Callender's chain, he also built a solid smoked-meats-and-suds rep with this barbecue–microbrewery. Carnivores show up in droves for fall-off-the-bone racks of ribs, pulled pork sandwiches, brisket-topped salads, and chops that are marinated overnight—all of which pair well with the IPAs, ales, and lagers brewed on site. **Known for:** Coachella Valley's oldest and most-acclaimed microbrewery; pinup girl art and bronze pigs; ribs smoked over hickory and pecan wood. [$] *Average main: $35* ✉ *71800 Hwy. 111, Rancho Mirage* ☎ *760/346–8738* 🌐 *www.babesbbqbrewery.com.*

Catalan

$$$$ | MEDITERRANEAN | At this restaurant, known for its beautifully prepared Mediterranean cuisine, you can dine inside or under the stars in the atrium. The service here is attentive, and the menu roams Spain, Italy, California, and beyond. **Known for:** house-made limoncello that stews for three months; cheese and charcuterie boards; tons of desert choices. [$] *Average main: $43* ✉ *70026 Hwy. 111, Rancho Mirage* ☎ *760/770–9508* 🌐 *catalanrestaurants.com.*

Las Casuelas Nuevas

$ | MEXICAN | FAMILY | Using his grandmother's passed-down family recipes from Mazatlán, Mexico, Florencio Delgado and his wife opened their original restaurant in 1973. Five decades later, the Delgado descendants are still pumping out hearty and traditional plates of fajitas, tacos, enchiladas, and harder-to-find stuffed-pepper dishes like *chile en nogada*. **Known for:** vast margarita menu; table-side guacamole presentation; lively happy hour. [$] *Average main: $16* ✉ *70–050 Hwy. 111, Rancho Mirage* ☎ *760/328–8844* 🌐 *www.lascasuelasnuevas.com* 🕑 *Closed Tues.*

🛏 Hotels

Agua Caliente Rancho Mirage

$$ | RESORT | This resort feels like a small-scale Sin City, thanks to a lobby-level casino, a 2,101-seat concert venue that welcomes household names, a cigar lounge, eight eateries (including a sports bar and a decadent steak house dishing up 32-ounce bone-in tomahawks), clubs and bars, a pool with cabanas, and a lavish spa. **Pros:** poolside cabanas with TVs, misters, and refrigerators; valet parking included; all spa massages include hot stones and foot exfoliation. **Cons:** casino ambience; not appropriate for kids; some live performances draw huge crowds. [$] *Rooms from: $349* ✉ *32–250 Bob Hope Dr., Rancho Mirage* ☎ *888/999–1995* 🌐 *aguacalientecasinos.com* 🛏 *340 rooms* 🍴 *No Meals.*

Omni Rancho Las Palmas

$$ | RESORT | FAMILY | Home to the Splashtopia water park—with a lazy river, two 100-foot waterslides, fountain and sprinkler zones, a cliff-side hot tub, and a sandy beach—this is probably the desert's most family-friendly resort, though guests without kids can escape to the adults-only pool, the spa, or the golf course. **Pros:** rooms have private balconies or patios; trails for hiking and jogging; all-day activities and entertainment. **Cons:** second-floor rooms accessed by steep stairs; golf course surrounds some rooms; often hosts conventions and weddings. [$] *Rooms from: $349* ✉ *41000 Bob Hope Dr., Rancho Mirage* ☎ *760/568–2727* 🌐 *www.omnihotels.com* 🛏 *444 rooms* 🍴 *No Meals.*

★ The Ritz-Carlton, Rancho Mirage
$$$$ | RESORT | FAMILY | High on a hill overlooking the Coachella Valley, this posh resort spoils guests with exemplary service and comforts that include two pools, one of the desert's finest full-service spas, complimentary fitness classes, and two restaurants. **Pros:** well-stocked club lounge; easy access to hiking and golfing; spa that's a destination in itself. **Cons:** very pricey; some airport noise; stores, attractions, and restaurants all require a drive. [$] *Rooms from: $950* ✉ *68900 Frank Sinatra Dr., Rancho Mirage* ☎ *760/321–8282* 🌐 *www.ritzcarlton.com* 🛏 *244 rooms* 🍴 *No Meals.*

The Westin Rancho Mirage Golf Resort & Spa
$$$ | RESORT | FAMILY | Set on 360 manicured acres that include an acclaimed Pete Dye golf course, the polished, service-oriented Westin offers bright and recently renovated rooms, several restaurants (a celebrity chef–driven "backyard kitchen" among them), and a slew of activities for all ages—from tennis, bike rentals, and swimming in three pools (one with dual waterslides) to full-moon hikes, guided meditations, and cacao ceremonies. **Pros:** first-class golf facilities; Halo IR sauna combines infrared heat and salt therapies; families will love minigolf, duckpin bowling, and the arcade. **Cons:** rooms lack sense-of-place design; crowded when a convention is booked; far from town. [$] *Rooms from: $399* ✉ *71333 Dinah Shore Dr., Rancho Mirage* ☎ *760/328–3198* 🌐 *www.marriott.com* 🛏 *512 rooms* 🍴 *No Meals.*

Nightlife

Agua Caliente Casino & The Show Theater
LIVE MUSIC | In addition to the expansive floor filled with all kinds of gambling options (e.g., slot machines, table games, a poker room), the casino/resort also has multiple places to wet your whistle, shake your (fingers-crossed) moneymaker, and see DJs or local acts. The Show, the resort's prized theater where none of the 2,101 seats are more than 125 feet from the stage, also books a full calendar of concerts by household names like Dolly Parton and Sting, as well as fashion shows and sporting events like boxing matches. ✉ *32–250 Bob Hope Dr., at E. Ramon Rd., Rancho Mirage* ☎ *800/514–3849* 🌐 *www.aguacalientecasinos.com.*

Shopping

Brandini Toffee
CANDY | FAMILY | What started as a fundraising endeavor for a high-school trip to Italy in 2006 has grown into a four-store, family-owned empire peddling the preservative-free, non-GMO, chocolate-topped toffee that has been touted by Oprah Winfrey and Martha Stewart. You can watch candy being made while enjoying toffee milk shakes, pretzels, popcorn, brownies, or ice-cream bars. You can also stock up on souvenir tins. (Good luck getting them all the way home.) ✉ *42250 Bob Hope Dr., Rancho Mirage* ☎ *760/200–1598* 🌐 *brandinitoffee.com.*

★ Rancho Relaxo
SOUVENIRS | FAMILY | It's easy to lose track of time in this female-owned, fabulously curated apparel, gift, and curios shop housed in the former Coachella Valley Repertory Theater, where wall murals feature positive messages, and staffers are sociable. Every table, shelf, nook, and cranny is filled with jewelry, art, graphic tees, stuffed animals, books, crystals, hats, candles, bags, toiletries, glasses,

and toys. Although the store carries some national brands, it also works hard to promote local makers and artists, often through limited-edition collaborations. A second smaller location at The Gardens on El Paseo in Palm Desert carries RR logo products and best-selling items. ☒ *The Atrium, 69930 Hwy. 111, Suite 116, Rancho Mirage ☎ 760/459–2569 ⊕ ranchorelaxoca.com.*

The River at Rancho Mirage

MALL | FAMILY | Fronting a man-made river and waterfalls, this complex has several beauty and fashion shops, as well as a Cinemark multiplex, a cigar lounge, and lots of eateries, including Acqua (sister to the popular Lulu California Bistro in Palm Springs). In addition, family-friendly events like dance parties and movie nights are held at the on-site amphitheater. ☒ *71800 Hwy. 111, at Bob Hope Dr., Rancho Mirage ☎ 760/341–2711 ⊕ www.theriveratranchomirage.com.*

 Activities

GOLF

Westin Rancho Mirage Golf Course

GOLF | The Pete Dye course here has amazing mountain views and wide fairways and is described as "potentially diabolical yet indescribably playable." If you are just getting started with the sport, the club offers equipment rentals and instruction. The resort typically has stay-and-play packages, including one that includes unlimited golf. ☒ *71333 Dinah Shore Dr., Rancho Mirage ☎ 760/328–3198 ⊕ www.westinranchomiragegolf.com ☎ The club uses real-time dynamic pricing to set tee time prices as low as $45. ⅃ 18 holes, 5525 yards, par 72.*

SPAS

★ The Ritz-Carlton Spa, Rancho Mirage

SPAS | Two hundred–plus suspended quartz crystals adorn the entranceway at one of the desert's premier spas. With private men's and women's areas, a coed outdoor soaking tub, a salon, 16 elegant

treatment rooms (many with private terraces), food service, and some of the kindest spa technicians around, you can expect pampering par excellence. The signature Spirit of the Mountains treatment, which includes a full-body exfoliation, a massage using desert botanicals, and a body wrap, is pure bliss. The gym, equipped with state-of-the-art machines, is open 24/7. Private trainers are available to guide your workout; wellness classes are also available. ☒ *68900 Frank Sinatra Dr., Rancho Mirage ☎ 760/202–6170 ⊕ www.ritzcarlton.com ☎ Massages from $195, facials from $205 ⊙ Closed Sun.*

The Spa at Rancho Mirage

SPAS | The emphasis at this 12-room spa in a quiet corner of the Westin Rancho Mirage is on comfort rather than glitz. Attentive therapists incorporate lemon balm, thyme, lavender, hydrating honey, and other botanicals into treatments that include massages, rubs and scrubs, facials, and nail services. Also on-site are a Halo IR sauna combining infrared heat and salt therapies, a steam room, a therapy pool, and a movement studio where yoga and other wellness classes are offered. ☒ *The Westin Rancho Mirage Golf Resort & Spa, 71333 Dinah Shore Dr., Rancho Mirage ☎ 760/770–2180 ⊕ www.marriott.com ☎ Massages from $170, facials and body wraps from $185.*

Sunstone Spa

SPAS | This full-service bastion of wellness with myriad spa and beauty treatments as well as a sauna, a steam room, and a pool, is the ideal place to spend your winnings from the adjacent Aqua Caliente Casino. Though pricey, massages here include many things that are add-ons at other spas like foot exfoliation, heated stones, heated infrared tables, and chromatic light mats embedded with crystals. Be sure to recalibrate in a grounding chair with complimentary mocktails and snacks from Shields Date Garden. ☒ *Agua Caliente Rancho Mirage,*

32–250 Bob Hope Dr., Rancho Mirage
☎ 760/202–2121 ⊕ aguacalientecasinos.
com/spa ✉ Massages from $280, facials
from $215, scrubs and wraps from $180.

Palm Desert

2 miles southeast of Rancho Mirage.

Palm Desert is a thriving residential, retail, and business community with popular restaurants, private and public golf courses, and premium shopping along its main commercial drag, El Paseo. It's ritzy but doesn't take itself too seriously as evidenced by the almost six-decades-old Palm Desert Golf Cart Parade, in which a theme procession of 80 golf cart "floats" launches "the season." Animal lovers and families shouldn't miss the singular Living Desert Zoo and Gardens.

GETTING HERE AND AROUND
Palm Desert stretches from north of I–10 to the hills south of Highway 111. West–east cross streets north to south are Frank Sinatra Drive, Country Club Drive (lined on both sides with gated golfing communities), and Fred Waring Drive. Monterey Avenue marks the western boundary, and Washington Street forms the eastern edge.

TOURS
Art in Public Places
SELF-GUIDED TOURS | Several self-guided tours cover the works in Palm Desert's 150-piece Art in Public Places collection. Each tour is walkable or drivable. Maps and information about the pieces and the routes are available online and at the city's visitor center, which also houses a community art gallery. ⊠ *Palm Desert Visitor Center, 73510 Fred Waring Dr., Palm Desert* ☎ 760/568–1441 ⊕ *discoverpalmdesert.com/public-art* ✉ *Free.*

◉ Sights

Faye Sarkowski Sculpture Garden
PUBLIC ART | FAMILY | Established in 2012 by the Palm Springs Art Museum, the 4-acre desert garden, open from sunrise to sunset, holds 14 cutting-edge works by contemporary sculptors, including Donald Judd, Betty Gold, Yehiel Shemi, Felipe Castañeda, Jesús Bautista Moroles, and Dan Namingha. ⊠ *72–567 Hwy. 111, Palm Desert* ☎ *760/322–4800* ⊕ *www.psmuseum.org/visit/palm-desert* ✉ *Free.*

★ The Living Desert Zoo and Gardens
ZOO | FAMILY | Come eye-to-eye with more than 600 animals including desert dwellers like wolves, coyotes, mountain lions, cheetahs, bighorn sheep, golden eagles, warthogs, naked mole rats, and owls at the Living Desert, which showcases the flora and fauna found in arid landscapes. Easy to challenging trails traverse terrain populated with plants of the Mojave, Colorado, and Sonoran deserts. In the African WaTuTu village, you'll find a traditional marketplace, as well as camels, hyenas, and other animals. Wallabies, emus, and kookaburras inhabit the immersive Australian Adventures area.

Get your bearings with a 30-minute shuttle tour. Pet domesticated creatures, including Nigerian dwarf goats, in a "petting kraal," attend zookeeper talks throughout the day. Crawl and climb all over the Gecko Gulch playground, ride a carousel, and check out a hall that holds ancient Pleistocene animal bones. ■TIP➔ **Time your visit to begin in the early morning to beat the heat and feed the giraffes.** ⊠ *47900 Portola Ave., south from Hwy. 111, Palm Desert* ☎ *760/346–5694* ⊕ *www.livingdesert.org* ✉ *$35; shuttle tour $15 extra.*

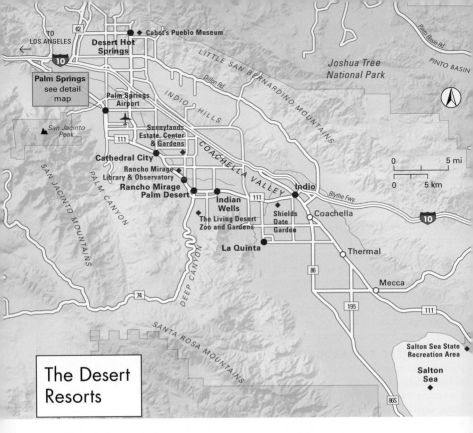

🍽 Restaurants

★ Chef Tanya's Kitchen

$ | **VEGETARIAN** | **FAMILY** | At her colorful flagship eatery and market, vegan chef Tanya Petrovna—who founded the first national plant-based chain, Native Foods, in the early '90s—pumps out filling, well-seasoned, and meat-free sandwiches and burgers, as well as salads, fries, and popular deli items. Dedicated to living cruelty-free, she prides herself on making all the "meat" (e.g., cultured tempeh, seitan, and tofu facon) in-house and also uses personal recipes to create the agua fresca, chai, and desserts—including what is easily the tastiest, least-grainy, vegan, soft-serve ice cream to have ever been swirled. **Known for:** communal tables and friendly devoted patrons; hearty vegan comfort food; the zingy Chupacabra. $ *Average main: $14*

✉ *72695 Hwy. 111, Suite A6, Palm Desert* ☎ *760/636–0863* ⊕ *cheftanyaskitchen. com.*

Pacifica Seafood

$$$$ | **SEAFOOD** | Yes, Palm Desert is land-locked, but there's no hesitation when it comes to recommending this seafood specialist, which has drawn residents and visitors for choice surf and turf for 15 years. Fish arrives daily from San Diego, is cooked to perfection, and is served on the rooftop and inside the dining room on the second floor of the Gardens of El Paseo shopping center. **Known for:** several cold dishes for hot summer nights; happy hour daily; reduced-price two-course sunset menu from 3:30 to 5. $ *Average main: $41* ✉ *73505 El Paseo, Palm Desert* ☎ *760/674–8666* ⊕ *www. pacificaseafoodrestaurant.com* ⊗ *No lunch June–Aug.*

☕ Coffee and Quick Bites

★ Perfect Pint

$ | ICE CREAM | FAMILY | A chef and a sommelier turned losing their jobs during the COVID shutdown into a pandemic silver lining by starting this French-style frozen-custard company out of an adorable chrome trailer. Not only do they collaborate with local coffee, toffee, honey, and date purveyors, but they also offer unique flavors like lemon-blackberry streusel, kaffir-lime piña colada, and peppermint cookies-n-cream—all served by the pint and half-pint out. **Known for:** no artificial colors or emulsifiers; high-quality ingredients; gluten-free options. $ *Average main: $10* ✉ *The Gardens on El Paseo, 73545 El Paseo, Palm Desert* ☎ *760/218–9458* ⊕ *www.perfectpint760.com.*

🛏 Hotels

Hotel Paseo

$$ | HOTEL | FAMILY | A half-block from El Paseo shopping strip, this hip, pet-friendly hotel (under Marriott's Autograph Collection umbrella) reflects the mid-century modern history and upscale, yet casual lifestyle of the desert. **Pros:** billiards guest suite has an in-room pool table; golf discount through partnership with Desert Willow; courtesy shuttle within a 3-mile radius. **Cons:** in a heavily trafficked neighborhood off a busy street; pool area can seem small and crowded; street parking unless you pay for valet. $ *Rooms from: $300* ✉ *45–400 Larkspur La., Palm Desert* ☎ *760/340–9001* ⊕ *hotelpaseo. com* ⇄ *149 rooms* ⦿ *No Meals.*

JW Marriott Desert Springs Resort & Spa

$$ | RESORT | FAMILY | Set on 450 landscaped acres, 18 of which are lakes and waterways, this crisp, contemporary resort is the size of a small village and attracts business travelers, couples, and families who appreciate the amenities that give it a "park once and never *have* to leave" vibe. **Pros:** commute by boat to restaurants; daily cocktail hour is homage

to Frank Sinatra; spa shop specializes in brands with a do-good components. **Cons:** very crowded in season; can feel corporate and short on character; long walk from lobby to rooms. $ *Rooms from: $279* ✉ *74–855 Country Club Dr., Palm Desert* ☎ *888/538–9459* ⊕ *www. marriott.com* ⇄ *884 rooms* ⦿ *No Meals.*

🎭 Performing Arts

Acrisure Arena

CONCERTS | New in 2022, this 300,000-plus-square-foot entertainment and sports venue has an 11,000-person capacity; an adjoining community ice skating facility; and multiple bars, restaurants, and portable food carts including Pizza by Giada De Laurentiis and Shaq's Big Chicken. In its inaugural year, it hosted concerts by the likes of Sting, Luis Miguel, Stevie Nicks, and Dierks Bentley, as well as Cirque du Soleil performances. It's also the home of the Coachella Valley Firebirds, an American Hockey League team affiliated with the Seattle Kraken. Other events held here have included WWE matches, monster-truck rallies, and preseason NBA games. ✉ *75702 Varner, Palm Desert* ☎ *888/695–8778* ⊕ *acrisurearena.com.*

🛍 Shopping

El Paseo

NEIGHBORHOODS | FAMILY | Parallel to Highway 111 lies "The Rodeo Drive of the Desert," a mile-long, Mediterranean-styled shopper's paradise lined with fountains, courtyards, and upscale boutiques, including those in the Gardens on El Paseo complex. You'll find shoe emporiums, jewelry boutiques, home goods stores, beauty salons, and children's shops as well as two dozen restaurants and nearly as many art galleries. It's a pleasant place to stroll, window-shop, and watch both people and the annual alfresco concert series. ■**TIP→ In winter and spring, a free shuttle ferries shoppers**

from store to store and back to their cars. ✉ *Between Monterey and Portola Aves., Palm Desert* ☎ *760/341–4058* 🌐 *www.elpaseocatalogue.com.*

Activities

BALLOONING

Fantasy Balloon Flights

BALLOONING | FAMILY | Sunrise excursions over the Coachella Valley lift off at 6 am and take from 60 to 90 minutes; a champagne toast follows the landing. Afternoon excursions, timed to touch down at sunset, are offered from November through February. ✉ *74181 Parosella St., Palm Desert* ☎ *760/568–0997* 🌐 *www.fantasyballoonflight.com* 🎟 *$230* 🕒 *Closed June–Aug.*

GOLF

Desert Willow Golf Resort

GOLF | Praised for its environmentally smart design, this top-rated, public golf resort planted water-thrifty turf and native vegetation, and doesn't use pesticides. The Mountain View course has eight tee selections, rolling fairways, and titular views. Firecliff is a slightly more-challenging course with five configurations and more than 100 bunkers/waste areas. Lessons are offered here through the Palm Desert Golf Academy. ✉ *38995 Desert Willow Dr., off Country Club Dr., Palm Desert* ☎ *760/346–0015* 🌐 *www.desertwillow.com* 🎟 *From $70* 🏌 *Mountain View: 18 holes, 6913 yards, par 72. Firecliff: 18 holes, 7056 yards, par 72.*

Indian Wells

5 miles east of Palm Desert.

A mostly quiet and exclusive residential enclave, Indian Wells hosts major tennis tournaments throughout the year, including the BNP Paribas Open, and is crawling with mega-resorts, three of which share access to a championship golf club and all of which cater to families and business travelers alike with fun water parks, noteworthy spas, and ample restaurants.

GETTING HERE AND AROUND

Indian Wells lies between Palm Desert and La Quinta, with most resorts, restaurants, and shopping set back from Highway 111.

Restaurants

Don Diego's of Indian Wells

$$ | MEXICAN | FAMILY | This is, and has been since 1981, exactly what most people look for in a casual, go-any-day-of-the-week, Mexican-American restaurant—big portions, reasonable prices, a variety of margaritas, and a massive menu with all the basics (tacos, fajitas, burritos, enchiladas) and some fancier dishes like *chile rellenos* (stuffed roasted peppers) or *carne asada* (marinated grilled steak). What's more, the waiters are friendly, and the atmosphere is festive yet still relaxed enough for kids and fur babies (the latter are welcome on the patio). **Known for:** strong margaritas and The Tower of Tequila; fried desserts including the original Peachorito; four kinds of fajitas (the house specialty). [$] *Average main: $22* ✉ *74969 Hwy. 111, Indian Wells* ☎ *760/340–5588* 🌐 *dondiegosindianwells.com.*

The Pink Cabana

$$$ | AMERICAN | FAMILY | The pink-and-green palette, botanical wallpaper, oversize globe pendants, gold trim, tile floor, and velvety banquettes draw the pretty people and those who follow them on social media to this Martyn Lawrence Bullard–designed gem at the Sands Hotel. But it's the Mediterranean-Moroccan cuisine—think lamb tagine or harissa chicken—and punchy drinks that keep them happy and snapping. **Known for:** retro-racquet-club aesthetic; chorizo shakshuka; cocktails inspired by the spice route. [$] *Average main: $40* ✉ *Sands Hotel & Spa, 44–985 Province*

Way, Indian Wells ☎ *760/321–3772* 🌐 *sandshotelandspa.com/dining-bar.*

Vue Grille and Bar

$$ | AMERICAN | This not-so-private restaurant at the Indian Wells Golf Resort offers a glimpse of how the country-club set lives. The service is impeccable, outdoor tables provide views of mountain peaks that seem close enough to touch, and happy hour is a lively scene of golfers bragging and griping about their day on the fairways. **Known for:** specialty nights like Prime Rib Friday and Sangria Sunday; house-roasted chicken daily; classed-up comfort food. [$] *Average main: $21* ✉ *44500 Indian Wells La., Indian Wells* ☎ *760/834–3800* 🌐 *www.indianwells-golfresort.com.*

Hotels

Hyatt Regency Indian Wells Resort & Spa

$$$ | RESORT | FAMILY | Spread across 45 acres, this behemoth resort adjacent to the Golf Resort at Indian Wells is one of the grandest in the desert (especially after a $21 million renovation in 2020), with its nine pools, two golf courses, a water park that has dueling 30-foot slides and a 450-foot lazy river, a marketplace with Starbucks, three restaurants, outdoor games, tennis/pickleball courts, and a full-service spa. **Pros:** excellent business services; new med-spa; very family- and pet-friendly. **Cons:** size makes it a tad impersonal; long walks between amenities; noisy public areas. [$] *Rooms from: $369* ✉ *44600 Indian Wells La., Indian Wells* ☎ *760/776–1234* 🌐 *www.hyatt.com* 🛏 *520 rooms* 🍴 *No Meals.*

Renaissance Esmeralda Resort & Spa

$$ | RESORT | FAMILY | Adjacent to the Indian Wells Golf Resort and with soothing water—pools, ponds, lakes, fountains, streams—everywhere, this luxurious resort is popular with business travelers as well as families, who appreciate amenities like an arcade with virtual-reality experiences, a pool that also has a sandy beach, and the Desert Glow zone, which features duckpin bowling. **Pros:** tennis and basketball court access with racket and ball rental; double-sink bathrooms; fitness center has Pelotons. **Cons:** higher noise level in rooms surrounding pool; somewhat corporate ambience; $38 resort fee. [$] *Rooms from: $300* ✉ *44-400 Indian Wells La., Indian Wells* ☎ *760/773–4444* 🌐 *www.marriott.com* 🛏 *560 rooms* 🍴 *No Meals.*

Tommy Bahama Miramonte Resort & Spa

$$$ | RESORT | It became the first Tommy Bahama resort in late 2023, and with the change came public spaces, guest quarters, and amenities that were refreshed and reimagined to reflect the laidback resort wear and island lifestyle brand for which it is named. **Pros:** three swimming pools; partnership with adjacent Indian Wells Golf Resort; spa uses property citrus to make essential oils for treatments. **Cons:** not quite as many kid-centered activities as its competitors; limited on-site resort facilities; long walk to lobby from some rooms. [$] *Rooms from: $320* ✉ *45000 Indian Wells La., Indian Wells* ☎ *442/305–4500* 🌐 *www.miramonteresort.com* 🛏 *215 rooms* 🍴 *No Meals.*

Activities

GOLF

Indian Wells Golf Resort

GOLF | Adjacent to the Hyatt Regency and within comfortable walking distance of the Renaissance and Tommy Bahama resorts, this complex includes The Celebrity course, designed by Clive Clark with so much water (streams, lakes, and waterfalls!) that it earned the nickname "Beauty," and the Players Course, a longer, more open "Beast" designed by John Fought to incorporate views of the surrounding mountain ranges. Both consistently rank among the best public courses in California and have hosted numerous PGA events including the Skins Game. There's also a smart Top Tracer Driving Range and a lit-up nighttime experience called Shots In The Dark. ■ **TIP→ It's a good idea to book tee times well in advance, up to 60 days.** ✉ *44500 Indian Wells La., Indian Wells* ☎ *760/346–4653* 🌐 *www.indianwells-golfresort.com* 🎫 *From $59* ⛳ *Celebrity Course: 18 holes, 7050 yards, par 72. Players Course: 18 holes, 7376 yards, par 72.*

SPAS

The WELL Spa

SPAS | Despite sitting in the central courtyard of a large resort, near the main pool and restaurant, this 12,000-square-foot, two-story facility is surprisingly serene, even if you're indulging in the hot-and-cold-soak circuit in the alfresco coed lounge. The silence is even more golden when holed up in the eucalyptus steam room or one of nine private rooms getting a facial, a scrub, or massage that might be enhanced with hot basalt rocks, crystals, dry brushes, or citrus oil distilled in-house using fruit collected from resort groves. Anyone can book an appointment, but hotel guests can also participate in yoga sessions or join guided bikes/walks in the surrounding neighborhood. ✉ *Tommy Bahama Miramonte Resort, 45000 Indian Wells La., Indian Wells* ☎ *442/305–4505* 🌐 *www.miramonteresort.com* 🎫 *Massages from $190, facials from $245, body therapies from $195.*

La Quinta

4 miles south of Indian Wells.

The desert became an old Hollywood hideout in the 1920s when La Quinta Hotel (now La Quinta Resort & Club) opened and introduced the Coachella Valley's first golf course. Dripping in showy bougainvillea, Old Town is a popular draw. Wander until one of the many eateries, shops, galleries, or pottery studio calls your name. Or picnic in one of the many community parks.

GETTING HERE AND AROUND

Most of La Quinta lies south of Highway 111. The main drag through town is Washington Street.

🍴 Restaurants

Arnold Palmer's

$$$$ | AMERICAN | From the photos, trophies, and other memorabilia to a menu filled with The King's favorite dishes like meatloaf and Latrobe banana splits, golf champ and restaurant namesake Arnold Palmer's essence infuses the spacious dining room and pub where families gather for new American cuisine and good times. It does brisk birthday and Sunday dinner business yet the service is always attentive. **Known for:** chopped BLT salad, double-cut pork chops, baked mac and cheese; top-notch wine list; entertainment most nights. [$] *Average main: $42* ✉ *78164 Ave. 52, near Desert Club Dr., La Quinta* ☎ *760/771–4653* 🌐 *www.arnoldpalmersrestaurant.com* 🕒 *Closed Sun. and late May–mid-Sept.*

Lavender Bistro

$$$$ | BISTRO | This romantic bistro with a spacious outdoor atrium decked out with flowers, twinkle lights, and pops of the namesake color has several weekly specials (e.g., no-corkage-fee Sunday) and a lengthy menu of fancy meats, seafood, and old-school salads. Always save room for dessert. **Known for:** live music on the patio and in the fireside lounge; prime rib Thursday; extensive locavore menu. [$] *Average main: $47* ✉ *78–073 Calle Barcelona, La Quinta* ☎ *760/564–5353* 🌐 *www.lavenderbistro.com* 🕒 *No lunch. Closed June–Sept.*

🛏 Hotels

The Chateau at Lake La Quinta

$ | HOTEL | Old-world French design, contemporary style, and luxe creature comforts make this lakeside inn a good choice for those who want intimate, upscale lodgings near La Quinta's main attractions. **Pros:** idyllic lakeside setting; restaurant serves breakfast, lunch, and dinner; outdoor pool, deck with firepits. **Cons:** two-story building with no elevator; some rooms not as posh as others; not ideal for families with children. $ *Rooms from: $199 ⊠ 78–120 Caleo Bay Dr., La Quinta ☎ 760/564–7332 ⊕ www.thechateau.com ⇨ 24 rooms �◎ No Meals.*

La Quinta Resort & Club

$$ | **RESORT** | **FAMILY** | Opened in 1926 and now a member of the Hilton's Curio Collection, the desert's oldest resort, a 45-acre oasis, feels like a small town made up of expansive lawns with quiet, flowery spots to sit and myriad adobe casitas, suites, and villas. **Pros:** some rooms have private plunge pools; gorgeous grounds; pet- and family-friendly. **Cons:** party atmosphere sometimes prevails; long distances between rooms and amenities; restaurants, spa, and pools can be crowded. $ *Rooms from: $249 ⊠ 49499 Eisenhower Dr., La Quinta ☎ 760/564–4111 ⊕ www.laquintaresort. com ⇨ 718 units �◎ No Meals.*

🏃 Activities

GOLF

★ PGA West

GOLF | The world-class golf destination, known as "The Western Home of Golf In America" and host of The American Express, has nine courses, five of which are open to nonmembers. The resort courses were designed by legends of the sport including Pete Dye, Jack Nicklaus, and Greg Norman. ⊠ *55–955 PGA Blvd., La Quinta ☎ 760/564–7101 Tournament Clubhouse ⊕ www.pgawest.com ☒ Greens fees vary by course, season, and time of day; book tee times online for most up-to-date rates.* ⚐ *Mountain Course: 18 holes, 6732 yards, par 72; Dunes: 18 holes, 6712 yards, par 72; Greg Norman: 18 holes, 7156 yards, par 72; TPC Stadium: 18 holes, 7300 yards, par 72; Jack Nicklaus Tournament: 18*

holes, 7204 yards, par 72 ☞ *Tee times are best booked through the website.*

SPAS

Spa La Quinta

SPAS | At this grand sanctuary, you can indulge in massages, wraps, facials, and salon and nail services. It's set in a beautiful garden with a large fountain, flowers galore, and plenty of nooks where you can inhale and exhale deeply. There's also a fitness center with classes and a Jacuzzi with a waterfall. A series of CBD and muscle recovery–focused treatments and innovative waterbeds are among the newer offerings. ⊠ *La Quinta Resort & Club, 49451 Av. Obregon, La Quinta ☎ 760/777–4800 ⊕ www.laquintaresort. com ☒ Massages from $255, facials from $195.*

Indio

5 miles east of Indian Wells.

Indio is the home of the annual Coachella music festival and the renowned date shake, an extremely thick and sweet milk shake made with locally grown dates. The city and surrounding countryside generate 95% of the dates grown and harvested in the United States.

GETTING HERE AND AROUND

Highway 111 runs right through Indio, and I–10 skirts it to the north.

👁 Sights

Shields Date Garden and Café

FARM/RANCH | **FAMILY** | Sample, select, and take home some of Shields's locally grown dates. Ten varieties are available, including the giant supersweet royal medjools, along with specialty date products such as date crystals, stuffed dates, confections, and local honey. At the Shields Date Garden Café you can try an iconic date shake, dig into date pancakes, or go exotic with a date burger. Breakfast and lunch are served daily.

For almost a century, Shields Family dates have been grown, sold, and enjoyed on this site, which now includes a 105-seat theater showing "The Romance & Sex Life of the Date" on a loop, a store where you can sample the 10 varieties, gulp down a date shake at the original 1960s counter, and purchase all kinds of snacks and sweets featuring the star fruit, a café serving breakfast and lunch, and a walk through a 17-acre date grove and botanical garden that features 23 biblical statues. ✉ *80225 Hwy. 111, Indio* ☎ *760/347–0996* 🌐 *shieldsdate-garden.com* 🎟 *$5 for garden walk* 🕒 *Café closed July 4–Aug. 6. Garden closes on very windy days.*

🍴 Restaurants

Ciro's Ristorante and Pizzeria
$ | **ITALIAN** | **FAMILY** | Since the 1960s, this Coachella Valley classic has served pizza, pasta, chicken parmigiana, and other entrées commonly ordered by mobsters in the movies. The booths are big; the lights are low; the soundtrack is soft rock; and the kitchen isn't stingy with cheese, salad dressing, or red sauce. **Known for:** wallet-friendly lunch combos; old-school Italian dishes; house-made, hand-tossed pizza dough. [$] *Average main: $16* ✉ *81963 Hwy. 111, Indio* ☎ *760/347–6503* 🌐 *www.cirosindio.com.*

Cork & Fork
$ | **MODERN AMERICAN** | **FAMILY** | Set on a corner lot of a crisp new strip mall, this woman-owned restaurant is a popular local hangout that focuses on matching wines and cocktails with its array of small and large plates meant to be shared. The globe-trotting menu changes with the seasons, but you might feast on tequila lime shrimp tacos, poke wonton nachos, veggie kale dumplings, Korean barbecue pork belly sliders, or Neapolitan-style pizzas. **Known for:** separate vegan menu (and many gluten-free options); eclectic list of affordable wines by the glass and bottle; casual fine dining. [$] *Average main: $17* ✉ *49890 Jefferson St., Suite 100, Indio* ☎ *760/777–7555* 🌐 *www.corkandfork-winebar.com* 🕒 *No lunch.*

Salton Sea

30 miles south of Indio on Highway 111, 3-hour drive from San Diego

The Salton Sea, one of the largest inland seas on Earth, is the product of both natural and artificial forces. It occupies the Salton Basin, a remnant of prehistoric Lake Cahuilla. Over the centuries, the Colorado River flooded the basin, and the water drained into the Gulf of California. In 1905, a flood crashed canal gates filling the Salton Basin while the exit to the gulf was blocked by sediment. It wasn't until 1907 that engineers could stop the breaching water and thus a saline lake 228 feet below sea level, 35 miles long, and 15 miles wide, with a surface area of nearly 380 square miles, was born.

The sea, which lies along the Pacific Flyway, has been visited by 400 species of birds. Fishing for tilapia, boating, camping, kayaking, and bird-watching are popular activities year-round.

GETTING HERE AND AROUND

Salton Sea State Recreation Area includes about 14 miles of coastline on the northeastern shore of the sea, about 30 miles south of Indio via Highway 111. The Sonny Bono Salton Sea National Wildlife Refuge fills the southernmost tip of the sea's shore. To reach it from the recreation area, continue south about 60 miles to Niland; continue south to Sinclair Road, and turn west following the road to the Refuge Headquarters.

👁 Sights

Salton Sea State Recreation Area
STATE/PROVINCIAL PARK | **FAMILY** | Each year, this huge recreation area on the sea's northeastern shore draws thousands of campers, hikers, anglers, paddlers, and

bird-watchers (the park is on the Pacific Flyway). Ranger-guided walking tours take place during the winter migration season (November to February) when up to 4 million birds visit daily. Fishing is best from June through September. ⊠ *100–225 State Park Rd., North Shore* ☎ *760/393–3059 park, 760/393–3810 visitor center* ⊕ *www.parks.ca.gov* ☞ *$7.*

Sonny Bono Salton Sea National Wildlife Refuge

WILDLIFE REFUGE | FAMILY | Named after pop star and area congressman Sonny Bono, the 37,900-acre wildlife refuge on the Pacific Flyway is a wonderful spot for viewing migratory birds. There are observation towers, photography blinds, and platforms, as well as numerous trails through desert scrub and wetlands along which you might view eared grebes, burrowing owls, great blue herons, ospreys, yellow-footed gulls, or any of the 400 species that have been documented on and around California's largest lake. ⚠ **Though the scenery is beautiful, the waters here give off an unpleasant odor, and the New River, which empties into the sea, is quite toxic.** ⊠ *906 W. Sinclair Rd., Calipatria* ☎ *760/348–5278* ⊕ *www. fws.gov/refuge/sonny_bono_salton_sea* ☞ *Free* ☉ *Visitor center closed Mar.–Oct.* ☞ *Birding is best Nov.–Feb.*

Desert Hot Springs

9 miles north of Palm Springs.

Desert Hot Springs's unique geology—superpure hot and cold mineral aquifers run deep underneath it as does the infamous San Andreas Fault—has long lured humans to this side of the valley in the foothills of the San Bernardino Mountains. Considered sacred by the Cahuilla Indians and a key part of survival for homesteaders in the late 1800s, the

springs eventually attracted droves of visitors who believed in the water's believed curative powers.

The first bathhouse was built in 1941. Many followed, adding accommodations and other amenities, thus earning the town its nickname Spa City. There's been a resurgence of its wellness rep of late, with new and rebooted spas once again making the area worthy of travelers' attention.

GETTING HERE AND AROUND

Desert Hot Springs lies due north of Palm Springs. Take Gene Autry Trail north to I–10, where the street name changes to Palm. Continue north to Pierson Boulevard, the town's center, and up to the Miracle Hill neighborhood to visit a cluster of spas.

◉ Sights

Cabot's Pueblo Museum

HISTORIC HOME | FAMILY | One of the first homesteaders in Desert Hot Springs, Cabot Yerxa, the man often credited with "discovering" the hot springs the Cahuilla Indians had known about for centuries, built a quirky, 35-room, Hopi-inspired pueblo by hand using reclaimed and found materials between 1941 and his death in 1965. Now a museum, the adobe structure is filled with memorabilia from Yerxa's wild life, including his encounters with Hollywood celebrities and his expedition to the Alaskan gold rush. The inside of the home can only be seen on self-guided audio tours, but grounds-only tickets are also available. ⊠ *67616 E. Desert View Ave., at Eliseo Rd., Desert Hot Springs* ☎ *760/329–7610* ⊕ *www. cabotsmuseum.org* ☞ *$13 for home tour, grounds-only $5* ☉ *Closed Mon. Oct.–May 31, Mon. and Sun. June–Sept. 30* ☞ *Tour slots available every ½ hr.*

🛏 Hotels

Azure Palm Hot Springs Resort & Day Spa Oasis

$$ | RESORT | It's fitting that this healthful haven is set on Miracle Hill—in 2021, using the bones of an old hotel, it was resurrected and revitalized as an adults-only boutique property with individually decorated rooms and suites, a full-service spa, a juice-cleanse program, a café, a 100-foot mineral-water pool (the longest in Southern California), saunas and jetted hot tubs, a cold chamber, a Himalayan salt room, and thatch-shaded soaking tubs that are continuously refilled with fresh mineral water. **Pros:** can reserve oasis tubs for private two-hour blocks; only overnight guests can use ice and salt rooms; spa suites have spring-fed in-room soaking tubs. **Cons:** day-pass program can make it a tad crowded; café with limited (though nutritious) menu is the only on-site dining option; towels and robes could be bigger and plusher. ⓢ *Rooms from: $269* ✉ *67589 Hacienda Ave., Desert Hot Springs* ☎ *760/251–2000* ⊕ *azurepalmhotsprings.com* ⤢ *40 rooms* ⎆ *No Meals.*

The Good House Hotel & Spa

$$ | HOTEL | Blink and you'll miss this Miracle Hill adults-only gem, the sole Black-owned hotel in the Greater Palm Springs area, which—with a tiny spa, a sizable yard, a springs-fed pool and hot tubs, a chaise-lined terrace, and a firepit—feels like a cross between an updated Joshua Tree hotel, a wellness camp, and your childhood friend's parent's ranch house. **Pros:** a house label Rosé; kitchenette-equipped rooms can help cut trip costs; welcoming and inclusive staff. **Cons:** limited parking; some amenities like sauna and firepit are self-service; dinner only offered Thursday–Sunday. ⓢ *Rooms from: $285* ✉ *12885 Eliseo Rd., Desert Hot Springs* ☎ *760/251–2885* ⊕ *www. welcometothegoodhouse.com* ⤢ *7 rooms* ⎆ *No Meals* ☞ *Hotel calendar is organized in 3-month seasonal blocks. Owners reserve the right to close during extremely hot summer weather.*

Two Bunch Palms

$$$ | RESORT | This resplendent, 72-acre resort, a ways off the road and behind a security gate and wall of vegetation, is equal parts historical property (Al Capone hid out here), hushed haven (no kids splashing in the grotto, no cars honking), high-end spa (treatment rooms look like they jumped from the pages of *Dwell* magazine), and hippie retreat (sage cleansing, sound baths, chakra balancing, tarot readings). **Pros:** restaurant serves vegetable-forward meals; digital detox rooms make it easy to unplug; full-service spa, popular since the 1940s. **Cons:** some rooms have no TV; no pets allowed; can give off elitist air. ⓢ *Rooms from: $395* ✉ *67425 Two Bunch Palms Trail, Desert Hot Springs* ☎ *760/676–5000* ⊕ *twobunchpalms.com* ⤢ *65 rooms* ⎆ *No Meals* ☞ *Reservations are only taken within 3-month windows.*

Chapter 8

JOSHUA TREE
NATIONAL PARK

Updated by
Carrie Bell

🏕 Camping	🛏 Hotels	🏃 Activities	👁 Scenery	👥 Crowds
★★★★★	★★★★☆	★★★★★	★★★★★	★★★★☆

WELCOME TO JOSHUA TREE NATIONAL PARK

TOP REASONS TO GO

★ **Rock climbing and bouldering:** Joshua Tree is a world-class site with challenges for climbers of every skill level.

★ **Peace and quiet:** Just three hours from Los Angeles, this great wilderness is the ultimate escape from traffic and technology.

★ **Stargazing:** Be mesmerized by the Milky Way flowing across the summer sky and shooting stars year-round. For spectacular natural fireworks, visit in mid-August during the Perseid meteor shower.

★ **Wildflowers:** In spring, the hillsides explode in a patchwork of color.

★ **Sunsets:** Twilight is magical here, especially in winter when the setting sun turns the landscape gold and the skies lavender.

★ **Quirky neighbors:** A strange and entertaining mix of hippies, cool kids, doomsday preppers, families, military personnel, and outdoorsy types comingle in unique and groovy surrounding towns.

1 **Park Boulevard.** Drive the paved road between the west and north entrances to explore many of the park's main sights like Skull Rock, Barker Dam, and the big boulders of Hidden Valley, which was once a cattle rustlers' hideout.

2 **Keys View Road.** Keys View is the park's most dramatic overlook as you can see Signal Mountain in Mexico on clear days.

3 **Highway 62.** Spot wildlife like desert tortoises and coyotes at Black Rock and Indian Cove. Near the north entrance, stroll the nature trail around Oasis of Mara, which the first settlers, the Serrano, dubbed "the place of little springs and much grass."

4 **Pinto Basin Road.** Pull out binoculars at Cottonwood Spring, one of the best birding spots in the park. Go to Cholla Cactus Garden in the late afternoon, when the spiky stalks of the cacti are backlit against an intense blue sky.

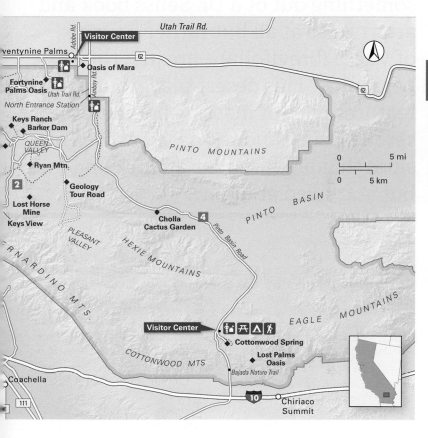

Although iconic, the park's spiky namesake trees—which look like something out of a Dr. Seuss book and aren't trees at all but rather a type of yucca (brevifolia)—are just the beginning. This desert playground also features piles of massive boulders and serene, palm-studded oases, as well as skies that are lavender at dusk and inky but star filled at night.

The country's eighth most visited national park (more than 3 million people come annually) occupies a remote area in southeastern California. Here, two distinct ecosystems meet: the arid Mojave Desert, which sits above 3,000 feet, and the more sparsely vegetated Colorado Desert, which is part of the larger Sonoran Desert that stretches into Arizona and northern Mexico.

Humans have inhabited the area for at least 5,000 years, starting with the Pinto and followed by the Cahuilla, Chemehuevi, Serrano, and Mojave peoples. Cattlemen, miners, and homesteaders arrived in the 1800s and early 1900s. By the 1920s, new roads lured developers and tourists. Pasadena resident and plant enthusiast Minerva Hoyt visited often and witnessed reckless poaching and pillaging of cacti and other plants. She spearheaded studies to prove the value of regional plants and wildlife. Thanks to her dedicated efforts, Joshua Tree National Monument was established in 1936.

The 29 Palms Corporation deeded part of the historic Oasis of Mara to the National Park Service in 1950. The monument then graduated to national park status on October 31, 1994. Today, the park encompasses almost 800,000 acres (nearly 600,000 of them designated as wilderness), with elevations that range from 536 feet to the peak of 5,814-foot Quail Mountain. The diverse habitats here protect more than 800 plant, 250 bird, 46 reptile, and 57 mammal species including the desert bighorn sheep and the endangered desert tortoise.

You can experience Joshua Tree National Park on several levels, even if time is short. It doesn't take long to drive the paved Park Boulevard or wander a self-guided nature trail for a taste of what makes the park special—from North American desert scenery with a staggering abundance of flora and fauna to remnants of wind-worn homesteads from a century ago. Be sure to stop by the newest visitor center in Twentynine Palms, not only to get your bearings but also to learn about the history and culture of the region's indigenous peoples.

As the park never closes, nightfall brings opportunities for stellar stargazing. In fact, Joshua Tree was made an official International Dark Sky Park in 2017. Park at any of the pullouts or lots to watch the sparkling show above. If rock climbing is your passion, answer the call of the many boulder heaps, gnarled rock formations, and craggy mountaintops. You can commune solo with nature on a pristine wilderness trek, camp in big groups, or make new friends in a photography workshop. Regardless of how you spend time here, be mindful of the heat, which can be extreme. Bring (and drink) plenty of water; dress in layers; and wear sunscreen, sunglasses, and a hat.

Planning

Getting Here and Around

AIR
Palm Springs International Airport is the closest major air gateway to Joshua Tree National Park. It's about 45 miles from the park. The drive from Los Angeles International Airport to Joshua Tree takes about two to three hours.

CAR
An isolated island of pristine wilderness—a rarity these days—Joshua Tree National Park is within a short drive of 11 million Southern California residents. Most visitors, in fact, make the two- to three-hour drive from the Los Angeles area to enjoy a weekend of solitude in 792,726 acres of untouched desert.

The urban sprawl of Palm Springs (home to the nearest airport) is 45 miles away, but gateway towns Joshua Tree, Yucca Valley, and Twentynine Palms are just north of the park. If you're staying in the Palm Springs area, you can enjoy the highlights of the park in one day, including a stop for a picnic at a scenic spot.

Within the park, passenger cars are fine for paved areas, but you'll need four-wheel drive for many of the rugged backcountry roadways. At the park's most popular sites, parking is limited. Joshua Tree does not have public transportation. ■TIP➜ **If you'd prefer not to drive, most Palm Springs area hotels can arrange a half- or full-day tour that hits the highlights of Joshua Tree National Park.**

Hotels

Area lodging choices consist primarily of roadside motels (some of which have been given cool, contemporary makeovers), historical inns, chain hotels, and glampgrounds, though there are a few slightly more upscale establishments in the gateway towns. Vacation rentals, especially those overseen by Homestead Modern (⊕ *homesteadmodern.com*), are the way to go if you desire something fancier, architecturally significant, or Instagram-worthy. For mega-resorts and luxury boutiques, bunk down in Palm Springs or the down valley resort communities.

■TIP➜ **Book far ahead for wildflower season, new-moon nights, and holiday weekends, especially in late fall or early spring.**

Park Essentials

ACCESSIBILITY
Black Rock, Indian Cove, and Jumbo Rocks campgrounds have one accessible campsite each. Nature trails at Oasis of Mara, Bajada, Keys View, and Cap Rock are accessible. Some trails at roadside viewpoints can be negotiated by those with limited mobility.

PARK FEES AND PERMITS
Park admission is $30 per car; $15 per person on foot, bicycle, or horse; and $25 per person by motorcycle. The Joshua Tree Pass, good for one year, is $55.

PARK HOURS

The park is open every day, around the clock, but visitor centers are staffed from approximately 8 am to 5 pm. The park is in the Pacific time zone.

CELL PHONE RECEPTION

Cell service is extremely limited in most areas of the park, and there are no pay phones in its interior.

Restaurants

Despite being slightly bigger than the state of Rhode Island, Joshua Tree National Park has zero dining outlets. But never fear going hungry as there are lots of great places to fill up bright and early, refuel after a long day, or buy provisions for picnics, camp dinners, and fireside happy hours in the gateway towns.

Although fast-food outlets and casual chains still maintain a strong presence, especially in Yucca Valley and Twentynine Palms, there are also plenty of comfort food–slinging diners, pizza parlors, restaurants that double as concert venues, plant-based eateries, quality bars, Mexican specialists, barbecue joints, and even a couple of eateries that serve fine-dining caliber food in laid-back environments. Foodies willing to head over the hill 40 minutes into the Coachella Valley quadruple their number of choices.

⇨ *Restaurant and hotel reviews have been shortened. For full information visit Fodors.com. Restaurant prices are the average cost of a main course at dinner, or if dinner is not served, at lunch. Hotel prices are the lowest cost of a standard double room in high season.*

What It Costs			
$	$$	$$$	$$$$
RESTAURANTS			
under $20	$20–$30	$31–$40	over $40
HOTELS			
under $200	$200–$350	$351–$500	over $500

Tours

Twentynine Palms Astronomy Club

SPECIAL-INTEREST TOURS | FAMILY | Book a private night sky experience for 2 to 10 people led by astrophotographer Steve Caron and others who have a passion for sharing the night sky. They bring high-powered telescopes and other equipment to a location of your choice in the Morongo Basin—from Morongo Valley in the west to Wonder Valley in the east, plus Pioneertown and Landers. ✉ *Twentynine Palms* ☎ *760/401–3004* ⊕ *www.29palmsastronomy.org* ✉ *From $250 for a 2-hr session.*

Visitor Information

CONTACTS Joshua Tree National Park.

✉ *74485 National Park Dr., Twentynine Palms* ☎ *760/367–5500* ⊕ *www.nps.gov/ jotr.*

When to Go

High season is October through May when desert temperatures are tolerable. Daytime temperatures range from the 70s in December and January to the high-80s in October and May. There is a wide diurnal shift and lows can dip to near freezing in winter. You may even encounter snow at higher elevations. Summers are torrid, with daytime temperatures often reaching 115°F.

AVERAGE HIGH/LOW TEMPERATURES					
Jan.	Feb.	Mar.	Apr.	May	June
62/32	65/37	72/40	80/50	90/55	100/65
July	Aug.	Sept.	Oct.	Nov.	Dec.
105/70	101/78	96/62	85/55	72/40	62/31

Park Boulevard

Well-paved Park Boulevard—the park's main artery—loops between the west entrance near the town of Joshua Tree and the north entrance just south of Twentynine Palms. If you have time only for a short visit, driving Park Boulevard is your best choice. It traverses the most scenic portions of the high-desert section. Along with some sweeping views, you'll see jumbles of giant boulders, stands of Joshua trees, and Hidden Valley and Barker Dam, remnants of the area's wild and woolly past.

⊙ Sights

HISTORIC SIGHTS
Hidden Valley
NATURE SIGHT | FAMILY | Lore claims that this 1-mile trail loops through a big-boulder valley often used by cattle rustlers as a hideout. Kids love to scramble on and around the rocks before sitting down for sammies at shaded picnic tables. ⊠ *Park Blvd., Joshua Tree National Park* ✛ *14 miles south of west entrance.*

★ Keys Ranch
HISTORIC HOME | FAMILY | This 150-acre 1910 ranch, which once belonged to William and Frances Keys and is now on the National Historic Register, illustrates one of the area's most successful attempts at homesteading. The couple raised five children under extreme desert conditions. Most of the original buildings, including the house, school, store, and workshop, have been restored to the way they were when William died in 1969. It's only open via ranger-guided, 90-minute, half-mile walking tours offered from October to May. Reservations are required. ⊠ *Joshua Tree National Park* ⊠ *$10.*

SCENIC DRIVES
Geology Tour Road
SCENIC DRIVE | FAMILY | Some of the park's most fascinating landscapes can be observed from this 18-mile dirt road. Parts of the journey are rough; a 4X4 vehicle is required after mile marker 9. Sights to see include a 100-year-old stone dam called Squaw Tank, defunct mines, and a large plain with an abundance of Joshua trees. Allow about two hours to complete the round-trip drive and explore all 16 stops. There are a few hiking trails and climbing routes that can be accessed from here as well. ⊠ *South of Park Blvd., west of Jumbo Rocks, Joshua Tree National Park.*

SCENIC STOPS
Barker Dam
DAM | FAMILY | Built around 1900 by ranchers and miners to hold water for cattle and mining operations, the dam now collects rainwater and is a good place to spot wildlife such as the elusive bighorn sheep. ⊠ *Barker Dam Rd., Joshua Tree National Park* ✛ *Off Park Blvd., 10 miles south of west entrance.*

TRAILS
Hidden Valley Trail
TRAIL | FAMILY | Crawl through the rocks surrounding Hidden Valley to see where cattle rustlers supposedly hid out on a 1-mile loop. *Easy.* ⊠ *Joshua Tree National Park* ✛ *Trailhead: At Hidden Valley Picnic Area.*

Joshua Tree in One Day

After stocking up on water, snacks, and lunch (you won't find supplies inside the park), head to the **Joshua Tree Visitor Center** to pick up maps, pick rangers' brains, and peruse exhibits, before entering the park itself at the **West Entrance Station** 10 minutes up the road. Continue driving along the highly scenic and well-maintained **Park Boulevard.** Stop first at **Hidden Valley** to relax at the picnic area or hike the easy, mile-long loop trail. After a few more miles, turn left onto the spur road to the trailhead for the **Barker Dam Trail.** Walk the easy 1.1-mile loop to view a water tank ranchers built to quench their cattle's thirst; along the way, you'll spot birds, cacti, and possibly bighorn sheep.

Return to Park Boulevard and head south; you'll soon leave the main road again for the drive to **Keys View.** The easy loop trail here is only ¼ mile, but the views extend for miles in every direction—look for the San Andreas Fault, the Salton Sea, and nearby mountains. Return to Park Boulevard, where you'll find **Cap Rock,** another short loop trail winding amid rock formations and Joshua trees.

Continuing along Park Boulevard, the start of the 18-mile self-guided **Geology Tour Road** will soon appear on your right. A brochure outlining its 16 stops is available at visitor centers; note that the round-trip will take about two hours, and high-clearance, four-wheel-drive vehicles are recommended after stop 9. ⚠ **Do not attempt this route if it has rained recently.**

Return to Park Boulevard and stop at the aptly named **Skull Rock.** This downright spooky formation is next to the parking lot; a nearby trailhead marks the beginning of a 1.7-mile nature loop. End your day with a stroll through the historical Oasis of Mara followed by a stop at the newest visitor center in Twentynine Palms, which specializes in the culture and history of the area's indigenous communities. ■ **TIP→ To avoid long lines of cars at the West Entrance, reverse this itinerary on weekends or anytime during high season.**

Ryan Mountain Trail

TRAIL | The payoff for hiking to the top of Ryan Mountain is one of Joshua Tree's best panoramas. From here, you can see Mt. San Jacinto, Mt. San Gorgonio, Lost Horse Valley, and the Pinto Basin. You'll need two to three hours to complete the 3-mile out-and-back trail with 1,062 feet of elevation gain. *Difficult.* ⊠ *Joshua Tree National Park* ⊕ *Trailhead: At Ryan Mountain parking area, 13 miles southeast of park's west entrance, or Sheep Pass, 16 miles southwest of Oasis Visitor Center.*

Skull Rock Trail

TRAIL | **FAMILY** | The 1.7-mile loop takes you through boulder piles, desert washes, and a rocky alley. It's named for the park's most famous rock formation, which resembles a human skull. Access the path from within Jumbo Rocks Campground or from a small parking area just east of the campground. *Easy.* ⊠ *Joshua Tree National Park* ⊕ *Trailhead: At Jumbo Rocks Campground.*

Split Rock Loop Trail

TRAIL | **FAMILY** | Experience rocky jumbles, Joshua trees, cacti, and geological wonders along this relatively flat 2½-mile loop trail that includes a short spur to Face Rock. Keep your eyes peeled for wildlife as this is a hot spot for birds and reptiles. *Moderate.* ⊠ *Joshua Tree National Park*

⊕ *Trailhead: Along dirt road off main Park Blvd. (signs point the way).*

VISITOR CENTERS
Joshua Tree Visitor Center

VISITOR CENTER | **FAMILY** | This visitor center, the most frequented of the park's four, has maps and interesting exhibits illustrating park geology, cultural and historic sites, and hiking and rock-climbing activities. There's also a small bookstore, café, restrooms with flush toilets, and rangers available to give advice. ⊠ *6554 Park Blvd., Joshua Tree* ☎ *760/366–1855* ⊕ *www.nps.gov/jotr.*

Keys View Road

Keys View Road travels south from Park Boulevard from Cap Rock up to Keys View, the best vista point in the park. The trailhead for the historic Lost Horse Mine hike is along the way.

◉ Sights

HISTORIC SIGHTS
Lost Horse Mine

MINE | The mine, one of about 300 developed within the current park boundaries, was among Southern California's most productive, generating 10,000 ounces of gold and 16,000 ounces of silver between 1894 and 1931. The 10-stamp mill is one of the best preserved of its type in the park system. The site is accessed via a moderately strenuous 4-mile hike. Mind the signs, and note that parking, which is at end of the dirt access road, is limited. ⊠ *Off Keys View Rd., Joshua Tree National Park* ⊕ *About 15 miles south of west entrance.*

SCENIC STOPS
★ Keys View

VIEWPOINT | **FAMILY** | At 5,185 feet, this point affords a sweeping view of the Coachella Valley, the San Andreas Fault, the peak of 11,500-foot Mt. San Gorgonio, the shimmering surface of the Salton Sea, and—on a very clear day—Signal Mountain in Mexico. Sunrise and sunset are magical times to head to the wheelchair-accessible crest lookout as the light throws rocks and trees into high relief before bathing the hills in fiery shades of red, orange, and gold. ⊠ *Keys View Rd., Joshua Tree National Park* ⊕ *16 miles south of park's west entrance.*

TRAILS
Cap Rock

TRAIL | **FAMILY** | This ½-mile, wheelchair-accessible loop—named after a boulder that sits atop a huge rock formation like a cap—winds through other fascinating rock formations and has signs that explain the geology of the Mojave Desert. *Easy.* ⊠ *Joshua Tree National Park* ⊕ *Parking lot at junction of Keys View Rd. and Park Blvd.*

Highway 62

Highway 62 stretches along the northern border of the park from Yucca Valley to Twentynine Palms. You can access the Black Rock, Indian Cove, Fortynine Palms, and Oasis of Mara sections of the park off this road, as well as the main visitor centers and park entrances in Joshua Tree and Twentynine Palms.

◉ Sights

SCENIC STOPS
Fortynine Palms Oasis

INDIGENOUS SIGHT | **FAMILY** | A short drive off Highway 62, this site is a bit of a preview of what the park's interior has to offer: a fan palm oasis, barrel cacti, interesting petroglyphs, and evidence of fires built by early Native Americans. Because animals frequent this area, you may spot a coyote, bobcat, or roadrunner. ⊠ *End of Canyon Rd. off Hwy. 62, Joshua Tree National Park* ⊕ *4 miles west of Twentynine Palms.*

Did You Know?

Found only in Arizona, California, Nevada, and Utah, the Joshua tree is actually a member of the yucca family. Native Americans used the hearty foliage like leather, forming it into everyday items like baskets and shoes. Later, early settlers used its core and limbs for building fences to contain livestock.

Indian Cove

NATURE SIGHT | FAMILY | The view from here is of rock formations that draw thousands of climbers to the park each year. This isolated area is reached via Twentynine Palms Highway and Indian Cove Road. You'll find a campground, picnic area, and an easy nature trail in the area. ⊠ *End of Indian Cove Rd. off Hwy. 62, Joshua Tree National Park.*

TRAILS

High View Nature Trail

TRAIL | Nestled in between campsites 20 and 21 in the Black Rock Canyon Campground, this 1.4-mile loop climbs up a steep ridge to score views of nearby Mt. San Gorgonio (snowcapped in winter). You can pick up a pamphlet describing the vegetation you'll see along the way at any visitor center. It is 2.1 miles if you start at the Black Rock Nature Center. *Moderate.* ⊠ *Joshua Tree National Park ✛ Trailhead: In Black Rock Canyon Campground.*

Indian Cove Trail

TRAIL | FAMILY | Look for lizards and roadrunners along this ½-mile loop that follows a desert wash. A walk along this well-signed trail reveals signs of Native American habitation, animals, and flora such as desert willow and yucca. *Easy.* ⊠ *Joshua Tree National Park ✛ Trailhead: At west end of Indian Cove Campground.*

Oasis of Mara Trail

TRAIL | FAMILY | A stroll along this ½-mile wheelchair-accessible trail in Twentynine Palms reveals how early area residents took advantage of this verdant oasis, which was first settled by the Serrano tribe. (*Mara* means "place of little springs and much grass" in their language.) The Serrano, who farmed the oasis until the mid-1850s, planted one palm tree for each male baby born during the first year of the settlement. *Easy.* ⊠ *Joshua Tree National Park ✛ Trailhead: On Utah Trail minutes from Hwy. 62.*

VISITOR CENTERS

★ **Joshua Tree National Park Visitor Center**

VISITOR CENTER | FAMILY | Many areas that fall under the auspices of the National Park Service are on what was Native American land and encompass spots of sacred, archaeological, historical, and cultural importance to indigenous tribes. This beautiful new 4,100-square-foot visitor center—which opened in 2022 in Freedom Plaza right in downtown Twentynine Palms—is indicative of a commitment by the park service in recent years to tell this side of park history. Displays and programs focus on the Maara'yam (Serrano), Nüwüwü (Chemehuevi), Kawiya (Cahuilla), and Aha Macave (Mojave) peoples whose traditional homelands or use areas fall within today's park borders.

The four original cultures who lived, farmed, worshipped, or hunted in this region have descendants in 15 modern-day bands, tribes, and nations, which worked in partnership with the park service, City of Twentynine Palms, Joshua Tree National Park Association, and Bureau of Land Management to create the permanent exhibition. The center also has an information desk, a bookstore, a gift shop, and restrooms with flush toilets. ⊠ *6533 Freedom Way, Twentynine Palms* ☎ *760/367–5535* ⊕ *nps.gov/jotr.*

Pinto Basin Road

This paved road runs from the main part of the park near Split Rock to I–10, traveling from the high Mojave desert to the low Colorado desert through an ecologically diverse transition zone that eventually leads to the Coachella Valley floor. The drive is slow but the views, scenery, and roadside exhibits make it worth the extra time.

About 5 miles from the north entrance, the road forks; take a left, and continue another 9 miles to the Cholla Cactus Garden. Past that are the Ocotillo Patch,

Turkey Flats, several hiking trails, and the Cottonwood Visitor Center. Note that side trips from this route require a 4X4.

👁 Sights

SCENIC STOPS
Cholla Cactus Garden
GARDEN | FAMILY | This stand of thousands of teddy-bear cholla (sometimes called jumping cholla because its hooked spines seem to jump at you) is best seen and photographed in the late afternoon, when the backlit spiky stalks stand out against a colorful sky, and in spring when they're most likely to bloom. Stay on the ¼-mile boardwalk, as the minuscule barbs easily detach and latch on, and they are very painful to remove. ⊠ *Pinto Basin Rd., Joshua Tree National Park* ✣ *20 miles north of Cottonwood Visitor Center.*

Cottonwood Spring
INDIGENOUS SIGHT | FAMILY | This area was home to the indigenous Cahuilla people for centuries, and its spring provided them, as well as travelers and early prospectors, with water. It still supports a large stand of fan palms and cottonwood trees and is one of the best spots in the park for bird-watching. There are some remains, including concrete pillars, of several gold mines that were located here. Numerous hikes begin here as well. ⊠ *Cottonwood Visitor Center, on Pinto Basin Rd., Pinto Basin Rd., Joshua Tree National Park.*

Lost Palms Oasis
NATURE SIGHT | Reachable by a challenging 7½-mile, round-trip hike, this oasis has more than 100 fan palms, the largest grouping of the exotic plants found in the park, and a spring that bubbles from between the rocks only to disappear into the sandy, boulder-strewn canyon. Visits are not recommended during the summer months. Parking is down the road from Cottonwood Visitor Center at Cottonwood Spring. ⊠ *Joshua Tree National Park* ✣ *1 mile east of the Cottonwood Visitor Center.*

Ocotillo Patch
NATURE SIGHT | FAMILY | Make this quick roadside stop to see a thriving grove of ocotillo, which has long spindly branches tipped by red flowers. These succulents are particularly colorful after a rain shower. ⊠ *Pinto Basin Rd., Joshua Tree National Park* ✣ *About 3 miles east of Cholla Cactus Gardens.*

TRAILS
Bajada
TRAIL | FAMILY | Learn all about what plants do to survive in the Colorado Desert on this ¼-mile loop. *Easy.* ⊠ *Joshua Tree National Park* ✣ *Trailhead: South of Cottonwood Visitor Center, ½ mile from park's south entrance.*

Mastodon Peak Trail
TRAIL | Boulder scrambling is optional on this 3-mile hike that loops past a gold mine and up to the 3,371-foot Mastodon Peak where you can get a glimpse of the Salton Sea in the distance. The peak draws its name from a large rock formation that early miners believed looked like the head of a prehistoric beast. *Moderate.* ⊠ *Joshua Tree National Park* ✣ *Trailhead: At Cottonwood Spring parking lot.*

VISITOR CENTERS
Cottonwood Visitor Center
VISITOR CENTER | FAMILY | The south entrance is the closest to I–10, the east–west highway from Los Angeles to Phoenix. Exhibits in this small center, staffed by rangers and volunteers, illustrate the region's natural history. The center also has a small bookstore, a water-filling station, and restrooms with flush toilets. ⊠ *Cottonwood Spring, Pinto Basin Rd., Joshua Tree National Park* ☎ *760/367–5500* ⊕ *www.nps.gov/jotr.*

Activities

BIKING

Covington Flat

BIKING | This 3.8-mile (one-way) ride takes you past impressive Joshua trees as well as pinyon pines, junipers, and areas of lush desert vegetation. It's tough going toward the end. But once you reach 5,518-foot Eureka Peak, you'll have great views of Palm Springs, the Morongo Basin, and surrounding mountains. ⊠ *Joshua Tree National Park ✛ At Covington Flat picnic area, 10 miles south of Rte. 62.*

Pinkham Canyon and Thermal Canyon Roads

BIKING | This challenging 20-mile route begins at the Cottonwood Visitor Center and loops through the Cottonwood Mountains. The unpaved trail follows Smoke Tree Wash through Pinkham Canyon, rounds Thermal Canyon, and loops back to the beginning. Rough and narrow in places, the road travels through soft sand and rocky floodplains. ⊠ *Joshua Tree National Park ✛ At Cottonwood Visitor Center.*

Queen Valley

BIKING | This 13.4-mile network of mostly level roads winds through one of the park's most impressive groves of Joshua trees and is backdropped by Queen Mountain. Bike racks are scattered about the area so you can hop off to explore on foot. ⊠ *Joshua Tree National Park ✛ Begin at Barker Dam or Big Horn Pass.*

BIRD-WATCHING

Between residents, migrants, nesters, and seasonal transients, Joshua Tree, located along the Pacific Flyway, hosts about 250 species of birds throughout the year, and thus the park is popular with birders. Reliable sighting areas include Barker Dam (white-throated swifts, several types of swallows, or red-tailed hawks), Cottonwood Spring (Lucy's warblers, flycatchers, and Anna's hummingbirds), Black Rock Canyon (pinyon jays, and warbling vireos), Covington Flat (mountain quail, La Conte's thrashers, ruby-crowned kinglets), Indian Cove (rufous hummingbirds, Pacific-slope flycatchers, various warblers), and Queen and Lost Horse valleys (woodpeckers, bushtits, and gnatcatchers).

Any of the palm oases are also good places to search the skies and trees. Bird lists, as well as information on recent sightings, are available at visitor centers.

CAMPING

The park's campgrounds, set at elevations from 3,000 to 4,500 feet, have mostly primitive facilities like pit toilets and fire grates; few have drinking water. Campsites at Belle, Hidden Valley, and White Tank are first-come, first-served. Black Rock, Cottonwood, Indian Cove, Jumbo Rocks, and Ryan require reservations (☎ 877/444–6777 ⊕ recreation. gov). ■TIP➔ **Campgrounds fill quickly, especially in the high season, so reserve well in advance.**

Belle and White Tank campgrounds, and parts of Black Rock Canyon, Cottonwood, and Indian Cove campgrounds, are closed from the day after Memorial Day to September. Sites cost between $15 and $25 per night.

EDUCATIONAL PROGRAMS

The Desert Institute

HIKING & WALKING | The Desert Institute, the educational arm of Joshua Tree National Park Association (the park's primary nonprofit partner), offers a full schedule of lectures, classes, field trips, retreats, and hikes covering topics that range from natural and cultural history to photography and other creative arts to survival skills. Offerings, which often take place within the park, are designed for adults, though the minimum age to enroll is 14. ⊠ *74485 National Park Dr., Twentynine Palms ☎ 760/367–5525 ⊕ www. joshuatree.org* 🖃 *Fees vary* ☞ *Joshua Tree National Park Association members receive a Desert Institute discount.*

8

Joshua Tree National Park ACTIVITIES

Learn about the park's flora and fauna by attending the ranger programs.

Evening Programs

HIKING & WALKING | FAMILY | Rangers present 30- to 45-minute-long programs, often on Friday or Saturday evenings, at Cottonwood Amphitheater, Indian Cove Amphitheater, and Jumbo Rocks Campground. Topics range from natural history to local lore. As times and days for such offerings aren't fixed, it's best to check the online schedule. Rangers also lead sunset strolls daily in the summer at Cap Rock. ⊠ *Joshua Tree National Park* ⊕ *www.nps.gov/jotr/planyourvisit/programs.htm* ▭ *Free.*

★ Stargazing

STARGAZING | FAMILY | Designated an International Dark Sky Park in 2017, Joshua Tree is a great spot for astrotourism, especially on new moon nights. The Milky Way can be seen, often with the naked eye, from June through September, and the Perseid meteor shower is a mid-August highlight. Rangers offer occasional stargazing programs as does the nearby Sky's the Limit Observatory (⊕ *www.skysthelimit29.org*) on the

Utah Trail. ⊠ *Joshua Tree National Park* ⊕ *www.nps.gov/jotr/planyourvisit/calendar.htm.*

HIKING

There are more than 190 miles of hiking trails in Joshua Tree, ranging from ¼-mile nature walks to 35-mile multiday treks. Some connect with each other, so you can design your own desert maze. Remember that drinking water is hard to come by—you won't find it in the park except at the entrances and a few of the campgrounds. Bring along at least a gallon per person for all but the shortest hikes, more if the weather is hot.

Roadside signage identifies hiking- and rock-climbing routes. Before striking out, though grab a map from a visitor center.

HORSEBACK RIDING

More than 250 miles of equestrian trails crisscross dry washes and canyon bottoms. You're welcome to bring your own animals, but you must stay on trails to avoid damaging the desert, bring water for your horses, and follow rules like no grazing. Trail maps are available at visitor centers. Ryan and Black Rock campgrounds have designated areas for horses that requires reservations (☎ 877/444–6777 ⊕ recreation.gov).

ROCK CLIMBING

With an abundance of weathered igneous boulder outcroppings, Joshua Tree is one of the nation's top winter-climbing destinations. There are more than 8,000 established routes offering a full menu of climbing experiences for all skill levels: bouldering (Wonderland of Rocks), crack, slab, steep-face, slacklining, and multi-ple-pitch climbs (Echo Rock and Saddle Rock). The monzogranite mecca even has a designated climbing ranger who holds court at Climber Coffee sessions at the Hidden Valley Campground on Saturday and Sunday mornings from mid-October to April. (Coffee, tea, and cocoa are provided for free, but you must bring your own mug.)

Vertical Adventures Rock Climbing School
ROCK CLIMBING | About 1,000 climbers each year learn the sport in Joshua Tree National Park through this school. Classes, offered September–May, meet at a designated location in the park, and all equipment is provided. The company also offers private instruction and guided climbs. ⊠ Joshua Tree National Park ☎ 800/514–8785 office, 949/322–6108 mobile/text ⊕ www.vertical-adventures. com ☙ From $165.

What's Nearby

Yucca Valley

21 miles northeast of Desert Hot Springs, 27 miles northeast of Palm Springs.

Yucca Valley has traditionally been the "middle child" of the region's desert outposts—more of a bedroom communi-ty and place to meet all the basic needs (groceries, gas, urgent care, Starbucks,

nuggets for the kids) than a destination unto itself. Recently, however, this has started to change owing to a run on real estate and an influx of cool bars, nonchain eateries, unique boutiques and vintage shops, and trendy rentals. Just up the road is Pioneertown, a Wild West movie set turned tourist attraction, as well as Pappy + Harriet's, a famed venue for top musical talent.

GETTING HERE AND AROUND

From I–10, the drive to Yucca Valley on Highway 62/Twentynine Palms Highway passes through the Painted Hills and drops down into Morongo Valley. Take Pioneertown Road north to the Old West outpost.

ESSENTIALS

VISITOR INFORMATION California Welcome Center Yucca Valley. ⊠ 56711 Twentynine Palms Hwy., Yucca Valley ☎ 760/365–5464 ⊕ californiawelcom-ecenter.com. **Yucca Valley Chamber of Commerce.** ⊠ 56711 Twentynine Palms Hwy., Yucca Valley ☎ 760/365–6323 ⊕ www.yuccavalley.org.

◉ Sights

Hi-Desert Nature Museum
SCIENCE MUSEUM | FAMILY | Natural and cultural history of the Morongo Basin and high desert are the focus here. A small live-animal display includes scorpions, snakes, lizards, and little mammals. You'll also find gems and minerals, fossils from the Paleozoic era, taxidermy, and Native American artifacts. There's also a children's area and art exhibits. ⊠ Yuc-ca Valley Community Center, 57090 Twentynine Palms Hwy., Yucca Valley ☎ 760/369–7212 ⊕ hidesertnaturemuse-um.org ☙ Free but donations welcome ⊙ Closed Sun.–Tues.

★ Pioneertown
TOWN | FAMILY | In 1946, Roy Rogers, Gene Autry, the Sons of the Pioneers (the music group for which the town is named), Russ Hayden, and various other

Did You Know?

Joshua Tree is one of the world's most popular rock-climbing and bouldering destinations, with more than 400 climbing formations (including Frigid Tower, pictured here) and 8,000 routes.

entertainers invested in Dick Curtis' dream of building a "living breathing movie set." The result was Pioneertown, an 1880s-style Wild West town on 32,000 acres, surrounded by mesas and rock formations. Its main street featured a mix of false-front buildings (jail, bathhouse, etc.) and fully functioning businesses including a bowling alley, motel, saloon, and post office. More than 50 films/shows including *Cisco Kid* were made there in the 1940s and '50s.

Although some photo shoots and productions still happen there, most folks roll into town as tourists to grab drinks at the reopened bar; look at the movie memorabilia in the small museum; catch a concert at Pappy + Harriet's; meet the mayor (which is usually a goat, horse, or dog); or shop for pottery, vintage duds, and skin-care products in the shops that now fill many of the wood-and-adobe structures on the pedestrian-only lane. Weekends are especially bustling, with staged gunfights, drive-in movies, food carts, and comedy shows. ✉ *53688 Pioneertown Rd., Pioneertown* ✣ *6 miles north of Yucca Valley* 🌐 *visitpioneertown.com* 🎫 *Free.*

🍴 Restaurants

Frontier Café

$ | CAFÉ | FAMILY | A cozy coffeehouse with a counterculture undercurrent, Frontier is a good place to stop before heading into the park—and a popular one, judging by the number of visiting Angelenos in line for prehike egg sandwiches and posthike Top Chico mineral water at any one time. Pair fancy coffee drinks with bagels and parfaits in the morning or salads and sandwiches if you're off to a late start. **Known for:** fresh bakery items; vegan, veggie, and gluten-free options; daily specials. [$] *Average main: $15* ✉ *55844 Twentynine Palms Hwy., Yucca Valley* ☎ *760/820–1360* 🌐 *www.cafefrontier.com* 🕒 *No dinner.*

★ La Copine

$$ | CONTEMPORARY | You're going to think you're lost, but resist the urge to turn around because the tiny speck of sand that is Flamingo Heights really is that far out there, and this gastronomical goldmine—a roadside diner elevated by a lesbian couple who came to the desert for their honeymoon and never left—will likely be the best meal you'll eat this side of the Little San Bernardinos. Expect seasonally inspired brunch and lunch plates served without pretense and made using farm-to-fork ingredients and bits of culinary wisdom cribbed from the South (fried chicken), France (buckwheat ham galette), the Middle East (citrus and beets, a labneh-doused burger), and Philly's top kitchens (where the chef once toiled). **Known for:** filling meals and decadent but not too sugary desserts; long waits and closed lists; charming host and capable waitstaff. [$] *Average main: $22* ✉ *848 Old Woman Springs Rd., Yucca Valley* ☎ *760/289–8537* 🌐 *www.lacopinekitchen.com* 🕒 *Closed Mon.–Wed. and July and Aug.*

The Red Dog Saloon

$ | SOUTHWESTERN | One of the founding businesses/set pieces of Pioneertown's movie colony and a legendary hangout of the Western actors and crews who worked on location there, the Red Dog has been reborn, and its second coming was worth the wait thanks to from-scratch Tex-Mex that's filtered through a California lens and takes full advantage of the Golden State's agricultural bounty. All three meals are available daily although the lunch and dinner menus are the same—chile relleno; tacos (mushroom asada with tomatillo salsa is simple but sapid!); and standard sides like chips and queso or salsa, street corn, and churros. **Known for:** Tex-Mex by way of Cali; an original Pioneertown business; margaritas and music. [$] *Average main: $7* ✉ *53539 Mane St., Pioneertown* ☎ *760/228–9047* 🌐 *www.reddogpioneertown.com* 🕒 *Closed Tues. and Wed.*

Hotels

Pioneertown Motel

$$ | HOTEL | When new owners took over this motel built in 1946 as a bunkhouse for film stars shooting in and around Pioneertown (like Gene Autry, who used Room 9 for late-night poker games), they gave it a much-needed rehab while respecting its cowboy movie roots, so, although there are still beat-up wood doors and exposed-beam ceilings, there are also new sink basins, tiled showers, air-conditioning, and property-wide Wi-Fi. **Pros:** Western movie time warp; walk to Pappy + Harriet's or hiking trails; surrounded by mesas and protected land. **Cons:** rooms on the smallish side; curvy, long drive to gas, groceries, and other services; too dusty when wind kicks up. [$] *Rooms from: $350* ✉ *5240 Curtis Rd., Pioneertown* ☎ *760/365–7001* 🌐 *www.pioneertown-motel.com* 🛏 *19 rooms* 🍴 *No Meals.*

Nightlife

AWE Bar

LIVE MUSIC | Not everyone who feels like having a drink and rocking out can fit into Pappy + Harriet's, so this live-music venue with two bars, an outdoor patio, and a restaurant slinging burgers and serving up tacos and chips with guacamole is a welcome addition to the valley's nightlife scene. It's set in a renovated historical Old Town building, and its wave-shape ceiling, wood-strip walls, and cork-backed flooring make for warm, open acoustics. ✉ *56193 Twentynine Palms Hwy., Yucca Valley* ☎ *760/853–0090* 🌐 *www.awe-bar.com* 🕒 *Closed Mon. and Tues.*

★ **Pappy + Harriet's Pioneertown Palace**

LIVE MUSIC | Smack in the middle of a Wild West main street movie set built in the 1940s, this haute–honky tonk saloon serves stiff drinks and hosts live music on two stages: one inside and intimate, the other out under the stars. Given that it's on the small side and in the middle of nowhere, you might be surprised at the caliber of talent it books—Paul McCartney, Robert Plant, Orville Peck, Lizzo, and Patti Smith have all made the pilgrimage—and the number of patrons it packs in on any given night. It also hosts surprise, drop-in performers, especially during the Coachella music festival. Bring your dancing shoes and come hungry, as the restaurant here dishes up open-fire, Santa Maria–style barbecue that's worth the inevitable wait for a table (reservations aren't accepted). ✉ *53688 Pioneertown Rd., Pioneertown* ☎ *760/228–2222* 🌐 *pappyandharriets.com* 🕒 *Closed Tues. and Wed.*

The Tiny Pony Tavern

BARS | A couple of transplants took what was at one time a gun shop and another time a beauty parlor—set in a run-down, retro strip mall—and created a small bar with a big personality that welcomes tourists but focuses on winning the hearts and minds (and hard-earned dollars) of locals. From the grandma-core art—one wall is devoted entirely to cat paintings and photos, another to black-velvet works—elevated bar food (loaded yuca fries, chilaquiles tacos), and numerous activities and theme nights (photo booth, pool table, karaoke, movies, prime-rib Thursdays), what's not to love? ✉ *57205 Twentynine Palms Hwy., Yucca Valley* ☎ *442/205–0163* 🌐 *www.thetinypony.com.*

Shopping

Acme 5 Lifestyle

HOUSEWARES | Owned by TV production designer/artist Anton Goss, who is a part-time high-dessert resident, this bright and airy boutique specializes in mid-century and bohemian-modern furniture and home decor, with pieces sourced locally as well as from Mexico, Mali, and elsewhere in the world. It's also a full-service nursery, making it handy if your days in the desert have inspired you to invest in some new succulents. Should you need time to contemplate potential purchases, stroll through the meditative green space out back. ⊠ *55870 Twentynine Palms Hwy., Yucca Valley* ☎ *760/853–0031* ⊕ *www.acme5lifestyle.com.*

Hoof & The Horn

GENERAL STORE | FAMILY | Given the name, you might assume that this is a pet shop or fancy feed store. But unless you want to pamper your pooch with Jenni Earle's positively inscribed bandanas, this is a store for free spirits of any gender or age who appreciate colorful and comfy clothes, candles, crystals, witty cards, cool tchotchkes, and the occasional hat customization pop-up. There's also a lot of park-theme paraphernalia and desert-inspired art. ⊠ *55840 Twentynine Palms Hwy, Yucca Valley* ☎ *760/365–6100* ⊕ *www.hoofandthehorn.com.*

Wine & Rock Shop

WINE/SPIRITS | Yes, you did just see an alien in a banana suit on Highway 62. It's the welcome wagon for what just might be the best retail representation of this desert area's alluring *je ne sais quoi.* Although it's a shop for serious imbibers, it's also a place for shoppers who don't take themselves too seriously. Here you can find a Pét-Nat and a pet rock, crystals and coffee table books, ceramic match strikers and Syrahs, and body care products and beer. ⊠ *59006 Twentynine Palms Hwy., Yucca Valley* ☎ *760/853–0012* ⊕ *wineandrockshop.com.*

Joshua Tree

12 miles east of Yucca Valley.

Artists, renegades, and adrenaline-seeking adventurers have long found acceptance and kindred spirits in this small quirky desert town, a gateway to the same-named national park. If you zip through town, you might wonder what all the hype is about. If, however, you slow down, sip a cup of Bali Kintamani on Joshua Tree Coffee's splendid patio,

browse racks at vintage shops, take in an art exhibit, strike up a conversation or two at the Saturday farmers' market, and silently watch a glorious sunset, you'll find much to love.

GETTING HERE AND AROUND

Highway 62 is the main route to and through Joshua Tree. Most businesses are here or along Park Boulevard as it heads toward the national park.

👁 Sights

The Integratron

OTHER ATTRACTION | More often than not, California's, and specifically the high desert's, reputation for being wacky and weird is blown out of proportion. But in the case of this woo-woo wellness offering—namely, a 60-minute sonic healing session/sound bath during which someone plays 20 quartz singing bowls keyed to each body chakra while you lie on the floor of a white, domed structure in the middle of nowhere—believe the hype. If you go in with an open mind, you might just find inner peace, a clear mind, and deep relaxation. Even if you don't, think of the tale you'll be able to share with relatives at the next holiday get-together. ⊠ *2477 Balfield Blvd., Landers* ☎ *760/364–3126* ⊕ *www.integratron.com* 🎟 *From $55* 🕐 *Closed Mon.–Wed. and July–mid-Sept.* 🔔 *Reservations highly suggested* 🔍 *Children must be at least 5 to participate in private sessions and at least 14 to attend public sound baths.*

★ Noah Purifoy Desert Art Museum of Assemblage Art

ART MUSEUM | FAMILY | This installation of "assemblage art" on a sandy 10-acre tract of land in town honors the work of artist Noah Purifoy, whose sculptures blend with the spare desert in an almost postapocalyptic way. Purifoy lived here for the last 25 years of his life until his death in 2004. He used found materials to create works that highlighted social issues, and his pieces have been displayed at the Los

Angeles County Museum of Art, J. Paul Getty Museum, Museum of Modern Art in New York, and elsewhere. ⊠ *63030 Blair La., Joshua Tree* ⊕ *www.noahpurifoy. com* 🖃 *Free but donations are appreciated* ⊙ *Closed dusk–dawn.*

World Famous Crochet Museum

OTHER MUSEUM | FAMILY | Another only-in-Joshua Tree spot not to be missed, this museum displays all kinds of crocheted creations inside a reimagined drive-through photo stand. Tucked off the street in Art Queen's courtyard, it earned global recognition when it appeared in an international advertising campaign. Before you get back in the car, detour around the front to see another eclectic collection at the Beauty Bubble Salon and Museum (⊕ *beautybubble.net*). The working salon displays more than 3,000 pieces of vintage equipment, toys, products, and advertising related to the hair/beauty industry. ⊠ *61855 Twentynine Palms Hwy., Joshua Tree National Park* ☎ *760/660–5672* ⊕ *www.sharielf. com/museum.html* 🖃 *Free but donations are welcome.*

🍴 Restaurants

Crossroads Cafe

$ | AMERICAN | FAMILY | Egg dishes, griddle items, and hearty Mexican breakfasts like huevos rancheros are the morning draw at this Joshua Tree institution, but plenty of people sing the praises of its sandwiches, burgers, salads, and tacos for lunch or early dinner. Taxidermy animals, framed newspaper clippings, old photos, and beer-can lights decorate the interior, and tattooed waitresses and the quirky regulars make it clear that the high desert is unlike anywhere else in San Bernardino County. **Known for:** great people-watching and eavesdropping; hearty and affordable meals; vegetarian and vegan dishes that use tofu, fake meat, or JUST Egg. $ *Average main: $15* ⊠ *61715 Twentynine Palms Hwy., Joshua Tree* ☎ *760/366–5414* ⊕ *crossroadscafejtree.com.*

The Natural Sisters Cafe

$ | VEGETARIAN | FAMILY | No matter the time of day or year, if this plant-based palate pleaser is open, there will be a wait, but when you finally arrive at the counter to order breakfast or lunch, you'll still be greeted with kind eyes and big smiles. The genuine, happy-hippie kindness will be extended to your digestive system, too, as the wraps, burgers, chia puddings, salads, and avo toasts are mostly organic and always nutritious and bursting with seasonal flavor. **Known for:** catering to vegetarian, vegan, gluten-free, dairy-free eaters; lines around the block perpetually; food that's easy to transport for park days. $ *Average main: $14* ⊠ *61695 Twentynine Palms Hwy., Joshua Tree National Park* ☎ *760/366–3600* ⊕ *naturalsisterscafe.com* ⊙ *No dinner.*

Sky High Pie

$ | PIZZA | FAMILY | When in doubt, order pizza from this tidy, tasty spot on the main drag, within walking distance of the national park visitor center, where toppings include things like smoked Gouda, Fresno chili, soppressata, or fried eggs. Sky also turns its ovens on early most mornings to prepare fresh quiche and pastries, which are served from a takeout window and can be enjoyed with a cup of Joe in the expansive courtyard that's shared with the neighboring Joshua Tree Coffee Company. **Known for:** personal pies made to order (and with amore); gluten-free crusts folks swear by; variety of toppings, including vegan meats and cheeses. $ *Average main: $19* ⊠ *61740 Twentynine Palms Hwy., Joshua Tree National Park* ☎ *760/974–1050* ⊕ *www. facebook.com/skyhighJT* ⊙ *Closed Tues.*

Hotels

★ AutoCamp Joshua Tree

$$ | **RESORT** | **FAMILY** | A stay at this pristine property, opened in 2022 by a trusted name in Golden State glamping, barely qualifies as roughing it thanks to refurbished Airstream and other more spacious RVs (four of them ADA accessible) that are done in calming neutral tones; filled with space-saving hacks; and equipped with panoramic windows, TVs, high-thread-count sheets on actual mattresses, kitchenettes, full bathrooms, and workhorse HVAC systems. **Pros:** bathrooms inside trailers means no midnight walks to communal toilets; Quonset hut lounge can be rented for events; café makes an awesome chicken potpie. **Cons:** have to carry or wagon luggage from parking lot to the trailers; no blackout shades, so morning light streams in; snack shop is pricey. $ *Rooms from: $220* ⊠ *62209 Verbena Rd., Joshua Tree* ☎ *844/366–9715* ⊕ *autocamp.com/joshua-tree* ⇄ *55 trailers* ⊙ *No Meals.*

The Bungalows

$$$$ | **RESORT** | Amid serene desert on a far corner of the 152-acre Joshua Tree Retreat Center, this adults-only property has three painstakingly restored mid-century-modern buildings containing suites that offer the architectural panache of Palm Springs (patterned masonry, breeze blocks, angular lines, slanted roofs, giant windows) and mod-cons like keyless entry, Parachute linens, and water filtered by reverse osmosis. **Pros:** great place to watch sunrises and sunsets; mellow, high-desert vibe; access to hiking trails where you will likely not see anyone else. **Cons:** no TVs; no on-site personnel; swimming pools haven't been updated and are hard to find. $ *Rooms from: $650* ⊠ *59700 Twentynine Palms Hwy., Joshua Tree* ⊕ *On grounds of Joshua Tree Retreat Center* ☎ *760/299–5010* ⊕ *retreat.homesteadmodern.com* ⇄ *14 suites* ⊙ *No Meals.*

The Joshua Tree Inn

$ | **B&B/INN** | Like the Harmony Motel in Twentynine Palms, this rustic roadside refuge will forever be a part of rock music lore, though, admittedly, it's tied to a darker moment—singer/guitarist and member of The Byrds Gram Parsons died in Room 8, which, despite its sad history and reports of paranormal activity, is still the most requested room. **Pros:** guitars to borrow during stay; all units have personal back patios; complimentary tea, coffee, and granola bars. **Cons:** rooms don't get much natural light; far from fancy with furnishings in a mishmash of styles; pool can get loud when kids are present. $ *Rooms from: $171* ⊠ *61259 Twentynine Palms Hwy., Joshua Tree* ☎ *760/366–1188* ⊕ *www.joshuatreeinn.com* ⇄ *12 rooms* ⊙ *No Meals.*

Nightlife

★ Más o Menos

COCKTAIL LOUNGES | Halfway between Joshua Tree and Twentynine Palms sits a gleaming white Spanish bungalow so striking and solitary and surrounded by sand that you're bound to do a double-take. But it's no mirage. In fact, it's an adorable, chill oasis where you can quench two types of thirst: the morning or afternoon-pick-me-up need for coffee (and pastries) and the anytime (post-work, post-hike, celebration) alcoholic fix. There's a great patio, where patrons sometimes do yoga but usually just sip selections from the Mexican-leaning cocktail menu of margaritas, Mezcal negronis, micheladas, Bloody Marias. ⊠ *66031 Twentynine Palms Hwy., Joshua Tree National Park* ☎ *442/370–2266* ⊕ *masomenosjt.com.*

🛍 Shopping

Joshua Tree Bottle Shop

WINE/SPIRITS | After a long day of hiking or rock climbing, you deserve a reward, and this well-curated bottle shop, which focuses mainly on small-batch wines for under $25, is a great place to do it. To make your selection you can read the well-researched tasting notes or ask for recommendations (staffers love diving deep!). There's also a range of craft spirits like amaro, mezcal, and sake, as well as beer, mead, canned cocktails, and nonalcoholic alternatives. ✉ *61707 Twentynine Palms Hwy., Joshua Tree* ☎ *760/465–0001* ⊕ *www.joshuatreebottleshop.com.*

Ricochet

SECOND-HAND | **FAMILY** | Throw a dart in any direction in any high desert city, and it's likely to end up at a vintage store. Even new-clothing proprietors usually have at least one rack of secondhand threads. This downtown business is filled with upcycled, good-condition Western wear (cowboy boots, scarves, belts with big buckles, leather cuffs, silver jewelry), as well as things like frilly 1950s TV mom aprons. ✉ *61731 Twentynine Palms Hwy., Joshua Tree* ☎ *760/366–1898* ⊕ *www.ricochetjoshuatree.com* ⊗ *Closed Tues. and Wed.*

★ The Station

SOUVENIRS | **FAMILY** | Find pop-star paraphernalia, graphic T-shirts, magazines, trinkets, snacks, and Mexican blankets in this wild shop set up in a converted 1949 Richfield gas station. Between the giant man statue, retro cars, and back patio, there's enough eye candy to warrant a stop even if you're not in the market for souvenirs. ✉ *61943 Twentynine Palms Hwy., Joshua Tree* ☎ *760/974–9050* ⊕ *thestationjoshuatree.com* ⊗ *Closed Tues. and Wed.*

Twentynine Palms

12 miles east of Joshua Tree.

A gateway town to Joshua Tree National Park, Twentynine Palms, known colloquially as 29, is also home to the U.S. Marine Corps Air Ground Task Force Training Command and Combat Center, the largest Marine base in the world. You can find services, supplies, and lodging in town. (Thanks to the military presence, there are also numerous tattoo parlors and barbers skilled in the ways of the high and tight.) Although it has historically been one of the least cool of the high-desert cities, it has seen a bit of a renaissance of late with new shops, restaurants, and a microbrewery.

GETTING HERE AND AROUND

Highway 62 is the main route to and through Twentynine Palms. Most businesses here center on it or Utah Trail, 3 miles north of Joshua Tree's entrance.

ESSENTIALS

VISITOR INFORMATION 29 Palms Visitor Center. ✉ *73484 Twentynine Palms Hwy., Twentynine Palms* ☎ *760/358–6324* ⊕ *visit29.org.*

👁 Sights

Oasis of Murals

PUBLIC ART | **FAMILY** | Twenty-six murals painted on the sides of buildings depict the pioneer history, military service, wildlife, and landscape of Twentynine Palms and its past and current residents. The public art project began in 1994 and the group behind it, Action Council for 29 Palms, restores them as needed. You can't miss the art on a drive around town, but you can also pick up a free map from the visitor center. ✉ *Twentynine Palms* ⊕ *www.action29palmsmurals.com.*

Sky's the Limit Observatory & Nature Center

OBSERVATORY | **FAMILY** | Run by a dedicated, local nonprofit, this volunteer-staffed 15-acre park near the northern entrance to Joshua Tree National Park educates visitors on the region's celestial and terrestrial attributes. It has an observatory dome with a 14-inch telescope, nature trails that feature desert plants, a meditation garden, numerous sculptures, and an orrery (a 20 billion–to-1 scaled model of the solar system). The campus is always open for walks or stargazing with your own equipment, but the big dome and telescope are only available during the free Night Sky Programs, which are held once a month on the Saturday night nearest the new moon. Programs usually start an hour after sunset and last two hours. The observatory also hosts an annual Night Sky Festival. ⊠ *9697 Utah Irail, Twentynine Palms* ☎ *760/490–9561* ⊕ *www.skysthelimit29.org* 🍴 *Free.*

🍴 Restaurants

Campbell Hill Bakery

$ | **BAKERY** | **FAMILY** | Prepare to wait in line at this tiny downtown eatery owned and operated by married New Yorkers who have years of Big Apple bakery experience. Also be prepared to finally reach the counter only to find that they've sold out of strawberry-poppy scones, cornbread loaves, or blueberry and cream-cheese brioche. **Known for:** hefty hot and cold sandwiches; sweets that sell out quickly; good place to pick up food for a park day. $ *Average main: $8* ⊠ *73491 Twentynine Palms Hwy., Twentynine Palms* ☎ *760/401–8284* ⊕ *campbellhillbakery.com* ⊗ *No dinner. Closed Sun.–Tues.*

grnd sqrl

$ | **AMERICAN** | Turns out you can go home again, and, sometimes, when you do, you also quit your day job and open up the kind of restaurant you'd like to hang out in—at least, that's the case with the ex-teacher behind this downtown den that promises (and delivers) "good eats, rad beer." In addition to having the best beer list for 100 miles (with 13 on tap and roughly 70 more in cans and bottles,

plus a few ciders, hard kombuchas, seltzers, and wine) it also has delicious food created by a Swedish chef (for real) who worked in big-name kitchens in Copenhagen, New York, and L.A. and who makes falafel so moist and zesty that it will leave carnivores rethinking their stance on veganism. **Known for:** elevated, scratch-made comfort food; experiments with pickling; open mike, trivia, and live music nights. $ *Average main: $14* ⊠ *73471 Twentynine Palms Hwy., Twentynine Palms* ☎ *760/800–1275* ⊕ *www.grndsqrl29p.com* ⊗ *Closed Aug. and Sun. in summer.*

🛏 Hotels

Campbell House

$$ | **B&B/INN** | **FAMILY** | When this stone mansion was built back in 1925 (by a WW I vet who married into a wealthy family before being sent to the desert as a remedy for mustard-gas exposure), no expense was spared, as evidenced by the 50-foot-long great room's planked-maple floor, the intricate carpentry, and the huge stone fireplaces that warm the house on cold nights. **Pros:** a/c and heating; access to amenities at sister property, 29 Palms Inn; perfect for family reunions or small-group retreats. **Cons:** somewhat isolated; no elevator in three-story main building; furniture and decor is a mixed bag. $ *Rooms from: $205* ⊠ *74744 Joe Davis Dr., Twentynine Palms* ☎ *760/367–3238* ⊕ *visitcampbellhouse.com* 🛏 *12 units* 🍴 *Free Breakfast.*

Harmony Motel

$ | **MOTEL** | In the late 1980s, while working on and taking photos for the now legendary album, *The Joshua Tree,* the rock band U2 found itself holed up at this circa-1952 roadside motel atop a hill overlooking town and beneath the national park's jagged peaks. **Pros:** cactus gardens and nature trail; outdoor pool and hot tub; a mile from 49 Palms Oasis trail. **Cons:** small property that books quickly; dated decor; on a busy highway. $ *Rooms*

from: $128 ⊠ 71161 Twentynine Palms
Hwy., Twentynine Palms ☎ 760/367–3351
⊕ www.harmonymotel.com ⇨ 8 units
⊖ No Meals.

★ 29 Palms Inn

$$ | B&B/INN | FAMILY | Accommodations
at the closest lodging to Joshua Tree
National Park's north entrance are in
adobe-and-wood-frame cottages, some
dating from the 1920s and '30s (indeed,
James Cagney was often found playing
the piano in the inn's bar back in the day),
set on 70 acres of grounds that include
the ancient Oasis of Mara, a popular
bird-watching spot, and the organic farm
that provides produce to the on-site
restaurant. **Pros:** restaurant is one of the
best in town; on-site pool and nearby
art gallery; gracious innkeepers. **Cons:**
homespun accommodations; limited
amenities; no in-room Wi-Fi. $ Rooms
from: $215 ⊠ 73950 Inn Ave., Twentynine
Palms ☎ 760/367–3505 ⊕ www.29palm-
sinn.com ⊘ Restaurant closed Mon. and
Tues. ⇨ 25 units ⊖ Free Breakfast.

🛍 Shopping

Desert General

GENERAL STORE | FAMILY | This contempo-
rary take on the old-timey general store
opened in 2022 and stocks an eclectic
array of gourmet food, books, games,
novelties, and canvas desert hats. It also
sells household necessities including a
lot of environmentally friendly cleaning
supplies and sustainable everyday items.
In addition, it emphasizes local vendors
and community involvement through
collaborations and exhibits. While you're
here, check out other occupants of Cor-
ner 62, a renovated retail complex, such
as Scorpion Lollipop (candy/gifts), Pisces
(swimwear), and The Moon and the Mat
(yoga studio). ⊠ Corner 62, 73552 Twen-
tynine Palms Hwy., Twentynine Palms
☎ 646/256–6640 ⊕ www.thedesertgen-
eralstore.com.

Habitat

HOUSEWARES | On the same strip as a
number of other must-shop stops, small,
veteran-owned Habitat specializes in
home decor, especially of the ceramic
variety (mugs, plant pots, plates, vases,
etc). There's also a wide range of whim-
sical and botanical prints and tea towels,
house plants, mirrors, and pillows—plen-
ty of which are made by local artisans.
⊠ 73519 Twentynine Palms Hwy., Suite
B, Twentynine Palms ☎ 760/865–0774
⊕ www.shophabitat29.com ⊘ Closed
Sun. and Mon.

Hi-Desert Daydream

SOUVENIRS | FAMILY | This nouveau-boho
boutique carrying a little bit of everything
is just the kind of shop you hope to
happen upon during a vacation. Between
apparel, candles, journals, art, coffee, tea,
cocktail kits, felt Coachella hats, jewelry,
dried flowers, and photos of desert
splendor and the nearby national park,
most of which are made by local crea-
tives, you'll likely find yourself in a "one
for them, two for me" souvenir scenario.
⊠ 73515 Twentynine Palms Hwy., Twen-
tynine Palms ⊕ hidesertdaydream.com.

White Label Vinyl

RECORDS | FAMILY | With black cement-
block walls and a white drop ceiling, this
no-frills record store isn't going to win
any awards for interior design, but what
it lacks in the looks department it makes
up for in inventory. Well-organized bins
of new and used vinyl teem with rock,
punk, rap, and jazz classics and recent
hits. There are also small sections of pre-
owned CDs and DVDs as well as a rack
of T-shirts. ⊠ 73517 Twentynine Palms
Hwy., Twentynine Palms ☎ 760/800–1234
⊕ www.whitelabelvinyl.com ⊘ Closed
Tues. and Wed.

Chapter 9

MOJAVE DESERT

Updated by
Marlise Kast-Myers

WELCOME TO THE MOJAVE DESERT

TOP REASONS TO GO

★ **Nostalgia:** Old neon signs, historic motels, and restored (or neglected but still striking) rail stations abound across this desert landscape. Don't miss the classic eateries along the way.

★ **Great ghost towns:** California's gold rush brought miners to the Mojave, and the towns they left behind have their own unique charms.

★ **Desert flora and fauna:** From fields of California poppies to Joshua trees, and from desert tortoises to cave-dwelling creatures, the natural world here is captivating and surprisingly diverse.

★ **Arid landscapes:** Visit the Mojave National Preserve to view volcanic cinder cones, huge sand dunes, and other geological wonders. Combine a visit to the Mojave with one to Death Valley to experience still more of the region's unique desert terrain.

1 Lancaster. Poppies and aerospace tech thrive in and near this western Mojave hub.

2 Red Rock Canyon State Park. Colorful formations, Native American heritage, and mining history converge in an eerily gorgeous setting.

3 Ridgecrest. A gateway to Death Valley, the northern Mojave's largest town is a welcome oasis near Trona Pinnacles and Petroglyph Canyons.

4 Randsburg. In this living ghost town, wander the well-preserved streets where miners struck gold.

5 Victorville. Experience the Mother Road at the California Route 66 Museum.

6 Barstow. Visit the Mojave's "capital" to explore museums (many in the restored Harvey House depot) and Calico Ghost Town.

7 Mojave National Preserve. Ancient lava beds, rare plants and animals, and towering dunes are among this 1.6-million-acre sanctuary's sights.

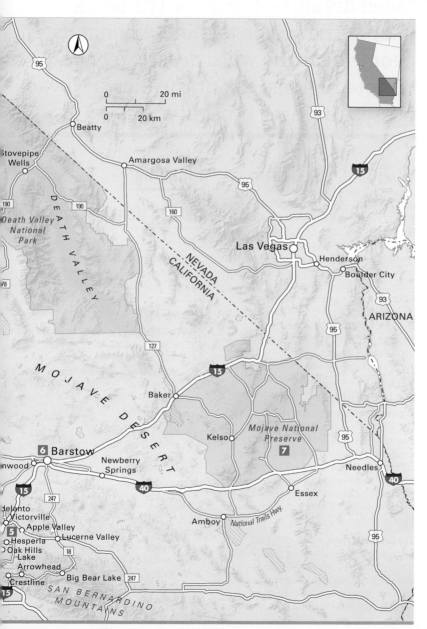

0   20 mi

0   20 km

95

Beatty

Stovepipe
Wells

Amargosa Valley

93

190

190

95

15

160

Death Valley
National
Park

DEATH VALLEY

78

127

Las Vegas

Henderson

NEVADA
CALIFORNIA

Boulder City

93

95

ARIZONA

MOJAVE DESERT

15

Baker

Kelso

Mojave National
Preserve

7

95

6 Barstow

Newberry
Springs

40

Essex

Needles

40

nwood

15

247

delanto
Victorville

Apple Valley

5

Hesperia

Oak Hills
Lake

Arrowhead

Crestline

15

SAN BERNARDINO
MOUNTAINS

Lucerne Valley

18

Big Bear Lake   247

Amboy   National Trails Hwy.

95

Dust and desolation, tumbleweeds and rattlesnakes, barren landscapes and failed dreams—these are the bleak images that come to mind when most people hear the word *desert*. Yet the remote regions east of the Sierra Nevada possess a singular beauty.

The vast spaces here are peppered with creosite bushes, spiky Joshua trees and cacti, undulating sand dunes, faulted mountains, and dramatic rock formations. The topography is extreme: the Mojave Desert, once part of an ancient inland sea, is one of the largest swaths of open land in Southern California, with elevations ranging from 3,000 to 5,000 feet, while Death Valley, to the north, drops to almost 300 feet below sea level and contains the lowest (and hottest) spot in North America. As abandoned homesteads can attest, the area is not heavily populated, with just a few communities separated by expanses in which visitors can both lose and find themselves.

MAJOR REGIONS

The Western Mojave. Lancaster, Red Rock Canyon State Park, Ridgecrest, and Randsburg are all in this vast area, where wildflowers bloom in spring and snow caps the mountain peaks year-round. The scenery is especially beautiful along U.S. 395, which runs north up to towns at the western edge of Death Valley National Park.

The Eastern Mojave. Here you'll find Victorville and Barstow, the main hubs of a region defined by majestic, wide-open spaces, and one of the state's most rewarding but demanding destinations: Mojave National Preserve.

Planning

Getting Here and Around

AIR

Harry Reid International in Las Vegas is the nearest airport to many eastern Mojave destinations. Hollywood Burbank is the largest and closest airport to the western Mojave region.

CONTACTS Harry Reid International Airport. ✉ *5757 Wayne Newton Blvd., Las Vegas* ☎ *702/261–5211* ⊕ *www.harryreidairport. com.* **Hollywood Burbank Airport.** ✉ *Burbank* ☎ *818/840–8840* ⊕ *www.hollywoodburbankairport.com.*

BUS

Greyhound provides bus service to Barstow and Victorville. Check with the chambers of commerce about local bus service, which is generally more useful to residents than to tourists.

CAR

Touring this region really requires a car. The major north–south route through the western Mojave, U.S. 395, intersects with I–15 between Cajon Pass and Victorville. Farther west, Highway 14 runs north–south between Inyokern (near Ridgecrest) and Lancaster.

To the north I–15 travels through the Mojave to Las Vegas, Nevada; to the south, I–40 heads to the Mojave National Preserve. At the intersection of the two interstates, in Barstow, I–15 veers south toward Victorville and Los Angeles, and I–40 gives way to Highway 58 west toward Bakersfield. ■TIP→ **Traffic can be especially troublesome Friday through Sunday, when thousands of Angelenos head to Las Vegas.**

Before heading out, make sure your vehicle is in good condition, and let someone know your route, destination, and estimated time of return. Carry water, a jack, tools, and towrope or chain. Mind your gas gauge, filling up whenever you can to keep the needle above half. Stay on main roads, and watch out for wildlife, horses, and cattle.

TRAIN
Amtrak trains traveling east and west stop in Victorville and Barstow, but the stations aren't staffed, so you'll have to purchase tickets in advance and handle your own bags. The Barstow station is served daily by Amtrak California motor coaches that stop in Los Angeles, Bakersfield, Las Vegas, and elsewhere. Amtrak buses also stop in Lancaster and Mojave. Metrolink's Antelope Valley line travels from Los Angeles north to Burbank Airport, Palmdale, and Lancaster.

CONTACTS Metrolink. ☎ *800/371–5465* ⊕ *metrolinktrains.com.*

Hotels

Chain hotels and roadside motels are the desert's primary lodging options. The tourist season runs from late May through September. Though rarely needed, reservations are still a good idea.

Restaurants

Dining is a fairly simple affair. There are chain establishments in Ridgecrest, Lancaster, Victorville, and Barstow, as well as some ethnic eateries.

⇨ *Restaurant and hotel reviews have been shortened. For full information, visit Fodors.com. Restaurant prices are the average cost of a main course at dinner, or if dinner is not served, at lunch. Hotel prices are the lowest cost of a standard double room in high season.*

What It Costs			
$	$$	$$$	$$$$
RESTAURANTS			
under $20	$20–$30	$31–$40	over $40
HOTELS			
under $200	$200–$350	$351–$500	over $500

Tours

Sierra Club
SPECIAL-INTEREST TOURS | The San Gorgonio Chapter of the Sierra Club and the chapter's Mojave Group conduct interesting field trips and desert excursions. Activities are often volunteer-run and free, but participants are sometimes required to cover parking and other expenses. ☎ *951/684–6203* ⊕ *sangorgonio2.sierraclub.org* ✉ *Some free; fee tour prices vary.*

Visitor Information

CONTACTS California Welcome Center Barstow. ✉ *2796 Tanger Way, Suite 100, Barstow* ✛ *Off Lenwood Rd.* ☎ *760/253–4782* ⊕ *www.visitcalifornia.com/experience/california-welcome-center-barstow.*

When to Go

Spring and fall are the best seasons to tour the desert. Winters are generally mild, but summers can be cruel. If you're on a budget, take advantage of room rates that drop as the temperatures rise.

Lancaster

70 miles north of Los Angeles.

Points of interest around Lancaster include a state poppy reserve that bursts to life in the spring and Edwards Air Force Base (open to those with base access), which many consider the birthplace of supersonic flight. Lancaster was founded in 1876, when the Southern Pacific Railroad arrived. Before that, several Native American tribes, some of whose descendants still live in the surrounding mountains, inhabited it.

The adjacent town of Palmdale (often included with Lancaster as part of the Antelope Valley region) evolved from a sleepy agricultural community into an aerospace and defense capital when Edwards Air Force Base and U.S. Air Force Plant 42 were established after World War II.

GETTING HERE AND AROUND

From the Los Angeles basin, take Highway 14, which proceeds north to Mojave and Highway 58, a link between Bakersfield and Barstow. Regional Metrolink trains serve Lancaster from the Los Angeles area.

ESSENTIALS

VISITOR INFORMATION Destination Lancaster. ⊠ *554 W. Lancaster Blvd., Lancaster* ☎ *661/948–4518* ⊕ *www. destinationlancasterca.org.*

◉ Sights

Antelope Valley California Poppy Reserve
NATURE PRESERVE | FAMILY | The California poppy, the state flower, can be spotted throughout the state, but this quiet park holds the densest concentration. Eight miles of trails wind through 1,745 acres of hills carpeted with poppies and other wildflowers, including a paved section that allows wheelchair access. Keep in mind that poppy flowers will curl up their petals if it's too windy or cold, so plan accordingly. Heed the rules and stay on the official trails when taking photos. ■ **TIP→ Blooming season is usually March through May.** On a clear day at any time of year, though, you'll be treated to sweeping valley views. Visit the website to watch the poppy cam, or call the wildflower hotline for the current bloom status. ⊠ *15101 Lancaster Rd., west off Hwy. 14, Ave. I Exit, Lancaster* ☎ *661/724–1180 wildflower hotline, 661/946–6092 administration* ⊕ *www.parks.ca.gov/poppyreserve* 🎫 *$10 per vehicle* ☉ *Visitor center closed mid-May–Feb.*

★ **Antelope Valley Indian Museum**
HISTORY MUSEUM | FAMILY | This museum got its start as a private collection of Native American antiquities gathered in the 1920s by artist and amateur naturalist Howard Arden Edwards. Today, his Swiss chalet–style home is a state museum known for one-of-a-kind artifacts from California, Southwest, and Great Basin native cultures, including tools, artwork, basketry, and rugs. The eclectic works are predominately focused on the people of Antelope Valley. A ¼-mile walking trail loops a portion of the property. To get here, exit north off Highway 138 at 165th Street East and follow the signs, or take the Avenue K exit off Highway 14. ⊠ *15701 E. Ave. M, Lancaster* ☎ *661/946–3055* ⊕ *www.avim.parks. ca.gov* 🎫 *$3* ☉ *Closed weekdays.*

Antelope Valley Winery

WINERY | Here, the high-desert sun and nighttime chill work their magic on wine grapes such as Merlot, Zinfandel, and Sangiovese. In addition to tastings, the winery hosts a Saturday farmers' market (from May through November between 9 and noon) and sells grass-fed buffalo and other game and exotic meats such as venison, pheasant, and wild boar. ✉ *42041 20th St. W, at Ave. M, Lancaster* ☎ *661/722–0145, 888/282–8332* 🌐 *www.avwinery.com* 🎟 *Winery free, tastings from $12* 🕒 *Closed Mon. and Tues.*

The BLVD

NEIGHBORHOOD | FAMILY | Lancaster's downtown arts and culture district and social hub, The BLVD, stretches for nine blocks along West Lancaster Boulevard from 10th Street West to Sierra Highway. Boeing Plaza anchors the east end and marks the start of the Aerospace Walk of Honor—a series of murals and monuments lauding 100 legendary figures, including Neil Armstrong and Chuck Yaeger. The district is also home to the Lancaster Performing Arts Center, the Lancaster Museum of Art & History, galleries, restaurants, boutiques, coffee and tea shops, craft breweries, and entertainment venues. ✉ *W. Lancaster Blvd., Lancaster* ✥ *10th St. W to Sierra Hwy. and Jackman to Milling Sts.* 🌐 *www.theblvdlancaster.com.*

Devil's Punchbowl Natural Area

NATURE SIGHT | FAMILY | A mile from the San Andreas Fault, this natural bowl-shape depression in the earth is framed by 300-foot rock walls. At the bottom is a stream, which you can reach via a moderately strenuous 1-mile hike. You also can detour on a short nature trail; at the top, an interpretive center has displays of native flora and fauna, including live animals such as snakes, lizards, and birds of prey. ✉ *28000 Devil's Punchbowl Rd., south of Hwy. 138, Pearblossom* ☎ *661/944–2743* 🌐 *parks.lacounty.gov* 🎟 *Free* 🕒 *Closed Mon.*

St. Andrew's Abbey

CHURCH | Nestled in the foothills of the Antelope Valley, this enclave is both Benedictine monastery and restful place for both day visitors and those participating in retreats. You can walk the lush tree-lined grounds, which include a shaded pond teeming with ducks and red-eared turtles, or browse the well-stocked gift shop. Ceramic tiles in the image of saints and angels by Father Maur van Doorslaer, a Belgian monk whose work U.S. and Canadian collectors favor, are among the items sold here to help sustain the monastery and its good works. ✉ *31001 N. Valyermo Rd., south of Hwy. 138, Valyermo* ☎ *661/944–2178 ceramics studio* 🌐 *saintandrewsabbey.com* 🎟 *Free.*

Hotels

★ DoubleTree By Hilton Palmdale

$ | HOTEL | FAMILY | From the moment you're greeted with a warm chocolate chip cookie, you know you're in for a good stay at this DoubleTree hotel just 10-minutes outside Lancaster. **Pros:** good restaurant; friendly staff; plenty of amenities. **Cons:** pool is not heated; sound carries between rooms; not centrally located in Lancaster. [$] *Rooms from: $149* ✉ *300 W. Palmdale Blvd., Palmdale* ☎ *661/265–1749* 🌐 *www.hilton.com* 🛏 *134 rooms* 🍴 *No Meals.*

Red Rock Canyon State Park

48 miles north of Lancaster.

On the stretch of Highway 14 that slices through Red Rock Canyon State Park, it's easy to become caught up in the momentum of rushing to your "real" destination. But it would be a shame not to stop for this deeply beautiful canyon, with its rich, layered colors and Native American heritage.

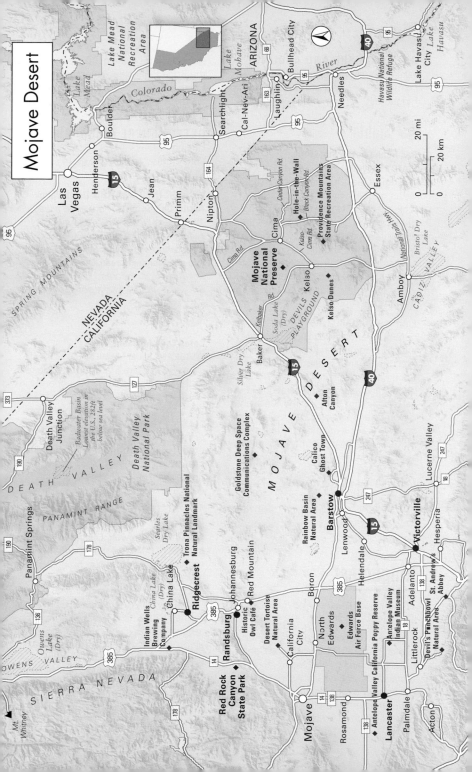

GETTING HERE AND AROUND

Take Highway 14 north from the Palmdale–Lancaster area or south from Ridgecrest.

👁 Sights

Red Rock Canyon State Park

STATE/PROVINCIAL PARK | FAMILY | A geological feast for the eyes with its layers of pink, white, red, and brown rock, this remote canyon is also a region of fascinating biological diversity—the ecosystems of the Sierra Nevada, the Mojave Desert, and the Basin Range all converge here. Native American known as the Kawaiisu lived here some 20,000 years ago. Later, Mojave Indians roamed the land for centuries.

From 1863 to 1893, the gold rush lured miners, eventually leading to an infrastructure comprised of a stagecoach station, the Ricardo settlement, and the Red Rock Railroad. You can still see remains of gold and ash mining operations in the park, and more than 150 movies such as *Silverado* and *Jurassic Park* have been shot here. For a quiet nature trail a little off the beaten path try the 0.75-mile loop at Red Cliffs Natural Preserve about about ⅓ of a mile off Highway 14, across from the entrance to the Ricardo Campground. ⊠ *Visitor Center, 37749 Abbott Dr., off Hwy. 14, Cantil* ☎ *661/946–6092, 442/247–5158* ⊕ *www.parks.ca.gov* ☞ *$6 per vehicle* ☞ *$25 camping.*

Ridgecrest

28 miles northeast of Red Rock Canyon State Park.

This town of about 29,000 residents serves the U.S. Naval Weapons Center to its north and has scores of stores, restaurants, and hotels. As it's the last community of any significant size that you'll encounter when heading northeast toward Death Valley National Park, it's a good base for visiting attractions such as the Trona Pinnacles. Note, though, that Ridgecrest's amenities aren't in a central district, but rather spread across about 21 square miles.

GETTING HERE AND AROUND

Driving here is via U.S. 395 or, from the Los Angeles area, Highway 14.

ESSENTIALS

VISITOR INFORMATION Death Valley Tourist Center. ⊠ *At Maturango Museum, 100 E. Las Flores Ave., at Hwy. 178, Ridgecrest* ☎ *760/375–6900* ⊕ *www. maturango.org.* **Ridgecrest Area Convention and Visitors Bureau.** ⊠ *880 N. China Lake Blvd., Ridgecrest* ☎ *760/375–8202, 800/847–4830* ⊕ *www.goridgecrest.com.*

👁 Sights

China Lake Museum

HISTORY MUSEUM | FAMILY | Since the Naval Air Warfare Station is now closed to the public, this museum—opened in 2018—gives an alternative glimpse into the history, technology, and weaponry at China Lake. More than 20 exhibits display missiles, aircraft, rockets, and other full-spectrum weapons. There is no charge to visit the gift shop and exterior fighter jets. ⊠ *130 E. La Flores Ave., Ridgecrest* ☎ *760/677–2866* ⊕ *chinalakemuseum.org* ☞ *$5* ☉ *Closed Sun. and Mon.*

Indian Wells Brewing Company

BREWERY | FAMILY | After driving through the hot desert, you'll surely appreciate a cold one at Indian Wells Brewing Company, where master brewer Rick Lovett lovingly crafts his Lobotomy Bock, Amnesia I.P.A., and Lunatic Lemonade, among others. If you have the kids along, grab a six-pack of his specialty root beer and soda pop available in more than 100 flavors. ⊠ *2565 N. Hwy. 14, 2 miles west of U.S. 395, Inyokern* ☎ *760/377–5989* ⊕ *www.facebook.com/ IndianWellsBrewingCompany.*

Did You Know?

Movies like *Jurassic Park* have been shot in Red Rock Canyon State Park in the Mojave Desert.

Maturango Museum

HISTORY MUSEUM | FAMILY | The museum contains interesting exhibits that survey the Upper Mojave Desert area's art, history, archaeology, and geology. It also sponsors art exhibits and cultural programs, and it contains an information center for Death Valley. ✉ *100 E. Las Flores Ave., at Hwy. 178, Ridgecrest* ☎ *760/375–6900* 🌐 *maturango.org* 🎟 *$5.*

Trona Pinnacles National Natural Landmark

NATURE SIGHT | FAMILY | Fantastic-looking formations of calcium carbonate, known as tufa, were formed underwater along fault lines in the bed of what is now Searles Dry Lake. Some of the more than 500 spires stand as tall as 140 feet, creating a landscape so surreal that it doubled for outer-space terrain in the film *Star Trek V.* The Pinnacles also served as the backdrop in *Planet of the Apes, Battlestar Galactica*, and music videos by Rihanna and Lady Gaga. An easy-to-walk ½-mile trail allows you to see the tufa up close, but wear sturdy shoes—tufa cuts like coral. It's located 45 minutes east of Ridgecrest, and the best road to the area can be impassable after a rainstorm. ✉ *Pinnacle Rd.* ✣ *5 miles south of Hwy. 178, 18 miles east of Ridgecrest* ☎ *760/384–5400 Ridgecrest BLM office* 🌐 *www.blm.gov/visit/trona-pinnacles.*

Hotels

Hampton Inn & Suites Ridgecrest

$ | HOTEL | FAMILY | Your best bet in Ridgecrest, the Hampton has a well-equipped exercise room; pool; impeccable Internet service, free breakfast; laundry facilities; early check-in/late check-out (based on availability); and rooms with microwaves, mini-refrigerators, and coffeemakers. **Pros:** attentive, friendly service; easy app for check in and check out; big rooms. **Cons:** a rather strong chain vibe; thin walls; basic breakfast. [$] *Rooms from: $170* ✉ *104 E. Sydnor Ave., Ridgecrest* ☎ *760/446–1968* 🌐 *www.hilton.com* 🛏 *93 rooms* 🍴 *Free Breakfast.*

Randsburg

21 miles south of Ridgecrest, 26 miles east of Red Rock Canyon State Park.

Randsburg and nearby Red Mountain and Johannesburg make up the Rand Mining District, which first boomed with the discovery of gold in the Rand Mountains in 1895. Rich tungsten ore, used in World War I to make steel alloy, was discovered in 1907, and silver was found in 1919.

The boom has gone bust, but the area still has some residents, a few antiques shops, and plenty of character that draws the biker crowd and off-roading fans. Butte Avenue is the main drag in Randsburg, whose tiny city jail, just off Butte, is among the original buildings still standing. An archetypal Old West cemetery perched on a hillside looms over Johannesburg.

GETTING HERE AND AROUND

From Red Rock Canyon, drive east on Redrock Randsburg Road. From Ridgecrest, drive south on South China Lake Road and U.S. 395.

Sights

Desert Tortoise Natural Area

WILDLIFE REFUGE | FAMILY | It's not easy to spot the elusive desert tortoise in this protected 40-square-mile habitat, but the area often blazes with wildflowers in the spring and early summer. It's also a great place to view desert kit fox, red-tailed hawks, cactus wrens, and Mojave rattlesnakes. Walking paths and a small interpretive center are part of the experience, and a naturalist is on hand March to June to provide information on the area's flowers and wildlife. ✉ *8 miles northeast of California City via Randsburg Mojave Rd.* ☎ *442/294–4258* 🌐 *tortoise-tracks.org* 🎟 *Free.*

General Store

RESTAURANT | FAMILY | Built as Randsburg's drug store in 1896, this is one of the area's few surviving ghost-town buildings. It has an original tin ceiling, light fixtures, and 1904-era marble-and-stained-glass soda fountain, where you can still enjoy a phosphate soda, malt, or shake. If you're hungry, there are sandwiches with sides, too. ✉ *35 Butte Ave., Randsburg* ☎ *760/374–2332* 🌐 *www.randsburggeneralstore.com* 🕓 *Closed weekdays.*

Historic Owl Café

HISTORY MUSEUM | **FAMILY** | Don't be fooled by the name. The Owl Café off Highway 395 just south of Randsburg contains a mining museum in a building that once served as a speakeasy saloon and brothel. The original 1930s bar remains, and there's plenty of memorabilia to keep you entertained, including prospecting supplies, old photographs, and newspaper clippings from the Prohibition era. Mining tours and gold-prospecting charters are offered by advance reservation. ✉ *701 Hwy. 395, Red Mountain, Randsburg* ☎ *760/374–2102* 🌐 *www.redmtnkelly-silver.com* 🎟 *Museum $3; tours $79* 🕓 *Closed Sun. and Tues.–Thurs.*

Rand Desert Museum

HISTORY MUSEUM | **FAMILY** | The colorful history of the Rand Mining District during its heyday of 1896 is celebrated in this small museum, with displays that include historical mining photographs, documents, and artifacts. Since the museum is only open weekends (11 am–2 pm) based on volunteer availability, it's best to email ahead regarding a visit. (The phone line is seldom answered.) ✉ *161 Butte Ave., Randsburg* ☎ *760/608–7776* ✉ *randdesertmuseum@gmail.com* 🌐 *www.randdesertmuseum.com* 🎟 *Free* 🕓 *Closed weekdays.*

🍴 Restaurants

The Joint

$ | **AMERICAN** | **FAMILY** | Off-roading enthusiasts and locals tend to congregate at The Joint, considered the center of the action (or maybe the only action) in town—with live music on weekends, pickleback shots, and a chalkboard menu reading "Soup of the Day: Whisky." Dating from 1905, the adobe building originally served as a German steam bakery, and today the bar/restaurant is operated by Neil and Hollie Shotwell, the third generation to keep the family-owned saloon alive since 1955. Stop by on Saturday for guest vendors serving tacos or burgers on the grill. **Known for:** live music; whisky and beer; burritos and salsa. [$] *Average main: $15* ✉ *165 Butte Ave., Randsburg* ☎ *760/608–9421* 🌐 *the-joint-randsburg-ca.business.site* 🕓 *Closed Mon.–Wed.*

Victorville

87 miles south of Ridgecrest.

At the southwest corner of the Mojave is sprawling Victorville, a town with a rich Route 66 heritage and a museum dedicated to the Mother Road. Victorville was named for Santa Fe Railroad pioneer Jacob Nash Victor, who drove the first locomotive through the Cajon Pass here in 1885. Once home to Native Americans, the town later became a stop for Mormons and missionaries. In 1941, George Air Force Base, now an airport and storage area, brought scores of military families to the area, many of whom stayed.

GETTING HERE AND AROUND

Follow I–15 from Los Angeles or Las Vegas; from the north, take U.S. 395. Amtrak and Greyhound serve the town, as do Victor Valley Transit buses, but driving is more practical.

ESSENTIALS

TRANSPORTATION INFORMATION Victor Valley Transit. ✉ *Hesperia* ☎ *760/948–3030* 🌐 *vvta.org.*

Sights

California Historic Route 66 Museum

HISTORY MUSEUM | When it comes to the history of road travel in America, it's hard not to think fondly of Historic Route 66, and this 4,500-square-foot museum is chock-full of memorabilia—maps and postcards, photographs, paintings, nostalgic displays—that brings the iconic highway to life. Highlights include a Studebaker horse carriage, a 1917 Model T Ford, and an original concession stand from Santa Monica Beach. Friendly volunteers are more than happy to answer questions and take your picture inside the flower-painted VW Love Bus. There's a large gift shop where you can sift through Mother Road souvenirs. ✉ *16825 S. D St., between 5th and 6th Sts., Victorville* ☎ *760/951–0436* 🌐 *www.califrt66museum.org* 🎟 *Free* 🕒 *Closed Tues. and Wed.* ☞ *Park in secure lot next to building instead of on street.*

Mojave Narrows Regional Park

CITY PARK | **FAMILY** | This 840-acre park is one of the few spots where the Mojave River flows aboveground, and the result is open pastures, wetlands, and two lakes surrounded by cottonwoods and cattails. Amenities include camping, fishing, equestrian/walking trails, and a large playground with splash zone (runs 8–3:30). The two lakes are stocked with catfish (May–September) and trout (November–April). A California state fishing license is required to fish. ✉ *18000 Yates Rd., north on Ridgecrest Rd. off Bear Valley Rd., Victorville* ☎ *760/245–2226* 🌐 *www.parks.sbcounty.gov/park/mojave-narrows-regional-park* 🎟 *$8 per car weekdays; $10 weekends; fishing $12* 🕒 *Closed Tues. and Wed.*

Restaurants

Emma Jean's Holland Burger Cafe

$ | **DINER** | **FAMILY** | The short-order cook and his grill are literally center stage in this tiny, family-owned, Route 66 restaurant that has changed little since it opened in 1947. Pick a barstool, and settle in for big portions of traditional diner food—although the peach cobbler, Brian burger, and fried chicken keep locals lining up at the door, anyone wanting a glimpse of 20th-century Americana can get their kicks here, too. **Known for:** Mother Road memorabilia; historical diner; hearty breakfasts. [$] *Average main: $15* ✉ *17143 N. D St., at Water Power Housing Dr., Victorville* ☎ *760/243–9938* 🌐 *www.hollandburger.com/home* 💳 *No credit cards* 🕒 *Closed Sun. No dinner.*

Molly Brown's Country Cafe

$ | **AMERICAN** | **FAMILY** | There's no mystery why this place is a locals' favorite—the cozy eatery offers a mouthwatering breakfast menu that includes everything from chicken fried steak to a sizzling garden skillet brimming with fresh vegetables. Lunch includes sandwiches, salads, and hot plates such as meat loaf with potatoes, veggies, and cornbread. **Known for:** hearty breakfasts; locals' favorite; homemade breads. [$] *Average main: $15* ✉ *15775 Mojave Dr., Victorville* ☎ *760/241–4900* 🌐 *www.mollybrownscountrycafe.com* 🕒 *No dinner.*

Hotels

Courtyard Marriott Victorville Hesperia

$ | **HOTEL** | **FAMILY** | Rooms are spacious and contemporary, and there is both an indoor pool and large outdoor patio and pool area ideal for large groups. **Pros:** convenient location off I–15; some rooms with desert views; two pools. **Cons:** breakfast only with certain room rates; not pet-friendly; some rooms close to freeway noise. [$] *Rooms from: $179* ✉ *9619 Mariposa Rd., Hesperia* ☎ *760/956–3876* 🌐 *www.marriott.com* 🛏 *131 rooms* 🍴 *No Meals.*

Many of the buildings in the popular Calico Ghost Town are authentic.

Barstow

32 miles northeast of Victorville.

Barstow was born in 1886, when a subsidiary of the Atchison, Topeka, and Santa Fe Railway began construction of a Harvey House depot and hotel here. The depot has been restored and includes three free museums, the family-friendly Calico Ghost Town is just north of town, and there are well-known chain motels and restaurants right off I–15 if you need to rest and refuel.

GETTING HERE AND AROUND

Driving here on I–15 from Los Angeles or Las Vegas is the best option, although you can reach Barstow via Amtrak or Greyhound. The local bus service, operated by Victor Valley Transit, is helpful for sights downtown.

ESSENTIALS

VISITOR INFORMATION Barstow Chamber of Commerce. ⊠ *229 E. Main St., Barstow* ☎ *760/256–8617* ⊕ *barstowchamber.*

com. **California Welcome Center Barstow.** ⊠ *2796 Tanger Way, Suite 100, Barstow* ⊹ *Off Lenwood Rd.* ☎ *760/253–4782* ⊕ *www.visitcalifornia.com/experience/ california-welcome-center-barstow.*

👁 Sights

Afton Canyon

CANYON | FAMILY | Because of its colorful, steep walls, Afton Canyon is often called the Grand Canyon of the Mojave. It was carved over thousands of years by the rushing waters of the Mojave River, which makes one of its few aboveground appearances here. The dirt road that leads to the canyon is ungraded in spots, so it is best to explore it in an all-terrain vehicle. There are 22 primitive campsites available on a first-come, first-served basis. ⊠ *Off Afton Rd., 36 miles northeast of Barstow via I–15, Barstow* ⊹ *From Barstow, take I–15 east for 35 miles. Take Afton exit south. Drive south 3 miles on dirt road to parking area for Afton Campground.* ⊕ *www.blm.gov/ visit/afton-canyon* 🏕 *Camping $6.*

★ Calico Ghost Town

GHOST TOWN | FAMILY | This former silver-mining boomtown was founded in 1881, and, within a few years, it had 500 mines and 22 saloons. Its reconstruction in 1951 by Walter Knott of Knott's Berry Farm makes it more about G-rated family entertainment than the town's gritty past, but that doesn't detract from the fun of panning for (fool's) gold, touring the original tunnels of Maggie Mine, or taking a leisurely ride on the Calico Odessa Railroad. Of the 33 structures, five are original buildings, such as the impressive Lane's General Store. The town's setting among the stark beauty of the Calico Hills can make a stroll along its once-bustling Main Street downright peaceful. Camping, cabins, and a bunkhouse are all available for overnight stays. ✉ *36600 Ghost Town Rd., off I–15, Yermo* ✛ *15 min from Barstow* ☎ *909/387–2757, 760/254–1123* ⊕ *parks.sbcounty.gov/park/calico-ghost-town-regional-park* ✉ *$8* ☞ *Camping from $30.*

Casa Del Desierto Harvey House

HISTORY MUSEUM | FAMILY | This historic train depot was built around 1911 (the first 1885 structure was destroyed by fire) and was one of the original Harvey Houses, providing dining and lodging for rail passengers. Waitresses at the depots were popularized in movies such as *The Harvey Girls* with Judy Garland. It now houses offices and three museums: the Western American Railroad, Route 66 Mother Road, and the NASA Goldstone Deep Space Visitor Center, but you can still walk along the porticos of the impressive Spanish Renaissance Classical building, or stroll into the restored lobby to see the original staircase, terrazzo floor, and copper chandeliers. ✉ *681 N. 1st Ave., near Riverside Dr., Barstow* ☎ *760/818–4400* ⊕ *barstowharveyhouse.com* ✉ *Free* ☽ *Closed Sun. NASA Goldstone Center also closed Tues. and Wed.*

★ Goldstone Deep Space Communications Complex

SCIENCE MUSEUM | FAMILY | Friendly and enthusiastic staffers conduct guided tours of this 53-square-mile complex at Fort Irwin Military Base, 35 miles north of Barstow. Tours start at the Goldstone Museum, where exhibits detail past and present space missions and Deep Space Network history. From there, you'll drive out to see the massive concave antennas, starting with those used for early manned space flights and culminating with the 24-story-tall "listening" device. This is one of only three complexes in the world that make up the Deep Space Network, tracking and communicating with spacecraft throughout our solar system. One-month advanced reservations are required for this 2½-hour driving tour (in your own vehicle); contact the complex to reserve a slot. The NASA Goldstone Deep Space Visitor Center at the Harvey House in Barstow offers a glimpse of what's in store. ✉ *NASA Goldstone Visitor Center, 681 N. 1st Ave., Barstow* ☎ *760/255–8688* ⊕ *www.gdscc.nasa.gov* ✉ *Free* ☽ *Closed Sun.*

Main Street Murals

PUBLIC ART | FAMILY | More than two dozen hand-painted murals in downtown Barstow depict the town's history, from prehistoric times and early explorers to pioneer caravans, mining eras, and Route 66. Self-guided walking tour maps are available at the Barstow Chamber of Commerce or on the Main Street Mural website. ✉ *E. Main St., Barstow* ✛ *Between 1st and 7th Sts.* ⊕ *www.mainstreetmurals.com.*

Mojave River Valley Museum

HISTORY MUSEUM | FAMILY | Considered "Barstow's attic," this museum has a floor-to-ceiling collection that highlights local history, both quirky and conventional. Items on display include Ice Age fossils such as a giant mammoth tusk dug up in 2006, Native American artifacts, 19th-century handmade quilts, and exhibits on early settlers. Entrance is free, and there's a little gift shop with a nice collection of more than 500 books about the area. **■TIP→ The story about Possum Trot and its population of folk-art dolls is not to be missed.** ✉ *270 E. Virginia Way, at Barstow Rd., Barstow* ☎ *760/256–5452* 🌐 *www.mrvmuseum.org* 🎫 *Free.*

Rainbow Basin Natural Area

NATURE SIGHT | **FAMILY** | Many science-fiction movies set on Mars have been filmed in this area 8 miles north of Barstow. Huge slabs of red, orange, white, and green stone tilt at crazy angles like ships about to capsize, and traces of ancient beasts such as mastodons and bear-dogs, which roamed the basin up to 16 million years ago, have been discovered in its fossil beds. The dirt road around the basin is narrow and bumpy so vehicles with higher clearance are recommended. Rain can quickly turn the road to mud so, at times, only four-wheel-drive vehicles are permitted. Owl Canyon has 22 primitive campsites. ✉ *Fossil Bed Rd., Barstow* ✣ *3 miles west of Fort Irwin Rd. (head north from I–15)* ☎ *760/252–6000* 🌐 *www.blm.gov/visit/rainbow-basin-natural-area* 🎫 *Camping $6.*

Skyline Drive-In Theatre

OTHER ATTRACTION | **FAMILY** | Check out a bit of surviving Americana at this dusty drive-in, where you can watch the latest Hollywood flicks among the Joshua trees and starry night sky. Keep in mind the old-time speakers are no more; sound is tuned in via car radio. ✉ *31175 Old Hwy. 58, Barstow* ☎ *760/256–3333* 🌐 *www.facebook.com/Skylinedriveinbarstowca* 🎫 *$12 per person* ⏲ *Closed Dec.–early Mar.* ☞ *Cash only; no ATMs nearby.*

Western America Railroad Museum

HISTORY MUSEUM | **FAMILY** | You can almost hear the murmur of passengers and rhythmic, metal-on-metal clatter as you stroll past the old cabooses, railcars, and engines, such as Sante Fe Number 95, that are on display outside the historic Barstow station housing this museum. Inside, the memorabilia includes a train simulator, rail equipment, a model railroad, items from the depot's Harvey House days, and period dining-car china from railways around the country. ✉ *Casa Del Desierto, 685 N. 1st Ave., near Riverside Dr., Barstow* ☎ *760/256–9276* 🌐 *barstowrailmuseums.com* 🎫 *Free* ⏲ *Closed Mon.–Thurs.*

🍴 Restaurants

Peggy Sue's 50s Diner

$ | **AMERICAN** | **FAMILY** | Checkerboard floors and life-size versions of Elvis and Betty Boop greet you at this funky '50s coffee shop and pizza parlor. It's the oldest diner on Highway 15, and the fare is basic American—fries, onion rings, burgers, pork chops—with some fun surprises such as deep-fried dill pickles. **Known for:** movie and TV memorabilia; over-the-top '50s vibe; gift shop, jukebox, soda fountain, and duck pond. [$] *Average main: $14* ✉ *35654 W. Yermo Rd., at Daggett-Yermo Rd., Yermo* ✣ *3 miles from Calico Ghost Town* ☎ *760/254–3370* 🌐 *www.peggysuesdiner.com.*

🛏 Hotels

Holiday Inn & Suites Barstow

$ | **HOTEL** | **FAMILY** | In a sea of chain hotels this one has a few homespun touches up its sleeves, such as the cozy living-room-style lobby and designated pet-friendly rooms. **Pros:** kids under 18 stay and eat free; entirely nonsmoking; Tesla charging stations. **Cons:** pricey for Barstow; near freeway; shared parking lot with other businesses. [$] *Rooms from: $150* ✉ *2812 Lenwood Rd., Barstow* ☎ *760/307–3121* 🌐 *www.ihg.com/holidayinn/hotels* 🔑 *92 rooms* 🍽 *Free Breakfast.*

Mojave National Preserve

64 miles northeast of Barstow via I–15, 80 miles southeast of Barstow via I–40.

The 1.6-million-acre Mojave National Preserve has a surprising abundance of plant and animal life—especially considering the elevation (nearly 8,000 feet in some areas). There are traces of human history, too, including abandoned army posts and vestiges of mining and ranching towns.

Don't miss the Soda Springs area in the unincorporated community of Zzyzx. In the 1940s, this was a mineral spring and health resort owned by Curtis Springer. It now operates as a Desert Studies Center under California State University. Here you can explore the pools and Lake Tuendae, which is ideal for birding.

The Cinder Cone Lava Beds area holds 75 inactive volcanoes; the youngest is 11,500 years old. North Cima Road passes a significant Joshua tree forest. Mojave National Preserve rangers also oversee the adjacent 20,920-acre Castle Mountains National Monument.

GETTING HERE AND AROUND

The preserve lies between I–15 and I–40. Kelbaker Road bisects the park from north to south. Northbound from I–40, Essex Road gets you to Hole-in-the-Wall on pavement but is graveled beyond there.

◉ Sights

Hole-in-the-Wall

NATURE SIGHT | Created millions of years ago by volcanic activity, Hole-in-the-Wall formed when gases were trapped between layers of deposited ash, rock, and lava; the gas bubbles left holes in the solidified material. ⊠ *Mojave National Preserve* ☎ *760/252–6104* ⊕ *www.nps. gov/moja* 🎫 *Free.*

★ Kelso Dunes

NATURE SIGHT | As you enter the Mojave National Preserve, you'll pass miles of open scrub brush, Joshua trees, and beautiful red-black cinder cones before encountering the Kelso Dunes. These golden, fine-sand slopes cover 45 square miles, reaching heights of 500 feet. You can reach them via a 1.5-mile walk from the main parking area, but be prepared for a serious workout. When you reach the top of a dune, kick a little bit of sand down the lee side and listen to the sand "sing" (or vibrate). North of the dunes, in the town of Kelso, is the Mission revival–style Kelso Depot Visitor Center, a striking building that dates from 1923. It's normally open everyday but Tuesday and Wednesday, but it's closed for renovation until 2025; check ahead for updates. ⊠ *Mojave National Preserve* ✛ *For Kelso Depot Visitor Center, take Kelbaker Rd. exit from I–15 (head south 34 miles) or I–40 (head north 22 miles)* ☎ *760/252–6100, 760/252–6108* ⊕ *www. nps.gov/moja* 🎫 *Free* ⌲ *Dunes 8 miles south of the Depot.*

Providence Mountains State Recreation Area (*Mitchell Caverns*)

CAVE | Drive around the area and marvel at the desert vistas, or overnight at one of five pack-in/pack-out campsites. The main attraction, however, is Mitchell Caverns. Access to them is via 1.5-mile round-trip hike and a two-hour, ranger-led tour, during which you'll encounter stalactites, flowstone, stalagmites, and possibly cave-dwelling animals. (Book campsites or cavern tours at ⊕ *www. reservecalifornia.com.*) ⊠ *Essex Rd., Mojave National Preserve* ✛ *16 miles north of I–40* ☎ *760/928–2586* ⊕ *www. parks.ca.gov* 🎫 *Day use $10; camping $27; tours $20* ⊗ *Park closed July and Aug. Closed Mon.–Thurs. except Mon. holidays* ⌲ *Tours 11 am and 2 pm Oct.– May; and 10 am June and Sept. Dogs not allowed.*

Chapter 10

DEATH VALLEY NATIONAL PARK

Updated by
Marlise Kast-Myers

🏕 Camping	🛏 Hotels	🏃 Activities	👁 Scenery	👥 Crowds
★★★☆☆	★★★★☆	★★★☆☆	★★★★★	★★☆☆☆

WELCOME TO
DEATH VALLEY NATIONAL PARK

TOP REASONS TO GO

★ **Roving rocks:** Death Valley's Racetrack is home to moving boulders, a rare phenomenon that until recently had scientists baffled. Drivers of all-terrain vehicles, who don't mind lack of cell service and sharp rocks, can view the rock 'n' roll show.

★ **Lay low:** Stand on the lowest spot on the continent at Badwater, 282 feet below sea level.

★ **Wildflower explosion:** In spring during a superbloom, this desert landscape is ablaze with greenery and colorful flowers, especially in low-elevation areas in March and high-elevation in June and July.

★ **Ghost towns:** Renowned for its Wild West heritage, the region is home to such crumbling settlements as Ballarat, Rhyolite, Chloride City, Greenwater, Harrisburg, Leadfield, Panamint City, and Skidoo.

★ **Geologically amazing:** From canyons and sand dunes to salt flats and dry lake beds, Death Valley serves up plenty of treasures.

1 Central Death Valley. Furnace Creek sits along Highway 190 in the heart of Death Valley. If time is limited, head here to visit gorgeous Golden Canyon, Zabriskie Point, and Artists Drive. To the southeast is Badwater Basin, which you can access on a 15-mile drive along Highway 178 from Furnace Creek or, if you're feeling adventurous, a much longer drive up from the park's southeastern entrance near Shoshone, CA.

2 Northern Death Valley. This region is uphill from Furnace Creek, which means marginally cooler temperatures. Be sure to stop by Rhyolite Ghost Town on Highway 374 before entering the park and exploring colorful Titus Canyon and the jaw-dropping Ubehebe Crater.

3 Western Death Valley. When entering the park from the west, stop at Panamint Springs Resort to grab a meal and get your bearings before moving on along Highway 190 to Father Crowley Vista Point, quaint Darwin Falls, and historic Stovepipe Wells Village. You can also access the beehive-shape Wildrose Charcoal Kilns off Highway 190 in this area of the park.

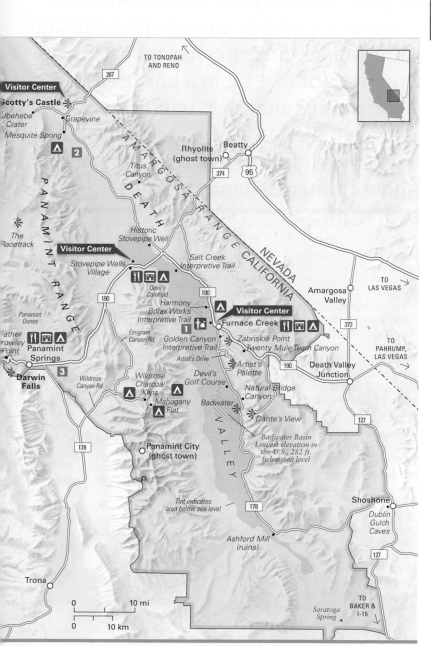

TO TONOPAH
AND RENO

267

Visitor Center
Scotty's Castle

Ubehebe
Crater

Grapevine

Mesquite Spring

2

Rhyolite
(ghost town)

Beatty

374

95

Titus
Canyon

The
Racetrack

Historic
Stovepipe Well

Salt Creek
Interpretive Trail

Visitor Center
Stovepipe Wells
Village

190

Devil's
Cornfield

190

Harmony
Borax Works
Interpretive Trail

Visitor Center
Furnace Creek

Amargosa
Valley

TO
LAS VEGAS

373

Panamint
Dunes

Emigrant
Canyon Rd.

Father
Crowley
Point
Panamint
Springs

3

Golden Canyon
Interpretive Trail

Zabriskie Point
Twenty Mule Team Canyon

Death Valley
Junction

TO
PAHRUMP,
LAS VEGAS

190

**Darwin
Falls**

Wildrose
Canyon Rd.

Artist's Drive

Devil's
Golf Course

Artist's
Palette

Wildrose
Charcoal
Kilns

Mahogany
Flat

Natural Bridge
Canyon

Badwater

Dante's View

127

178

Panamint City
(ghost town)

Badwater Basin
Lowest elevation in
the U.S., 282 ft.
below sea level

Tint indicates
area below sea level

178

Shoshone

Dublin
Gulch
Caves

127

Ashford Mill
(ruins)

Trona

0   10 mi

0   10 km

Saratoga
Spring

TO
BAKER &
I-15

AMARGOSA RANGE

DEATH

PANAMINT RANGE

VALLEY

NEVADA

CALIFORNIA

The natural riches of Death Valley—the largest national park outside Alaska—are overwhelming: rolling waves of sand dunes, black cinder cones thrusting up hundreds of feet from a blistered desert floor, riotous sheets of wildflowers, bizarrely shaped Joshua trees basking in the orange glow of a sunset, tiny pupfish, and a dramatic silence.

This is a land of extremes of climate (hottest and driest) and geography. The park centers on the valley, which extends 156 miles from north to south and includes Badwater Basin, the lowest point in the USA (282 feet below sea level). Two mountain ranges border the valley: the Panamint to the west, where Telescope Peak juts more than 11,000 feet up from the valley floor, and the Amargosa to the east. Salt basins, spring-fed oases, sand dunes, deep canyons, and more than a thousand miles of paved and dirt roads punctuate the barren landscapes.

Humans first roamed this once-lush region around 10,000 years ago. The Timbisha Shoshone have lived here for more than a thousand years, originally along the shores of a 30-foot-deep lake. They called the area Timbisha for the red-hue rocks in the hillsides. Gold-rush pioneers looking for a shortcut to California traversed the barren expanse in 1849; some met their demise in the harsh environment, and those who survived named the place Death Valley. Silver, gold, and borax mining companies soon arrived on the scene. They didn't last long (most had stopped operations by 1910), but they left ghost towns and ramshackle mines as evidence of their dreams.

In 1933, President Herbert Hoover proclaimed the area a national monument to protect both its natural beauty and its scientific importance. In 1994, Congress passed the California Desert Protection Act, adding 1.3 million acres and designating the region a national park. Today, Death Valley National Park encompasses nearly 3.4 million acres, 93% of which is designated wilderness.

Despite its moniker, Death Valley teems with life. More than a million visitors a year come here to view plants and animals that reveal remarkable adaptations to the desert environment, hike through deep canyons and up mountain trails, gaze at planets and stars in a vast night sky, and follow in the footsteps of ancient cultures and pioneers. They come to explore an outstanding, exceptionally diverse outdoor natural history museum, filled with excellent examples of the planet's geological history. Most of all, they come to experience peace, quiet, and solitude in a stark, surreal landscape found nowhere else on Earth.

Planning

Getting Here and Around

AIR

The closest airport with commercial service, Las Vegas's Harry Reid International Airport, is 130 miles east, so you'll still need to drive a couple of hours to reach the park. Roughly 160 miles to the west, Burbank's Bob Hope Airport is the second-closest airport.

CAR

It can take more than three hours to cross from one side of the park to another, so it's important to choose an entrance point that makes sense for what you want to see. If you're driving from Los Angeles, enter through the western portion off Highway 395; from Las Vegas, enter from the north at Beatty, Nevada, or via the central entrance at Death Valley Junction on the 190. Travelers from Orange County, San Diego, and the Inland Empire should access the park via I–15 North at Baker.

Distances can be deceiving: what seems close can be very far away. Much of the park can be viewed on regularly scheduled bus tours, but these often don't allow time for hikes to sites not seen from the road, such as Salt Creek, Golden Canyon, and Natural Bridge. The best option is to drive to a number of the sites, get out of the car, and walk.

When driving in Death Valley, reliable maps are important, as signage is often limited or, in a few places, nonexistent. Bring a phone, but don't rely on cell coverage exclusively in every remote area, and pack plenty of food and water (3 gallons per person per day is recommended). Cars, especially in summer, should be prepared for the hot, dry weather, too. Some of the park's most spectacular canyons are accessible only via four-wheel-drive vehicles, but make

sure the trip is well planned, and use a backcountry map.

Be aware of possible winter closures or driving restrictions because of snow. The park's website stays up-to-date on road closures during the wet (and popular) months. **⚠ One of the park's signature landmarks, Scotty's Castle, and the 8-mile road connecting it to the park border is closed until 2025 due to damage from floods.**

Hotels

It's difficult to find lodging anywhere in Death Valley that doesn't have breathtaking views of the park and surrounding mountains. Most accommodations, aside from the Inn at Death Valley, are homey and rustic. Rooms fill up quickly during the fall and spring seasons, and reservations are required about three months in advance for the prime weekends.

Outside the park, head to Beatty, Pahrump, or Amargosa Valley in Nevada for a bit of nightlife and casino action. The western side of Death Valley, along the eastern Sierra Nevada, is a gorgeous setting, though it's quite a distance from Furnace Creek. Here, you can stay in the historic Dow Villa Motel, where John Wayne spent many a night.

Park Essentials

ACCESSIBILITY

All of Death Valley's visitor centers, contact stations, and museums are accessible to all visitors. The campgrounds at Furnace Creek, Sunset, and Stovepipe Wells have wheelchair-accessible sites. Highway 190, Badwater Road, and paved roads to Dante's View provide access to the major scenic viewpoints and historic points of interest. Dogs are not permitted on trails, but are allowed in the park in developed areas such as campgrounds and along roads.

PARK FEES AND PERMITS

The entrance fee is $30 per vehicle, $25 for motorcycles, and $15 for those entering on foot or bike. The payment, valid for seven consecutive days, is collected at the park's ranger stations, self-serve fee stations, and the visitor center at Furnace Creek. Annual park passes, valid only at Death Valley, are $55.

A permit is not required for groups of 14 or fewer, but if you're planning an overnight visit to the backcountry, complete a registration form at the Furnace Creek Visitor Center. Backcountry camping is allowed in areas that are at least 1 mile from maintained campgrounds and the main paved or unpaved roads and 100 yards from water sources. Most abandoned mining areas are restricted to day use.

PARK HOURS

The park is open day or night year-round. Most facilities operate daily 8–5.

AUTOMOBILE SERVICE STATIONS

CONTACTS Furnace Creek Fuel. ✉ *Hwy. 190, Furnace Creek* ☎ *760/786–2345.* **Panamint Springs Gas Station & General Store.** ✉ *40440 Hwy. 190, Death Valley National Park* ☎ *775/482–7680.* **Stovepipe Wells General Store Gas Station.** ✉ *Hwy. 190, Stovepipe Wells* ☎ *760/786–7090.*

CELL PHONE RECEPTION

Results vary, but in general you should be able to get fairly good reception on the valley floor. In the surrounding mountains, however, don't count on it. During peak season, the signal weakens as more users connect.

RESTROOMS

Flush toilets are available at many of the campgrounds throughout the park. There are public restrooms at Furnace Creek Visitor Center and Stovepipe Wells Ranger Station.

Restaurants

Inside the park, if you're looking for a special evening out, head to the Inn at Death Valley Dining Room, which is also a great spot to start the day with a hearty gourmet breakfast. Most other eateries within the park are mom-and-pop-type places with basic American fare.

Outside the park, dining choices are much the same, with little cafés and homey diners serving up coffee shop–style burgers, chicken, and steaks. If you're vegetarian or vegan, BYOB (bring your own beans).

⇨ *Hotel and restaurant reviews have been shortened. For full information visit Fodors.com. Hotel prices are the lowest cost of a standard double room in high season. Restaurant prices are the average cost of a main course at dinner, or if dinner is not served, at lunch.*

What It Costs			
$	$$	$$$	$$$$
RESTAURANTS			
under $20	$20–$30	$31–$40	over $40
HOTELS			
under $200	$200–$350	$351–$500	over $500

Tours

Furnace Creek Visitor Center

GUIDED TOURS | This center has many programs, including ranger-led hikes that explore natural wonders such as Golden Canyon, nighttime stargazing parties with telescopes, and evening ranger talks. ✉ *Furnace Creek Visitor Center, Hwy. 190, 30 miles northwest of Death Valley Junction, Death Valley* ☎ *760/786–2331* ⊕ *www.nps.gov/thingstodo/visit-the-furnace-creek-visitor-center.htm* 🎟 *Free.*

AVERAGE HIGH/LOW TEMPERATURES					
Jan.	Feb.	Mar.	Apr.	May	June
68/41	75/48	84/57	93/65	99/73	113/85
July	Aug.	Sept.	Oct.	Nov.	Dec.
118/91	116/89	108/79	93/64	78/49	66/41

Visitor Information

In addition to selling a variety of books on the area, the **Death Valley Natural History Association** (☎ 760/786–2146 or 800/478–8564 ⊕ www.dvnha.org) sells a waterproof, tear-proof topographical map of the entire park. Additional topo maps covering select areas are also available from the association or the visitor center.

■TIP→ **Before your trip, download the free Death Valley National Park app. It works offline and offers access to weather, webcams, park entrance times, fees, tours, trails, and more.**

CONTACTS Death Valley National Park. ✉ Death Valley National Park ☎ 760/786–3200 ⊕ www.nps.gov/deva.

When to Go

Most of the park's 1.7 million annual visitors come between late fall and early spring, taking advantage of moderate temperatures and the lack of rainfall. During these cooler months, you will need to book a room in advance, but don't worry: the park never feels crowded.

If you visit in summer, believe everything you've ever heard about desert heat—it can be brutal, with temperatures often topping 130°F. The dry air wicks moisture from the body without causing a sweat, so drink plenty of water. Bring sunglasses, a hat, and sufficient clothing to block the sun's rays and the wind.

Flash floods are fairly common. Sections of roadway can be washed away, as they were after major floods in recent years.

Central Death Valley

East-central entrance: on Hwy. 190, 18 miles northwest of Death Valley Junction, California; Furnace Creek Visitor Center is another 12 miles northwest. Southeastern entrance: on Hwy. 178, 1 mile north of Shoshone, California.

Furnace Creek village (194 feet below sea level) was once the center of mining operations for the Pacific Coast Borax Company. Today, it's the hub of Death Valley National Park, home to park headquarters and the main visitor center; the Timbisha Indian Village; and the Oasis at Death Valley hotels, golf course, restaurants, and market. Many major park sites are a short drive north or south from here, including Zabriskie Point, Artists Drive, and Dantes View.

Highway 178 accesses Badwater Basin from the park's southeastern entrance near Shoshone. Portions of this slow-going route are fairly desolate, however, and you can more readily access the basin on a 20-minute drive southeast from Furnace Creek.

■TIP→ **If you're following Highway 190 across the park from east to west, be sure to stop for gas at Stovepipe Wells Village, which lies 25 miles northwest of Furnace Creek.**

◉ Sights

HISTORIC SIGHTS
Harmony Borax Works
MINE | FAMILY | Death Valley's mule teams hauled borax from here to the railroad town of Mojave, 165 miles away.

Death Valley in One Day 👁

If you begin the day in Furnace Creek, you can readily see several sights. Just be sure to bring plenty of water and some food, too. Rise early and make the 20-minute drive south to **Badwater Basin**, which looks out on the lowest point in North America and is a dramatic place to watch the sunrise.

Return north, and stop at **Natural Bridge**, a conglomerate rock formation that has been hollowed at its base to form a span across the canyon, and then **Devil's Golf Course**, with its large pinnacles of salt. Detour to the right onto **Artists Drive**, a 9-mile one-way, northbound route that passes **Artists Palette**, where minerals have given the rocks their red, yellow, orange, and green colorations.

Four miles north of Artists Drive is the **Golden Canyon Interpretive Trail**, a 2-mile round-trip that winds through a canyon with colorful rock walls. Just before Furnace Creek, take Highway 190 3 miles east to **Zabriskie Point**, overlooking dramatic, furrowed red-brown hills and the **Twenty Mule Team Canyon.** Return to Furnace Creek, where you can grab a meal and visit the museum at the visitor center. Heading north from Furnace Creek, pull off the highway and take a look at the historic **Harmony Borax Works**, and the **Mesquite Flat Sand Dunes** to view the wind-rippled hills.

They plied the route until 1889, when the railroad finally arrived in Zabriskie. Constructed in 1883, one of the oldest buildings in Death Valley houses the Borax Museum, 2 miles south of the borax works at the Ranch at the Oasis at Death Valley (between the restaurants and the post office). Originally a miners' bunkhouse, the building once stood in Twenty Mule Team Canyon. Now it displays mining machinery and historical exhibits. The adjacent structure is the original mule-team barn. ✉ *Harmony Borax Works Rd., west of Hwy. 190 at Ranch at Death Valley, Death Valley National Park* ⊕ *www.nps.gov/deva/historyculture/harmony.htm.*

Stovepipe Wells Village

TOWN | FAMILY | This tiny 1926 town, the first resort in Death Valley, takes its name from the stovepipe that an early prospector left to indicate where he found water. Although the area has a hotel (rooms from $180), restaurant, convenience store, gas station (fill the tank here

if you're heading across the park to its western edge), swimming pool, and RV hookups, you're better off staying in Furnace Creek, which is more central to the park's natural attractions. Off Highway 190, on a 3-mile gravel road immediately southwest, are the multicolor walls of Mosaic Canyon. ✉ *Hwy. 190, Death Valley* ⊕ *2 miles from Sand Dunes, 77 miles east of Lone Pine* ☎ *760/786–7090* ⊕ *www.deathvalleyhotels.com.*

SCENIC DRIVE
★ Artists Drive

SCENIC DRIVE | FAMILY | Don't rush this quiet, lonely 9-mile paved route that skirts the foothills of the Black Mountains and provides intimate views of a changing landscape. About 4 miles in, a short side road veers right to a parking lot that's a few hundred feet from one of Death Valley's signature sights: Artists Palette, so called for the contrasting colors (including shades of green, gold, and pink) of its volcanic deposits and sedimentary layers. ◼ TIP➔ **The drive is one-way, heading north**

off Badwater Road, so if you're visiting Bad-water Basin from Furnace Creek, come here on the way back. ⊠ *South on Badwater Rd. from Rte. 190 intersection, Death Valley National Park.*

SCENIC STOPS

★ Badwater Basin

NATURE SIGHT | **FAMILY** | At 282 feet below sea level, Badwater is the lowest spot of land in North America—and also one of the hottest. Stairs and wheelchair ramps descend from the parking lot to a wooden platform that overlooks a spring-fed pool, a small but remarkably persistent reminder that the valley floor used to contain a lake. Be sure to look across to Telescope Peak, which towers more than 2 miles above the landscape. You can continue past the platform on a broad, white path that peters out after 1 mile. Bring water and a hat since there's no shade whatsoever. ⊠ *Badwater Rd., Death Valley* ✛ *19 miles south of Furnace Creek.*

★ Dantes View

VIEWPOINT | **FAMILY** | This lookout is 5,450 feet above sea level in the Black Mountains. The view is astounding: in the dry desert air, you can see across most of 160-mile-long Death Valley. Take a 10-minute, mildly strenuous walk from the parking lot toward a series of rocky overlooks, where, with binoculars, you can spot some signature sites. A few interpretive signs point out the highlights below in the valley and across to the Panamint Range. Getting here from Fur-nace Creek takes about an hour—time well invested. ⊠ *Dante's View Rd., Death Valley* ✛ *Off Hwy. 190, 35 miles from Badwater, 20 miles south of Twenty Mule Team Canyon.*

Devil's Golf Course

NATURE SIGHT | **FAMILY** | Thousands of min-iature salt pinnacles carved into surreal shapes by the desert wind dot this wildly varied landscape. The salt was pushed up to the surface by pressure created as underground salt- and water-bearing gravel crystallized. ⊠ *Badwater Rd., Death Valley* ✛ *13 miles south of Furnace Creek. Turn right onto dirt road and drive 1 mile.*

Mesquite Flat Sand Dunes

NATURE SIGHT | These dunes, made up of minute pieces of quartz and other rock, are ever-changing products of the wind-rippled hills, with curving crests and a sun-bleached hue. Among the park's most photographed features, the dunes are at their best at sunrise and sunset. Keep your eyes open for animal tracks— you may even spot a coyote or fox. Bring plenty of water, and note where you parked your car: it's easy to become dis-oriented in this ocean of sand. If you lose your bearings, climb to the top of a dune, and scan the horizon for the parking lot. ⊠ *Death Valley* ✛ *19 miles north of Hwy. 190, northeast of Stovepipe Wells Village.*

Zabriskie Point

VIEWPOINT | **FAMILY** | Although only about 710 feet in elevation, this is one of the park's most scenic spots, overlooking a striking panorama of wrinkled, multi-color hills. It's a great place to watch the sunrise, but it can be bustling any time of day. From the parking lot, there's a short walk up a paved trail. ■**TIP**➔ **Pair your Zabriskie Point visit with a drive out to magnificent Dantes View.** ⊠ *Hwy. 190, Death Valley* ✛ *5 miles south of Furnace Creek.*

TRAILS

Golden Canyon Trail

TRAIL | **FAMILY** | Just south of Furnace Creek, these glimmering mountains are perhaps best known for their role in the original *Star Wars.* The canyon is a fine hiking spot, with a 3-mile out-and-back route offering gorgeous views of the Pan-amint Mountains, ancient dry lake beds, and alluvial fans. *Moderate.* ⊠ *Hwy. 178, Death Valley* ✛ *Trailhead: From Furnace Creek Visitor Center, drive 2 miles south on Hwy. 190, then 2 miles south on Hwy. 178 to parking area.*

The Mesquite Flat Sand Dunes

Mosaic Canyon Trail

TRAIL | FAMILY | A gradual uphill trail (4 miles round-trip) winds through the smoothly polished, marbleized limestone walls of this narrow canyon. There are dry falls to climb at the upper end. *Moderate.* ⊠ *Death Valley* ✛ *Trailhead: Access road off Hwy. 190, ½ mile west of Stovepipe Wells Village.*

Natural Bridge Canyon Trail

TRAIL | FAMILY | A rough 2-mile access road from Badwater Road leads to a trailhead. From there, set off to see interesting geological features in addition to the bridge, which is a half-mile away. The one-way trail continues for a few hundred yards, but scenic returns diminish quickly, and eventually you're confronted with climbing boulders. *Easy.* ⊠ *Death Valley* ✛ *Trailhead: Access road off Badwater Rd., 15 miles south of Furnace Creek.*

VISITOR CENTERS

★ Furnace Creek Visitor Center and Museum

VISITOR CENTER | FAMILY | Here, exhibits, artifacts, a 20-minute film, and live presentations on cultural and natural history provide a broad overview of how Death Valley formed. This is also the place to find out about ranger programs (available November through April) and pick up free Junior Ranger booklets—packed with games and info on the park and its critters—for the kids. In addition, you can purchase maps at the bookstore run by the Death Valley Natural History Association. ■**TIP➔ There are water filling stations outside the restrooms.** ⊠ *Hwy. 190, Death Valley* ✛ *30 miles northwest of Death Valley Junction* ☎ *760/786–3200* ⊕ *www.nps.gov/deva.*

Stovepipe Wells Ranger Station
VISITOR CENTER | Like most amenities in the village of Stovepipe Wells, this station is basic but convenient, with a ranger on hand to answer questions and provide information and maps. You can also pay entrance fees here. Hours are variable; if it's closed, there's a pay station outside the building. ✉ *Hwy. 190, Stovepipe Wells* ☎ *760/786–2342.*

🍴 Restaurants

★ The Inn at the Oasis at Death Valley Dining Room
$$$$ | **AMERICAN** | Fireplaces, beamed ceilings, and spectacular views provide a visual feast to match this fine-dining restaurant's ambitious menu. Dinner entrées include salmon, free-range chicken, filet mignon, and seasonal vegetarian dishes; breakfast is also served here. **Known for:** views of surrounding desert; old-school charm; dinner reservations are a good idea. [$] *Average main: $54* ✉ *Inn at the Oasis at Death Valley, Hwy. 190, Furnace Creek* ☎ *760/786–3385* 🌐 *www.oasisatdeathvalley.com/dine* 🕒 *No lunch.*

Last Kind Words Saloon
$$ | **AMERICAN** | **FAMILY** | Swing through wooden doors and into a spacious dining room that re-creates an authentic Old West saloon, decked out with a wooden bar and furniture, mounted animal heads, fugitive wanted fliers, film posters, and other memorabilia. The traditional steakhouse menu includes ribs, filet mignon, flat iron steak, along with crab cakes, salmon, pizzas, and pasta. **Known for:** hefty steaks, ribs, and fish dishes; extensive drinks menu, from local craft beer to whiskeys and wines; patio with fireplace. [$] *Average main: $29* ✉ *The Ranch at the Oasis at Death Valley, Hwy. 190, Furnace Creek* ☎ *760/786–3335* 🌐 *www.oasisatdeathvalley.com/dine.*

🛏 Hotels

★ The Inn at the Oasis at Death Valley
$$$$ | **HOTEL** | Built in 1927 and most recently renovated over a five-year period ending in 2022, this adobe-brick-and-stone lodge in a green oases offers Death Valley's most luxurious accommodations, including brand-new, one- or two-bedroom casitas. **Pros:** spa and tennis courts; chemical-free pool fed by a warm mineral stream; great views. **Cons:** services reduced during low season (July and August); expensive; resort fee of $28. [$] *Rooms from: $599* ✉ *Furnace Creek Village, near intersection of Hwy. 190 and Badwater Rd., Death Valley* ☎ *760/786–2345* 🌐 *www.oasisatdeathvalley.com* 🛏 *88 rooms* 🍴 *No Meals.*

The Ranch at the Oasis at Death Valley
$$$ | **RESORT** | **FAMILY** | Originally the crew headquarters for the Pacific Coast Borax Company, this ranch-turned-resort is more like a town, with two restaurants, an ice-cream parlor, general store, saloon, golf course, riding stables, and comfortable rooms that are great for families. **Pros:** good family atmosphere; central location; cottages that sleep four. **Cons:** rooms can get hot in summer despite a/c; resort fee ($22); thin walls and ceilings in some rooms. [$] *Rooms from: $400* ✉ *Hwy. 190, Furnace Creek* ☎ *760/786–2345* 🌐 *www.oasisatdeathvalley.com* 🛏 *304 rooms* 🍴 *No Meals* ☞ *Nonguest day passes to pool and showers available for $14.*

Stovepipe Wells Village Hotel
$ | **HOTEL** | **FAMILY** | If you prefer quiet nights and an unfettered view of the starry sky and nearby Mesquite Flat Sand Dunes and Mosaic Canyon, this property is for you. **Pros:** intimate and relaxed; restaurant, full-hookup RV campsites, and nice pool; authentic desert-community ambience. **Cons:** isolated; cheapest patio rooms very small; limited Wi-Fi access. [$] *Rooms from: $161* ✉ *51880 Hwy. 190, Stovepipe Wells* ☎ *760/786–7090*

⊕ www.deathvalleyhotels.com ↩ 83 rooms ⦿ No Meals.

🛍 Shopping

Experienced desert travelers carry a cooler stocked with food and beverages. You're best off replenishing your food stash in Lone Pine, Ridgecrest, Barstow, or Pahrump, larger towns that have a better selection and nontourist prices.

Northern Death Valley

6 miles west of Beatty, Nevada, via Nevada Hwy. 374, 54 miles north of Furnace Creek via Hwy. 190 and Scotty's Castle Rd.

Venture into the remote northern region of the park to travel along the 27-mile Titus Canyon scenic drive, visit the Ube-hebe Crater, and hike along Fall Canyon and Titus Canyon trails. Scotty's Castle, one of the park's main northern sights, and the 8-mile road that connects it to the park border, is currently closed to repair damage from floods in 2015 and 2022; it's expected to reopen in 2025. Check the park website for updates before you visit.

👁 Sights

SCENIC DRIVES
Titus Canyon

SCENIC DRIVE | FAMILY | This popular, one-way, 27-mile drive starts at Nevada Highway 374 (Daylight Pass Road), 2 miles from the park's boundary. Highlights include a hike along the Fall Canyon Trail (from the parking area), the Leadville Ghost Town, and the spectacular lime-stone and dolomite narrows. Toward the end of the route, a two-way section of gravel road leads you into the mouth of the canyon from northern Highway 190. This dirt road is steep, bumpy, and nar-row, so high-clearance, four-wheel-drive vehicles are strongly recommended.

✉ Death Valley National Park ✛ Access road off Nevada Hwy. 374, 6 miles west of Beatty, NV.

SCENIC STOPS
Racetrack

NATURE SIGHT | Getting here involves a 28-mile journey over a washboard dirt road, but the reward is well worth the trip. Where else in the world do rocks move on their own? This mysterious phenomenon, which baffled scientists for years, now appears to have been "settled." Research has shown that the movement merely involves a rare confluence of conditions: rain and then cold to create a layer of ice along which gusty winds can readily push the rocks—sometimes for several hundred yards. When the ice melts and the mud dries, a telltale trail remains. The trek to the Race-track can be made in a truck or SUV with thick tires (including spares) and high clearance; other types of vehicles aren't recommended as sharp rocks can slash tires. The nearest tow companies are in Lone Pine, outside the park to the west, and they charge upward from $1,000 for service out of Death Valley. ✉ *Death Valley ✛ 27 miles west of Ubehebe Crater via rough dirt road.*

Ubehebe Crater

VOLCANO | At 500 feet deep and ½ mile across, this crater resulted from under-ground steam and gas explosions, some as recently as 300 years ago. Volcanic ash spreads out over most of the area, and the cinders lie as deep as 150 feet near the crater's rim. Trek down to the crater's floor or walk around the 2-mile rim counterclockwise to avoid the steep uphill climb. Either way, you need about an hour and will be treated to fantastic views. The hike from the floor can be strenuous, especially because of loose terrain. ✉ *N. Death Valley Hwy., Death Valley ✛ 8 miles northwest of Scotty's Castle.*

TRAILS
Fall Canyon Trail

TRAIL | This is a 6-mile, roundtrip hike from the Titus Canyon parking area. First, walk ½ mile north along the base of the mountains to a large wash, then go 2½ miles up the canyon to a dry fall. For something more technical and steep, continue by climbing around to the falls on the south side. *Moderate.* ⊠ *Death Valley National Park ⊹ Trailhead: Access road off Scotty's Castle Rd., 33 miles northwest of Furnace Creek.*

Western Death Valley

Panamint Springs is on Hwy. 190, 50 miles southeast of Lone Pine (via U.S. Hwy. 395 and California Hwy. 136), and 30 miles southwest of Stovepipe Wells

Panamint Springs, a tiny burg with a rustic resort and restaurant, as well as a market and gas station, anchors the western portion of the park and is a good base for hiking several trails. Pull over at Father Crowley Vista Point for exceptional views of the Panamint Valley. Ballarat Canyon ghost town, with just one permanent resident, lies just a few miles from the park's southwestern border.

◉ Sights

HISTORIC SIGHTS
Ballarat Ghost Town

GHOST TOWN | Although not officially in Death Valley, Ballarat—a crusty, dusty town that saw its heyday between 1897 and 1917—might make an interesting stop during a visit to the park's western reaches. Situated 30 miles south of the Panamint Springs Resort, it has a small store (open afternoons and weekends only) where you can grab a cold soda before venturing out to explore the crumbling landscape. The town itself has just one full-time resident, Rocky Novak. For years Ballarat's more infamous draw was Barker Ranch, where convicted murderer Charles Manson and his "family" were captured after the 1969 Sharon Tate murder spree; the house burned down in 2009. ⊠ *Death Valley ⊹ From Hwy. 395, Exit SR-178 and travel 45 miles to historic marker; Ballarat is 3½ miles from pavement.*

Charcoal Kilns

MINE | FAMILY | Ten well-preserved stone kilns, each 25 feet high and 30 feet wide, stand as if on parade. The kilns, built by laborers for the Modock Consolidated Mining Company in 1877, were used to burn wood from pinyon pines to turn it into charcoal. The charcoal was then transported to the Argus Range west of Panamint Valley—and later to the towns of Darwin and Lookout—where it was used to extract lead and silver from the ore mined there. Nearby is the trailhead for the difficult, 8.4-mile hike to Wildrose Peak. ⊠ *Wildrose Canyon Rd., 37 miles south of Stovepipe Wells, West along Emigrant Canyon Road, 28 miles from Highway 190., Death Valley ⊹ Last 2.1 miles are gravel.*

SCENIC STOPS
★ Father Crowley Vista Point

VIEWPOINT | FAMILY | Pull off Highway 190 in Western Death Valley into the vista point parking lot to gaze at the remnants of eerie volcanic flows down to Rainbow Canyon. Stroll a short distance to catch a sweeping overview of northern Panamint Valley. This is also an excellent site for stargazing. ⊠ *Death Valley National Park.*

TRAILS
★ Darwin Falls

TRAIL | FAMILY | Although some scrambling is involved, this 2-mile round-trip hike rewards you with a refreshing year-round waterfall surrounded by thick vegetation and a rocky gorge. No swimming or bathing is allowed, but it's a beautiful place for a picnic. Adventurous hikers can climb higher toward more rewarding views of the falls. The trail is unmarked so follow the water's edge. ⚠ **Some sections of the trail are not passable for those with mobility** issues. *Moderate.* ⊠ *Death Valley National Park* ⊹ *Trailhead: Access the 2-mile graded dirt road and parking area off Hwy. 190, 1 mile west of Panamint Springs Resort* ☞ *No dogs allowed.*

🛏 Hotels

Panamint Springs Resort

$$ | **HOTEL** | **FAMILY** | Ten miles inside the park's west entrance, overlooking Panamint Valley's sand dunes and unusual geological formations, this rustic, mom-and-pop-style resort has a wraparound porch, as well as a restaurant and bar, a gas station, and a general store. **Pros:** slow-paced; friendly; peaceful and quiet after sundown. **Cons:** far from the park's main attractions; limited Wi-Fi and cell service; rooms don't have TV. $ *Rooms from: $226* ⊠ *Hwy. 190, Death Valley* ⊹ *28 miles west of Stovepipe Wells* ☎ *775/482–7680* ⊕ *www.panamintsprings.com* ⇨ *25 units* ◎ *No Meals.*

Activities

BIKING

Mountain biking is forbidden on hiking trails but allowed on any of the back roads and roadways open to the public. Visit the park website for a list of suggested routes for all levels of ability.

Bicycle Path, a 4-mile round-trip trek from the visitor center to Mustard Canyon, is a good place to start. Bike rentals are available at the Oasis at Death Valley, by the hour or by the day.

Escape Adventures

BIKING | **FAMILY** | Ride into the heart of Death Valley on the Death Valley & Red Rock Mountain Bike Tour, a five-day trip through the national park, or on a customizable two-day journey (on single-track trails and jeep roads). Tours are available February–April and October only. Bikes, tents, and other gear may be rented for an additional price. ⊠ *Death Valley National Park* ☎ *800/596–2953, 702/596–2953* ⊕ *escapeadventures.com* ⊠ *From $1,699.*

BIRD-WATCHING

Approximately 400 bird species have been identified in Death Valley. You can download a complete park bird checklist, divided by season, from the park website.

Along the fairways at Furnace Creek Golf Course, you can see kingfishers, peregrine falcons, hawks, Canada geese, yellow warblers, and the occasional golden eagle. Other good spots to find birds are at Wildrose, the springs near Furnace Creek, Saratoga Springs, Mesquite Springs, and Travertine Springs.

CAMPING

Most of the park's developed campgrounds are open seasonally and are first-come, first-served. The exception is Furnace Creek, which requires reservations (☎ *877/444–6777* ⊕ *www.recreation.gov*) at least two days in advance but allows them to be made up to six months in advance. It's best to book way ahead for one of the 18 RV sites that have full hookups. Alternatively, you could try your luck at Panamint Springs Resort, which is in but not overseen by the park and also has RV sites (six with full hookups).

To find out where you can camp in the backcountry, pick up a copy of the backcountry map at the visitor center, or check the website, which also has information on the free backcountry camping permits that are required in some areas and recommended in others. In most cases, though, you'll need a high-clearance or 4X4 vehicle to reach the backcountry.

Note that camping is prohibited in historic sites; mining areas; use spots; and on the valley floor from Ashford Mill in the south to 2 miles north of Stovepipe Wells, on the Eureka Dunes, or in Greenwater Canyon. It is also not allowed in Titus Canyon, Mosaic Canyon, West Side, Wildrose, Skidoo, Aguereberry Point, Cottonwood Canyon (first 8 miles only), Grotto Canyon, Racetrack (from Teakettle Junction to Homestake Dry Camp), Natural Bridge Canyon, Desolation Canyon, Pinion Mesa, and Big Pine.

You can only build fires in the metal fire grates that are available at most campgrounds, though fires may be restricted in summer (check with rangers about current conditions). Wood gathering is prohibited at all campgrounds. A limited supply of firewood is available at general stores in Furnace Creek and Stovepipe Wells, but because prices are high and supplies limited, you're better off bringing your own if you intend to have a campfire.

FOUR-WHEELING

Driving off established roads, and off-road vehicles including ATVs, are strictly prohibited in the park, which only allows street-legal vehicles. Maps and guidebooks for four-wheel-drive and other backcountry roads (including the popular Cottonwood/Marble canyons, Racetrack, Eureka Dunes, Saline Valley, Saratoga Springs, and Warm Springs Canyon) are available at the Furnace Creek Visitor Center.

■TIP➔ **Check backroad conditions on the park website before heading out, never travel alone, and bring plenty of water and snacks.**

GOLF

Furnace Creek Golf Course at Death Valley

GOLF | Golfers rave about how their drives carry at altitude, so what happens on the lowest golf course in the world (214 feet below sea level)? Its improbably green fairways are lined with date palms and tamarisk trees, and its level of difficulty is rated surprisingly high. You can rent clubs and carts, and there are golf packages available for resort guests. In fall and winter, reservations are essential. ⊠ *Hwy. 190, Furnace Creek* 🖀 *760/786–3373* ⊕ *www.oasisatdeathvalley.com/furnace-creek-golf-course* 🖃 *From $50* 🏌 *18 holes, 6215 yards, par 70* ☞ *Collared or mock golf shirts required (no denim or swim wear).*

HIKING

The park has about 20 developed trails, ranging from easy jaunts like the 0.4-mile mostly paved walk to Harmony Borax Works to the difficult 14-mile trek (with an elevation gain of 3,000 feet) to Telescope Peak. Plan to hike before or after midday in the spring, summer, or fall, unless you're in the mood for a masochistic baking. Carry plenty of water and snacks; use sunscreen; wear protective clothing, including a hat and sunglasses; and keep an eye out for scorpions, snakes, and other potentially dangerous creatures.

HORSEBACK RIDING
Furnace Creek Stables

HORSEBACK RIDING | FAMILY | Set off on a one- or two-hour guided horseback ride from Furnace Creek Stables. The one-hour outing drops into the valley floor, while the two-hour trek traverses the foothills of the Funeral Mountains. Evening full-moon rides and 40-minute carriage excursions are also available. ⊠ *Hwy. 190, Furnace Creek* 🖀 *760/614–1018* ⊕ *www.oasisatdeathvalley.com/plan/horseback-wagon-rides* 🖃 *From $98* ☾ *Closed May–Sept.*

What's Nearby

Beatty

7 miles east of Death Valley National Park Hells Gate entrance.

The tiny, Old West, Nevada town of Beatty has a well-preserved historic downtown district that's worth exploring. It's also a good place to relax and refresh thanks to its cluster of affordable hotels, restaurants, and other services. Hundreds of hiking, biking, and off-highway vehicle roads stretch out from here in all directions. Beatty is also home to the Death Valley Nut and Candy Company, Nevada's largest candy store, and the Rhyolite Ghost Town is just 5 miles west of downtown.

GETTING HERE AND AROUND

From Highway 190 in Death Valley, take the Beatty Cutoff toward Daylight Pass Road, where you'll follow long open two-lane stretches. As you approach the eastern park boundary, the road drops and curves all the way to Beatty. Keep an eye out for wild burros as you near the town.

ESSENTIALS
VISITOR INFORMATION Beatty Chamber of Commerce. ⊠ *119 E. Main St., Beatty* ☎ *775/553–2424* ⊕ *www.beattynevada. org.*

◉ Sights

Beatty Museum

HISTORY MUSEUM | FAMILY | Dedicated to the Bullfrog Mining District and the heritage of Beatty, this museum displays fossils, Native American artifacts, and clothing, tools, and bottles from miners. ⊠ *417 Main St., Beatty* ☎ *775/553–2303* ⊕ *www.beattymuseum.org* 🎫 *Free.*

Rhyolite

GHOST TOWN | FAMILY | This Nevada ghost town, named for the silica volcanic rock nearby, is a big draw. Around 1904, Rhyolite's Montgomery Shoshone Mine caused a financial boom, and fancy buildings sprang up all over town. Today you can still explore many of the crumbling edifices. The Bottle House, built by miner Tom Kelly out of almost 50,000 Adolphus Busch beer bottles, is a must-see. ⊠ *Hwy. 374* ✛ *5 miles west of Beatty and 35 miles north of Death Valley National Park's Furnace Creek Visitor Center* 🖼 ⊕ *www.nps.gov/deva/learn/historycul-ture/rhyolite-ghost-town.htm.*

Restaurants

Happy Burro

$ | AMERICAN | FAMILY | The menu is simple, but the backstory is rich—in 2008, the owners visited Beatty for a chili cook-off, which they won and which led to them to open this saloon, where bikers stop in for cold beer and chili, and trophies and plaques honor the talents of the owners, whose kindness shines light on this small Nevada town. Menu options are on point but limited, consisting only of bowls of chili, chili dogs, hot dogs, and Frito boats. **Known for:** cheap and cold beers; award-winning chili made with Angus beef; small bar and funky patio. 🖻 *Average main: $8* ⊠ *100 W. Main St., Beatty* ☎ *775/553–9099.*

Smokin J's BBQ

$ | BARBECUE | FAMILY | A local favorite, this barbecue joint slow cooks brisket, pulled pork, jalapeño cheddar sausage, and rib tips on an oak-fired grill and serves them with heaping sides of coleslaw, beans, and mac and cheese. Pick up meats by the pound to feast on at your lodgings later on. **Known for:** tender and juicy smoked meats; homemade banana pudding; hearty and flavorful sides. 🖻 *Average main: $18* ⊠ *107 W. Main St., Beatty*

☎ *775/553–5160* ⊕ *www.facebook. com/Smokinjsbarbecue* ☽ *Closed Mon.* ☞ *Open noon–8.*

🛏 Hotels

Atomic Inn

$ | MOTEL | FAMILY | Built in 1979, this retro-style motel is the most afforda-ble and reliable lodging in Beatty, with rooms 1–18 being your best options for a comfortable stay. **Pros:** great rates when call hotel directly; 100% smoke-free facility; quiet side road off Main Street. **Cons:** basic property; no in-room coffee; no blackout curtains. **$** *Rooms from: $77* ✉ *350 S. 1st St., Beatty* ☎ *775/553–2250* ⊕ *atomicinnbeatty.com* ⇆ *54 rooms* ⦿ *No Meals.*

Shoshone

1 mile from Death Valley National Park's Badwater entrance.

A prospector founded this tiny burg in 1910, hoping to build businesses around a new rail stop. He and his family eventually developed the town, and his descendants still run Shoshone Village, which encompasses a hotel, general store, gas station, museum, spring-fed swimming pool, restaurant, campground, and RV park. Nearby nature trails wind through wetlands, pupfish ponds, and bird and endangered-species habitats.

GETTING HERE AND AROUND

Just 45 minutes from Death Valley Junc-tion, Shoshone is one of the last stops before entering the park. You can literally see from one side of town to the other, with the General Store at its center. If traveling from Death Valley, get the most out of scenery by taking Highway 190 east with stops at Zabriskie Point and Twenty Mule Team Canyon toward Death Valley Junction. Alternatively, you travel to Shoshone from Badwater Road. The routes are clearly marked.

👁 Sights

Dublin Gulch

CAVE | FAMILY | A series of caves, carved into the caliche soil by miners during the 1920s, is a great spot for exploring and is a hit with kids. You aren't allowed to walk inside, but you can view the cells—with their stone walls, sleeping platforms, garages, and stovepipe chimneys—from the exterior. ✉ *Shoshone* ⊹ *0.3 miles southwest of Shoshone Village off Hwy. 127* ⊕ *www.shoshonevillage.com/ explore-shoshone.*

Marta Becket's Amargosa Opera House

PERFORMANCE VENUE | FAMILY | An artist and dancer from New York, Marta Becket first visited the former railway town of Death Valley Junction while on tour in 1967. Later that year, she returned to town and leased a boarded-up social hall that sat amid a group of run-down mock-Spanish-colonial buildings. The nonprofit she formed in the early 1970s eventually purchased the property, where she performed for nearly 50 years. To compensate for the sparse audienc-es in the early days, Becket painted a Renaissance-era Spanish crowd on the walls and ceiling, turning the theater into a trompe-l'oeil masterpiece. Despite her passing in 2017, a simple hotel still operates in her name beside the opera house open daily for tours at 9 am and 6 pm for $15 per person. Within the hotel lobby, you can see Marta's hats, books, and works of art on display. ✉ *Rte. 127, Death Valley Junction* ⊹ *27 miles north of Shoshone* ☎ *760/852–4441* ⊕ *www. amargosaoperahouse.org* ⬚ *Varies.*

Shoshone Museum

HISTORY MUSEUM | FAMILY | Housed in a 1906 building, this museum chronicles the history of the Southern Amargosa Val-ley and has a unique collection of period items, minerals, and rocks. A highlight is a mammoth skeleton found in the area. The museum also offers historical walking-tour maps of Shoshone Village, birding trails, culture walks, and local hikes. ✉ *Rte. 127, Shoshone* ☎ *760/852–4524* 🎟 *Free.*

🍴 Restaurants

Crowbar Café and Saloon

$ | **AMERICAN** | **FAMILY** | Built in the 1930s, the diner-esque Crowbar—where antique photos adorn the walls and mining equipment stands in the corners—serves enormous helpings of regional dishes such as steak and taco salads. Home-baked fruit pies make fine desserts, and frosty beers are surefire thirst quenchers. **Known for:** home-baked fruit pies; finger foods like hot fries and chips and salsa; great breakfast spot. [$] *Average main: $18* ✉ *Rte. 127, Shoshone* ☎ *760/852–4123* 🌐 *www.shoshonevillage.com/crowbar-cafe-and-saloon.*

🛏 Hotels

Shoshone Inn

$ | **HOTEL** | **FAMILY** | Built in 1956, the Shoshone Inn has simple, modern rooms with TVs, microwaves, refrigerators, and Keurig coffee machines; there are also six rooms with kitchenettes, a two-room bunkhouse, and a bungalow with a full kitchen and living room. **Pros:** walk to market, restaurant, and museum; courtyard with firepit; peaceful retreat. **Cons:** an hour's drive to main park sights; not dog-friendly; no room phones, spotty cell service. [$] *Rooms from: $184* ✉ *Rte. 127, Shoshone* ☎ *760/852–4335* 🌐 *www.shoshonevillage.com* 🛏 *18 units* 🍽 *Free Breakfast.*

Chapter 11

THE CENTRAL COAST

Updated by
Cheryl Crabtree

👁 **Sights**
★★★★★

🍴 **Restaurants**
★★★★☆

🛏 **Hotels**
★★★★★

🛍 **Shopping**
★★☆☆☆

🍸 **Nightlife**
★☆☆☆☆

WELCOME TO
THE CENTRAL COAST

TOP REASONS TO GO

★ **Incredible nature:** The wild and wonderful Central Coast is home to Channel Islands National Park, two national marine sanctuaries, state parks and beaches, and the rugged Los Padres National Forest.

★ **Edible bounty:** Land and sea provide enough fresh regional foods to satisfy the most sophisticated foodies. Get your fill at countless farmers' markets, wineries, and restaurants.

★ **Outdoor activities:** Kick back and revel in the California lifestyle. Surf, golf, kayak, hike, play tennis—or just hang out and enjoy the gorgeous scenery.

★ **Small-town charm, big-city culture:** With all the amazing cultural opportunities—museums, theater, music, and festivals—you might start thinking you're in L.A. or San Francisco.

★ **Wine tasting:** Central Coast wines earn high critical praise. Sample them in urban tasting rooms, dusty crossroads towns, and at high- and low-tech rural wineries.

1 Ventura. A walkable city with miles of beaches.

2 Channel Islands National Park. North America's Galapagos.

3 Ojai. Lush site of the film *Lost Horizon.*

4 Santa Barbara. The American Riviera.

5 Santa Ynez. An 1880s frontier town preserved.

6 Los Olivos. Has tasting rooms galore.

7 Solvang. America's "Little Denmark."

8 Buellton. Gateway to Santa Barbara wine country.

9 Pismo Beach. Classic California coastal city.

10 Avila Beach. A tiny village in a sunny cove.

11 San Luis Obispo. A busy university town.

12 Paso Robles. A small city amid a booming wine region.

13 Morro Bay. Outdoor activities reign here.

14 Cambria. A historic village with scenic shores and towering pines.

15 San Simeon. Home to Hearst Castle.

16 Big Sur Coast. A bucket-list road trip.

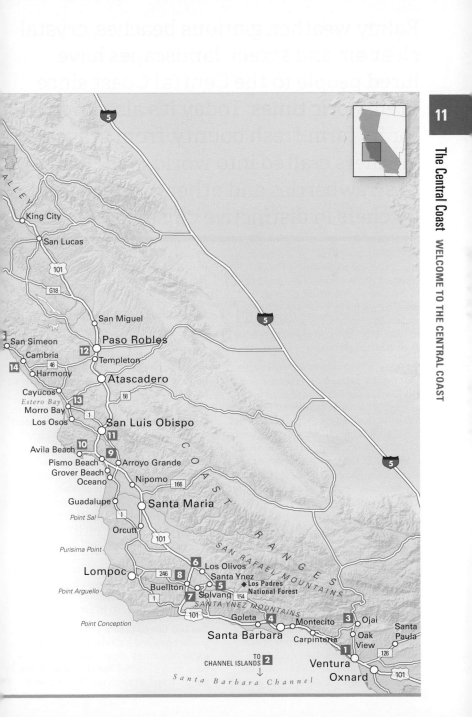

Balmy weather, glorious beaches, crystal clear air, and serene landscapes have lured people to the Central Coast since prehistoric times. Today it's also known for its farm-fresh bounty, from grapes vintners crafted into world-class wines, to strawberries and other produce used by chefs in distinctive cuisine.

The scenic variety along the Pacific coast is equally impressive—you'll see everything from dramatic cliffs and grass-tufted bluffs to wildlife estuaries and miles of dunes. It's an ideal place to relax, slow down, and appreciate the abundant natural beauty.

Offshore, a pristine national park and a vast marine sanctuary protect the wild, wonderful underwater resources of this incredible corner of the planet. But not all of the Central Coast's top attractions are natural: Ventura, Santa Barbara, and San Luis Obispo are filled with sparkling examples of Spanish-Mediterranean architecture, bustling shopping districts, and first-rate restaurants showcasing regional foods and wines.

MAJOR REGIONS

Ventura County. Ventura County was first settled by the Chumash Indians. Spanish missionaries were the first Europeans to arrive, followed by Americans and other Europeans, who established towns, transportation networks, and farms. Since the 1920s, agriculture has been steadily replaced as the area's main industry—first by the oil business and more recently by tourism. Accessible via boat or plane from Ventura (as well as Santa Barbara), Channel Islands National

Park consists of five protected islands just 11 miles offshore where hiking, kayaking, and wildlife viewing abound.

Santa Barbara County. The Santa Ynez Mountains divide the county geographically; U.S. 101 passes through a mountain tunnel leading inland. The South Coast includes the city of Santa Barbara and other coastal towns and small cities. Northern Santa Barbara County, which includes the communities of Buellton, Solvang, Santa Ynez, and Los Olivos, used to be known for sprawling ranches and strawberry and broccoli fields. Today, its nearly 300 wineries and 15,000 acres of vineyards stretch from the Santa Ynez Valley in the south to Santa Maria in the north. More than 70 grape varietals grow here, but over half the vineyards are planted with Chardonnay, Pinot Noir, and Syrah. Two-lane Highway 154 over San Marcos Pass is the shortest and most scenic route from Santa Barbara into the Santa Ynez Valley. Alternatively, U.S. 101 travels north 43 miles to Buellton, then 7 miles east through Solvang to Santa Ynez.

San Luis Obispo County. The area's pristine landscapes and abundant wildlife areas, especially those around Morro Bay, have long attracted nature lovers. In the south, coastal towns like Pismo Beach have great sand and surf. An inland wine region stretches from the Edna, Arroyo Grande, and Avila valleys and Nipomo in the south to Paso Robles in the north. A good way to explore the county is to follow the 101-mile California Highway 1 Road Trip route (⊕ *highway1roadtrip. com*), which travels off the beaten track through 10 small communities, from to Oceano/Nipomo, Arroyo Grande, Avila Beach, and Edna Valley in the south to Los Osos/Baywood Park, Cayucos, Cambria, San Simeon, and Ragged Point in the north.

Big Sur Coast. Long a retreat of artists and writers, Big Sur is a place of ancient forests and rugged shores that stretch 90 miles from San Simeon to Carmel. Residents have protected it from over-development, and much of the region lies within state parks and the more than 165,000-acre Ventana Wilderness, itself part of the Los Padres National Forest.

Planning

Getting Here and Around

AIR
Alaska Air, American, Southwest, and United fly to Santa Barbara Airport (SBA), 9 miles from downtown. United, Alaska, and American provide service to San Luis Obispo County Regional Airport (SBP), 3 miles from downtown San Luis Obispo.

Santa Barbara Airbus shuttles travelers between Santa Barbara and Los Angeles for $65 one-way. The Santa Barbara Metropolitan Transit District Bus 11 ($1.75) runs every 30 minutes from the airport to the downtown transit center. A taxi between the airport and the hotel districts costs between $22 and $40.

AIRPORT CONTACTS San Luis Obispo County Regional Airport. (*SBP*) ⊠ *901 Airport Dr., off Hwy. 227, San Luis Obispo* ☎ *805/781–5205* ⊕ *www.sloairport.com.*

Santa Barbara Airbus. ⊠ *Santa Barbara* ☎ *805/964–7759* ⊕ *www.sbairbus.com.*
Santa Barbara Airport. (*SBA*) ⊠ *500 Fowler Rd., off U.S. 101 Exit 104B, Santa Barbara* ☎ *805/967–7111* ⊕ *flysba.santabarbaraca. gov.*

BUS
Greyhound provides service from Los Angeles and San Francisco to San Luis Obispo, Ventura, and Santa Barbara. In addition to serving these three cities, several local transit companies provide regional service, including Gold Coast Transit (Ventura and Ojai); Santa Barbara Metropolitan Transit District (the city and the county's south coast, from Goleta in the west to Carpinteria in the east); Santa Ynez Valley Transit (Santa Ynez, Los Olivos, Ballard, Solvang, and Buellton); and San Luis Obispo Regional Transit Authority (SLORTA; San Luis Obispo, Paso Robles, and Pismo Beach and other coastal towns).

BUS CONTACTS Gold Coast Transit. ⊠ *Ojai* ☎ *805/487–4222* ⊕ *www.gctd.org.* **San Luis Obispo Regional Transit Authority.** ⊠ *San Luis Obispo* ☎ *805/541–2228* ⊕ *www.slorta.org.* **Santa Barbara Metropolitan Transit District.** ⊠ *Santa Barbara* ☎ *805/963–3366* ⊕ *sbmtd.gov.* **Santa Ynez Valley Transit.** ⊠ *Santa Ynez* ☎ *805/688– 5452* ⊕ *www.syvt.com.*

CAR
Driving is the easiest way to experience the Central Coast. The main north–south routes to and through the Central Coast from Los Angeles and San Francisco are U.S. 101, which travels inland, and highly scenic Highway 1, which hugs the coast.

■ **TIP→ A great way to see the region is by following the California Highway 1 Road Trip, a 101-mile designated road trip that takes you off the beaten track through 10 small towns and cities.**

Note that, between Ventura County and northern Santa Barbara County, U.S. 101 and Highway 1 are the same road. Highway 1 separates from U.S. 101 north of Gaviota, rejoining it again at Pismo Beach. Along any stretch where these two highways are separate, U.S. 101 is the quicker route.

The most dramatic section of the Central Coast is the 70 miles between San Simeon and Big Sur. The road is narrow and twisting, with a single lane in each direction. In fog or rain the drive can be downright nerve-racking; in wet seasons mudslides can close portions of the road. Other routes into the Central Coast include Highway 46 and Highway 33, which head, respectively, west and south from I–5 near Bakersfield.

CONTACTS California Highway 1 Road Trip. ⊕ *highway1roadtrip.com.*

TRAIN
The Amtrak *Coast Starlight,* which runs between Los Angeles and Seattle via Oakland, stops in Paso Robles, San Luis Obispo, Santa Barbara, and Oxnard. Amtrak also runs several *Pacific Surfliner* trains and buses daily between San Luis Obispo, Santa Barbara, Los Angeles, and San Diego. Metrolink Regional Rail Service trains connect Ventura and Oxnard with Los Angeles and points between.

TRAIN CONTACTS Metrolink. ☎ *800/371–5465* ⊕ *metrolinktrains.com.*

Hotels

Expect to pay top dollar for rooms along the shore, especially in summer. Moderately priced hotels and motels do exist—most just a short drive inland from their higher-price counterparts. Make your reservations as early as possible, and take advantage of midweek specials to get the best rates. It's common for lodgings to require two-day minimum stays on holidays and some weekends, especially in summer, and to double rates during festivals and other events.

Restaurants

The cuisine in Ventura and Santa Barbara is every bit as eclectic as it is in California's bigger cities; fresh seafood is a standout. A foodie renaissance has overtaken the entire region from Ventura to Paso Robles, spawning dozens of restaurants touting locavore cuisine made with fresh organic produce and meats. Dining attire on the Central Coast is generally casual, though slightly dressy casual wear is the custom at pricier restaurants.

⇨ *Restaurant and hotel reviews have been shortened. For full information, visit Fodors.com. Restaurant prices are the average cost of a main course at dinner, or if dinner is not served, at lunch. Hotel prices are the lowest cost of a standard double room in high season.*

What It Costs			
$	$$	$$$	$$$$
RESTAURANTS			
under $20	$20–$30	$31–$40	over $40
HOTELS			
under $200	$200–$350	$351–$500	over $500

Tours

Many tour companies will pick you up at your hotel or central locations; ask about this when booking.

Central Coast Food Tours
FOOD AND DRINK TOURS | Food and wine destinations are the focus of this outfit's walking tours of shops, restaurants, wineries, and other spots in San Luis Obispo, Paso Robles, and elsewhere. ☎ *844/337–1686* ⊕ *www.centralcoastfoodtours.com* ◺ *From $117.*

Cloud Climbers Jeep and Wine Tours

SPECIAL-INTEREST TOURS | This outfit conducts trips in open-air, six-passenger jeeps to the Santa Barbara/Santa Ynez mountains and Wine Country. Tour options include wine tasting, mountain, sunset, and a discovery adventure for families. The company also offers a four-hour All Around Ojai Tour and arranges horseback riding and trap-shooting tours. ☎ 805/646–3200 ⊕ ccjeeps.com 🖃 From $500 for exclusive jeep tour with driver-guide.

Grapeline Wine Tours

FOOD AND DRINK TOURS | Wine and vineyard picnic tours in Paso Robles and the Santa Ynez Valley are Grapeline's specialty. ☎ 951/693–5755 ⊕ gogrape.com 🖃 From $159.

Santa Barbara Adventure Company

ADVENTURE TOURS | This outfit provides coastal kayak tours, bike tours, and surf and SUP lessons. Sister company Santa Barbara Wine Country Tours shuttles guests on tasting adventures in the Santa Ynez Valley. ✉ 32 E. Haley St., Santa Barbara ☎ 805/884–9283 ⊕ www.sbadventureco.com 🖃 From $55.

Santa Barbara Wine Country Cycling Tours

BICYCLE TOURS | The company leads half- and full-day tours of the Santa Ynez wine region, conducts hiking and cycling tours, and rents bicycles and e-bikes. ☎ 888/557–8687, 805/686–9490 ⊕ www.winecountrycycling.com 🖃 From $180.

Stagecoach Co. Wine Tours

FOOD AND DRINK TOURS | Locally owned and operated, Stagecoach runs daily wine-tasting excursions and group and private tours to smaller boutique wineries through the Santa Ynez Valley in Sprinter vans or a minicoach. ✉ Solvang ☎ 805/686–8347 ⊕ www.winetourssantaynez.com 🖃 From $190.

Sustainable Vine Wine Tours

FOOD AND DRINK TOURS | This green-minded company specializes in eco-friendly Santa Ynez Valley wine tours in luxury vans and Tesla SUVs. Trips include tastings at limited-production wineries committed to sustainable practices. An organic picnic lunch is served. ☎ 805/698–3911 ⊕ www.sustainablewinetours.com 🖃 From $197.

TOAST Tours

FOOD AND DRINK TOURS | Owned and operated by a sommelier couple with extensive guiding experience in Europe, Napa, and Sonoma before relocating to Paso Robles, TOAST leads customized private tours to Central Coast tasting rooms at wineries, distilleries, and breweries, and to Hearst Castle. It also offers a group walking tour of Tin City in Paso Robles, as well as custom packages that include local hotel accommodations. ☎ 805/400–3141 ⊕ toasttours.com 🖃 From $150.

Visitor Information

CONTACTS Central Coast Tourism Council. ⊕ centralcoast-tourism.com. **Santa Barbara Vintners.** ☎ 805/688–0881 ⊕ sbcountywines.com. **SLO Coast Wine.** ☎ 805/550–2506 ⊕ slocoastwine.com. **Visit Santa Barbara.** ☎ 805/966–9222 ⊕ santabarbaraca.com. **Visit the Santa Ynez Valley.** ⊕ www.visitsyv.com. **Visit SLO CAL.** ✉ San Luis Obispo ☎ 805/541–8000 ⊕ www.slocal.com.

When to Go

The Central Coast climate is mild year-round. If you like to swim in warmer (if still nippy) ocean waters, July and August are the best months to visit. Be aware that this is also high season. Fog often rolls in along the coastal areas in early summer; you'll need a jacket, especially after sunset, close to the shore. It usually rains from December through March. From April to early June and early fall the weather is almost as fine as in high season, and the pace is less hectic.

FESTIVALS AND EVENTS

Festival Mozaic. San Luis Obispo's classical music concerts are held intermittently from midsummer to early spring. ⊕ *www.festivalmozaic.com*

I Madonnari. Artists of all ages create 150 large-scale pastel drawings on the pavement near the Old Mission steps during an Italian street-painting festival held Memorial Day weekend. ⊕ *ccp.sbceo. org/i-madonnari/welcome*

Ojai Music Festival. Since 1947, this early/mid-June event draws internationally known progressive and traditional musicians for concerts in Libbey Park. ⊕ *www.ojaifestival.org*

Old Spanish Days Fiesta. Santa Barbara celebrates its Spanish, Mexican, and Chumash heritage in early August with music, dancing, an all-equestrian parade, a carnival, and a rodeo. ⊕ *www.sbfiesta. org*

Paso Robles Wine Festival. Most local wineries pour at this mid-May outdoor festival with winery open houses, winemaker dinners, live bands, and food vendors. ⊕ *pasowine.com*

Santa Barbara International Film Festival. The 10-day festival in February attracts film enthusiasts and major stars to downtown venues for screenings, panels, and tributes. ⊕ *sbiff.org*

Summer Solstice Celebration. More than 100,000 revelers celebrate the arts at this mid-June Santa Barbara event featuring a parade of costumed participants who dance, drum, and ride people-powered floats up State Street. ⊕ *www. solsticeparade.com*

Ventura

60 miles north of Los Angeles.

Ventura Harbor is home to myriad fishing boats, restaurants, and water-activity centers where you can rent boats and take harbor cruises. The city is also very walkable. If you drive here, park your car in one of the city's free 24-hour parking lots, and explore on foot.

The most popular outdoor activities in Ventura are beach-going and whale-watching. California gray whales migrate offshore through the Santa Barbara Channel from late December through March; giant blue and humpback whales feed here from mid-June through September. The channel teems with marine life year-round, so tours, which depart from Ventura Harbor, include more than just whale sightings. The harbor is also home to the Channel Islands National Park visitor center and to Island Packers, which transports visitors to the park's islands.

GETTING HERE AND AROUND

U.S. 101 is the north–south main route into town, but for a scenic drive, take Highway 1 north from Santa Monica. The highway merges with U.S. 101 just south of Ventura. On weekends, traffic is generally fine except southbound on U.S. 101 between Santa Barbara and Ventura on Sunday late afternoon and early evening.

■TIP→ **Traveling north to Ventura from Los Angeles on weekdays, it's best to depart before 6 am, between 10 and 2, or after 7 pm, or you'll get caught in the extended rush-hour traffic. Coming south from Santa Barbara, depart before 1 or after 6 pm.**

ESSENTIALS

VISITOR INFORMATION Ventura Visitors and Convention Bureau. ✉ *Downtown Visitor Center, 101 S. California St., Ventura* ☎ *805/641–1400* 🌐 *visitventuraca.com.*

Sights

Lake Casitas Recreation Area

BODY OF WATER | **FAMILY** | Lunker largemouth bass, rainbow trout, crappie, redears, and channel catfish live in the waters at this park, one of the country's best bass-fishing areas. Nestled below the Santa Ynez Mountains' Laguna Ridge, Lake Casitas is also a beautiful spot for pitching a tent or having a picnic. The Casitas Water Adventure, which has two water playgrounds and a lazy river for tubing and floating, provides kids with endless diversions in summer. ✉ *11311 Santa Ana Rd., off Hwy. 33, 13 miles northwest of Ventura, Ventura* ☎ *805/649–2233, 805/649–1122 campground and water park reservations* 🌐 *www.casitaswater.org/recreation* 🎫 *From $10 per vehicle, $15 per boat; water adventure $23.*

Mission San Buenaventura

HISTORIC SIGHT | **FAMILY** | The ninth of the 21 California missions, Mission San Buenaventura was established in 1782, and the current church was rebuilt and rededicated in 1809. A self-guided tour takes you through a small museum, a quiet courtyard, and a chapel with 250-year-old paintings. ✉ *211 E. Main St., at Figueroa St., Ventura* ☎ *805/648–4496 gift shop* 🌐 *www.sanbuenaventuramission.org* 🎫 *$5.*

Museum of Ventura County

HISTORY MUSEUM | **FAMILY** | Exhibits in a contemporary complex of galleries and a sunny courtyard plaza tell the story of Ventura County from prehistoric times to the present. A highlight is the gallery that contains Ojai artist George Stuart's historical figures, dressed in exceptionally detailed, custom-made clothing reflecting their particular eras. In the courtyard, eight panels made with 45,000 pieces of cut glass form a history time line. ✉ *100 E. Main St., at S. Ventura Ave., Ventura* ☎ *805/653–0323* 🌐 *venturamuseum.org* 🎫 *$5* 🕒 *Closed Mon.–Wed.*

★ Ventura Oceanfront

PROMENADE | **FAMILY** | Four miles of gorgeous coastline stretch from the county fairgrounds at the northern border of the city of San Buenaventura, through San Buenaventura State Beach, down to Ventura Harbor Village in the south. The main attraction here is the San Buenaventura City Pier, a landmark built in 1872 and restored in 1993. Surfers rip the waves just north of the pier, and sunbathers relax on white-sand beaches on either side. The mile-long promenade and the Omer Rains Bike Trail north of the pier attract scores of joggers, surrey cyclers, and bikers throughout the year. ✉ *California St., at ocean's edge, Ventura.*

Restaurants

Andria's Seafood

$$ | **SEAFOOD** | The specialties at this casual, family-oriented restaurant in Ventura Harbor Village are fresh fish-and-chips and homemade clam chowder. After placing your order at the counter, you can sit outside on the patio and enjoy the view of the harbor and marina. **Known for:** harbor views; plates with locally caught grilled fish; wide-ranging menu of salads, burgers, chicken, and sides. [$] *Average main: $24* ✉ *1449 Spinnaker Dr., Suite A, Ventura* ☎ *805/654–0546* 🌐 *andriasseafood.com.*

★ Café Zack

$$$ | **AMERICAN** | A local favorite for anniversaries and other celebrations, Zack's serves classic European dishes in an intimate, two-room 1930s cottage adorned with local art. Entrées of note include seafood specials (depending on the local catch), slow-roasted boar shank, and filet mignon, the latter typically crusted in peppercorns or topped with

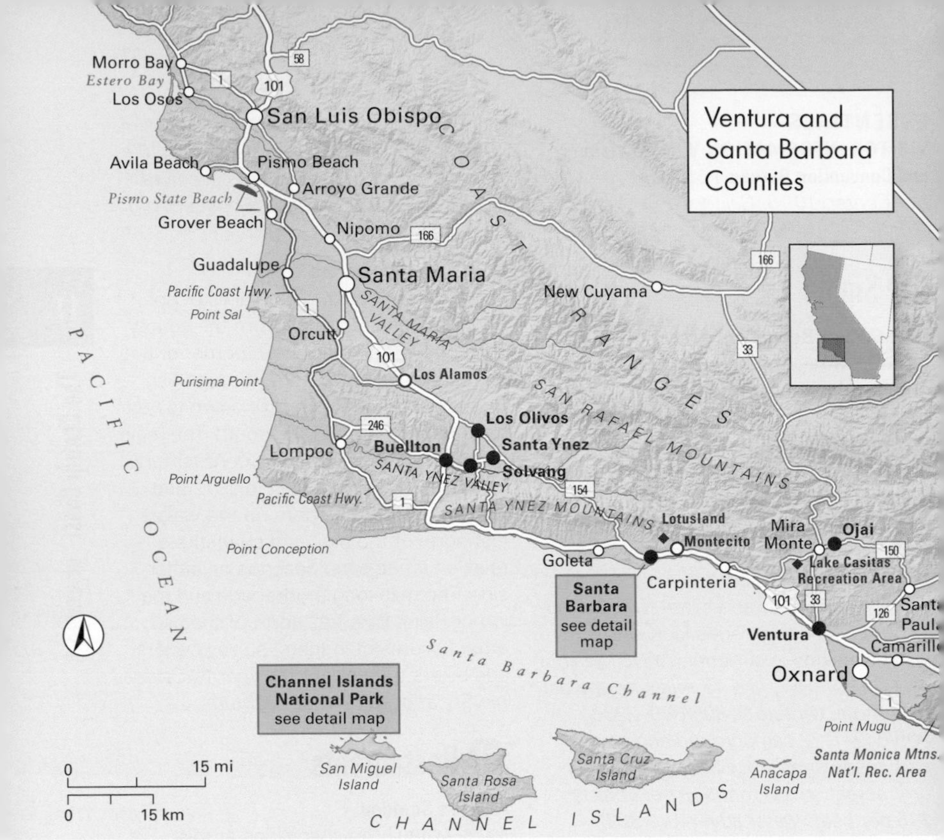

porcini mushrooms. **Known for:** personal service; house-made desserts; excellent California wines. [$] *Average main: $38* ✉ *1095 E. Thompson Blvd., at S. Ann St., Ventura* ☎ *805/643–9445* 🌐 *cafezack.com* 🕓 *Closed Sun. No lunch Sat.*

Harbor Cove Café

$ | CAFÉ | FAMILY | Waterfront views (from beside the Channel Islands National Park Robert J. Lagomarsino Visitor Center), hearty, cooked-to-order meals, and boxed picnic lunches make this casual dockside eatery a popular spot for island travelers and beachgoers. Fill up on a breakfast burrito before boarding the boat; take a boxed deli-sandwich along; and refuel posttrip with a hefty Angus burger, chowder, or fish-and-chips. **Known for:** hearty breakfasts; harbor views; seafood tacos. [$] *Average main: $18* ✉ *1867 Spinnaker Dr., Ventura* ☎ *805/658–1639* 🌐 *harborcovecafe.net* 🕓 *No dinner.*

Lure Fish House

$$ | SEAFOOD | Fresh, sustainably caught seafood charbroiled over a mesquite grill, a well-stocked oyster bar, specialty cocktails, and a wine list heavy on local vintages lure diners into this slick, nautical-theme space downtown. The menu, which emphasizes the use of organic vegetables alongside the local catches, includes tacos, sandwiches, and salads. **Known for:** shrimp-and-chips; cioppino; charbroiled oysters. [$] *Average main: $26* ✉ *60 S. California St., Ventura* ☎ *805/567–4400* 🌐 *www.lurefishhouse.com.*

Rumfish y Vino

$$ | CARIBBEAN | The sibling of a popular namesake restaurant in Placencia, Belize, Rumfish y Vino serves up zesty Caribbean fare with a California Wine Country twist in a courtyard venue just off Main Street near the mission. Eat in the beach-chic dining room or on the heated patio with a roaring fireplace, and perhaps enjoy one of the live music shows offered several nights a week. **Known for:** delectable fish tacos and flatbreads; happy hour and creative cocktails; Caribbean fish stew. [$] *Average main: $26* ✉ *434 N. Palm St., Ventura* ☎ *805/667–9288* 🌐 *rumfishyvino-ventura.com.*

Hotels

Four Points by Sheraton Ventura Harbor Resort
$$ | **RESORT** | An on site restaurant, spacious rooms, and a slew of amenities make this 17-acre property—which includes sister hotel Holiday Inn Express—a popular and practical choice for Channel Islands visitors. **Pros:** close to island transportation; quiet location; short drive to historic downtown. **Cons:** not in the heart of downtown; noisy seagulls sometimes congregate nearby; service can be spotty. [$] *Rooms from: $309* ✉ *1050 Schooner Dr., Ventura* ☎ *805/658–1212, 888/236–2427* 🌐 *four-points.marriott.com* 🛏 *106 rooms* 🍴 *No Meals.*

Holiday Inn Express Ventura Harbor
$$ | **HOTEL** | **FAMILY** | A favorite among Channel Islands visitors, this quiet, comfortable, lodge-inspired property sits right at the Ventura Harbor entrance. **Pros:** quiet at night; easy access to harbor restaurants and activities; five-minute drive to downtown. **Cons:** busy area on weekends; complaints of erratic service; fee for parking. [$] *Rooms from: $239* ✉ *1080 Navigator Dr., Ventura* ☎ *805/856–9533, 888/465–4329* 🌐 *hiexpress.com* 🛏 *109 rooms* 🍴 *Free Breakfast.*

Ventura Beach Marriott
$$ | **HOTEL** | Spacious, contemporary rooms, a peaceful location just steps from San Buenaventura State Beach, and easy access to downtown arts and culture make the Marriott a popular choice. **Pros:** walk to beach, biking/jogging trails, and restaurants; a block from historic pier; great value for location. **Cons:** close to highway; near busy intersection; special event noise some evenings. [$] *Rooms from: $239* ✉ *2055 E. Harbor Blvd., Ventura* ☎ *805/643–6000, 888/236–2427* 🌐 *www.marriott.com* 🛏 *285 rooms* 🍴 *No Meals.*

Waypoint Ventura
$$ | **HOTEL** | **FAMILY** | Stay in a meticulousy restored vintage Airstream or Spartan trailer in a landscaped park on a bluff overlooking Ventura State Beach. **Pros:** a block from Ventura Pier and a short walk to downtown; access to firepits, barbecues, lawn games, and house bikes; walk to craft brewery (sister business). **Cons:** near the train tracks; can be difficult to find; near several ongoing construction sites. [$] *Rooms from: $241* ✉ *398 S. Ash St., Unit E, Ventura* ☎ *805/888–5750* 🌐 *waypointventura.com* 🛏 *19 vintage trailers* 🍴 *No Meals.*

Channel Islands National Park

Via boat, Santa Cruz Island is 32 miles southwest of Ventura Harbor and 28 miles south of Santa Barbara.

On crystal clear days the craggy peaks of the Channel Islands are easy to see from the mainland, jutting from the Pacific in such sharp detail it seems you could reach out and touch them. A high-speed boat will whisk you to the closest ones in less than an hour—yet very few people ever visit them. Those who do will experience one of the most splendid land-and sea wilderness areas on the planet.

Camping is your only lodging choice on the islands, but it's a fantastic way to experience the park's natural beauty and isolation. Campsites are primitive, with no water (except on Santa Rosa and Santa Cruz) or electricity, and they cost

$15 per night. You must arrange your transportation before you reserve your site (☎ 877/444–6777 ⊕ www.recreation.gov) up to six months in advance.

Channel Islands National Park includes five of the eight Channel Islands and the 1 nautical mile of ocean that surrounds them. Six nautical miles of surrounding channel waters are designated a National Marine Sanctuary and are teeming with life, including giant kelp forests, 345 fish species, dolphins, whales, seals, sea lions, and seabirds. To maintain the integrity of their habitats, pets are not allowed in the park.

GETTING HERE AND AROUND

Most visitors access the Channel Islands via an Island Packers boat from Ventura Harbor. To reach the harbor by car, exit U.S. 101 in Ventura at Seaward Boulevard or Victoria Avenue and follow the signs to Ventura Harbor/Spinnaker Drive. An Island Packers boat also heads to Anacapa Island from Oxnard's Channel Islands Harbor, which you can reach from Ventura Harbor by following Harbor Boulevard south about 6 miles and continuing south on Victoria Avenue. Private vehicles are not permitted on the islands.

BOAT TOURS

Channel Islands Expeditions

CRUISE EXCURSIONS | FAMILY | Channel Islands Expeditions runs kayaking, paddleboarding, hiking, snorkeling, and scuba excursions to the National Marine Sanctuary and Channel Islands National Park. Boats depart from Santa Barbara Harbor and Channel Islands Harbor in Oxnard, south of Ventura. ✉ Santa Barbara Harbor, Santa Barbara ☎ 805/899–4925 ⊕ explorechannelislands.com ✍ From $99.

Island Packers

BOAT TOURS | FAMILY | Sailing on high-speed catamarans from Ventura or a monohull vessel from Oxnard, Island Packers goes to Santa Cruz Island daily most of the year, weather permitting. The boats also go to Anacapa several days a week and to the outer islands from April through November. They also cruise along Anacapa's north shore on three-hour wildlife tours (no disembarking) several times a week. Rates start at $44 for whale-watching and wildlife cruises; other types of trips start at $65. ✉ 1691 Spinnaker Dr., Ventura ☎ 805/642–1393 ⊕ islandpackers.com.

PARK ESSENTIALS

The islands are open every day of the year. Channel Islands National Park Robert J. Lagomasino Visitor Center in Ventura is closed on Thanksgiving and Christmas. Channel Islands National Park is in the Pacific time zone.

There are no fees to enter the park, but boat excursions to reach them start at about $44 per person. Also, there is a $15-per-day fee for staying in one of the park's campgrounds.

Cell phone reception is spotty, varying by location and provider. There are public telephones on the mainland near the visitor center, which also has restrooms. The islands themselves have only pit toilets.

VISITOR INFORMATION

Channel Islands National Park Robert J. Lagomarsino Visitor Center

VISITOR CENTER | The park's fully accessible visitor center has a three-story observation tower with telescopes, a bookstore, and a museum. A 24-minute film, Treasure in the Sea, provides an engaging overview of the islands, and, in the marine life exhibit, sea stars cling to rocks, and a brilliant orange Garibaldi darts around. Also on display are full-size reproductions of a male northern elephant seal and the pygmy mammoth skeleton unearthed on Santa Rosa Island in 1994.

On weekends and holidays at 11 am and 3 pm, rangers lead various free public programs describing park resources, and, from Wednesday through Saturday in summer, the center screens live ranger

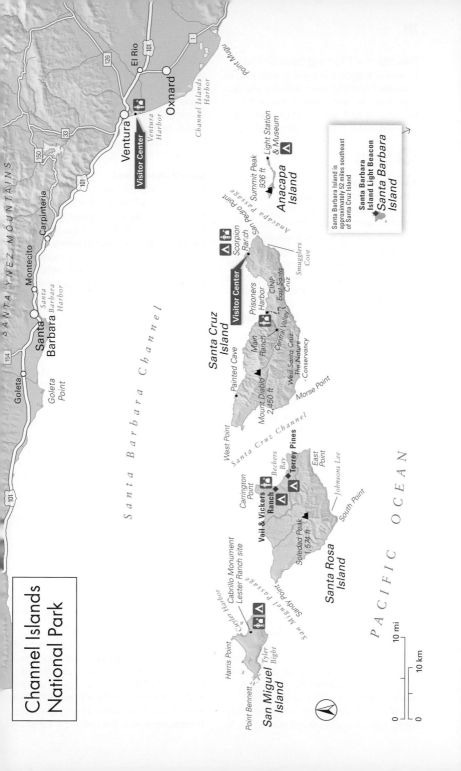

Channel Islands National Park

Santa Ynez Mountains

101
El Rio
126
Ventura
Visitor Center
Ventura Harbor
Oxnard
Channel Islands Harbor
Point Mugu
1

33
150
Montecito
Carpinteria
101
Santa Barbara
Santa Barbara Harbor
154
Goleta
Goleta Point

Santa Barbara Channel

Light Station & Museum
Summit Peak 936 ft
Anacapa Island

Santa Barbara Island is approximately 52 miles southeast of Santa Cruz Island

Santa Barbara Island Light Beacon
Santa Barbara Island

Scorpion Ranch
Visitor Center
Prisoners Harbor
CINP
East Santa Cruz
Smugglers Cove

San Pedro Point
Anacapa Passage

Santa Cruz Island
Main Ranch
Painted Cave
Central Valley
Mount Diablo 2,450 ft
West Santa Cruz: The Nature Conservancy
Morse Point
West Point

Santa Cruz Channel

Carrington Point
Bechers Bay
Torrey Pines
East Point
Vail & Vickers Ranch
Johnsons Lee
Soledad Peak 1,574 ft
South Point
Santa Rosa Island

PACIFIC OCEAN

Harris Point
Cuyler Harbor
Cabrillo Monument
Lester Ranch site
Tyler Bight
Sandy Point
San Miguel Passage
Point Bennett
San Miguel Island

10 mi
10 km

0
0

broadcasts of hikes and dives on Anacapa Island. Webcam images of bald eagles and other land and sea creatures are also shown at the center and on the park's website. ✉ *1901 Spinnaker Dr., Ventura* ☎ *805/658–5730* ⊕ *www.nps.gov/chis.*

◉ Sights

Anacapa Island
ISLAND | FAMILY | Most people think of Anacapa as an island, but it's actually comprised of three narrow islets. Although the tips of these volcanic formations nearly touch, the islets are inaccessible from one another except by boat. All three have towering cliffs, isolated sea caves, and natural bridges; Arch Rock, on East Anacapa, is one of the best-known symbols of Channel Islands National Park.

Wildlife viewing is the main activity on East Anacapa, particularly in summer when seagull chicks are newly hatched and sea lions and seals lounge on the beaches. Exhibits at East Anacapa's compact **museum** include the original lead-crystal Fresnel lens from the 1932 lighthouse.

On West Anacapa, depending on the season and the number of desirable species lurking about here, boats travel to **Frenchy's Cove.** On a voyage here you might see anemones, limpets, barnacles, mussel beds, and colorful marine algae in the pristine tide pools. The rest of West Anacapa is closed to protect nesting brown pelicans. ✉ *Channel Islands National Park.*

San Miguel Island
ISLAND | FAMILY | The westernmost of the Channel Islands, San Miguel Island is frequently battered by storms sweeping across the North Pacific. The 15-square-mile island's wild windswept landscape is lush with vegetation. Point Bennett, at the western tip, offers one of the world's most spectacular wildlife displays when more than 30,000 pinnipeds hit its beach. Explorer Juan Rodríguez Cabrillo was the first European to visit this island; he claimed it for Spain in 1542. Legend holds that Cabrillo died on one of the Channel Islands—no one knows where he's buried, but there's a memorial to him on a bluff above Cuyler Harbor. ✉ *Channel Islands National Park.*

Santa Barbara Island
ISLAND | FAMILY | At about 1 square mile, Santa Barbara Island is the smallest of the Channel Islands and well south of the others. Triangular in shape, Santa Barbara's steep cliffs—which offer a perfect nesting spot for the Scripps's murrelet, a rare seabird—are topped by twin peaks. In spring you can enjoy a brilliant display of yellow coreopsis. Learn about the wildlife on and around the islands at the island's small museum. ✉ *Channel Islands National Park.*

★ Santa Cruz Island
ISLAND | FAMILY | Five miles west of Anacapa, 96-square-mile Santa Cruz Island is the largest of the Channel Islands. The National Park Service manages the easternmost 24% of the island; the rest is owned by the Nature Conservancy, which requires a permit to land. When your boat drops you off on a portion of the 70 miles of craggy coastline, you see two rugged mountain ranges with peaks soaring to 2,500 feet and deep canyons traversed by streams. This landscape is the habitat of a remarkable variety of flora and fauna—more than 600 types of plants, 140 kinds of land birds, 11 mammal species, five varieties of reptiles, and three amphibian species live here. Bird-watchers may want to look for the endemic island scrub jay, which is found nowhere else in the world.

One of the largest and deepest sea caves in the world, **Painted Cave** lies along the northwest coast of Santa Cruz. Named for the colorful lichen and algae that cover its walls, Painted Cave is nearly ¼ mile long and 100 feet wide. In spring a waterfall cascades over the entrance. Kayakers may encounter seals or sea lions cruising alongside their boats inside the cave. The Channel Islands hold some of the richest archaeological resources in North America; all artifacts are protected within the park. Remnants of a dozen Chumash villages can be seen on the island. The largest of these villages, at the eastern end, occupied the area now called **Scorpion Ranch.** The Chumash mined extensive chert deposits on the island for tools to produce shell-bead money, which they traded with people on the mainland. You can learn about Chumash history and view artifacts, tools, and exhibits on native plant and wildlife at the interpretive visitor center near the landing dock. Visitors can also explore remnants of the early-1900s ranching era in the restored historic adobe and outbuildings. ✉ *Channel Islands National Park.*

Santa Rosa Island

ISLAND | FAMILY | Between Santa Cruz and San Miguel, Santa Rosa is the second largest of the Channel Islands. The terrain along the coast varies from broad, sandy beaches to sheer cliffs—a central mountain range, rising to 1,589 feet, breaks the island's relatively low profile. Santa Rosa is home to about 500 species of plants, including the rare Torrey pine, and three unusual mammals, the island fox, the spotted skunk, and the deer mouse. They hardly compare, though, to their predecessors: a nearly complete skeleton of a 6-foot-tall pygmy mammoth was unearthed in 1994.

From 1901 to 1998, cattle were raised at the island's **Vail & Vickers Ranch.** The route from Santa Rosa's landing dock to the campground passes by the historic ranch buildings, barns, equipment, and the wooden pier where cattle were brought onto the island. ✉ *Channel Islands National Park.*

⚡ Activities

Channel Islands Adventure Company leads guided sea cave kayak and snorkel tours at Scorpion Anchorage in the national park. Snorkel equipment is also available for rent on the island. Various concessionaires at Ventura Harbor Village (☎ *805/477–0470* ⊕ *www.venturaharborvillage.com*) arrange diving, paddling, kayaking, and other Channel Islands excursions out of Ventura. Island Packers provides public transportation to the islands and conducts whale-watching and wildlife cruises.

DIVING

Some of the best snorkeling and diving in the world can be found in the cool waters surrounding the Channel Islands. In the relatively warm water around Anacapa and eastern Santa Cruz, photographers can get great shots of rarely seen giant black bass swimming among the kelp forests. Here you also find a reef covered with red brittle starfish. If you're an experienced diver, you might swim among five species of seals and sea lions, or try your hand at spearing rockfish or halibut near San Miguel and Santa Rosa. The best time to scuba dive is in summer and fall, when the water is often clear up to a 100-foot depth.

KAYAKING

The most remote parts of the Channel Islands are accessible only by a sea kayak. Some of the best kayaking in the park can be found on Anacapa, Santa Barbara, and the eastern tip of Santa Cruz. It's too far to kayak from the mainland out to the islands, but outfitters have tours that take you to the islands. Tours are offered year-round, but high seas may cause trip cancellations between December and March. ⚠ **Channel waters can be unpredictable and challenging. Guided trips are highly recommended.**

WHALE-WATCHING

About a third of the world's cetacean species (27 to be exact) can be seen in the Santa Barbara Channel. In July and August, humpback and blue whales feed off the north shore of Santa Rosa. From late December through March, up to 10,000 gray whales pass through the Santa Barbara Channel on their way from Alaska to Mexico and back again; if you go on a whale-watching trip during this time frame you're likely to spot one or more of them. Other types of whales, but fewer in number, swim the channel from June through August.

Ojai

15 miles northeast of Ventura.

The Ojai Valley, which director Frank Capra used as a backdrop for his 1936 film *Lost Horizon,* sizzles in the summer when temperatures routinely reach 90°F. The acres of orange and avocado groves here evoke postcard images of long-ago agricultural Southern California. Many artists and celebrities have sought refuge from life in the fast lane in lush Ojai.

GETTING HERE AND AROUND

From northern Ventura, Highway 33 veers east from U.S. 101 and climbs inland to Ojai. From Santa Barbara, exit U.S. 101 at Highway 150 in Carpinteria, then travel east 20 miles on a twisting, two-lane road that is not recommended at night or during poor weather. You can also access Ojai by heading west from I–5 on Highway 126. Exit at Santa Paula and follow Highway 150 north for 16 miles to Ojai.

Ojai can be easily explored on foot; you can also hop on the Ojai Trolley ($1.50, or $4 day pass), which, until about 5 pm, follows two routes around Ojai and neighboring Miramonte on weekdays and one route on weekends.

ESSENTIALS

BUS CONTACTS Ojai Trolley. ⊠ *Ojai* ☎ *805/646–5581* ⊕ *ojaitrolley.com.*

VISITOR INFORMATION Ojai Visitors Bureau. ⊠ *Ojai* ⊕ *www.ojaivisitors.com.*

◉ Sights

Ojai Art Center

ARTS CENTER | California's oldest nonprofit, multipurpose arts center exhibits visual art from various disciplines and presents theater, dance, and other performances. ⊠ *113 S. Montgomery St., near E. Ojai Ave., Ojai* ☎ *805/646–0117* ⊕ *www. ojaiartcenter.org* ⊗ *Closed Mon.*

Ojai Avenue

STREET | **FAMILY** | The work of local artists is displayed in the Spanish-style shopping arcade along the avenue downtown. On Sunday between 9 and 1, organic and specialty growers sell their produce at the outdoor market behind the arcade. ⊠ *Ojai Ave., Ojai.*

Ojai Valley Museum

HISTORY MUSEUM | **FAMILY** | The museum collects, preserves, and presents exhibits about the art, history, and culture of Ojai and Ojai Valley. Walking tours of Ojai depart from here. ⊠ *130 W. Ojai Ave., Ojai* ☎ *805/640–1390* ⊕ *www.ojaivalley-museum.org* ⊠ *Museum $5, walking tours from $7* ⊗ *Closed Mon.–Thurs.*

Ojai Valley Trail

TRAIL | **FAMILY** | The 18-mile trail is open to pedestrians, joggers, equestrians, bikers, and others on nonmotorized vehicles. You can access it anywhere along its route. ⊠ *Ojai* ✛ *Parallel to Hwy. 33 from Soule Park in Ojai to ocean in Ventura.*

🍴 Restaurants

The Dutchess

$$ | **BURMESE** | A bakery, shop, and café by day, this lively locals hub, run by longtime friends, morphs into a Burmese-Californian restaurant and bar by night. Menu items range from croissants, flatbreads, sandwiches, and salads to tandoori chicken or seafood dishes, and most ingredients used to make them come from eco-minded purveyors within 50 miles (some from a co-owner's family farm). **Known for:** live music Thursday night, happy hour specials weeknights; spicy Burmese rice bowls; nearly everything made in-house. $ *Average main: $28* ⊠ *457 E. Ojai Ave, Ojai* ☏ *805/640–7987* ⊕ *www.thedutchessojai.com* ⊘ *Closed Tues.*

Farmer and the Cook

$ | **AMERICAN** | **FAMILY** | An organic farmer and his chef-wife run this funky café/bakery/market in Meiners Oaks, just a few miles west of downtown Ojai. Order a wood-fired pizza, bento box, sandwich, or a daily special, and then grab a table indoors or out on the patio. **Known for:** many veggie, vegan, and gluten-free options; grab-and-go meals; Mexican-focused menu. $ *Average main: $16* ⊠ *339 W. El Roblar, Ojai* ☏ *805/640–9608* ⊕ *www.farmer-and-the-cook.com.*

★ Nocciola

$$$ | **ITALIAN** | Authentic northern Italian dishes with a California twist, a cozy fireplace dining room in a century-old Craftsman-style house, and a covered patio amid the oaks draw locals and visitors alike to this popular eatery, owned by an Italian chef and his American wife (the family lives upstairs). The menu changes seasonally, but regular stars include seared sea scallops with Parmesan fondue and truffle shavings, homemade pastas made with organic egg yolks, and *tagliatelle* with grass-fed Wagyu beef. **Known for:** great wild fish and game; Moment Pink signature cocktail; six-course tasting menu. $ *Average main: $40* ⊠ *314 El Paseo Rd., Ojai* ☏ *805/640–1648* ⊕ *www.nocciolaojai.com* ⊘ *Closed Wed. No lunch.*

🛏 Hotels

The Iguana Inns of Ojai

$$ | **B&B/INN** | Artists own and operate these two bohemian-chic inns—the Blue Iguana, a cozy Southwestern-style hotel about 2 miles west of downtown, and the Emerald Iguana, which has art nouveau rooms, suites, and cottages in a secluded residential setting near downtown. **Pros:** colorful art everywhere; secluded; pet-friendly (Blue Iguana). **Cons:** 2 miles from downtown; on a highway; no children under 14 (or pets) at Emerald Iguana. $ *Rooms from: $209* ⊠ *11794 N. Ventura Ave., Ojai* ☏ *805/646–5277* ⊕ *www.iguanainnsofojai.com* ⇗ *20 units* ⊙ *Free Breakfast.*

Ojai Rancho Inn

$$ | **HOTEL** | A collection of one-story buildings and cottages tucked between Ojai Avenue and the bike trail, this ranch-style motel attracts hipsters and those who appreciate a rustic getaway with modern comforts and a laid-back vintage vibe. **Pros:** free loaner cruiser bikes; small on-site bar; nice pool area with lounge chairs. **Cons:** not fancy or luxurious; rooms could use soundproofing; some road noise in rooms close to the road. $ *Rooms from: $250* ⊠ *615 W. Ojai Ave., Ojai* ☏ *805/646–1434* ⊕ *www.ojairancho-inn.com* ⇗ *17 rooms* ⊙ *No Meals.*

★ Ojai Valley Inn & Spa

$$$ | **RESORT** | This outdoorsy, golf-oriented resort and spa is set on 220 beautifully landscaped, oak-studded acres, with hillside views in nearly all directions. **Pros:** championship golf course, separate family and adult pools, exceptional outdoor activities; spa with 24 treatment rooms and two pools; multiple restaurants serving regional cuisine. **Cons:** high room rates for the region; areas near restaurants can be noisy; not an easy walk to downtown Ojai. $ *Rooms from: $500* ⊠ *905 Country Club Rd., Ojai* ☏ *855/697–8780* ⊕ *www.ojaivalleyinn.com* ⇗ *303 rooms* ⊙ *No Meals.*

Su Nido Inn

$$ | **B&B/INN** | This posh, Mission Revival–style inn sits in a quiet neighborhood a few blocks from Libbey Park and a short walk from downtown. **Pros:** walking distance from sights and restaurants; homey feel; soaking tubs and private patios or balconies in some rooms. **Cons:** no pool (and can get hot in summer); too quiet for some; two-night minimum stay on weekends. $ *Rooms from: $249* ✉ *301 N. Montgomery St., Ojai* ☎ *805/754–3513, 866/646–7080* ⊕ *suni-doinn.com* ⇌ *12 rooms* ⦾ *No Meals.*

Santa Barbara

27 miles northwest of Ventura and 29 miles west of Ojai.

Santa Barbara has long been an oasis for Los Angelenos seeking respite from big-city life. The attractions begin at the ocean and end in the foothills of the Santa Ynez Mountains. The waterfront here is beautiful, with palm-studded promenades and plenty of sand.

In the few miles between the beaches and the hills are downtown, Mission Santa Barbara, and the Santa Barbara Botanic Garden. For spectacular views of the city and the Santa Barbara Channel, drive along Alameda Padre Serra, a hillside road that begins near the mission and continues to Montecito.

GETTING HERE AND AROUND

U.S. 101 is the main route into Santa Barbara. If you're staying in town, a car is handy but not essential; the beaches and downtown are easily explored by bicycle or on foot. Visit the Santa Barbara Car Free website for bike-route and walking-tour maps, suggestions for car-free vacations, and transportation discounts.

CONTACTS Santa Barbara Car Free. ⊕ *santabarbaracarfree.org.*

TOURS

Land and Sea Tours

SPECIAL-INTEREST TOURS | This outfit conducts 90-minute narrated tours in an amphibious 49-passenger vehicle nicknamed the Land Shark. The adventure begins with a drive through the city, followed by a plunge into the harbor for a cruise along the coast. ✉ *10 E. Cabrillo Blvd., at Stearns Wharf, Santa Barbara* ☎ *805/683–7600* ⊕ *out2seesb.com* ⦿ *From $45.*

Santa Barbara Trolley Company

SPECIAL-INTEREST TOURS | Loop past major hotels, shopping areas, and attractions on a 90-minute tour ($28) aboard a motorized, San Francisco–style cable car. The company sometimes offers a hop-on-hop-off option, but days when this option is offered vary, so check ahead. ☎ *805/965–0353* ⊕ *www.sbtrolley.com* ⦿ *$28.*

Segway Tours of Santa Barbara

SPECIAL-INTEREST TOURS | After a brief training session, a guide leads you around town on electric-powered personal balancing transporters. Tour options for ages 12-plus include the waterfront (one hour) and Butterfly Beach (two hours), and self-guided rentals (you can also rent a Polaris Slingshot) to cruise around at your own pace. ✉ *122 Gray Ave., at E. Mason St., Santa Barbara* ☎ *805/963–7672* ⊕ *segwayofsb.com* ⦿ *From $65.*

ESSENTIALS

VISITOR INFORMATION Garden Street Visitor Center. ✉ *1 Garden St., at Cabrillo Blvd., Santa Barbara* ☎ *805/965–3021* ⊕ *santabarbaraca.com/plan-your-trip/know-before-you-go/visitors-center.* **State Street Visitor Center.** ✉ *120 State St., Santa Barbara* ☎ *805/869–2632* ⊕ *santabarbaraca.com/plan-your-trip/know-before-you-go/visitors-center.*

⊙ Sights

Andrée Clark Bird Refuge

WILDLIFE REFUGE | FAMILY | This peaceful lagoon and its gardens sit north of East Beach. Bike trails and footpaths, punctuated by signs identifying native and migratory birds, skirt the lagoon. ⊠ *1400 E. Cabrillo Blvd., near zoo, Santa Barbara* 🖾 *Free.*

Bellosguardo

HISTORIC HOME | In 1923, copper king and Montana senator William Andrews Clark bought the 24-acre Bellosguardo (Beautiful Lookout) estate on a bluff between East Beach and Butterfly Beach. After his death, his widow, Anna, built her own summer residence there, designed by famed architect Reginald Johnson and completed in 1937. When she died in 1963, the property passed on to daughter Huguette. (The Clarks' other daughter, Andrée, died as a teenager, and the family donated funds to create the adjacent Andrée Clark Bird Refuge in her honor.)

Although Huguette, a recluse in New York who died in 2011 at age 104, hadn't visited Bellosguardo in more than 50 years, she kept it maintained as if she and her family would walk through the door at any moment. Huguette willed the estate to a foundation so that it could become an arts and culture center, and today, Bellosguardo is slowly opening to the public.

For now, access is only via 90-minute, docent-led tours, conducted several times a day, of the garden and the ground floor of the main house. Of particular note are the carved wood panels in several of the rooms and the European art and antiques that once adorned the Clark luxury town house in New York. To book tours, which sell out quickly, click on the "Become a Supporter" option of the website, and subscribe to the mailing list for the latest information on ticket releases. ⊠ *1407 E. Cabrillo Blvd., Santa Barbara* 🕿 *805/969–3220* ⊕ *www. bellosguardo.org* 🖾 *Tours $100.*

Carriage and Western Art Museum

HISTORY MUSEUM | FAMILY | The country's largest collection of old horse-drawn vehicles—painstakingly restored—is exhibited here, with everything from polished hearses to police buggies to old stagecoaches and circus vehicles. In August, the Old Spanish Days Fiesta borrows many of the vehicles for a jaunt around town. Docents lead free tours from 1 to 4 pm the third Sunday of the month. ⊠ *Pershing Park, 129 Castillo St., Santa Barbara* 🕿 *805/962–2353* ⊕ *carriagemuseum.org* 🖾 *Free* ◷ *Closed weekends (except for tours on 3rd Sun. of month).*

El Presidio State Historic Park

MILITARY SIGHT | FAMILY | Founded in 1782, El Presidio was one of four military strongholds established by the Spanish along the coast of California. The park encompasses much of the original site in the heart of downtown. El Cuartel, the adobe guardhouse, is the oldest building in Santa Barbara and the second oldest in California. ⊠ *123 E. Canon Perdido St., at Anacapa St., Santa Barbara* 🕿 *805/965–0093* ⊕ *www.sbthp.org* 🖾 *$5.*

Funk Zone

NEIGHBORHOOD | FAMILY | A formerly run-down industrial neighborhood near the waterfront and train station, the Funk Zone has evolved into a hip hangout filled with wine-tasting rooms, arts-and-crafts studios, murals, breweries, distilleries, restaurants, and small shops. It's fun to poke around the three-square-block district. ■**TIP➜ Street parking is limited, so leave your car in a nearby city lot and cruise up and down the alleys on foot.** ⊠ *Santa Barbara* ✛ *Between State and Garden Sts. and Cabrillo Blvd. and U.S. 101* ⊕ *www.funkzone.net.*

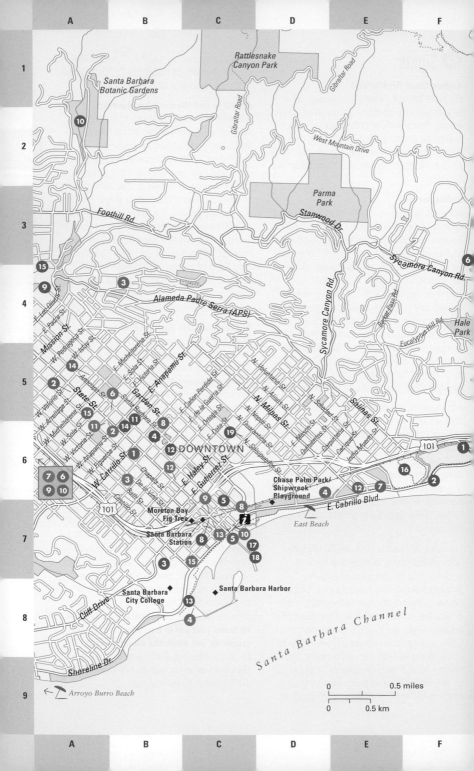

11

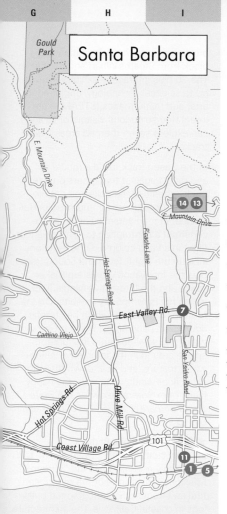

Santa Barbara

KEY

1 *Exploring Sights*
1 *Restaurants*
1 *Hotels*
i *Tourist information*

★ Lotusland

GARDEN | FAMILY | The 37-acre estate—
with gardens that are often ranked
among the world's 10 best—once
belonged to the Polish opera singer Gan-
na Walska, who purchased it in 1941 and
lived here until her death in 1984. Many
of the exotic trees and other subtropical
flora were planted in 1882 by horticultur-
ist R. Kinton Stevens. On the docent-led
or self-guided tour—the only options for
visiting unless you're a member (reserve
well ahead as spots fill fast)—you'll see
an outdoor theater, a topiary garden,
a lotus pond, and a huge collection of
rare cycads, an unusual plant genus
that has been around since the time
of the dinosaurs. ⊠ *695 Ashley Rd.,
off Sycamore Canyon Rd. (Hwy. 192),
Montecito* ✛ *Visitor entrance gate is on
Cold Spring Rd., at Sycamore Canyon Rd.*
☎ *805/969–9990* ⊕ *www.lotusland.org*
🖃 *$50* ⊗ *Closed mid-Nov.–mid-Feb. No
tours Sun.–Tues., except every 3rd Sun.
of month.*

Montecito

TOWN | FAMILY | Since the late 1800s,
the tree-studded hills and valleys of this
town have attracted the rich and famous:
Hollywood icons, business tycoons, tech
moguls, and old-money families. Shady
roads wind through the community,
which consists mostly of gated estates.
Swank boutiques line Coast Village Road,
where well-heeled residents such as
Oprah Winfrey, Katy Perry, and Prince
Harry and Meghan Markle find peaceful
refuge from the paparazzi. Residents
also hang out in the Upper Village, a chic
shopping area with restaurants and cafés
at the intersection of San Ysidro and East
Valley roads. ⊠ *Montecito.*

★ MOXI–The Wolf Museum of Exploration and Innovation

SCIENCE MUSEUM | FAMILY | It took more
than two decades of unrelenting community advocacy to develop this exceptional
science hub, which opened in early 2017
in a three-story, Spanish-Mediterranean
building next to the train station and a
block from Stearns Wharf and the beach.
The 70-plus interactive exhibits—devoted to science, technology, engineering,
arts, and mathematics (STEAM)—are
integrated so curious visitors of all ages
can explore seven themed areas (called
tracks).

In the Speed Track, build a model car
and race it against two others on a test
track—then use the collected data to
reconfigure your car for improved performance. In the Fantastic Forces space,
construct a contraption to send on a test
flight in a wind column. Other sections
include the Light, Tech, and Sound Tracks,
plus the Innovation Workshop maker
space and the Interactive Media Track,
which hosts temporary exhibits. On the
rooftop Sky Garden, which has terrific
downtown panoramas, make music with
wind- and solar-powered instruments,
splash around in the interactive White-
water feature, and peer down through
glass floor windows to view the happy
faces of explorers below. ⊠ *125 State St.,
Santa Barbara* ☎ *805/770–5000* ⊕ *moxi.
org* 🖃 *$18.*

★ Old Mission Santa Barbara

HISTORIC SIGHT | FAMILY | Dating from 1786
and widely referred to as the "Queen of
Missions," this is one of the most beautiful and frequently photographed buildings in coastal California. The architecture
evolved from adobe-brick buildings with
thatch roofs to more permanent edifices
as the mission's population burgeoned.
An 1812 earthquake destroyed the third
church built on the site. Its replacement,
the present structure, is still a functioning Catholic church. Old Mission
Santa Barbara has a splendid Spanish/
Mexican colonial art collection, as well as
Chumash sculptures and the only Native
American–made altar and tabernacle left
in the California missions. ⊠ *2201 Laguna
St., at E. Los Olivos St., Santa Barbara*
☎ *805/682–4149 gift shop, 805/682–4713*

tours ⊕ *www.santabarbaramission.org* ⊠ *From $15 self-guided tour.*

Santa Barbara Botanic Garden

GARDEN | FAMILY | Five miles of scenic trails meander through the garden's 78 acres of native plants. The Mission Dam, built in 1806, stands just beyond the redwood grove and above the restored aqueduct that once carried water to the Old Mission Santa Barbara. More than a thousand plant species thrive in various themed sections, including mountains, deserts, meadows, redwoods, and Channel Islands. ■TIP➔ **A conservation center dedicated to rare and endangered plant species presents rotating exhibitions.** ⊠ *1212 Mission Canyon Rd., north of Foothill Rd. (Hwy. 192), Santa Barbara* 🕾 *805/682–4726* ⊕ *www.sbbg.org* ⊠ *$20* ♿ *Reservations required.*

★ Santa Barbara County Courthouse

GOVERNMENT BUILDING | FAMILY | Hand-painted tiles and a spiral staircase infuse the courthouse, a national historic landmark, with the grandeur of a Moorish palace. This magnificent building was completed in 1929. An elevator rises to an arched observation area in the tower that provides a panoramic view of the city. Before or after you take in the view, you can (if it's open) visit an engaging gallery devoted to the workings of the tower's original, still operational Seth Thomas clock. The murals in the second-floor ceremonial chambers were painted by an artist who did backdrops for some of Cecil B. DeMille's films. Take a self-guided tour, or join a free one-hour docent-led tour, daily at 2 pm and weekdays at 10:30 am. ⊠ *1100 Anacapa St., at E. Anapamu St., Santa Barbara* 🕾 *805/962–6464* ⊕ *sbcourthouse.org.*

Santa Barbara Historical Museum

HISTORY MUSEUM | FAMILY | The historical society's museum exhibits decorative and fine arts, furniture, costumes, and documents from the town's past. Adjacent to it is the Gledhill Library, a collection of books, photographs, maps, and manuscripts. Tours are by appointment only. ⊠ *136 E. De La Guerra St., at Santa Barbara St., Santa Barbara* 🕾 *805/966–1601* ⊕ *www.sbhistorical.org* ⊠ *Free* ⊗ *Closed Mon. and Tues.*

Santa Barbara Maritime Museum

HISTORY MUSEUM | FAMILY | California's seafaring history is the focus here. High-tech, hands-on exhibits, such as a virtual sportfishing activity that lets participants haul in a "big one" and a local surfing history retrospective, make this a fun stop for families. In 2018, the museum introduced a fascinating History of Oil in the Santa Barbara Channel exhibit that traces the Chumash Indians' use of natural seeps to the infamous 1969 oil spill that spawned the modern environmental movement. The museum's shining star is a rare, 17-foot-tall Fresnel lens from the historic Point Conception Lighthouse. Ride the elevator to the fourth-floor observation area for great harbor views. ⊠ *113 Harbor Way, off Shoreline Dr., Santa Barbara* 🕾 *805/962–8404* ⊕ *sbmm.org* ⊠ *$10* ⊗ *Closed Wed.*

Santa Barbara Museum of Art

ART MUSEUM | The highlights of this museum's permanent collection include ancient sculpture, Asian art, impressionist paintings, contemporary art, photography, and American works in several mediums. ⊠ *1130 State St., at E. Anapamu St., Santa Barbara* 🕾 *805/963–4364* ⊕ *www.sbma.net* ⊠ *$10, free Thurs. 5–8* ⊗ *Closed Mon.*

Santa Barbara Museum of Natural History

SCIENCE MUSEUM | FAMILY | A gigantic blue whale skeleton greets you at the entrance to this 17-acre complex, whose major draws include its planetarium, paleo and marine life exhibits, and gem and mineral displays. Startlingly alive-looking stuffed specimens in the Mammal and Bird Halls include a smiling grizzly bear and nesting California condors. A room of dioramas illustrates Native American Chumash history and culture while a Santa Barbara Gallery showcases the region's unique biodiversity. Outdoors, nature trails wind through the serene oak woodlands, a Chumash plant garden, and a summer butterfly pavilion. ⊠ *2559 Puesta del Sol Rd., off Mission Canyon Rd., Santa Barbara* ☎ *805/682–4711* ⊕ *www.sbnature.org* 🖃 *$19* ⊗ *Closed Tues.*

Santa Barbara Zoo

ZOO | FAMILY | This compact zoo's gorgeous grounds shelter elephants, gorillas, Australian wildlife, exotic birds, and big cats, and has many exhibits that educate visitors on conservation efforts to save endangered species like the California condor and the red-legged frog. For small children, there's a scenic railroad and barnyard area where they can feed domestic sheep. Kids especially love feeding the giraffes from a view deck overlooking the beach. One-hour walking tours that focus on conservation and animal care are offered weekends at 11:45 and 3:15. ■**TIP**➔ **The palm-studded lawns on a hilltop overlooking the beach are perfect spots for family picnics.** ⊠ *500 Niños Dr., off El Cabrillo Blvd., Santa Barbara* ☎ *805/962–5339 main line, 805/962–6310 info line* ⊕ *www.sbzoo.org* 🖃 *Zoo $25, parking $11* ⚠ *Reservations required.*

Sea Center

SCIENCE MUSEUM | FAMILY | A branch of the Santa Barbara Museum of Natural History, the center specializes in Santa Barbara Channel marine life and conservation. Though small compared to aquariums in Monterey and Long Beach, this is a fascinating, hands-on marine science laboratory that lets you participate in experiments, projects, and exhibits, including touch pools. The two-story glass walls here open to stunning ocean, mountain, and city views. ⊠ *211 Stearns Wharf, Santa Barbara* ☎ *805/962–2526* ⊕ *www.sbnature.org* 🖃 *$14.*

Stearns Wharf

MARINA/PIER | FAMILY | Built in 1872, Stearns Wharf is Santa Barbara's most visited landmark. Expansive views of the mountains, cityscape, and harbor unfold from every vantage point on the three-block-long pier. Although it's a nice walk from the Cabrillo Boulevard parking areas, you can also park on the pier and then wander through the shops or stop for a meal at one of the wharf's restaurants. ⊠ *Cabrillo Blvd. and State St., Santa Barbara* ⊕ *stearnswharf.org.*

Urban Wine Trail

TRAIL | More than 30 winery tasting rooms in five neighborhoods form the Urban Wine Trail. Most are within walking distance of the waterfront and the lower State Street shopping and restaurant district. Santa Barbara Winery (⊠ *28 Anacapa St.*), The Valley Project (⊠ *116 E. Yanonali St.*), and Grassini Family Vineyards (⊠ *24 El Paseo*) are good places to start your oenological trek. ⊠ *Santa Barbara* ⊕ *urbanwinetrailsb.com.*

🏖 Beaches

★ Arroyo Burro Beach

BEACH | FAMILY | The beach's usually gentle surf makes it ideal for families with young children. It's a local favorite because you can walk for miles in both directions when tides are low. Leashed dogs are allowed on the main stretch of beach and westward; they are allowed to romp off-leash east of the slough at the beach entrance. The parking lots fill early on weekends and throughout the summer, but the park is relatively quiet at other times. Walk along the beach just a few hundreds yards away from the main steps at the entrance to escape crowds on warm-weather days. Surfers, swimmers, stand-up paddlers, and boogie boarders regularly ply the waves, and photographers come often to catch the vivid sunsets. **Amenities:** food and drink;

Be sure to visit Santa Barbara's beautiful—and usually uncrowded—beaches.

lifeguard (in summer); parking; showers; toilets. **Best for:** sunset; surfing; swimming; walking. ✉ *Cliff Dr. and Las Positas Rd., Santa Barbara* 🌐 *www.countyofsb.org/810/Arroyo-Burro-Beach.*

★ East Beach

BEACH | **FAMILY** | The wide swath of sand at the east end of Cabrillo Boulevard is a great spot for people-watching. East Beach has sand volleyball courts, summertime lifeguard and sports competitions, and arts-and-crafts shows on Sunday and holidays, plus Saturday on holiday weekends. You can use showers, a weight room, and lockers (bring your own towel) and rent umbrellas and boogie boards at the Cabrillo Bathhouse. Next door, there's an elaborate jungle-gym play area for kids. Hotels line the boulevard across from the beach. **Amenities:** food and drink; lifeguards (in summer); parking (fee); showers; toilets; water sports. **Best for:** surfing; swimming; walking. ✉ *1118 Cabrillo Blvd., at Ninos Dr., Santa Barbara* ☎ *805/897–2680.*

🍴 Restaurants

★ AMA Sushi

$$$$ | **JAPANESE** | Named for the Japanese women free divers who collected seafood for their villages, AMA (tucked in a courtyard at the Rosewood Miramar Resort) offers two fine-dining experiences—omakase at the 13-seat sushi bar (a two-hour feast—you must arrive promptly or risk missing a course or two) or prix-fixe (three or four courses total). You can combine meals with sake pairings for an additional fee; alternatively, the Japanese-inspired cocktails are especially popular. **Known for:** Japanese-style interiors with furnishings that honor the AMA heritage; outdoor dining in the lush, lantern-lit patio garden by the koi pond; extensive sake list. [$] *Average main: $145* ✉ *1759 S. Jameson La., Montecito* ☎ *805/900–8388* 🌐 *www.rosewoodhotels.com/en/miramar-beach-montecito/dining/ama-sushi* 🕒 *Closed Mon. No lunch.*

Arigato Sushi

$$ | **JAPANESE** | Locals flock to this two-story restaurant and sushi bar—famed for its wildly creative combination rolls and other delectables. Fans of authentic Japanese food sometimes disagree about the quality of the seafood, but all dishes are fresh and artfully presented. **Known for:** innovative creations; lively atmosphere; patio and second-floor balcony seating. $ *Average main: $30* ✉ *1225 State St., near W. Victoria St., Santa Barbara* ☎ *805/965–6074* ⊕ *www.arigatosb.com* ⊘ *No lunch.*

Barbareño

$$$ | **MODERN AMERICAN** | Determined to push the boundaries of farm-to-table, Barbareño combines Santa Barbara and Central Coast history and traditions with fresh local ingredients to create inventive dishes, for example, uni caesar salad, acorn tagliatelle, local black cod in a pinquito miso sauce with wild onion and blackberries, and crispy Brussels sprouts in a sauce infused with Bragg vinegar and Ojai honey. It churns its own butter; bakes its own breads; makes condiments from scratch; and forages mushrooms, eucalyptus leaves, and other ingredients from the wild. **Known for:** youthful, sophisticated vibe; extensive wine list focused on local, natural wines; seasonal menu. $ *Average main: $35* ✉ *205 W. Canon Perdido St., at De La Vina St., Santa Barbara* ☎ *805/963–9591* ⊕ *www.barbareno.com* ⊘ *Closed Tues. No lunch.*

Brophy Bros

$$ | **SEAFOOD** | **FAMILY** | The outdoor tables at this casual harborside restaurant have perfect views of the marina and mountains. Staffers serve enormous, exceptionally fresh fish dishes, and if you walk in without a reservation, which are very limited, they will text you when your table's ready so you can stroll along the breakwater and explore the harbor while you wait. **Known for:** seafood salad and chowder; stellar clam bar; waitlist for walk-ins. $ *Average main: $30* ✉ *119 Harbor Way, off Shoreline Dr., Santa Barbara* ☎ *805/966–4418* ⊕ *www.brophybros.com.*

★ Caruso's

$$$$ | **ITALIAN** | A special-occasion destination and treat for multiple senses, Caruso's combines exceptional views (perched on the sand at Rosewood Miramar Beach resort), sophisticated design (the ocean-inspired decor is as high-end as Santa Barbara gets), and romantic ambience (soft lighting, soft music) with Michelin-starred, Italian-California coastal cuisine. Options include three- and four-course prix-fixe menus (there's a vegan one, too) and a chef's tasting menu, which you can augment with wine pairings for an additional fee. **Known for:** inventive handcrafted cocktails; Michelin star and Green Star in 2022, James Beard Foundation Smart-Catch designation in 2023; deck dining at one of the region's only restaurants on the beach. $ *Average main: $145* ✉ *1759 S. Jameson La., Montecito* ☎ *805/900–8388* ⊕ *www.rosewoodhotels.com/en/miramar-beach-montecito/dining/carusos* ⊘ *No lunch.*

Corazón Comedor

$ | **MEXICAN** | **FAMILY** | Born from the hankerings for food from the owner's childhood haunts—the streets, markets, home–in Guadalajara, Mexico, this casual eatery (order from the counter) in the Arts District serves authentic south-of-the-border soul food, much of it derived from longtime family recipes and made with fresh local ingredients. Feast on everything from huevos rancheros, chilaquiles, and churro French toast for breakfast to tacos, tamales, enchiladas, and pozole for lunch and dinner. **Known for:** excellent service; house-made salsas; specialty ice creams and other desserts. $ *Average main: $19* ✉ *29 E. Victoria St., Santa Barbara* ☎ *805/679–5397* ⊕ *corazoncomedor.com* ⊘ *Closed Mon.*

Jeannine's

$ | **AMERICAN** | **FAMILY** | Take a break from waterfront and State Street explorations at Jeannine's, revered locally for its wholesome sandwiches, salads, and baked goods, made from scratch with organic and natural ingredients. Dine in the expansive dining room or on the patio, or pick up a turkey cranberry or chicken pesto sandwich to go and picnic on the beach or nearby Chase Palm Park. Jeannine's also has outlets in Montecito, Uptown, and Goleta. **Known for:** fantastic pastries; hearty, healthful breakfasts; turkey roasted or smoked in-house. $ *Average main: $16* ⊠ *1 State St., at Cabrillo Blvd., Santa Barbara* ☎ *805/770–3344* ⊕ *jeannines.com* ☾ *No dinner.*

★ The Lark

$$$ | **AMERICAN** | Shared dining—small plates and larger—and a seasonal menu showcasing local ingredients are the focus at this urban-chic restaurant named for an overnight all-Pullman train that chugged into the nearby railroad station for six decades. Sit at the 24-seat communal table set atop vintage radiators or at tables and booths crafted from antique Spanish church pews and other repurposed or recycled materials. **Known for:** social environment; wines curated by a master sommelier; handcrafted locavore cocktails. $ *Average main: $35* ⊠ *131 Anacapa St., at E. Yanonali St., Santa Barbara* ☎ *805/284–0370* ⊕ *www.thelarksb.com* ☾ *No lunch.*

Loquita

$$$ | **SPANISH** | In a cozy space on a prime corner at the gateway to the Funk Zone near Stearns Wharf, Loquita honors Santa Barbara's heritage by serving up authentic Spanish dishes, wines, and cocktails made with fresh, sustainably sourced local ingredients. The menu covers all bases, from tapas to wood-fired seafood and grilled meats to Spanish wines, vermouth, gin and tonics, and sangria. **Known for:** multiple types of paella; counter and takeaway items; great gin and tonic. $ *Average main: $34* ⊠ *202 State St., Santa Barbara* ☎ *805/880–3380* ⊕ *www.loquitasb.com.*

Oku

$$ | **ASIAN** | Locals and visitors alike flock to this sleek, Asian-inspired restaurant across from Stearns Wharf and East Beach (reserve a second-story table for killer views). The eclectic menu focuses mostly on small plates of classic dishes meant for sharing—sushi, sashimi, yakisoba, ramen soup with pork belly, black-garlic filet mignon—but it also has creative surprises like the halibut-crab-avocado "lollipop" or the lobster-tempura-Wagyu beef roll. **Known for:** two cocktail bars and a sushi bar; crispy Korean cauliflower with yuzu-shiso aioli, kalbi-style short ribs; craft cocktails, extensive wine and sake list. $ *Average main: $30* ⊠ *29 E. Cabrillo Blvd., Santa Barbara* ☎ *805/690–1650* ⊕ *www.okurestaurant.com.*

Olio e Limone

$$$ | **ITALIAN** | **FAMILY** | Sophisticated Italian cuisine with an emphasis on Sicily is served at this restaurant near the Arlington. The veal scaloppine is popular, but surprises abound here, with unusual dishes such as the duck ravioli or the ribbon pasta with quail and sausage in a mushroom ragout. **Known for:** prix-fixe menus; cozy white-tablecloth dining room; adjacent casual breakfast/lunch space and pizzeria. $ *Average main: $32* ⊠ *17 W. Victoria St., at State St., Santa Barbara* ☎ *805/899–2699* ⊕ *www.olioelimone.com* ☾ *No lunch Sun.*

Palace Grill

$$$ | **AMERICAN** | Mardi Gras energy, team-style service, lively music, and great Cajun, creole, and Caribbean food have made the Palace a Santa Barbara icon. Be prepared to wait for a table on Friday and Saturday night, though the live entertainment and free appetizers, sent out front when the line is long, will whet your appetite for the feast to come. **Known for:** blackened fish and meats;

Louisiana bread pudding soufflé; Cajun martini served in a mason jar. $ *Average main: $36* ⊠ *8 E. Cota St., at State St., Santa Barbara* ☎ *805/963–5000* ⊕ *palace-grill.com.*

Santo Mezcal

$$ | **MODERN MEXICAN** | Authentic flavors of coastal Mexico and fresh local ingredients make for packed indoor and outdoor tables at this eatery a block from the train station. For breakfast, fill up on huevos rancheros or chilaquiles; for lunch or dinner feast on seafood ceviches, grilled chicken breast with authentic mole poblano, or Mexican shrimp in a creamy mezcal sauce. **Known for:** weekday happy hour; fresh crab enchiladas and quesadillas, grilled rib-eye tacos; good selection of tequila, mezcal, cocktails. $ *Average main: $28* ⊠ *119 State St., Santa Barbara* ☎ *805/883–3593* ⊕ *santomezcalsb.com.*

★ The Stonehouse

$$$$ | **AMERICAN** | The elegant Stonehouse—consistently lauded as one of the nation's top restaurants—is inside a century-old granite former farmhouse at the San Ysidro Ranch resort. The menu changes constantly but might include pan-seared abalone or classic steak Diane flambéed table-side, and the Plow & Angel pub downstairs serves casual bistro fare. **Known for:** ingredients from on-site garden; heated ocean-view deck with fireplace; elegant dining room. $ *Average main: $63* ⊠ *900 San Ysidro La., off San Ysidro Rd., Montecito* ☎ *805/565–1720* ⊕ *www.sanysidroranch.com.*

★ Toma

$$$ | **ITALIAN** | Seasonal, locally sourced ingredients and softly lit muted-yellow walls evoke the flavors and charms of Tuscany and the Mediterranean at this rustic-romantic restaurant across from the harbor and West Beach. Ahi sashimi tucked in a crisp sesame cone is a popular appetizer, after which you can proceed, perhaps, to rock-shrimp gnocchi. **Known for:** house-made pastas and gnocchi; wines from Italy and California's Central Coast; romantic waterfront setting. $ *Average main: $34* ⊠ *324 W. Cabrillo Blvd., near Castillo St., Santa Barbara* ☎ *805/962–0777* ⊕ *www.tomarestaurant.com* ☽ *No lunch.*

🛏 Hotels

Canary Hotel

$$$$ | **HOTEL** | A full-service hotel in the heart of downtown, this Kimpton property blends a casual, beach-getaway feel with contemporary California style. **Pros:** upscale local cuisine at on-site Finch & Fork restaurant; evening wine hour; adjacent fitness center. **Cons:** across from transit center; a mile from the beach; valet parking only. $ *Rooms from: $515* ⊠ *31 W. Carrillo St., Santa Barbara* ☎ *805/884–0300, 800/546–7866* ⊕ *www.canarysantabarbara.com* ⤴ *97 rooms* ⫪ *No Meals.*

Courtyard by Marriott Santa Barbara Downtown

$$ | **HOTEL** | This sparkling Spanish Colonial Revival–style hotel in the heart of the Arts District, formerly a classic 1959 motor inn, opened in fall 2022 as a sophisticated refuge with spacious, seaside-theme rooms, hip Euro-contemporary interior spaces, and a stellar Mediterranean-centric restaurant, St. Rémy, open all day and evening. **Pros:** walk to public market, art museum, theaters; courtyard with a pool and hot tub; roof deck with city and ocean views. **Cons:** not in city's busy nightlife district; fee for parking; no pets allowed. $ *Rooms from: $279* ⊠ *1601 State St., Santa Barbara* ☎ *800/321–2211 reservations, 805/975–0660* ⊕ *www.marriott.com* ⤴ *62 rooms* ⫪ *Free Breakfast.*

★ El Encanto, a Belmond Hotel

$$$$ | **HOTEL** | Built in 1915 and following more than $100 million of extensive renovations a century later, this Santa Barbara icon lives on to thrill a new generation of guests with its relaxed-luxe bungalow rooms, lush gardens, and personalized service. **Pros:** dining terrace with panoramic city and ocean views; stellar spa; infinity pool with ocean views. **Cons:** long walk to downtown; pricey; guests staying for more than a few days may find the restaurant menus limited. $ *Rooms from: $1,060* ✉ *800 Alvarado Pl., Santa Barbara* ☎ *805/845–5800, 800/393–5315* ⊕ *www.belmond.com* ⤶ *92 rooms* ⫿⨀⫿ *No Meals.*

Hilton Santa Barbara Beachfront Resort

$$$ | **RESORT** | A full-scale resort with seven buildings spread over 24 landscaped acres across from East Beach, this hotel was founded by the late TV actor Fess Parker, best known for playing Davy Crockett and Daniel Boone. **Pros:** numerous amenities; right across from the beach; free shuttle to train station and airport. **Cons:** train noise filters into some rooms; too spread out for some; pricey. $ *Rooms from: $475* ✉ *633 E. Cabrillo Blvd., Santa Barbara* ☎ *800/879–2929, 805/564–4333* ⊕ *www.hilton.com* ⤶ *360 rooms* ⫿⨀⫿ *No Meals.*

★ Hotel Californian

$$$$ | **HOTEL** | A sprawling collection of Spanish-Moorish buildings that opened in 2017 at the site of the historic 1925 Hotel Californian, this sophisticated property with a hip youthful vibe occupies nearly three full blocks just steps from Stearns Wharf and the harbor. **Pros:** steps from the waterfront, Funk Zone, MOXI, and beaches; resort-style amenities; on-site parking. **Cons:** area gets crowded in summer and holiday weekends; must walk or bike to downtown attractions; train whistle noise in rooms close to station. $ *Rooms from: $747* ✉ *36 State St., Santa Barbara* ☎ *805/882–0100* ⊕ *www.hotelcalifornian.com* ⤶ *121 rooms* ⫿⨀⫿ *No Meals.*

The Leta Santa Barbara Goleta

$$ | **HOTEL** | A vintage Woody car, a silver Airstream trailer, and a lobby record shop are among the elements that bring 1960s California surf culture to life at this cool, casual Tapestry Collection by Hilton hotel in Goleta. **Pros:** free wine-and-beer social hour and s'mores by the fireside; live music or DJs several evenings a week; rate includes gym pass. **Cons:** not close to downtown; some rooms on the small side; thin walls allow for noise transfer from neighboring rooms. $ *Rooms from: $243* ✉ *5650 Calle Real, Goleta* ☎ *844/382–7378 reservations, 805/964–6241* ⊕ *www.hilton.com* ⤶ *158 rooms* ⫿⨀⫿ *No Meals.*

Mar Monte Hotel

$$$ | **HOTEL** | A complex of five buildings on 3 landscaped acres across from East Beach, the Mar Monte, part of the Hyatt family of properties, is an appealing lodging option, where the historic main building (circa 1931) reflects old Santa Barbara—Spanish tiles, wrought-iron chandeliers, and vintage black-and-white photos. **Pros:** steps from the beach; many room types and rates; restaurant, pool, bar/café. **Cons:** not in the heart of downtown; busy area in summer; no on-site self-parking, only valet service (fee). $ *Rooms from: $340* ✉ *1111 E. Cabrillo Blvd., Santa Barbara* ☎ *805/882–1234, 800/643–1994* ⊕ *www.hyatt.com* ⤶ *174 rooms* ⫿⨀⫿ *No Meals.*

Palihouse Santa Barbara

$$$$ | **HOTEL** | A half-block from the Presidio in the heart of downtown, this secluded retreat celebrates Santa Barbara style and design, from the Spanish-Mediterranean exterior with wrought-iron balconies to the interior's Palisociety signature hipster interpretation of local character (e.g., bright colors throughout, a custom playlist that sets an upbeat mood, a bowl of bright yellow tennis balls in the lobby lounge). **Pros:** walk to downtown; indoor parking beneath the hotel; spacious rooms. **Cons:** resort fee (includes parking); not on the waterfront; might be too small and serene for some. $ *Rooms from: $585* ✉ *915 Garden St., Santa Barbara* ☎ *805/564–4700* ⊕ *www.palisociety.com/hotels/santa-barbara* ⤶ *24 rooms* ⫿⨀⫿ *No Meals.*

Ramada by Wyndham Santa Barbara

$$ | **MOTEL** | **FAMILY** | While not a fancy place, this hidden oasis has many perks that merit a stay, including a convenient location between the airport/UCSB and downtown; lush gardens around a lagoon with ducks, turtles, and koi; a solar-heated outdoor pool and hot tub; a fitness center; free parking and Wi-Fi; and relatively affordable rates for the region. **Pros:** excellent customer service; free airport shuttle; EV charging stations. **Cons:** can be noisy in pool area; motel vibe; basic breakfast. $ *Rooms from: $219* ✉ *4770 Calle Real, Santa Barbara* ☎ *805/319–4314, 800/854–9517 reservations* ⊕ *www.wyndhamhotels.com/ramada* ⤴ *126 rooms* ❯❮ *Free Breakfast.*

★ The Ritz-Carlton Bacara, Santa Barbara

$$$$ | **RESORT** | A luxury resort with four restaurants and a 42,000-square-foot spa and fitness center with 36 treatment rooms, the Ritz-Carlton Bacara provides a gorgeous setting for relaxing retreats. **Pros:** many diversions including hiking and stargazing; three zero-edge pools; three golf courses nearby. **Cons:** resort and parking fees extra; not close to downtown; sand on beach not pristine enough for some. $ *Rooms from: $1029* ✉ *8301 Hollister Ave., Goleta* ☎ *805/968–0100* ⊕ *www.ritzcarlton.com* ⤴ *358 rooms* ❯❮ *Free Breakfast.*

★ Rosewood Miramar Beach

$$$$ | **RESORT** | Sprawling across 16 lush acres on one of the area's most scenic and exclusive beaches, this luxury resort was built from scratch on the site of the former Miramar by the Sea hotel, where generations of fashionable SoCal residents vacationed for decades. **Pros:** two cabana-lined pools; six restaurants and bars; steps to the beach. **Cons:** too expensive for some; next to a busy freeway and train tracks; popular weekend wedding site with lively partiers. $ *Rooms from: $1,650* ✉ *1759 S. Jameson La., Montecito*

☎ *805/900–8388* ⊕ *www.rosewoodhotels.com* ⤴ *160 rooms* ❯❮ *No Meals.*

★ Santa Barbara Inn

$$$ | **HOTEL** | This full-service, family-owned, Spanish-Mediterranean hotel occupies a prime waterfront corner across from East Beach. **Pros:** many rooms have ocean views; suites come with whirlpool tubs; delicious on-site restaurant Convivo. **Cons:** on a busy boulevard; limited street parking; not within easy walking distance of downtown. $ *Rooms from: $475* ✉ *901 E. Cabrillo Blvd., Santa Barbara* ⊕ *At Milpas St.* ☎ *800/231–0431, 805/966–2285* ⊕ *www.santabarbarainn.com* ⤴ *70 rooms* ❯❮ *No Meals.*

★ San Ysidro Ranch

$$$$ | **RESORT** | At this romantic hideaway on a historic property in the Montecito foothills—where John and Jackie Kennedy spent their honeymoon and Oprah sends her out-of-town visitors—guest cottages are scattered among groves of orange trees and flower beds. **Pros:** rooms have private outdoor spas; 17 miles of hiking trails nearby; home to iconic Plow & Angel Bistro and Stonehouse restaurant. **Cons:** ultra-expensive; too remote for some; noise from bridal parties travels to some suites. $ *Rooms from: $2,745* ✉ *900 San Ysidro La., Montecito* ☎ *805/565–1760, 800/368–6788* ⊕ *www.sanysidroranch.com* ⤴ *38 units* ❯❮ *All-Inclusive* ✆ *2-day minimum stay on weekends, 3 days on holiday weekends.*

★ Simpson House Inn

$$$ | **B&B/INN** | If you're a fan of traditional bed-and-breakfast inns, this property, with its beautifully appointed Victorian main house and acre of lush gardens, is for you. **Pros:** elegant furnishings; impeccable landscaping; within walking distance of downtown. **Cons:** some rooms in main building are small; two-night minimum stay on weekends May–October; no pets allowed. $ *Rooms from: $409* ✉ *121 E. Arrellaga St., Santa*

Barbara ☎ 805/963–7067 🌐 *www.simpsonhouseinn.com* 🛏 *15 rooms* 🍴 *Free Breakfast.*

The Upham

$$ | B&B/INN | Built in 1871, this downtown Victorian has been restored as a full-service hotel, with several one- and two-story buildings containing rooms that vary in size from small to spacious. **Pros:** 1-acre garden; easy walk to theaters; excellent restaurant. **Cons:** some rooms are small; not near beach or waterfront; no in-room safes. $ *Rooms from: $315* ✉ *1404 De la Vina St., Santa Barbara* ☎ *805/962–0058* 🌐 *uphamhotel.com* 🛏 *50 rooms* 🍴 *No Meals* ☞ *2-night minimum stay on weekends.*

Nightlife

The bar, club, and live music scene centers on lower State Street, between the 300 and 800 blocks.

Draughtsmen Aleworks

BREWPUBS | A low-key taproom with board and card games for entertainment, Draughtsmen pours its own craft beer, wine, cider, and hop tea. At the main taproom in Goleta, you can view the brewing facilities and sometimes take a tour. ✉ *1131 State St., in Mosaic Locale, Santa Barbara* ☎ *805/259–4356* 🌐 *www.draughtsmenaleworks.com.*

The Good Lion

BARS | The cocktail menu at this intimate neighborhood bar near The Granada Theatre changes seasonally, depending on what's available at the local produce markets. All juices are organic and squeezed fresh daily, and all syrups are made in-house with organic produce and sweeteners. ✉ *1212 State St., Santa Barbara* ☎ *805/845–8754* 🌐 *www.goodlioncocktails.com.*

M. Special Brewing Company

BREWPUBS | A favorite stop on the local beer trail, this lively taproom has more than a dozen craft beers and live music on weekends. A second taproom (and the main brewery) is in Goleta, near UCSB. ✉ *634 State St., Santa Barbara* ☎ *805/968–6500* 🌐 *www.mspecialbrewco.com.*

Milk & Honey

COCKTAIL LOUNGES | Artfully prepared tapas, mango mojitos, and exotic cocktails lure trendy crowds to swank M&H, despite high prices and a reputation for inattentive service. ✉ *30 W. Anapamu St., at State St., Santa Barbara* ☎ *805/275–4232* 🌐 *milknhoneytapas.com* 🕓 *Closed Sun.*

SOhO

LIVE MUSIC | A lively restaurant, bar, and music venue, SOhO books all kinds of musical acts, from jazz to blues to rock. ✉ *1221 State St., at W. Victoria St., Santa Barbara* ☎ *805/962–7776* 🌐 *www.sohosb.com.*

Performing Arts

The Arts District, with theaters, restaurants, and cafés, starts around the 900 block of State and continues north to the 1300 block. To see what's scheduled around town, pick up the free weekly *Santa Barbara Independent* newspaper, or visit its website (🌐 *www.independent.com*).

Arlington Theatre

ARTS CENTERS | This Moorish-style auditorium presents touring performers and films throughout the year. ✉ *1317 State St., at Arlington Ave., Santa Barbara* ☎ *805/963–4408* 🌐 *thearlingtontheatre.com.*

Center Stage Theatre

ARTS CENTERS | This venue hosts plays, music, dance, and readings. ✉ *Paseo Nuevo Center, Chapala and De la Guerra Sts., 2nd fl., Santa Barbara* ☎ *805/963–0408* 🌐 *centerstagetheater.org.*

Ensemble Theatre Company (ETC)

THEATER | The company stages classic and contemporary comedies, musicals, and dramas. ⊠ *33 W. Victoria St., at Chapala St., Santa Barbara* ☎ *805/965–5400* ⊕ *etcsb.org.*

The Granada Theatre

THEATER | A restored, modernized landmark that dates from 1924, the Granada hosts Broadway touring shows and dance, music, and other cultural events. ⊠ *1214 State St., at E. Anapamu St., Santa Barbara* ☎ *805/899–2222* ⊕ *www. granadasb.org.*

Lobero Theatre

THEATER | A state landmark, the Lobero hosts community theater groups and touring professionals. ⊠ *33 E. Canon Perdido St., at Anacapa St., Santa Barbara* ☎ *805/963–0761* ⊕ *www.lobero.org.*

🛍 Shopping

BOOKS

Book Den

BOOKS | Bibliophiles have browsed for new, used, and out-of-print books at this independent shop since 1933. ⊠ *15 E. Anapamu St., at State St., Santa Barbara* ☎ *805/962–3321* ⊕ *www.bookden.com.*

Chaucer's Bookstore

BOOKS | This well-stocked independent shop is a favorite of many locals. ⊠ *Loreto Plaza, 3321 State St., at Los Positas Rd., Santa Barbara* ☎ *805/682–6787* ⊕ *www.chaucersbooks.com.*

CLOTHING

DIANI

WOMEN'S CLOTHING | This upscale, European-style women's boutique dresses clients in designer clothing from around the world. Sibling shoe and home-and-garden shops are nearby. ⊠ *1324 State St., at Arlington Ave., Santa Barbara* ☎ *805/966–3114, 805/966–7175 shoe shop* ⊕ *www.dianiboutique.com.*

Wendy Foster

WOMEN'S CLOTHING | This store sells casual-chic women's fashions at its flagship store downtown and four other outlets around the county. ⊠ *1220 State St., at E. Victoria St., Santa Barbara* ☎ *805/966–2276* ⊕ *www.wendyfoster. com.*

FOOD AND WINE

Santa Barbara Public Market

WINE/SPIRITS | A dozen food and beverage vendors occupy this spacious arts district galleria. Stock up on gourmet goodies; sip on handcrafted wines and beers while watching sports events; and nosh on noodle bowls, sushi, artisanal ice cream, and savory street tacos. ⊠ *38 W. Victoria St., at Chapala St., Santa Barbara* ☎ *805/770–7702* ⊕ *www.sbpublicmarket. com.*

SHOPPING AREAS

★ El Paseo

NEIGHBORHOODS | Wine-tasting rooms, shops, art galleries, and studios share the courtyard and gardens of this historic arcade. ⊠ *Canon Perdido St., between State and Anacapa Sts., Santa Barbara.*

★ State Street

NEIGHBORHOODS | Between Cabrillo Boulevard and Sola Street, State Street is a shopper's paradise. Chic malls, quirky storefronts, antiques emporia, elegant boutiques, and funky thrift shops abound. Numerous community activities take place at **Paseo Nuevo,** an open-air mall in the 700 block. Shops, restaurants, galleries, and fountains line the tiled walkways of **La Arcada,** a small complex of landscaped courtyards in the 1100 block designed by architect Myron Hunt in 1926.

Summerland

NEIGHBORHOODS | Serious antiques hunters head southeast of Santa Barbara to Summerland, which is full of shops and markets. Several good ones are along Lillie Avenue and Ortega Hill Road. ⊠ *Summerland.*

SHOES
SeaVees

SHOES | FAMILY | Santa Barbara–based SeaVees makes and sells casual, comfortable, '60s-style California sneakers that have a classy, dressed-up flair. ✉ *24 E. Mason St., Santa Barbara* ☎ *805/456–9798* ⊕ *www.seavees.com* ⊗ *Closed Tues.*

SPORTING GOODS
Channel Islands Surfboards

SPORTING GOODS | Come here for top-of-the-line surfboards and the latest in California beachwear, sandals, and accessories. ✉ *36 Anacapa St., at E. Mason St., Santa Barbara* ☎ *805/966–7213* ⊕ *cisurfboards.com.*

Surf N Wear's Beach House

SPORTING GOODS | This shop carries surf clothing, gear, and collectibles; it's also the home of Santa Barbara Surf Shop and the exclusive local dealer of Surfboards by Yater. ✉ *10 State St., at Cabrillo Blvd., Santa Barbara* ☎ *805/963–1281* ⊕ *surfnwearbeachhouse.com.*

🏃 Activities

BIKING
Cabrillo Bike Path

BIKING | FAMILY | The level, two-lane, 3-mile Cabrillo Bike Path passes the Santa Barbara Zoo, the Andree Clark Bird Refuge, beaches, and the harbor. Stop for a meal at one of the restaurants along the way, or for a picnic along the palm-lined path looking out on the Pacific.

Mad Dogs & Englishmen

BIKING | FAMILY | Tucked in a storefront near Butterfly Beach, Andree Clark Bird Refuge, and miles of bike lanes, Mad Dogs & Englishmen rents and sells premium e-bikes and custom sidecars (great for kids and pets). It also provides self-guided, private, and guided cycling tours in Santa Barbara and at sister shops in downtown Carmel, Monterey, and Mill Valley. ✉ *1080 Coast Village Rd.,*
Santa Barbara ☎ *805/837–0033* ⊕ *www.maddogsandenglishmen.com.*

Wheel Fun Rentals

BIKING | FAMILY | You can rent bikes (electric, cruiser, and regular), quadricycles, electric vehicles, and skates here. ✉ *24 E. Mason St., Santa Barbara* ☎ *805/966–2282* ⊕ *wheelfunrentalssb.com.*

BOATS AND CHARTERS
Celebration Cruises

WILDLIFE-WATCHING | FAMILY | Board the *Azure Seas,* a luxury 70-foot multilevel yacht, for seasonal whale-watching, coastal, sunset, or happy-hour cruises. ✉ *237 Stearns Wharf, Santa Barbara* ☎ *805/465–6676* ⊕ *celebrationsantabarbara.com* 🚲 *From $30.*

★ Condor Express

BOATING | FAMILY | From Santa Barbara Landing, the *Condor Express,* a 75-foot, high-speed catamaran, whisks up to 149 passengers toward the Channel Islands on whale-watching excursions and sunset or dinner cruises. ✉ *301 W. Cabrillo Blvd., Santa Barbara* ☎ *805/882–0088, 888/779–4253* ⊕ *www.condorexpress.com* 🚲 *From $125.*

Paddle Sports Center

KAYAKING | FAMILY | This full-service center in the harbor guides kayak tours in and around the harbor and rents kayaks, stand-up paddleboards, surfboards, boogie boards, and water-sports gear. ✉ *117 B Harbor Way, off Shoreline Dr., Santa Barbara* ☎ *805/617–3425 rentals* ⊕ *www.paddlesportsca.com* 🚲 *Tours from $69, rentals from $25.*

Santa Barbara Landing

FISHING | This outfit operates surface and deep-sea fishing charters year-round. ✉ *Cabrillo Blvd., at Bath St., and breakwater in Santa Barbara Harbor, Santa Barbara* ☎ *805/963–3564* ⊕ *www.sealanding.net.*

Santa Barbara Sailing Center

BOATING | FAMILY | The center offers sailing instruction, rents and charters sailboats, kayaks, and stand-up paddleboards, and organizes dinner and sunset champagne cruises, island excursions, and whale-watching trips. ⊠ *Santa Barbara Harbor launching ramp, Santa Barbara* ☎ *805/962–2826* ⊕ *sbsail.com* ⊠ *Cruises from $65.*

Santa Barbara Water Taxi

BOATING | FAMILY | Children beg to ride *Lil' Toot,* a cheery yellow water taxi that cruises from the harbor to Stearns Wharf and back again. ⊠ *237 Stearns Wharf, Santa Barbara* ☎ *805/465–6676* ⊕ *celebrationsantabarbara.com/lil-toot-water-taxi* ⊠ *$5 per kid, $10 per adult one-way* ⊙ *Runs daily June–Aug., weekends only rest of year.*

GOLF
Sandpiper Golf Club

GOLF | This public course sits on the ocean bluffs and combines superscenic views with a challenging game. ⊠ *7925 Hollister Ave., Santa Barbara* ✛ *14 miles north of downtown off U.S. 101* ☎ *805/968–1541* ⊕ *www.sandpipergolf.com* ⊠ *$160 Mon.–Thurs., $195 Fri.–Sun. and holidays* ⅄ *18 holes, 7000 yards, par 72.*

Santa Barbara Golf Club

GOLF | The well-maintained public club—among the area's most affordable—occupies a hilltop site with sweeping views of mountains, ocean, and islands. ⊠ *3500 McCaw Ave., at Las Positas Rd., Santa Barbara* ☎ *805/687–7087* ⊕ *www.playsantabarbara.com* ⊠ *Nonresidents $51 weekdays, $61 weekends* ⅄ *18 holes, 6037 yards, par 70.*

Santa Ynez

31 miles northeast of Santa Barbara.

Founded in 1882, the tiny town of Santa Ynez still has many of its original frontier buildings. You can walk through its three-block downtown in a few minutes, shop for antiques, and hang around the old-time saloon. At some of the Santa Ynez

Valley's best restaurants, you just might bump into one of the celebrities who own nearby ranches.

GETTING HERE AND AROUND
Take Highway 154 over San Marcos Pass or U.S. 101 north 43 miles to Buellton, then drive 7 miles east.

◉ Sights
Gainey Vineyard

WINERY | The 1,800-acre Gainey Ranch, straddling the banks of the Santa Ynez River, includes about 100 acres of organic vineyards: Sauvignon Blanc, Merlot, Cabernet Sauvignon, and Cabernet Franc. The winery also makes wines from Chardonnay, Pinot Noir, and Syrah grapes from the Santa Rita Hills. You can taste the latest releases—the estate Pinot Noir is especially good—in a Spanish-style hacienda overlooking the ranch. Gainey's Evans Ranch tasting room in Los Olivos showcases their six limited-production wines from the Sta. Rita Hills AVA. ⊠ *3950 E. Hwy. 246, Santa Ynez* ☎ *805/688–0558* ⊕ *gaineyvineyard.com* ⊠ *Tastings from $25.*

★ Santa Ynez Chumash Museum and Cultural Center

INDIGENOUS SIGHT | FAMILY | This stunning 14,000-square-foot facility and 3½-acre cultural park, completed in 2023, has a welcome center; heritage exhibits; an amphitheater; and spaces devoted to the indigenous Samala language, storytelling, basket weaving, and other cultural activities. Landscaping includes 11,000 California native plants, including 140 species used by the Chumash in their daily lives. ⊠ *3500 Numancia St., Santa Ynez* ⊕ *chumash.gov/museum.*

🍴 Restaurants
Ellie's Tap+Vine

$$ | AMERICAN | Chef-owner Joy Reinhart opened this locals-favorite restaurant to honor her deceased mom, Ellie, a colorful, full-of-life character who enjoyed life to the max. The intimate, clublike dining room and deck invite socialization, and the seasonal, farm-to-fork menu is filled with Ellie's favorites, including liver pâté, crab cake atop creamy, sweet-potato-to-bacon-spinach hash, and slow-cooked beef short ribs. **Known for:** extensive local and international wine list; partnerships with local purveyors; Tuesday Asian food night with '80s music, daily happy hour. $ *Average main: $28* ⊠ *3640 Sagunto St., Santa Ynez* ☎ *916/390–3595* ⊕ *elliestapandvine.com* ⊘ *Closed Sun.*

S.Y. Kitchen

$$ | **ITALIAN** | The owners of Toscana, a popular eatery in L.A.'s Brentwood neighborhood, run this rustic-chic restaurant with an Italy-meets-California-Wine-Country vibe. Chef and co-owner Luca Crestanelli, a native of Verona, Italy, typically offers multiple seasonal daily specials. **Known for:** wood-fired pizzas and oak-grilled entrées; creative craft cocktails; gelatos and "not-so-classic" tiramisu. $ *Average main: $30* ⊠ *1110 Faraday St., at Sagunto St., Santa Ynez* ☎ *805/691–9794* ⊕ *www.sykitchen.com.*

🛏 Hotels

ForFriends Inn & Village

$$ | **B&B/INN** | This luxury, family-owned B&B—designed as a casual place where friends can gather to enjoy good wine, food, and music—has rooms and suites in the main building or cottages, as well as a "village: of six studio-layout bungalows with private porches and parking. **Pros:** three-course breakfast (basket delivered to bungalows); evening wine and appetizers included; friendly innkeepers; "Friendship Pass" provides perks and savings at restaurants and wineries. **Cons:** not designed for children; no pets allowed; must climb stairs to second-floor rooms. $ *Rooms from: $315* ⊠ *1121 Edison St., Santa Ynez* ☎ *805/693–0303* ⊕ *forfriendsinn.com* ⤴ *14 units* ⏿ *Free Breakfast.*

Los Olivos

4 miles north of Santa Ynez.

This pretty village was once on Spanish-built El Camino Real (Royal Road) and later a stop on major stagecoach and rail routes. Tasting rooms, art galleries, antiques stores, and country markets line Grand Avenue and intersecting streets for several blocks.

GETTING HERE AND AROUND

From U.S. 101 north or south, exit at Highway 154 and drive east about 8 miles. From Santa Barbara, travel 30 miles northwest on Highway 154.

👁 Sights

Blair Fox Cellars

WINERY | Blair Fox, a Santa Barbara native, crafts small-lot Rhône-style wines made from organic grapes. The bar in his rustic Los Olivos tasting room, where you can sample exceptional vineyard-designated Syrahs and other wines, was hewn from Australian white oak reclaimed from an old Tasmanian schoolhouse. ⊠ *2477 Alamo Pintado Ave., Los Olivos* ☎ *805/691–1678* ⊕ *www.blairfoxcellars.com* ⤳ *Tastings $25* ⊘ *Closed Tues. and Wed.*

Coquelicot Estate Vineyard

WINERY | Named for the vivid red poppy flowers that blanket the French countryside and appear on all its labels, this limited-production winery focuses on handcrafted Bordeaux wines made from grapes at its certified organic 58-acre Santa Ynez Valley vineyard. Don't miss samples of the flagship wines: Sixer (a Syrah and Viogner blend), Mon Amour (a Bordeaux blend), and the estate Sauvignon Blanc and Rosé. ⊠ *2884 Grand Ave., Los Olivos* ☎ *805/688–1500* ⊕ *www.coquelicotwines. com* ⤳ *Tastings from $20.*

Firestone Vineyard

WINERY | Heirs to the Firestone tire fortune developed (but no longer own) this winery known for its Chardonnay,

Gewürztraminer, Cabernet Sauvignon, and Syrah and for the fantastic valley views from its tasting room (reservations required) and picnic area. ✉ *5017 Zaca Station Rd., off U.S. 101, Los Olivos* ☎ *805/688–3940* 🌐 *www.firestonewine.com* 🎟 *Tastings from $25* 🕒 *Closed Tues. and Wed.*

Roblar Winery & Vineyard

WINERY | Stop at this 40-acre estate to sip wines under the wisteria-covered pergola, nosh on farm-to-table dishes (so fresh the organic veggies still have their greens attached), and gaze at the vineyard views. Winemaker Max Marshak specializes in Rhone varieties, unusual white wines, and deep reds. ✉ *3010 Roblar Ave., Los Olivos* ☎ *805/686–2603* 🌐 *roblarwinery.com* 🎟 *Tastings $25.*

🍴 Restaurants

Bar Le Côte

$$ | **SPANISH** | Spanish flavors and seafood combine with coastal California flair at this trendy downtown eatery. Menu items change with the season, but perennial favorites include dry-aged branzino, paella, or saffron buns with Santa Barbara sea urchin butter. **Known for:** small-farm oysters; scallop crudo; fried-chicken sandwich. [$] *Average main: $30* ✉ *2375 Alamo Pintado Ave., Los Olivos* 🌐 *www.barlecote.com* 🕒 *Closed Mon. and Tues.*

★ Mattei's Tavern

$$$ | **AMERICAN** | Housed in a renovated 1886 building, erected during the stagecoach era, Mattei's encompasses several sophisticated, light-filled dining rooms with leather seats and benches, exposed brick walls, and high ceilings with wooden beams. The seasonal menu features California ranch–inspired dishes, many of which are cooked over a wood fire in the open kitchen and all of which use local and regional ingredients. **Known for:** stellar service; historic saloon-style bar and lounge; extensive list of local wines, flavor-packed cocktails. [$] *Average main: $38* ✉ *2350 Railway Ave., Los Olivos* ☎ *888/218–4941* 🌐 *www.the-tavernrestaurant.com* 🕒 *Closed Mon. and Tues. No lunch.*

🛏 Hotels

Fess Parker's Wine Country Inn

$$$$ | **B&B/INN** | This luxury inn's elegant, tree-shaded main building occupies a prime downtown corner, and its spacious accommodations, all completely updated in 2023, have fireplaces and include a complimentary wine tasting for two at Parker family tasting rooms. **Pros:** convenient wine-touring base; walking distance from restaurants and galleries; Nella restaurant. **Cons:** pricey for the area; not pet-friendly; thin walls between some rooms. [$] *Rooms from: $695* ✉ *2860 Grand Ave., Los Olivos* ☎ *805/688–7788, 800/446–2455* 🌐 *www.fessparker.com/inns-and-cabins* 🛏 *19 rooms* 🍽 *Free Breakfast.*

★ The Inn at Mattei's Tavern

$$$$ | **HOTEL** | In the stagecoach days, Mattei's Tavern provided wayfarers with hearty meals and warm beds; in the early 2020s, new owners restored the 1886 building and four cottages (historic artifacts, paintings, and photos are on display everywhere) and added clapboard, cottage-style buildings with guest rooms sprinkled over the 6-acre property with winding paths and gardens amid old-growth palm and olive trees. **Pros:** pool and hot tub with food and beverage service; spa with six treatment rooms, gym and exercise studio, daily yoga; walk to restaurants, tasting rooms, shops. **Cons:** some rooms face highway and can be noisy; $50 resort fee; pathway gravel can stick in shoes and roller wheels. [$] *Rooms from: $1,195* ✉ *2350 Railway Ave., Los Olivos* ☎ *844/837–2999* 🌐 *aubergeresorts.com/matteistavern* 🛏 *71 units* 🍽 *No Meals.*

Solvang

5 miles south of Los Olivos.

You'll know you've reached the town of Solvang when the architecture suddenly changes to half-timber buildings and windmills. Danish educators settled the town in 1911—the flatlands and rolling green hills reminded them of home. Solvang has attracted tourists for decades, but it's lately become more sophisticated, with smorgasbords giving way to galleries, upscale restaurants, and wine-tasting rooms by day and wine bars by night.

GETTING HERE AND AROUND

Highway 246 West (Mission Drive) traverses Solvang, connecting with U.S. 101 to the west and Highway 154 to the east. Alamo Pintado Road connects Solvang with Ballard and Los Olivos to the north. Park your car in one of the free public lots and stroll the town. Or take the bus: Santa Ynez Valley Transit shuttles run between Solvang and nearby towns.

ESSENTIALS

VISITOR INFORMATION Solvang Visitors Center. ✉ *1637 Copenhagen Dr., at 2nd St., Solvang* ☎ *805/465–7298* 🌐 *www.solvangusa.com.*

👁 Sights

Alma Rosa Winery

WINERY | Pioneering winemaker Richard Sanford helped put Santa Barbara County on the international wine map with a 1989 Pinot Noir, and founded Alma Rosa Winery in 2005. Today, Alma Rosa winemaker Sara Morris crafts wines from grapes grown on 100-plus acres of sustainable farmed vineyards in the Sta. Rita Hills AVA. The Pinot Noirs and Chardonnays are exceptional. Vineyard tours and tastings are available by appointment. ✉ *623 Mission Dr., off Hwy. 246, west of U.S. 101, Solvang* ☎ *805/691–9395* 🌐 *almarosawinery.com* 🎟 *Tastings from $25, vineyard tour $95.*

Mission Santa Inés

HISTORIC SIGHT | **FAMILY** | The mission holds an impressive collection of paintings, statuary, vestments, and Chumash and Spanish artifacts in a serene bluff-top setting. You can tour the museum, sanctuary, and gardens. ✉ *1760 Mission Dr., at Alisal Rd., Solvang* ☎ *805/688–4815* 🌐 *missionsantaines.org* 🎟 *$8.*

🍴 Restaurants

★ First & Oak

$$$ | **AMERICAN** | Savor the chef's carefully curated tasting menu with five different groups of eclectic California-French dishes paired with local wines at this elegant farm-to-table restaurant inside the Mirabelle Inn. The seasonal menu changes constantly, but regular dishes include smoked sweet-and-spicy duck wings, truffle-roasted cauliflower, local spot prawns, short rib bourguignonne, and pears poached in red wine from the sommelier-owner's organic Coceliquot Estate Vineyard. **Known for:** intimate fine-dining setting; sommelier-owner selected wine list; complex dishes and presentation. [$] *Average main: $39* ✉ *409 1st St., at Oak St., Solvang* ☎ *805/688–1703* 🌐 *firstandoak.com* 🕑 *No lunch.*

peasants FEAST

$$ | **MODERN AMERICAN** | **FAMILY** | This low-key, family-friendly eatery in the heart of town serves up made-from-scratch dishes that showcase seasonal local bounty sourced from trusted fishers and farmers. Feast on soups, beef-and-cheese smash burgers, and various salads and sandwiches in the casual interior or in the cozy brick patio. **Known for:** tacos with rockfish, gourmet mushrooms, or slow-cooked pork; house-cured and smoked bacon, pickled organic veggies, pastrami-smoked salmon; arcade and deli/market attached to restaurant. [$] *Average main: $29* ✉ *487 Atterdag Rd., Solvang* ☎ *805/686–4555* 🌐 *www.peasantsfeast.com* 🕑 *Closed Mon. and Tues. No dinner Wed. or Sun.*

Hotels

★ Alisal Guest Ranch and Resort

$$$$ | RESORT | Since 1946, celebrities and plain folk alike have come to this 10,000-acre ranch to join in a slew of activities, including horseback riding, tennis, golf, archery, boating, and fishing. **Pros:** Old West atmosphere; breakfast and dinner included in the rate; free Wi-Fi. **Cons:** no in-room phones or TVs; not close to downtown; jacket required for dinner. [$] *Rooms from: $925* ✉ *1054 Alisal Rd., Solvang* ☎ *805/693–4208, 800/425–4725* 🌐 *www.alisalranch.com* 🛏 *73 rooms* 🍴 *All-Inclusive.*

★ Corque Hotel

$$ | HOTEL | Owned by the Santa Ynez Band of Chumash Indians, this hotel offers a full slate of upscale amenities and public areas that feature mahogany, oak, and maple floors and furnishings; stone tiles; granite countertops; and textured walls and color schemes that reflect a chic, contemporary vibe. **Pros:** friendly, professional staff; short walk to shops, tasting rooms and restaurants; refurbished, upscale pool area. **Cons:** no kitchenettes or laundry facilities; some rooms need updating; not pet-friendly. [$] *Rooms from: $239* ✉ *400 Alisal Rd., Solvang* ☎ *805/688–8000, 800/248–6274* 🌐 *corquehotel.com* 🛏 *132 rooms* 🍴 *No Meals.*

The Landsby

$$ | B&B/INN | FAMILY | New owners transformed the former old-world-style Petersen Village Inn into a cozy, contemporary Scandinavian retreat that feels like a residence in downtown Copenhagen. **Pros:** in the heart of Solvang; easy parking; courtyard with fire pits. **Cons:** on highway; unusual hallway configuration can be confusing; thin walls in some rooms. [$] *Rooms from: $279* ✉ *1576 Mission Dr., Solvang* ☎ *805/688–3121* 🌐 *thelandsby.com* 🛏 *51 rooms* 🍴 *No Meals.*

★ Mirabelle Inn

$$ | B&B/INN | French, Danish, and American flags at the entrance and crystal chandeliers, soaring ceilings, and skylights in the lobby set the tone from the get-go in this elegant four-story inn a few blocks from the main tourist hub. **Pros:** excellent farm-to-table restaurant (dinner only); concierge and sommelier; away from noisy crowds. **Cons:** some rooms on the small side; not in the heart of town; restaurant noise travels to nearby rooms. [$] *Rooms from: $260* ✉ *409 1st St., at Oak St., Solvang* ☎ *805/688–1703, 800/786–7925* 🌐 *mirabelleinn.com* 🛏 *12 rooms* 🍴 *No Meals.*

Buellton

3 miles west of Solvang.

At the intersection of U.S. 101 and Highway 246, Buellton has evolved from a sleepy, crossroads, gas-and-coffee stop into an enclave of wine-tasting rooms, beer gardens, and restaurants. It's also a gateway to the Santa Rita Hills Wine Trail to the west and to Solvang, Santa Ynez, and Los Olivos to the east.

GETTING HERE AND AROUND

Driving is the easiest way to get to Buellton. From Santa Barbara, follow U.S. 101 north to the Highway 246 exit. Santa Ynez Valley Transit serves Buellton with shuttle buses from Solvang and nearby towns.

ESSENTIALS

VISITOR INFORMATION Discover Buellton. ✉ *597 Ave. of the Flags, Suite 101, Buellton* ☎ *805/688–7829* 🌐 *discoverbuellton.com.* **Santa Rita Hills Wine Trail.** 🌐 *sbcountywines.com/region/areas-avas.*

Sights

Industrial Way

NEIGHBORHOOD | A half-mile west of U.S. 101, head south from Highway 246 on Industrial Way to explore a hip and happening collection of food and drink destinations. Top stops include Industrial Eats (a craft butcher shop and restaurant),

Figueroa Mountain Brewing Company, and the Buscador Winery tasting room. ✉ *Industrial Way, off Hwy. 246, Buellton* 🌐 *www.industrialwaysbc.com.*

Lafond Winery and Vineyards

WINERY | A rich, concentrated Pinot Noir is the main attention-getter at this winery that also produces noteworthy Chardonnays and Syrahs. Bottles with Lafond's SRH (Santa Rita Hills) label are an especially good value. The winery also has a tasting room (✉ *28 Anacapa St.*) in Santa Barbara's Funk Zone. ✉ *6855 Santa Rosa Rd., west off U.S. 101, Exit 139, Buellton* ☎ *805/688–7921* 🌐 *www.lafondwinery.com* 🎟 *Tastings $20.*

La Purísima Mission State Historic Park

HISTORIC SIGHT | **FAMILY** | The state's most fully restored mission, founded in 1787, stands in a stark and still remote location that powerfully evokes the lives and isolation of California's Spanish settlers. Docents lead tours Wednesday to Sunday (daily June to August), and vivid displays illustrate the secular and religious activities that formed mission life. ✉ *2295 Purisima Rd., off Hwy. 246, 14 miles west of Buellton, Lompoc* ☎ *805/733–3713* 🌐 *www.lapurisimamission.org* 🎟 *$6 per vehicle.*

Los Alamos

TOWN | **FAMILY** | A tiny stagecoach town founded in 1876, Los Alamos is a fun, Old West stopover when driving along Highway 101. Many of its original structures, including the 1880 Union Hotel, still line several blocks of Bell Street, the main drag. In recent years Los Alamos has evolved into a hip food-and-wine destination with first-rate tasting rooms and restaurants within the western-style buildings. Standouts include Bell's Restaurant, Plenty on Bell, Bob's Well Bread, and Casa Dumetz Wines. ✉ *On Hwy. 101, 15 miles north of Buellton, Los Alamos* 🌐 *www.visitsyv.com/discover-syv/los-alamos.*

Vega Vineyard & Farm

WINERY | **FAMILY** | Taste wines by famed local vintner Steve Clifton (known for his Chardonnay, Pinot Noir, and Italian varietals like Barbera), feast on lunch and snacks at the on-site restaurant, and visit with farm animals (chickens, goats, llamas, sheep, miniature donkeys, and more) at this family-oriented tasting room, farm stand, and event center at an historic estate, established in 1853. If the weather's balmy, sit on the patio overlooking the vineyard and listen to live music, which typically plays on weekends. ✉ *9496 Santa Rosa Rd., Buellton* ☎ *805/688–2415* 🌐 *www.vegavineyardandfarm.com* 🎟 *Tastings $25.*

🍴 Restaurants

The Hitching Post II

$$$ | **AMERICAN** | You'll find everything from grilled artichokes to quail at this casual eatery, but most people come for the smoky Santa Maria–style barbecue. Be sure to try a glass of owner-chef-winemaker Frank Ostini's signature Highliner Pinot Noir, a star in the film *Sideways*. **Known for:** entrées grilled over local red oak; chef-owner makes his own wines; classic cocktails. $ *Average main: $38* ✉ *406 E. Hwy. 246, off U.S. 101, Buellton* ☎ *805/688–0676* 🌐 *www.hitchingpost2.com* 🕘 *No lunch.*

🛏 Hotels

Inn at Zaca Creek

$$$ | **HOTEL** | Originally built by descendants of Buellton's founding family and reinvented as a rustic luxury resort after decades of dormancy, this elegant collection of suites, a restaurant, and secluded, multitiered spaces on 3 tree-studded acres pays homage to the land's historical roots and pastoral setting. **Pros:** fine-dining restaurant and bar; secluded site near ranches and a residential area; attentive, personal service. **Cons:** next to Highway 101; popular wedding venue with lively guests; not in the heart of town. [$] *Rooms from: $360* ✉ *1297 Jonata Park Rd., Buellton* ☎ *805/688–2412* 🌐 *zaca-creek.com* 🛏 *6 suites* 🍴 *No Meals.*

Activities

Highline Adventures

ZIP LINING | FAMILY | Enjoy sweeping views of the Santa Ynez Valley while soaring 1½ miles along a ridge and down 1,000 feet of vertical on three tandem zip lines. Alternatively, you can join a guided walk through protea flower fields, clamber around an adventure park amid an ancient stand of oak trees with 65 different challenge elements in a Via Ferrata–style harness system (minimum 65 pounds, 4′2″ tall), or hang out in the air-conditioned visitor center. ✉ *700 E. Hwy. 246, Buellton* ☎ *805/556–4049* 🌐 *highlineadventures.com* 🎟 *From $100.*

Santa Ynez Horseback Riding

HORSEBACK RIDING | FAMILY | Ride along the banks of the Santa Ynez River and view wildlife (eagles, deer, beavers) in their natural habitats during 60- to 90-minute horseback adventures. Children age two and older can sign up for pony encounters, and the whole family can enjoy the picnic area, children's play area, petting zoo, and cornhole. ✉ *151 Sycamore Dr., Buellton* ☎ *805/693–4600* 🌐 *www.syvhorsebackrides.com* 🎟 *From $119.*

Pismo Beach

51 miles northwest of Buellton.

About 20 miles of sandy shoreline begins at the town of Pismo Beach. The southern end of town runs along sand dunes, some of which are open to cars and off-road vehicles. Sheltered by the dunes, a grove of eucalyptus trees attracts thousands of migrating monarch butterflies from November through February. A long, broad beach fronts the center of town, where a municipal pier extends into the sea at the foot of shop-lined Pomeroy Street. To the north, hotels and homes perch atop chalky oceanfront cliffs. Fewer than 10,000 people live in this quintessential surfer haven, but Pismo Beach has a slew of hotels and restaurants with great views of the Pacific Ocean.

GETTING HERE AND AROUND

Pismo Beach straddles both sides of U.S. 101. If you're coming from the south and have time for a scenic drive, exit U.S. 101 in Santa Maria and take Highway 166 west for 8 miles to Guadalupe and follow Highway 1 north 16 miles to Pismo Beach. South County Area Transit (SCAT) buses run throughout San Luis Obispo and connect the city with nearby towns. On summer weekends, the free Avila Trolley extends service to Pismo Beach.

ESSENTIALS

VISITOR INFORMATION California Welcome Center. ✉ *333 5 Cities Dr., Pismo Beach* ☎ *805/668–7354* 🌐 *www.visitcalifornia.com.* **Pismo Beach Visitor Information Center.** ✉ *Dolliver St./Hwy. 1, at Hinds Ave., Pismo Beach* ☎ *800/443–7778, 805/556–7397* 🌐 *www.experiencepismobeach.com.*

Beaches

★ Oceano Dunes State Vehicular Recreation Area

BEACH | FAMILY | Part of the spectacular Guadalupe-Nipomo Dunes, this 3,600-acre coastal playground is one of the few places in California where you can drive or ride off-highway vehicles on the beach and sand dunes. Hike, ride horses, kiteboard, join a Hummer tour, or rent an ATV or a dune buggy and cruise up the white-sand peaks for spectacular views. At Oso Flaco Lake Nature Area—3 miles west of Highway 1 on Oso Flaco Road—a 1½-mile boardwalk over the lake leads to a platform with views up and down the coast. Leashed dogs are allowed in much of the park except Oso Flaco and Pismo Dunes Natural Reserve. **Amenities:** food and drink; lifeguards (seasonal); parking (fee); showers; toilets; water sports. **Best for:** sunset; surfing; swimming; walking. ⊠ *West end of Pier Ave., off Hwy. 1, Oceano* 🕾 *805/773–7170* ⊕ *www.parks. ca.gov* 🖾 *$5 per vehicle.*

Pismo State Beach

BEACH | **FAMILY** | Hike, surf, ride horses, swim, fish in a lagoon or off the pier, and dig for Pismo clams at this busy state beach. One of the day-use parking areas is off Highway 1 near the Monarch Butterfly Grove, where from November through February monarch butterflies nest in eucalyptus and Monterey pines. The other parking area is about 1½ miles south at Pier Avenue. **Amenities:** food and drink; lifeguards (seasonal); parking (fee); showers; toilets; water sports. **Best for:** sunset; surfing; swimming; walking. ⊠ *555 Pier Ave., off Hwy. 1, 3 miles south of downtown Pismo Beach, Oceano* 🕾 *805/473–7220* ⊕ *www.parks. ca.gov* 🖾 *Day-use $15 per vehicle if parking at beach.*

🍴 Restaurants

Cracked Crab

$$$ | **SEAFOOD** | **FAMILY** | This traditional New England–style crab shack imports fresh seafood daily from Australia, Alaska, and the East Coast. Fish is line-caught, much of the produce is organic, and everything is made from scratch. **Known for:** shellfish meals in a bucket, dumped on the table; casual setting; daily specials. 🆂 *Average main: $32* ⊠ *751 Price St., near Main St., Pismo Beach* 🕾 *805/773–2722* ⊕ *www.crackedcrab. com.*

★ Ember

$$$ | **AMERICAN** | A barn-style restaurant with high ceilings and an open kitchen, Ember enjoys a red-hot reputation for Italian-inflected dishes prepared in an authentic Tuscan fireplace or a wood-burning oven. Chef-owner Brian Collins, a native of Arroyo Grande, the town bordering Pismo Beach, honed his culinary skills at Berkeley's legendary Chez Panisse Restaurant. **Known for:** seasonal menu changes monthly; wood-fired flatbread pizzas; craft cocktails, local wines, local craft beer on tap. 🆂 *Average main: $34* ⊠ *1200 E. Grand Ave., at Brisco Rd., Arroyo Grande* 🕾 *805/474–7700* ⊕ *www.emberwoodfire.com* 🕙 *Closed Mon. and Tues. No lunch.*

Giuseppe's Cucina Italiana

$$$ | **ITALIAN** | **FAMILY** | The classic flavors of southern Italy are highlighted at this lively downtown spot. Most recipes originate from Bari, a seaport on the Adriatic; the menu includes breads and pizzas baked in the wood-burning oven, hearty dishes such as dry-aged steak and rack of lamb, and homemade pastas. **Known for:** lively family-style atmosphere; daily specials; most fruits and veggies come from owner's 12-acre farm. 🆂 *Average main: $32* ⊠ *891 Price St., at Pismo Ave., Pismo Beach* 🕾 *805/773–2870* ⊕ *www. giuseppesrestaurant.com* 🕙 *No lunch weekdays.*

The Spoon Trade

$$ | **AMERICAN** | **FAMILY** | A silver spoon display at the entrance reflects this casual eatery's mission to "spoon food and trade stories" with diners who indulge in traditional American comfort food that's given a modern twist. Perennial menu faves include tri-tip tartare, grilled artichoke, duck ramen, and fried chicken with sourdough waffles; save room for a root beer float or brown sugar pot de crème for dessert. **Known for:** pet-friendly patio; house-made pastas; lively dining room with open kitchen. 🆂 *Average main: $30* ⊠ *295 W. Grand Ave., Grover Beach* 🕾 *805/904–6773* ⊕ *thespoontrade. com* 🕙 *Closed Mon. and Tues. No lunch.*

Ventana Grill

$$ | **FUSION** | Perched on a bluff at the northern edge of Pismo Beach, Ventana Grill offers ocean views from nearly every

San Luis Obispo County and Big Sur Coast

table, unusual seafood-centered Latin American–California fusion dishes, and more than 50 tequilas plus craft cocktails at the bar. Reservations are essential—this place is almost always packed, especially during the weekday happy hour. **Known for:** happy hour with sunset views; Sunday brunch buffet; house-made tortillas. $ *Average main: $30* ✉ *2575 Price St., Pismo Beach* ☎ *805/773–0000* ⊕ *ventanagrill.com.*

🛌 Hotels

The Cliffs Hotel & Spa

$$ | **RESORT** | Lawns and palm trees surround this full-service resort that's perched dramatically on an oceanfront cliff. **Pros:** beach access via short downhill path; oceanfront spa, restaurant and lounge; bluff-top walking trail. **Cons:** not close to downtown; rooms near service areas and elevator can be noisy; resort fee. $ *Rooms from: $259* ✉ *2757 Shell Beach Rd., Pismo Beach* ☎ *805/773–5000, 800/826–7827* ⊕ *cliffshotelandspa. com* ⤳ *160 rooms* ❯❮ *No Meals.*

Dolphin Bay Resort & Spa

$$$$ | **RESORT** | On grass-covered bluffs overlooking Shell Beach, this luxury resort looks and feels like an exclusive community of villas; choose among sprawling one- or two-bedroom suites, each with a gourmet kitchen, laundry room with washer and dryer, and contemporary furnishings. **Pros:** lavish apartment units; Lido farm-to-table restaurant; many suites have ocean views. **Cons:** no a/c; no 24-hour room service; not close to downtown. $ *Rooms from: $579* ✉ *2727 Shell Beach Rd., Pismo Beach* ☎ *805/773–4300, 800/516–0112 reservations, 805/773–8900 restaurant*

🌐 *www.thedolphinbay.com* 🛏 *60 suites* 🍴 *No Meals.*

Inn at the Pier

$$$ | **HOTEL** | The luxe Inn at the Pier, part of Hilton's Curio collection, covers a prime city block just steps from the sand and across from the pier. **Pros:** walk to downtown restaurants, sights, and shops; fitness center and cruiser bike rentals; new building. **Cons:** daily resort fee; valet parking only; bar noise travels to some rooms. [$] *Rooms from: $379* ✉ *601 Cypress St., Pismo Beach* ☎ *805/295–5565* 🌐 *www.theinnatthepier.com* 🛏 *104 rooms* 🍴 *No Meals.*

Pismo Lighthouse Suites

$$ | **HOTEL** | **FAMILY** | Each of the well-appointed two-room, two-bath suites at this oceanfront hotel has a private balcony or patio. **Pros:** open-air play deck with badminton, Ping-Pong, and life-size chess board; nautical-style furnishing; nice pool area. **Cons:** not easy to walk to main attractions; some units are next to busy road; first-floor units can hear footsteps from suites above. [$] *Rooms from: $269* ✉ *2411 Price St., Pismo Beach* ☎ *805/773–2411, 800/245–2411* 🌐 *www.pismolighthousesuites.com* 🛏 *70 suites* 🍴 *Free Breakfast.*

Vespera Resort

$$$ | **HOTEL** | This stylish, yet casual Marriott Autograph Collection resort, on the town's famed boardwalk just steps from the beach and the Pismo Pier, feels like a luxury beach house, with a swank living room–style lobby-lounge, a pool and hot tub, an outdoor bar, and a lawn with firepits—all overlooking the ocean. **Pros:** bar with many tequila options; seafood-centric restaurant with Baja California flair; daily well-being classes. **Cons:** resort fee ($35); valet parking only; lots of traffic in area in summer and holiday weekends. [$] *Rooms from: $367* ✉ *147 Stimson Ave., Pismo Beach* ☎ *805/773–1011* 🌐 *vesperapismobeach.com* 🛏 *124 rooms* 🍴 *No Meals.*

Avila Beach

4 miles north of Pismo Beach.

Because the village of Avila Beach and the sandy, cove-front shoreline for which it's named face south into the Pacific Ocean, they get more sun and less fog than any other stretch of coast in the area. With its fortuitous climate and protected waters, Avila's public beach draws sunbathers and families; summer weekends are very busy. Downtown Avila Beach has a lively seaside promenade and some shops and hotels, but for real local color, head to the far end of the cove and watch the commercial fishers off-load their catch on the old Port San Luis wharf. On Friday from mid-April through mid-September, a fish and farmers' market livens up the beach area with music, fresh local produce and seafood, and children's activities.

GETTING HERE AND AROUND

Exit U.S. 101 at Avila Beach Drive and head 3 miles west to reach the beach. The free Avila Trolley operates weekends year-round, plus Friday afternoon and evening from April to September. The minibuses connect Avila Beach and Port San Luis to Shell Beach, with multiple stops along the way. Service extends to Pismo Beach in summer.

ESSENTIALS

VISITOR INFORMATION Avila Beach Tourism Alliance. ✉ *Avila Beach* 🌐 *visitavilabeach.com.*

👁 Sights

Avila Valley Barn

FARM/RANCH | **FAMILY** | An old-fashioned country store jam-packed with local fruits and vegetables, prepared foods, and gifts, Avila Valley Barn also offers the chance to experience rural American traditions. You can pet farm animals and savor homemade ice cream and pies daily, and on weekends ride ponies or a hay wagon out to the fields to pick your own produce. ✉ *560 Avila Beach Dr., San Luis Obispo* ☎ *805/595–2816* 🌐 *www.avilavalleybarn.com* 🕑 *Closed Tues. and Wed. Jan.–Mar.*

Point San Luis Lighthouse
LIGHTHOUSE | **FAMILY** | Docents lead hikes along scenic Pecho Coast Trail (3½ miles round-trip) to see the historic 1890 lighthouse and its rare Fresnel lens. ■ **TIP→ If you'd prefer a lift out to the lighthouse, join a shuttle tour. Hikes and tours require reservations.** ✉ *Port San Luis* ✥ *1¾ miles west of Harford Pier* ☎ *805/540–5771* 🌐 *www.pointsanluislighthouse.org* 🎟 *Shuttle tours $27; hikes free ($10 to enter lighthouse).*

Beaches

Avila City Beach
BEACH | **FAMILY** | At the edge of a sunny cove next to downtown shops and restaurants, Avila's ½-mile stretch of white sand is especially family-friendly, with a playground, barbecue and picnic tables, volleyball and basketball courts, and lifeguards on watch in summer and on many holiday weekends. The free beachfront parking fills up fast, but there's a nearby pay lot ($8 for the day, $3 after 4 pm). Dogs aren't allowed on the beach from 10 to 5. **Amenities:** food and drink; lifeguards (seasonal); parking; showers; toilets; water sports. **Best for:** sunset; surfing; swimming; walking. ✉ *Avila Beach Dr., at 1st St., Avila Beach* 🌐 *www.visitavilabeach.com* 🎟 *Free.*

Restaurants

Mersea's
$ | **SEAFOOD** | **FAMILY** | Walk down the pier to this casual crab shack where you can order at the counter, grab a drink at the bar, and find a seat on the deck or in the casual indoor dining area to gaze at spectacular Avila Bay views while you dine. The menu includes chowder bowls, burgers, sandwiches, seafood, and salads, plus bowls of fish, shrimp, or chicken served over rice pilaf and veggies. **Known for:** clam chowder in sourdough bread bowls; fish tacos; fresh local ingredients. [$] *Average main: $16* ✉ *3985 Port San Luis Pier, Avila Beach* ✥ *At Port San Luis* ☎ *805/548–2290* 🌐 *www.merseas.com.*

Ocean Grill
$$$ | **SEAFOOD** | Across from the promenade, beach, and pier, Ocean Grill serves up fresh seafood to diners who typically arrive before sunset to enjoy the views. Boats anchored in the bay provide much of the seafood, which pairs well with the mostly regional wines on the list. **Known for:** fantastic ocean views; wood-fired pizzas; gluten-free and vegetarian options. [$] *Average main: $32* ✉ *268 Front St., Avila Beach* ☎ *805/595–4050* 🌐 *oceangrillavila.com* 🕑 *Closed Tues. and Wed. No lunch.*

Hotels

Avila La Fonda
$$ | **HOTEL** | Modeled after a village in early California's Mexican period—with a facade that replicates eight different casitas, including several famous historical homes in Mexico—Avila La Fonda surrounds you with rich jewel tones, fountains, and upscale comfort. **Pros:** one-of-a-kind theme and artwork; flexible room combinations; a block from the beach. **Cons:** pricey for the area; most rooms don't have an ocean view; spotty Wi-Fi. [$] *Rooms from: $329* ✉ *101 San Miguel St., Avila Beach* ☎ *805/595–1700* 🌐 *www.avilalafonda.com* 🛏 *28 rooms* 🍴 *No Meals.*

Avila Lighthouse Suites
$$ | **HOTEL** | **FAMILY** | Families, honeymooners, and business travelers all find respite at this two-story oceanfront hotel, where some of the stylish nautical-theme suites have fireplaces and ocean views and all have private patios and balconies. **Pros:** directly across from sand; easy walk to restaurants and shops; free underground

parking. **Cons:** noise from passersby can be heard in room; some ocean-view rooms have limited vistas; basic breakfast. ⓢ *Rooms from: $349* ✉ *550 Front St., Avila Beach* ☎ *805/627–1900, 800/372–8452* ⊕ *www.avilalighthousesuites.com* ⤳ *54 suites* ⊙ *Free Breakfast.*

Sycamore Mineral Springs Resort & Spa
$$ | RESORT | This wellness resort's hot mineral springs bubble up into private outdoor tubs on an oak-and-sycamore-forest hillside. **Pros:** great place to rejuvenate; nice hiking nearby; incredible spa with yoga classes, integrative healing arts, and many treatments. **Cons:** rooms vary in quality; 2½ miles from the beach; road noise can travel to certain areas of property. ⓢ *Rooms from: $259* ✉ *1215 Avila Beach Dr., San Luis Obispo, Avila Beach* ☎ *805/595–7302* ⊕ *www.sycamoresprings.com* ⤳ *72 rooms* ⊙ *No Meals.*

San Luis Obispo

8 miles north of Avila Beach.

About halfway between San Francisco and Los Angeles, San Luis Obispo spreads out below gentle hills and rocky extinct volcanoes. Its main appeal lies in its architecturally diverse, pedestrian-friendly downtown, which bustles with shoppers, restaurant goers, and students from California Polytechnic State University, known as Cal Poly. On Thursday evening from 6 to 9 the city's famed farmers' market fills Higuera Street with local produce, entertainment, and food stalls.

San Luis Obispo is the commercial center of a south-county wine region whose appellations (SLO Coast and such sub-appellations as Edna Valley and Arroyo Grande Valley) stretch west toward the coast and east toward the inland mountains. Many of the nearly 30 wineries here line Highway 227 and connecting roads. The region is known for Chardonnay and Pinot Noir, although

many wineries experiment with other varietals and blends. Wine-touring maps are available around San Luis Obispo. Most wineries charge a tasting fee and close at 5.

GETTING HERE AND AROUND
U.S. 101/Highway 1 traverses the city for several miles. From the north, Highway 1 merges with U.S. 101 when it reaches the city limits. The wineries of the Edna Valley and Arroyo Grande Valley wine regions lie south of town off Highway 227, the parallel (to the east) Orcutt Road, and connecting roads.

SLO City Transit buses operate daily. The Downtown Trolley provides evening service to the city's hub every Thursday, on Friday from June to early September, and Saturday from April through October.

ESSENTIALS
VISITOR INFORMATION San Luis Obispo Chamber of Commerce. ✉ *895 Monterey St., San Luis Obispo* ☎ *805/781–2777* ⊕ *slochamber.org.* **San Luis Obispo City Visitor Information.** ✉ *San Luis Obispo* ☎ *877/756–8696* ⊕ *visitslo.com.*

◉ Sights

Biddle Ranch Vineyard
WINERY | Glass doors and walls in a converted dairy barn fill the Biddle Ranch Vineyard tasting room with light and sweeping valley, mountain, and vineyard views. The small-production winery focuses on estate Chardonnay (the adjacent 17-acre vineyard is planted exclusively to the grape), plus Pinot Noir and various red blends. ✉ *2050 Biddle Ranch Rd., at Hwy. 227, San Luis Obispo* ☎ *805/543–2399* ⊕ *www.biddleranch. com* 🍷 *Tastings $30 (reservations recommended)* ⊙ *Closed Tues. and Wed.*

Claiborne & Churchill
WINERY | An eco-friendly winery built from straw bales, C&C makes small lots of aromatic Alsatian-style wines such as dry Riesling and Gewürztraminer, plus Pinot

Noir blends, Syrah, and Chardonnay. ✉ *2649 Carpenter Canyon Rd., at Price Canyon Rd., San Luis Obispo* ☎ *805/544–4066* 🌐 *www.clairbornechurchill.com* 🎟 *Tastings from $24.*

Mission San Luis Obispo de Tolosa
HISTORIC SIGHT | FAMILY | Sun-dappled Mission Plaza fronts the fifth mission established in 1772 by Franciscan friars. A small museum exhibits artifacts of the Chumash Indians and early Spanish settlers. Guided tours are offered Wednesday–Sunday at 1:15 pm and Sunday at 2 pm. ✉ *751 Palm St., at Chorro St., San Luis Obispo* ☎ *805/543–6850* 🌐 *missionsanluisobispo.org* 🎟 *$5* 🕒 *Closed Mon. and Tues.*

San Luis Obispo Children's Museum
CHILDREN'S MUSEUM | FAMILY | Activities at this facility geared to children under age 10 include an "imagination-powered" elevator that transports visitors to a series of underground caverns. Kids can pick rubber fruit at a farmers' market and race in a fire engine to fight a fire. ✉ *1010 Nipomo St., at Monterey St., San Luis Obispo* ☎ *805/544–5437* 🌐 *www.slocm.org* 🎟 *$10* 🕒 *Closed Tues. and Wed.*

Talley Vineyards
WINERY | Acres of Chardonnay and Pinot Noir, plus smaller parcels of Sauvignon Blanc, Syrah, and other varietals blanket Talley's mountain-ringed dell in the Arroyo Grande Valley. Enjoy stunning estate views in the sleek interior and on the adjacent patio. Standout wines include the single-vineyard Rosemary's Pinot Noir and Chardonnay. ✉ *3031 Lopez Dr., off Orcutt Rd., Arroyo Grande* ☎ *805/489–0446* 🌐 *talleyvineyards.com* 🎟 *Tastings from $30.*

Wolff Vineyards
WINERY | Syrah, Petite Sirah, and Riesling join the expected Pinot Noir and Chardonnay as the stars at this family-run winery 6 miles south of downtown. The pourers are friendly, and you'll often meet one of the owners or their children in the tasting room. With its hillside views, the outdoor patio is a great place to enjoy an afternoon picnic. ✉ *6238 Orcutt Rd., near Biddle Ranch Rd., San Luis Obispo* ☎ *805/781–0448* 🌐 *wolffvineyards.com* 🎟 *Tastings $20.*

🍴 Restaurants

Big Sky Café
$$ | ECLECTIC | FAMILY | Family-friendly Big Sky turns local and organically grown ingredients into global dishes, starting with breakfast. Just pick your continent—braised Brazilian lamb shanks, Southeast Asian noodle bowls and crispy tempura cauliflower, Middle Eastern shakshuka, Spanish paella, Nashville fried chicken sandwich. **Known for:** artsy, creative vibe; ample choices for vegetarians; house-cured Reuben sandwich. [$] *Average main: $25* ✉ *1121 Broad St., at Higuera St., San Luis Obispo* ☎ *805/545–5401* 🌐 *www.bigskycafe.com.*

★ Giuseppe's Cucina Rustica
$$ | ITALIAN | The younger sibling of the hugely popular Guiseppe's restaurant in Pismo Beach, this lively downtown eatery serves up authentic southern Italian fare in the historic Sinsheimer Bros. building, constructed in 1884. Dine in the spacious main restaurant amid high ceilings, fireplaces, and the bar or in the courtyard beneath strings of twinkling lights. **Known for:** bread, sauce, pasta, and gelato and other desserts made in-house; organic ingredients from the owner's 12-acre farm or local purveyors; historic ambience. [$] *Average main: $27* ✉ *849 Monterey St., San Luis Obispo* ☎ *805/541–9922* 🌐 *www.giuseppesrestaurant.com.*

Luna Red
$$ | INTERNATIONAL | A spacious, contemporary space with a festive outdoor patio, this restaurant near Mission Plaza serves creative tapas and cocktails. The small plates include birria-braised beef tacos, avocado-tuna ceviche, and crispy

Brussels sprouts. **Known for:** excellent Valencian paellas; craft cocktails; lively music scene. $ *Average main: $27* ⊠ *1023 Chorro St., at Monterey St., San Luis Obispo* ☎ *805/540–5243* ⊕ *www. lunaredslo.com.*

Novo Restaurant & Lounge

$$ | **ECLECTIC** | In the colorful dining room or on the large creek-side deck, this animated downtown eatery will take you on a culinary world tour. The salads, small plates, and entrées come from nearly every continent. **Known for:** patio seating; savory curry and noodle dishes; local farmers' market ingredients. $ *Average main: $25* ⊠ *726 Higuera St., at Broad St., San Luis Obispo* ☎ *805/543–3986* ⊕ *www.novorestaurant.com.*

SLO Provisions

$$ | **AMERICAN** | **FAMILY** | Stop at this casual café–market in the Upper Monterey neighborhood for a sit-down or takeaway meal all day. In addition to full meals, you can order specialty sandwiches, farm-fresh salads, and baked goods, or hang out and taste wine or beer at the casual tasting bar. **Known for:** house-roasted rotisserie meats; family-style dinners; daily specials. $ *Average main: $20* ⊠ *1255 Monterey St., San Luis Obispo* ☎ *805/439–4298* ⊕ *www.sloprovisions. com* ☾ *Closed Sun.*

🛏 Hotels

Garden Street Inn

$$ | **B&B/INN** | From this restored 1887 Italianate Queen Anne downtown, you can walk to many restaurants and attractions; uniquely decorated rooms, each with private bath, are filled with antiques, and some rooms have stained-glass windows, fireplaces, and decks. **Pros:** lavish homemade breakfast; convenient location; complementary wine-and-cheese reception. **Cons:** city noise filters into some rooms; not great for families; no elevator. $ *Rooms from: $249* ⊠ *1212 Garden St., San Luis Obispo*

☎ *805/545–9802* ⊕ *www.gardenstreet-inn.com* ⇌ *13 rooms* ⦿⦿ *Free Breakfast.*

Granada Hotel & Bistro

$$ | **HOTEL** | Built in 1922 in the heart of downtown and still sparkling, the two-story Granada is a vintage-style retreat with hardwood floors, redbrick walls, and antique rugs. **Pros:** one of a few full-service downtown hotels; easy walk to restaurants, shops, and sights; farm-to-table bistro, cocktail bar, and grab-and-go restaurant. **Cons:** some rooms are tiny; sometimes noisy near restaurant kitchen; late-night bar noise travels to some rooms. $ *Rooms from: $279* ⊠ *1126 Morro St., San Luis Obispo* ☎ *805/544–9100* ⊕ *www.granadahotelandbistro.com* ⇌ *17 rooms* ⦿⦿ *No Meals.*

★ Hotel Cerro

$$ | **HOTEL** | San Luis Obispo's Chumash, mission, and 19th-century industrial eras blend with urban sophistication in this eco-friendly, four-story complex, which opened in 2019. **Pros:** restaurant, café, and lobby lounge; tree-lined outdoor terrace; designed and built to meet LEED Silver status. **Cons:** in the heart of the downtown bar scene; limited on-site valet parking only; room designs not ideal for families with small children. $ *Rooms from: $275* ⊠ *1125 Garden St., San Luis Obispo* ☎ *805/548–1000* ⊕ *www.hotelcerro.com* ⇌ *65 rooms* ⦿⦿ *No Meals.*

★ Hotel San Luis Obispo

$$$ | **HOTEL** | Just a block from the mission and steps from restaurants, shops, and night spots, this sleek, three-story hotel has custom-furnished rooms with light wood floors, high ceilings, and either a private balcony or terrace—often with a view of the garden courtyard and mountains. **Pros:** spa and other upscale amenities; park the car and walk to most attractions; contemporary styling. **Cons:** valet parking only; some rooms overlook a parking garage; too pet-friendly for some guests. $ *Rooms from:*

$459 ✉ *877 Palm St., San Luis Obispo* ☎ *805/235–0700* 🌐 *hotel-slo.com* 🛏 *78 rooms* 🍴 *No Meals.*

Madonna Inn

$$ | **HOTEL** | From its rococo bathrooms to its pink-on-pink froufrou steak house, the Madonna Inn is fabulous or tacky, depending on your point of view. **Pros:** fun, one-of-a-kind experience; infinity pool, exercise room, and day spa; each room has its own distinct identity (e.g., Safari Room). **Cons:** rooms vary widely; must appreciate kitsch; no elevator. [$] *Rooms from: $229* ✉ *100 Madonna Rd., San Luis Obispo* ☎ *805/543–3000, 800/543–9666* 🌐 *www.madonnainn.com* 🛏 *110 rooms* 🍴 *No Meals.*

Petit Soleil

$$ | **B&B/INN** | A cobblestone courtyard and country-French custom furnishings evoke a Provençal mood at this cheery inn. **Pros:** includes wine and appetizers at cocktail hour; includes scrumptious breakfasts; cozy rooms with luxury touches. **Cons:** sits on a busy avenue; cramped parking; some rooms are tiny. [$] *Rooms from: $209* ✉ *1473 Monterey St., San Luis Obispo* ☎ *805/549–0321, 800/676–1588* 🌐 *www.petitsoleilslo.com* 🛏 *16 rooms* 🍴 *Free Breakfast.*

Nightlife

SLO's club scene is centered on Higuera Street, off Monterey Street.

The Libertine Brewing Company

BREWPUBS | Come to Libertine to savor 76 craft beers and wines on tap, house-made brews of kombucha and cold brew coffee, and pub food infused with the brewery's own wild ales. ✉ *1234 Broad St., San Luis Obispo* ☎ *805/548–2337* 🌐 *libertinebrewing.com/san-luis-obispo.*

Nightcap

COCKTAIL LOUNGES | Indulge in craft and vintage cocktails at the Granada Hotel's artsy cocktail lounge, decked out in velvet, mirrored ceilings, and marble tables and countertops. ✉ *1130 Morro St., San Luis Obispo* ☎ *805/544–9100* 🌐 *www.granadahotelandbistro.com.*

The Rock

BEER GARDENS | Home to SLO Brew's 30-barrel brewing and tasting facility near the airport, the Rock has a beer garden, restaurant, and regular live-music performances. ✉ *855 Aerovista Pl., San Luis Obispo* ☎ *844/756–2739* 🌐 *slobrew.com/the-rock.*

Shopping

Many of San Luis Obispo's locally owned and operated shops cluster around downtown's Higuera Street in the blocks east of the mission. Also head up Monterey Street just north of the mission to find more small stores with one-of-a-kind treasures.

Paso Robles

30 miles north of San Luis Obispo, 25 miles northwest of Morro Bay.

In the 1860s, tourists began visiting this ranching outpost to "take the cure" in a bathhouse fed by underground mineral hot springs. An Old West town emerged, and grand Victorian homes went up, followed in the 20th century by Craftsman bungalows. These days, the wooded hills of Paso Robles west of U.S. 101 and the flatter, more open land to the freeway's east have more than 200 wineries, many with tasting rooms. Hot summer days, cool nights, and varied soils and microclimates allow growers to cultivate an impressive array of Bordeaux, Rhône, and other grape types.

Cabernet Sauvignon grows well in the Paso Robles AVA—40,000 of its 600,000-plus acres are planted to grapes—as do Petit Verdot, Grenache, Syrah, Viognier, and Zinfandel. In recognition of the diverse growing conditions, the AVA has been divided into 11 subappellations.

Pick up a wine-touring map at lodgings, wineries, and attractions around town. The fee at most tasting rooms is between $20 and $40; many lodgings pass out discount coupons.

Upscale restaurants, bars, antiques stores, and little shops fill the streets around oak-shaded City Park, where special events of all kinds—custom car shows, an olive festival, Friday-night summer concerts—take place. Despite its increasing sophistication, Paso (as the locals call it) retains a small-town vibe. The city celebrates its cowboy roots in late July and early August with the two-week California Mid-State Fair, complete with livestock auctions, carnival rides, and corn dogs.

GETTING HERE AND AROUND
U.S. 101 runs north–south through Paso Robles. Highway 46 West links Paso Robles to Highway 1 and Cambria on the coast. Highway 46 East connects Paso Robles with I–5 and the San Joaquin Valley. Public transit is not convenient for wine touring and sightseeing.

ESSENTIALS
VISITOR INFORMATION Paso Robles CAB Collective. ⊠ *Paso Robles* ☎ *805/543–2288* ⊕ *www.pasoroblescab.com.* **Paso Robles Wine Country Alliance.** ⊠ *Paso Robles* ☎ *805/239–8463* ⊕ *pasowine. com.* **Rhone Rangers/Paso Robles.** ⊕ *www. rhonerangers.org.* **Travel Paso.** ⊠ *1225 Park St., near 12th St., Paso Robles* ☎ *805/238–0506* ⊕ *www.travelpaso.com.*

 ## Sights

Brecon Estate
WINERY | Small-batch superpremium wines sold exclusively in the tasting room are the focus of this much-lauded, 40-acre, Westside estate winery. Specialties include Albariño, Cabernet Franc, and Rhone blends. Brecon also crafts Bordeaux varietals, including the reserve Old Vine Cabernet Sauvignon, with estate grapes from one of the

oldest vines in Paso Robles. Taste wines within the urban-chic cedar barn, which combines Scandinavian and Australian design elements, or at tables on the shady patio. ⊠ *7450 Vineyard Dr., Paso Robles* ☎ *805/239–2200* ⊕ *breconestate. com* ⊠ *Tastings $20.*

★ Calcareous Vineyard
WINERY | Elegant wines, a stylish tasting room, and knockout hilltop views make for a winning experience at this winery along winding Peachy Canyon Road. Cabernet Sauvignon, Syrah, and Zinfandel grapes thrive in the summer heat and limestone soils of the two vineyards near the tasting room. A third vineyard on cooler York Mountain produces Pinot Noir, Chardonnay, and a Cabernet with a completely different character from the Peachy Canyon edition. Food is available for purchase daily. ⊠ *3430 Peachy Canyon Rd., Paso Robles* ☎ *805/239–0289* ⊕ *www.calcareous.com* ⊠ *Tastings $30; tour and tasting (reservations required) from $90.*

Denner Vineyards
WINERY | The sloping roof of this winery's tasting room and production facility mimics the gently rolling, limestone-laden landscape it occupies. The respect for the terrain that the architecture exhibits repeats itself in the farming and cellar techniques used to create Denner's mostly Rhône-style wines, which—along with Zinfandel, Cabernet Sauvignon, and a few other reds—routinely receive mid-90s scores from major critics. Appointment-only tastings indoors or out take advantage of hilltop views of Willow Creek District trees, vines, and pastures. ⊠ *5414 Vineyard Dr., Paso Robles* ☎ *805/239–4287* ⊕ *www.dennervineyards.com* ⊠ *Tastings $30.*

Eberle Winery
WINERY | Stop here to join a tour (reservations essential) of the huge wine caves beneath the vineyards and to participate in various types of seated tastings. Eberle produces wines from Bordeaux,

Rhône, and Italian varietals and makes intriguing blends including Côte-du-Rôbles Blanc and Rouge and Cabernet Sauvignon—Syrah. ✉ *3810 Hwy. 46 E, 3½ miles east of U.S. 101, Paso Robles* ☏ *805/238–9607* ⊕ *www.eberlewinery. com* 🍷 *Cave tour and tasting $20 by appointment, VIP tour and tasting $50 by appointment.*

Firestone Walker Brewing Company

BREWERY | At this working craft brewery you can sample medal-winners such as the Double Barrel Ale and learn about the beer-making process on 45-minute guided tours of the brewhouse and cellar. ✉ *1400 Ramada Dr., east side of U.S. 101; exit at Hwy. 46 W/Cambria, but head east, Paso Robles* ☏ *805/296–7454 visitor center* ⊕ *www.firestonebeer.com* 🍷 *Tastings from $2 per sample, tour $13 (includes 4 samples).*

Halter Ranch Vineyard

WINERY | A good place to learn about contemporary Paso Robles wine making, this ultramodern operation produces high-quality wines from estate-grown Bordeaux and Rhône grapes grown in sustainably farmed vineyards. The gravity-flow winery, which you can view on tours, is a marvel of efficiency. Ancestor, the flagship wine, a potent Bordeaux-style blend of Cabernet Sauvignon, Petit Verdot, and Malbec, is named for the ranch's huge centuries-old coast oak tree. ✉ *8910 Adelaida Rd., at Vineyard Dr., Paso Robles* ☏ *888/367–9977* ⊕ *www.halterranch.com* 🍷 *Tastings from $35.*

JUSTIN Vineyards & Winery

WINERY | This suave winery built its reputation on Isosceles, a hearty Bordeaux blend, usually of Cabernet Sauvignon, Cabernet Franc, and Merlot. JUSTIN's Cabernet Sauvignon is also well regarded, as is the Right Angle blend of Cab and three other varietals. Tastings here take place in the expansive outdoor patio overlooking the hillside vineyards. ✉ *11680 Chimney Rock Rd., Paso Robles*

⊹ *15 miles west of U.S. 101's Hwy. 46 E exit; take 24th St. west and follow road (name changes along the way) to Chimney Rock Rd.* ☏ *805/238–6932* ⊕ *www.justinwine.com* 🍷 *Tastings $49, tour and tasting $80* ☞ *Tours 10 and 2:30 (reservations recommended).*

★ Niner Wine Estate

WINERY | A family-owned winery in the Willow Creek district, Niner is known equally for its range of estate wines (especially powerful reds) and its farm-fresh lunches designed to complement tasting flights. For a special treat, sign up for a private tour of the solar-powered, gravity-fed winery, followed by a tasting flight of current releases. The option to order lunch is available with tasting reservations, which are required. ✉ *2400 Hwy. 46 W, Paso Robles* ☏ *805/239–2233* ⊕ *www.ninerwine.com* 🍷 *Tasting $40, reserve tasting $100, tour and tasting $150.*

★ Pasolivo

OTHER ATTRACTION | While touring the idyllic west side of Paso Robles, take a break from wine tasting by stopping at Pasolivo. Find out how the artisans here make their Tuscan-style olive oils on a high-tech Italian press, and test the acclaimed results. If you're in downtown Paso Robles, stop by Pasolivo's urban tasting room at 1229 Park Street. ✉ *8530 Vineyard Dr., Paso Robles* ⊹ *West off U.S. 101 (Exit 224) or Hwy. 46 W (Exit 228)* ☏ *805/227–0186* ⊕ *www.pasolivo. com* 🍷 *Tastings $15.*

Re:Find Handcrafted Spirits

DISTILLERY | The owners of Villicana Winery in west Paso Robles launched the first local distillery in 2011, aiming to repurpose the saignée (free-run juice) that's typically tossed out during the wine-making process. They ferment and distill the high-quality juices into premium spirits, thus reclaiming about 70 acres of premium wine grapes. Taste vodka (including kumquat and cucumber versions), gin, whiskey, bourbon, and limoncello in the tiny barrel-room tasting space or outdoors under the oaks. ☒ *2725 Adelaida Rd., Paso Robles* ☏ *805/239–9456* ⊕ *refinddistillery.com* ☕ *Tastings $25* ⊙ *Closed Mon.*

River Oaks Hot Springs & Spa

HOT SPRING | The lakeside spa, on 240 hilly acres near the intersection of U.S. 101 and Highway 46 East, is a great place to relax after wine tasting or festival-going. Soak in a private indoor or outdoor hot tub fed by natural mineral springs, or indulge in a massage or facial. ☒ *800 Clubhouse Dr., Paso Robles* ⊹ *Off River Oaks Dr., just north of River Oaks Golf Course* ☏ *805/238–4600* ⊕ *riveroakshotsprings.com* ☕ *From $16 per hr.*

Robert Hall Winery

WINERY | In recent years, Robert Hall Winery—known for its Bordeaux-based reds, Rhone-based reds and whites, and sparkling wines— has become a regional leader in sustainable and regenerative viticulture at its 130-acre estate. The pet-friendly, kid-friendly property has an on-site kitchen with a seasonal menu, and you can taste wine (from $25) and sign up online in advance for various tours, including the Sustainability Tour and Tasting ($75), Cavern Tour and Barrel Tasting ($75), and Paired Culinary Experience ($75). ☒ *3443 Mill Rd., at Hwy. 46E, 3 miles east of U.S. 101, Paso Robles* ☏ *805/239–1616* ⊕ *www.roberthallwinery.com* ☕ *Tastings $20; tour and tasting $55.*

★ Sensorio

PUBLIC ART | This multi-acre outdoor adventure honors the natural topography and engages the senses with amusing, mystical, and kinetic experiences. Here you can walk through internationally renowned artist Bruce Munro's installation, *Field of Light,* a huge array of stemmed spheres with solar-powered fiber-optic lights that morph into different hues. More than 17,000 wine bottles were used to create the 69 colorful structures of *Light Towers,* an installation whose fiber-optic illumination ripples to a musical score. Nearby the towers are two new-in-2023 attractions: the magical *Fireflies* display with more than 10,000 flickering points of light and the reflective *Gone Fishing* exhibit, which offers a playful interpretation of a contemplative pastime.

A visit begins in the predusk hours to capture the changing light of the landscape and the installations as darkness descends. A hospitality area offers live entertainment by local musicians, as well as wine, beer, and meals or snacks in the casual, indoor–outdoor Mercado Sensorio dining space. Sign up for the Terrace Experience to gain exclusive access to an Airstream bar, private tables, and firepits on a terrace overlooking *Field of Light.* Reserve tickets well in advance: Sensorio is phenomenally popular. ☒ *4380 E. Hwy. 46, Paso Robles* ☏ *805/226–4287* ⊕ *sensoriopaso.com* ☕ *General admission $43, Terrace Experience $87* ⊙ *Hrs vary; check website.*

★ Sixmilebridge Vineyards

WINERY | In a cutting-edge facility on a 95-acre Westside estate, Sixmilebridge (named for the owner's ancestral home in Ireland), produces limited-production Cabernet Sauvignon and Bordeaux blends crafted mostly from organically grown estate fruit. A spacious terrace surrounding a 150-year-old coastal oak tree is reserved for those who purchase a glass or bottle of wine (picnics welcome). ☒ *5120 Peachy Canyon Rd., Paso Robles* ☏ *805/239–5844* ⊕ *www.sixmilebridge.com* ☕ *Tastings from $30.*

Studios on the Park

ARTS CENTER | A 1951 Hudson Hornet (a nod to the building's automotive past) greets you at the entrance to this nonprofit, open-studios arts center on the east side of City Park. Interact with professional artists as they work on their latest pieces, browse the four galleries and gift shop, and, on the first Saturday evening of the month, sip wine and listen to music while viewing the center's latest exhibit. ✉ *1130 Pine St., Paso Robles* ☎ *805/238–9800* 🌐 *studiosonthepark.org.*

SummerWood Winery

WINERY | Rhône varietals do well in the Paso Robles AVA, where many wineries, including this one, produce GSM (Grenache, Syrah, Mourvèdre) red blends, along with whites such as Viognier, Marsanne, and Grenache Blanc. Winemaker Mauricio Marchant displays a subtle touch with Rhône whites and reds, as well as Sentio, a Petit Verdot–heavy Bordeaux red blend. Tastings here are relaxed and informal, and there's a patio from which you can enjoy the vineyard views. ✉ *2175 Arbor Rd., off Hwy. 46W, Paso Robles* ☎ *805/227–1365* 🌐 *www.summerwoodwine.com* 🎟 *Tastings $20, reserve $40.*

Tablas Creek Vineyard

WINERY | Tucked in the western hills of Paso Robles, Tablas Creek is known for its blends of certified biodynamically grown, hand-harvested Rhône varietals. Roussanne and Viognier are the standout whites; the Mourvèdre-heavy blend called Panoplie (it also includes Grenache and Syrah) has received high praise in recent years. A free guided tour of the cellar and vineyard starts every day at 10:15; reservations are required. ■ **TIP→ There's a fine picnic area here.** ✉ *9339 Adelaida Rd., west of Vineyard Dr., Paso Robles* ☎ *805/237–1231* 🌐 *tablascreek.com* 🎟 *Tasting $25, tour free.*

★ Tin City

MARKET | This industrial park on the southern border of Paso Robles houses a collection of wineries, craft breweries, distilleries, and specialty shops where you can pick up sheep's milk ice cream, fresh pasta, and other local wares. Good places to start your explorations include Giornata Winery, Levo Winery, and TinCity Cider Co. Dine upscale (dinner only) at Michelin-starred Six Test Kitchen. ✉ *Limestone Way, Paso Robles* ✣ *East of Ramada Dr. via Marquita Ave.* 🌐 *www.tincitypasorobles.com.*

SIP Certification

Many wineries in Paso Robles take pride in being SIP (Sustainability in Practice) Certified, for which they undergo a rigorous third-party audit of their entire operations. Water and energy conservation practices are reviewed, along with pest management and other aspects of farming. Also considered are the wages, benefits, and working conditions of the employees, and the steps taken to mitigate the impact of grape growing and wine production on area habitats.

🍴 Restaurants

BL Brasserie

$$$ | **FRENCH** | Owner-chef Laurent Grangien's handsome, welcoming French bistro occupies an 1890s brick building across from City Park. He focuses on traditional dishes such as duck confit, rack of lamb, and onion soup, but always prepares a few au courant daily specials as well. **Known for:** classic French dishes; locally sourced ingredients; good selection of local and international wines. [$] *Average main: $34* ✉ *1202 Pine St., at 12th St., Paso Robles* ☎ *805/226–8191* 🌐 *www.bistrolaurent.com* 🕓 *Closed Mon. No lunch Sun.*

The Hatch

$$ | **AMERICAN** | A wood-fire rotisserie in an open kitchen, simple but tasty comfort foods, and a lively bar scene attract locals and visitors alike to this cozy, casual space in an historic brick building a block north of the main square. Although reservations are recommended, bar seating with access to full dinner menu is available for walk-ins. **Known for:** rotisserie chicken, weekly specials; market-inspired cocktails, extensive whiskey collection; intimate, friendly atmosphere. [$] *Average main: $22* ✉ *835 13th St., Paso Robles* ☎ *805/221–5727* 🌐 *www.hatchpasorobles.com* 🕓 *Closed Sun. and Mon. No lunch.*

Il Cortile

$$$ | **ITALIAN** | One of two Paso establishments owned by chef Santos MacDonal and his wife, Carole, this Italian restaurant entices diners with complex flavors and a contemporary space featuring art deco overtones. Consistent crowd-pleasers often on the menu include the beef carpaccio with white truffle cream sauce and shaved black truffles and the pappardelle with wild boar ragù. **Known for:** house-made pastas; excellent wine pairings; ingredients from chef's garden. [$] *Average main: $38* ✉ *608 12th St., near Spring St., Paso Robles* ☎ *805/226–0300* 🌐 *ilcortileristorante.com* 🕓 *Closed Mon. and Tues. No lunch.*

Jeffry's Wine Country BBQ

$ | **AMERICAN** | **FAMILY** | Award-winning local chef Jeff Wiesinger and his wife Kathleen opened this casual eatery, tucked in a hidden courtyard a block from downtown City Park. Feast indoors or out on made-to-order sandwiches, hearty mac-and-cheese bowls, house-made potato chips, fresh salads, craft beer, and local wines while listening to throwback soundtracks from the '60s and '70s. **Known for:** delectable mac-and-cheese dishes; smoked tri-tip and other meats; savory paella. [$] *Average main: $18* ✉ *819 12th St., Suite B, Paso Robles* ✥ *In alley between 12th and 13th Sts.* ☎ *805/369–2132* 🌐 *jeffryswinecountrybbq.com* 🕓 *Closed Wed.*

La Cosecha

$$$ | **SOUTH AMERICAN** | At barlike, tin-ceilinged La Cosecha (Spanish for "the harvest"), Honduran-born chef Santos MacDonal faithfully re-creates dishes from Spain and South America. Noteworthy starters include *pastelitos catracho,* Honduran-style empanadas in a light tomato sauce served with *queso fresco* (fresh cheese) and micro cilantro. **Known for:** fusion of Latin spices and fresh local fare; daily paella special; artisanal cocktails. [$] *Average main: $38* ✉ *835 12th St., near Pine St., Paso Robles* ☎ *805/237–0019* 🌐 *www.lacosechabr.com* 🕓 *Closed Mon. and Tues.*

McPhee's Grill

$$$$ | **AMERICAN** | Just south of Paso Robles in tiny Templeton, this casual chophouse in an 1860s wood-frame storefront serves sophisticated, contemporary versions of traditional Western fare such as oak-grilled filet mignon and fresh seafood tostadas. The house-label wines, made especially for the restaurant, are quite good. **Known for:** meats grilled over red oak; local seasonal menu; excellent wine selections. [$] *Average main: $42* ✉ *416 S. Main St., at 5th St., Templeton* ☎ *805/434–3204* 🌐 *mcpheesgrill.com* 🕓 *Closed Mon. and Tues. No lunch.*

★ Six Test Kitchen

$$$$ | **AMERICAN** | Tucked in a tiny space in the heart of Tin City, this Michelin-starred restaurant offers an intimate gastronomical experience nonpareil in SLO County—12 guests sit at a wooden counter that wraps around an open kitchen and dine on small plates, followed by a seasonal 12-course chef's tasting menu (two seatings per night). **Known for:** ingredient-driven dishes that showcase Central Coast bounty; does not welcome kids under 12; no accommodations for special dietary needs. [$] *Average main: $215* ✉ *3075 Blue Rock Rd., Unit B, Paso Robles* ☎ 🌐 *sixtestkitchen.com* 🕓 *Closed Mon. and Tues.*

Hotels

★ Allegretto Vineyard Resort

$$ | **RESORT** | This swank, 20-acre, Tuscan-style resort amid estate vineyards is also a private museum (nonguests are welcome to walk around) where owner Douglas Ayres displays hundreds of

artworks and artifacts collected on his world travels, including things like ancient Indian river stones and statues, a massive cross section from a giant sequoia, and Russian and California impressionist paintings. **Pros:** yoga in medieval chapel; full-service restaurant Cello and spa; bocce ball, firepit, pool, and other diversions. **Cons:** not close to downtown square; pricey; some rooms close to courtyard music. Ⓢ *Rooms from: $349* ✉ *2700 Buena Vista Dr., Paso Robles* ☎ *805/369–2500* ⊕ *www.allegrettovineyardresort. com* ⌫ *171 rooms* ⦿ *No Meals.*

★ Hotel Cheval

$$$ | **HOTEL** | Equestrian themes surface throughout this intimate European-style boutique hotel a half block from the main square and near some of Paso's best restaurants. **Pros:** most rooms have fireplaces; sip wine and champagne at the on-site Pony Club and zinc bar; extremely personalized service. **Cons:** views aren't great; no pool or hot tub; no elevator. Ⓢ *Rooms from: $410* ✉ *1021 Pine St., Paso Robles* ☎ *805/226–9995, 866/522–6999* ⊕ *www.hotelcheval.com* ⌫ *16 rooms* ⦿ *Free Breakfast.*

JUST Inn

$$$$ | **B&B/INN** | Fine wines, a destination restaurant, and a vineyard's-edge setting make a stay at the Justin winery's inn an exercise in sophisticated seclusion. **Pros:** amazing night skies; vineyard views; destination restaurant. **Cons:** half-hour drive to town; location may be too secluded for some; spotty cell service. Ⓢ *Rooms from: $620* ✉ *11680 Chimney Rock Rd., Paso Robles* ☎ *805/238–6932, 800/726–0049* ⊕ *www.justinwine.com/visit/just-inn* ⌫ *4 suites* ⦿ *Free Breakfast.*

Paso Robles Inn

$$ | **HOTEL** | **FAMILY** | On the site of an old spa hotel of the same name, this inn has various buildings clustered around a lush, shaded garden with a pool. **Pros:** private hot tubs in many rooms; special touches like unique photography in each room; across from town square. **Cons:**

fronts a busy street; rooms vary in size and amenities; some areas could use an upgrade. Ⓢ *Rooms from: $209* ✉ *1103 Spring St., Paso Robles* ☎ *800/676–1713* ⊕ *www.pasoroblesinn.com* ⌫ *98 rooms* ⦿ *No Meals.*

★ SummerWood Inn

$$ | **B&B/INN** | Easygoing hospitality, vineyard-view rooms, and elaborate breakfasts make this inn a mile west of U.S. 101 worth seeking out. **Pros:** convenient wine-touring base; elaborate breakfasts; free tastings at associated winery. **Cons:** some noise from nearby highway during the day; no elevator; not close to downtown restaurants. Ⓢ *Rooms from: $350* ✉ *2130 Arbor Rd., Paso Robles* ✛ *1 mile west of U.S. 101, at Hwy. 46W* ☎ *805/227–1111* ⊕ *www. summerwoodwine.com/inn* ⌫ *9 rooms* ⦿ *Free Breakfast.*

ⓨ Nightlife

1122 Speakeasy

COCKTAIL LOUNGES | Press the doorbell and request permission to enter this elegant, 1930s-era cocktail lounge and speakeasy on the back patio of Pappy McGregor's Pub on the main square. It has just 28 seats, so be prepared to wait in line on weekend nights. ✉ *1122 Pine St., Paso Robles* ✛ *Entrance on Railroad St. or walk through pub* ☎ *805/238–7070 info line* ⊕ *www.eleven-twentytwo.com* ☽ *Closed Mon.* ☞ *No reservations Fri. and Sat.*

ⓧ Performing Arts

Vina Robles Amphitheatre

CONCERTS | At this 3,300-seat, Mission-style venue with good food, wine, and sight lines, you can enjoy acclaimed musicians in concert. ✉ *Vina Robles winery, 3800 Mill Rd., off Hwy. 46, Paso Robles* ☎ *805/286–3680* ⊕ *www.vinaroblesamphitheatre.com* ☞ *Performances Apr.–Nov.*

🛍 Shopping

Paso Robles Market Walk

MARKET | **FAMILY** | Taste wine and craft beer, feast on ramen bowls, burgers, and sweet treats, and shop for one-of-a-kind gifts in this upscale public market in a residential area six blocks north of City Park. The eclectic collection of purveyors showcases the products of local chefs, vintners, and makers—all committed to sustainable business practices. ■TIP➔ **Book a room in one of the six luxury lofts on the market's second floor for convenient dining and shopping before or after wine touring.** ✉ *1803 Spring St., Paso Robles* ☎ *805/720–1255* ⊕ *www. pasomarketwalk.com.*

Morro Bay

30 miles southwest of Paso Robles, 14 miles north of San Luis Obispo.

Commercial fishermen slog around Morro Bay in galoshes, and beat-up fishing boats bob in the bay's protected waters. Nature-oriented activities take center stage here: kayaking, hiking, biking, fishing, and wildlife-watching around the bay and national marine estuary and along the state beach.

GETTING HERE AND AROUND

From U.S. 101 south or north, exit at Highway 1 in San Luis Obispo and head west. Scenic Highway 1 passes through the eastern edge of town. From Atascadero, two-lane Highway 41 West treks over the mountains to Morro Bay. San Luis Obispo RTA Route 12 buses travel year-round between Morro Bay, San Luis Obispo, Cayucos, Cambria, San Simeon, and Hearst Castle ($1.75 to $3.25, $5.50 regional day pass).

ESSENTIALS

VISITOR INFORMATION Morro Bay
Tourism. ✉ *695 Harbor St., at Piney Way, Morro Bay* ☎ *805/225–7411* ⊕ *www. morrobay.org.*

👁 Sights

Embarcadero

PROMENADE | **FAMILY** | The center of Morro Bay action on land is the Embarcadero, where vacationers pour in and out of souvenir shops and seafood restaurants and stroll or bike along the scenic half-mile Harborwalk to Morro Rock. From here, you can get out on the bay in a kayak or tour boat. ✉ *Morro Bay* ✛ *On waterfront from Beach St. to Tidelands Park.*

Montaña de Oro State Park

STATE/PROVINCIAL PARK | **FAMILY** | West of San Luis Obispo, Los Osos Valley Road winds past farms and ranches to this state park whose miles of nature trails traverse rocky shoreline, wild beaches, and hills overlooking dramatic scenery. Check out the tide pools, watch the waves roll into the bluffs, and picnic in the eucalyptus groves. From Montaña de Oro you can reach Morro Bay by following the coastline along South Bay Boulevard 8 miles through the quaint residential villages of Los Osos and Baywood Park. ✉ *San Luis Obispo* ✛ *West about 13 miles from downtown San Luis Obispo on Madonna Rd., to Los Osos Valley Rd., to Pecho Valley Rd.; to continue on to Morro Bay, backtrack east to Los Osos Valley Rd., then head north on S. Bay Blvd., and west on State Park Rd.* ☎ *805/772–6101* ⊕ *www.parks.ca.gov.*

Morro Bay State Park
Museum of Natural History

SCIENCE MUSEUM | **FAMILY** | The museum's entertaining interactive exhibits explain the natural environment and how to preserve it—in the bay and estuary and on the rest of the planet. ■TIP➔ **Kids age 17 and under are admitted free.** ✉ *20 State Park Rd., south of downtown, Morro Bay* ☎ *805/772–2694* ⊕ *centralcoastparks. org* 🎟 *$3.*

Morro Rock

NATURE SIGHT | **FAMILY** | At the mouth of Morro Bay stands 576-foot-high Morro Rock, one of nine small volcanic peaks, or morros, in the area. A short walk leads to a breakwater, with the harbor on one side and crashing ocean waves on the other. You may not climb the rock, where endangered falcons and other birds nest. Sea lions and otters often play in the water below the rock. ⊠ *Northern end of Embarcadero, Morro Bay.*

🍴 Restaurants

Dorn's Original Breakers Cafe

$$ | **SEAFOOD** | **FAMILY** | This restaurant overlooking the harbor has satisfied local appetites since 1942 and serves straight-ahead dishes such as cod or shrimp fish-and-chips or calamari tubes sautéed in butter and wine. **Known for:** sweeping views of Morro Rock and the bay; fresh local seafood; friendly, efficient service. ⓢ *Average main: $23* ⊠ *801 Market Ave., at Morro Bay Blvd., Morro Bay* ☎ *805/772–4415* ⊕ *www.dornscafe.com.*

Taco Temple

$ | **AMERICAN** | **FAMILY** | This family-run diner serves some of the freshest food around. The seafood-heavy menu includes salmon burritos, Alaskan cod tostadas, superb fish tacos with mango salsa, and other dishes hailing from somewhere between California and Mexico. **Known for:** freshly made salsas; hefty portions; daily specials. ⓢ *Average main: $16* ⊠ *2680 Main St., at Elena St., just north of Hwy. 1/Hwy. 41 junction, Morro Bay* ☎ *805/772–4965* ⊕ *tacotemple.com.*

★ Tognazzini's Dockside

$$ | **SEAFOOD** | **FAMILY** | Captain Mark Tognazzini catches seasonal seafood and delivers the bounty to his family's collection of down-home, no-frills, harbor-side enterprises—a fish market with patio dining and up-close views of Morro Rock (Dockside Too) and the original Dockside restaurant. Local musicians play live music nearly every day at the outdoor patio at Dockside Too. **Known for:** fresh-as-it-gets seafood; live music nearly every day; front-row seats to Morro Rock

views. ⓢ *Average main: $25* ⊠ *1245 Embarcadero, Morro Bay* ☎ *805/772–8100 restaurant, 805/772–8120 fish market and patio dining* ⊕ *www.morrobay-dockside.com.*

Windows on the Water

$$$$ | **SEAFOOD** | Diners at this second-floor restaurant view the sunset through giant picture windows. Meanwhile, fresh fish and other dishes incorporating local ingredients emerge from the wood-fired oven in the open kitchen, and oysters on the half shell beckon from the raw bar. **Known for:** sustainably sourced seafood; 20-plus wines by the glass; menu changes nightly. ⓢ *Average main: $45* ⊠ *699 Embarcadero, at Pacific St., Morro Bay* ☎ *805/772–0677* ⊕ *www.windowsmb.com* ⊗ *Closed Sun. and Mon. No lunch.*

🛏 Hotels

★ Anderson Inn

$$ | **B&B/INN** | Friendly, personalized service and an oceanfront setting keep guests returning to this Embarcadero inn, which features well-appointed rooms with state-of-the-art tiled bathrooms and cozy comforters atop king beds. **Pros:** walk to restaurants and sights; spacious rooms; oceanfront rooms have fireplaces and private balconies. **Cons:** not low-budget; waterfront area can get crowded; need to book well in advance—fills quickly. ⓢ *Rooms from: $315* ⊠ *897 Embarcadero, Morro Bay* ☎ *805/772–3434* ⊕ *andersoninnmorrobay.com* ⤸ *8 rooms* ⚏ *No Meals.*

The Inn at Morro Bay

$$ | **RESORT** | Surrounded by eucalyptus trees, this inn abuts a heron rookery and Morro Bay State Park. **Pros:** great for wild-life lovers; stellar views from restaurant and some rooms; nearby golf course, on-site wellness center. **Cons:** some rooms on the small side; birds and seals can wake you early; remote location, not close to the Embarcadero. ⓢ *Rooms* *from: $209 ✉ 60 State Park Rd., Morro Bay ☎ 805/772–5651 ⊕ innatmorrobay. com ⤻ 98 rooms ⌾ No Meals.*

🏃 Activities

Lost Isle Adventures
BOATING | Offerings include 45-minute jaunts around Morro Bay ($25) or adults-only sunset cruises ($30) aboard a tiki-themed boat. A faster adventure boat is used for 90-minute whale-watching excursions ($85). ✉ *Giovanni's Fish Market, 1001 Front St., on the Embarcadero, Morro Bay* ☎ *805/440–8170* ⊕ *morrobay-tikiboat.com.*

Sub-Sea Tours & Kayaks
BOATING | FAMILY | You can view sea life aboard this outfit's glass-bottom boat; cruise the bay or watch whales from its two larger vessels; or rent a kayak, canoe, or stand-up paddleboard. ✉ *699 Embarcadero, Morro Bay* ☎ *805/772–9463* ⊕ *morrobaywhalewatching.com* ✉ *From $60.*

Virg's Landing
FISHING | Virg's conducts deep-sea-fishing and whale-watching trips. ✉ *1169 Market Ave., Morro Bay* ☎ *805/772–1222* ⊕ *www.virgslanding.com* ✉ *From $89.*

Cambria

28 miles west of Paso Robles, 20 miles north of Morro Bay.

Cambria, set on piney hills above the sea, was settled by Welsh miners in the 1890s. In the 1970s, the isolated setting attracted artists and other independent types, and although the town now caters to tourists, it still bears the imprint of its bohemian past. Both of Cambria's downtowns, the original East Village and the newer West Village, are packed with art and crafts galleries, antiques shops, cafés, restaurants, and B&Bs.

Two diverting detours lie between Morro Bay and Cambria. In the laid-back beach town of Cayucos, 4 miles north of Morro Bay, you can stroll the long pier, feast on chowder (at Duckie's), and sample the namesake delicacies of the Brown Butter Cookie Co. Over in Harmony, a quaint former dairy town 7 miles south of Cambria (population 18), you can take in the glassworks, pottery, and other artsy enterprises.

GETTING HERE AND AROUND
Highway 1 leads to Cambria from the north and south. Highway 246 West curves from U.S. 101 through the mountains to Cambria. San Luis Obispo RTA Route 12 buses stop in Cambria (and Hearst Castle).

ESSENTIALS
VISITOR INFORMATION Cambria Chamber of Commerce. ✉ *767 Main St.* ☎ *805/927–3624* ⊕ *www.cambriachamber.org.*

👁 Sights

Covell Ranch Clydesdale Horses
FARM/RANCH | FAMILY | Come to the 2,000-acre Covell Ranch to see one of the world's largest private stands of endangered Monterey pines and witness herds of gentle Clydesdales roaming the range. Much of the ranch is in a conservation easement that will never be developed. The 1½-hour guided vehicle tours take you through pastures and pine groves to the barn. The ranch also offers trail rides. ✉ *5694 Bridge St., Cambria* ☎ *805/975–7332* ⊕ *www.covellsclydesdaleranch.com* ✉ *Tours $200 for up to 5 persons* ⊙ *Tours and trail rides by appointment only.*

Fiscalini Ranch Preserve
NATURE PRESERVE | FAMILY | Walk down a mile-long coastal bluff trail to spot migrating whales, otters, and shorebirds at this 450-acre public preserve. Miles of additional scenic trails crisscross the protected habitats of rare and endangered species of flora and fauna, including a Monterey pine forest, western pond

turtles, monarch butterflies, and burrowing owls. Dogs are permitted on-leash everywhere and off-leash on all trails except the bluff. ✉ *Hwy. 1* ✥ *Between Cambria Rd. and Main St. to the north and Burton Dr. and Warren Rd. to the south; access either end of bluff trail off Windsor Blvd.* ☎ *805/927–2856* 🌐 *www.fiscaliniranchpreserve.org.*

Leffingwell Landing

VIEWPOINT | FAMILY | This state picnic ground is a good place for examining tidal pools and watching otters frolic in the surf. ✉ *Cambria* ✥ *North end of Moonstone Beach Dr.* ☎ *805/927–2070.*

Moonstone Beach Drive

SCENIC DRIVE | FAMILY | The drive runs along a bluff above the ocean, paralleled by a 3-mile boardwalk that winds along the beach. On this photogenic walk you might glimpse sea lions and sea otters, and perhaps a gray whale during winter and spring. Year-round, birds fly about, and tiny creatures scurry amid the tidepools. ✉ *Off Hwy. 1.*

★ Stolo Family Vineyards

WINERY | Just 3 miles from the ocean and a short drive from Cambria's East Village, the 52-acre Stolo estate produces about 4,000 cases of premium wine each year. Its Syrahs consistently win top awards; sample these and other wines, including Pinot Noir, dry Gewurztraminer, Sauvignon Blanc, and Chardonnays, in the hilltop tasting room on the site of a former dairy farm. If the weather's nice, sit out on the sprawling lawn near a 1920s barn and 1895 farmhouse. ✉ *3776 Santa Rosa Creek Rd., Cambria* ☎ *805/924–3131* 🌐 *www.stolofamilyvineyards.com* 🎟 *Tasting $25 by reservation.*

🍴 Restaurants

Brydge

$$ | AMERICAN | The fresh bounty of the Central Coast takes center stage at this hyperlocal eatery in a Victorian-era home in Cambria's Old Village. Soups, salads, burgers, sandwiches, and small plates to share predominate here, but you can also order large comfort-food meals (roast chicken, eggplant cassoulet, Wagyu rib eye) for two persons. **Known for:** almost everything can be made gluten-free and dairy-free (just ask!); tiny spicy meatballs, salt cod brandade; patio seating available. [$] *Average main: $26* ✉ *4286 Bridge St., Cambria* ☎ *805/203–5381* 🌐 *www.brydgerestaurant.com* 🕒 *Closed Tues. and Wed.*

Linn's Restaurant

$$ | AMERICAN | FAMILY | Homemade soups, potpies, and other farmhouse comfort foods share the menu at this spacious East Village restaurant with fancier farm-to-table dishes such as organic, free-range chicken topped with raspberry-orange-cranberry sauce. Also on-site are a bakery, a café serving more casual fare (take-out available), and a gift shop that sells gourmet foods. **Known for:** olallieberry pie; numerous gluten-free and vegan options; family-owned and -operated for decades. [$] *Average main: $30* ✉ *2277 Main St., at Wall St., Cambria* ☎ *805/927–0371* 🌐 *www.linnsfruitbin.com.*

★ Madeline's

$$$ | FRENCH FUSION | Dine on stellar French-American delights at a romantic, candlit table in this tiny restaurant within a tasting room and wineshop in Cambria's West Village. The menu changes seasonally, but you might start with diver scallops or stuffed quail, move on to Louisiana seafood gumbo or Long Island duck breast, and then finish with bananas foster or crème brûlée. **Known for:** lamb osso buco, octopus, and other unusual dishes; excellent selection of local wines; house-made desserts. [$] *Average main: $35* ✉ *788 Main St., Cambria* ☎ *805/927–4175* 🌐 *madelinescambria.com.*

Robin's

$$ | ECLECTIC | An international, vegetarian-friendly dining experience awaits you at this cozy East Village cottage. Dinner choices include chiles relents, grilled Skuna Bay salmon, lamb curry, and grilled pork chops. **Known for:** savory curries; top-notch salmon bisque; secluded (heated) garden patio. [$] *Average main: $28* ✉ *4095 Burton Dr., at Center St., Cambria* ☎ *805/927–5007* 🌐 *www.robins-restaurant.com.*

★ Sea Chest Oyster Bar and Restaurant

$$$ | **SEAFOOD** | Cambria's best place for seafood fills up soon after it opens at 5:30 (no reservations taken, but you can put your name on a waitlist at 5:30). Those in the know grab seats at the oyster bar and take in spectacular sunsets while watching the chefs broil fresh halibut, steam garlicky clams, and fry crispy calamari steaks; if you arrive to a wait, play cribbage or checkers in the game room. **Known for:** New England chowder house vibe; savory cioppino; waiting areas in wine bar, game room, and patio with firepit. [$] *Average main: $35* ✉ *6216 Moonstone Beach Dr., near Weymouth St., Cambria* ☎ *805/927–4514* 🌐 *seachestoysterbar.com* 💳 *No credit cards* ⏲ *Closed Tues. mid-Sept.–May. No lunch.*

🛏 Hotels

Cambria Pines Lodge

$$ | **RESORT** | **FAMILY** | Accommodations at this 25-acre retreat up the hill from the East Village range from basic fireplace cabins to motel-style standard rooms to large fireplace suites and deluxe suites with spa tubs. **Pros:** short walk from downtown; live music nightly in the lounge; verdant gardens. **Cons:** service and housekeeping not always top-quality; some units need updating; thin walls in some units. [$] *Rooms from: $269* ✉ *2905 Burton Dr., Cambria* ☎ *805/927–4200, 800/966–6490* 🌐 *www.cambria-pineslodge.com* 🛏 *152 rooms* 🍴 *Free Breakfast.*

Moonstone Landing

$$ | **HOTEL** | This up-to-date motel's amenities, reasonable rates, and accommodating staff make it a Moonstone Beach winner. **Pros:** Mission-style furnishings; across from the beach; cheery lounge. **Cons:** narrow property; some rooms overlook a parking lot; noise occasionally travels from next-door restaurant machinery. [$] *Rooms from: $209* ✉ *6240 Moonstone Beach Dr., Cambria* ☎ *805/927–0012, 800/830–4540* 🌐 *moonstonelanding.com* 🛏 *29 rooms* 🍴 *Free Breakfast.*

★ Olallieberry Inn

$$ | **B&B/INN** | The second-oldest home in Cambria (built in 1875) and a national historic monument, this painstakingly restored B&B inn offers luxurious creature comforts in a pristine, English-garden setting on the banks of Santa Rosa Creek. **Pros:** gourmet three-course breakfast; wine hour with homemade appetizers; walk to East Village restaurants and shops. **Cons:** no elevator; no children under 12; some rooms front busy road. [$] *Rooms from: $240* ✉ *2476 Main St., Cambria* ☎ *805/927–3222* 🌐 *www.olallieberry.com* 🛏 *9 rooms* 🍴 *Free Breakfast.*

★ White Water Cambria

$$$ | **HOTEL** | A fascinating design that blends beach-boho 1970s California with Scandinavian modern elements (clean lines, light woods, natural accents), an inviting lobby lounge with sweeping ocean views, and cozy rooms that evoke unfussy luxury make White Water stand out among Moonstone Beach lodgings. **Pros:** lobby lounge with small bites and shared plates, cocktails, wine, and craft beer; steps to the beach and walking trails; fleet of complimentary Linus bikes. **Cons:** not in downtown; some rooms on the small side; fog sometimes obscures ocean views. [$] *Rooms from: $399* ✉ *6736 Moonstone Beach Dr., Cambria* ☎ *805/927–1066* 🌐 *whitewatercambria.com* 🛏 *25 rooms* 🍴 *Free Breakfast.*

⚡ Activities

Vyana Wellness Collective

SPAS | Drop in at Vyana, in the heart of the Old Village, for various services, including massage therapy (from $115), infrared-sauna sessions ($35 for 45 minutes), and wellness classes (from $15). ✉ *4090 Burton Dr., Suite 6, Cambria* ☎ *805/235–8785* ⊕ *www.vyana.life.*

San Simeon

9 miles north of Cambria, 65 miles south of Big Sur.

Whalers founded San Simeon in the 1850s but had virtually abandoned it by 1865, when Senator George Hearst began purchasing most of the surrounding ranch land. Hearst turned San Simeon into a bustling port, and his son, William Randolph Hearst, further developed the area while erecting Hearst Castle (one of the many remarkable stops you'll encounter when driving along Highway 1). Today San Simeon is basically a strip of unremarkable gift shops and so-so motels that straddle Highway 1 about 4 miles south of the castle's entrance, but Old San Simeon, right across from the entrance, is worth a peek. Julia Morgan, William Randolph Hearst's architect, designed some of the village's Mission Revival–style buildings.

GETTING HERE AND AROUND

Highway 1 is the only way to reach San Simeon. Connect with the highway off U.S. 101 directly or via rural routes such as Highway 41 West (Atascadero to Morro Bay) and Highway 46 West (Paso Robles to Cambria).

ESSENTIALS

VISITOR INFORMATION San Simeon Chamber of Commerce Visitor Center.
✉ *250 San Simeon Ave., San Simeon* ☎ *805/927–3500* ⊕ *visitsansimeonca. com.*

◉ Sights

★ Hearst Castle

CASTLE/PALACE | **FAMILY** | Officially known as Hearst San Simeon State Historical Monument, Hearst Castle sits in solitary splendor atop La Cuesta Encantada (the Enchanted Hill). Its buildings and gardens spread over 127 acres that were the heart of newspaper magnate William Randolph Hearst's 250,000-acre ranch. Hearst commissioned renowned California architect Julia Morgan to design the estate, but he was very much involved with the final product, a blend of Italian, Spanish, and Moorish styles. The 115-room main structure and three huge "cottages" are connected by terraces and staircases and surrounded by pools, gardens, and statuary. In its heyday the castle, whose buildings hold about 22,000 works of fine and decorative art, was a playground for Hearst and his guests—Hollywood celebrities, political leaders, scientists, and other well-known figures. Construction began in 1919 and was never officially completed. Work was halted in 1947 when Hearst had to leave San Simeon because of failing health. The Hearst Corporation donated the property to the State of California in 1958, and it is now part of the state park system.

Access to the castle is through the visitor center at the foot of the hill, where you can view educational exhibits and a 40-minute film about Hearst's life and the castle's construction. Buses from the center zigzag up to the hilltop estate, where guides conduct several daytime tours, each with a different focus: Grand Rooms, Upstairs Suites, Designing the Dream, Cottages and Kitchen, Julia Morgan, Art of San Simeon, Hearst and Hollywood. These tours take about three hours and include a movie screening and time at the end to explore the castle's exterior and gardens. In spring and fall, docents in period costume portray Hearst's guests and staff for the Evening Tour, which begins around sunset.

Reservations are recommended for all tours, which include a ½-mile walk and between 150 and 400 stairs. ■TIP→ Be sure to check the website in advance of your visit for any updates. ⊠ *San Simeon State Park, 750 Hearst Castle Rd., San Simeon* ☎ *800/444–4445, 518/218–5078 international reservations* ⊕ *hearstcastle.org* ⊠ *Daytime tours from $30, evening tours $41.*

Hearst Ranch Winery

WINERY | Old whaling equipment and Hearst Ranch and Hearst Castle memorabilia decorate this winery's casual Old San Simeon outpost. The tasting room occupies a historic warehouse building with a gift shop, deli, and an outdoor deck and umbrella-shaded tables overlooking San Simeon Cove. The flagship wines include the Bunkhouse Cabernet Sauvignon, named after the historic Hearst Ranch building designed by Julia Morgan, and Rhône-style white and red blends. Malbec and Tempranillo are two other strong suits. ⊠ *442 SLO San Simeon Rd., off Hwy. 1, San Simeon* ☎ *805/927–4100* ⊕ *www.hearstranchwinery.com* ⊠ *Tastings from $30.*

Piedras Blancas Elephant Seal Rookery

WILDLIFE REFUGE | FAMILY | A large colony of elephant seals (at last count 25,000) gathers every year at this rookery on the beaches near Piedras Blancas Lighthouse. The huge males with their pendulous, trunklike noses typically start appearing on shore in late November, and the females begin to arrive in December to give birth—most babies are born in the last two weeks of January. The newborn pups spend about four weeks nursing before their mothers head out to sea, leaving them on their own; the "weaners" leave the rookery when they are about 3½ months old. The seals return in the spring and summer months to molt or rest, but not en masse as in winter. You can watch them from a boardwalk along the bluffs just a few feet above the beach; do not attempt to approach them

as they are wild animals. The nonprofit Friends of the Elephant Seal runs a small visitor center and gift shop (⊠ *250 San Simeon Ave.*) in San Simeon. ⊠ *San Simeon* ✛ *Off Hwy. 1, 4½ miles north of Hearst Castle, just south of Piedras Blancas Lighthouse* ☎ *805/924–1628* ⊕ *www.elephantseal.org.*

Piedras Blancas Light Station

LIGHTHOUSE | FAMILY | If you think traversing craggy, twisting Highway 1 is tough, imagine trying to navigate a boat up the rocky coastline (*piedras blancas* means "white rocks" in Spanish) near San Simeon before lighthouses were built. Captains must have cheered wildly when the beam began to shine here in 1875. Try to time a visit to include the 9:45 am tour held on Tuesday, Thursday, and Saturday year-round, as well as on Monday and Friday in summer. ■TIP→ Do not meet your guide at the gate to the lighthouse—you'll miss the tour. Meet instead at the former Piedras Blancas Motel, 1½ miles north of the light station. ⊠ *15950 Cabrillo Hwy., San Simeon* ☎ *877/444–6777* ⊕ *www.piedrasblancas.org* ⊠ *$10* ⚠ *Advance reservations and online ticket purchase required* ☞ *No pets allowed.*

⊕ Beaches

William Randolph Hearst Memorial Beach

BEACH | FAMILY | This wide, sandy beach edges a protected cove on both sides of San Simeon Pier. Fish from the pier or from a charter boat, picnic and barbecue on the bluffs, or boogie board or bodysurf the relatively gentle waves. In summer you can rent a kayak and paddle out into the bay for close encounters with marine life and sea caves. The NOAA Coastal Discovery Center, next to the parking lot, has interactive exhibits and hosts educational activities and events. **Amenities:** food and drink; parking; toilets; water sports. **Best for:** sunset; swimming; walking. ⊠ *750 Hearst Castle Rd., off Hwy. 1, west of Hearst Castle entrance,*

San Simeon ☎ *805/927–2035* ⊕ *www. parks.ca.gov* 🖰 *Free.*

🛏 Hotels

Cavalier Oceanfront Resort
$ | HOTEL | Reasonable rates for the area, an oceanfront location, evening bonfires, and well-equipped rooms—some with wood-burning fireplaces and private patios—make this motel a great choice. **Pros:** on the bluffs; fantastic views; close to Hearst Castle. **Cons:** room amenities and sizes vary; pools are small and sometimes crowded; some rooms need updating. Ⓢ *Rooms from: $199* ⊠ *9415 Hearst Dr., San Simeon* ☎ *805/927–4688, 800/826–8168* ⊕ *www.cavalierresort.com* ⇥ *90 rooms* ᵀᴼ� *No Meals.*

Big Sur Coast

76 miles north along Hwy. 1 from San Simeon to Bixby Creek Bridge.

The countercultural spirit of Big Sur—a loose string of coast-hugging properties along Highway 1—is alive and well. Its few residents include the very wealthy, the enthusiastically outdoorsy, and the utterly evolved, as, since the 1960s, the Esalen Institute, a center for alternative education and East–West philosophical study, has attracted seekers of higher consciousness and devotees of the property's hot springs. Today, posh and rustic resorts amid the redwoods cater to visitors drawn by the scenery and the serenity. Southern Big Sur, the 52-mile stretch between San Simeon and Julia Pfeiffer Burns State Park, is especially rugged—a rocky world of mountains, cliffs, and beaches.

GETTING HERE AND AROUND
To explore Southern Big Sur from the south, access Highway 1 from U.S. 101 in San Luis Obispo; from the north, take rural route Highway 46 West (Paso Robles to Cambria) or Highway 41 West (Atascadero to Morro Bay). Nacimiento-to-Fergusson Road snakes through mountains and forest from U.S. 101 at Jolon about 25 miles to Highway 1 at Kirk Creek, about 4 miles south of Lucia; this curving, sometimes precipitous road is a motorcyclist favorite, not recommended for the faint of heart or during inclement weather. To reach Central Big Sur, head north from Julia Pfeiffer Burns State Park on Highway 1 or follow Highway 1 south out of Carmel.

ESSENTIALS
Stop by Big Sur Station to talk to staff, get information on activities and road conditions, and take advantage of public restrooms and fairly reliable cell service.

VISITOR INFORMATION Big Sur Chamber of Commerce. ⊠ *Big Sur* ☎ *831/667–2100* ⊕ *bigsurcalifornia.org.* **Big Sur Station.** ⊠ *47555 California Hwy. 1, ¼ mile south of Pfeiffer Big Sur State Park entrance, Big Sur* ☎ *831/667–2315* ⊕ *lpforest.org/ big-sur-station.*

◉ Sights

Bixby Creek Bridge
BRIDGE | FAMILY | The graceful arc of Bixby Creek Bridge is a photographer's dream. Built in 1932, the bridge spans a deep canyon, more than 100 feet wide at the bottom. From the north-side parking area you can admire the view or walk the 550-foot structure. The parking area is very small. ■ **TIP→ Follow all signs regarding how (e.g., single-file, parallel to the bluff) and where to park. If there are no spots, cross the bridge to one of the pullouts to the south.** ⊠ *Hwy. 1, 6 miles north of Point Sur State Historic Park, 13 miles south of Carmel, Big Sur.*

★ Highway 1
SCENIC DRIVE | FAMILY | One of California's most spectacular drives snakes up the coast north of San Simeon. Numerous pullouts offer tremendous views and photo ops. On some beaches, huge elephant seals lounge nonchalantly, seemingly

Did You Know?

McWay Cove at Julia Pfeiffer Burns State Park is a renowned spot on the Big Sur Coast.

oblivious to the attention of rubberneckers. Heavy rain can cause mudslides that block the highway north and south of Big Sur, so sections of the route are sometimes closed for repairs or general maintenance. ■TIP➔ **Before traveling, visit ⊕ *bigsurcalifornia.org* and click on the Highway 1 Conditions and Information link.** ⊕ *www.dot.ca.gov.*

Julia Pfeiffer Burns State Park

STATE/PROVINCIAL PARK | FAMILY | The park provides fine hiking, from an easy ½-mile stroll with marvelous coastal views to a strenuous 6-mile trek through redwoods. The big draw here, an 80-foot waterfall that drops into the ocean, gets crowded in summer; still, it's an astounding place to contemplate nature. Migrating whales, harbor seals, and sea lions can sometimes be spotted just offshore. ■TIP➔ **Trails east of Highway 1 and beach access to McWay Falls were closed in 2023 due to storm damage; check the website for updates.** ⊠ *Hwy. 1, 15 miles north of Lucia* ☏ *831/667–1112* ⊕ *www.parks. ca.gov* ⊠ *$10.*

Pfeiffer Big Sur State Park

STATE/PROVINCIAL PARK | FAMILY | Among the many hiking trails at Pfeiffer Big Sur, a short route through a redwood-filled valley leads to a waterfall. You can double back or continue on the more difficult trail along the valley wall for views over miles of treetops to the sea. ⊠ *47231 Hwy. 1, Big Sur* ☏ *831/667–1112* ⊕ *www.parks. ca.gov* ⊠ *$10 per vehicle.*

★ Pfeiffer Canyon Bridge

BRIDGE | FAMILY | In 2017, heavy winter rains caused an old concrete bridge built in 1968 to crack and slip downhill at Pfeiffer Canyon, in the heart of Big Sur. Engineers deemed the old bridge irreparable, and auto and pedestrian access to Highway 1 south of the bridge was cut off indefinitely. CalTrans quickly made plans to construct a new, $24-million bridge to span the deep canyon. Normally, such a massive project would take at least seven years, but CalTrans accelerated the project and completed it in less than a year. The new bridge—a 21st-century engineering marvel—stretches 310 feet across the ravine without the need for column support. It's made of 15 steel girders, each weighing 62 tons and connected by steel plates holding 14,000 bolts. ⊠ *Hwy. 1, Big Sur* ⊹ *0.7 mile south of Big Sur Station.*

Point Sur State Historic Park

STATE/PROVINCIAL PARK | FAMILY | The 1889 lighthouse at this state park still stands watch from atop a large volcanic rock. Four lighthouse keepers lived here with their families until 1974, when the station became automated. Their homes and working spaces are open to the public only on three-hour ranger-led tours. Considerable walking, including up two stairways, is involved. Strollers are not allowed. ⊠ *Hwy. 1, 7 miles north of Pfeiffer Big Sur State Park, Big Sur* ☏ *831/625–4419* ⊕ *www. parks.ca.gov* ⊠ *$15* ☞ *Call or visit website for current tour schedule.*

🏖 Beaches

Pfeiffer Beach

BEACH | FAMILY | Through a hole in one of the gigantic boulders at secluded Pfeiffer Beach, you can watch the waves break first on the seaside and then on the beach side. Keep a sharp eye out for the unsigned, nongated road to the beach: it branches west of Highway 1 between the post office and Pfeiffer Big Sur State Park. The 2-mile, one-lane road descends sharply. **Amenities:** parking (fee); toilets. **Best for:** solitude; sunset. ⊠ *Off Hwy. 1, 1 mile south of Pfeiffer Big Sur State Park, Big Sur* ⊕ *www.fs.usda.gov* ⊠ *$12 per vehicle.*

🍴 Restaurants

COAST Big Sur

$$ | AMERICAN | FAMILY | Feast on ocean views and farm-fresh food at this casual café on a terrace atop three redwood water tanks and an art gallery. Lunch options include pizzas, vegan bowls, salads, mix-and-match dips, breads, and snacks—all made from organic, locally and ethnically sourced ingredients. **Known for:** savory seed and oat bread and other baked goods; organic soft-serve ice cream; on-site shop for picnic provisions. $ *Average main: $20* ⊠ *49901 Hwy. 1, Big Sur* ☎ *831/667–2301* ⊕ *coastbigsur. com* ☾ *Closed Tues. and Wed. No dinner.*

★ Deetjen's Big Sur Inn

$$$ | **AMERICAN** | The candle-lighted, creaky-floor restaurant in the main house at the historic inn of the same name is a Big Sur institution. It serves spicy seafood paella, grass-fed filet mignon, and rack of lamb for dinner and flavorful eggs Benedict for breakfast. **Known for:** rustic, romantic setting; ingredients from sustainable purveyors; stellar daily breakfast. $ *Average main: $32* ⊠ *48865 Hwy. 1, Big Sur* ☎ *831/667–2378* ⊕ *www. deetjens.com* ☾ *Closed Wed. and Thurs. No lunch.*

★ Nepenthe

$$$ | **AMERICAN** | The coastal views are utterly spectacular from Nepenthe, named for an opiate mentioned in Greek literature that would induce a state of "no sorrow." For the best vistas, settle on the terraced deck in the late afternoon, order a glass from the extensive wine list, and watch the sun slip into the Pacific Ocean. **Known for:** ambrosia burger, fresh fish, hormone-free steaks; multiple view decks; brunch and lunch at casual outdoor Café Kevah. $ *Average main: $40* ⊠ *48510 Hwy. 1, 2½ miles south of Big Sur Station, Big Sur* ☎ *831/667–2345* ⊕ *www.nepenthe.com.*

★ Sierra Mar

$$$$ | **AMERICAN** | At cliff's edge 1,200 feet above the Pacific at the ultrachic Post Ranch Inn, Sierra Mar serves cutting-edge American cuisine made from mostly organic, seasonal ingredients, some from the on-site chef's garden. The four-course prix-fixe option always shines. **Known for:** stunning ocean panoramas;

one of the nation's most extensive wine lists; iconic Big Sur farm-to-table experience. $ *Average main: $145* ⊠ *47900 Hwy. 1, Big Sur* ☎ *831/667–2800* ⊕ *www.postranchinn.com/dine.*

★ The Sur House

$$$$ | **AMERICAN** | The Alila Ventana Big Sur's restaurant sits high on a ridge, and magnificent terraces offer stunning ocean views and a full-service outdoor bar. Regional and international wines on a comprehensive list pair well with the California-inspired dishes, many of whose ingredients are sourced from local purveyors, and the bar serves seasonal specialty cocktails and California craft beers. **Known for:** stunning views; Pacific-sourced seafood and local free-range meats and produce; excellent wine list. $ *Average main: $45* ⊠ *48123 Hwy. 1, Big Sur* ☎ *831/667–2331* ⊕ *www. ventanabigsur.com/dining/the-sur-house.*

🛏 Hotels

★ Alila Ventana Big Sur

$$$$ | **HOTEL** | Hundreds of celebrities have escaped to this romantic resort on 160 tranquil acres 1,200 feet above the Pacific, where you can participate in a range of activities, workshops, and programs; sunbathe; hike in the nearby hills; or pamper yourself with mind-and-body treatments in the spa or your own private quarters. **Pros:** secluded; nature trails everywhere; rates include daily guided hike, yoga, and wine and cheese hour. **Cons:** ultra-expensive; some rooms lack an ocean view; not family-friendly. $ *Rooms from: $1,900* ⊠ *48123 Hwy. 1, Big Sur* ☎ *831/667–2331, 800/628–6500* ⊕ *www.ventanabigsur.com* ⇥ *74 units* ⍟ *All-Inclusive.*

Big Sur Lodge

$$ | **HOTEL** | **FAMILY** | The lodge's modern, motel-style cottages with Mission-style furnishings and vaulted ceilings sit in a meadow surrounded by redwood trees and flowering shrubbery. **Pros:** secluded

setting near trailheads; good camping alternative; rates include state parks pass. **Cons:** basic rooms; walk to main lodge; thin common walls in some units. [$] *Rooms from: $299* ✉ *Pfeiffer Big Sur State Park, 47225 Hwy. 1, Big Sur* ☎ *855/238–6950 reservations* 🌐 *www.bigsurlodge.com* 🛏 *62 rooms* 🍴 *No Meals.*

Big Sur River Inn

$$ | **B&B/INN** | **FAMILY** | In summer at this rustic property you can sip drinks beside—or in—the Big Sur River fronted by the inn's wooded grounds, and, if you're here on a Sunday afternoon between May and September, you can enjoy live music on the restaurant's deck. **Pros:** riverside setting complete with outdoor pool; next to a restaurant and small market; recently renovated baths. **Cons:** standard motel rooms across the road; not pet-friendly; fronts busy road. [$] *Rooms from: $345* ✉ *46800 Hwy. 1, Big Sur* ☎ *831/667–2700, 800/548–3610* 🌐 *www.bigsurriverinn.com* 🛏 *22 rooms* 🍴 *No Meals.*

Deetjen's Big Sur Inn

$$ | **B&B/INN** | This 1930s Norwegian-style property is endearingly rustic, with its village of cabins nestled in the redwoods; many of the very individual rooms have their own fireplaces. **Pros:** tons of character; wooded grounds; excellent food and wine in on-site restaurant. **Cons:** thin walls; some rooms don't have private baths; no TVs or Wi-Fi, limited cell service. [$] *Rooms from: $250* ✉ *48865 Hwy. 1, Big Sur* ☎ *831/667–2377* 🌐 *www.deetjens.com* 🛏 *20 rooms* 🍴 *No Meals* ☞ *2-night minimum stay on weekends.*

Glen Oaks Big Sur

$$$ | **HOTEL** | At this rustic-modern complex of adobe-and-redwood buildings, you can choose between motel-style rooms, cabins, and cottages in the woods. **Pros:** in the heart of town; natural river-rock radiant-heated tiles; restaurant across the street. **Cons:** near busy road and parking lot; no TVs; some cabins are tiny. [$] *Rooms from: $385* ✉ *47080 Hwy. 1, Big Sur* ☎ *831/667–2105* 🌐 *glenoaksbigsur.com* 🛏 *29 units* 🍴 *No Meals.*

★ Post Ranch Inn

$$$$ | **RESORT** | The redwood guesthouses at this luxurious retreat blend almost invisibly into a wooded cliff 1,200 feet above the ocean and have views of the sea or the mountains. **Pros:** units come with fireplaces and private decks; activities like yoga and stargazing; gorgeous property with trails. **Cons:** expensive; austere design; not a good choice if you're afraid of heights. [$] *Rooms from: $1,750* ✉ *47900 Hwy. 1, Big Sur* ☎ *831/667–2200, 800/527–2200* 🌐 *www.postranchinn.com* 🛏 *41 units* 🍴 *Free Breakfast.*

Ragged Point Inn

$$ | **HOTEL** | At this cliff-top resort—the only inn and restaurant for miles around—glass walls in most rooms open to awesome ocean views. **Pros:** on the cliffs; good burgers and locally made ice cream; idyllic views. **Cons:** busy road stop during the day; often booked for weekend weddings; spotty cell phone service. [$] *Rooms from: $279* ✉ *19019 Hwy. 1, Ragged Point* ☎ *805/927–4502, 805/927–5708 restaurant, 888/584–6374* 🌐 *www.raggedpointinn.com* 🛏 *39 rooms* 🍴 *No Meals.*

Treebones Resort

$$$ | **RESORT** | Perched on a hilltop surrounded by national forest and stunning, unobstructed ocean views, this yurt resort provides a stellar back-to-nature experience along with creature comforts. **Pros:** luxury yurts with cozy beds; lodge with fireplace and games; local food at Wild Coast Restaurant and decked sushi bar. **Cons:** steep paths; no private bathrooms; not good for families with young children. [$] *Rooms from: $390* ✉ *71895 Hwy. 1, Willow Creek Rd., 32 miles north of San Simeon, 1 mile north of Gorda* ☎ *805/927–2390, 877/424–4787* 🌐 *www.treebonesresort.com* 🛏 *23 yurts* 🍴 *Free Breakfast* ☞ *2-night minimum.*

Chapter 12

MONTEREY BAY AREA

Updated by
Cheryl Crabtree

⦿ Sights   🍴 Restaurants   🛏 Hotels   🛍 Shopping   🍸 Nightlife
★★★★★   ★★★★☆   ★★★★★   ★★☆☆☆   ★☆☆☆☆

WELCOME TO THE MONTEREY BAY AREA

TOP REASONS TO GO

★ **Marine life:** Monterey Bay is the location of the world's third-largest marine sanctuary, home to whales, otters, and other underwater creatures.

★ **Getaway central:** For more than a century, urbanites have come to the Monterey Bay area to unwind, relax, and have fun. It's a great place to browse unique shops and galleries, ride a giant roller coaster, or play a round of golf on a world-class course.

★ **Nature preserves:** The region has nearly 30 state parks, beaches, and preserves—all of them fantastic places for walking, jogging, hiking, or biking.

★ **Wine and dine:** The area's rich agricultural bounty translates into abundant fresh produce, great wines, and fabulous dining. It's no wonder more than 300 culinary events take place here every year.

★ **Small-town vibes:** Even the cities here are friendly, walkable places where you'll feel like a local.

1 Carmel-by-the-Sea. Galleries and cobblestone streets are among its charms.

2 Carmel Valley. An esteemed wine region marks this celebrity enclave.

3 Pebble Beach. This world-class golf destination also has the stunning 17-Mile Drive.

4 Pacific Grove. A picturesque city known for its migrating butterflies.

5 Monterey. The state's first capital is rich in history and marine life.

6 Salinas. The heart of Steinbeck country is also known for its fruits and veggies.

7 Pinnacles National Park. A volcano with jagged spires and caves.

8 Moss Landing. This tiny fishing port is near marine preserves.

9 Aptos. A charming village that edges redwood forests and stellar beaches.

10 Capitola and Soquel. Seaside gateways to mountain wine country.

11 Santa Cruz. World-famous surf and a university are among its draws.

0 — 5 mi
0 — 5 km

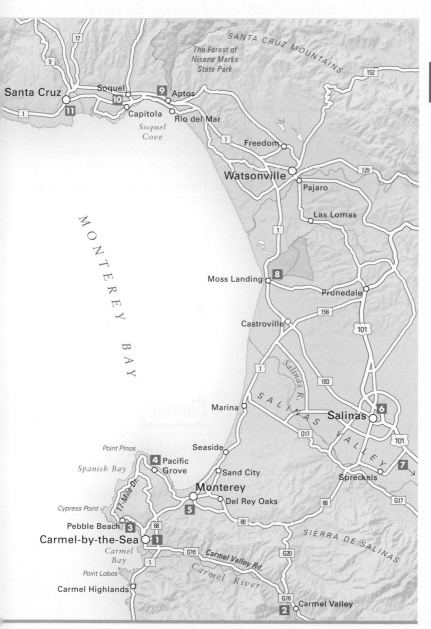

North of Big Sur, the coastline softens into lower bluffs, windswept dunes, pristine estuaries, and long, sandy beaches bordering one of the world's most amazing marine environments—Monterey Bay.

The bay itself is protected by the Monterey Bay National Marine Sanctuary, which holds the nation's largest undersea canyon—bigger and deeper than the Grand Canyon. Sunny coastal communities such as Aptos, Capitola, Soquel, and Santa Cruz offer miles of sand and surf. On-the-water activities abound, from whale-watching and kayaking to sailing and surfing. Bay cruises from Monterey and Moss Landing almost always encounter other enchanting sea creatures, among them sea otters, sea lions, and porpoises.

Land-based activities include hiking, ziplining in the redwood canopy, and wine tasting along urban and rural trails. Golf has been an integral part of the Monterey Peninsula's social and recreational scene since the Del Monte Golf Course opened in 1897. Today, Pebble Beach's championship courses host prestigious tournaments. Quaint, walkable towns such as Carmel-by-the-Sea and Carmel Valley Village are dotted with smart restaurants and galleries that encourage culinary and cultural immersion. Monterey's well-preserved waterfront invites historical exploration. Of course, whatever activity you pursue, natural splendor appears at every turn.

MAJOR REGIONS
The Monterey Peninsula. On the peninsula at the bay's southern end are Carmel-by-the-Sea—a good jumping-off point for the Carmel Valley wine region—Pebble Beach, Pacific Grove, and Monterey itself, home to a world-famous aquarium.

East and North of the Monterey Peninsula. Inland from the bay, amid a rich agricultural area that many refer to as Steinbeck Country, is Salinas, with Pinnacles National Park farther to the southeast. North of Monterey, Highway 1 cruises along the curving coastline, passing windswept beaches piled high with dunes, as well as wetlands and artichoke and strawberry fields. Here you'll find Moss Landing, where otters and seals play; classic seaside villages such as Aptos, Soquel, and Capitola; and Santa Cruz, home of surf legends, a historic boardwalk, and UC Santa Cruz.

Planning

Getting Here and Around

AIR
Monterey Regional Airport, 3 miles east of downtown Monterey off Highway 68, is served by Alaska, Allegiant, American, JSX, and United. Taxi service costs from $14 to $16 to downtown and from $23 to $25 to Carmel. Monterey Airbus service between the region and the San Jose and San Francisco airports starts at $53; the Early Bird Airport Shuttle costs from $220 to $250 ($270 from Oakland).

AIRPORT CONTACTS Monterey Regional Airport. *(MRY)* ✉ *200 Fred Kane Dr., at Olmsted Rd., off Hwy. 68, Monterey* ☎ *831/648–7000* ⊕ *www.montereyairport.com.*

GROUND TRANSPORTATION Central Coast Cab Company. ☎ *831/626–3333.* **Early Bird Airport Shuttle.** ☎ *831/462–3933* ⊕ *www.earlybirdairportshuttle.com.* **Monterey Airbus.** ☎ *831/373–7777* ⊕ *www.montereyairbus.com.* **Yellow Cab.** ☎ *831/333–1234* ⊕ *www.yellowcab1234.com.*

BUS

Greyhound serves Santa Cruz and Salinas from San Francisco (4½ hours) and San Jose (3 hours). Monterey-Salinas Transit (MST) provides frequent service in Monterey County (from $2; day pass $6), and Santa Cruz METRO ($2; day pass from $6 to $14) buses operate throughout Santa Cruz County. You can switch between the lines in Watsonville.

BUS CONTACTS Monterey-Salinas Transit. ☎ *888/678–2871* ⊕ *mst.org.* **Santa Cruz METRO.** ☎ *831/425–8600* ⊕ *scmtd.com.*

CAR

Highway 1 runs south–north along the coast, linking the towns of Carmel-by-the-Sea, Monterey, and Santa Cruz; some sections have only two lanes. The freeway, U.S. 101, lies to the east, roughly parallel to Highway 1. The two roads are connected by Highway 68 from Pacific Grove to Salinas; Highway 156 from Castroville to Prunedale; Highway 152 from Watsonville to Gilroy; Highway 129 from near San Juan Bautista to Watsonville; and Highway 17 from Santa Cruz to San Jose.

■TIP➔ **Traffic near Santa Cruz can crawl to a standstill during commuter hours. Avoid traveling between 7 and 9 am and between 4 and 7 pm.**

The drive south from San Francisco to Monterey can be made comfortably in three hours or less. The most scenic way is to follow Highway 1 down the coast.

A generally faster route is I–280 south to Highway 85 to Highway 17 to Highway 1. The drive from the Los Angeles area takes five or six hours. Take U.S. 101 to Salinas, and head west on Highway 68. You can also follow Highway 1 up the coast.

TRAIN

Amtrak's *Coast Starlight* runs between Los Angeles, Oakland, and Seattle. You can also take the *Pacific Surfliner* to San Luis Obispo and connect to Amtrak buses to Salinas or San Jose. From the train station in Salinas you can connect with buses serving Carmel and Monterey, and from the train station in San Jose with buses to Santa Cruz.

Hotels

Accommodations in the Monterey area range from no-frills motels to luxurious hotels. Pacific Grove, amply endowed with ornate Victorian houses, is the region's bed-and-breakfast capital; Carmel also has charming inns. Lavish resorts cluster in exclusive Pebble Beach and pastoral Carmel Valley.

High season runs from May through October. Rates in winter, especially at the larger hotels, may drop by 50% or more, and smaller inns often offer midweek specials. Whatever the month, some properties require a two-night stay on weekends.

■TIP➔ **Many of the fancier accommodations aren't suitable for children; if you're traveling with kids, ask before you book.**

Restaurants

The Monterey Bay area is a culinary paradise. The surrounding waters are full of fish, wild game roams the foothills, and the inland valleys are some of the most fertile in the country. Local chefs draw on this bounty for their fresh, truly Californian cuisine. Except at beachside stands and inexpensive eateries, where anything goes, casual but neat dress is the norm.

⇨ *Restaurant and hotel reviews have been shortened. For full information, visit Fodors.com. Restaurant prices are the average cost of a main course at dinner, or if dinner is not served, at lunch. Hotel prices are the lowest cost of a standard double room in high season*

What It Costs

	$	$$	$$$	$$$$
RESTAURANTS				
	under $20	$20–$30	$31–$40	over $40
HOTELS				
	under $200	$200–$350	$351–$500	over $500

Tours

Ag Venture Tours & Consulting
GUIDED TOURS | Crowd-pleasing half-day wine tasting, sightseeing, walking, and agricultural tours are Ag Venture's specialty. Tastings are at Monterey and Santa Cruz Mountains wineries; sightseeing opportunities include the Monterey Peninsula, Big Sur, and Santa Cruz; and the agricultural forays take in the Salinas and Pajaro valleys. Customized and full-day itineraries can be arranged. ☎ 831/761–8463 ⊕ agventuretours.com ☑ From $65 (½-day walking tour) and $100 (½-day van tour).

California Pacific Excursions
BUS TOURS | This outfit operates motorcoach tours in Monterey and Carmel, and from those towns and San Jose to Big Sur. The company's two-day San Jose–Los Angeles tours include stops in Monterey and Carmel. ☎ 415/228–9865 ⊕ californiapacificexcursions.com ☑ From $278 (day) and $418 (overnight).

Monterey Guided Wine Tours
SPECIAL-INTEREST TOURS | The company's guides lead customized wine tours in Monterey, Carmel, and Carmel Valley, along with the Santa Lucia Highlands, the Santa Cruz Mountains, and the Paso Robles area. Tours, which typically last from four to six hours, take place in a town car, a Lincoln Navigator, or a party bus and can accommodate groups of one to 100. ☎ 831/920–2792 ⊕ www.montereyguidedwinetours.com ☑ From $175.

Visitor Information

CONTACTS **Monterey County Convention & Visitors Bureau.** ✉ 419 Webster St., Suite 100, Monterey ☎ 888/221–1010 ⊕ www.seemonterey.com. **Monterey Wine Country.** ✉ Monterey ☎ 831/375–9400 ⊕ montereywines.org. **Santa Cruz Mountains Winegrowers Association.** ✉ 335 Spreckels Dr., Suite B, Aptos ☎ 831/685–8463 ⊕ winesofthesantacruzmountains.com. **Visit Santa Cruz County.** ✉ 303 Water St., Suite 100, Santa Cruz ☎ 831/425–1234, 800/833–3494 ⊕ www.santacruz.org.

When to Go

Summer is peak season; mild weather brings in big crowds. In this coastal region a cool breeze generally blows and fog often rolls in from offshore; you will frequently need a sweater or windbreaker. Off-season, from November through April, fewer people visit and the mood is mellower. Rainfall is heaviest in January and February. Fall and spring days are often clearer than those in summer.

FESTIVALS AND EVENTS
Carmel Bach Festival. This three-week, mid-July festival has presented the works of Johann Sebastian Bach and his contemporaries since 1935. ⊕ bachfestival.org

Jazz Bash by the Bay. Bands play early jazz, big band, swing, ragtime, blues, zydeco, and gypsy jazz at waterfront venues during this festival, held on the first full weekend of March. ⊕ *jazzbashmonterey. com*

Monterey Jazz Festival. The world's oldest jazz festival, held the third full weekend in September, attracts top-name performers and their fans to the Monterey Fairgrounds. ⊕ *montereyjazzfestival.org*

Santa Cruz Shakespeare. This six-week festival in July and August occasionally includes a modern dramatic performance. Most performances are outdoors under the redwoods in Delaveaga Park. ⊕ *santacruzshakespeare.org*

Carmel-by-the-Sea

26 miles north of Big Sur.

Even when its population quadruples with tourists on weekends and in summer, Carmel-by-the-Sea, commonly referred to as Carmel, retains its identity as a quaint village. Self-consciously charming, the town is populated by many celebrities, major and minor, and has its share of quirky ordinances. For instance, women wearing high heels do not have the right to pursue legal action if they trip and fall on the cobblestone streets, and drivers who hit a tree and leave the scene are charged with hit-and-run.

Buildings have no street numbers—street names are written on discreet white posts—and consequently no mail delivery. One way to commune with the locals: head to the post office. Artists started this community, and their legacy is evident in the numerous galleries.

GETTING HERE AND AROUND
From north or south follow Highway 1 to Carmel. Head west at Ocean Avenue to reach the main village hub.

TOURS
Carmel By-the-Sea Wine Walk
SPECIAL-INTEREST TOURS | Download a free, mobile Wine Walk Guide with a map to tasting rooms and other venues where you can redeem exclusive offers like discounted flights and free tapas plates. (It's not an app—it's downloaded via text or email.) Check in at each tasting room (just pull up the venue in the guide) to redeem the offers. ⊠ *Carmel Chamber of Commerce Visitor Center, San Carlos St., between 5th and 6th Aves., Carmel* ☏ *831/624–2522* ⊕ *www.carmelcalifornia.com/carmel-by-the-sea-wine-walk. htm* ⌫ *$100.*

Carmel Food Tours
SPECIAL-INTEREST TOURS | Taste your way through Carmel-by-the-Sea culinary delights on this guided walking tour to restaurants and shops that serve small portions of standout offerings, from empanadas and ribs to honey and chocolate. Along the way, guides share colorful tales about local culture, history, and architecture. The Classic Tour (which departs from the Sunset Cultural Center) includes five to six tasting stops and lasts three hours. The five-hour Bikes, Bites, & Bevs Tour combines a morning e-bike tour from Carmel through Pebble Beach with four food and wine/cocktail destinations in the afternoon. Tickets must be purchased in advance. ⊠ *Sunset Cultural Center, 9th Ave. at San Carlos St., Carmel* ☏ *831/216–8161 tickets* ⊕ *carmelfoodtour.com* ⌫ *From $119.*

Carmel Walks
WALKING TOURS | For insight into Carmel's history and culture, join one of these guided two-hour ambles through hidden courtyards, gardens, and pathways. Tours depart from the Pine Inn courtyard, on Lincoln Street. Call or visit the website to reserve a spot. ⊠ *Lincoln St. at 6th Ave., Carmel* ☏ *831/223–4399* ⊕ *gaelgallagher. com/carmel-walks.html* ⌫ *From $35.*

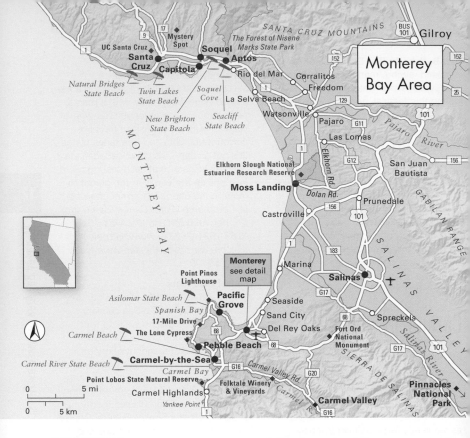

Monterey
Bay Area

ESSENTIALS

VISITOR INFORMATION Carmel Chamber of Commerce. ⊠ *Visitor center, in Carmel Plaza, Ocean Ave. between Junipero and Mission Sts., Carmel* ☎ *831/624–2522* ⊕ *carmelchamber.org.*

👁 Sights

Carmel Mission

RELIGIOUS BUILDING | FAMILY | Long before it became a shopping and browsing destination, Carmel was an important religious center during the establishment of Spanish California. That heritage is preserved in the Mission San Carlos Borroméo del Rio Carmelo, more commonly known as the Carmel Mission. Founded in 1771, it served as headquarters for the mission system in California under Father Junípero Serra. Adjoining the stone church is a tranquil garden planted with California poppies. Museum rooms at the mission include an early kitchen, Serra's spartan sleeping quarters and burial shrine, and the first college library in California. ⊠ *3080 Rio Rd., at Lasuen Dr., Carmel* ☎ *831/624–1271* ⊕ *carmelmission.org* 🖾 *$13* 🕑 *Closed Mon. and Tues.*

★ Ocean Avenue

STREET | FAMILY | Downtown Carmel's chief lure is shopping, especially along its main street, Ocean Avenue, between Junipero Avenue and Camino Real. The architecture here is a mishmash of ersatz Tudor, Mediterranean, and other styles. ⊠ *Carmel.*

★ Point Lobos State Natural Reserve

NATURE PRESERVE | FAMILY | A 350-acre headland harboring a wealth of marine life, the reserve lies a few miles south of Carmel. The best way to explore here is to walk along one of the many trails.

The Cypress Grove Trail leads through a forest of Monterey cypress (one of only two natural groves remaining) that clings to the rocks above an emerald-green cove. Sea Lion Point Trail is a good place to view sea lions. From those and other trails, you might also spot otters, harbor seals, and (in winter and spring) migrating whales. An additional 750 acres of the reserve is an undersea marine park open to qualified scuba divers. No pets are allowed. **■ TIP→ Arrive early (or in late afternoon) to avoid crowds; the parking lots fill up.** ✉ *Hwy. 1, Carmel* ☎ *831/624–4909* 🌐 *www.pointlobos.org* 🎫 *$10 per vehicle.*

Tor House

HISTORIC HOME | Scattered throughout the pines of Carmel-by-the-Sea are houses and cottages originally built for the writers, artists, and photographers who discovered the area decades ago. Among the most impressive dwellings is Tor House, a stone cottage built in 1919 by poet Robinson Jeffers on a craggy knoll overlooking the sea. Portraits, books, and unusual art objects fill the low-ceilinged rooms. The highlight of the small estate is Hawk Tower, a detached edifice set with stones from the Carmel coastline—as well as one from the Great Wall of China. The docents who lead tours (six people maximum) are well informed about the poet's work and life. Reservations (by phone or online) are required. ✉ *26304 Ocean View Ave., Carmel* ☎ *831/624–1813 direct docent office line, Mon.–Thurs. only* 🌐 *www.torhouse.org* 🎫 *$15* ☞ *No children under 12.*

Beaches

Carmel Beach

BEACH | **FAMILY** | Carmel-by-the-Sea's greatest attraction is its rugged coastline, with pine and cypress forests and countless inlets. Carmel Beach, an easy walk from downtown shops, has sparkling white sands and magnificent sunsets. **■ TIP→ Dogs are allowed to romp off-leash here. Amenities:** parking (no fee); toilets. **Best for:** sunset; surfing; walking. ✉ *End of Ocean Ave., Carmel* ☎ *831/620–2020.*

🍴 Restaurants

Anton and Michel

$$$$ | **AMERICAN** | Carefully prepared California cuisine is the draw at this airy restaurant, where the rack of lamb is carved at the table, the grilled Halloumi cheese and tomatoes are meticulously stacked and served with basil and Kalamata olive tapenade, and the desserts are set aflame before your eyes. For lighter fare with a worldwide flair, head to the bar, where small plates such as Dungeness crab ravioli and brochette of filet mignon with chimichurri sauce are served. **Known for:** romantic courtyard with fountain; elegant interior with fireplace lounge; flambé desserts. [$] *Average main: $46* ✉ *Mission St. and 7th Ave., Carmel* ☎ *831/624–2406* 🌐 *www.antonand-michel.com.*

★ Aubergine

$$$$ | **AMERICAN** | To eat and sleep at luxe L'Auberge Carmel is an experience in itself, but even those staying elsewhere can splurge at the inn's intimate restaurant, which was awarded a Michelin star in 2022. Chef Justin Cogley's eight-course prix-fixe tasting menu (your only option at dinner, $265 per person) is a gastronomical experience unrivaled in the region. **Known for:** exceptional chef's choice tasting menu; expert wine pairings (extra fee); intimate nine-table dining room. [$] *Average main: $265* ✉ *Monte Verde at 7th Ave., Carmel* ☎ *831/624–8578* 🌐 *auberginecarmel.com* 🕒 *Closed Mon. and Tues. No lunch.*

★ Basil

$$ | **AMERICAN** | Eco-friendly Basil was Monterey County's first restaurant to achieve a green-dining certification, recognition of its commitment to using organic, sustainably cultivated ingredients in creative dishes such as black

Point Lobos State Natural Reserve offers stunning vistas of sea and sky.

squid linguine with sea urchin sauce, charred octopus, and smoked venison and other house-made charcuterie. **Known for:** organic ingredients; creative cocktails; year-round patio dining. [$] *Average main: $30* ✉ *Paseo Sq., San Carlos St., between Ocean Ave. and 7th Ave., Carmel* ☎ *831/626–8226* 🌐 *basilcarmel.com.*

Casanova

$$$ | MEDITERRANEAN | This restaurant inspires European-style celebration and romance in an intimate French-country setting. Feast on authentic dishes from southern France and northern Italy—think beef tartare and escargot. **Known for:** house-made pastas and gnocchi; private dining at antique Van Gogh's table; romantic candlelight dining room and outdoor patio. [$] *Average main: $34* ✉ *5th Ave., between San Carlos and Mission Sts., Carmel* ☎ *831/625–0501* 🌐 *www.casanovacarmel.com.*

The Cottage Restaurant

$ | AMERICAN | FAMILY | This family-friendly spot serves sandwiches, pizzas, and homemade soups at lunch, but the best meal is breakfast (good thing it's served all day). The menu offers six variations on eggs Benedict and all kinds of crepes. **Known for:** artichoke soup; sweet or savory crepes; daily specials. [$] *Average main: $17* ✉ *Lincoln St. between Ocean and 7th Aves., Carmel* ☎ *831/625–6260* 🌐 *www.cottagerestaurant.com* 🕓 *No dinner.*

Flying Fish Grill

$$ | SEAFOOD | Simple in appearance yet bold with its flavors, this Japanese–California seafood restaurant is one of Carmel's most inventive eateries. The warm, wood-lined dining room is broken up into very private booths. **Known for:** almond-crusted sea bass served with Chinese cabbage and rock shrimp stir-fry; clay pot dinners for two cooked at the table; authentic Asian decor. [$] *Average main: $30* ✉ *Carmel Plaza, Mission St. between Ocean and 7th Aves., Carmel* ☎ *831/625–1962* 🌐 *www.flyingfishgrill.com* 🕓 *No lunch.*

Grasing's Coastal Cuisine

$$$ | **AMERICAN** | Chef Kurt Grasing draws from fresh Carmel Coast and Central Valley ingredients to whip up contemporary adaptations of European-provincial and American dishes. Longtime menu favorites include fresh farm-raised abalone, a savory sausage and seafood paella, and grilled steaks and chops. **Known for:** artichoke and fontina ravioli; grilled steaks; bar, patio lounge, and rooftop deck. $ *Average main: $39* ⊠ *6th Ave. and Mission St., Carmel* ☎ *831/624–6562* ⊕ *grasings.com.*

★ The Pocket

$$$ | **MODERN ITALIAN** | In surf lingo, "the pocket" is a perfect riding spot within a barrel-shape wave, and this Italian–Californian restaurant is likewise a perfect (casual and unfussy) gathering spot for those who seek first-rate food, wine, and cocktails. The chefs craft seasonal menus that focus on seafood, fresh pastas, curries, steaks, and braised meats. **Known for:** sleek marble, wood, and slate dining room; spacious garden seating; full bar, extensive list of more than 400 wines; lively atmosphere, especially during the daily happy hour. $ *Average main: $35* ⊠ *Lincoln St., between 5th and 6th Ave., Carmel* ☎ *831/626–8000* ⊕ *www.thepocketcarmel.com* ⊗ *Closed Mon. and Tues. No lunch.*

Stationaery

$$ | **ECLECTIC** | This cozy neighborhood restaurant serves one of Carmel's most popular brunches every day, plus dinner several nights a week. The eclectic seasonal menu focuses on elegant comfort food with an international flair—options vary, but might include caviar with crème fraiche and kettle chips, shakshuka, chilaquiles, or poke bowls for brunch and soft-shell crab with fava bean puree for dinner. **Known for:** specialty coffee, natural wines; fresh, locally sourced ingredients; takeout window. $ *Average main: $30* ⊠ *San Carlos St., between 5th and 6th Aves., Carmel* ☎ *831/250–7183*

⊕ *www.thestationaery.com* ⊗ *No dinner Sun.–Wed.*

Vesuvio

$$$ | **ITALIAN** | Chef and restaurateur Rich Pèpe heats up the night with this lively trattoria downstairs and swinging rooftop terrace, the Star Bar. Pèpe's elegant take on traditional Italian cuisine yields dishes such as risotto made with local seafood, spicy Calabrian sausage, and lobster reduction sauce, crab ravioli, and velvety limoncello mousse cake. **Known for:** traditional cuisine of Campania, Italy; two bars with pizzas and small plates; live music on rooftop terrace in summer. $ *Average main: $32* ⊠ *6th and Junipero Aves., Carmel* ☎ *831/625–1766* ⊕ *chefpepe.com/restaurants/vesuvio* ⊗ *No lunch* ⌐ *Cash not accepted.*

🛏 Hotels

Carmel Mission Inn

$ | **HOTEL** | A multimillion-dollar renovation completed in the early 2020s transformed this 1970s motel, conveniently located near the intersection of Highway 1 and Rio Road, into a hip haven that evokes the region's natural environment (sand, sea, mountains, pines) and artsy past (mosaic floors, local art, vintage doors). **Pros:** near two shopping centers with many services; fitness center with Peleton bikes; pool and hot tub, free parking. **Cons:** some rooms have limited storage space; no guest laundry; noise from outdoor gathering areas filters to some rooms. $ *Rooms from: $191* ⊠ *3665 Rio Rd., Carmel* ☎ *855/235–3915, 831/624–1841* ⊕ *www.carmelmissioninn.com* ⌐ *165 rooms* ❏ *No Meals.*

Cypress Inn

$$ | **B&B/INN** | This luxurious inn has a fresh, Mediterranean ambience with Moroccan touches. **Pros:** luxury without snobbery; popular lounge and restaurant; live music on the patio. **Cons:** not for the pet-phobic; some rooms and baths are tiny; basic amenities. $ *Rooms*

from: $299 ✉ Lincoln St. and 7th Ave., Carmel ☎ 831/624–3871, 800/443–7443 🌐 cypress-inn.com 🛏 44 rooms 🍴 Free Breakfast.

Hyatt Carmel Highlands

$$$ | **HOTEL** | High on a hill overlooking the Pacific, this place has superb views and accommodations that include king rooms with fireplaces, suites with personal whirlpool tubs, and full town houses with many perks. **Pros:** killer views; romantic getaway; great food. **Cons:** thin walls; must drive to the center of town; some rooms and buildings need update. [$] *Rooms from: $499 ✉ 120 Highlands Dr., Carmel ☎ 831/620–1234 🌐 www.hyatt.com 🛏 48 rooms 🍴 No Meals.*

La Playa Carmel

$$$$ | **HOTEL** | A historic complex of lush gardens and Mediterranean-style buildings, La Playa has light and airy interiors done in Carmel Bay beach-cottage style. **Pros:** historical restaurant and bar; manicured gardens; two blocks from the beach. **Cons:** four stories (no elevator); busy lobby; some rooms are on the small side. [$] *Rooms from: $549 ✉ Camino Real at 8th Ave., Carmel ☎ 800/582–8900, 831/293–6100 🌐 laplayahotel.com 🛏 75 rooms 🍴 Free Breakfast.*

★ L'Auberge Carmel

$$$$ | **B&B/INN** | Stepping through the doors of this elegant inn is like being transported to a little European village. **Pros:** in town but off the main drag; four blocks from the beach; full-service luxury. **Cons:** touristy area; not a good choice for families; no a/c. [$] *Rooms from: $549 ✉ Monte Verde at 7th Ave., Carmel ☎ 831/624–8578 🌐 laubergecarmel.com 🛏 20 rooms 🍴 Free Breakfast.*

Mission Ranch

$$ | **HOTEL** | Movie star Clint Eastwood owns this sprawling property where accommodations include rooms in a converted barn and several cottages, some with fireplaces. **Pros:** farm setting; pastoral views; great for tennis buffs. **Cons:** busy parking lot; must drive to the heart of town; old buildings. [$] *Rooms from: $270 ✉ 26270 Dolores St., Carmel ☎ 831/624–6436, 800/538–8221, 831/625–9040 restaurant 🌐 www.missionranchcarmel.com 🛏 31 rooms 🍴 No Meals.*

Pine Inn

$$ | **HOTEL** | A favorite with generations of visitors, the Pine Inn is four blocks from the beach and has Victorian-style furnishings, complete with a grandfather clock, padded fabric wall panels, antique tapestries, and marble tabletops. **Pros:** elegant; close to shopping and dining; Carmel institution. **Cons:** on the town's busiest street; public areas a bit dark; limited parking. [$] *Rooms from: $289 ✉ Ocean Ave. and Monte Verde St., Carmel ☎ 831/624–3851, 800/228–3851 🌐 www.pineinn.com 🛏 49 rooms 🍴 No Meals.*

Tally Ho Inn

$$ | **B&B/INN** | This inn is nearly all suites, many of which have fireplaces and floor-to-ceiling glass walls that open onto ocean-view patios. **Pros:** within walking distance of shops, restaurants, and beach; free parking; spacious rooms. **Cons:** small property; busy area; basic breakfast. [$] *Rooms from: $299 ✉ Monte Verde St. and 6th Ave., Carmel ☎ 831/624–2232, 800/652–2632 🌐 www.tallyho-inn.com 🛏 12 rooms 🍴 No Meals.*

Tickle Pink Inn

$$$$ | **B&B/INN** | Atop a towering cliff, this inn has views of the Big Sur coastline, which you can contemplate from your private balcony. **Pros:** close to great hiking; intimate; dramatic views. **Cons:** close to a big hotel; lots of traffic during the day; basic breakfast. [$] *Rooms from: $429 ✉ 155 Highland Dr., Carmel ☎ 831/624–1244, 800/635–4774 🌐 www.ticklepink-inn.com 🛏 34 units 🍴 Free Breakfast.*

Nightlife

Barmel

BARS | Al Capone and other Prohibition-era legends once sidled up to this hip nightspot's carved wooden bar. Rock to DJ music and sit indoors, or head out to the pet-friendly patio. Some menu items pay homage to California's early days. ✉ *San Carlos St., between Ocean and 7th Aves., Carmel* ☎ *831/626–3400* ⊕ *barmel.com* ☽ *Closed Mon.*

Mulligan Public House

PUBS | A sports bar with seven TV screens, 12 beers on tap, and extensive menu packed with hearty American pub food, Mulligan usually stays open until midnight. ✉ *5 Dolores St. at Ocean* ☎ *831/250–5910* ⊕ *www.mulliganscarmel.com.*

Shopping

ART GALLERIES
Carmel Art Association

ART GALLERIES | Carmel's oldest gallery, established in 1927, exhibits original paintings and sculptures by local artists. ✉ *Dolores St., between 5th and 6th Aves., Carmel* ☎ *831/624–6176* ⊕ *carmel-art.org* ☽ *Closed Tues. and Wed.*

★ Weston Gallery

ART GALLERIES | Run by the family of the late Edward Weston, this is hands down the best photography gallery around, with contemporary color photography and classic black-and-whites. ✉ *6th Ave., between Dolores and Lincoln Sts., Carmel* ☎ *831/624–4453* ⊕ *www.westongallery.com* ☽ *Open by appointment only.*

MALLS
Carmel Plaza

MALL | FAMILY | Tiffany & Co. and Anthropologie are among the name brands doing business at this mall on Carmel's east side, but what makes it worth a stop are homegrown enterprises such as Carmel Honey Company for local honey; Monterey Design Center for home decor;

and J. Lawrence Khaki's for debonair menswear. Flying Fish Grill, Alvarado Street Brewery, and several other restaurants are here, along with Wrath, Hahn, and Blair Estate wine tasting rooms. The Carmel Visitor Center (open daily) is on the second floor. ✉ *Ocean Ave. and Mission St., Carmel* ☎ *831/624–1385* ⊕ *carmelplaza.com.*

SPECIALTY SHOPS
elizabethW

SOUVENIRS | Named after the designer and owner's pioneering great-grandmother, elizabethW handcrafts fragrances, essential oils, candles, silk eye pillows, and other soul-soothing goods for bath, body, and home. ✉ *Ocean Ave., between Monte Verde and Lincoln, Carmel* ☎ *831/626–3892* ⊕ *www.elizabethw.com.*

★ Foxy Couture

SECOND-HAND | Shop for one-of-a-kind treasures at this curated collection of gently used luxury couture and vintage clothes and accessories—think Chanel, Hermes, and Gucci—without paying a hefty price tag. ✉ *San Carlos St., in Vanervort Court, between Ocean and 7th Aves., Carmel* ☎ *831/625–9995* ⊕ *foxy-couturecarmel.com* ☽ *Closed Tues. and Wed.*

Jan de Luz

HOUSEWARES | This shop monograms and embroiders fine linens (including bathrobes) while you wait. ✉ *Dolores St., at 6th Ave. NE, Carmel* ☎ *831/622–7621* ⊕ *jandeluzlinens.com.*

Carmel Valley

10 miles east of Carmel.

Carmel Valley Road, which heads inland from Highway 1 south of Carmel, is the main thoroughfare through this valley, a secluded enclave of horse ranchers and other well-heeled residents who prefer the area's sunny climate to coastal fog and wind. Once thick with dairy farms, the valley has evolved into an esteemed wine appellation. Carmel Valley Village has crafts shops, art galleries, and the tasting rooms of numerous local wineries.

GETTING HERE AND AROUND

From U.S. 101 north or south, exit at Highway 68 and head west toward the coast. Scenic, two-lane Laureles Grade winds southwest over the mountains to Carmel Valley Road west of the village.

An incredible bargain ($6 for an all-day pass), the Carmel Valley Grapevine Express—aka MST's Bus 24—travels between Carmel Valley Village and downtown Monterey, with stops near wineries, restaurants, and shopping centers.

Sights

Bernardus Tasting Room

WINERY | At the tasting room of Bernardus—known for its Bordeaux-style red blend, called Marinus, and its Chardonnays—you can sample current releases and reserve wines. ✉ *5 W. Carmel Valley Rd., at El Caminito Rd., Carmel Valley* ☎ *831/298–8021, 800/223–2533* 🌐 *www.bernardus.com* 🎟 *Tastings from $30.*

Earthbound Farm

FARM/RANCH | **FAMILY** | Pick up fresh vegetables, ready-to-eat meals, gourmet groceries, flowers, and gifts at Earthbound Farm, the world's largest grower of organic produce. You can also take a romp in the kids' garden, cut your own herbs, and stroll through the chamomile aromatherapy labyrinth. ✉ *7250 Carmel Valley Rd., Carmel* ☎ *831/625–6219* 🌐 *www.earthboundfarm.com* 🎟 *Free.*

★ Folktale Winery & Vineyards

WINERY | The expansive winery on a 15-acre estate offers daily tastings, live music on weekends (plus Friday in summer and fall), and special events and programs such as Sunday yoga in the vineyard. Best-known wines include the estate Pinot Noir, Sparkling Rosé, and Le Mistral Joseph's Blend. Chefs in the on-site restaurant cook up small plates with wine pairing suggestions. Tours of the winery and organically farmed vineyards are available by appointment. ✉ *8940 Carmel Valley Rd., at Schetter Rd.* ☎ *831/293–7500* 🌐 *www.folktalewinery.com* 🎟 *Tastings from $40; tours $30 (includes tasting)* 🕒 *Closed Tues. and Wed.*

★ Holman Ranch Vineyards Tasting Room

WINERY | Estate-grown Chardonnay and Pinot Noir are among the standout wines made by Holman Ranch, which pours samples in its chic tasting room and on two patios in the historic Will's Fargo tavern building. The 15-acre ranch itself is just up the road, set amid rolling hills that were once part of the Carmel mission's land grant. You can take winery and vineyard tours by appointment ✉ *18 W. Carmel Valley Rd., Carmel Valley* ☎ *831/659–2640* 🌐 *www.holmanranch.com* 🎟 *Tastings from $35* 🕒 *Closed Tues. and Wed.*

Restaurants

Café Rustica

$$$ | **EUROPEAN** | European country cooking is the focus at this lively roadhouse, where specialties include roasted meats, seafood, pastas, and thin-crust pizzas from the wood-fired oven. It can get noisy inside; for a quieter meal, request a table outside. **Known for:** Tuscan-flavored dishes from Alsace; open kitchen with wood-fired oven; outdoor patio seating. [$] *Average main: $34* ✉ *10 Delfino Pl., at Pilot Rd., off Carmel Valley Rd., Carmel Valley* ☎ *831/659–4444* 🌐 *caferusticacv.com* 🕒 *Closed Mon. No lunch Tues. and Wed.*

Corkscrew Café

$$ | **MODERN AMERICAN** | Farm-fresh food is the specialty of this casual, Old Monterey–style bistro, where the herbs and seasonal produce come from its own organic gardens, the catch of the day comes from local waters, and the meats are hormone-free. Don't miss the collection of corkscrews dating from the 17th century to the present. **Known for:** wood-fired pizzas; fantastic regional wine list; garden patio. $ *Average main: $23* ✉ *55 W. Carmel Valley Rd., Carmel Valley* ☎ *831/659–8888* ⊕ *www.corkscrewcafe. com* ☉ *Closed Jan.*

Roux

$$$$ | **MODERN FRENCH** | Chef Fabrice Roux,. who hails from France, worked at lauded Parisian restaurants for more than a decade before coming to Carmel Valley to wow diners with his contemporary takes on traditional French-Mediterranean cuisine. The eclectic menu, with mostly small and large plates meant for sharing, focuses on local ingredients procured that week—perhaps crispy duck leg confit, tuna tartare, or braised wild-boar bourguignon. **Known for:** expert food and wine pairings; European-style cottage with private room for dining and tastings; extensive wine list with more than 400 labels. $ *Average main: $41* ✉ *6 Pilot Rd., Carmel Valley* ☎ *831/659–5020* ⊕ *rouxcarmel.com* ▭ *No credit cards* ☉ *Closed Tues. No lunch Wed. and Thurs.*

🛏 Hotels

★ Bernardus Lodge & Spa

$$$$ | **RESORT** | The spacious guest rooms at this luxury spa resort have vaulted ceilings, French oak floors, featherbeds, fireplaces, patios, and bathrooms with heated-tile floors and soaking tubs for two. **Pros:** exceptional personal service; outstanding food and wine; serene, cushy full-service spa. **Cons:** hefty rates; can feel a little snooty; resort fee. $ *Rooms from: $535* ✉ *415 W. Carmel Valley Rd., Carmel Valley* ☎ *831/658–3400* ⊕ *www.bernarduslodge.com* ⇆ *73 rooms* ⦿ *No Meals.*

★ Carmel Valley Ranch

$$$$ | **RESORT** | **FAMILY** | The activity options at this luxury ranch are so varied that the resort provides a program director to guide you through them. **Pros:** stunning natural setting; upscale on-site restaurant, Valley Kitchen; River Ranch center with a pool, splash zone, boccie courts, and fitness center. **Cons:** must drive several miles to shops and nightlife; high rates; footsteps from neighboring rooms easy to hear in some buildings. $ *Rooms from: $707* ✉ *1 Old Ranch Rd., Carmel* ☎ *831/625–9500, 855/687–7262 toll-free reservations* ⊕ *carmelvalleyranch.com* ⇆ *181 suites* ⦿ *No Meals.*

Quail Lodge & Golf Club

$$$ | **HOTEL** | **FAMILY** | A sprawling collection of ranch-style buildings on 850 acres of meadows, fairways, and lakes, Quail Lodge offers luxury rooms and outdoor activities at surprisingly affordable rates. **Pros:** on the golf course; on-site restaurant; spacious rooms. **Cons:** service sometimes spotty; 5 miles from the beach and Carmel Valley Village; basic amenities. $ *Rooms from: $395* ✉ *8205 Valley Greens Dr., Carmel* ☎ *866/675–1101 reservations, 831/624–2888* ⊕ *www.quaillodge.com* ⇆ *93 rooms* ⦿ *No Meals.*

★ Stonepine Estate

$$$ | **RESORT** | Set on 407 pastoral acres, the former estate of the Crocker banking family has been converted to a luxurious inn. **Pros:** supremely exclusive; close to Carmel Valley Village; attentive, personalized service. **Cons:** not suitable for children under 12; far from the coast; expensive rates. $ *Rooms from: $375* ✉ *150 E. Carmel Valley Rd., Carmel Valley* ☎ *831/659–2245* ⊕ *stonepineestate.com* ⇆ *16 units* ⦿ *Free Breakfast.*

⚡ Activities

GOLF
Quail Lodge & Golf Club

GOLF | Robert Muir Graves designed this championship, semiprivate, 18-hole course that provides challenging play for golfers of all skill levels. The scenic course, which is set next to Quail Lodge and incorporates five lakes and edges the Carmel River, was completely renovated in 2015 by golf architect Todd Eckenrode to add extra challenge to the golf experience, white sand bunkers, and other enhancements. For the most part flat, the walkable course is well maintained, with stunning views, lush fairways, and ultrasmooth greens. ⊠ *8000 Valley Greens Dr., Carmel* ☎ *831/620–8808 golf shop, 831/620–8866 club concierge* ⊕ *www.quaillodge.com/golf* ⊡ *$236* ⅄ *18 holes, 6500 yards, par 71.*

SPAS
★ Refuge

SPAS | At this coed, European-style center on 2 serene acres you can recharge without breaking the bank. Heat up in the eucalyptus steam room or cedar sauna, plunge into cold pools, and relax indoors in zero-gravity chairs or outdoors in Adirondack chairs around firepits. Repeat the cycle a few times, then lounge around the thermal waterfall pools. Talk is not allowed, and bathing suits are required. ⊠ *27300 Rancho San Carlos Rd., south off Carmel Valley Rd., Carmel* ☎ *831/620–7360* ⊕ *www.refuge.com* ⊡ *$44* ⌖ *$55 admission; $175 50-min massage (includes Refuge admission), $12 robe rental, hot tubs (outdoor), sauna, steam room. Services: aromatherapy, hydrotherapy, massage.*

Pebble Beach

Off North San Antonio Ave. in Carmel-by-the-Sea or off Sunset Dr. in Pacific Grove.

In 1919, the Pacific Improvement Company acquired 18,000 acres of prime land on the Monterey Peninsula, including the entire Pebble Beach coastal region and much of Pacific Grove. Pebble Beach Golf Links and The Lodge at Pebble Beach opened the same year, and the private enclave evolved into a world-class golf destination with three posh lodges, five golf courses, hiking and riding trails, and some of the West Coast's ritziest homes. Pebble Beach has hosted major international golf tournaments, including the U.S. Open in 2019. The annual Pebble Beach Food & Wine, a four-day event in late April with 100 celebrity chefs, is one of the West Coast's premier culinary festivals.

GETTING HERE AND AROUND

If you drive south from Monterey on Highway 1, exit at 17-Mile Drive/Sunset Drive in Pacific Grove to find the northern entrance gate. Coming from Carmel, exit at Ocean Avenue and follow the road almost to the beach; turn right on North San Antonio Avenue to the Carmel Gate. You can also enter through the Highway 1 Gate off Highway 68. Monterey–Salinas Transit (MST) buses provide regular service in and around Pebble Beach.

⊙ Sights

★ The Lone Cypress

NATURE SIGHT | FAMILY | The most-photographed tree along 17-Mile Drive is the weather-sculpted Lone Cypress, which grows out of a precipitous outcropping above the waves about 1½ miles up the road from Pebble Beach Golf Links. You can't walk out to the tree, but you can stop for a view of it at a small parking area off the road. ⊠ *Pebble Beach.*

★ 17-Mile Drive

SCENIC DRIVE | **FAMILY** | Primordial nature resides in quiet harmony with palatial, mostly Spanish Mission–style estates along 17-Mile Drive, which winds through an 8,400-acre microcosm of the Pebble Beach coastal landscape. Dotting the drive are rare Monterey cypresses, trees so gnarled and twisted that Robert Louis Stevenson described them as "ghosts fleeing before the wind." The most famous of these is the Lone Cypress.

Other highlights include Bird Rock and Seal Rock, home to harbor seals, sea lions, cormorants, and pelicans and other sea creatures and birds, and the Crocker Marble Palace, inspired by a Byzantine castle and easily identifiable by its dozens of marble arches. ■**TIP→** If **you spend $35 or more on dining in Pebble Beach and show a receipt upon exiting, you'll receive a refund off the drive's $11.75 per-car fee.** ⊠ Hwy. 1 Gate, 17-Mile Dr., at Hwy. 68, Pebble Beach ⊠ $12 per car, free for bicyclists.

Hotels

★ Casa Palmero

$$$$ | RESORT | This exclusive boutique hotel evokes a stately Mediterranean villa, where rooms are decorated with sumptuous fabrics and fine art. **Pros:** ultimate in pampering; sumptuous decor; more private than sister resorts. **Cons:** rates out of reach for most visitors; not the best views compared to sister lodges; some showers on the small side. $ Rooms from: $1,290 ⊠ 1518 Cypress Dr., Pebble Beach ☎ 831/622–6650, 800/877–0597 reservations ⊕ www.pebblebeach.com ⇨ 24 rooms ⧦ Free Breakfast.

The Inn at Spanish Bay

$$$$ | RESORT | This resort sprawls along a breathtaking stretch of shoreline and has plush, 600-square-foot rooms. **Pros:** attentive service; many amenities; spectacular views. **Cons:** huge hotel; 4 miles from other Pebble Beach Resorts

facilities; atmosphere too snobbish for some. $ Rooms from: $960 ⊠ 2700 17-Mile Dr., Pebble Beach ☎ 831/647–7500, 800/877–0597 ⊕ www.pebble-beach.com ⇨ 269 rooms ⧦ No Meals.

The Lodge at Pebble Beach

$$$$ | RESORT | Most rooms have wood-burning fireplaces, and many have wonderful ocean views at this circa-1919 resort, which includes the much newer, 38-room Fairway One complex. **Pros:** world-class golf; borders the ocean and fairways; fabulous facilities. **Cons:** some rooms are on the small side; very pricey; not many activities if you don't golf. $ Rooms from: $1,100 ⊠ 1700 17-Mile Dr., Pebble Beach ☎ 831/624–3811, 800/877–0597 ⊕ www.pebblebeach.com ⇨ 199 rooms ⧦ No Meals.

Activities

GOLF

The Hay

GOLF | The only 9-hole, par-3 course on the Monterey Peninsula open to the public attracts golfers of all skill levels. It's an ideal place for warm-ups, practicing short games, and for those who don't have time to play 18 holes. ⊠ 17-Mile Dr. and Portola Rd., Pebble Beach ☎ 800/877–0597 ⊕ www.pebblebeach.com ⊠ $65 ⅃ 9 holes, 725 yards, par 27.

Links at Spanish Bay

GOLF | This course, which hugs a choice stretch of shoreline, was designed by Robert Trent Jones Jr., Tom Watson, and Sandy Tatum in the rugged manner of traditional Scottish links, with sand dunes and coastal marshes interspersed among the greens. A bagpiper signals the course's closing each day. ■**TIP→ Nonguests of the Pebble Beach Resorts can reserve tee times up to two months in advance.** ⊠ 17-Mile Dr., north end, Pebble Beach ☎ 800/877–0597 ⊕ www.pebblebeach.com ⊠ $335 ⅃ 18 holes, 6821 yards, par 72.

Did You Know?

The Lone Cypress has stood on this rock for more than 250 years. The tree is the official symbol of the Pebble Beach Company.

★ Pebble Beach Golf Links

GOLF | Each February, show-business celebrities and golf pros team up at this course, the main site of the glamorous AT&T Pebble Beach National Pro-Am tournament. On most days the rest of the year, tee times are available to guests of the Pebble Beach Resorts who book a minimum two-night stay. Nonguests can reserve a tee time only one day in advance on a space-available basis; resort guests can reserve up to 18 months in advance. ⊠ *17-Mile Dr., near The Lodge at Pebble Beach, Pebble Beach* ☎ *800/877–0597* ⊕ *www.pebblebeach.com* ⛳ *$625* 🏌 *18 holes, 6828 yards, par 72.*

Poppy Hills

GOLF | An 18-hole course designed in 1986 by Robert Trent Jones Jr., Poppy Hills reopened in 2014 after a yearlong renovation that Jones supervised. Each hole was restored to its natural elevation along the forest floor, and all 18 greens were rebuilt with bent grass. Individuals may reserve up to a month in advance. ■TIP→ **Poppy Hills, owned by a golfing nonprofit, represents good value for this area.** ⊠ *3200 Lopez Rd., at 17-Mile Dr., Pebble Beach* ☎ *831/622–8239* ⊕ *poppy-hillsgolf.com* ⛳ *$300* 🏌 *18 holes, 7002 yards, par 73.5.*

Spyglass Hill

GOLF | With three holes rated among the toughest on the PGA tour, Spyglass Hill, designed by Robert Trent Jones Sr. and Jr., challenges golfers with its varied terrain but rewards them with glorious views. The first 5 holes border the Pacific, and the other 13 reach deep into the Del Monte Forest. Reservations are essential and may be made up to one month in advance (18 months for resort guests). ⊠ *Stevenson Dr. and Spyglass Hill Rd., Pebble Beach* ☎ *800/877–0597* ⊕ *www.pebblebeach.com* ⛳ *$465* 🏌 *18 holes, 6960 yards, par 72.*

Pacific Grove

3 miles north of Carmel-by-the-Sea.

This picturesque town, which began as a summer retreat for church groups more than a century ago, recalls its prim and proper Victorian heritage in a host of tiny board-and-batten cottages and stately mansions. However, long before the church groups flocked here the area received thousands of annual pilgrims—in the form of bright orange-and-black monarch butterflies. They still come, migrating south from Canada and the Pacific Northwest to take residence in pine and eucalyptus groves from October through March. In Butterfly Town USA, as Pacific Grove is known, the sight of a mass of butterflies hanging from the branches like a long, fluttering veil is unforgettable.

A prime way to enjoy Pacific Grove is to walk or bicycle the 3 miles of city-owned shoreline along Ocean View Boulevard, a cliff-top area landscaped with native plants and dotted with benches meant for sitting and gazing at the sea. You can spot many types of birds here, including the web-footed cormorants that crowd the massive rocks rising out of the surf. Two Victorians of note along Ocean View are the Queen Anne–style Green Gables, at No. 301—erected in 1888, it's now an inn—and the 1909 Pryor House, at No. 429, a massive, shingled, private residence with a leaded- and beveled-glass doorway.

GETTING HERE AND AROUND

Reach Pacific Grove via Highway 68 off Highway 1, just south of Monterey. From Cannery Row in Monterey, head north until the road merges with Ocean Boulevard and follow it along the coast. MST buses travel within Pacific Grove and surrounding towns.

Sights

Lovers Point Park

CITY PARK | FAMILY | The coastal views are gorgeous from this waterfront park whose sheltered beach has a children's pool and a picnic area. The main lawn has a volleyball court and a snack bar. ✉ *Ocean View Blvd., northwest of Forest Ave., Pacific Grove* 🌐 *www.cityofpacificgrove.org.*

Monarch Grove Sanctuary

NATURE PRESERVE | FAMILY | The sanctuary is a reliable spot for viewing monarch butterflies between November and February. ■ **TIP→ The best time to visit is between noon and 3 pm.** ✉ *250 Ridge Rd., off Lighthouse Ave., Pacific Grove* 🌐 *www.pgmuseum.org/monarch-viewing* 🎟 *Free.*

Pacific Grove Museum of Natural History

HISTORY MUSEUM | FAMILY | The museum, a good source for the latest information about monarch butterflies, has permanent exhibitions about the butterflies, birds of Monterey County, biodiversity, and plants. There's a native plant garden, and a display documents life in Pacific Grove's 19th-century Chinese fishing village. ✉ *165 Forest Ave., at Central Ave., Pacific Grove* ☎ *831/648–5716* 🌐 *www.pgmuseum.org* 🎟 *$10* 🕐 *Closed Mon. and Tues.*

Point Pinos Lighthouse

LIGHTHOUSE | FAMILY | At this 1855 structure, the West Coast's oldest continuously operating lighthouse, you can learn about the lighting and foghorn operations and wander through a small museum containing U.S. Coast Guard memorabilia. ✉ *Asilomar Ave., between Lighthouse Ave. and Del Monte Blvd., Pacific Grove* ☎ *831/648–5722* 🌐 *www.cityofpacificgrove.org* 🎟 *$5* 🕐 *Closed Mon.–Thurs.*

Beaches

Asilomar State Beach

BEACH | FAMILY | A beautiful coastal area, Asilomar State Beach stretches between Point Pinos and the Del Monte Forest. The 100 acres of dunes, tidal pools, and pocket-size beaches form one of the region's richest areas for marine life—including surfers, who migrate here most winter mornings. Leashed dogs are allowed on the beach. **Amenities:** none. **Best for:** sunrise; sunset; surfing; walking. ✉ *Sunset Dr. and Asilomar Ave., Pacific Grove* ☎ *831/646–6440* 🌐 *www.parks.ca.gov.*

Restaurants

Beach House

$$$ | AMERICAN | Patrons of this bluff-top perch sip classic cocktails, sample California fare, and watch the otters frolic on Lovers Point Beach below. The sunset discounts between 4 and 5:30 (reservations recommended) are a great value. **Known for:** sweeping bluff-top views; heated patio; seafood and organic pastas. [$] *Average main: $31* ✉ *620 Ocean View Blvd., Pacific Grove* ☎ *831/375–2345* 🌐 *beachhousepg.com* 🕐 *No lunch.*

★ Fandango

$$$ | MEDITERRANEAN | The menu here is mostly Mediterranean and southern French, with such dishes as osso buco and paella. The decor follows suit—stone walls and country furniture lend the restaurant the earthy feel of a European farmhouse. **Known for:** wood-fire-grilled rack of lamb, seafood, and beef; convivial residential vibe; traditional European flavors. [$] *Average main: $38* ✉ *223 17th St., south of Lighthouse Ave., Pacific Grove* ☎ *831/372–3456* 🌐 *fandangorestaurant.com* 🕐 *No lunch Mon.–Sat.*

★ Passionfish

$$$ | MODERN AMERICAN | South American artwork and artifacts decorate Passionfish, and Latin and Asian flavors infuse the dishes. The chef shops at local farmers' markets several times a week to find the best produce, fish, and meat available and then pairs it with creative sauces like a caper, raisin, and walnut relish. **Known for:** sustainably sourced and organic ingredients; reasonably priced wine list that supports small producers; slow-cooked meats. [$] *Average main: $32* ✉ *701 Lighthouse Ave., Pacific Grove* ☎ *831/655–3311* 🌐 *www.passionfish.net* 🕒 *No lunch.*

Red House Café

$$ | **AMERICAN** | **FAMILY** | When it's nice out, sun pours through the big windows of this cozy restaurant and across tables on the porch; when fog rolls in, the fireplace is lit. The American menu changes with the seasons, but grilled lamb chops atop mashed potatoes are often on offer for dinner, and a grilled calamari steak might be served for lunch, either in a salad or as part of a sandwich. **Known for:** cozy homelike dining areas; comfort food; stellar breakfast and brunch. [$] *Average main: $24* ✉ *662 Lighthouse Ave., at 19th St., Pacific Grove* ☎ *831/643–1060* 🌐 *redhousecafe.com* 🕒 *Closed Mon. No dinner Sun.*

Wild Fish

$$$ | **SEAFOOD** | Inventive dishes—made with 100% organic and locally sourced ingredients—live music, and a friendly staff are among the reasons why this intimate, ocean-to-table eatery is packed on weekends. Everything is fresh as it gets, from fish-and-chips, Monterey Bay bouillabaisse, and whole roasted fish of the day to local greens with spicy vinaigrette. **Known for:** cured house-smoked sablefish; jazz quartet on Friday and Saturday nights; smoked fish chowder. [$] *Average main: $34* ✉ *545 Lighthouse Ave., Pacific Grove* ☎ *831/373–8523* 🌐 *www.wild-fish.com.*

Hotels

Gosby House Inn

$$ | **B&B/INN** | This turreted Queen Anne Victorian was completely remodeled and updated in early 2023, and although rooms still have things like vintage armoires and headboards, they now also have a swanky, contemporary vibe and modern amenities. **Pros:** peaceful; homey; within walking distance of shops and restaurants. **Cons:** not cozy enough for some; area is busy during the day; limited parking. [$] *Rooms from: $200* ✉ *643 Lighthouse Ave., Pacific Grove* ☎ *831/375–1287* 🌐 *www.gosbyhouseinn.com* 🛏 *22 rooms* 🍴 *Free Breakfast.*

★ Green Gables Inn

$$$ | **B&B/INN** | Stained-glass windows, ornate interior details, and sophisticated modern amenities (the inn completed a top-to-bottom remodel in early 2023) compete with spectacular ocean views at this Queen Anne–style mansion. **Pros:** exceptional views; impeccable attention to historic detail; afternoon wine and cheese served in the parlor. **Cons:** some rooms are small; thin walls; breakfast room can be crowded. [$] *Rooms from: $365* ✉ *301 Ocean View Blvd., Pacific Grove* ☎ *831/375–2095* 🌐 *www.greengablesinnpg.com* 🛏 *11 rooms* 🍴 *Free Breakfast.*

Martine Inn

$$ | **B&B/INN** | The glassed-in parlor and many guest rooms at this 1899 Mediterranean-style villa have stunning ocean views. **Pros:** romantic; exquisite antiques; ocean views. **Cons:** not child-friendly; sits on a busy thoroughfare; inconvenient parking. [$] *Rooms from: $309* ✉ *255 Ocean View Blvd., Pacific Grove* ☎ *831/373–3388* 🌐 *www.martineinn.com* 🛏 *25 rooms* 🍴 *Free Breakfast.*

★ Seven Gables Inn

$$$ | **B&B/INN** | This luxe collection of seven buildings and flower-filled gardens on a bluff overlooking Monterey Bay includes the main mansion, built in 1886,

a carriage house, guesthouse, and beach house. **Pros:** great location across from Lover's Point, a short walk to area restaurants, and a short drive to Cannery Row and Monterey aquarium; cooked-to-order breakfast in solarium; concierge services. **Cons:** small parking lot; not pet-friendly; most rooms aren't child-friendly. [$] *Rooms from: $390* ✉ *555 Ocean View Blvd., Pacific Grove* ☎ *831/372–4341* 🌐 *thesevengablesinn.com* 🛏 *25 rooms* 🍴 *Free Breakfast* ☞ *2-night minimum on weekends.*

Activities

GOLF

Pacific Grove Golf Links

GOLF | One of the best golf values in the region, this course has spectacular ocean views on its links-style back nine, which borders 17-Mile Drive. Jack Neville designed this section in 1960. Golfers with a sense of history will appreciate that H. Chandler Egan, a giant of early-20th-century course architecture, designed the front nine. Tee times may be reserved up to 60 days in advance. ✉ *77 Asilomar Ave., Pacific Grove* ☎ *831/648–5775* 🌐 *www.playpacificgrove.com* 🎟 *From $62* ⛳ *18 holes, 5800 yards, par 70.*

Monterey

2 miles southeast of Pacific Grove, 2 miles north of Carmel.

Monterey is a scenic city filled with early California history: adobe buildings from the 1700s, Colton Hall, where California's first constitution was drafted in 1849, and Cannery Row, made famous by author John Steinbeck. Thousands of visitors come each year to mingle with otters and other sea creatures at the world-famous Monterey Bay Aquarium and in the protected waters of the national marine sanctuary that hugs the shoreline.

GETTING HERE AND AROUND

From San Jose or San Francisco, take U.S. 101 south to Highway 156 West at Prunedale. Head west about 8 miles to Highway 1 and follow it about 15 miles south. From San Luis Obispo, take U.S. 101 north to Salinas and drive west on Highway 68 about 20 miles.

Many MST bus lines connect at the Monterey Transit Center, at Pearl Street and Munras Avenue. In summer (daily from 10 until at least 7), the free MST Monterey Trolley travels from downtown Monterey along Cannery Row to the Aquarium and back.

TOURS

Old Monterey Walking Tour

WALKING TOURS | **FAMILY** | Learn all about Monterey's storied past by joining a guided walking tour through the historic district. Tours begin at the Custom House in Custom House Plaza, across from Fisherman's Wharf and are typically offered Thursday through Sunday at 11, 1, and 3. ✉ *Monterey* 🌐 *www.parks.ca.gov/?page_id=951* 🎟 *$10.*

The Original Monterey Walking Tours

WALKING TOURS | **FAMILY** | Learn more about Monterey's past, primarily the Mexican period until California statehood, on a guided tour through downtown Monterey. You can also join a guided walking tour of Cannery Row in the morning. Tours last 1½ to 2 hours and are offered Thursday–Sunday at 10 am and 2. Reservations are essential. ✉ *Monterey* ☎ *831/521–4884* 🌐 *walkmonterey.com* 🎟 *From $25.*

ESSENTIALS

VISITOR INFORMATION Monterey Peninsula Chamber of Commerce. ✉ *353 Camino El Estero, Monterey* ☎ *831/648–5350* 🌐 *www.montereychamber.com.*

Sights

Cannery Row
STREET | FAMILY | When John Steinbeck published the novel *Cannery Row* in 1945, he immortalized a place of rough-edged working people. The waterfront street, edging a mile of gorgeous coastline, once was crowded with sardine canneries processing, at their peak, nearly 200,000 tons of the smelly silver fish a year. During the mid-1940s, however, the sardines disappeared from the bay, causing the canneries to close. Through the years the old tin-roof canneries have been converted into restaurants, art galleries, and malls with shops selling T-shirts, fudge, and plastic sea otters. Recent tourist development along the row has been more tasteful, however, and includes stylish inns and hotels, wine tasting rooms, and upscale specialty shops. ⊠ *Between Reeside and David Aves., Monterey* ⊕ *canneryrow.com.*

Colton Hall
HISTORY MUSEUM | FAMILY | A convention of delegates met here in 1849 to draft the first state constitution. The stone building, which has served as a school, a courthouse, and the county seat, is a city-run museum furnished as it was during the constitutional convention. The extensive grounds outside the hall surround the Old Monterey Jail. ⊠ *570 Pacific St., between Madison and Jefferson Sts., Monterey* ☎ *831/646–5640* ⊕ *www.monterey.org/museums* ⌖ *Free* ⊙ *Closed Mon.–Wed.*

Cooper-Molera Adobe
HISTORIC HOME | FAMILY | The restored 2-acre complex includes a house dating from the 1820s, a gift shop, bakery, and a large garden enclosed by a high adobe wall. The mostly Victorian-era antiques and memorabilia that fill the house provide a glimpse into the life of a prosperous sea merchant's family. The museum is open weekends for self-guided tours; docents are available to answer

Steinbeck's Cannery Row

"Cannery Row in Monterey in California is a poem, a stink, a grating noise, a quality of light, a tone, a habit, a nostalgia, a dream. Cannery Row is the gathered and scattered, tin and iron and rust and splintered wood, chipped pavement and weedy lots and junk heaps, sardine canneries of corrugated iron, honky tonks, restaurants and whore houses, and little crowded groceries, and laboratories and flophouses." — John Steinbeck, *Cannery Row*

questions. If the house is closed, you can still pick up walking-tour maps and stroll the grounds. ⊠ *Monterey State Historic Park, 506 Munras Ave., Monterey* ☎ *800/944–6847* ⊕ *coopermolera.org* ⌖ *$5 tour* ⊙ *Museum closed weekdays.*

Fisherman's Wharf
PEDESTRIAN MALL | FAMILY | The mournful barking of sea lions provides a steady soundtrack all along Monterey's waterfront, but the best way to actually view the whiskered marine mammals is to walk along one of the two piers across from Custom House Plaza. Lined with souvenir shops, the wharf is undeniably touristy, but it's lively and entertaining. At Wharf No. 2, a working municipal pier, you can see the day's catch being unloaded from fishing boats on one side and fishermen casting their lines into the water on the other. The pier has a couple of low-key restaurants, from whose seats lucky customers might spot otters and harbor seals. ⊠ *At end of Calle Principal, Monterey* ⊕ *www.montereywharf.com.*

Fort Ord National Monument
NATIONAL PARK | FAMILY | Scenic beauty, biodiversity, and miles of trails make this former U.S. Army training grounds

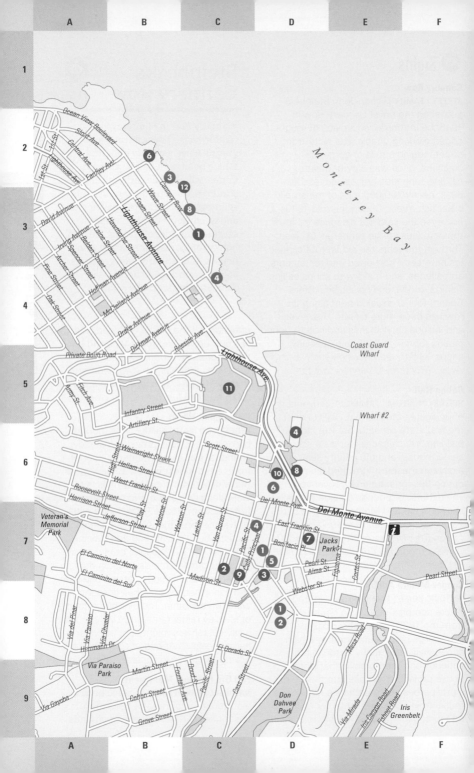

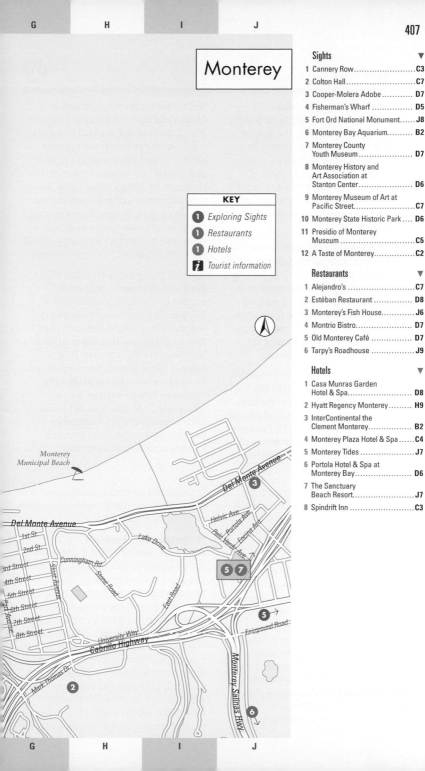

Monterey

KEY

- ① Exploring Sights
- ① Restaurants
- ① Hotels
- 𝒊 Tourist information

The Marine Sanctuary

Although Monterey's coastal landscapes are stunning, their beauty is more than equaled by the wonders that lie offshore. The Monterey Bay National Marine Sanctuary—which stretches 276 miles, from north of San Francisco almost down to Santa Barbara—teems with abundant life, and has topography as diverse as that aboveground.

The preserve's 5,322 square miles include vast submarine canyons, which reach down 10,663 feet at their deepest point. They also encompass dense forests of giant kelp—a kind of seaweed that can grow more than a hundred feet from its roots on the ocean floor. These kelp forests are especially robust off Monterey.

The sanctuary was established in 1992 to protect the habitat of the many species that thrive in the bay. Some animals can be seen quite easily from land. In summer and winter you might glimpse the offshore spray of gray whales as they migrate between their summer feeding grounds in Alaska and their breeding grounds in Baja. Clouds of marine birds—including white-faced ibis, three types of albatross, and more than 15 types of gull—skim the waves, or roost in the rock islands along 17-Mile Drive. Sea otters dart and gambol in the calmer waters of the bay; and of course, you can watch the sea lions—and hear their round-the-clock barking—on the wharves in Santa Cruz and Monterey.

The sanctuary supports many other creatures, however, that remain unseen by most on-land visitors. Some of these are enormous, such as the giant blue whales that arrive to feed on plankton in summer; others, like the more than 22 species of red algae in these waters, are microscopic. So whether you choose to visit the Monterey Bay Aquarium, take a whale-watch trip, or look out to sea with your binoculars, remember you're seeing just a small part of a vibrant underwater kingdom.

a haven for nature lovers and outdoor enthusiasts. The 7,200-acre park, which stretches east over the hills between Monterey and Salinas, is also protected habitat for 35 species of rare and endangered plants and animals. There are 86 miles of single-track, dirt, and paved trails for hiking, biking, and horseback riding. The main trailheads are the Creekside, off Creekside Terrace near Portola Road, and Badger Hills, off Highway 68 in Salinas. Maps are available at the various trail-access points and on the park's website. ■ TIP→ **Dogs are permitted on trails, but should be leashed when other people are nearby.** ⊠ *Monterey* ✛ *Bordered by Hwy. 68 and Gen. Jim Moore and Reservation Rds.* ☎ *831/582–2200*

⊕ *www.blm.gov/programs/national-conservation-lands/california/fort-ord-national-monument* 🎫 *Free*.

★ Monterey Bay Aquarium

AQUARIUM | FAMILY | Playful otters and other sea creatures surround you the minute you enter this extraordinary facility, where all the exhibits convey what it's like to be in the water with the animals. Leopard sharks swim in a three-story, sunlit kelp forest exhibit; sardines swim around your head in a circular tank; and jellyfish drift in and out of view in dramatically lighted spaces that suggest the ocean depths. A petting pool puts you literally in touch with bat rays, and the million-gallon Open Seas exhibit illustrates the variety of creatures—from hammerhead sharks to placid-looking turtles—that live in the eastern Pacific. Splash Zone's 45, interactive, bilingual exhibits let kids commune with African penguins, clownfish, and other marine life. The only drawback to the aquarium experience is that it must be shared with the throngs that congregate daily, but most visitors think it's worth it. ⊠ *886 Cannery Row, Monterey* ☎ *831/648–4800 info* ⊕ *www.monterey-bayaquarium.org* ⊠ *$60.*

Monterey County Youth Museum
(*MY Museum*)

CHILDREN'S MUSEUM | FAMILY | Monterey Bay comes to life from a child's perspective in this fun-filled, interactive indoor exploration center. The seven galleries showcase the science and nature of the Big Sur coast, theater arts, Pebble Beach golf, and beaches. Also here are a live performance theater, a creation station; a hospital emergency room; and an agriculture corner where kids follow artichokes, strawberries, and other fruits and veggies on their evolution from sprout to harvest to farmers' markets. ⊠ *425 Washington St., between E. Franklin St. and Bonifacio Pl., Monterey* ☎ *831/649–6444* ⊕ *mymuseum.org* ⊠ *$10* ⊗ *Closed Mon. and Tues.*

Monterey History and Art Association at Stanton Center

ART MUSEUM | This two-story museum in Custom House Plaza showcases works by well-known contemporary artists, as well as artifacts relating to Monterey's maritime history. Featured artists include Salvador Dali, Armin Hansen, Paul Whitman, and Jo Mora. Exhibits focusing on a local artist rotate every three months. ⊠ *5 Custom House Plaza, Monterey* ☎ *831/372–2608* ⊕ *montereyhistory.org/ stanton-center* ⊠ *$20* ⊗ *Closed Fri.*

Monterey Museum of Art at Pacific Street

ART MUSEUM | Photographs by Ansel Adams and Edward Weston and works by other artists who have spent time on the peninsula are on display here, along with international folk art, from Kentucky hearth brooms to Tibetan prayer wheels.

⊠ *559 Pacific St., across from Colton Hall, Monterey* ☎ *831/372–5477* ⊕ *montereyart.org* ⊠ *$15* ⊗ *Closed Mon.–Wed.*

★ Monterey State Historic Park

HISTORY MUSEUM | FAMILY | You can glimpse Monterey's early history in several well-preserved adobe buildings in Custom House Plaza and the downtown area. Although most are only open via guided tours (check ahead for details), some also have beautiful gardens to explore. Set in what was once a hotel and saloon, the Pacific House Museum now houses a visitor center and exhibits of gold-rush relics; photographs of old Monterey; and Native American baskets, pottery, and other artifacts. The adjacent Custom House, built by the Mexican government in 1827 and now California's oldest standing public building, was the first stop for sea traders whose goods were subject to duties. (In 1846 Commodore John Sloat raised the American flag over this adobe structure and claimed California for the United States.)

Exhibits at Casa Soberanes (1842), once a customs-house guard's residence, survey Monterey life from Mexican rule to the present. A veranda encircles the second floor of Larkin House (1835), whose namesake, an early California statesman, brought many of the antique furnishings inside from New Hampshire. Stevenson House was named in honor of author Robert Louis Stevenson, who boarded here briefly in a tiny upstairs room that's now furnished with items from his family's estate. Other rooms include a gallery of memorabilia and a children's nursery with Victorian toys.

■ **TIP→ If the buildings are closed, you can access a cell-phone tour 24/7 (**☎ *831/998–9458*) **or download an app.** ⊠ *10 Custom House Plaza, Pacific House Museum visitor center, Monterey* ☎ *831/649–2907* ⊕ *www.parks.ca.gov/?page_id=575* ⊠ *Free–$5, 1-hr history walk $10.*

California sea lions are intelligent, social animals that live (and sleep) close together in groups.

Presidio of Monterey Museum

HISTORY MUSEUM | **FAMILY** | This spot has been significant for centuries. Its first incarnation was as a Native American village for the Rumsien tribe. The Spanish explorer Sebastián Vizcaíno landed here in 1602, and Father Junípero Serra arrived in 1770. Notable battles fought here include the 1818 skirmish in which the corsair Hipólito Bruchard conquered the Spanish garrison that stood on this site and claimed part of California for Argentina. The indoor museum tells the stories; plaques mark the outdoor sites. ✉ *Corporal Ewing Rd., Monterey* ✣ *Off Lighthouse Ave.* ☎ *831/646–3456* 🌐 *www.monterey.org/museums* 🎟 *Free* 🕒 *Closed weekdays.*

A Taste of Monterey

WINERY | Without driving the back roads, you can taste the wines of nearly 100 area vintners (craft beers, too) while taking in fantastic bay views. Bottles are available for purchase, and food is served from 11:30 until closing. ✉ *700 Cannery Row, Suite KK, Monterey* ☎ *831/646–5446* 🌐 *atasteofmonterey.com* 🎟 *Tastings from $23.*

🍴 Restaurants

Alejandro's

$$ | **MEXICAN** | **FAMILY** | A stylish Mexican eatery in the heart of downtown, Alejandro's is designed to feel like a Yucatán holiday getaway. Options, many of them cooked in the wood-fired oven, include seafood tostadas and ceviches, *birria* (meat stew), bone-marrow tacos, and roast chicken wrapped in banana leaves. **Known for:** housemade tortillas; extensive salsa selection; creative cocktails and list of wines from Baja and Alta California. [$] *Average main: $30* ✉ *474 Alvarado St., Monterey* ☎ *831/717–4781* 🌐 *www.alejandros.co* 🕒 *No lunch.*

Estéban Restaurant

$$$ | **SPANISH** | **FAMILY** | A festive dining room with a fireplace at the Casa Munras hotel is the setting for meals featuring modern and classic versions of empanadas, crispy Spanish octopus, flash-fried wild Gulf prawns, and five types of paella. Midweek specials abound—on Tuesday night, feast on a three-course prix-fixe paella dinner ($38 per person), bottles of wine are half off on Monday, and Wednesday wine flights are just $16 for three tastes. **Known for:** daily tapas happy hour from 4:30 to 6; patio with firepit; special menus for kids and pups. $ *Average main: $35* ⊠ *700 Munras Ave., Monterey* ☎ *831/375–0176* ⊕ *www. hotelcasamunras.com/dining* ☾ *No lunch.*

Monterey's Fish House

$$ | **SEAFOOD** | Casual yet stylish and always packed, this seafood restaurant is removed from the hubbub of the wharf. The bartenders and waitstaff will gladly advise you on the perfect wine to go with your poached, blackened, or oak-grilled seafood. **Known for:** seafood, steaks, house-made pasta; festive atmosphere; oyster bar. $ *Average main: $25* ⊠ *2114 Del Monte Ave., at Dela Vina Ave., Monterey* ☎ *831/373–4647* ⊕ *monterey-fishhouse.com.*

★ Montrio Bistro

$$$$ | **AMERICAN** | This quirky converted firehouse, with its rawhide walls and iron indoor trellises, has a wonderfully sophisticated menu. Organic produce and meats and sustainably sourced seafood are used in imaginative dishes that reflect the area's agriculture—crispy artichoke hearts with Mediterranean baba ghanoush, for instance, and hamachi crudo with passion-fruit vinaigrette. **Known for:** green-certified restaurant; extensive international wine list; inventive cocktails. $ *Average main: $44* ⊠ *414 Calle Principal, at W. Franklin St., Monterey* ☎ *831/648–8880* ⊕ *www. montrio.com* ☾ *No lunch.*

Old Monterey Café

$ | **AMERICAN** | **FAMILY** | Breakfast here gets constant local raves thanks to familiar favorites such as a dozen kinds of omelets and pancakes options that range from blueberry to cinnamon-raisin-pecan. The lunch menu has good soups, salads, and sandwiches. **Known for:** seven types of eggs Benedict; upbeat, team-style service; all meals cooked to order. $ *Average main: $16* ⊠ *489 Alvarado St., at Munras Ave., Monterey* ☎ *831/646–1021* ⊕ *www.oldmontereycafeca.com* ☾ *No dinner.*

Tarpy's Roadhouse

$$$ | **AMERICAN** | **FAMILY** | Fun, dressed-up American favorites—a little something for everyone—are served in this renovated early-1900s stone farmhouse several miles east of town. The kitchen cranks out everything from Cajun-spiced prawns to meat loaf with marsala-mushroom gravy to grilled ribs and steaks. **Known for:** American comfort food with a California twist; rustic dining near an indoor fireplace or out in a garden courtyard; generous portions. $ *Average main: $34* ⊠ *2999 Monterey–Salinas Hwy., Hwy. 68, Monterey* ☎ *831/647–1444* ⊕ *www. tarpys.com.*

🛏 Hotels

Casa Munras Garden Hotel & Spa

$ | **HOTEL** | **FAMILY** | A cluster of Spanish-theme buildings in the heart of downtown, Casa Munras pays homage to Monterey's roots and the legacy of Spanish diplomat Don Estéban Munras, who built a residence on the site in 1824. **Pros:** full-service spa and salon, heated pool, and fitness room; excellent tapas restaurant; walk to downtown sights and restaurants; rate includes bike usage. **Cons:** $17 parking fee; pool area can get noisy; thin walls. $ *Rooms from: $199* ⊠ *700 Munras Ave., Monterey* ☎ *831/375–2411, 800/222–2446* ⊕ *www. hotelcasamunras.com* ⇆ *154 rooms* ⑩ *No Meals.*

Hyatt Regency Monterey

$$ | **RESORT** | **FAMILY** | A 22-acre resort amid cypress forests on the Del Monte Golf Course, the Hyatt Regency Monterey is a good choice for business travelers and families (especially those with pets)

seeking relatively affordable lodgings with numerous on-site services. **Pros:** half the rooms overlook the golf course; six tennis courts, firepits, two pools and hot tubs, hammocks, and swings on property; restaurant with live weekend entertainment. **Cons:** not in heart of downtown; sprawling resort that can seem packed during busy seasons; not ideal for pet-phobic guests. [$] *Rooms from: $264* ✉ *1 Old Golf Course Rd., Monterey* ☎ *831/372–1234* 🌐 *www.hyatt.com* 🛏 *560 rooms* 🍴 *No Meals.*

InterContinental the Clement Monterey
$$$ | **HOTEL** | **FAMILY** | Spectacular bay views, upscale amenities, assiduous service, and a superb location next to the aquarium propelled this luxury hotel to immediate stardom. **Pros:** a block from the aquarium; fantastic waterfront views from some rooms; great for families. **Cons:** a tad formal; not budget; Cannery Row crowds everywhere on weekends and holidays. [$] *Rooms from: $365* ✉ *750 Cannery Row, Monterey* ☎ *831/375–4500* 🌐 *www.ictheclementmonterey.com* 🛏 *208 rooms* 🍴 *No Meals.*

Monterey Plaza Hotel & Spa
$$ | **HOTEL** | Guests at this Cannery Row hotel can see frolicking sea otters from its wide outdoor patio and many room balconies. **Pros:** on the ocean; many amenities; attentive service. **Cons:** touristy area; heavy traffic; parking fee. [$] *Rooms from: $306* ✉ *400 Cannery Row, Monterey* ☎ *831/920–6710* 🌐 *montereyplazahotel.com* 🛏 *290 rooms* 🍴 *No Meals.*

Monterey Tides
$$ | **RESORT** | One of the area's best values, this hotel has a great waterfront location—2 miles north of Monterey, with views of the bay and the city skyline—and offers a surprising array of amenities. **Pros:** on the beach; large pool; family-friendly. **Cons:** several miles from major attractions; big-box mall neighborhood; most rooms on the small side. [$] *Rooms from: $249* ✉ *2600 Sand Dunes Dr., Monterey* ☎ *831/394–3321, 800/242–8627* 🌐 *montereytides.com* 🛏 *196 rooms* 🍴 *No Meals.*

Portola Hotel & Spa at Monterey Bay
$$ | **HOTEL** | **FAMILY** | One of Monterey's largest hotels, and locally owned and operated for more than 40 years, the coastal-theme Portola anchors a prime city block between Custom House Plaza and the Monterey Conference Center. **Pros:** walk to sights and downtown restaurants and shops; three on-site restaurants and coffee shop; pet- and family-friendly. **Cons:** crowded when conferences convene; no limit on dog size; parking fee. [$] *Rooms from: $316* ✉ *2 Portola Plaza, Monterey* ☎ *831/649–4511, 888/222–5851* 🌐 *www.portolahotel.com* 🛏 *379 rooms* 🍴 *No Meals.*

The Sanctuary Beach Resort
$$$ | **HOTEL** | **FAMILY** | Walk to the sand from spacious, luxurious bungalows furnished in contemporary, ocean-theme style at this 19-acre, wellness-centered resort next to Marina Dunes Preserve and a secluded stretch of Marina State Beach. **Pros:** easy access to hiking and biking trails; heated pool, on-site spa services; each bungalow has two rooms that can combine for families and groups. **Cons:** not in the heart of town; parking lot relatively far from rooms; area weather is often cooler than other parts of the bay. [$] *Rooms from: $429* ✉ *3295 Dunes Dr., Seaside* ☎ *855/693–6583* 🌐 *www.thesanctuarybeachresort.com* 🛏 *60 rooms* 🍴 *No Meals.*

Spindrift Inn
$$ | **HOTEL** | This boutique hotel on Cannery Row has beach access and a rooftop garden that overlooks the water. **Pros:** close to aquarium; steps from the beach; friendly staff. **Cons:** throngs of visitors outside; can be noisy; not good for families. [$] *Rooms from: $315* ✉ *652 Cannery Row, Monterey* ☎ *831/646–8900, 800/841–1879* 🌐 *www.spindriftinn.com* 🛏 *45 rooms* 🍴 *Free Breakfast.*

▼ Nightlife

BARS
Cibo

LIVE MUSIC | An Italian restaurant and event venue with a big bar area, Cibo brings live jazz and other music to downtown five nights a week. ✉ *301 Alvarado St., at Del Monte Ave., Monterey* ☎ *831/649–8151* ⊕ *cibo.com.*

LindaRose Bar & Grill

BARS | Head up to the rooftop bar at Hotel 1110 for sweeping bay views, craft cocktails, local wine and beer, and an array of Mediterranean-centric dishes— from kebabs and lamb fries to mezze. Check the event schedule for live music and other special happenings. ✉ *1110 Del Monte Ave., Monterey* ☎ *831/655–0515* ⊕ *www.hotel1110.com/lindarose.*

Turn 12 Bar & Grill

BARS | The motorcycles and vintage photographs at this downtown watering hole pay homage to nearby 11-turn Laguna Seca Raceway. The large-screen TVs, heated outdoor patio, happy-hour specials, and live entertainment keep the place jumpin' into the wee hours. ✉ *400 Tyler St., at E. Franklin St., Monterey* ☎ *831/372–8876* ⊕ *www.turn12barand-grill.com.*

BREWPUBS
Alvarado Street Brewery & Grill

BREWPUBS | Housed in an historic Beaux Arts building that dates from 1916, this craft brewery lures locals and visitors alike with a full bar and 20 craft beers on tap, decent gastropub menu, beer garden, and shaded sidewalk patio. The company also has a brewery, bistro, and wine bar in Carmel Plaza in Carmel-by-the-Sea. ✉ *426 Alvarado St., Monterey* ☎ *831/655–2337* ⊕ *www.alvaradostreet-brewery.com.*

Peter B's Brewpub

BREWPUBS | House-made beers, 18 HDTVs, a decent pub menu, and a pet-friendly patio ensure lively crowds at this craft brewery in back of the Portola Hotel & Spa. ✉ *2 Portola Plaza, Monterey* ☎ *831/649–2699* ⊕ *www.portolahotel. com/dining/peter-bs-brewpub* ⊘ *Closed Mon. and Tues.*

PUBS
Crown & Anchor

PUBS | An authentic British pub, downtown Crown & Anchor has 20 beers on tap, classic cocktails, and a full menu, including 18 daily specials available in the restaurant and heated patio until midnight. ✉ *150 W. Franklin St., Monterey* ☎ *831/649–6496* ⊕ *crownandanchor.net.*

🛍 Shopping

Alvarado and nearby downtown streets are good places to start a Monterey shopping spree, especially if you're interested in antiques and collectibles.

Cannery Row Antique Mall

ANTIQUES & COLLECTIBLES | Bargain hunters can sometimes find little treasures at the mall, which houses more than 100 local vendors under one roof. ✉ *471 Wave St., Monterey* ☎ *831/655–0264* ⊕ *www. canneryrowantiquemall.com.*

🏃 Activities

Monterey Bay waters never warm to the temperatures of their Southern California counterparts—the warmest they get is the low 60s. That's one reason why the marine life here is so diverse, which in turn brings out the fishers, kayakers, and whale-watchers. During the rainy winter, the waves grow larger, and surfers flock to the water. On land pretty much year-round, bikers find opportunities to ride, and walkers have plenty of waterfront to stroll.

BIKING
Adventures by the Sea

BIKING | **FAMILY** | You can rent surreys plus tandem, standard, and electric bicycles from this outfit that also conducts bike and kayak tours, and rents kayaks and stand-up paddleboards. There are multiple locations along Cannery Row and Custom House Plaza as well as branches at Lovers Point in Pacific Grove and 17-Mile Drive in Pebble Beach. ⊠ *299 Cannery Row, Monterey* ☎ *831/372–1807, 800/979–3370 reservations* ⊕ *adventuresbythesea.com.*

FISHING
J&M Sport Fishing
FISHING | FAMILY | This outfit takes beginning and experienced fishers out to sea to catch rock cod, ling cod, sand dabs, mackerel, halibut, salmon (in season), albacore, squid, Dungeness crab, and other species. ⊠ *66 Fisherman's Wharf, Monterey* ☎ *831/372–7440* ⊕ *jmsportfishing.com* ⊠ *Trips from $115.*

GOLF
Del Monte Golf Course
GOLF | Though overshadowed by its higher-profile Pebble Beach siblings, this classic course that golf champion Johnny Miller once described as "sneaky hard" predates them all. Designed by Charles Maud in 1897 (the first nine) and 1903 (the back nine) and redesigned in 1920 by W. Herbert Fowler, the course has wide fairways—many of them with wicked doglegs—flanked by oak, pine, and cypress trees. Many golfers find the par-5 13th hole their unluckiest: long (512 yards) and straight, it narrows sharply just before the green. ⊠ *1300 Sylvan Rd., Monterey* ☎ *800/877–0597* ⊕ *pebblebeach.com* ⊠ *$125* ⅃. *18 holes, 6365 yards, par 72.*

HIKING
Monterey Bay Coastal Recreation Trail
HIKING & WALKING | FAMILY | From Custom House Plaza, you can walk along the coast in either direction on this 18-mile-long trail and take in spectacular views of the sea. The trail runs from north of Monterey in Castroville south to Pacific Grove, with sections continuing around Pebble Beach. Much of the path follows an old Southern Pacific Railroad route. *Easy–moderate.* ⊠ *Monterey* ☎ *888/221–1010*

⊕ *www.seemonterey.com/things-to-do/outdoors/hiking/coastal-trail.*

KAYAKING
★ Monterey Bay Kayaks
KAYAKING | FAMILY | For many visitors the best way to see the bay is by kayak. This company rents equipment and conducts classes and natural-history tours. ⊠ *693 Del Monte Ave., Monterey* ☎ *831/373–5357* ⊕ *www.montereybaykayaks.com* ⊠ *4-hr rentals from $35 per person.*

WHALE-WATCHING
Thousands of gray whales pass close by the Monterey Coast on their annual migration between the Bering Sea and Baja California, and a whale-watching cruise is the best way to see these magnificent mammals close up. The migration south takes place from December through March; January is prime viewing time. The whales migrate north from March through June. Blue whales and humpbacks also pass the coast; they're most easily spotted in late summer and early fall.

Fast Raft Ocean Safaris
RAFTING | FAMILY | Naturalists lead whale-watching and sightseeing tours of Monterey Bay aboard the 33-foot *Ranger,* a six-passenger, rigid-hull, inflatable boat. The speedy craft slips into coves inaccessible to larger vessels, and its quiet engines enable intimate marine experiences without disturbing wildlife. Children ages eight and older are welcome to participate. From April to November, the boat departs from Moss Landing Harbor North Boat Launching Ramp. ⊠ *32 Cannery Row, Suite F2, Monterey* ☎ *408/659–3900* ⊕ *www.fastraft.com* ⊠ *From $195.*

Monterey Bay Whale Watch
WILDLIFE-WATCHING | FAMILY | The marine biologists here lead three- to five-hour whale-watching tours. ⊠ *84 Fisherman's Wharf, Monterey* ☎ *831/375–4658* ⊕ *montereybaywhalewatch.com* ⊠ *From $79.*

Princess Monterey Whale Watching

WILDLIFE-WATCHING | FAMILY | Tours are offered daily on a 100-passenger high-speed cruiser and a large 100-foot boat. ⊠ *96 Fisherman's Wharf, Monterey* ☎ *831/372–2203* ⊕ *montereywhale-watching.com* 🎫 *From $70.*

Salinas

17 miles east of Monterey on Hwy. 68.

Salinas, a hardworking city surrounded by vineyards and fruit and vegetable fields, honors the memory and literary legacy of John Steinbeck, its most famous native, with the National Steinbeck Center. The facility is in Old Town Salinas, where renovated turn-of-the-20th-century stone buildings house shops and restaurants.

GETTING HERE AND AROUND

From San Francisco, take Highway 101 south to Salinas, exit at Market Street for downtown/Old Town Salinas. Highway 68 connects Salinas to Monterey; Highway 183 is the main route to Castroville and Santa Cruz County. Both routes eventually connect with Highway 1.

Greyhound buses stop at the main depot (⊠ *11 Station Pl. at Market St.*), as does Amtrak's *Coast Starlight.* From there it's a short walk to the Salinas Transit Center (⊠ *110 Salinas St. at Central Ave.*), with connections to public transit throughout Monterey Bay and Central California. You can purchase day passes for Monterey-Salinas Transit (MST) buses here.

ESSENTIALS

TRAIN INFORMATION Salinas Amtrak Station. ⊠ *11 Station Pl., Salinas* ☎ *800/872–7245* ⊕ *www.amtrak.com.*

VISITOR INFORMATION California Welcome Center. ⊠ *1A Station Pl., Salinas* ☎ *831/757–8687* ⊕ *www.visitcalifornia.com.*

◉ Sights

★ National Steinbeck Center

HISTORY MUSEUM | FAMILY | The center's exhibits document the life of Pulitzer- and Nobel-prize winner John Steinbeck and the history of the nearby communities that inspired novels such as *East of Eden.* Highlights include reproductions of the green pickup-camper from *Travels with Charley* and the bunk room from *Of Mice and Men.* Steinbeck House, the author's Victorian birthplace, is two blocks from the center at 132 Central Avenue. Now a popular (lunch-only) restaurant and gift shop with docent-led tours, it also displays memorabilia. ⊠ *1 Main St., Salinas* ☎ *831/775–4721* ⊕ *www.steinbeck.org* 🎫 *$15.*

San Juan Bautista State Historic Park

HISTORIC SIGHT | FAMILY | With the low-slung, colonnaded Mission San Juan Bautista as its drawing card, this park 20 miles northeast of Salinas is about as close to early-19th-century California as you can get. Historic buildings ring the wide green plaza, among them an adobe home furnished with Spanish-colonial antiques, a hotel frozen in the 1860s, a blacksmith shop, a pioneer cabin, and a jailhouse. The mission's cemetery contains the unmarked graves of more than 4,300 Native American converts. ■TIP➔ **On the first Saturday of the month, costumed volunteers engage in quilting bees, tortilla making, and other frontier activities, and sarsaparilla and other non-alcoholic drinks are served in the saloon.** ⊠ *19 Franklin St., San Juan Bautista* ☎ *831/623–4881* ⊕ *www.parks.ca.gov* 🎫 *$3 park, $4 mission* ⊗ *Mission closed Tues.*

Pinnacles National Park

38 miles southeast of Salinas.

It was Teddy Roosevelt who recognized the uniqueness of this ancient volcano—its jagged spires and monoliths thrusting upward from chaparral-covered mountains—when he made it a national monument in 1908. Though only about two hours from the bustling Bay Area, the outside world seems to recede well before you even reach the park's gates.

GETTING HERE AND AROUND

One of the first things you need to decide when visiting Pinnacles is which entrance—east or west—you'll use, because there's no road connecting the two rugged peaks separating them. Entering from Highway 25 on the east is straightforward. The gate is only a mile or so from the turnoff. From the west, once you head east out of Soledad on Highway 146, the road quickly becomes narrow and hilly, with many blind curves. Drive slowly and cautiously along the 10 miles or so before you reach the west entrance.

ESSENTIALS

Pinnacles Visitor Center

VISITOR CENTER | At the park's main visitor center, near the eastern entrance, you'll find a helpful selection of maps, books, and gifts. The adjacent campground store sells light snacks. ✉ *5000 Hwy. 146, Paicines* ☎ *831/389–4485* ⊕ *www.nps. gov/pinn.*

West Pinnacles Visitor Contact Station

VISITOR CENTER | This small ranger station is just past the park's western entrance, about 10 miles east of Soledad. Here you can get maps and information, watch a 13-minute film about Pinnacles, and view interpretive exhibits. No food or drink is available here. ✉ *Hwy. 146, Soledad* ☎ *831/389–4427* ⊕ *www.nps.gov/pinn.*

◉ Sights

Pinnacles National Park

NATIONAL PARK | FAMILY | The many attractions at Pinnacles include talus caves, 30 miles of hiking trails, and hundreds of rock-climbing routes. A mosaic of diverse habitats supports an amazing variety of wildlife species: 160 birds, 48 mammals, 70 butterflies, and nearly 400 bees. The park is also home to some of the world's remaining few hundred condors in captivity and release areas. Fourteen of California's 25 bat species live in caves and other habitats in the park. President Theodore Roosevelt declared this remarkable 26,000-acre geologic and wildlife preserve a national monument in 1908. President Barack Obama officially designated it a national park in 2013.

The pinnacles are believed to have been created when two major tectonic plates collided and pushed a smaller plate down beneath the earth's crust, spawning volcanoes in what's now called the Gabilan Mountains, southeast of Salinas and Monterey. After the eruptions ceased, the San Andreas Fault split the volcanic field in two, carrying part of it northward to what is now Pinnacles National Park. Millions of years of erosion left a rugged landscape of rocky spires and crags, or pinnacles. Boulders fell into canyons and valleys, creating talus caves and a paradise for modern-day rock climbers.

Spring is the most popular time to visit, when colorful wildflowers blanket the meadows; the light and scenery can be striking in fall and winter; the summer heat is often brutal. The park has two entrances—east and west—but they are not connected. Amenities and attractions on the park's east side include the Pinnacles Visitor Center, Bear Gulch Nature Center, the park headquarters, Pinnacles Campground, and the Bear Gulch Cave and Reservoir. The Chaparral Parking Area is on the west side, where you can feast on fantastic views of the Pinnacles High

Peaks from the parking area. Dogs are not allowed on hiking trails.

■**TIP→** **The east entrance is 32 miles southeast of Hollister via Highway 25. The west entrance is about 12 miles east of Soledad via Highway 146.** ⊠ *5000 Hwy. 146, Paicines* ☎ *831/389–4486* ⊕ *www. nps.gov/pinn* ☎ *$30 per vehicle, $15 per visitor if biking or walking.*

Activities

HIKING
Hiking is the most popular activity at Pinnacles, with more than 30 miles of trails for every interest and level of fitness. Because there isn't a road through the park, hiking is also the only way to experience its interior, including the High Peaks, the talus caves, and the reservoir.

★ **Balconies Cliffs–Cave Loop**
TRAIL | **FAMILY** | Grab your flashlight before heading out from the Chaparral Trailhead parking lot for this 2.4-mile loop that takes you through the Balconies Caves. This trail is especially beautiful in spring, when wildflowers carpet the canyon floor. About 0.6 mile from the start of the trail, turn left to begin ascending the Balconies Cliffs Trail, where you'll be rewarded with close-up views of Machete Ridge and other steep, vertical formations; you may run across rock climbers testing their skills before rounding the loop and descending back through the cave. *Easy–Moderate.* ⊠ *Pinnacles National Park* ⊹ *Trailhead: Chaparral Parking Area.*

★ **Bear Gulch Cave–Moses Spring–Rim Trail Loop**
TRAIL | **FAMILY** | Perhaps the most popular hike at Pinnacles, this relatively short (2.2-mile) loop trail is fun for kids and adults. It leads to the Bear Gulch cave system, and if your timing is right, you'll pass by several seasonal waterfalls inside the caves (flashlights are required). If it's been raining, check with a ranger, as the caves can flood. The upper side of the cave is usually closed in spring and

early summer to protect the Townsend's big-ear bats and their pups. *Easy.* ⊹ *Trailhead: Bear Gulch Day Use Area.*

Moss Landing

12 miles northwest of Salinas.

Moss Landing is not much more than a couple of blocks of cafés and restaurants, art galleries, and studios, plus a busy fishing port, but therein lies its charm. It's a fine place to overnight or stop for a meal and get a dose of nature.

GETTING HERE AND AROUND
From Highway 1 north or south, exit at Moss Landing Road on the ocean side. MST buses serve Moss Landing.

TOURS
Elkhorn Slough Safari Nature Boat Tours
BOAT TOURS | **FAMILY** | This outfit's naturalists lead two-hour tours of Elkhorn Sough aboard a 27-foot pontoon boat. Reservations are required. ⊠ *Moss Landing Harbor, Moss Landing* ☎ *831/633–5555* ⊕ *elkhornslough.com* ☎ *From $43.*

ESSENTIALS
VISITOR INFORMATION Moss Landing Chamber of Commerce. ⊠ *Moss Landing* ☎ *831/633–4501* ⊕ *mosslandingchamber. com.*

Sights

Elkhorn Slough National Estuarine Research Reserve
NATURE PRESERVE | **FAMILY** | The reserve's 1,700 acres of tidal flats and salt marshes form a complex environment that supports some 300 species of birds. A walk along the meandering waterways and wetlands can reveal hawks, white-tailed kites, owls, herons, and egrets. Also living or visiting here are sea otters, sharks, rays, and many other animals. ⊠ *1700 Elkhorn Rd., Watsonville* ☎ *831/728–2822* ⊕ *www.elkhornslough. org* ☎ *Free* ☉ *Closed Mon. and Tues.*

🍴 Restaurants

Haute Enchilada

$$ | SOUTH AMERICAN | FAMILY | Part of a complex that includes art galleries and an events venue, the Haute adds bohemian character to the seafaring village of Moss Landing. The inventive Latin American–inspired dishes include shrimp and black corn enchiladas topped with a citrus cilantro cream sauce, and roasted *pasilla* chilies stuffed with mashed plantains and caramelized onions. **Known for:** extensive cocktail and wine list; many vegan and gluten-free options; artsy atmosphere. [$] *Average main: $26* ✉ *7902 Moss Landing Rd., Moss Landing* ☎ *831/633–5843* 🌐 *www.hauteenchilada.com* ⏲ *Closed Tues. and Wed.*

🛏 Hotels

Captain's Inn

$ | B&B/INN | Commune with nature and pamper yourself with upscale creature comforts at this green-certified complex in the heart of town. **Pros:** walk to restaurants and shops; tranquil natural setting; closest Monterey Bay hotel to Pinnacles National Park. **Cons:** rooms in historic building don't have water views; far from urban amenities; not appropriate for young children. [$] *Rooms from: $129* ✉ *8122 Moss Landing Rd., Moss Landing* ☎ *831/889–0815* 🌐 *www.captainsinn.com* 🛏 *10 rooms* 🍽 *No Meals.*

🏃 Activities

KAYAKING

Monterey Bay Kayaks

KAYAKING | FAMILY | Rent a kayak to paddle out into Elkhorn Slough for up-close wildlife encounters. ✉ *2390 Hwy. 1, at North Harbor, Moss Landing* ☎ *831/373–5357* 🌐 *www.montereybaykayaks.com* 🎟 *4-hr rentals from $35 per person.*

Aptos

17 miles north of Moss Landing.

Backed by a redwood forest and facing the sea, downtown Aptos—known as Aptos Village—is a place of wooden walkways and false-fronted shops, as well as a "new" village complex of restaurants, shops, and services. Antiques dealers cluster along Trout Gulch Road, off Soquel Drive east of Highway 1.

GETTING HERE AND AROUND

Use Highway 1 to reach Aptos from Santa Cruz or Monterey. Exit at State Park Drive to reach the main shopping hub and Aptos Village. You can also exit at Freedom Boulevard or Rio del Mar. Soquel Drive is the main artery through town.

ESSENTIALS

VISITOR INFORMATION Aptos Chamber of Commerce. ✉ *7605–A Old Dominion Ct., Aptos* ☎ *831/688–1467* 🌐 *aptoschamber.com.*

⛱ Beaches

★ Seacliff State Beach

BEACH | FAMILY | Sandstone bluffs tower above this popular beach, whose long fishing pier was, unfortunately, demolished in 2023 following devastating winter storm damage. The 1.5-mile walk north to adjacent New Brighton State Beach in Capitola is one of the nicest on the bay. Leashed dogs are allowed on the beach. **Amenities:** food and drink; lifeguards; parking (fee); showers; toilets. **Best for:** sunset; swimming; walking. ✉ *201 State Park Dr., Aptos* ☎ *831/685–6500* 🌐 *www.parks.ca.gov* 🎟 *$10 per vehicle.*

🍴 Restaurants

Bittersweet Bistro

$$$ | MEDITERRANEAN | A large old tavern with cathedral ceilings houses this popular bistro, where the Mediterranean–California menu changes seasonally, but regular highlights include paella, seafood puttanesca, and pepper-crusted rib-eye steak with Cabernet demi-glace. **Known for:** value-laden happy hour; seafood specials; house-made desserts. $ *Average main: $38 ⊠ 787 Rio Del Mar Blvd., off Hwy. 1, Aptos* ☎ *831/662–9799* ⊕ *www. bittersweetbistro.com* ⊗ *Closed Mon. and Tues. No lunch, but open at 2 for dinner.*

★ **Mentone**

$$ | **ITALIAN** | This spacious restaurant with soaring ceilings and floor-to-ceiling windows serves dishes featuring the authentic flavors of the French/Italian Riviera, from Nice to Genoa. The menu changes often, depending on ingredients acquired from local purveyors, but, in addition to house-made pizzas and traditional pastas, it might offer black-truffle cappellini in an Armagnac and truffle butter sauce, Dungeness crab gnocchi, or pork belly with squash and fennel in a scallop sauce. **Known for:** seasonal cocktails; wood-oven-fired pizzas; house-made pastas. $ *Average main: $30 ⊠ 174 Aptos Village Way, Aptos* ☎ *831/708–4040* ⊕ *www. mentonerestaurant.com* ⊗ *Closed Tues. No lunch weekdays.*

🛏 **Hotels**

Seacliff Inn, Tapestry Collection by Hilton

$ | **HOTEL** | **FAMILY** | Families and business travelers like this 6-acre property near Seacliff State Beach that's more resort than hotel. **Pros:** walking distance to the beach; family-friendly; on-site restaurant and bar. **Cons:** close to freeway; occasional nighttime bar noise; no elevator. $ *Rooms from: $180 ⊠ 7500 Old Dominion Ct., Aptos* ☎ *831/688–7300, 800/367–2003* ⊕ *www.seacliffinn.com* ⇨ *158 rooms* ⦿ *No Meals.*

Seascape Beach Resort

$$$ | **RESORT** | **FAMILY** | It's easy to unwind at this full-fledged resort on a bluff overlooking Monterey Bay. The spacious suites sleep from two to eight people. **Pros:** time share–style apartments; access to miles of beachfront; superb views. **Cons:** far from city life; most bathrooms are small; some rooms need updating. $ *Rooms from: $387 ⊠ 1 Seascape Resort Dr., Aptos* ☎ *831/662–7171, 866/867–0976* ⊕ *www.seascaperesort. com* ⇨ *285 suites* ⦿ *No Meals.*

Capitola and Soquel

4 miles northwest of Aptos.

On the National Register of Historic places as California's first seaside resort town, the village of Capitola has been in a vacation mood since the late 1800s. Casual eateries, surf shops, and ice-cream parlors pack its walkable downtown. Inland, across Highway 1, antiques shops line Soquel Drive in the town of Soquel. Wineries dot the Santa Cruz Mountains beyond.

GETTING HERE AND AROUND

From Santa Cruz or Monterey, follow Highway 1 to the Capitola/Soquel (Bay Avenue) exit about 7 miles south of Santa Cruz and head west to reach Capitola and east to access Soquel Village. On summer weekends, park for free in the lot behind the Crossroads Center, a block west of the freeway, and hop aboard the free Capitola Shuttle to the village.

ESSENTIALS

VISITOR INFORMATION Capitola-Soquel Chamber of Commerce. ⊠ *1855 41st Ave., Suite J06, Capitola* ☎ *831/475–6522* ⊕ *www.capitolachamber.com.*

⊕ **Beaches**

★ **New Brighton State Beach**

BEACH | **FAMILY** | Once the site of a Chinese fishing village, New Brighton is now a popular surfing and camping spot. Its Pacific Migrations Visitor Center traces the history of the Chinese and other peoples who settled around Monterey Bay. It also documents the migratory patterns of the area's wildlife, such as monarch

Did You Know?

Soquel Cove in Santa Cruz is surrounded by New Brighton State Beach and Seacliff State Beach, where a WWI concrete ship sits partially submerged in the water.

butterflies and gray whales. Leashed dogs are allowed in the park. New Brighton connects with Seacliff Beach, and at low tide you can walk or run along this scenic stretch of sand for nearly 16 miles south (though you might have to wade through a few creeks). ■ TIP➔ **The 1½-mile stroll from New Brighton to Seacliff's concrete ship is a local favorite.** **Amenities:** parking (fee); showers; toilets. **Best for:** sunset; swimming; walking. ✉ *1500 State Park Dr., off Hwy. 1, Capitola* ☎ *831/464–6329* ⊕ *www.parks.ca.gov* ✈ *$10 per vehicle.*

🍴 Restaurants

Carpo's

$ | SEAFOOD | FAMILY | Locals love this casual restaurant where seafood predominates, but you can also order burgers, salads, and steaks. Baskets of battered snapper are among the favorites, along with calamari, prawns, seafood kebabs, fish-and-chips, and homemade olallieberry pie. **Known for:** large portions of healthy comfort food; lots of options under $14; soup and salad bar. $ *Average main: $14* ✉ *2400 Porter St., at Hwy. 1, Soquel* ☎ *831/476–6260* ⊕ *www.carposrestaurant.com.*

Gayle's Bakery & Rosticceria

$$ | CAFÉ | FAMILY | Whether you're in the mood for an orange-olallieberry muffin, a wild rice and chicken salad, or tri-tip on garlic toast, this bakery-deli's varied menu is likely to satisfy. Munch on your lemon meringue tartlet or chocolate brownie on the shady patio, or dig into the daily blue-plate dinner—teriyaki grilled skirt steak with edamame-shiitake sticky rice, perhaps, or roast turkey breast with Chardonnay gravy—amid the whirl of activity inside. **Known for:** prepared meals to go; on-site bakery and rosticceria; deli and espresso bar. $ *Average main: $23* ✉ *504 Bay Ave., Capitola* ☎ *831/462–1200* ⊕ *www.gaylesbakery.com.*

Shadowbrook

$$$ | EUROPEAN | To get to this romantic spot overlooking Soquel Creek, you can take a cable car or walk the stairs down a steep, fern-lined bank beside a running waterfall. Dining room options include the rooftop Redwood Room, the wood-paneled Wine Cellar, the creekside, glass-enclosed Greenhouse, the Fireplace Room, and the airy Garden Room. **Known for:** romantic creek-side setting; prime rib and grilled seafood; local special-occasion favorite for nearly 70 years. $ *Average main: $38* ✉ *1750 Wharf Rd., at Lincoln Ave., Capitola* ☎ *831/475–1511* ⊕ *www.shadowbrook-capitola.com.*

VinoCruz Wine Bar & Kitchen

$ | AMERICAN | In a lively contemporary space with a patio in the heart of Soquel Village, VinoCruz offers more than 50 wines by the glass, with a focus on Santa Cruz Mountains but also other California and international regions; it also has local cider and beer on tap. Nosh on artisanal burgers, tacos, flatbread pizzas, salads, and cheese and charcuterie plates. **Known for:** weekend brunch; weekday happy hour and weekly live music; fresh food, made in-house. $ *Average main: $18* ✉ *4901 Soquel Dr., Soquel* ☎ *831/426–8466* ⊕ *vinocruz.com* ☾ *No lunch weekdays.*

🛏 Hotels

Inn at Depot Hill

$$ | B&B/INN | This inventively designed B&B in a former rail depot views itself as a link to the era of luxury train travel, and each double room or suite, complete with fireplace and featherbeds, is inspired by a different destination— Italy's Portofino, France's Côte d'Azur, Japan's Kyoto. **Pros:** short walk to beach and village; historic charm; excellent service. **Cons:** fills quickly; hot-tub conversation audible in some rooms; not suitable for children. $ *Rooms from: $319* ✉ *250 Monterey Ave., Capitola*

☎ *831/462–3376, 800/572–2632* ⊕ *www. innatdepothill.com* ⤵ *13 rooms* ⫤ *Free Breakfast.*

Santa Cruz

5 miles west of Capitola, 48 miles north of Monterey.

The big city on this stretch of the California coast, Santa Cruz (pop. 63,364) is less manicured than Carmel or Monterey. Long known for its surfing and its amusement-filled beach boardwalk, the town is an eclectic mix of grand Victorian-era homes, beachside inns, and multimillion-dollar compounds owned by tech gurus. The opening of the University of California campus in the 1960s swung the town sharply to the left politically, and the counterculture more or less lives on here. At the same time, a revitalized downtown and an insane real-estate market reflect the city's proximity to Silicon Valley, which is just a 30-minute drive to the north, and to a growing wine region in the surrounding mountains.

Amble around downtown's Santa Cruz Farmers' Market (Wednesday afternoon year-round) to experience the local culture, which derives much of its character from close connections to food and farming. The market covers a city block and includes not just the expected organic produce, but also live music and booths with local crafts and prepared food.

GETTING HERE AND AROUND

From the San Francisco Bay area, take Highway 17 south over the mountains to Santa Cruz, where it merges with Highway 1. Use Highway 1 to get around the area. The Santa Cruz Transit Center is at 920 Pacific Avenue, at Front Street, a short walk from the wharf and boardwalk, with connections to public transit throughout the Monterey Bay and San Francisco Bay areas. You can purchase day passes for Santa Cruz METRO buses here.

ESSENTIALS

VISITOR INFORMATION Visit Santa Cruz County. ⊠ *303 Water St., Suite 100, Santa Cruz* ☎ *831/425–1234, 800/833–3494* ⊕ *www.santacruz.org.*

◉ Sights

Monterey Bay National Marine Sanctuary Exploration Center
VISITOR CENTER | FAMILY | The interactive and multimedia exhibits at this fascinating interpretive center reveal and explain the treasures of the nation's largest marine sanctuary. The two-story building, across from the main beach and municipal wharf, has films and exhibits about migratory species, watersheds, underwater canyons, kelp forests, and intertidal zones. The second-floor deck has stellar ocean views and an interactive station that provides real-time weather, surf, and buoy reports. ⊠ *35 Pacific Ave., near Beach St., Santa Cruz* ☎ *831/421–9993* ⊕ *montereybay.noaa.gov/vc/sec* ⤵ *Free* ◷ *Closed Mon. and Tues.*

Mystery Spot
OTHER ATTRACTION | FAMILY | Hokey tourist trap or genuine scientific enigma? Since 1940, curious throngs baffled by the Mystery Spot have made it one of the most visited attractions in Santa Cruz. The laws of gravity and physics don't appear to apply in this tiny patch of redwood forest, where balls roll uphill and people stand on a slant. ■**TIP→ On weekends and holidays, it's wise to purchase tickets online in advance.** ⊠ *465 Mystery Spot Rd., off Branciforte Dr. (north off Hwy. 1), Santa Cruz* ☎ *831/423–8897* ⊕ *www. mysteryspot.com* ⤵ *$10, parking $5.*

Pacific Avenue
STREET | FAMILY | When you've had your fill of the city's beaches and waters, take a stroll in downtown Santa Cruz, especially on Pacific Avenue between Laurel and Water streets. Vintage boutiques and mountain-sports stores, sushi bars, and Mexican restaurants, day spas, and

nightclubs keep the main drag and the surrounding streets hopping from midmorning until late evening.

★ Santa Cruz Beach Boardwalk

AMUSEMENT PARK/CARNIVAL | FAMILY | This boardwalk has entertained beachgoers for more than a century. Its Looff carousel and classic wooden Giant Dipper roller coaster, both dating from the early 1900s, are surrounded by high-tech thrill rides and easygoing kiddie rides with ocean views. Video and arcade games, a minigolf course, and a laser-tag arena pack one gigantic building, which is open daily even if the rides aren't running. You have to pay to play, but you can wander the entire boardwalk for free while sampling carnival fare such as corn dogs and garlic fries. ⊠ *Along Beach St., Santa Cruz* ☎ *831/423–5590 info line* ⊕ *beachboardwalk.com* 🎟 *$40 day pass for unlimited rides, or pay per ride* ⏱ *Some rides closed Sept.–May.*

Santa Cruz Mission State Historic Park

HISTORY MUSEUM | FAMILY | On the northern fringes of downtown is the site of California's 12th Spanish mission, built in the 1790s and destroyed by an earthquake in 1857. A museum in a restored 1791 adobe and a half-scale replica of the mission church are part of the complex. ⊠ *144 School St., at Adobe St., Santa Cruz* ☎ *831/425–5849* ⊕ *www.parks. ca.gov* 🎟 *Free* ⏱ *Closed Tues. and Wed.*

Santa Cruz Municipal Wharf

MARINA/PIER | FAMILY | Jutting half a mile into the ocean near one end of the boardwalk, the century-old Municipal Wharf is lined with seafood restaurants, a wine bar, souvenir shops, and outfitters offering bay cruises, fishing trips, and boat rentals. A salty soundtrack drifts up from under the wharf, where barking sea lions lounge in heaps on the crossbeams. ⊠ *Beach St. and Pacific Ave., Santa Cruz* ☎ *831/420–5725* ⊕ *www.santacruzwharf.com.*

Santa Cruz Surfing Museum

HISTORY MUSEUM | FAMILY | This museum inside the Mark Abbott Memorial Lighthouse chronicles local surfing history. Photographs show old-time surfers, and a display of boards includes rarities such as a heavy redwood plank predating the fiberglass era and the remains of a modern board chomped by a great white shark. Surfer docents reminisce about the good old days. ⊠ *Lighthouse Point Park, 701 W. Cliff Dr. near Pelton Ave., Santa Cruz* ☎ *831/420–6289* ⊕ *www.facebook. com/santacruzsurfingmuseum* 🎟 *$3 suggested donation* ⏱ *Closed Tues. and Wed. except open Tues. July–early Sept.*

Seymour Marine Discovery Center

AQUARIUM | FAMILY | Part of the Long Marine Laboratory at the University of California Santa Cruz's Institute of Marine Sciences, the center looks more like a research facility than a slick aquarium. Interactive exhibits demonstrate how scientists study the ocean, and the aquarium displays creatures of interest to marine biologists. The 87-foot blue whale skeleton is one of the world's largest. ⊠ *100 Shaffer Rd., end of Delaware Ave., west of Natural Bridges State Beach, Santa Cruz* ☎ *831/459–3800* ⊕ *seymourcenter.ucsc. edu* 🎟 *$12* ⏱ *Closed Mon.*

Surf City Vintners

WINERY | A dozen tasting rooms of limited-production wineries occupy renovated warehouse spaces west of the beach. MJA, Sones Cellars, Santa Cruz Mountain Vineyard, and Equinox are good places to start. Also here are the Santa Cruz Mountain Brewing Company and El Salchichero, popular for its homemade sausages, jams, and pickled and candied vegetables. ⊠ *Swift Street Courtyard, 334 Ingalls St., at Swift St., off Hwy. 1 (Mission St.), Santa Cruz* ☎ ⊕ *www. surfcityvintners.com.*

UC Santa Cruz

COLLEGE | FAMILY | The 2,000-acre University of California Santa Cruz campus nestles in the forested hills above town.

Its sylvan setting, ocean vistas, and redwood architecture make the university worth a visit, as does its arboretum ($10, open daily from 9 to 5), whose walking path leads through areas dedicated to the plants of California, Australia, New Zealand, and South Africa. **■TIP➔ Free shuttles help students and visitors get around campus, and you can join a guided tour (online reservation required).** ✉ *Santa Cruz* ✣ *Main entrance at Bay and High Sts. (turn left on High for arboretum)* ☎ *831/459–0111* 🌐 *www.ucsc.edu/visit.*

★ West Cliff Drive

SCENIC DRIVE | FAMILY | The road that winds along an oceanfront bluff from the municipal wharf to Natural Bridges State Beach makes for a spectacular drive, but it's even more fun to walk or bike the paved path that parallels the road. Surfers bob and swoosh in Monterey Bay at several points near the foot of the bluff, especially at a break known as **Steamer Lane.** Named for a surfer who died here in 1965, the nearby Mark Abbott Memorial Lighthouse stands at Point Santa Cruz, the cliff's major promontory. From here you can watch pinnipeds hang out, sunbathe, and frolic on Seal Rock. ✉ *Santa Cruz.*

Beaches

Natural Bridges State Beach

BEACH | FAMILY | At the end of West Cliff Drive lies this stretch of soft sand edged with tide pools and sea-sculpted rock bridges. **■TIP➔ From September to early January a colony of monarch butterflies roosts in the eucalyptus grove. Amenities:** lifeguards; parking (fee); toilets. **Best for:** sunrise; sunset; surfing; swimming. ✉ *2531 W. Cliff Dr., Santa Cruz* ☎ *831/423–4609* 🌐 *www.parks.ca.gov* 🎟 *Beach free, parking $10.*

Twin Lakes State Beach

BEACH | FAMILY | Stretching ½ mile along the coast on both sides of the small-craft jetties, Twin Lakes is one of Monterey Bay's sunniest beaches. It encompasses Seabright State Beach (with access in a residential neighborhood on the upcoast side) and Black's Beach on the downcoast side. Families often come here to sunbathe, picnic, and hike the nature trail around adjacent Schwann Lake. Parking is tricky from May through September—you need to pay for a $10 day-use permit at a kiosk and the lot fills quickly—but you can park all day in the harbor pay lot and walk here. Leashed dogs are allowed. **Amenities:** food and drink; lifeguards (seasonal); parking; showers; toilets; water sports (seasonal). **Best for:** sunset; surfing; swimming; walking. ✉ *7th Ave., at East Cliff Dr., Santa Cruz* ☎ *831/427–4868* 🌐 *www.parks.ca.gov.*

Restaurants

Bad Animal

$$ | ECLECTIC | By day, Bad Animal mostly sells rare and used books, but, at 5 pm, it morphs into a wine bar and restaurant, where you're encouraged to order a glass of wine while browsing the stacks. The menu depends on who is the current Culinary Artist in residence, a position that rotates every year or so. **Known for:** extensive list of natural, primarily French and California wines; interesting intellectual staff and clientele; emphasis on local, organic ingredients. [$] *Average main: $29* ✉ *1011 Cedar St., Santa Cruz* ☎ *831/900–5031* 🌐 *www.badanimalbooks.com* 🕒 *Closed Mon. and Tues. No lunch.*

Crow's Nest

$$ | SEAFOOD | FAMILY | Vintage surfboards and local surf photography line the walls, and nearly every table overlooks sand and surf at this restaurant on the Santa Cruz Harbor. For sweeping ocean views and fish tacos, burgers, and other casual fare, head upstairs to the Breakwater Bar & Grill. **Known for:** house-smoked salmon and calamari apps; crab-cake eggs Benedict and olallieberry pancakes; on-site market with pizzas, sandwiches, soups, and salads. [$] *Average main: $29* ✉ *2218 E. Cliff Dr., west* of 7th Ave., Santa Cruz ☎ 831/476–4560 ⊕ crowsnest-santacruz.com.

★ Laili Restaurant

$$ | **MEDITERRANEAN** | Exotic Mediterranean flavors with an Afghan twist take center stage at this artsy, stylish space with soaring ceilings. In the evening, locals come to relax over wine and soft jazz at the blue-concrete bar, on the seasonal heated patio with twinkly lights, or at a communal table near the open kitchen. **Known for:** house-made pastas and numerous vegetarian and vegan options; fresh naan, chutneys, and dips with every meal; traditional dishes like pomegranate eggplant and maushawa soup. $ *Average main: $24* ⊠ 101–B Cooper St., near Pacific Ave., Santa Cruz ☎ 831/423–4545 ⊕ lailirestaurant.com ⊗ Closed Sun. and Mon. No lunch.

La Posta Via

$$ | **ITALIAN** | Authentic Italian fare made with fresh local produce lures diners into this cozy, modern-rustic restaurant. Nearly everything is made in-house, from the pizzas and breads baked in the brick oven to the pasta and the vanilla-bean gelato. **Known for:** seasonal wild-nettle lasagna; braised lamb shank; in the heart of the Seabright neighborhood. $ *Average main: $30* ⊠ 538 Seabright Ave., at Logan St., Santa Cruz ☎ 831/457–2782 ⊕ www.lapostarestaurant.com ⊗ Closed Mon. and Tues. No lunch.

Oswald

$$$ | **EUROPEAN** | Sophisticated yet unpretentious European-inspired California cooking is the order of the day at this intimate and stylish bistro, whose seasonal menu might include such items as seafood risotto or crispy duck breast in a pomegranate reduction sauce. The creative concoctions poured at the slick marble bar include whiskey mixed with apple and lemon juice or tequila with celery juice and lime. **Known for:** excellent burgers and fries; crab appetizers; dark-chocolate soufflé and other tasty desserts. $ *Average main: $34* ⊠ 121 Soquel Ave., at Front St., Santa Cruz ☎ 831/423–7427 ⊕ www.oswaldrestaurant.com ⊗ Closed Sun.–Tues.

🛏 Hotels

Babbling Brook Inn

$$ | **B&B/INN** | Though it's in the middle of Santa Cruz, this inn has lush gardens, a running stream, and tall trees that make you feel as if you're in a secluded wood. **Pros:** close to UCSC; within walking distance of downtown shops; woodsy feel. **Cons:** near a high school; some rooms close to a busy street; many stairs and no elevator. $ *Rooms from: $280* ⊠ 1025 Laurel St., Santa Cruz ☎ 831/427–2437 ⊕ www.babblingbrookinn.com ⤷ 13 rooms ⊠ No Meals.

★ Chaminade Resort & Spa

$$ | **RESORT** | **FAMILY** | Secluded on 300 hilltop acres of redwood and eucalyptus forest laced with hiking trails, this Mission-style complex also features a lovely terrace restaurant with expansive views of Monterey Bay. Guest rooms are furnished in an eclectic, bohemian style that pays homage to the artsy local community and the city's industrial past. **Pros:** peaceful, verdant setting; full-service spa and large pool; ideal spot for romance and rejuvenation. **Cons:** not within walking distance of downtown; not near the ocean; resort fee. $ *Rooms from: $289* ⊠ 1 Chaminade La., Santa Cruz ☎ 800/283–6569, 831/475–5600 ⊕ www.chaminade.com ⤷ 156 rooms ⊠ No Meals.

Courtyard by Marriott Santa Cruz

$$ | **HOTEL** | **FAMILY** | This sparkling hotel, set in the heart of the tourist district and opened in fall 2022, is a warm, welcoming, haven filled with custom-designed furnishings and local art that reflects the beachy Santa Cruz vibe. **Pros:** two blocks from the beach and boardwalk, easy walk to the wharf and downtown; on-site café; spa with four treatment rooms. **Cons:** no rooms with beach views; valet parking only (fee); summer traffic may cause slow arrival to hotel. $ *Rooms from:*

$249 ✉ *313 Riverside Ave., Santa Cruz* ☎ *831/419–8700* ⊕ *www.marriott.com* 🛏 *151 rooms* ⏍ *No Meals.*

★ Dream Inn Santa Cruz

$$$ | HOTEL | A short stroll from the boardwalk and wharf, this full-service luxury hotel is the only lodging in Santa Cruz directly on the beach, and its rooms all have private balconies or patios overlooking Monterey Bay. Accommodations have contemporary furnishings, muted retro-chic colors, and upscale linens, but the main draw here is having the ocean at your doorstep. **Pros:** restaurant with sweeping bay views; cool mid-century modern design; walk to boardwalk and downtown. **Cons:** expensive; area gets congested on summer weekends; pool area and hallways can be noisy. $ *Rooms from: $499* ✉ *175 W. Cliff Dr., Santa Cruz* ☎ *831/740–8069* ⊕ *www.dreaminnsantacruz.com* 🛏 *165 rooms* ⏍ *No Meals.*

Hotel Paradox

$$ | HOTEL | About a mile from the ocean and two blocks from Pacific Avenue, this stylish, forest-theme complex (part of the Marriott Autograph Collection) is among the few full-service hotels in town. **Pros:** close to downtown and main beach; spacious pool area with cabanas, firepits, hot tub, and dining and cocktail service; farm-to-table restaurant. **Cons:** pool area can get crowded; some rooms on the small side; thin walls. $ *Rooms from: $297* ✉ *611 Ocean St., Santa Cruz* ☎ *831/425–7100, 888/236–2427 reservations* ⊕ *www.hotelparadox.com* 🛏 *172 rooms* ⏍ *No Meals.*

★ West Cliff Inn

$$$ | B&B/INN | On bluffs across from Cowell Beach, this three-story, Italianate property, built in 1877, exudes classic California beach style. **Pros:** killer bay and boardwalk views; walking distance of the beach; close to downtown. **Cons:** boardwalk noise; outdoor hot tub has limited privacy; street traffic. $ *Rooms from: $348* ✉ *174 W. Cliff Dr., Santa Cruz* ☎ *831/457–2200* ⊕ *www.westcliffinn.com* 🛏 *9 units* ⏍ *Free Breakfast.*

☿ Nightlife

Catalyst

LIVE MUSIC | This huge, grimy, and fun club books rock, indie rock, punk, death-metal, reggae, and other acts. ✉ *1011 Pacific Ave., Santa Cruz* ☎ *831/713–5492* ⊕ *catalystclub.com.*

Moe's Alley

LIVE MUSIC | Blues, salsa, reggae, funk: delightfully casual Moe's presents it all (and more). ✉ *1535 Commercial Way, Santa Cruz* ☎ *831/479–1854* ⊕ *moesalley.com* ☉ *Closed Mon.*

🎟 Performing Arts

Kuumbwa Jazz Center

MUSIC | The center draws top performers such as Lee Ritenour, Chris Potter, and the Dave Holland Trio. A café serves meals an hour before most shows. ✉ *320–2 Cedar St., Santa Cruz* ☎ *831/427–2227* ⊕ *www.kuumbwajazz.org.*

Tannery Arts Center

ARTS CENTERS | The former Salz Tannery now contains nearly 30 studios and live-work spaces for artists whose disciplines range from ceramics and glass to film and digital media; most have public hours of operation. Performances also take place at the on-site Colligan Theater, and the center hosts assorted arts events on weekends and, occasionally, on weekdays. ✉ *1060 River St., at intersection of Hwys. 1 and 9, Santa Cruz* ⊕ *www.tanneryartscenter.org.*

🛍 Shopping

Bad Animal Books

BOOKS | An eclectic independent shop in downtown Santa Cruz, Bad Animal has shelves packed with rare and used books, mostly representing the humanities: literature, philosophy, and theology, among them the favorite picks of the owner, a friend of famed poet Lawrence Ferlenghetti who earned a PhD in the History of Consciousness from UC Santa Cruz. ⊠ *1011 Cedar St., Santa Cruz* ☎ *831/900–5031* ⊕ *www.badanimalbooks.com* ⊙ *Closed Mon. and Tues.*

Bookshop Santa Cruz

BOOKS | FAMILY | In 2021, the town's best and most beloved independent bookstore celebrated its 55th anniversary of selling new, used, and remaindered titles. The children's section is especially comprehensive, and the shop's special events calendar is packed with readings, social mixers, book signings, and discussions. ⊠ *1520 Pacific Ave., Santa Cruz* ☎ *831/423–0900* ⊕ *www.bookshopsantacruz.com.*

Botanic + Luxe

OTHER SPECIALTY STORE | Come here to browse a carefully curated collection of goods, many from local craftspeople, including items for the home, jewelry, personal care, and plants—all that you need to inspire soulful living. ⊠ *110 Cooper St., Suite 100F, Santa Cruz* ☎ *831/515–7710* ⊕ *botanicandluxe.com.*

O'Neill Surf Shop

SPORTING GOODS | FAMILY | Local surfers get their wetties (wet suits) and other gear at this O'Neill store or the one in Capitola (⊠ *1115 41st Ave.*). There's also a satellite shop on the Santa Cruz Boardwalk. ⊠ *110 Cooper St., Santa Cruz* ☎ *831/469–4377* ⊕ *us.oneill.com.*

Santa Cruz Downtown Farmers' Market

MARKET | FAMILY | Santa Cruz is famous for its long tradition of organic growing and sustainable living, and its downtown market (one of five countywide) reflects the incredible diversity and quality of local agriculture and the synergistic daily life of community-minded residents. The busy market, which always has live music, happens every Wednesday from 1 to 6, rain or shine. The stalls cover much of an entire city block near Pacific Avenue and include fresh produce plus everything from oysters, beer, bread, and charcuterie to arts and crafts to prepared foods made from ingredients sourced from on-site vendors. ⊠ *Cedar St. at Lincoln St., Santa Cruz* ☎ *831/454–0566* ⊕ *santacruzfarmersmarket.org.*

🏃 Activities

BICYCLING

Another Bike Shop

BIKING | FAMILY | Mountain bikers should head here for tips on the best area trails and to browse cutting-edge gear made and tested locally. ⊠ *2361 Mission St., at King St., Santa Cruz* ☎ *831/427–2232* ⊕ *www.anotherbikeshop.com.*

BOATS AND CHARTERS

Chardonnay Sailing Charters

BOATING | The 70-foot *Chardonnay II* departs year-round from Santa Cruz yacht harbor on whale-watching, sunset, and other cruises around Monterey Bay. Most regularly scheduled excursions cost $75; food and drink are served on many of them. Reservations are essential. ⊠ *Santa Cruz West Harbor, 790 Mariner Park Way, Santa Cruz* ☎ *831/423–1213* ⊕ *www.chardonnay.com.*

Stagnaro Sport Fishing, Charters & Whale Watching Cruises

BOATING | FAMILY | Stagnaro (aka Santa Cruz Whale Watching) offers salmon, albacore, and rock-cod fishing expeditions (fees include bait) as well as whale-watching, dolphin, and sea-life cruises year-round. ⊠ *1718 Brommer St., near Santa Cruz Harbor, Santa Cruz* ☎ *831/427–0230* ⊕ *stagnaros.com* 🎫 *From $48.*

GOLF

DeLaveaga Golf Course

GOLF | Woodsy DeLaveaga, a public course set in a hilly park, overlooks Santa Cruz and the bay. With its canyons, tree-lined fairways, and notoriously difficult par-5, dogleg 10th hole, the course challenges novices and seasoned golfers. ⊠ *401 Upper Park Rd., Santa Cruz*

☎ *831/423–7214* ⊕ *www.delaveagagolf.com* ✉ *$60 weekdays, $80 weekends/holidays* ⌘ *18 holes, 5700 yards, par 70.*

Pasatiempo Golf Club

GOLF | Designed by famed golf architect Dr. Alister MacKenzie in 1929, this semiprivate course, set amid undulating hills just above the city, is among the nation's top championship courses. Golfers rave about the spectacular views and challenging terrain. According to the club, MacKenzie, who designed Pebble Beach's exclusive Cypress Point course and Augusta National in Georgia, the home of the Masters Golf Tournament, declared this his favorite layout. ✉ *20 Clubhouse Rd., Santa Cruz* ☎ *831/459–9155* ⊕ *www.pasatiempo.com* ✉ *From $345* ⌘ *18 holes, 6125 yards, par 72.*

KAYAKING

Kayak Connection

KAYAKING | FAMILY | From March through May, participants in this outfit's tours mingle with gray whales and their calves on their northward journey to Alaska. Throughout the year, the company rents kayaks and paddleboards and conducts tours of Natural Bridges State Beach, Capitola, and Elkhorn Slough. ✉ *Santa Cruz Harbor, 413 Lake Ave., Suite 3, Santa Cruz* ☎ *831/479–1121* ⊕ *kayakconnection.com* ✉ *From $85 for scheduled tours.*

Venture Quest Kayaking

KAYAKING | FAMILY | Explore hidden coves and kelp forests on guided two-hour kayak tours that depart from Santa Cruz Wharf. The tours include a kayaking lesson. Venture Quest also rents kayaks (and wet suits and gear) and arranges tours at other Monterey Bay destinations, including Elkhorn Slough. ✉ *2 Santa Cruz Wharf, Santa Cruz* ☎ *831/427–2267 kayak hotline, 831/425–8445 rental office* ⊕ *www.santacruzkayak.com* ✉ *From $40 for rentals, $70 for tours.*

SURFING

Club-Ed Surf School and Camps

SURFING | FAMILY | Find out what all the fun is about at Club-Ed. Your first private or group lesson ($120 and up) includes all equipment. ✉ *Cowell's Beach, at Dream Inn Santa Cruz, Santa Cruz* ☎ *831/464–0177* ⊕ *club-ed.com.*

Cowell's Surf Shop

SURFING | FAMILY | This shop sells gear, clothing, and swimwear; rents surfboards, stand-up paddleboards, and wet suits; and offers lessons. ✉ *30 Front St., Santa Cruz* ☎ *831/427–2355* ⊕ *www.facebook.com/cowellssurfshop.*

Richard Schmidt Surf School

SURFING | FAMILY | Since 1978, Richard Schmidt has shared the stoke of surfing and the importance of ocean awareness and conservation with legions of students of all ages. Today, the outfit offers surfing and stand-up paddleboard lessons (equipment provided) as well as marine adventure tours in Santa Cruz and elsewhere on the bay. Locations depend on where the waves are breaking or the wind's a'blowing, but outings typically convene at Cowell's Beach or Pleasure Point. ✉ *Santa Cruz* ☎ *831/423–0928* ⊕ *richardschmidt.com* ✉ *From $120.*

ZIPLINING

Mount Hermon Adventures

ZIP LINING | FAMILY | Zipline through the redwoods at this adventure center in the Santa Cruz Mountains. On some weekends there's an aerial adventure course with obstacles and challenges in the redwoods. ■**TIP**➜ **To participate (reservations essential), you must be at least 10 years old and at least 54 inches tall, and weigh between 75 and 250 pounds.** ✉ *17 Conference Dr., 9 miles north of downtown Santa Cruz near Felton, Mount Hermon* ☎ *831/430–4357* ⊕ *mounthermonadventures.com* ✉ *From $90* ⊘ *Closed Tues.–Thurs.*

Index

Photo Credits

Front Cover: Karry Huang/500px **[Descr.:** Aerial view of people at beach,Santa Monica,California,United States,USA**]. Back cover, from left to right:** Valhalla/Design & Conquer. Kimberly Beck Rubio/iStockphoto. Salvador Ceja/Dreamstime. **Spine:**Ken Wolter/Shutterstock. **Interior, from left to right:**Matt Gush/Shutterstock (1). LHBLLC/Shutterstock (2-3). Lequint/Dreamstime (5). **Chapter 1: Experience Southern California:** Sean Xu/Shutterstock (6-7). Choness/iStockphoto (8-9) Jill Krueger (9). Charlie Blacker/iStockphoto (9). Hamilton Pytluk/Universal Studios Hollywood (10). Chris Martin/Dreamstime (10). Julia Hiebaum/Alamy Stock Photo (10). Sebastien Burel/Shutterstock (10). Melanie Stocker/Courtesy of San Diego.org (11). Courtesy of San Diego.org (11). Jose Angel Astor Rocha/Shutterstock (12). Kelly vanDellen/iStockphoto (12) Bongo/Visit California (12). Sergey Didenko/Shutterstock. (12). Michele Kemper/Dreamstime (13). Briana Edwards/Paramount Studios (13). Ryan J. Thompson/Shutterstock (14). Robert Holmes/Visit California (14). Jamie Williams/Visit California (14). Blaise/Visit California (14). Blaise/Visit California (15). Nisimo/Shutterstock (20). Christian Heinz/Shutterstock (21). Dancestrokes/Shutterstock (22). Joseph S Giacalone/Alamy (22). Sebastien Burel/Shutterstock (22). Julia Hiebaum/Alamy (23). Marcel Fuentes/Shutterstock (23). Travelview/Shutterstock (24). NicholasNicholas.com (24). LMWH/Shutterstock (24). Pinz Bowling Center (24). Henry Hargreaves (25). Catch Hospitality Group (25). Rob Stark/Toscana Restaurant (25). Chateau Marmont (25). **Chapter 3: Southern California's Best Road Trips:** PauloZimmermann/iStockphoto (37). **Chapter 4: San Diego:** Dancestrokes/Shutterstock (49).Americanspirit/Dreamstime (69). Alisafarov/Shutterstock (69). Steve Snodgrass/Flickr (71). Robert Holmes/San Diego Zoo (71). FPat/Flickr (72). FPat/Flickr (72). Edward Fielding/Shutterstock (72). Chris Gotz/Shutterstock (72). Lequint/Dreamstime (72). Jose Angel Astor Rocha/Shutterstock (73). Howard Sandler/iStockphoto (92). **Chapter 5: Disneyland and Orange County:** Beach Media/Shutterstock (99). Ericcastro.biz/Flickr (110). Robert Holmes (121). f00sion/iStockphoto (124). Rwongphoto.com/Alamy (127). Brett Shoaf/Artistic Visuals Photography (131). Lowe Llaguno/Shutterstock (135). Steve Heap/Shutterstock (140). **Chapter 6: Los Angeles:** Jill Krueger (145). Paper Cat/Shutterstock (153). Carl Yu (168). Adam Latham (178). **Chapter 7: Palm Springs:** Carol M. Highsmith/Visit California (215). Danielschreurs/Dreamstime (227). David Falk/iStockphoto (238). **Chapter 8: Joshua Tree National Park:** Eric Foltz/iStockphoto (255). Dennis Silvas/Shutterstock (264). Miroslav_1/iStockphoto (268). Greg Epperson/Shutterstock (270). **Chapter 9: Mojave Desert:** Sierralara/Shutterstock (279). Mlgb/Fodors Member (285). DebsG/Shutterstock (289). Maksershov/Dreamstime (293). **Chapter 10: Death Valley National Park:** Bryan Brazil/Shutterstock (297). Kavram/Shutterstock (306). **Chapter 11: The Central Coast:** Jamesh1977/iStockphoto (315). Davidmschrader/Dreamstime (339). Aimee M Lee / Shutterstock (375). Lucky-photographer/iStockphoto (378-379). **Chapter 12: Monterey Bay Area:** Haveseen/Shutterstock (383). Nadezhdasarkisian/Dreamstime (392). Artyart/Shutterstock (400). Wolterk/Dreamstime (410). Mike Brake/Dreamstime (420). **About Our Writers:** All photos are courtesy of the writers.

*Every effort has been made to trace the copyright holders, and we apologize in advance for any accidental errors. We would be happy to apply the corrections in the following edition of this publication.

Notes

Notes